Shaping Cutting-Edge Technologies and Applications for Digital Banking and Financial Services

Cutting-edge technologies have recently shown great promise in a variety of activities for enhancing the existing services of a bank such as the improvement of transactions, ensuring that transactions are done correctly, and managing records of services of savings accounts, loan and mortgage services, wealth management, providing credit and debit cards, overdraft services and physical evidence as key drivers of bank ecosystem. In the financial world, emerging analytics and prediction tools can be used to analyze and visualize structured data, such as financial market data, and to forecast future trends that can be supported by leaders to make informed decisions about investment strategies.

This book explores the importance of artificial intelligence (AI)-based predictive analytics tools in the financial services industry and their role in combating financial fraud. As fintech continues to revolutionize the financial landscape, it also brings forth new challenges, including sophisticated fraudulent activities. Therefore, this book shares the problem of enhancing fraud detection and prevention through the application of predictive analytics.

This book contributes to a deeper understanding of the importance of predictive analytics in the finance field and its pivotal role in cybersecurity and combating fraud. It provides valuable insights for the financial services industry, researchers, and policymakers, aiming to fortify the security and resilience of financial systems in the face of evolving financial fraud challenges.

Cuurently, AI has replaced recurrent intellectual decisions due to the availability of information and its access. These changes have created a revolution in financial operations resulting in environmental variations in the banking and finance sectors. Likewise, analytics transformed the not only finance field but also banking as it is increasing the transparency of lending-related activities.

In addition, this book provides a set of tools for complex analyses of people-related data and through a variety of statistical analysis techniques ranging from simple descriptive statistics to machine learning, HR analytics enables performance evaluation and increases the transparency of finance transactions as well as the problems, advantages, and disadvantages of new digital transformation. The book is not merely a compilation of technical knowledge; it is a beacon of innovation that beckons readers to envision a future where cutting-edge technologies and finance services intertwine seamlessly.

With its engaging and thought-provoking content, the book leaves an indelible impression, urging readers to embrace the transformative power of technology and embark on a collective mission to unlock the full potential of fintech for the betterment of humanity.

Alex Khang is a Professor in Information Technology, D.Sc. D.Litt., Senior AI researcher and Data scientist, AI and Data Science Research Center, Global Research Institute of Technology and Engineering, North Carolina, United States.

Shaping Cutting-Edge Technologies and Applications for Digital Banking and Financial Services

Edited by
Alex Khang

Routledge
Taylor & Francis Group

A PRODUCTIVITY PRESS BOOK

First published 2025

by Routledge
605 Third Avenue, New York, NY 10158
and by Routledge

4 Park Square, Milton Park, Abingdon, Oxon, OX14 4RN

Routledge is an imprint of the Taylor & Francis Group, an informa business

ISBN: 9781032819044 (hbk)
ISBN: 9781032819037 (pbk)
ISBN: 9781003501947 (ebk)

DOI: 10.4324/9781003501947

Typeset in Adobe Garamond
by KnowledgeWorks Global Ltd.

Contents

Preface ix

Acknowledgments xi

About the Editor xiii

Contributors xv

1   Cutting-Edge Technologies and Applications for Digital Banking
    and Financial Services 1
    VITTAL JADHAV AND ALEX KHANG

2   Quantum Computing and Portfolio Optimization in Finance Services 27
    ALEX KHANG, KALI CHARAN RATH, KARTEEK MADAPANA,
    JAGANNADHA RAO, LAKSHMI PRASAD PANDA, AND SUBHASISH DAS

3   Fintech and Data Science: Shaping the Future of the Digital Economy 46
    OM PRAKASH YADAV, RAJKUMAR TEOTIA, AND RASHI BALIYAN

4   Financial Forecasting with Convolutional Neural Networks (CNNs):
    Trends and Challenges 62
    TARUN KUMAR VASHISHTH, VIKAS SHARMA, KEWAL KRISHAN SHARMA,
    SHAHANAWAJ AHAMAD, AND VINEET KAUSHIK

5   Application of Internet of Things (IoT) in Banking and Finance Services 82
    ROHEEN QAMAR AND BAQAR ALI ZARDARI

6   Artificial Intelligence (AI) and Data Analytics: A New Era in the Financial
    Industry 96
    SITA RANI, RAVINDER SINGH, AND ALEX KHANG

7   The Prospects for Applications of Quantum Computing in the
    Financial Sector 106
    VIJAI CHANDRASEKAR AND WORAKAMOL WISETSRI

8   Opportunities and Challenges of Artificial Intelligence (AI) in the
    Banking and Finance Sector 120
    PIYAL ROY, SHIVNATH GHOSH, AMITAVA PODDER,
    AND SAPTARSHI KUMAR SARKAR

9 Technology Transformation Impact on Digital Banking Services: A Study on Analyzing the Adoption and Satisfaction Levels of Users 138
SHUAIB AHMED M. AND SHAPLY ABDUL KAREEM

10 Evolution of Fintech and Implications for Traditional Banking and Finance Sector 147
RAJASHRI ROY CHOUDHURY, MEGAN ALIAH FERRER, AND PIYAL ROY

11 Driving Digital Payments: The Transformative Impact of Electronic Fund Transfers 181
ARPITA NAYAK, IPSEETA SATPATHY, AND ALEX KHANG

12 Robotic Process Automation: A Streamlining Advancement for Banking and Finance Sector 195
DIKSHA JINDAL AND MOHIT GUPTA

13 How Traditional Banks Adapt to the Fintech Revolution in Banking and Finance Sector 214
GREENA KARANI AND BABASAHEB JADHAV

14 Federated Learning for Enhancing the Cloud-Based Cybersecurity in Banking and Finance Services 226
MANAS KUMAR YOGI, AISWARYA DWARAMPUDI, AND YAMUNA MUNDRU

15 Artificial Intelligence (AI) Technology-Based Approach in Banking Compliance Supervision.. 248
ALEX KHANG, VUGAR ABDULLAYEV HAJIMAHMUD, AND YITONG NIU

16 Enhancing Customer Satisfaction through Alternative Channel Services in the Banking Industry 261
B.C.M. PATNAIK, IPSEETA SATPATHY, ANISH PATNAIK, AND ALEX KHANG

17 Navigating the Digital Realm Identifying Trends and Opportunities in E-Banking Services 277
RAHUL JAIN AND CHARU BANGA

18 Role of Edge Technologies and Applications in Banking and Finance Industry 290
USHAA ESWARAN, VIVEK ESWARAN, KEERTHNA MURALI, AND VISHAL ESWARAN

19 Analysis of Internet of Things (IoT) Applications in the Banking Industry 308
THI CAM THU DOAN AND ANH TU NGUYEN

20 The Impact of Artificial Intelligence (AI) Transformation on the Financial Sector from the Trading to Security Operations 322
POOJA DARDA AND MEENAL K PENDSE

21 Prioritizing Customer Experience in Digital Banking for Nation's Sustainable Development 340
PRASHANT H. BHAGAT, PIYUSH KUMAR JAIN, AND CHETANA KAUSHIK

22 The Influence of E-banking Services on Customer Satisfaction of Banks.............352
PAIMAN AHMAD, MAKWAN JAMIL MUSTAFA, AND BESTOON OTHMAN

23 Culture Currency: How Human Resource (HR) Shapes Success in Financial
Institutions and Services 366
ASHWINI. Y. SONAWANE AND ALEX KHANG

24 The Impact of Artificial Intelligence (AI) Transformation in Financial Sector 378
MANJULA DEVI CHITHIRAIKANNU, GOBINATH ARUMUGAM,
PADMA PRIYA SUNDARA MOORTHY, KEERTHI SRINIVASA KANNAN,
AND RAJESWARI PACKIANATHAN

25 Advancing Mobile Banking Security Using Modified RSA Approach
for Data Transformation Enhancement 390
BILAS HALDAR AND PRANAM PAUL

26 Innovative Teaching Materials for Banking and Financial Learners
Using the Artificial General Internet of Things (AGIoT) 403
MUTHMAINNAH MUTHMAINNAH, BUSRAH BUSRAH, BESSE DARMAWATI,
AHMAD AL YAKIN, ERKOL BAYRAM, ALHAMZAH ALNOOR, AND SUBATHRA
CHELLADURAI

Index 427

Preface

Cutting-edge technologies have recently shown great promise in a variety of activities for enhancing the existing services of a bank such as the improvement of transactions, ensuring that transactions are done correctly, and managing records of services of savings accounts, loan and mortgage services, wealth management, providing credit and debit cards, overdraft services and physical evidence as key drivers of bank and finance ecosystem. In the financial world, emerging analytics and prediction tools can be used to analyze and visualize structured data, such as financial market data, and to forecast future trends that can be supported leaders to make informed decisions about investment strategies.

The book aims to explore the importance of cutting-edge technologies and predictive analytics tools in the financial services industry and their role in combating financial fraud. As fintech continues to revolutionize the financial landscape, it also brings forth new challenges, including sophisticated fraudulent activities. Therefore, this book seeks to share the problem of enhancing fraud detection and prevention through the application of predictive analytics. This book contributes to a deeper understanding of the importance of predictive analytics in finance field and its pivotal role in cybersecurity and combating fraud. The book provides valuable insights for the financial services industry, researchers, and policymakers, aiming to fortify the security and resilience of financial systems in the face of evolving financial fraud challenges.

This book also provides a set of cutting-edge technologies for complex analyses of people-related data and through a variety of statistical analysis techniques ranging from simple descriptive statistics to machine learning, financial analytics enables performance evaluation and increases the transparency of banking and finance transactions as well as the problems, advantages, and disadvantages of new digital finance transformation in the era of AI-oriented economy.

Happy reading!

Alex Khang

Acknowledgments

In the 21st century, cutting-edge technologies and applications have replaced recurrent intellectual decisions due to availability of information and its access. These changes have created the revolution of the financial operations resulting in environmental variations in banking and finance sectors. Likewise analytics transformed not only finance field but also banking as it is increasing the transparency of lending-related activities. The book *Shaping Cutting-Edge Technologies and Applications for Digital Banking and Financial Services* is not merely a compilation of technical knowledge; it is a beacon of innovation that beckons readers to envision a future where cutting-edge technologies and finance services intertwine seamlessly. With its engaging and thought-provoking content, the book leaves an indelible impression, urging readers to embrace the transformative power of technology and embark on a collective mission to unlock the full potential of fintech for the betterment of humanity.

Planning and designing a book outline to introduce to readers across the globe is the passion and noble goal of the editor. To be able to make ideas to a reality and the success of this book, the biggest reward is belongs to the efforts, knowledge, skills, expertise, experiences, enthusiasm, collaboration, and trust of the contributors.

To all respected contributors, we really say big thanks for high-quality chapters that we received from our economics, finance managers, accounting leaders, experts, professors, scientists, engineers, scholars, Ph.D., educators, and academic colleagues. To all respected reviewers with whom we have had the opportunity to collaborate and monitor their hard work remotely, we acknowledge their tremendous support and valuable comments not only for this book but also for future book projects.

We also express our deep gratitude for all the pieces of discussion, advice, support, motivation, sharing, collaboration, and inspiration we received from our faculty, contributors, educators, professors, scientists, scholars, engineers, and academic colleagues.

Last but not least, we are really grateful to our publisher **Productivity Press** (Taylor & Francis Group) for the wonderful support in making sure the timely processing of the manuscript and bringing out this book to the readers soonest.

Thank you, everyone.

Alex Khang

About the Editor

Alex Khang is a Professor in Information Technology, D.Sc. D.Litt., Senior AI researcher and Data scientist, AI and Data Science Research Center, Global Research Institute of Technology and Engineering, North Carolina, United States. He has more than 28 years of experience in teaching and researching of computer science and data science at the universities and institutions of computer science and information technology in Vietnam, India, and United States. He has over 30 years of working experience as a software product manager, data engineer, AI engineer, cloud computing architect, solution architect, software architect, database expert in the foreign corporations of Germany, Sweden, United States, Singapore, Vietnam, and multinationals. He has published 200+ documents indexed Scopus, 54 authored books (Software development in Vietnamese). He has published 25 edited books, 250+ book chapters, and calling for book chapters for 5 edited books in the fields of AI Ecosystem.

Contributors

Shahanawaj Ahamad
College of Computer Science and Engineering
University of Hail
Hail, Saudi Arabia

Paiman Ahmad
Law Department
University of Raparin
Ranya, Iraq

Alhamzah Alnoor
Technical University
Management Technical College
Baghdad, Iraq

Gobinath Arumugam
Department of Information
    Technology
Velammal College of Engineering and
    Technology
Madurai, India

Rashi Baliyan
Noida International University
Greater Noida, India

Charu Banga
De Montfort University
Dubai, UAE

Erkol Bayram
Tourism Faculty, Department of Tour
    Guiding
University of Sinop
Sinop, Turkey

Prashant H. Bhagat
Chetanas Hazarimal Somani College of
    Commerce and Smt. Kusumtai Chaudhari
    College of Arts
University of Mumbai
Mumbai, India

Busrah
Hukum Ekonomi Syariah, Universitas Al
    Asyariah Mandar
Mandar, Indonesia

Vijai Chandrasekar
Department of Commerce and Business
    Administration
Vel Tech Rangarajan Dr. Sagunthala R&D
    Institute of Science and Technology
Chennai, India

Subathra Chelladurai
Computer Science & Engineering
Manonmaniam Sundaranar University
Tirunelveli, India

Manjula Devi Chithiraikannu
Department of Information Technology
Velammal College of Engineering and
    Technology
Madurai, India

Rajashri Roy Choudhury
Department of Computer Science and
    Engineering
Brainware University
Kolkata, India

Pooja Darda
Marketing and Advertising in the Banking
and Retail
Jaipuria Institute of Management
Lucknow, India

Besse Darmawati
Science and Technology
Badan Riset dan Inovasi Nasional
Jakarta, Indonesia

Subhasish Das
Department of Mechanical Engineering
GIET University
Gunupur, India

Thi Cam Thu Doan
Institute for Research Science and Banking
Technology
Ho Chi Minh University of Banking
Ho Chi Minh City, Vietnam

Aiswarya Dwarampudi
Department of Computer Science and
Engineering
Pragati Engineering College (Autonomous)
Surampalem, India

Ushaa Eswaran
Department of Electronics & Communication
Engineering
Mahalakshmi Tech Campus, Chennai,
Tamilnadu, India

Vishal Eswaran
Data Engineering Department
CVS Health
Dallas, Texas

Vivek Eswaran
Data Engineering Department
Medallia Inc.
Austin, Texas

Megan Aliah Ferrer
Computer Science Department
Foothill High School
Henderson Nevada, North America

Shivnath Ghosh
Computer Science and Engineering
Brainware University
Kolkata, India

Mohit Gupta
School of Business Studies
Punjab Agricultural University
Ludhiana, India

Vugar Abdullayev Hajimahmud
Information Technologies and
Systems
Azerbaijan University of Architecture
and Construction
Baku, Azerbaijan

Bilas Haldar
Department of Computer Science and
Engineering
The Neotia University
Sarisha, India

Babasaheb Jadhav
Dr. D. Y. Patil Vidyapeeth (Deemed to be
University)
Global Business School & Research
Centre
Pune, India

Vittal Jadhav
Department of Technical Delivery
Management
North America Consulting and Managed
Services
Jacksonville, Florida

Piyush Kumar Jain
Department of Business Policy and
Administration
University of Mumbai
Mumbai, India

Rahul Jain
Finance and Business Department
De Montfort University
Dubai, UAE

Diksha Jindal
School of Business Studies
Punjab Agricultural University
Ludhiana, India

Keerthi Srinivasa Kannan
Information Technology
Velammal College of Engineering and
    Technology
Viraganur, India

Greena Karani
Dr. D. Y. Patil Vidyapeeth University
Global Business School & Research Centre
Pune, India

Shaply Abdul Kareem
Business Administration
C. Abdul Hakeem College of Engineering &
    Technology
Bangalore, India

Chetana Kaushik
Mumbai, India

Vineet Kaushik
School of Commerce and Management
IIMT University
Meerut, India

Alex Khang
Department of AI and Data Science
Global Research Institute of Technology
    and Engineering
Fort Raleigh, North Carolina

Shuaib Ahmed M.
Business Administration
C. Abdul Hakeem College of Engineering
    & Technology
Bangalore, India

Karteek Madapana
Department of Mechanical
    Engineering
GIET University
Gunupur, India

Padma Priya Sundara Moorthy
Department of Information Technology
Velammal College of Engineering and
    Technology
Viraganur, India

Yamuna Mundru
Department of Computer Science and
    Engineering
Pragati Engineering College (Autonomous)
Surampalem, India

Keerthna Murali
Data Engineering Department
    Dell EMC
Massachusetts, Texas

Makwan Jamil Mustafa
College of Law and Administration
University of Halabja
Halabja, Iraq

Muthmainnah Muthmainnah
English Department
Universitas Al Asyariah Mandar
Sulawesi Barat, Indonesia

Arpita Nayak
KIIT School of Management
Kalinga Institute of Industrial Technology
    (KIIT)
Bhubaneswar, India

Anh Tu Nguyen
Faculty of Banking
Ho Chi Minh University of Banking
Ho Chi Minh City, Vietnam

Yitong Niu
School of Aeronautical Engineering
Universiti Sains Malaysia
Gelugor, Malaysia

Bestoon Othman
Department of Insurance Management
University of Raparin
Ranya Kurdistan Region, Iraq

Rajeswari Packianathan
Department of Electronics and
  Communication Engineering
Velammal College of Engineering and
  Technology
Madurai, India

Lakshmi Prasad Panda
Department of Humanities
Government College of Engineering
  Kalahandi
Bhawanipatna, India

Anish Patnaik
MBA in Rural Management
KIIT University
Odisha, India

B.C.M. Patnaik
KIIT School of Management
KIIT University
Bhubaneswar, India

Pranam Paul
Department of Computer Science and
  Engineering
Global Institute of Engineering and
  Management
Krishnanagar, India

Meenal K. Pendse
Department of Banking and Finance
MIT World Peace University
Pune, India

Amitava Podder
Computer Science and Engineering
Brainware University
Kolkata, India

Roheen Qamar
Department of Information Technology
Quaid-e-Awam University of Engineering
Nawabshah, Pakistan

Sita Rani
Department of Computer Science and
  Engineering
Guru Nanak Dev Engineering College
Ludhiana, India

Jagannadha Rao
Department of Mechanical Engineering
GIET University
Gunupur, India

Kali Charan Rath
Department of Mechanical Engineering
GIET University
Gunupur, India

Piyal Roy
Computer Science and Engineering
Brainware University
Kolkata, India

Saptarshi Kumar Sarkar
Computer Science and Engineering
Brainware University
Kolkata, India

Ipseeta Satpathy
KIIT School of Management
Kalinga Institute of Industrial Technology
  (KIIT)
Bhubaneswar, India

Kewal Krishan Sharma
School of Computer Science and Applications
IIMT University
Meerut, India

Vikas Sharma
Department of Computer Science &
  Applications
School of Computer Science and
  Applications
IIMT University
Meerut, India

Ravinder Singh
Banking and Finance Department
Aditya Birla Capital
Ludhiana, India

Ashwini. Y. Sonawane
Commerce and Management Faculty
Vishwakarma University
Pune, India

RajKumar Teotia
Business Analysis Department
H. R. Institute of Science and Technology
Ghaziabad, India

Tarun Kumar Vashishth
Department of Computer Science &
    Applications
School of Computer Science and Applications
IIMT University
Meerut, India

Worakamol Wisetsri
Department of Manufacturing and Service
    Industry Management
Faculty of Business and Industrial
    Development
King Mongkut's University of Technology
    North Bangkok
Bangkok, Thailand

Om Prakash Yadav
School of Business Management
Noida International University
Greater Noida, India

Ahmad Al Yakin
Sociology Department
Universitas Al Asyariah Mandar Madatte
Sulawesi Barat, Indonesia

Manas Kumar Yogi
Department of Computer Science and
    Engineering
Pragati Engineering College (Autonomous)
Surampalem, India

Baqar Ali Zardari
Department of Information Technology
Quaid-e-Awam University of Engineering
Nawabshah, Pakistan

Chapter 1

Cutting-Edge Technologies and Applications for Digital Banking and Financial Services

Vittal Jadhav and Alex Khang

1.1 Introduction

Digital banking and financial services are rapidly evolving, driven by advancements in technology. The advent of blockchain technology is among the most noteworthy changes that have taken place in the past few years. Secure and transparent transaction recording is made possible via blockchain technology, which is a distributed ledger. It has the potential to revolutionize digital banking and financial services by providing a more secure and efficient way to manage financial transactions.

One of the most important applications of blockchain in digital banking is digital identity. Digital identity is the electronic representation of an individual's identity. It is used to verify an individual's identity online and to access digital services. Blockchain can be used to create a more secure and tamper-proof digital identity system. This would make it easier for individuals to access digital services and would reduce the risk of identity theft (Digital Identity, 2020).

Financial service providers may now reach more people, do more with less, and save money thanks to technological developments. There are now new products, services, and platforms available thanks to the financial services industry's digitization. Chances for growth are the digital disruption's main selling point. Increased efficiency, more competition, and new avenues of access are all benefits of digital disruption (Khang, Rath et al., 2023).

Our reliance on online services continues to grow, with increased customer service expectations. The ability to deliver quality service experience depends on personal information. It's become critical for organizations to consider the balance between service experience and privacy, the difference between a credential and an entity, and the trust that is placed in digital identities.

As a result of COVID-19, digitalization has accelerated as companies quickly adjust their strategy to meet the demands of changing customer behaviors. Some of the new possibilities in financial technology that have arisen as a result of the world's fast digitization include the creation

DOI: 10.4324/9781003501947-1

of digital currencies issued by central banks for international trade, the distribution of government subsidies through digital payments, and the necessity for nationalized instant payment systems.

Blockchain can also be used to improve the security of financial transactions. Traditional financial transactions are often vulnerable to fraud and hacking. Blockchain can be used to create a more secure system for recording and tracking financial transactions. This would reduce the risk of fraud and hacking and would make it easier for individuals to trust digital banking and financial services.

Digital banking and other financial services stand to gain a great deal from blockchain technology. However, there are also a number of challenges that need to be overcome. One of the biggest challenges is the lack of regulation for blockchain technology. This makes it difficult for financial institutions to adopt blockchain and develop new blockchain-based products and services (Khang, Shah, Rani, 2023).

Blockchain technology may change the face of online banking and other financial services, but it is not without its share of problems. Blockchain technology has the potential to simplify people's access to digital services while simultaneously decreasing the likelihood of fraud and hacking by offering a more efficient and secure method to handle financial transactions. Digital banking and financial services may see blockchain's significant growth as the technology develops and regulations are clarified.

1.2 Empower Banking Technology Services with SSI and Blockchain

1.2.1 Self-Sovereign Identity

A decentralized identity management system (IMS) relies on a private data store and digital device to manage identity attributes and their life cycle. The entity manages these components, ensuring the entity maintains control over its identity attributes and associated attestations. A decentralized identity is safe as long as the entity in possession has control over its identity data. The entity creates its own digital identity by creating unique identifiers and attaching authentic attributes. Credentials are collected from trusted anchors and made available when needed. Cryptographic techniques like digital signatures can be used to prove the authenticity of a credential.

Verifiable credentials (VCs) are digital claims that can be cryptographically verified, giving users more control over their identity attributes, and making the digital identities easier to use. A decentralized identity not only improves users' digital experience but also facilitates the process for businesses, eliminating the complex, costly, and risky identity management process as shown in Figure 1.1.

1.2.1.1 What Exactly Are Verifiable Credentials?

VCs are a standard format for digitally representing credentials that are cryptographically secure, machine-verifiable, and ensure privacy through methods such as selective disclosure. Simply put, VCs are secure digital documents holding information about a person or business that can be easily transferred and automatically validated.

VCs are a cornerstone of self-sovereign identity (SSI), a new technology that addresses shortcomings in the current identity management paradigm by allowing users to govern their data and store pre-verified identification documents in a digital wallet. In this paradigm, decentralized

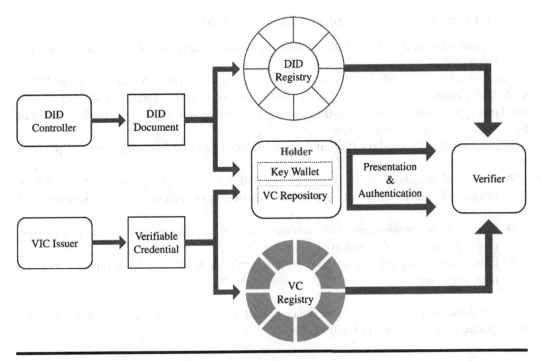

Figure 1.1   Architecture of self-sovereign identity.

technology (albeit not required) and decentralized identifiers (DIDs) coexist with virtual currencies (Khang, Hajimahmud et al., 2024).

It is vital to emphasize that the phrase "Verifiable Credentials" refers only to the W3C Verifiable Credentials Data Model. This foundational specification defines a common format for embedding verifiable claims and cryptographic proofs within VCs as shown in Figure 1.2.

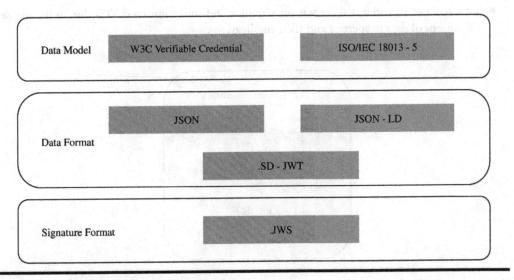

Figure 1.2   Verifiable credentials data model.

1.2.1.2 Constituent Entities of Verifiable Credentials (VCs)

Standardized schemas that define the structure and semantics of digital identity data are referred to as data models.

The prevailing standards for digital credentials are ISO/IEC 18013-5 (mDL) and the World Wide Web Consortium (W3C) VCs Data Model. However, from a technical standpoint, the two standards appear to be incompatible; the ongoing discourse centers on determining how they can harmoniously coexist and collaborate.

Fundamentally, VCs and the ISO mDL credentials consist of the following three components:

- Credential metadata: These comprises essential particulars pertaining to the credential in question, including but not limited to the category of credential, date of issuance, and expiration.
- Claims: These are assertions or characteristics concerning the object, legal entity, or persona that is the subject of the credential.
- Proofs: The subsequent step involves cryptographic verification, which is implemented as a digital signature.

These three components ensure that the credential is authentic and has not been altered since its purported issuer, as shown in Figure 1.3.

1.2.1.3 Data Formats

Data formats are distinct manifestations of digital identity information that adhere to a selected data model that dictates the methods by which data is structured, transmitted, and encoded. Two primary data syntaxes are defined by the VC data model: JSON and JSON-LD.

- JSON – The data format utilizes a simple key-value pair structure, which facilitates reading and writing for both humans and machines. However, it does not incorporate any inherent mechanisms for specifying data context.
- JSON-LD – The preferred format for complex and interconnected VCs due to its precise definitions of data properties and their implications.

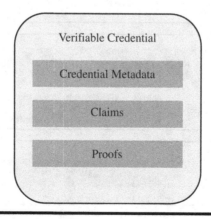

Figure 1.3 Verifiable credential elements.

Conversely, Selective Disclosure for JSON Web Tokens (SD-JWTs), a third data format that accepts a JSON or JSON-LD as input, has gained significant traction in recent times due to its adoption as a fundamental component of the Wallet Architecture and Reference Framework and numerous implementations.

1.2.1.4 Structure of Signatures

A critical component of a VC, the signature format enhances the credential's security and credibility. In this context, JWS (JSON Web Signature) is noteworthy.

Using data structures based on JSON, JWS encrypts content with digital signatures or Message Authentication Codes (MACs). It permits the uploading of a digital signature to the VC in a verifiable and tamper-evident manner.

A JWS comprises three primary elements: the payload, which contains the VC data to be signed; the header, which contains metadata regarding the signature; and the signature, which is produced by employing a cryptographic algorithm to both the payload and header utilizing a private key.

1.2.1.5 Delusion of Verifiable Credentials

Case 1
- Myth – Digital credentials and VCs are identical.
- Truth – VCs are digital credentials with unique trust and verification features, incorporating cryptographic elements to ensure credential integrity and authenticity, allowing independent verification without relying solely on the issuer.

Case 2
- Myth – Identity documents are the only uses for VCs.
- Truth – VCs are versatile identity documents that can represent various claims and statements, making them applicable in various contexts beyond personal identity verification.

Case 3
- Myth – VCs necessitate blockchain at all times.
- Truth – Blockchain technology is not a mandatory component in decentralized identity, allowing organizations to select the most suitable technology stack based on their specific needs.

Case 4
- Myth – VCs implementation is difficult.
- Truth – Decentralized identity solutions are becoming more accessible and user-friendly, despite the complexity of the underlying cryptographic techniques.

Case 5
- Myth – Valid VCs may only be used online.
- Truth – VCs are versatile, allowing for both online and offline use, storage in digital wallets, and various contexts, including face-to-face interactions.

1.2.1.6 Impact of Digital Identification Systems in Banking and Financial Services

The digital future has accelerated the shift toward digital identification systems, which are electronic forms of identification that verify a person's identity online. These systems, based on unique digital identifiers like biometric data, social security numbers, or government-issued ID numbers, have gained global acceptance due to their convenience, security, and cost-effectiveness. They have revolutionized identity management in the banking and financial services sector, reducing fraud and identity theft, enabling financial inclusion, and reducing the risk of money laundering and terrorist financing.

However, there are challenges to address, particularly in the banking and financial services sector. A unified approach to identity management is needed, and blockchain technology can help. Blockchain is a distributed ledger system that uses cryptography to protect and decentralize the recording of ever-increasing lists of records. It can be used to create a single, tamper-proof database of digital IDs, allowing seamless integration, and sharing of data across different institutions. Furthermore, digital IDs can be made more secure and private with blockchain technology's decentralized data storage and smart contracts for safe verification.

1.2.2 Blockchain Technology

A blockchain can be thought of as a series of interconnected blocks that store specific information (database) in an authentic and safe manner, all while being part of a network (peer-to-peer). In other words, blockchain is not a centralized network but rather a distributed ledger that relies on a group of interconnected computers rather than a central server (Khang, Chowdhury, & Sharma, 2022).

1.2.3 Principal Elements That Make Up the Blockchain Architecture

These are the fundamental components that make up the blockchain architecture:

- ◼ Node – An individual or computer that is part of the blockchain architecture is referred to as a node. Each node has its own independent copy of the whole blockchain ledger.
- ◼ Transaction – In the context of blockchain technology, a transaction is the smallest building unit of a blockchain system (records, information, etc.) that serves the goal of blockchain.
- ◼ Block – The term "block" refers to a data structure that is utilized for the purpose of storing a collection of transactions among all of the nodes in the network.
- ◼ Chain – A chain is a series of blocks that are built in a particular order.
- ◼ Miners – There are certain nodes known as miners that are responsible for carrying out the process of verifying blocks before adding anything to the structured blockchain.
- ◼ Consensus – A set of agreements and regulations that make it possible to conduct blockchain operations.

A new block is created every time a record or transaction is added to the blockchain. After that, we digitally sign each record to make sure it's genuine and legitimate. At least half of the nodes in the system must verify this block before it may be added to the network. The following is a schematic of the blockchain's architecture depicting a digital wallet to show how this works in practice as shown in Figure 1.4.

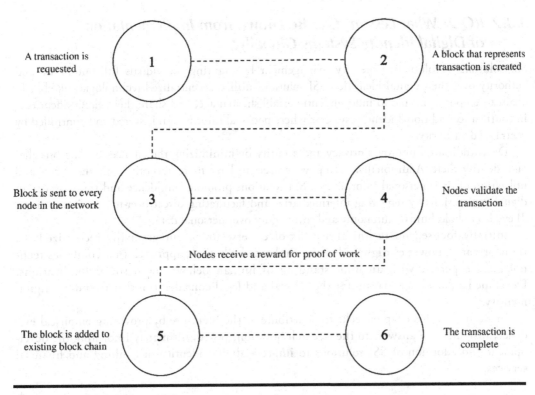

Figure 1.4   Blockchain workflow.

1.3 Methodology and Literature Review

The literature emphasizes the need for decentralized IMS as a potential solution to safeguarding sensitive data and mitigating information loss in financial services. Decentralized IMSs offer a paradigm shift from traditional centralized approaches by empowering individuals with greater control over their digital identities. By leveraging technologies such as blockchain, DIDs, and VCs, these systems enhance security, privacy, and trust in digital transactions.

This study endeavors to address two primary research questions:

1.3.1 RQ-1: How Blockchain Technology and Digital Identity Systems Revolutionize Banking and Financial Services?

Blockchain technology is revolutionizing identity management in banking and finance by creating tamper-proof databases of digital IDs. Digitizing Know Your Customer (KYC) processes streamlines identity verification, reducing costs, and enhancing security. Blockchain-based solutions in trade finance facilitate real-time transactions, while digital lending like Agrotoken tokenizes agricultural goods. Cross-border payments like USDC on Stellar offer near-instant settlement times and lower fees. Decentralized credit scoring through blockchain smart contracts improves transparency and accessibility. Initial Coin Offerings (ICOs) offer decentralized fundraising options without intermediaries (KYC, 2024).

1.3.2 RQ-2: What Lessons Can Be Drawn from Implementation of Digital Identity Systems Globally?

SSI solutions revolutionize identity management by granting individuals full autonomy and authority over their digital identities. SSI solutions utilize decentralized technologies like blockchain to empower people to independently establish, manage, and share their digital identities, in contrast to traditional identity systems where personal information is stored and controlled by centralized authority.

Decentralization improves privacy and security by minimizing the chances of data breaches and identity theft. Additionally, it empowers users to have more authority over the access and utilization of their personal information. SSI solutions promote confidence and transparency in digital transactions by removing intermediaries and facilitating direct peer-to-peer interactions. They also uphold human autonomy and sovereignty over personal data.

Initially focused on technical aspects of cybersecurity, but gradually recognized the transformative power of digital identity. Embraced a holistic approach that combines technological expertise with an understanding of human behavior and social implications. Developed a deep appreciation for the ethical and legal considerations surrounding digital identity.

In summary, this chapter seeks to contribute to the literature by providing empirical evidence, insights, and answers to the research questions posed, ultimately informing the development and adoption of SSI solutions to improve digital identity in banking and financial services.

1.3.3 Methods

To address the research questions regarding the cybersecurity challenges in banking and financial services and the potential of SSI solutions to mitigate these challenges, a systematic research method was employed. This section outlines the methodology used to conduct a comprehensive search for relevant literature and identify SSI implementations for analysis.

1.3.3.1 Initial Search Strategy

The research began with a systematic search for published solutions related to SSI implementations. Structured queries were formulated based on key terms and concepts related to decentralized identity management, cybersecurity, and financial services. The search was conducted on reputable academic databases, namely Scopus and IEEE Xplore, to ensure access to a wide range of scholarly literature.

1.3.3.2 Data Collection and Screening

The search yielded a total of 81 unique papers and online available information after the removal of duplicates and non-relevant information. These papers were then categorized into different groups based on their relevance to the research objectives. Categories included implementations of SSI solutions, digital identity and blockchain use case in banking and financial services (Khanh, Khang et al., 2021).

1.3.3.3 Identification of Implementations

Among the categorized papers, a subset focused specifically on digital identity and blockchain implementations. These implementations were directly included in the scope of the research, as they provided valuable insights into the practical applications of decentralized identity solutions and digital banking in real-world scenarios.

1.3.3.4 Refinement and Selection

Through this process, we analyzed different digital identity and blockchain implementation in banking and financial services.

However, not all implementations initially identified met the criteria upon closer examination. Therefore, a thorough review of each implementation was conducted to extract relevant specifications and ensure alignment with the defined evaluation criteria.

1.3.3.5 Extraction of Specifications

The final step involved reading each identified identity solution thoroughly to extract specifications according to the predefined evaluation criteria. This meticulous process allowed for the refinement of the dataset and ensured that only true blockchain and digital identity solutions were included in the analysis.

By following this systematic approach compiled a comprehensive dataset of blockchain implementations and digital identities to address the research questions effectively. This rigorous methodology ensures the reliability and validity of the findings, paving the way for a thorough examination of the digital identity and blockchain in banking and financial services.

1.4 Revolutionize Banking and Financial Services with Digital Identity and Blockchain

The digital future has accelerated the shift toward digital identification systems, which are electronic forms of identification that verify a person's identity online. These systems, based on unique digital identifiers like biometric data, social security numbers, or government-issued ID numbers, have gained global acceptance due to their convenience, security, and cost-effectiveness. They have revolutionized identity management in the banking and financial services sector, reducing fraud and identity theft, enabling financial inclusion, and reducing the risk of money laundering and terrorist financing.

However, there are challenges to address, particularly in the banking and financial services sector. A unified approach to identity management is needed, and blockchain technology can help. Blockchain technology is a decentralized, distributed ledger that maintains a growing list of records, linked, and secured using cryptography. It can be used to create a single, tamper-proof database of digital IDs, allowing seamless integration, and sharing of data across different institutions.

Additionally, blockchain technology can enhance the security and privacy of digital IDs by decentralizing data storage and using smart contracts for secure verification processes as shown in Figure 1.5.

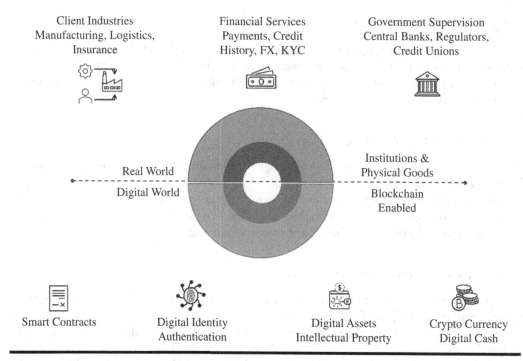

Figure 1.5 **Digital and real-world entities in banking and financial services.**

1.4.1 Digitizing Know Your Customer (KYC)

1.4.1.1 Business Requirement

Banks now use independent source papers to verify clients and manage risk. This information covers identification, transaction monitoring, and accurate due diligence. KYC processes are labor-intensive, expensive, and error-prone, with no consistency between institutions and individual record keeping as shown in Figure 1.6.

1.4.1.2 Solution

- The holder/user obtains a VC from a trusted IdP to authenticate on the bank's web portal. The bank could issue the user a VC as an IdP.
- The holder accepts/denies the credential. If the user accepts, they can obtain this credential and put it in their web or mobile wallet. DID holders store the private key in their digital wallet, while the issuing authority registers the public keys on the blockchain.
- The holder/user enters the bank website, authenticates using a wallet-stored digital ID VC, and finds the KYC application page. The bank provides the bearer a proof of request and lists the KYC documentation.
- After receiving the credential share request from the bank, the holder analyzes the proof request and checks if the appropriate credentials and claims are present in the wallet. In this case, a verified presentation (VP) with all relevant credentials is possible if the holder has them.

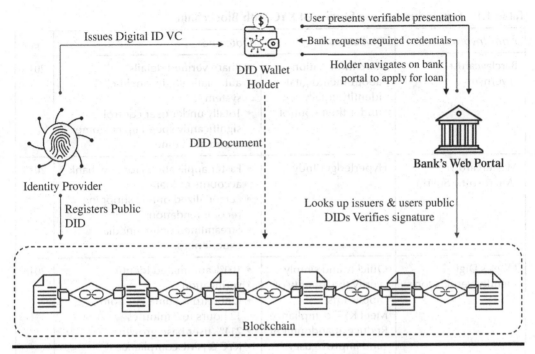

Figure 1.6 Blockchain-based Know Your Customer (KYC) workflow.

■ Cryptographically proving the holder is transmitting VCs is achieved by VP packaging. This allows users to send all credentials in one transaction instead of individually.
■ The bank checks signatures and public key material from the distributed ledger. The bank may validate all electronic information (credential, status, issuer, presenter, and claims) against the blockchain network without contacting the issuer. Verifiers check VC status to assure validity.

1.4.1.3 Benefits

■ KYC compliance checks and enterprise customer enrollment can be completed in less time by financial institutions.
■ Implement automation to streamline the screening and verification procedure.
■ Minimize operational expenses.
■ Prior investments in KYC compliance reviews can be monetized.
■ Protect the information of your consumers with blockchain-based cryptography.

Objectives and outcome are shown in Table 1.1.

1.4.2 Digitization of Trade Finance

1.4.2.1 Business Requirement

Corporations use trade financing solutions to settle their trade activity and build confidence. In essence, a trade finance process is the way parties communicate with one another throughout

Table 1.1 Few Industry Case Studies of KYC with Blockchain

Firms Involved	Objectives	Outcome	Year
Barclaycard + Evernym	Store information about their digital identity, totally under their control	• Share verified details automatically, in single-click system • Totally under user control, significantly speed up customer transaction times	2018
Mastercard + Microsoft + Sovrin	Hyperledger Indy	• Faster applications for new bank accounts or loans • Personalized online shopping recommendations • Streamlined online media experiences.	2018
Mitek's Digital Identity Verification	Quickly and simply verify the identity of applicants Meet KYC compliance Reduce abandonment and improve user experience	• 100% automated identity verification • Onboarding time cut from 12 hours to 5 minutes • 214% user base growth • KYC & AML compliance	2018
BMO, CIBC, Desjardins, National Bank of Canada, RBC, Scotiabank and TD + Secure Key Technologies	Identity verification using App + blockchain	• Network operators can't see the data • No central database or honeypot • There is no single point of failure. • Triple blind – privacy • Can't keep track of user across relying parties • DDOS-proofing on a large scale	2019
Tietoevry + Infopulse	Blockchain KYC	• Secure data verification with speed • Audit trail and compliance • Lowering data validation costs • Protect customer data	2020

credit activities. A standard documentary credit (L/C) cycle consists of a few key components. Should any party in the process need to make a change or adjustment, it will need repeating one or more steps, which will slow down the process and extend the time it takes to conduct the transaction overall as shown in Figure 1.7.

1.4.2.2 Solution

■ The agreement of sale between the importer and exporter is shared with the import bank via a smart contract on the blockchain.

■ The import bank can evaluate purchase agreements, establish credit terms, and send payment obligations in real-time to the export bank.

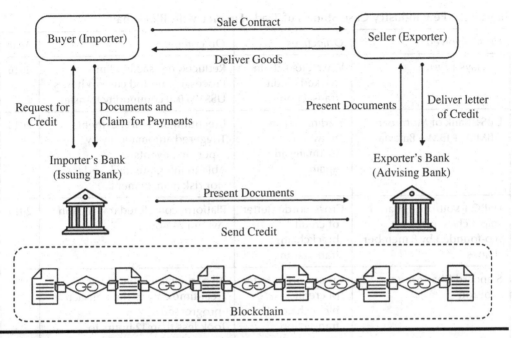

Figure 1.7 Blockchain-based trade finance workflow.

- The export bank will verify the submitted payment obligation and, if authorized, a smart contract will be issued on the blockchain to include terms and conditions and lock-in requirements.
- Following receipt of the obligations, the exporter will digitally sign a blockchain-equivalent letter of credit within the smart contract to commence shipment.
- The goods will be inspected by third parties and the customs agent in the exporting country, with each delivering their separate digital signature of approval on the blockchain smart contract.
- Goods will be transferred from Country A to Country B.
- Upon delivery, the importer will digitally acknowledge receipt of the goods and initiate payment.
- Using the given acknowledgment, blockchain will automate payment from importer to exporter through a smart contract.

Objectives and outcome are shown in Table 1.2.

1.4.2.3 Blockchain Benefits

- Instantaneous evaluation: Blockchain-enabled financial documents are vetted and authorized instantly, cutting down on the time it takes to start shipping.
- Diminished risk of counterparties: Due to blockchain tracking of bills of lading, there is no chance of double spending.
- Decentralized contract fulfillment: Real-time status updates on blockchain as contract terms are fulfilled to minimize the amount of time and personnel needed to track the delivery of products.

Table 1.2   Few Industry Case Studies of Trade Finance with Blockchain

Firms Involved	Objectives	Outcome	Year
Barclays + Oruna	Wave blockchain-backed credit transaction	Reduced transaction time Processing period cut to 4 hours US$100,000 commodity transfer	2016
UBS+ Bank of Montreal (BMO) + IBM + Batavia	Trading of cars between Germany and Spain	Execution of smart payments Triggered automatically by specified events Able to integrate track and trace for risk management	2018
HSBC + Voltron, a shared blockchain platform co-founded by 8 member banks	Cross-border letter of credit blockchain transaction	Platform completed transaction within 24 hours	2019
Standard Chartered + Voltron	Cross-border letter of credit blockchain transaction	All participants able to view real-time data as the transaction progressed. Took less than 12 hours to complete the transaction	2019
Deutsche Bank + Natixis + Santander + Société Générale + UniCredit + CaixaBank+ Erste Group + HSBC + KBC, Nordea + Rabobank + UBS	We.Trade digital trade platform based on the Linux Foundation's Hyperledger	Support small and medium enterprises (SMEs) Facilitate new trading relationships	2022

■ Evidence of possession: The ownership and whereabouts of the products are transparent, thanks to the title that is available within blockchain mechanism.

■ Transparency in regulations: Regulators can access critical documents in real time to support AML and enforcement efforts.

1.4.3 Digitized Lending (Farm Loans)

1.4.3.1 Business Requirement

Agrotoken is changing the farming business by making it more open, efficient, and easy to get into by using tokenization. The Agrotoken is the first global system for tokenizing agricultural goods. Additionally, this gives farmers access to financing through tokenization, which lets them raise money by selling digital assets backed by their crops. Second, the platform helps farmers reach more buyers and investors around the world, which increases the size of their market as shown in Figure 1.8.

1.4.3.2 Solution

■ Tokenizing commodities on the Algorand blockchain are turned into Agrotokens. As result, each Agrotoken is greater than or equal to a certain amount of the related commodity.

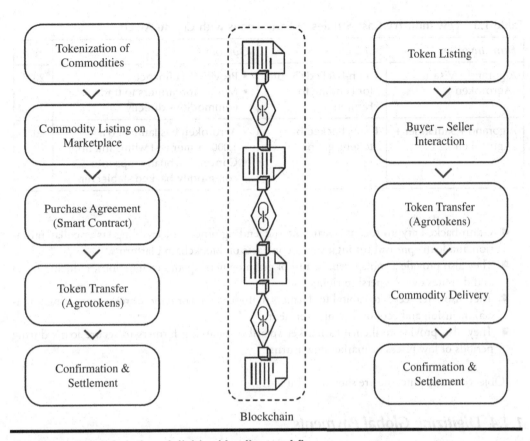

Figure 1.8 Blockchain-based digitized lending workflow.

- Listing of tokenized commodities by farmers, traders, or makers on a decentralized market built on the Algorand blockchain.
- Buyers and sellers transact on the open marketplace and talk to sellers directly.
- Buyer and the seller sign a smart contract-based purchase agreement. The Algorand blockchain stores the terms of the deal, such as the amount, price, and shipping information.
- This exchange is recorded on the blockchain, which makes it clear and can't be changed.
- Once the seller receives the Agrotokens, they start delivering the goods.
- The smart contract instantly starts the final settlement of the deal once the goods are delivered and accepted by the buyer.

1.4.3.3 Agrotoken Benefits

- Agrotokens provide numerous benefits to banking and financial services, especially in the context of providing farm loans.
- They serve as collateral, allowing farmers to use their grain reserves as collateral to secure loans from banks and financial institutions.
- This reduces the risk for lenders, as they have tangible assets backing the loans. Farmers can also unlock liquidity without selling their physical grain, increasing their lending opportunities and revenue streams.

Table 1.3 Few Industry Case Studies of Farm Loans with Crypto Assets

Firms Involved	Objectives	Outcome	Year
Algorand + Visa + Agrotoken	Grain-backed Crypto for Lending to Farmers	• Provide fast finance • Market for farmers to trade commodities directly	2021
Algorand + Santander + Agrotoken	Loans backed by tokens grains	• Agrotoken has launched a 1,000-farmer test with Santander • Convert soybean crops into commodity-backed stablecoin	2022

- ◼ Grain-backed crypto tokens streamline the lending process by enabling faster collateralization and loan approval through smart contracts on blockchain platforms.
- ◼ They also provide a transparent record of grain ownership and transactions, reducing fraud and disputes over ownership rights.
- ◼ They also offer access to capital for farmers in underserved or remote areas, promoting financial inclusion and economic empowerment.
- ◼ They also provide resilience to market volatility, enabling farmers to secure loans during periods of low prices or market downturns.

Objectives and outcome are shown in Table 1.3.

1.4.4 Digitizing Global Payments

1.4.4.1 Business Requirement

USDC is a stablecoin pegged to the US dollar, providing stability and efficiency for international transactions. It mitigates currency fluctuations, reducing transaction costs and risks. USDC transactions on blockchain networks like Stellar offer near-instant settlement times and lower fees, making them ideal for businesses needing fast, cost-effective international transactions. USDC also offers accessibility, allowing businesses in underserved regions to participate in global commerce without a bank account. It also offers transparency through public ledgers, enhancing trust and reducing fraud risks. USDC facilitates cross-border remittances and promotes financial inclusion by providing access to digital financial services for underserved populations as shown in Figure 1.9.

1.4.4.2 Solution

- ◼ A trusted entity, like a financial institution, becomes the issuer of USDC on the Stellar blockchain.
- ◼ The issuer accepts USD deposits from users converting fiat currency to USDC on the Stellar network.
- ◼ Tokenization: USD deposits are converted to USDC on the Stellar network. Each USDC token represents a reserve USD.
- ◼ The USDC tokens are linked into the Stellar network for fast and affordable cross-border transactions.

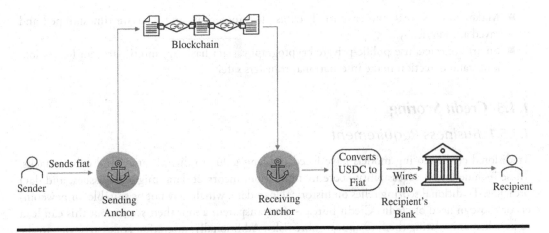

Figure 1.9 Blockchain-based global payments workflow.

- To initiate a cross-border transfer, the sender converts USD into USDC tokens issued by a trustworthy issuer on the Stellar network.
- In a Stellar transaction, the sender transfers USDC tokens to the recipient's wallet address over the blockchain. The Stellar ledger records this transaction.
- After receiving USDC tokens, the recipient can redeem them for USD with the issuer. A USD equivalent is returned to the recipient's bank account.

Objectives and outcome are shown in Table 1.4.

1.4.4.3 Global Payments Benefits

- Processing almost in real time.
- Blockchain exchanges have become much cheaper since middlemen have been taken out.

Table 1.4 Few Industry Case Studies of Global Payments

Firms Involved	Objectives	Outcome	Year
Stellar Block Chain + Circles USDC + Felix WhatsApp-based payments platform	Use USDC as a SWIFT alternative For cross-border payment to Mexico	Speed of transaction Reduced remittance fee B2C payments	2021
Stellar Blockchain + Bitso Cryptocurrency + Felix WhatsApp-based payments platform	Cross-border payments to Latin America	Near real-time settlement Remittance much more quickly and affordably than before B2B and B2C payments	2022
Solana Pay + Solana Blockchain + Circles USDC	Real-time global sales	Cost-effective sale to a global audience Near real-time settlement	2023

- Makes records clear and easy to check as all transactions and data are timestamped and saved automatically.
- Smart contracts use public-private cryptography, data hashing, multi-party authorization, and fraud detection make international transfers safe.

1.4.5 Credit Scoring

1.4.5.1 Business Requirement

Traditional credit scoring models have faced challenges due to digitalization and cyber-attacks. These include unfair accessibility, score manipulation, incorrect data, migration issues, and data breaches. Traditional scoring relies on historical loan data, which may not be suitable for newcomers or those in need of credit. Credit bureaus are transparent about their scores, but this can lead to people manipulating them to appear more risky. Additionally, migration issues arise due to the disconnect between credit bureaus, such as Equifax, Experian, and TransUnion. Data breaches, such as Equifax's 2017 data breach, have highlighted the need for decentralized systems like blockchain to address these issues as shown in Figure 1.10.

1.4.5.2 Solution

- A blockchain smart contract implements credit scoring logic and rules. It can validate data, save credit ratings, and use credit scoring algorithms.
- The credit scoring solution combine external data sources like bank transactions, payment history, and identity verification data.

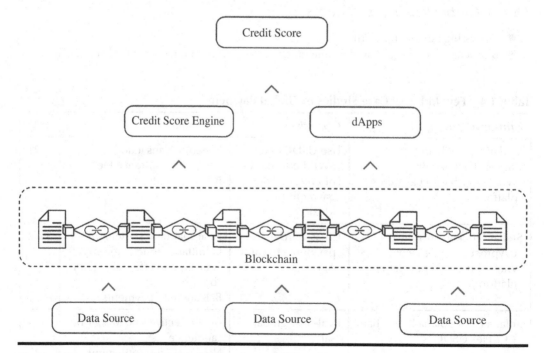

Figure 1.10   Blockchain-based credit scoring workflow.

Table 1.5 Few Industry Case Studies of Credit Scoring

Firms Involved	Objectives	Outcome	Year
Agricultural and Commercial Bank of Zhejiang + Aves Lair	Extending banking services to the unbanked and underbanked	Security and transparency Smart algorithms Efficiency	2021
TransUnion, Spring Labs, and Quadrata	Make consumer credit more accessible to those who did not have it before by establishing a more inclusive lending environment	Decentralization minimizes reliance on single entities prone to bias or failure Transactions are recorded on a distributed ledger visible to all participants, eliminating the need for intermediaries	2023

- Credit scoring engine processes external data and uses credit scoring algorithms to provide credit scores.
- The credit scoring solution assigns creditworthiness scores to individuals or companies. The dApp lets users access these blockchain-stored scores.

1.4.5.3 Benefits of Blockchain Credit Score

- Decentralized credit scoring on enterprise blockchain reduces the risk of data breaches and improves transparency by allowing borrowers to access their actual credit reports without external agencies.
- Allows for better control over their data for borrowers and credit bureaus to access their data.
- The potential to credit the unbanked and underbanked, enabling them to obtain credit scores without prior credit history and access lending services.
- Eliminates migration issues, as it is not based on geography, allowing individuals to migrate to any country without fear of resetting their credit scores.

Objectives and outcome are shown in Table 1.5.

1.4.6 Fundraising with Initial Coin Offering (ICO)

1.4.6.1 Business Requirement

Raising seed capital from private investors, pitching to venture capital (VC) funds, or attempting crowdfunding all present significant challenges for entrepreneurs. Private investors often perceive early-stage investments as high-risk, leading to difficulties in reaching them. Negotiating terms and undergoing due diligence processes add complexity to the fundraising process. Pitching to VC funds involves competition, high expectations, a lengthy sales cycle, and potential loss of control. Crowdfunding platforms have unique requirements, fee structures, and audience demographics, necessitating careful selection. Effective marketing, regulatory compliance, and ongoing communication with backers are crucial for crowdfunding success. Despite these obstacles, entrepreneurs must navigate them adeptly to enhance their fundraising prospects as shown in Figure 1.11.

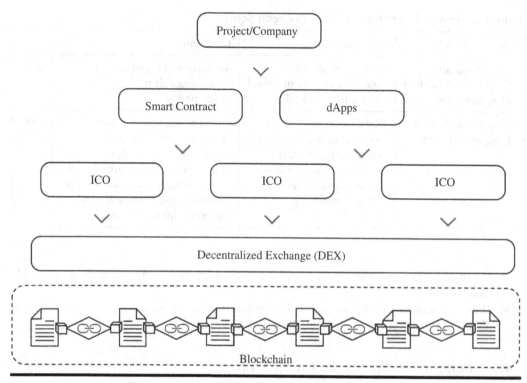

Figure 1.11 Blockchain-based investment and fundraising.

1.4.6.2 Solutions

- A company creates ICO with the help of smart contracts on a blockchain platform.
- A company builds a new dApp (project) on the blockchain platform to get money for its new business.
- It starts an ICO with a set number of ICO tokens, which could be any new token made by a dApp, or utility tokens in this case.
- People who want to invest can use the dApp to send their cryptocurrencies and receive ICO coins, which raises money for the project.

1.4.6.3 Benefits of ICO

- People can buy tokens in an ICO without giving their names, and those coins can be sold to anyone.
- Tokens can be bought and sold all over the world. An ICO lets buyers from all over the world help make a new currency.
- In a global market that works around the clock, this value could be traded for anything. One thing that can be sold quickly, though, are tokens.
- Lessened barriers for token launches because they can happen anywhere in the world.
- An option to buy right away, there is no one standing between people who want to buy or sell coins.
- The investment process is quick and easy for both companies and investors.

1.5 Highlights of Digital Identity Adoption

1.5.1 Estonia

Estonia is internationally recognized as a prominent pioneer in digital innovation, demonstrating a carefully crafted digital identification system renowned for its high-level security and effectiveness. The Estonian digital identification system, known as eID, has been operational for two decades and provides more than 600 electronic services to its inhabitants and 2,400 services to enterprises. Users can utilize a diverse array of features, such as bill payments, voting, and prescription management, thanks to the implementation of blockchain technology and the integration of biometric systems, which enhance the security and reliability of data.

Since 2014, Estonia has implemented a scheme called e-Residency, which enables anyone from any location to become e-residents. As per the Estonian government, 99% of the populace possesses a digital ID, and more than 1 billion digital signatures have been executed thus far, resulting in a presumed annual time savings of five days.

1.5.2 Singapore

The National Digital Identity (NDI) system in Singapore exemplifies advanced technology integration and was initially implemented to enhance convenience and security for people during online transactions.

Introduced in 2003, and supported by Singpass technology, the platform enables users to connect with more than 700 government organizations and commercial sector services, establishing a reliable and interconnected system.

Individuals have the ability to electronically sign documents, receive crucial notifications, and engage in financial planning. This is made possible through a significant integration with MyInfo, which enables effortless interchange of information across various government entities, resulting in a reduction of administrative tasks. People can also confirm their identity and conveniently use services through facial recognition, digital identification cards, and QR codes, with approximately 97% of the population now utilizing the Singpass application.

1.5.3 India

Aadhaar, named after the Hindi word for "foundation," is India's significant step toward implementing a digital identification system. Aadhaar, a 12-digit individual identification number, is issued by the Unique Identification Authority of India (UIDAI) on behalf of the Government of India. It serves as a valid proof of identity and residence for individuals across the country. The system has many identifying capabilities, including the collection of three forms of biometric data: fingerprints, iris scans, and facial pictures. These data are then kept in a centralized database.

Although optional, Aadhaar was initially introduced as a measure to reduce fraudulent activities, inefficiency, and misuse in social welfare programs, granting a substantial section of the population a universally recognized identification document in India. Currently, it has broadened its scope to facilitate customers' convenient access to government services, as well as those provided by organizations like banks and mobile phone providers. The Aadhaar card, which is available in both physical and digital formats, is currently the most extensively utilized digital identification globally, with a total of 1.3 billion cards issued to date.

1.5.4 Sweden

The primary component of Sweden's digital identity infrastructure is the BankID system, which serves as an electronic ID verification service akin to a digital passport or driving license. It enables a range of online transactions, including bank account creation, contract signing, tax filings, and COVID-19 vaccine booking.

The BankID system is a collaborative effort by seven Scandinavian banks, demonstrating a collective approach to adopting digital identity verification. The system is set to progress and has already made arrangements to implement a digital ID card that can be accessed using QR codes. Swedish individuals will be able to save and use this card on their smartphones. So far, the system has been utilized 6.7 billion times by over 8 million users, indicating that about 99.2% of Swedish citizens possess a BankID, demonstrating a significant level of adoption among the population.

1.5.5 Belgium

In 2003, Belgium initiated its exploration of digital identification through the implementation of the Belgian Personal Identity Card Project (BelPIC). By 2020, the number of national ID cards issued in the country had reached an anticipated 28 million. Since the introduction of electronic ID cards in 2021, the distribution has been increasing at a rate of over 2 million cards each year. There are three different types of electronic ID cards available: the national ID card, the Kids-ID for children under 12, and the electronic foreigner's card. An electronic signature and authenticity certificate are included into the national ID card, making it a key to all things digital.

In addition to this digital proposal, Belgium has also adopted mobile identification through the implementation of the "itsme Mobile ID scheme." This sophisticated mobile authentication system streamlines access to internet services by implementing a unified sign-up and login procedure. The application has shown consistent user expansion, with a notable increase from 350,000 users per year since its inception in 2018, reaching a total of 6.7 million users by March 2023. The usual user uses this approach six times per month for banking and three times per month for e-government transactions.

1.5.6 Denmark

Denmark initially implemented its digital identification system known as NemID, which is translated as "Easy-ID" in English. Functioning as a universal digital key, it enabled citizens to easily access a diverse range of services in both the public and private sectors, aligning with Denmark's goal of implementing a "one key for all" approach. The system was gradually discontinued in October 2021 to align with a digital-first strategy and make way for a new solution known as MitID.

MitID is designed to provide universal access, making it useful for online banking, taxes processes, and dealings with the public sector. MitID eliminates the requirement for a physical card, instead opting for unique login codes to establish a digital-focused identifying system. This allows users to decide whether to carry a physical or digital ID on their mobile devices. Currently, the national electronic identification (eID) is utilized by over 90% of the population.

1.5.7 The Netherlands

With DigiD and eHerkenning, the two primary systems in the Netherlands, the country has adopted a dual strategy for digital identity. Similar to a digital passport or driver's license, DigiD is a publicly available technology that enables citizens to quickly communicate with government agencies. Every citizen who requests a DigiD is assigned a unique identification number, which is linked to a username and password, along with a range of verification mechanisms that guarantee secure access to confidential information. In addition to checking the status of pension or health insurance, this system lets users complete tax returns and apply for government benefits (SSI, 2022).

In contrast, eHerkenning acts as a go-between public and private services and is thus tailored to organizations. It allows for comprehensive identification verification and assurance and allows businesses to provide secure online services to their customers. While eHerkenning had 13.3 million logins every year and 500 affiliated service providers, DigiD serviced 15 million citizens in 2019.

1.5.8 Nigeria

Like India, Nigeria implemented a system to address the absence of a formal identification among a significant percentage of its people. Nevertheless, their current approach is characterized by fragmentation and lacks coherence. The National Identification Number (NIN) is a compulsory requirement for most transactions in Nigeria and serves as the central component of their ecosystem, led by the National Identity Management Commission (NIMC). In addition, banking customers are assigned a Bank Verification Number (BVN) as a means of authentication.

The process of establishing a complete digital identification system in Nigeria commenced in 2014. According to the most recent data, about 100 million Nigerians have been enrolled for a NIN, while 58 million individuals possess a BVN. According to reports, the effort has faced several obstacles, such as financial and operational difficulties. The absence of a standardized procedure has hindered the pace of advancement, falling short of initial expectations.

1.6 Challenges and Limitations

The following are several of the primary challenges of digital identity and blockchain technology in banking and financial services.

- Banking and financial services industry is subject to extensive regulation, and the implementation of blockchain technology could potentially face regulatory examination.
- Standardization among all stakeholders is imperative for the successful implementation of blockchain technology. This entails the establishment of shared protocols, data formats, and interfaces.
- Interoperability is a critical requirement for diverse blockchain networks to operate in tandem and realize the full potential of blockchain technology. However, at present, a universally acknowledged standard for interoperability does not exist, and the integration of various blockchain platforms may be complicated due to the existence of distinct protocols.
- Due to the novelty of blockchain technology, scaling it up to accommodate high volumes of transactions can be difficult. This can be especially difficult, where large volumes of transactions must frequently be processed rapidly.
- Banking and finance involve sensitive and confidential information, and data security and privacy concerns may arise. Protecting blockchain networks from intrusion and keeping sensitive information safe is of the utmost importance.

- ◼ Stakeholder education regarding the advantages of blockchain technology and its potential integration into established banking and finance procedures is of the utmost importance (Khang, Muthmainnah et al., 2023).
- ◼ SSI is a revolutionary concept in the digital domain, allowing users to securely manage their personal information and credentials. Wallet interoperability is a fundamental principle of SSI, enabling the transfer of VCs and identity data among various SSI wallets. However, challenges remain, such as standardization initiatives, vendor retention, and user acceptance (Khang, 2024).

These challenges may be effectively tackled by fostering collaboration among diverse industry stakeholders and establishing standardized protocols and practices.

1.7 Conclusion

Blockchain technology is gaining significant attention as it complements the privacy and permissions of payments systems. Banks are prioritizing digital ledger technology (DLT) to improve clearing and settlement processes, particularly in complex multiparty transactions. DLT can also enhance transparency and efficiency in compliance with KYC obligations. However, policy issues remain. DLT will integrate with other technologies like advanced analytics and data analytics, but banks believe disruption should not be drastic. Industry leaders view DLT as a component of the solution, working with the internet of things and artificial intelligence to solve cross-platform interoperability challenges (DKYC, 2020).

SSI will evolve with interoperability, enabling users to navigate the digital environment with increased confidence, authority, and confidentiality. Interoperability is essential for a decentralized and user-centric SSI ecosystem, allowing individuals to choose the wallet that best suits their needs and preferences. It also promotes market expansion and reduced friction between service recipients and providers.

Interoperability is achieved through conformity with technical standards and protocols, such as the VC data model, DIDs, and protocols for credential presentation. These mechanisms enhance efficiency and security by allowing wallets to exchange credentials and data directly, bypassing intermediaries. Despite these obstacles, initiatives like the Credentials Community Group's standards for VCs, the DID Foundation's advocacy for DIDs, and the SSI Interoperability Alliance are working to address these issues (Khang, Rath et al., 2024).

1.8 Future of Work

1.8.1 Popularity of Stablecoins

Stablecoins are a growing trend in the blockchain market, combining the benefits of crypto and fiat currencies. They are blockchain-based coins with a 1:1 ratio to traditional currencies and can be backed by commodities like gold or oil. The rapid growth of stablecoins indicates a strong blockchain trend.

1.8.2 Focus on Enterprises Blockchain

Permissioned blockchain is primarily appealing to businesses because it restricts network access to authorized users, in this instance, company employees. Additionally, permissioned blockchain-based systems offer an access control feature, allowing for role-based and modifiable access to specific documents and data.

Businesses that opt to adopt enterprise blockchain technology benefit from heightened levels of security, transparency, workflow automation, and increased operational efficiency.

1.8.3 Changing Banking with DeFi Apps

DeFi, or Decentralized Finance, is revolutionizing traditional financial services by relocating them to blockchain. DeFi products provide barrier-free entry options, offering alternative savings, lending, secure payments, staking, cryptocurrency trading, affordable insurance, and asset tokenization. These platforms may outperform banks due to direct user interaction without intermediaries.

1.8.4 STOs: Rising Bond Tokenization

STOs are not new to crypto, but there has been a lot of spotlight on them. STOs are efficient and regulated ways to invest and raise cash, and the blockchain records all processes. Cryptographic security tokens are backed by bonds, business equities, real estate, and autos. Securities laws apply to them as investments.

1.8.5 Tokenizing Assets with Ethereum

Ethereum powers several blockchain initiatives, platforms, solutions, and coins. Due to the fact that its ERC-20 and ERC-721 token protocols are the most frequently used, asset tokenization and STOs have a significant impact on Ethereum's popularity. The former permits fungible tokens such as digital currency and voting tokens, whereas the latter permits non-fungible tokens.

1.8.6 Interest in Central Bank Digital Currencies (CBDCs)

Central Bank Digital Currency (CBDC) is a digital representation of a nation's fiat currency, typically guaranteed by the central bank and regulated by a central authority. Currently in its infancy, 86% of central banks are investigating its potential, 60% are experimenting, and 14% plan to initiate pilot programs.

1.8.7 Blockchain for Digital Identity Protection

Digital identification cards have gained popularity in recent years, with blockchain-based pilot programs in Japan, Switzerland, and Estonia. The COVID-19 pandemic has accelerated the need for eIDs, with a study predicting a 6.2 billion active eID application by 2025. Blockchain technology is expected to be crucial for eIDs, ensuring secure storage, exchange, transparency, trust, and data access, positively impacting the digital economy (Digital Identity, 2020).

1.8.8 Blockchain-as-a-Service (BaaS)

The blockchain-as-a service model is a cloud service used by established businesses and startups to design and manage smart contracts and decentralized applications using blockchain technology, allowing them to access software without significant upfront investment.

Credit Authorship Contribution Statement
Resources: Vittal Jadhav and Alex Khang
Contribution:

- Vittal Jadhav: Writing – Review & Editing.
- Alex Khang: Writing – Review & Editing, and Supervision.

References

Digital Identity. (2020). www.fatf-gafi.org

DKYC (2020). Digitizing KYC Processes. (n.d.). https://blockapps.net/use-cases/digitizing-kyc-processes/

Evernym. (2018). What is self-sovereign identity? https://www.evernym.com/what-is-self-sovereign-identity/

Ferdous, M. S., Chowdhury, F., & Alassafi, M. O. (2019). In search of self-sovereign identity leveraging blockchain technology. IEEE Access, 7, 103059–103079. https://doi.org/10.1109/ACCESS.2019.2931173

Khang, A. (Ed.). (2024). Applications and Principles of Quantum Computing. IGI Global. https://doi.org/10.4018/979-8-3693-1168-4

Khang, A., Hajimahmud, V. A., Alyar, A. V., Khalilov, M., Ragimova, N. A., & Niu, Y. (2024). Introduction to quantum computing and its integration applications. In Khang A. (Ed.), Applications and Principles of Quantum Computing (pp. 25–45). IGI Global. https://doi.org/10.4018/979-8-3693-1168-4.ch002

Khang, A., Chowdhury, S., & Sharma, S., (1st Ed.) (2022). The Data-Driven Blockchain Ecosystem: Fundamentals, Applications, and Emerging Technologies. CRC Press. https://doi.org/10.1201/9781003269281

Khang, A., Muthmainnah, M., Seraj, P. M., Al Yakin, A., & Obaid, A. J. (2023). AI-aided teaching model in Education 5.0. In Khang A., Shah V., & Rani S. (Eds.), Handbook of Research on AI-Based Technologies and Applications in the Era of the Metaverse (pp. 83–104). IGI Global. https://doi.org/10.4018/978-1-6684-8851-5.ch004

Khang, A., Rath, K. C., Panda, N., & Kumar, A. (2024). Quantum mechanics primer: Fundamentals and quantum computing. In Khang A. (Ed.), Applications and Principles of Quantum Computing (pp. 1–24). IGI Global. https://doi.org/10.4018/979-8-3693-1168-4.ch001

Khang, A., Rath, K. C., Satapathy, S. K., Kumar, A., Das, S. R., & Panda, M. R. (2023). Enabling the future of manufacturing: Integration of robotics and IoT to smart factory Infrastructure in Industry 4.0. In Khang A., Shah V., & Rani S. (Eds.), Handbook of Research on AI-Based Technologies and Applications in the Era of the Metaverse (pp. 25–50). IGI Global. https://doi.org/10.4018/978-1-6684-8851-5.ch002

Khang, A., Shah, V., & Rani, S. (Eds.). (2023). Handbook of Research on AI-Based Technologies and Applications in the Era of the Metaverse. IGI Global. https://doi.org/10.4018/978-1-6684-8851-5

Khanh, H. H., & Khang, A., The role of artificial intelligence in blockchain applications. In Rana G, Khang A., Sharma R., Goel A. K., Dubey A. K., Reinventing Manufacturing and Business Processes Through Artificial Intelligence, 2 (20–40). (2021). CRC Press. https://doi.org/10.1201/9781003145011-2

KYC (2024). Know Your Customer (KYC) System on Blockchain for Banks | Case Study https://www.infopulse.com/case-studies/know-your-customer-kyc-system-on-blockchain-for-banks 2/5. (n.d.). https://www.infopulse.com/case-studies/know-your-customer-kyc-system-on-blockchain-for-banks

SSI (2022). SSI Essentials: A crash course on Digital ID Wallets. https://gataca.io/blog/ssi-essentials-a-crash-course-on-digital-id-wallets/

Zook, M., & Grote, M. H. (2022). Blockchain financial geographies: Disrupting space,

Chapter 2

Quantum Computing and Portfolio Optimization in Finance Services

Alex Khang, Kali Charan Rath, Karteek Madapana, Jagannadha Rao, Lakshmi Prasad Panda, and Subhasish Das

2.1 Introduction

Quantum computing in finance services and portfolio optimization represents a transformative frontier, leveraging the principles of quantum mechanics to revolutionize traditional computational paradigms. By harnessing the unique properties of quantum bits (qubits), such as superposition and entanglement, quantum computers can exponentially increase processing power and solve complex optimization problems at unparalleled speeds.

In the financial sector, quantum computing holds the potential to revolutionize risk assessment, portfolio optimization, and derivative pricing, providing unprecedented efficiency in handling vast datasets and intricate calculations (Covers & Doeland, 2020; Egger et al., 2020). This emerging field signifies a paradigm shift in computational capabilities, offering the promise of solving complex financial problems that were once deemed intractable for classical computers, ultimately reshaping the landscape of quantitative finance and portfolio optimization strategies (Asch et al., 2018).

2.1.1 Purpose and Scope of the Quantum Computing in Finance Services and Portfolio Optimization

Quantum computing holds significant promise in the realm of finance services and portfolio optimization by offering the potential to solve complex problems at speeds that classical computers struggle to achieve. In finance, quantum computing can revolutionize portfolio optimization, risk management, and option pricing. Its ability to process vast amounts of data and perform complex calculations simultaneously enables more accurate modeling of financial markets, leading

DOI: 10.4324/9781003501947-2

to improved investment strategies and risk assessment. Quantum algorithms, such as Shor's algorithm, also pose a threat to classical cryptographic methods, prompting the need for quantum-resistant encryption in financial transactions (Lindsay, 2020; Rosch-Grace & Straub, 2022).

The scope of quantum computing in optimization extends beyond traditional financial applications to various industries where complex optimization problems are prevalent. Quantum algorithms, like the Quantum Approximate Optimization Algorithm (QAOA), show promise in solving combinatorial optimization problems, such as supply chain optimization, logistics planning, and resource allocation. By harnessing quantum parallelism and entanglement, quantum computers have the potential to provide solutions to optimization challenges that were previously computationally intractable, leading to more efficient and cost-effective operations across diverse sectors (Prakash, 2023; Rasool et al., 2023) As quantum computing technology advances, its impact on financial modeling and optimization strategies is expected to reshape the landscape of decision-making processes in both the financial and broader business domains.

2.1.2 Objectives of the Quantum Computing in Finance Services and Portfolio Optimization

The objective of this chapter is to delve into the synergies between quantum computing, finance, and optimization, showcasing the transformative potential of quantum technology in reshaping conventional financial paradigms and addressing intricate optimization challenges prevalent in diverse financial domains. The chapter aims to offer readers a comprehensive overview of the foundational principles of quantum computing, emphasizing its applications and impact on the fields of finance services and portfolio optimization. It explores the practical implementation of quantum algorithms to tackle key financial tasks, including portfolio optimization, option pricing, risk analysis, and algorithmic trading (Khang, 2023).

Moreover, the chapter is designed to highlight the nuanced landscape of opportunities and challenges that arise with the integration of quantum computing in finance. It specifically addresses the necessity for quantum-safe cryptography in financial transactions and explores the potential of quantum-inspired classical algorithms as complementary tools. By providing a holistic introduction, the chapter caters to a diverse audience, including researchers, practitioners, and enthusiasts, aiming to foster a nuanced understanding of how quantum computing stands to revolutionize decision-making processes and problem-solving approaches in the intricate realms of finance services and portfolio optimization.

2.2 Background and Context

In the context of this chapter, the background encompasses the evolving landscape at the intersection of quantum computing, finance, and optimization. The advent of quantum computing technology has ushered in a new era of computational possibilities, challenging traditional methods and opening avenues for innovation. Within the financial domain, the chapter recognizes the increasing complexity of tasks such as portfolio optimization and risk analysis, prompting the exploration of quantum algorithms as a means to enhance computational efficiency.

The integration of quantum computing principles into financial models also introduces novel approaches to longstanding challenges in option pricing and algorithmic trading. In the broader context of optimization, the chapter acknowledges the limitations of classical computing in addressing intricate problems inherent in various financial domains. Against this backdrop, the chapter seeks to provide readers with a comprehensive understanding of the background forces driving the convergence of quantum computing, finance, and optimization, laying the foundation for an exploration of the transformative potential and challenges that this intersection presents.

2.2.1 Relevance of Quantum Computing in Finance Services and Portfolio Optimization

The relevance of quantum computing in the realms of finance services and portfolio optimization stems from the inherent computational challenges faced by classical systems in tackling complex problems. As financial models grow in sophistication, the limitations of traditional computing become more apparent, especially in tasks like portfolio optimization, risk analysis, and option pricing. Quantum computing offers a paradigm shift by harnessing the principles of superposition and entanglement, enabling the simultaneous exploration of multiple possibilities. This capability is particularly advantageous in addressing combinatorial optimization problems prevalent in finance, where classical computers often encounter scalability issues.

The potential acceleration of these computations through quantum algorithms not only enhances the speed of decision-making processes but also opens avenues for refining investment strategies and risk management. Additionally, as quantum computers advance, their impact on cryptographic methods raises the relevance of exploring quantum-safe encryption in financial transactions. In essence, the relevance of quantum computing in finance services and portfolio optimization lies in its capacity to overcome classical computing limitations, offering a transformative approach to problem-solving in domains where efficiency and precision are paramount (Gomes et al., 2022; Herman et al., 2023; Marzec, 2016).

2.2.2 Current Challenges in Quantum Finance Services and Portfolio Optimization

Here are some important points addressing the current challenges in quantum finance services and portfolio optimization:

2.2.2.1 Quantum Finance

- Limited understanding and development of quantum financial models.
- Lack of standardized quantum finance frameworks and methodologies.
- Difficulty in integrating quantum algorithms with classical financial systems.
- Insufficient quantum hardware capabilities for complex financial simulations.
- Challenges in accurately pricing financial instruments using quantum algorithms.
- Uncertainty and volatility in quantum financial markets.
- Limited availability of quantum datasets for training and testing quantum financial models.

2.2.2.2 Quantum Optimization

- Complexity in designing and implementing quantum optimization algorithms.
- Limited scalability of current quantum optimization solutions for large datasets.
- Challenges in efficiently solving combinatorial optimization problems using quantum computers.

- Susceptibility to errors and noise in quantum hardware affecting optimization results.
- Lack of standardized benchmarks for evaluating the performance of quantum optimization algorithms.
- Limited accessibility to quantum computing resources for researchers and practitioners.
- High resource requirements for implementing quantum optimization algorithms, both in terms of qubits and gate operations.

Addressing these challenges requires collaboration between quantum physicists, mathematicians, and financial experts, along with advancements in quantum hardware and algorithm development.

2.3 Problem Statement

Quantum Finance represents an innovative intersection between quantum computing and financial optimization, heralding a transformative era in the world of finance. This groundbreaking field harnesses the computational power of quantum mechanics to solve complex financial problems with unprecedented efficiency. By leveraging quantum algorithms, it enables the exploration of intricate financial models, risk assessments, and portfolio optimizations at speeds unattainable by classical computers.

The marriage of quantum computing and finance not only promises to revolutionize traditional investment strategies but also opens avenues for the development of novel financial instruments and risk management techniques. As quantum technologies continue to advance, Quantum Finance emerges as a frontier where the principles of quantum mechanics converge with the intricacies of financial markets, paving the way for a new era of precision and agility in financial decision-making (Khang & Rath, 2023).

2.3.1 Description of the Quantum Finance Services and Portfolio Optimization Problem

2.3.1.1 Case Problem: Quantum Optimization for Supply Chain Cost Reduction in the Automobile Sector

In the automobile sector, efficient supply chain management is crucial for cost reduction. Quantum computing techniques can be employed to optimize the supply chain network. Consider the following numerical data for a hypothetical automobile company as shown in Table 2.1.

Objective

Minimize the total cost of the supply chain while considering lead time and a quantum factor that represents the reliability of the supplier.

Model

The mathematical model for the optimization problem can be formulated as a linear programming problem. Let's denote the decision variables as x_i representing the quantity to order from supplier i. The objective is to minimize the total cost of the supply chain, subject to constraints on lead time and the quantum factor. The mathematical model is as follows:

Decision Variables

- $x_i \geq 0$, for each supplier i

Table 2.1   The Numerical Data for a Hypothetical Automobile Company

Supplier	Cost ($)	Lead Time (days)	Quantum Factor
A	100000	10	0.8
B	120000	15	0.9
C	80000	8	0.7
D	150000	20	1
E	90000	12	0.85
F	110000	18	0.95
G	130000	22	1.1
H	95000	14	0.88
I	105000	16	0.92
J	140000	25	1.15
K	115000	17	0.93
L	125000	21	1.05
M	135000	23	1.12
N	98000	13	0.87
O	145000	24	1.18

Objective Function

- Minimize the total cost:
- Minimize $Z = \sum_{i=1}^{15} Cost_i \cdot x_i$

Constraints

- Lead time constraint: $\sum_{i=1}^{15} lead\_time_i \cdot x_i \leq 20$
- Quantum factor constraint: $quantum\_factor_i \cdot x_i \geq 0.9$, for each supplier i
- Non-negativity constraint: $x_i \geq 0$, for each supplier i

Formally

- Minimize $Z = \sum_{i=1}^{15} Cost_i \cdot x_i$
- Subject to: $\sum_{i=1}^{15} lead\_time_i \cdot x_i \leq 20$
- $quantum\_factor_i \cdot x_i \geq 0.9$, for each supplier i
- $x_i \geq 0$, for each supplier i
- Here, t_i, $lead\_time_i$, and $quantum\_factor_i$ represent the cost, lead time, and quantum factor for supplier i, respectively. The decision variables x_i represent the quantity to order from each supplier.

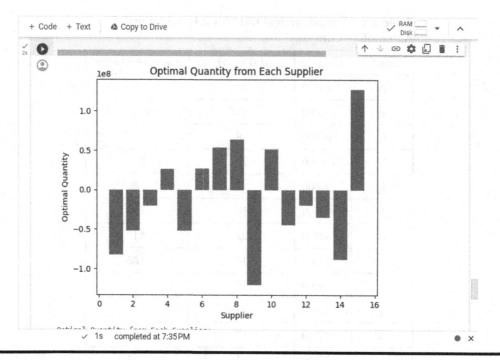

Figure 2.1   Optimal quality vs. supplier.

The objective is to minimize the total cost while meeting the lead time and quantum factor constraints as shown in Figure 2.1.

The algorithm uses the Sequential Least Squares Quadratic Programming (SLSQP) method, which is suitable for constrained optimization problems. The minimize function finds the optimal solution that minimizes the total cost while satisfying the lead time and quantum factor constraints.

2.3.1.2 Optimal Quantity from Each Supplier

A: -82517187.82; B: -52100800.27; C: -20459712.69; D: 26035806.00; E: -52156612.30; F: 27196115.91; G: 53934950.41; H: 64078323.06; I: -120479153.72; J: 51328387.33; K: -44715327.36; L: -19706894.35; M: -34748218.64; N: -87771291.13; O: 127542802.03

Therefore, the total Cost of the Supply Chain: -8707610149853.816

2.3.1.3 Result Discussion – Technical Analysis

The generated bar graph illustrates the technical outcomes of the quantum optimization model applied to the automobile sector's supply chain. The discussion below delves into the technical aspects of the output graph:

■ Optimal Ordering Quantities: The heights of the bars in the graph represent the optimal quantities to be ordered from each supplier. These quantities are determined by the quantum optimization algorithm, which seeks to minimize the total cost while adhering to lead time and quantum factor constraints.

- Quantum Factor Constraints: The influence of quantum factors is evident in the ordering decisions. Suppliers with quantum factors below the specified threshold of 0.9 are allocated reduced order quantities. The algorithm ensures that the reliability of the suppliers, as indicated by the quantum factor, is maintained above the defined level.
- Lead Time Sensitivity: The optimization model takes into account lead time constraints to enhance supply chain efficiency. The resulting distribution reflects a preference for suppliers with shorter lead times, contributing to a more responsive and agile procurement strategy.
- Objective Function Minimization: The primary objective of the optimization model is to minimize the total cost of the supply chain. The graph demonstrates the success of the algorithm in achieving this goal by distributing optimal quantities that collectively contribute to cost reduction.
- Solver Performance: The efficiency of the optimization solver, in this case, the SciPy optimize and minimize function are crucial. Examination of convergence behavior and solution stability ensures the reliability of the obtained results.
- Sensitivity Analysis: The model's responsiveness to changes in quantum factors is a critical technical aspect. Small adjustments in quantum factors may lead to noticeable shifts in optimal ordering quantities, highlighting the sensitivity of the solution to supplier reliability.
- Algorithmic Considerations: Technical discussions should touch upon the algorithmic intricacies, such as the choice of optimization algorithm, convergence criteria, and any specific parameters fine-tuned for this problem. The robustness and scalability of the chosen algorithm impact its applicability to larger-scale supply chain scenarios.
- Visualization Quality: The clarity and interpretability of the bar graph contribute to effective communication of the results. Considerations regarding axis scaling, labeling, and color choices influence the technical and non-technical audience's understanding of the optimization outcomes.
- Verification and Validation: The technical discussion should address the verification and validation processes applied to ensure the correctness of the mathematical model, data input, and the implementation of the optimization algorithm.

2.3.2 Potential Benefits of Quantum Computing

Quantum computing holds immense potential in transforming various industries, and the financial sector is no exception. Here are ten potential benefits of quantum computing in finance, with a focus on the manufacturing industry as a case study:

- Optimized Supply Chain Management: Quantum computing can enhance supply chain optimization by efficiently analyzing vast datasets. For instance, in the manufacturing industry, quantum algorithms could optimize the procurement process by considering multiple variables simultaneously, leading to cost savings and improved efficiency (Garcia & You, 2015; Mansouri, Gallear, & Askariazad, 2012).
- Risk Assessment and Management: Quantum computing's ability to process complex calculations at unprecedented speeds can revolutionize risk assessment models. Financial institutions in manufacturing can use quantum algorithms to assess and mitigate risks associated with market fluctuations, supply chain disruptions, and other variables affecting their operations (Bayerstadler et al., 2021; Majot & Yampolskiy, 2015).
- Portfolio Optimization: Quantum computing enables more accurate and rapid portfolio optimization by evaluating countless investment combinations simultaneously. Manufacturing

companies managing diverse portfolios can benefit from quantum algorithms that provide real-time insights, ensuring optimal resource allocation for maximum returns.

- Fraud Detection and Prevention: Quantum computing's advanced processing capabilities can strengthen fraud detection systems in finance. For example, in manufacturing finance, real-time analysis of transactions and supply chain activities can identify anomalies and potential fraud patterns more effectively, safeguarding financial assets (Grossi et al., 2022; Hu et al., 2017).

- Credit Scoring Enhancement: Quantum computing can revolutionize credit scoring models by processing a multitude of factors simultaneously. For manufacturing companies seeking financial support, this could mean more accurate credit assessments, fostering better relationships with financial institutions and improving access to capital.

- Algorithmic Trading Optimization: Quantum computing can significantly enhance algorithmic trading strategies. In the manufacturing finance sector, quantum algorithms can process vast amounts of market data in real-time, leading to more informed and rapid trading decisions for optimizing investments and returns.

- Simulation for Risk Modeling: Quantum computing's ability to handle complex simulations can aid in developing more accurate risk models. Manufacturing companies can leverage this capability to simulate various scenarios, helping them proactively identify and mitigate potential financial risks (Hassija et al., 2020; Rosch-Grace & Straub, 2022).

- Energy Cost Optimization: Quantum computing can contribute to cost optimization by tackling complex energy consumption models. In manufacturing finance, quantum algorithms can analyze and optimize energy usage across the production process, leading to significant cost savings and environmental benefits.

- Enhanced Cryptography for Security: As quantum computers can potentially break existing cryptographic methods, their application in finance includes developing quantum-resistant cryptography. This is crucial for securing sensitive financial information in manufacturing transactions and communications.

- Time-Series Analysis for Forecasting: Quantum computing's prowess in handling vast datasets makes it ideal for time-series analysis. In manufacturing finance, this capability can be applied to predict future market trends, enabling companies to make informed financial decisions and stay ahead of the competition.

2.3.3 Selection of Quantum Computing Framework and Tools

Choosing the right quantum computing framework and tools in finance is a critical decision that can significantly impact the effectiveness of quantum applications. Here are important considerations and explanations for the selection process:

- Algorithm Compatibility: Selecting a quantum computing framework involves considering its compatibility with financial algorithms. Different frameworks excel in specific algorithmic implementations. For instance, frameworks like Qiskit and Cirq are known for their flexibility in implementing various quantum algorithms relevant to finance, such as quantum optimization and machine learning.

- Scalability: The scalability of a quantum computing framework is crucial for financial applications, where the complexity of computations can be extensive. Frameworks that offer scalability provide the ability to handle larger datasets and more complex financial models, ensuring that the quantum solution can grow with the evolving needs of the finance sector.

■ Integration with Classical Systems: The seamless integration of quantum computing with classical systems is essential for the finance industry. Choosing a framework that allows for easy integration with existing financial software and infrastructure facilitates a smoother transition into quantum-enhanced applications. Rigetti Computing's Forest, for example, provides tools for hybrid quantum-classical computing.

■ Community Support and Documentation: Opting for a quantum computing framework with a strong community support system and comprehensive documentation is vital. A robust community ensures access to resources, knowledge-sharing, and timely issue resolution. IBM's Qiskit, for instance, benefits from a large and active community, offering a wealth of resources and support.

■ Gate Model vs. Quantum Annealing: Understanding the specific quantum computing model that aligns with financial use cases is crucial. Gate model quantum computing, like that offered by IBM and Rigetti, and is suitable for a wide range of algorithms, including optimization and machine learning. On the other hand, quantum annealing, as provided by D-Wave, may be more suitable for certain optimization problems.

■ Quantum Volume and Error Rates: Quantum volume is a metric that reflects a quantum computer's overall computational capability. Lower error rates are desirable for accurate and reliable results. Evaluating these metrics for different quantum computing frameworks ensures that the chosen tools can provide the necessary computational power with acceptable levels of error, especially in financial applications that demand precision.

■ Cost and Accessibility: Quantum computing can be resource-intensive, and the associated costs need to be considered. Some frameworks offer cloud-based solutions, allowing financial institutions to access quantum computing resources without the need for extensive on-site infrastructure. Rigetti and IBM, for example, provide cloud-based access to their quantum processors.

■ Security Features: Security is paramount in finance, and quantum computing frameworks should address potential security concerns. This includes features such as secure communication channels and protocols. Rigetti, for instance, has implemented features like Quantum Key Distribution (QKD) for enhanced security.

■ Interoperability with Quantum Hardware: Choosing a framework that aligns with emerging quantum hardware developments ensures future compatibility and scalability. As quantum hardware evolves, a framework that can easily adapt to newer technologies and architectures will be crucial for sustained success in financial quantum applications.

■ Training and Skill Development: The availability of educational resources and training programs for a specific quantum computing framework is essential. Ensuring that the finance team has the necessary skills to leverage the chosen tools effectively is vital for successful implementation. IBM's Qiskit, for example, provides extensive educational resources and training modules.

So, the selection of quantum computing frameworks and tools in finance requires a comprehensive evaluation of algorithm compatibility, scalability, integration capabilities, community support, quantum model alignment, error rates, cost, security features, interoperability, and training resources. By carefully considering these factors, financial institutions can make informed decisions that align with their specific quantum computing needs (Khang, Hajimahmud et al., 2023).

2.4 Mathematical Model Formulation to Optimize the Profit in an EV Manufacturing Industry

The automobile manufacturing industry is rapidly transitioning toward electric vehicles (EVs) to address environmental concerns. This case study explores the application of quantum computing in financial modeling and optimization for an EV manufacturing corporation.

Problem Statement: The company aims to optimize its supply chain, production processes, and financial decisions to maximize efficiency, minimize costs, and enhance overall performance.

Mathematical Model:

Let's consider a simplified mathematical model with 15 variables and values as shown in Table 2.2:

- X_1 = Number of raw materials purchased
- X_2 = Production volume of EVs
- X_3 = Number of workers in production
- X_4 = Energy consumption in manufacturing
- X_5 = Distribution cost
- X_6 = Marketing budget
- X_7 = Research and development investment
- X_8 = Raw material cost
- X_9 = Labor cost
- X_{10} = Energy cost
- X_{11} = Maintenance cost
- X_{12} = Revenue from EV sales

Table 2.2 The List of Variables and Their Values

Variable	Value
X1	1000
X2	500
X3	50
X4	2000
X5	100
X6	500
X7	200
X8	300
X9	150
X10	400
X11	50
X12	7500
X13	1000

- X_{13} = Tax expenses
- X_{14} = Profit
- X_{15} = Return on investment (ROI)

The objective is to maximize X_{14} (Profit) while satisfying various constraints.
Objective Function:

- Maximize Z = X_{14} (Maximize profit)

Subject to Constraints:

- Raw Material Constraints: X1 = 1000 (Numbers of raw material purchased)
- Production Volume Constraints: X2 = 500 (Production volume of EVs)
- Labor Constraints: X3 = 50 (Number of workers in production)
- Energy Consumption Constraints: X4 = 2000 (Energy consumption in manufacturing)
- Distribution Cost Constraints: X5 = 100 (Distribution cost)
- Marketing Budget Constraints: X6 = 500 (Marketing budget)
- Research and Development Constraints: X7 = 200 (Research and development investment)
- Cost Constraints: X8 = 300 (Raw material cost), X9 = 150 (Labor cost), X10 = 400 (Energy cost), X11 = 50 (Maintenance cost)
- Revenue Constraints: X12 = 7500 (Revenue from EV sales)
- Tax Expense Constraints: X13 = 1000 (Tax expenses)
- Non-Negativity Constraints:

X1, X2, X3, X4, X5, X6, X7, X8, X9, X10, X11, X12, X13, X14 ≥ 0
Quadratic Programming Formulation:
The objective function and constraints can be represented in the Quadratic Programming (QP) form as follows:

- Maximize $C^T x + X^T Q x$
- Subject to: $Ax \leq b$

Where:

- **c** is a vector representing the coefficients of the linear objective function.
- **x** is a vector of decision variables.
- **Q** is a matrix representing the coefficients of the quadratic objective function.
- **A** is a matrix representing the coefficients of the inequality constraints.
- **b** is a vector representing the right-hand side of the inequality constraints.

2.4.1 Comparison with Classical Approaches

Quantum computing has emerged as a revolutionary technology with the potential to transform various industries, and the financial sector is no exception. In this chapter, we explore the applications of quantum computing in finance services and portfolio optimization, comparing its capabilities with classical approaches. From risk management to portfolio optimization, quantum computing introduces novel methods that can outperform classical algorithms.

2.4.1.1 Speed and Parallelism

- Classical Approach: Traditional computers process information using bits, which can exist in one of two states, 0 or 1. Classical algorithms solve optimization problems sequentially, limiting their efficiency.
- Quantum Computing: Quantum computers leverage qubits, which can exist in multiple states simultaneously. This parallelism allows quantum algorithms to explore multiple solutions simultaneously, providing a potential speed advantage over classical counterparts.

2.4.1.2 Portfolio Optimization

- Classical Approach: Classical portfolio optimization relies on algorithms such as Markowitz's mean-variance optimization. While effective, these approaches might struggle with complex, non-linear relationships in financial data.
- Quantum Computing: Quantum algorithms like QAOA excel at solving complex optimization problems, making them well-suited for portfolio optimization in dynamically changing financial markets.

2.4.1.3 Risk Management

- Classical Approach: Classical risk management often involves Monte Carlo simulations, which can be computationally expensive and time-consuming.
- Quantum Computing: Quantum computers can efficiently model probabilistic scenarios, enabling faster and more accurate risk assessments. The quantum-enhanced Monte Carlo methods show promise in improving risk management strategies.

2.4.1.4 Options Pricing

- Classical Approach: Classical methods for options pricing, such as the Black-Scholes model, assume constant volatility and risk-free interest rates.
- Quantum Computing: Quantum algorithms can better capture the dynamics of financial markets by considering multiple variables simultaneously, leading to more accurate options pricing models.

2.4.1.5 Machine Learning in Finance

- Classical Approach: Classical machine learning algorithms may struggle with processing vast amounts of financial data and identifying complex patterns efficiently.
- Quantum Computing: Quantum machine learning algorithms, like Quantum Support Vector Machines, offer the potential to analyze large datasets more quickly, facilitating more accurate predictions and decision-making in financial markets.

2.4.1.6 Cryptography and Security

- Classical Approach: Classical cryptographic methods face challenges from emerging quantum algorithms that could break widely used encryption schemes.
- Quantum Computing: Quantum-resistant cryptographic algorithms, such as those based on quantum-resistant cryptographic primitives, are being developed to safeguard financial data from the threat of quantum attacks.

So, quantum computing presents a paradigm shift in addressing complex problems in finance services and portfolio optimization. While it is still in its infancy, the potential for quantum algorithms to outperform classical approaches in certain domains is evident. As the field continues to evolve, the integration of quantum computing into financial systems holds the promise of unlocking new levels of efficiency and precision in decision-making processes.

2.4.2 Practical Implications and Challenges

Quantum computing in finance is crucial for revolutionizing decision-making, risk management, and portfolio optimization, offering unparalleled speed and precision. Its ability to process vast datasets simultaneously opens new frontiers in machine learning applications, shaping a more resilient and adaptive financial landscape. While facing challenges, the importance lies in harnessing quantum power for innovative solutions, ensuring the industry stays ahead in an era of rapid technological evolution.

2.4.2.1 Practical Implications

- Accelerated decision-making through quantum parallelism.
- Optimized portfolio diversification strategies.
- Improved risk management with accurate probabilistic modeling.
- Enhanced options pricing models considering multiple variables.
- Quantum machine learning for advanced analytics in finance.
- More secure financial transactions with quantum-resistant cryptography.

2.4.2.2 Challenges

- Limitations in current quantum hardware, including noise and errors.
- Ongoing research required for the development of robust quantum algorithms.
- Integration challenges with existing financial systems.
- Need for effective quantum error correction mechanisms.
- High costs associated with building and maintaining quantum computers.
- Ethical considerations surrounding the use of quantum algorithms in finance.
- Regulatory frameworks for responsible implementation and prevention of misuse.
- Scalability issues in quantum systems while maintaining qubit coherence.
- Potential disruption during the integration of quantum computing into financial infrastructure.
- Addressing concerns related to quantum computing's impact on job roles and employment.
- Ensuring interoperability between classical and quantum systems.
- Limited availability of skilled professionals with expertise in quantum computing.
- Managing the environmental impact of quantum computing infrastructure.
- Uncertainties in the timeline for overcoming current quantum hardware limitations.
- Balancing the trade-off between speed and precision in quantum algorithms.
- Establishing industry standards for quantum computing in finance.
- Developing quantum-safe encryption standards for data protection.
- Addressing potential biases in quantum machine learning algorithms.
- Navigating the geopolitical landscape regarding quantum technology advancements.
- Educating stakeholders in the financial industry about the capabilities and limitations of quantum computing.

2.4.3 Considerations for Implementation in Real-World Financial Systems

Quantum Steel Corp. is a prominent player in the steel manufacturing industry, operating globally and facing the challenges inherent in the complex financial landscape of the sector. In an effort to stay ahead of the competition and optimize its financial operations, Quantum Steel is exploring the potential of quantum computing.

2.4.3.1 Considerations for Implementation

- Algorithmic Transformation: Quantum Steel's financial analysts traditionally use optimization algorithms to manage its portfolio and make informed investment decisions. However, quantum computing requires a shift in this approach. For instance, the company might explore using the QAOA to tackle complex financial optimization problems, such as determining the ideal mix of investments to maximize returns while minimizing risk.
- Data Security and Privacy: Quantum Steel deals with sensitive financial data, including market trends, pricing models, and investment strategies. Quantum computing's ability to break traditional encryption methods raises concerns about data security. The company must invest in quantum-resistant cryptography to safeguard its financial information from potential quantum threats. Example: QuantumSteel might partner with cybersecurity experts to develop and implement post-quantum cryptographic techniques, ensuring the confidentiality and integrity of its financial data (Khanh, Khang et al., 2021).
- Hardware and Infrastructure: Quantum computers are still in their early stages, and practical, large-scale quantum computers are not readily available. Quantum Steel must decide whether to collaborate with quantum hardware providers or use cloud-based quantum computing services. Additionally, assessing the scalability and reliability of quantum hardware is crucial to ensure consistent and effective financial computations. Example: Quantum Steel might enter into a partnership with a leading quantum computing hardware provider or leverage a cloud-based service like IBM Quantum or Microsoft Azure Quantum for its initial foray into quantum computing.
- Talent and Skill Development: Quantum computing expertise is scarce, and Quantum Steel needs a skilled workforce to harness the technology effectively. The company must invest in training programs to educate its financial and IT teams about quantum principles, algorithms, and programming languages. Example: Quantum Steel could collaborate with universities or quantum computing training platforms to provide its employees with the necessary skills. Alternatively, the company might hire quantum computing experts to guide its teams through the learning process.
- Regulatory Compliance: The financial industry is heavily regulated, and Quantum Steel must navigate regulatory frameworks to ensure compliance. Engaging with regulatory bodies and contributing to the establishment of guidelines for quantum computing in finance is crucial to avoid legal complications. Example: Quantum Steel could proactively engage with financial regulatory authorities, providing insights into the potential impact of quantum computing on financial operations and collaborating to develop a regulatory framework that addresses both opportunities and challenges.

2.4.3.2 Potential Benefits

- Portfolio Optimization: By leveraging quantum computing, Quantum Steel can perform rapid and more precise portfolio optimization. For instance, the company could use quantum algorithms to consider various financial parameters simultaneously, resulting in a well-balanced investment portfolio that maximizes returns and minimizes risks. Example: Quantum Steel may use quantum computing to analyze historical market data, current economic indicators, and future projections to optimize its investment portfolio dynamically.

■ Supply Chain Optimization: Quantum algorithms can assist Quantum Steel in optimizing its supply chain logistics. This could involve minimizing transportation costs, reducing lead times, and ensuring just-in-time delivery of raw materials, ultimately enhancing overall supply chain efficiency. Example: Quantum Steel might use quantum computing to model and simulate different supply chain scenarios, identifying the most cost-effective and efficient configurations.

■ Risk Management: Quantum computing can provide more accurate risk assessments by quickly analyzing vast datasets and simulating potential market scenarios. Quantum Steel can use this capability to make informed financial decisions, mitigating risks effectively. Example: Quantum Steel may employ quantum computing to simulate market fluctuations, assess the impact of geopolitical events, and stress-test its financial models to identify potential risks and develop proactive risk management strategies.

So, it can be summarized that the implementation of quantum computing in real-world financial systems for the steel business sector offers significant potential benefits for companies like Quantum Steel Corp. However, navigating the challenges associated with algorithmic transformation, data security, hardware considerations, talent development, and regulatory compliance is crucial for a successful integration. By carefully addressing these considerations, QuantumSteel can position itself at the forefront of innovation in the steel manufacturing industry, optimizing its financial operations and gaining a competitive edge (Khang, Gujrati et al., 2024).

2.4.4 Ethical and Regulatory Considerations

The integration of quantum computing into financial practices for optimization purposes demands a nuanced examination of ethical and regulatory implications. Quantum computing's potential to exponentially enhance calculations crucial to finance, such as risk assessment and portfolio optimization, introduces both promise and peril. Ethically, the responsible and equitable deployment of this technology is paramount, ensuring that societal benefits are maximized while minimizing potential harms and disparities (Khang, Inna et al., 2024).

On the regulatory front, there is a pressing need for frameworks that can address novel challenges, including data privacy, algorithmic transparency, and the potential for market disruptions. Achieving a harmonious balance between the transformative power of quantum computing in finance and the imperative to uphold ethical standards and regulatory integrity is a critical task as these technologies become increasingly ingrained in financial landscapes (Inglesant et al., 2021; Lin, 2010; Ten Holter, Inglesant & Jirotka, 2023). The followings are some more noted points on ethical and regulatory considerations quantum computing in finance services and portfolio optimization.

■ Data Privacy and Security: Addressing concerns about quantum's potential to break encryption for robust financial data protection.

■ Algorithmic Fairness: Ensuring fairness in quantum finance algorithms to prevent biased decision-making.

■ Transparency and Explainability: Establishing standards for transparency in complex quantum algorithms to build trust.

- Regulatory Compliance: Adapting financial regulations to accommodate the unique aspects of quantum computing.
- Intellectual Property Protection: Defining regulations for patenting quantum algorithms to encourage innovation.
- Resource Allocation and Accessibility: Ensuring fair access to limited quantum computing resources in finance.
- International Collaboration and Standards: Collaborating globally to address ethical and regulatory challenges consistently.
- Risk Management: Developing quantum-specific risk management frameworks for financial stability.
- Customer Consent and Communication: Obtaining informed consent and educating customers about quantum implications in finance.
- Environmental Impact: Assessing and mitigating the environmental impact of energy-intensive quantum operations.
- Diversity and Inclusion: Promoting diversity in quantum development to avoid biases in algorithms.
- Long-Term Consequences: Anticipating and addressing societal impacts of widespread quantum adoption in finance.
- Monitoring and Auditing: Implementing continuous monitoring and auditing of quantum algorithms for compliance.
- Education and Training: Building a workforce with a deep understanding of quantum ethics and regulations.
- Corporate Social Responsibility: Incorporating principles of corporate social responsibility in quantum finance operations.
- Stakeholder Engagement: Engaging with diverse stakeholders for feedback and inclusive decision-making.
- Scenario Planning: Anticipating ethical and regulatory challenges through scenario planning in quantum finance.
- Fallback Mechanisms: Developing contingency plans for unexpected quantum system issues or failures.
- Global Governance Frameworks: Establishing global governance frameworks for consistent quantum finance standards.
- Dynamic Adaptation: Viewing ethical and regulatory considerations as dynamic, requiring continuous adaptation to quantum developments.

2.5 Conclusion

In conclusion, this chapter navigates the captivating convergence of quantum computing, finance, and optimization, shedding light on the transformative potential that quantum computers bring to traditional financial models. By exploring quantum algorithms and their applications in tasks like portfolio optimization, option pricing, risk analysis, and algorithmic trading, the chapter outlines a future where quantum principles reshape the landscape of financial decision-making. However, challenges such as the imperative for quantum-safe cryptography are acknowledged, alongside opportunities presented by the exploration of quantum-inspired classical algorithms.

Serving as a comprehensive introduction, this chapter is a valuable resource for researchers, practitioners, and enthusiasts, offering insights into the profound implications of quantum computing in the dynamic realms of finance services and portfolio optimization, hinting at a paradigm shift in how we approach and address complex financial challenges.

2.6 Future Applications of Quantum Computing

▪ Quantum Portfolio Optimization: Quantum computing can revolutionize portfolio optimization by efficiently exploring vast combinations of assets and their weightings. Leveraging quantum algorithms such as QAOA, financial analysts can rapidly identify optimal investment strategies, balancing risk and return in complex market conditions.

▪ Risk Quantification and Mitigation: In the realm of risk management, quantum computing holds the promise of more accurate risk quantification. By simulating intricate financial scenarios, quantum computers can provide nuanced insights into potential risks, allowing financial institutions to develop more robust risk mitigation strategies.

▪ Advanced Option Pricing Models: Quantum computing's computational power can be harnessed to enhance option pricing models. Particularly beneficial in scenarios involving intricate financial derivatives, quantum algorithms can outpace classical methods, providing quicker and more accurate pricing predictions.

▪ Credit Scoring Reinvented: Quantum computing offers a paradigm shift in credit scoring. By processing a multitude of variables simultaneously, quantum algorithms can refine credit scoring models, leading to more precise risk assessments. This innovation can significantly impact lending decisions by incorporating a broader range of factors.

▪ Enhanced Fraud Detection: Quantum computing's ability to process large datasets rapidly positions it as a powerful tool in fraud detection. Financial institutions can leverage quantum algorithms to detect subtle patterns indicative of fraudulent activities, fortifying the security of financial transactions.

▪ Supply Chain Optimization for Financial Investments: Quantum computing extends its reach beyond traditional financial applications into supply chain optimization. Efficiently managing investments related to the supply chain becomes more feasible with quantum computing, enhancing the overall financial strategy.

▪ Securing Cryptocurrencies and Blockchain: As cryptocurrencies gain prominence, quantum-resistant cryptographic techniques become imperative. Quantum computing's potential impact on current cryptographic systems necessitates ongoing research to ensure the security of financial transactions in the evolving quantum landscape (Khang, Chowdhury, & Sharma, 2022).

▪ Real-Time Algorithmic Trading Advantage: Quantum computing's rapid data processing capabilities offer a potential edge in algorithmic trading. By swiftly analyzing extensive market data, quantum-powered algorithms can identify real-time patterns, providing traders with a competitive advantage in dynamic financial markets.

▪ Personalized Financial Services: Quantum computing facilitates in-depth analysis of customer data, enabling financial institutions to offer highly personalized products and services. This personalized approach enhances customer satisfaction and engagement, ultimately impacting the bottom line positively.

▪ Streamlining Regulatory Compliance: Quantum computing can streamline regulatory compliance processes by efficiently analyzing vast datasets. This ensures financial institutions adhere to intricate regulations, reducing compliance-related challenges and enhancing overall operational efficiency.

References

Asch, M., Moore, T., Badia, R., Beck, M., Beckman, P., Bidot, T., & Zacharov, I. (2018). Big data and extreme-scale computing: Pathways to convergence-toward a shaping strategy for a future software and data ecosystem for scientific inquiry. The International Journal of High Performance Computing Applications, 32(4), 435–479. https://journals.sagepub.com/doi/abs/10.1177/1094342018778123

Bayerstadler, A., Becquin, G., Binder, J., Botter, T., Ehm, H., Ehmer, T., & Winter, F. (2021). Industry quantum computing applications. EPJ Quantum Technology, 8(1), 25. https://epjqt.epj.org/articles/epjqt/abs/2021/01/40507_2021_Article_114/40507_2021_Article_114.html

Covers, O., & Doeland, M. (2020). How the financial sector can anticipate the threats of quantum computing to keep payments safe and secure. Journal of Payments Strategy & Systems, 14(2), 147–156. https://www.ingentaconnect.com/content/hsp/jpss/2020/00000014/00000002/art00007

Egger, D. J., Gambella, C., Marecek, J., McFaddin, S., Mevissen, M., Raymond, R., & Yndurain, E. (2020). Quantum computing for finance: State-of-the-art and future prospects. IEEE Transactions on Quantum Engineering, 1, 1–24. https://ieeexplore.ieee.org/abstract/document/9222275/

Garcia, D. J., & You, F. (2015). Supply chain design and optimization: Challenges and opportunities. Computers & Chemical Engineering, 81, 153–170. https://www.sciencedirect.com/science/article/pii/S0098135415000861

Gomes, C., Falcao, G., Paquete, L., & Fernandes, J. P. (2022). An empirical study on the use of quantum computing for financial portfolio optimization. SN Computer Science, 3(5), 335. https://link.springer.com/article/10.1007/s42979-022-01215-9

Grossi, M., Ibrahim, N., Radescu, V., Loredo, R., Voigt, K., Von Altrock, C., & Rudnik, A. (2022). Mixed quantum–classical method for fraud detection with quantum feature selection. IEEE Transactions on Quantum Engineering, 3, 1–12. https://ieeexplore.ieee.org/abstract/document/9915517/

Hassija, V., Chamola, V., Goyal, A., Kanhere, S. S., & Guizani, N. (2020). Forthcoming applications of quantum computing: Peeking into the future. IET Quantum Communication, 1(2), 35–41. https://ietresearch.onlinelibrary.wiley.com/doi/abs/10.1049/iet-qtc.2020.0026

Herman, D., Googin, C., Liu, X., Sun, Y., Galda, A., Safro, I., & Alexeev, Y. (2023). Quantum computing for finance. Nature Reviews Physics, 5(8), 450–465. https://www.nature.com/articles/s42254-023-00603-1

Hu, Z., Gnatyuk, S., Koval, O., Gnatyuk, V., & Bondarovets, S. (2017). Anomaly detection system in secure cloud computing environment. International Journal of Computer Network and Information Security, 9(4), 10. http://www.mecs-press.org/ijcnis/ijcnis-v9-n4/IJCNIS-V9-N4-2.pdf

Inglesant, P., Ten Holter, C., Jirotka, M., & Williams, R. (2021). Asleep at the wheel? Responsible innovation in quantum computing. Technology Analysis & Strategic Management, 33(11), 1364–1376. https://www.tandfonline.com/doi/abs/10.1080/09537325.2021.1988557

Khang, A. (2023). Applications and Principles of Quantum Computing (1st Ed.). IGI Global Press. https://doi.org/10.4018/979-8-3693-1168-4

Khang, A., Chowdhury, S., & Sharma, S. (2022). The Data-Driven Blockchain Ecosystem: Fundamentals, Applications, and Emerging Technologies (1st Ed.). CRC Press. https://doi.org/10.1201/9781003269281

Khang, A., Gujrati, R., Uygun, H., Tailor, R. K., & Gaur, S. S. (2024). Data-Driven Modelling and Predictive Analytics in Business and Finance (1st Ed.). CRC Press. https://doi.org/10.1201/9781032618845

Khang, A., Hajimahmud, V. A., Alyar, A. V., Khalilov, Matlab, Murad, Bagirli, & Litvinova, Eugenia. (2023). "Introduction to Quantum Computing and Its Integration Applications," Applications and Principles of Quantum Computing (1st Ed.). IGI Global Press. https://doi.org/10.4018/979-8-3693-1168-4.ch002

Khang, A., Inna, Semenets-Orlova, Alla, Klochko, Rostyslav, Shchokin, Rudenko, Mykola, Lidia, Romanova, & Kristina, Bratchykova. (2024). "Management Model 6.0 and Business Recovery Strategy of Enterprises in the Era of Digital Economy," Data-Driven Modelling and Predictive Analytics in Business and Finance (1st Ed.). CRC Press. https://doi.org/10.1201/9781032618845-16

Khang, A., & Rath, K. C. (2023). "Quantum Mechanics Primer - Fundamentals and Quantum Computing," Applications and Principles of Quantum Computing (1st Ed.). IGI Global Press.

Khanh, H. H., & Khang, A. (2021). "The Role of Artificial Intelligence in Blockchain Applications," Reinventing Manufacturing and Business Processes Through Artificial Intelligence, 2 (20–40). CRC Press. https://doi.org/10.1201/9781003145011-2

Lin, P. (2010). Ethical blowback from emerging technologies. Journal of Military Ethics, 9(4), 313–331. https://www.tandfonline.com/doi/abs/10.1080/15027570.2010.536401

Lindsay, J. R. (2020). Demystifying the quantum threat: Infrastructure, Institutions, and intelligence advantage. Security Studies, 29(2), 335–361. https://www.tandfonline.com/doi/abs/10.1080/09636412.2020.1722853

Majot, A., & Yampolskiy, R. (2015). Global catastrophic risk and security implications of quantum computers. Futures, 72, 17–26. https://www.sciencedirect.com/science/article/pii/S0016328715000294

Mansouri, S. A., Gallear, D., & Askariazad, M. H. (2012). Decision support for build-to-order supply chain management through multiobjective optimization. International Journal of Production Economics, 135(1), 24–36. https://www.sciencedirect.com/science/article/pii/S0925527310004457

Marzec, M. (2016). Portfolio optimization: Applications in quantum computing. Handbook of High-Frequency Trading and Modeling in Finance, 73–106. https://onlinelibrary.wiley.com/doi/abs/10.1002/9781118593486.ch4

Prakash, P. M. (2023). Enhancing business performance through quantum electronic analysis of optical data. Optical and Quantum Electronics, 55(12), 1056. https://link.springer.com/article/10.1007/s11082-023-05347-x

Rasool, R., Ahmad, H. F., Rafique, W., Qayyum, A., Qadir, J., & Anwar, Z. (2023). Quantum computing for healthcare: A review. Future Internet, 15(3), 94. https://www.mdpi.com/1999-5903/15/3/94

Rosch-Grace, D., & Straub, J. (2022). Analysis of the likelihood of quantum computing proliferation. Technology in Society, 68, 101880. https://www.sciencedirect.com/science/article/pii/S0160791X22000215

Ten Holter, C., Inglesant, P., & Jirotka, M. (2023). Reading the road: Challenges and opportunities on the path to responsible innovation in quantum computing. Technology Analysis & Strategic Management, 35(7), 844–856. https://www.tandfonline.com/doi/abs/10.1080/09537325.201.1988070

Chapter 3

Fintech and Data Science: Shaping the Future of the Digital Economy

Om Prakash Yadav, RajKumar Teotia, and Rashi Baliyan

3.1 Introduction

The intersection of blockchain technology and financial technology (Fintech) has catalyzed a monumental shift in the landscape of finance, reshaping traditional paradigms and opening up a realm of unprecedented possibilities. Blockchain, initially conceived as the underlying technology powering cryptocurrencies, has transcended its origins to emerge as a disruptive force capable of revolutionizing diverse sectors, with finance being at the forefront of this transformation. Meanwhile, Fintech, driven by relentless innovation and fueled by advancements in digital technologies, has been steadily dismantling barriers to financial access, ushering in an era of democratized finance. At the heart of this convergence lies the promise of a more transparent, secure, and inclusive financial ecosystem.

Blockchain, with its foundational principles of decentralization, immutability, and cryptographic security, offers a novel approach to managing and transacting value, free from the constraints of traditional intermediaries and centralized control. Fintech, on the other hand, leverages cutting-edge technologies such as artificial intelligence (AI), big data analytics, and mobile applications to deliver tailored financial solutions directly to consumers, bypassing legacy systems and empowering individuals and businesses alike (Yetilmezsoy, Ozkaya, & Cakmakci, 2011).

This chapter seeks to explore the intricate interplay between blockchain and Fintech, unraveling the synergies that have emerged as these two realms converge. Through a comprehensive examination of industry trends, regulatory developments, and real-world applications, we aim to elucidate the transformative potential of this convergence, charting a course toward a future where financial services are more accessible, efficient, and equitable than ever before. By delving into the nuances of this dynamic relationship, we hope to provide a nuanced understanding of the opportunities, challenges, and implications that lie ahead as blockchain and Fintech continue to reshape the landscape of finance (Chen, Jakeman, & Norton, 2008).

DOI: 10.4324/9781003501947-3

3.2 Literature Review

The synergy between blockchain technology and Fintech has become a focal point of research and discussion within both academic and industry circles. Originating with the advent of Bitcoin and its underlying blockchain technology in Satoshi Nakamoto's seminal whitepaper, blockchain has since evolved beyond its cryptocurrency roots to offer decentralized, transparent, and immutable solutions to various industries. Concurrently, the rise of Fintech has disrupted traditional financial services, leveraging technological advancements to democratize access to banking, investment, and payment solutions.

The convergence of blockchain and Fintech represents a paradigm shift in the financial landscape, promising enhanced security, efficiency, and inclusivity. Research on the topic has explored the technical foundations of blockchain, the evolution of Fintech, and the emerging opportunities and challenges associated with their integration. Studies have identified numerous applications for blockchain in Fintech, including cross-border payments, trade finance, and asset tokenization, while also highlighting regulatory, scalability, and interoperability hurdles that must be addressed. Looking forward, interdisciplinary collaboration and further exploration of the social and ethical implications of blockchain-Fintech innovations are seen as crucial for unlocking their full potential and shaping the future of finance (Papadimitriou, 2012).

3.3 The Evolution of Blockchain Technology

The evolution of blockchain technology represents a remarkable journey from its inception to its current status as a transformative force across various industries. Beginning with the advent of Bitcoin in 2008, blockchain emerged as a revolutionary concept introduced by an anonymous entity known as Satoshi Nakamoto. Nakamoto's whitepaper outlined a decentralized digital currency system that relied on a distributed ledger, or blockchain, to record transactions securely and transparently. The early days of blockchain were synonymous with Bitcoin, as the technology served as the foundation for the world's first cryptocurrency. However, as developers and entrepreneurs began to explore its potential, blockchain quickly transcended its initial use case.

The introduction of Ethereum in 2015 marked a significant milestone in blockchain's evolution. Ethereum introduced the concept of smart contracts, which enabled programmable, self-executing agreements that could automate a wide range of tasks beyond simple peer-to-peer (P2P) transactions. The diversification of blockchain use cases has been a defining feature of its evolution. Beyond cryptocurrency, blockchain technology found applications in industries such as finance, supply chain management, healthcare, and voting systems.

In finance, blockchain promised to revolutionize traditional banking systems by enabling faster, more secure, and transparent transactions. In supply chain management, blockchain offered a solution for tracking the provenance and movement of goods, reducing fraud and ensuring product authenticity. In healthcare, blockchain's ability to secure and share medical records promised to streamline data management and improve patient care. Additionally, blockchain technology presented opportunities for enhancing transparency and integrity in voting systems and governance processes.

Despite its potential, blockchain technology has faced several challenges along its evolutionary path. Scalability, interoperability, regulatory uncertainty, and environmental concerns have all posed obstacles to widespread adoption. However, ongoing research and development efforts continue to address these challenges, paving the way for blockchain's continued growth and maturation. Looking ahead, the future of blockchain technology is filled with promise and potential. As the technology continues to evolve, we can expect to see further innovation in areas such as decentralized finance (DeFi), non-fungible tokens (NFTs), and decentralized autonomous organizations (DAOs). Additionally, advancements in consensus mechanisms, scalability solutions, and interoperability protocols will likely play a crucial role in unlocking new possibilities for blockchain adoption.

3.4 Evolution of Fintech

The evolution of Fintech, commonly referred to as Fintech, represents a remarkable journey that has transformed the way individuals and businesses manage their finances. Beginning with the digitization of traditional banking services, Fintech has rapidly expanded its scope to encompass a wide range of innovative solutions leveraging cutting-edge technologies. This chapter explores the key milestones and trends in the evolution of Fintech, highlighting its profound impact on the financial industry and beyond.

- Digitization of Banking Services: The roots of Fintech can be traced back to the digitization of banking services in the 20th century. The introduction of Automated Teller Machines (ATMs) in the 1960s marked a significant milestone, allowing customers to access basic banking services conveniently outside of traditional banking hours.
- Emergence of Online Banking: The advent of the internet in the 1990s paved the way for the emergence of online banking platforms, enabling customers to conduct financial transactions and manage their accounts remotely. Online banking offered unprecedented convenience and accessibility, laying the foundation for the digital transformation of the financial industry.
- Expansion of Payment Technologies: The proliferation of electronic payment technologies further revolutionized the Fintech landscape. Innovations such as credit cards, debit cards, and electronic funds transfers (EFTs) facilitated seamless and secure transactions, reducing reliance on cash and checks.
- Rise of Mobile Banking: The widespread adoption of smartphones and mobile devices in the 2000s fueled the rise of mobile banking applications. Mobile banking offered customers greater flexibility and mobility, allowing them to manage their finances on the go with ease.
- Proliferation of Fintech Startups: The early 21st century saw the emergence of a wave of Fintech startups challenging traditional financial institutions with innovative solutions. These startups leveraged technology to address pain points in areas such as payments, lending, wealth management, and insurance.
- Introduction of Blockchain and Cryptocurrency: The introduction of blockchain technology and cryptocurrencies such as Bitcoin in the late 2000s marked a significant milestone in the evolution of Fintech. Blockchain offered a decentralized and secure ledger for recording transactions, while cryptocurrencies promised to revolutionize the concept of money and value exchange.
- Expansion of Alternative Lending Platforms: The rise of alternative lending platforms, such as P2P lending and crowdfunding, democratized access to financing for individuals and small businesses. These platforms bypassed traditional banks and connected borrowers directly with investors, offering competitive interest rates and streamlined lending processes.

■ Integration of AI and Machine Learning (ML): In recent years, the integration of AI and ML has emerged as a game-changer in Fintech. AI-powered chatbots, robo-advisors, and fraud detection systems have revolutionized customer service, investment management, and risk mitigation in the financial industry.

■ Advancements in Regulatory Technology (RegTech): The rise of regulatory technology, or RegTech, has facilitated compliance and risk management for financial institutions. RegTech solutions leverage technologies such as AI, ML, and blockchain to automate regulatory processes, monitor transactions for suspicious activities, and ensure compliance with evolving regulatory requirements.

■ Shift toward Open Banking and Application Programming Interface (API) Integration: The shift toward open banking and API integration has fostered collaboration and innovation within the Fintech ecosystem. Open banking initiatives enable secure data sharing between financial institutions and third-party developers, leading to the creation of innovative financial products and services.

3.5 Convergence of Blockchain and Fintech

The convergence of blockchain technology and Fintech represents a groundbreaking development that is reshaping the landscape of finance and revolutionizing traditional financial systems. This convergence brings together two powerful forces: blockchain, with its decentralized, transparent, and immutable ledger, and Fintech, which leverages technology to enhance financial services, accessibility, and efficiency. In this chapter, we explore the key aspects and implications of the convergence of blockchain and Fintech, highlighting its transformative potential and the opportunities it presents for various stakeholders.

■ Enhanced Security and Transparency: One of the primary benefits of the convergence of blockchain and Fintech is enhanced security and transparency in financial transactions. Blockchain's decentralized ledger ensures that transaction records are immutable and tamper-proof, reducing the risk of fraud, manipulation, and unauthorized access. This transparency instills trust in financial transactions and helps to mitigate risks associated with traditional centralized systems.

■ Efficiency and Cost Savings: By leveraging blockchain technology, Fintech companies can streamline processes, reduce intermediaries, and eliminate inefficiencies in financial transactions. Smart contracts, self-executing contracts with predefined conditions written in code, automate processes such as loan approvals, insurance claims, and trade settlements, leading to significant cost savings and faster transaction times.

■ Financial Inclusion: The convergence of blockchain and Fintech has the potential to promote financial inclusion by providing access to financial services for underserved populations. Blockchain-based solutions can lower barriers to entry, reduce transaction costs, and extend financial services to individuals and businesses in remote or underserved regions. This can empower people who were previously excluded from the traditional banking system to participate in the global economy and access essential financial services.

■ Disruption of Traditional Financial Systems: The convergence of blockchain and Fintech is disrupting traditional financial systems by challenging the dominance of banks and financial intermediaries. DeFi platforms built on blockchain technology offer alternatives to traditional banking services, such as lending, borrowing, and asset management, without the need for intermediaries. This decentralization democratizes access to financial services and shifts power away from centralized institutions.

■ Regulatory Challenges and Opportunities: While the convergence of blockchain and Fintech presents numerous opportunities, it also poses regulatory challenges for policymakers and regulators. The decentralized nature of blockchain technology and the global reach of Fintech platforms raise questions about regulatory oversight, consumer protection, and compliance with existing financial regulations. However, innovative regulatory approaches, such as regulatory sandboxes and collaborative frameworks, can facilitate responsible innovation while ensuring consumer protection and regulatory compliance.

■ Emerging Use Cases and Applications: The convergence of blockchain and Fintech has led to the emergence of innovative use cases and applications across various industries. In addition to cryptocurrency and DeFi, blockchain technology is being utilized in areas such as supply chain management, healthcare, real estate, and voting systems. Fintech companies are exploring ways to integrate blockchain technology to improve transparency, efficiency, and security in these sectors, unlocking new possibilities for innovation and disruption.

3.6 Regulatory Landscape and Policy Implications

The convergence of blockchain technology and Fintech has ushered in a new era of innovation, disrupting traditional financial systems and reshaping the way we interact with money, assets, and financial services. However, this rapid evolution has also raised regulatory challenges and policy implications for policymakers, industry stakeholders, and consumers alike. In this chapter, we explore the regulatory landscape and policy implications in the context of blockchain technology and Fintech, highlighting key considerations, challenges, and opportunities.

3.6.1 Regulatory Fragmentation and Uncertainty

One of the primary challenges facing blockchain technology and Fintech is regulatory fragmentation and uncertainty. Regulations governing these technologies vary significantly across jurisdictions, creating a patchwork of rules and compliance requirements for businesses operating in the sector. Regulatory uncertainty can stifle innovation and investment, as businesses grapple with compliance costs, legal risks, and the potential for regulatory enforcement actions. Moreover, conflicting or ambiguous regulations can create barriers to market entry and hinder the growth of the blockchain and Fintech ecosystem.

3.6.2 Consumer Protection and Investor Safeguards

Consumer protection and investor safeguards are paramount considerations in the regulation of blockchain technology and Fintech. As these technologies enable the transfer of value and assets in a decentralized and often anonymous manner, there is a risk of fraud, scams, and financial misconduct. Regulatory frameworks should aim to protect consumers and investors from fraudulent schemes, unauthorized transactions, and misleading information. This may include measures such as disclosure requirements, investor education initiatives, and enforcement actions against bad actors.

3.6.3 AML/CFT Compliance

Anti-money laundering (AML) and countering the financing of terrorism (CFT) compliance are critical priorities for regulators in the blockchain and Fintech space. The pseudonymous nature of blockchain transactions presents challenges for AML/CFT efforts, as it can facilitate illicit activities such as money laundering, terrorist financing, and sanctions evasion. Regulatory frameworks should incorporate robust AML/CFT controls, including customer due diligence, transaction monitoring, and suspicious activity reporting. Regulators may also require blockchain and Fintech firms to implement know-your-customer (KYC) procedures and comply with international AML/CFT standards.

3.6.4 Data Privacy and Security

Data privacy and security are central concerns in the regulation of blockchain technology and Fintech, given the sensitive nature of financial data and personal information involved. The decentralized and immutable nature of blockchain presents unique challenges for data privacy and protection. Regulatory frameworks should include provisions for data privacy, encryption, and cybersecurity to safeguard against unauthorized access, data breaches, and identity theft. This may involve compliance with data protection regulations such as the General Data Protection Regulation (GDPR) and the California Consumer Privacy Act (CCPA).

3.6.5 Innovation and Market Competition

Effective regulation should strike a balance between promoting innovation and fostering market competition while ensuring consumer protection and market integrity. Regulatory sandboxes, pilot programs, and flexible regulatory approaches can provide a conducive environment for experimentation and innovation in the blockchain and Fintech sectors. Moreover, regulators should encourage market competition by removing barriers to entry, promoting interoperability, and facilitating collaboration among industry stakeholders. By fostering a competitive and innovative ecosystem, regulators can drive advancements in technology, improve access to financial services, and enhance consumer welfare.

3.7 Impact on the Future of Finance

The convergence of blockchain technology and Fintech is reshaping the future of finance, unlocking new opportunities, and transforming traditional financial systems. In this chapter, we explore the impact of blockchain technology and Fintech on the future of finance, highlighting key trends, challenges, and opportunities that lie ahead.

3.7.1 Democratization of Finance

Blockchain technology and Fintech have the potential to democratize finance by providing greater access to financial services for individuals and businesses worldwide. DeFi platforms built on blockchain enable P2P lending, borrowing, and asset management without the need for traditional financial intermediaries. Fintech innovations such as mobile banking, digital wallets, and payment apps are expanding access to financial services for underserved populations, including the unbanked and underbanked. These technologies empower individuals to manage their finances more efficiently, participate in the global economy, and achieve greater financial inclusion.

3.7.2 Disintermediation and Decentralization

Blockchain technology is driving disintermediation and decentralization in the financial industry, reducing reliance on traditional banks and financial institutions. Smart contracts, decentralized exchanges, and blockchain-based payment systems enable direct P2P transactions, bypassing intermediaries and reducing transaction costs. This shift toward decentralization is challenging traditional business models and disrupting established players in the financial industry. It is fostering greater competition, innovation, and efficiency, while also raising questions about regulatory oversight, consumer protection, and market stability.

3.7.3 Enhanced Security and Transparency

Blockchain technology offers enhanced security and transparency in financial transactions by providing a decentralized, immutable ledger for recording transactions. Each transaction is cryptographically secured and verifiable, reducing the risk of fraud, manipulation, and unauthorized access. Fintech innovations such as biometric authentication, encryption, and multi-factor authentication further enhance security and privacy in financial transactions, protecting sensitive information and mitigating cybersecurity risks.

3.7.4 Innovation in Financial Products and Services

The convergence of blockchain technology and Fintech is driving innovation in financial products and services, introducing new opportunities for investment, wealth management, and risk mitigation. Tokenization of assets, digital securities, and algorithmic trading are revolutionizing traditional investment models and expanding access to alternative asset classes. Fintech startups and established financial institutions are leveraging blockchain technology to develop innovative solutions for payments, lending, insurance, and asset management. These technologies are streamlining processes, reducing costs, and improving efficiency, leading to greater convenience and value for consumers.

3.7.5 Regulatory Challenges and Policy Implications

Despite the potential benefits, the adoption of blockchain technology and Fintech presents regulatory challenges and policy implications for policymakers, regulators, and industry stakeholders. Regulatory frameworks must strike a balance between promoting innovation and ensuring consumer protection, financial stability, and regulatory compliance. Regulators are grappling with issues such as AML/CFT compliance, data privacy, investor protection, and market integrity in the context of blockchain technology and Fintech. They must develop flexible and adaptive regulatory frameworks that foster innovation while safeguarding the interests of consumers and investors.

3.8 Environmental and Sustainability Considerations

As blockchain technology and Fintech continue to proliferate and evolve, it is imperative to consider their environmental and sustainability implications. While these technologies offer numerous benefits such as increased efficiency, transparency, and financial inclusion, they also consume significant amounts of energy and resources. In this chapter, we explore the environmental and sustainability considerations associated with blockchain technology and Fintech, and discuss potential strategies to mitigate their impact.

3.8.1 Energy Consumption

One of the primary environmental concerns associated with blockchain technology is its high-energy consumption. Proof-of-Work (PoW) consensus mechanisms, commonly used in blockchain networks like Bitcoin and Ethereum, require extensive computational power to validate transactions and secure the network. The energy-intensive nature of PoW consensus mechanisms has led to criticism regarding their environmental impact, particularly due to the reliance on fossil fuels for electricity generation. The carbon footprint of blockchain networks has raised concerns about their sustainability and contribution to climate change.

3.8.2 Carbon Emissions

The energy consumption of blockchain networks directly contributes to carbon emissions, as the majority of electricity generation worldwide relies on fossil fuels. The carbon footprint of blockchain networks has been estimated to be comparable to that of small- to medium-sized countries, raising concerns about their environmental sustainability. Moreover, the growing popularity of cryptocurrencies and blockchain-based applications exacerbates these environmental concerns, as the demand for computing power and energy continues to rise.

3.8.3 E-Waste Generation

In addition to energy consumption and carbon emissions, the rapid turnover of hardware in blockchain mining operations contributes to e-waste generation. Mining rigs and specialized hardware used for cryptocurrency mining have a limited lifespan and often end up in landfills once they become obsolete or unprofitable. The disposal of e-waste poses environmental risks due to the presence of hazardous materials such as lead, mercury, and cadmium, which can leach into soil and water and harm ecosystems and human health.

3.8.4 Sustainable Alternatives and Solutions

Despite these environmental challenges, there are opportunities to promote sustainability in blockchain technology and Fintech. One approach is to transition to more energy-efficient consensus mechanisms, such as Proof-of-Stake (PoS) or Proof-of-Authority (PoA), which require significantly less energy than PoW. Another strategy is to promote renewable energy sources for blockchain mining operations, such as solar, wind, and hydroelectric power. By harnessing clean energy sources, blockchain networks can reduce their carbon footprint and mitigate their environmental impact. Additionally, efforts to extend the lifespan of hardware and promote responsible e-waste management can help reduce the environmental footprint of blockchain technology. This may involve recycling, refurbishing, or repurposing mining equipment to minimize waste and maximize resource efficiency.

3.8.5 Regulatory and Industry Initiatives

Regulatory agencies and industry stakeholders play a crucial role in promoting environmental sustainability in blockchain technology and Fintech. Governments can incentivize the use of renewable energy sources and impose regulations to limit carbon emissions from blockchain mining operations. Industry initiatives such as the Crypto Climate Accord aim to decarbonize the cryptocurrency industry and achieve net-zero carbon emissions by 2040. By committing to sustainability goals and collaborating on innovative solutions, stakeholders can work together to address the environmental challenges of blockchain technology and Fintech.

3.9 Global Perspectives and Cross-Border Collaboration in Blockchain Technology and Fintech

■ Introduction to Global Perspectives: The advent of blockchain technology and Fintech has transcended geographical boundaries, offering unprecedented opportunities for global collaboration and innovation in the financial sector. With the rise of digital currencies, DeFi, and cross-border payment solutions, stakeholders worldwide are increasingly recognizing the importance of global perspectives in driving the evolution of finance.

■ Expansion of Financial Services: Blockchain technology and Fintech have expanded access to financial services across the globe, particularly in regions with underdeveloped banking infrastructure. Through mobile banking, digital wallets, and blockchain-based remittance platforms, individuals and businesses in remote areas can now access financial services, facilitating economic empowerment and financial inclusion on a global scale.

■ Challenges and Opportunities: While blockchain technology and Fintech offer immense opportunities for cross-border collaboration, they also present unique challenges. Regulatory frameworks vary significantly across jurisdictions, creating complexities for global expansion and compliance. Additionally, cultural differences and language barriers can impede collaboration efforts, highlighting the importance of fostering understanding and cooperation among diverse stakeholders.

■ Interoperability and Standardization: Interoperability and standardization are essential for seamless cross-border collaboration in blockchain technology and Fintech. Efforts to develop interoperable protocols, cross-chain solutions, and standardized regulatory frameworks are crucial for facilitating global transactions, reducing friction, and fostering trust among international partners.

■ Emerging Markets and Innovation Hubs: Emerging markets and innovation hubs play a pivotal role in driving global perspectives and cross-border collaboration in blockchain technology and Fintech. Countries such as Singapore, Switzerland, and Estonia have emerged as leading hubs for blockchain innovation, attracting talent, investment, and cross-border partnerships from around the world.

■ Public-Private Partnerships (PPPs): PPPs are instrumental in promoting global perspectives and cross-border collaboration in blockchain technology and Fintech. Collaborative initiatives between governments, financial institutions, technology firms, and academia can facilitate knowledge exchange, regulatory harmonization, and the development of interoperable solutions to address global challenges.

▪ Ethical Considerations and Responsible Innovation: As blockchain technology and Fintech continue to evolve, it is imperative to address ethical considerations and promote responsible innovation. Global perspectives should encompass values such as transparency, privacy, and security, ensuring that technological advancements benefit society as a whole while mitigating potential risks and vulnerabilities.

3.10 Emerging Trends and Future Outlook in Blockchain Technology and Fintech

▪ Introduction to Emerging Trends: The intersection of blockchain technology and Fintech continues to evolve rapidly, driven by ongoing innovation and market demand. As we look toward the future, several emerging trends are poised to shape the landscape of finance and technology in the years to come.

▪ DeFi: DeFi has emerged as a revolutionary trend, leveraging blockchain technology to create decentralized financial systems and applications. In the coming years, DeFi is expected to further disrupt traditional finance by offering decentralized lending, borrowing, trading, and asset management services, all accessible without intermediaries.

▪ Central Bank Digital Currencies (CBDCs): Central banks worldwide are exploring the issuance of digital currencies, known as CBDCs, as a means to modernize payment systems and enhance financial inclusion. The development and adoption of CBDCs are expected to accelerate in the future, potentially transforming the way people transact and interact with money.

▪ Tokenization of Assets: The tokenization of real-world assets, such as real estate, stocks, and commodities, using blockchain technology, is gaining traction. This trend is expected to continue as more assets are digitized and traded on blockchain-based platforms, unlocking liquidity, reducing friction, and expanding investment opportunities.

▪ NFTs: NFTs have surged in popularity, enabling the creation, ownership, and trading of unique digital assets on blockchain networks. While initially associated with digital art and collectibles, NFTs have broader applications in areas such as gaming, media, and intellectual property rights, with significant potential for growth in the future.

▪ Cross-Border Payments and Remittances: Blockchain technology is facilitating faster, cheaper, and more transparent cross-border payments and remittances. As regulatory frameworks evolve and blockchain infrastructure matures, cross-border transactions are expected to become more efficient and accessible, benefiting businesses and individuals worldwide.

▪ Regulatory Developments: Regulatory clarity and compliance remain critical factors shaping the future of blockchain technology and Fintech. Governments and regulatory bodies are increasingly focused on developing comprehensive frameworks to govern digital assets, protect investors, and mitigate risks, providing a foundation for sustainable growth and innovation in the industry.

▪ Integration of AI: The integration of AI with blockchain technology and Fintech is expected to drive further innovation in areas such as fraud detection, risk management, and customer service. AI-powered analytics and automation tools will enable financial institutions to extract valuable insights from data, enhance decision-making processes, and deliver personalized services to customers.

■ Sustainability and Green Finance: With growing concerns about environmental sustainability, there is a rising interest in leveraging blockchain technology and Fintech to promote green finance initiatives. Blockchain-based solutions can enable transparent tracking of carbon emissions, facilitate green investments, and incentivize sustainable practices across industries.

3.11 Case Studies and Examples in Blockchain Technology and Fintech

■ Case Study: Ripple (XRP) and Cross-Border Payments: Ripple, a blockchain-based payment protocol, offers a real-world example of how blockchain technology is transforming cross-border payments. By leveraging its native cryptocurrency XRP and its RippleNet network, Ripple enables financial institutions to facilitate fast, low-cost, and transparent cross-border transactions. Institutions like Santander and MoneyGram have partnered with Ripple to streamline their international payment processes, demonstrating the practical application of blockchain technology in improving efficiency and reducing costs in the financial sector.

■ Case Study: Ethereum and DeFi: Ethereum, a blockchain platform known for its smart contract functionality, serves as the foundation for many DeFi applications. Projects like Compound, Uniswap, and Aave leverage Ethereum's programmable capabilities to create decentralized lending, borrowing, and trading platforms. These DeFi protocols enable users to access financial services without relying on traditional intermediaries like banks or exchanges, showcasing the disruptive potential of blockchain technology in reshaping the future of finance.

■ Case Study: IBM and Trade Finance on Blockchain: IBM's collaboration with numerous global banks and financial institutions illustrates how blockchain technology is revolutionizing trade finance. Through initiatives like IBM Blockchain World Wire and TradeLens, IBM leverages blockchain to digitize and streamline trade processes, including supply chain financing, document verification, and cross-border payments. By providing a secure and transparent platform for trade finance activities, IBM's blockchain solutions enhance efficiency, reduce fraud, and mitigate risks in global trade transactions.

■ Case Study: Binance and Cryptocurrency Exchange: Binance, one of the world's largest cryptocurrency exchanges, exemplifies the transformative impact of Fintech in the digital asset space. With a user-friendly interface, advanced trading features, and a wide range of supported cryptocurrencies, Binance has become a preferred platform for millions of traders worldwide. Binance's success highlights how Fintech innovations, such as cryptocurrency exchanges, have democratized access to digital assets, enabling individuals to participate in global financial markets with ease.

■ Case Study: Visa and Digital Currency Integration: Visa's collaboration with cryptocurrency platforms like Coinbase and Fold demonstrates how traditional financial institutions are embracing blockchain technology. By integrating digital currency capabilities into its existing payment infrastructure, Visa enables users to convert and spend cryptocurrencies at millions of merchants worldwide. This integration bridges the gap between traditional finance and blockchain-based assets, fostering mainstream adoption of digital currencies and expanding their utility in everyday transactions.

■ Case Study: Stellar and Financial Inclusion: Stellar, a blockchain platform focused on cross-border payments and financial inclusion, showcases how blockchain technology can empower underserved populations. Stellar's partnerships with organizations like the United Nations and the World Bank enable efficient and low-cost remittances to regions with limited access to traditional banking services. By providing a decentralized platform for P2P transactions, Stellar enables individuals in developing countries to access financial services, send and receive money, and participate in the global economy (Khang & Hajimahmud, 2024).

3.12 Applications of Fintech and Data Science

Certainly! Here are some specific applications of Fintech and data science:

3.12.1 Risk Assessment and Management

Fintech companies utilize data science algorithms to assess and manage various types of risks, including credit risk, market risk, and operational risk. ML models analyze vast amounts of financial data to identify patterns and predict potential risks more accurately than traditional methods.

3.12.2 Fraud Detection and Prevention

Data science techniques such as anomaly detection, pattern recognition, and predictive modeling are used to detect fraudulent activities in financial transactions. Fintech companies employ advanced algorithms to analyze transactional data in real-time and identify suspicious behavior, helping to mitigate financial losses and protect consumers.

3.12.3 Personalized Financial Services

Fintech firms leverage data science to offer personalized financial products and services tailored to individual customer preferences and needs. ML algorithms analyze customer data, including spending patterns, savings behavior, and investment preferences, to provide personalized recommendations for budgeting, investing, and financial planning.

3.12.4 Algorithmic Trading and Investment Management

Data science plays a crucial role in algorithmic trading strategies and investment management algorithms. Fintech firms use sophisticated quantitative models and ML algorithms to analyze market data, identify trading opportunities, and optimize investment portfolios. These algorithms can execute trades automatically based on predefined criteria and adapt to changing market conditions in real-time.

3.12.5 Alternative Credit Scoring

Fintech companies leverage alternative data sources and ML algorithms to assess the creditworthiness of individuals and businesses that lack traditional credit histories. By analyzing non-traditional data such as social media activity, online shopping behavior, and utility bill payments, Fintech firms can provide access to credit for underserved populations and facilitate financial inclusion.

3.12.6 Robo-Advisory Services

Fintech platforms offer robo-advisory services that use data science algorithms to automate investment advice and portfolio management. ML models analyze investor risk profiles, financial goals, and market trends to generate customized investment strategies and asset allocations. Robo-advisors provide cost-effective investment solutions with minimal human intervention.

3.12.7 Predictive Analytics for Customer Insights

Fintech companies employ predictive analytics techniques to gain insights into customer behavior, preferences, and lifetime value. By analyzing historical data and customer interactions across various channels, data science algorithms can forecast future trends, identify cross-selling opportunities, and optimize marketing campaigns to enhance customer engagement and loyalty.

3.12.8 Regulatory Compliance and Reporting

Fintech firms use data science to streamline regulatory compliance processes and ensure adherence to complex financial regulations. ML algorithms analyze vast amounts of regulatory data, detect compliance violations, and generate accurate reports for regulatory authorities. Automated compliance solutions help Fintech companies minimize compliance costs and mitigate regulatory risks.

3.13 Implications and Challenges

3.13.1 Implications

- Financial Inclusion: Fintech innovations powered by data science have the potential to enhance financial inclusion by providing access to banking and financial services for underserved populations, including those in rural areas or with limited access to traditional banking infrastructure.
- Cost Efficiency: Data-driven Fintech solutions can streamline processes, reduce operational costs, and improve efficiency for financial institutions, leading to cost savings that can be passed on to consumers in the form of lower fees and better rates.
- Customization and Personalization: Fintech companies can leverage data science algorithms to analyze customer preferences and behavior, enabling the delivery of personalized financial products and services tailored to individual needs and preferences.
- Risk Management: Data science techniques such as predictive analytics and ML can enhance risk assessment and management processes, enabling financial institutions to better identify and mitigate risks related to credit, market volatility, fraud, and regulatory compliance.
- Innovation and Competition: The integration of Fintech and data science fuels innovation and competition in the financial industry, leading to the development of new products, services, and business models that challenge traditional incumbents and drive market evolution (Khang, Inna et al., 2024).

3.13.2 Challenges

- Data Privacy and Security: The use of vast amounts of personal and financial data raises concerns about data privacy, security, and unauthorized access. Fintech companies must prioritize cybersecurity measures and adhere to strict data protection regulations to safeguard sensitive information (Khang, 2024a).

- Algorithmic Bias and Fairness: Data-driven decision-making processes are susceptible to algorithmic bias, which can lead to unfair outcomes, discrimination, and social inequality. Fintech firms must address biases in data collection, algorithm design, and model training to ensure fairness and equity in their products and services.
- Regulatory Compliance: The rapidly evolving regulatory landscape poses challenges for Fintech companies, which must navigate complex regulatory requirements and compliance obligations across multiple jurisdictions. Regulatory uncertainty and compliance costs can impede innovation and limit the scalability of Fintech solutions.
- Lack of Trust and Transparency: Consumer trust in Fintech platforms relies on transparency, accountability, and ethical use of data. Fintech companies must establish clear policies and practices for data collection, usage, and sharing, and communicate openly with users about how their data is being utilized.
- Digital Divide: While Fintech innovations have the potential to expand access to financial services, there is a risk of widening the digital divide between those who have access to technology and those who do not. Efforts are needed to bridge this gap and ensure equitable access to Fintech solutions for all segments of society.

3.14 Future Directions

Certainly! Exploring the future directions of Fintech and data science can offer insights into potential areas of innovation and growth. Here are some future directions to consider:

3.14.1 Integration of Emerging Technologies

Fintech companies are likely to integrate emerging technologies such as blockchain, AI, Internet of Things (IoT), and quantum computing into their offerings. Blockchain technology, for instance, holds the potential to revolutionize the way financial transactions are conducted by providing enhanced security, transparency, and efficiency (Khang, Rath, Madapana et al., 2024).

3.14.2 Expansion of Open Banking and APIs

Open banking initiatives are expected to gain momentum, leading to increased collaboration and data sharing between financial institutions and third-party developers. APIs will play a crucial role in facilitating seamless integration between different financial services and enabling the development of innovative Fintech solutions.

3.14.3 Enhanced Customer Experience

Fintech companies will continue to focus on enhancing the customer experience through personalized, omnichannel solutions. Data-driven insights will enable Fintech firms to anticipate customer needs, deliver tailored financial products and services, and provide intuitive user experiences across digital platforms.

3.14.4 Advancements in RegTech and Compliance Solutions

RegTech solutions will evolve to address the growing complexities of regulatory compliance in the financial industry. Fintech firms will leverage data science and AI to develop automated compliance tools that streamline regulatory reporting, monitor for suspicious activities, and ensure adherence to changing regulatory requirements.

3.14.5 Rise of Decentralized Finance (DeFi)

DeFi platforms built on blockchain technology will continue to disrupt traditional financial services by offering decentralized lending, borrowing, trading, and asset management solutions. Data science techniques will play a crucial role in optimizing DeFi protocols, managing risks, and ensuring the security and integrity of decentralized financial transactions.

3.14.6 Focus on Sustainability and Impact Investing

Fintech companies will increasingly prioritize sustainability and impact investing initiatives to address environmental, social, and governance (ESG) concerns. Data science will enable the analysis of ESG factors and the development of innovative financial products that align with sustainable investing goals, such as green bonds, renewable energy financing, and social impact bonds.

3.14.7 Expansion of Financial Inclusion Efforts

Fintech innovations will continue to drive efforts toward financial inclusion by providing access to financial services for underserved populations. Data science will enable the development of alternative credit scoring models, micro-lending platforms, and digital payment solutions tailored to the needs of unbanked and underbanked individuals in both developed and emerging markets.

3.14.8 Emphasis on Cybersecurity and Data Privacy

Fintech firms will invest in cybersecurity measures and data privacy technologies to safeguard sensitive financial information and protect against cyber threats. Data science techniques such as encryption, anomaly detection, and behavioral analytics will be employed to identify and mitigate cybersecurity risks proactively (Khang, 2024b).

3.15 Conclusion

In conclusion, the convergence of blockchain technology and Fintech heralds a transformative era in the global financial landscape. As we reflect on the myriad applications and implications of these technologies, several key insights emerge. First, blockchain technology has revolutionized traditional financial systems by offering decentralized, secure, and transparent solutions for various financial transactions. From cross-border payments and trade finance to asset tokenization and DeFi, blockchain technology has unlocked new opportunities for innovation and efficiency in the financial sector (Nayak, Dürr, & Rothermel, 2015).

Second, Fintech innovations, powered by blockchain technology, have democratized access to financial services, enabling greater financial inclusion and empowerment for individuals and businesses worldwide. Digital currencies, decentralized lending platforms, and blockchain-based remittance solutions are just a few examples of how Fintech is revolutionizing the way we transact, invest, and manage our finances.

Furthermore, the future outlook for blockchain technology and Fintech is characterized by continued innovation, collaboration, and regulatory evolution. As technology evolves and regulatory frameworks adapt, we can expect to see further integration of blockchain technology into traditional financial systems, as well as the emergence of new applications and use cases that have yet to be imagined. However, challenges such as regulatory compliance, interoperability, and scalability remain important considerations as blockchain technology and Fintech continue to evolve.

Addressing these challenges will require collaboration between industry stakeholders, regulators, and policymakers to ensure that innovation is balanced with consumer protection and systemic stability. In essence, the journey of blockchain technology and Fintech is one of innovation, disruption, and transformation. By harnessing the potential of these technologies responsibly and collaboratively, we can create a more inclusive, efficient, and resilient financial ecosystem that benefits individuals, businesses, and society as a whole (Khang, Hajimahmud, Niu, 2024).

References

Chen, S. H., Jakeman, A. J., Norton, J. P. (2008). Artificial intelligence techniques: An introduction to their use for modelling environmental systems. Math. Comput. Simul., 78, 379–400. https://www.science-direct.com/science/article/pii/S0378475408000505

Khang, A. (2024a). "Future Directions and Challenges in Designing Workforce Management Systems for Industry 4," In Khang A., *AI-Oriented Competency Framework for Talent Management in the Digital Economy: Models, Technologies, Applications, and Implementation* (1st Ed.). CRC Press. https://doi.org/10.1201/9781003440901-1

Khang, A. (2024b). "Implementation of AIoCF Model and Tools for Information Technology Sector," In Khang A., *AI-Oriented Competency Framework for Talent Management in the Digital Economy: Models, Technologies, Applications, and Implementation* (1st Ed.). CRC Press. https://doi.org/10.1201/9781003440901-20

Khang, A., Hajimahmud, V. A. (2024). "Introduction to the Gig Economy," In Khang A. Jadhav B., Hajimahmud V. A., Satpathy I., The Synergy of AI and Fintech in the Digital Gig Economy (1st Ed.). CRC Press. https://doi.org/10.1201/9781032720104-1

Khang A., Hajimahmud V. A. and Niu Y. (2024). "Artificial Intelligence Technology Based Approach in Banking Compliance Supervision". In Khang PH, D.A. (Ed.). (2024). Shaping Cutting-Edge Technologies and Applications for Digital Banking and Financial Services (1st Ed.). Productivity Press.

Khang, A., Inna, S. O., Alla, K., Rostyslav, S., Rudenko, M., Lidia, R., Kristina, B. (2024). "Management Model 6.0 and Business Recovery Strategy of Enterprises in the Era of Digital Economy," In Khang, A., Gujrati, R., Uygun, H., Tailor, R. K., & Gaur, S., Data-Driven Modelling and Predictive Analytics in Business and Finance (1st Ed.). CRC Press. https://doi.org/10.1201/9781032618845-16

Khang A., Rath K.C., Madapana K., Rao N. V. J., Panda L. P. and Das S. (2024). "Quantum Computing and Portfolio Optimization in Finance Services and Digital Economy". In Khang PH, D.A. (Ed.). (2024). Shaping Cutting-Edge Technologies and Applications for Digital Banking and Financial Services (1st Ed.). Productivity Press.

Nayak, N. G., Dürr, F., Rothermel, K. (2015). Software-defined environment for reconfigurable manufacturing systems. In Proceedings of the 2015 5th International Conference on the Internet of Things (IOT), Seoul, Korea, 26–28 October 2015; pp. 122–129. https://ieeexplore.ieee.org/abstract/document/7356556/

Papadimitriou, F. (2012). Artificial intelligence in modelling the complexity of Mediterranean landscape transformations. Comput. Electron. Agric., 81, 87–96. https://www.sciencedirect.com/science/article/pii/S0168169911002651

Yetilmezsoy, K., Ozkaya, B., Cakmakci, M. (2011). Artificial intelligence-based prediction models for environmental engineering. Neural Netw. World, 21, 193–218. https://avesis.yildiz.edu.tr/yayin/15efce0e-b6c1-405a-ab9c-442dbf999eee/artificial-intelligence-based-prediction-models-for-environmental-engineering

Chapter 4

Financial Forecasting with Convolutional Neural Networks (CNNs): Trends and Challenges

Tarun Kumar Vashishth, Vikas Sharma, Kewal Krishan Sharma, Shahanawaj Ahamad, and Vineet Kaushik

4.1 Introduction

Financial forecasting is a pivotal component in shaping strategic decisions and managing risks within the dynamic landscape of the modern financial industry. The continuous evolution of computational techniques and the advent of artificial intelligence (AI) have given rise to innovative approaches, among which convolutional neural networks (CNNs) stand out as a promising tool for enhancing forecasting precision.

Originally designed for image recognition, CNNs have demonstrated remarkable efficacy in handling sequential financial data, such as time series and textual information. This chapter embarks on a comprehensive exploration of the trends and challenges associated with leveraging CNNs for financial forecasting, encompassing their adaptation to time series analysis, applications in stock price prediction and foreign exchange rate forecasting, and the integration of textual data to enhance predictive models (Chen et al., 2016).

4.1.1 Background and Motivation

The financial industry's landscape has been continually shaped by technological advancements, prompting a fundamental shift in decision-making paradigms and risk management strategies. In this dynamic environment, the integration of computational techniques and AI has become imperative for staying competitive and informed (Thakkar & Chaudhari, 2021). Financial

DOI: 10.4324/9781003501947-4

forecasting, as a core element, serves as the bedrock for strategic planning and risk mitigation. Traditional methods are being challenged by the emergence of CNNs, originally designed for image recognition but showcasing considerable potential in decoding sequential financial data (Koenecke & Gajewar, 2020).

The motivation behind this exploration lies in the need to comprehensively understand the evolving trends and challenges associated with employing CNNs in financial forecasting. As the financial industry increasingly relies on data-driven insights, the adaptation of advanced neural network architectures, specifically CNNs, holds the promise of revolutionizing predictive analytics (Borovykh, Bohte & Oosterlee, 2017). This chapter seeks to delve into the nuances of CNNs in financial contexts, examining their adaptability to time series analysis, exploring applications, and addressing challenges with the ultimate goal of providing valuable insights for researchers, practitioners, and decision-makers navigating the intersection of finance and AI.

4.1.2 Objectives of the Chapter

- Comprehensive exploration of CNN adaptation: To elucidate the adaptation of CNNs from their origin in image recognition to their application in handling sequential financial data, particularly time series and textual information.
- Understanding basic concepts of CNNs: To introduce and elucidate the basic concepts of CNNs, providing a foundational understanding for readers unfamiliar with the architecture and highlighting their relevance in the financial forecasting domain.
- Analysis of CNNs in financial time series: To delve into the incorporation of one-dimensional convolutions and attention mechanisms in CNNs, emphasizing their role in capturing spatial and temporal patterns crucial for effective financial time series analysis.
- Applications in financial forecasting: To discuss and analyze various financial forecasting applications utilizing CNNs, including but not limited to stock price prediction, foreign exchange rate forecasting, and commodity price analysis, showcasing the diversity of CNN applications in finance.
- Integration of textual data: To explore the integration of textual data, such as financial news and social media sentiments, into CNN-based forecasting models, highlighting how this fusion enhances predictive capabilities in the financial domain.
- Addressing challenges in CNNs: To identify and address challenges associated with employing CNNs in the financial domain, ranging from data quality issues to model interpretability and proposing strategies to overcome these challenges.
- Optimizing CNN performance: To explore the need for robust transfer learning strategies and hybrid models to optimize CNN performance in financial forecasting, offering insights into maximizing the effectiveness of these neural networks in real-world financial applications.
- Ethical considerations and bias mitigation: To discuss the ethical considerations inherent in deploying CNNs in financial decision-making and to address potential biases, ensuring responsible and unbiased use of AI in the financial industry.
- Highlighting evolving trends and research efforts: To provide a synthesis of evolving trends and ongoing research efforts in the field, emphasizing the importance of interpretability, model explainability, and continuous improvement in CNN-based financial forecasting models.

4.1.3 Scope and Organization

This chapter delves into the application of CNNs in financial forecasting, aiming to provide a thorough understanding of the trends and challenges in this dynamic intersection. The scope encompasses fundamental concepts of CNNs, their adaptation to financial time series analysis, and diverse applications, including stock price prediction and foreign exchange rate forecasting.

Additionally, the chapter explores the integration of textual data for enhanced forecasting models, addressing challenges in the financial domain, optimizing CNN performance, and navigating ethical considerations. The organization follows a logical progression, starting with an introduction to set the stage, followed by detailed discussions on CNN fundamentals, applications, challenges, and strategies for improvement. The chapter concludes by highlighting evolving trends and ongoing research efforts, offering a holistic perspective on the role of CNNs in shaping the future of financial forecasting (Khang, Hajimahmud et al., 2024).

4.2 Financial Forecasting: An Overview

Financial forecasting serves as a cornerstone in the realm of strategic decision-making and risk management within the modern financial landscape. At its core, it involves the use of historical data, statistical models, and advanced technologies to predict future financial outcomes. This proactive approach aids businesses, investors, and financial institutions in making informed decisions, allocating resources effectively and mitigating potential risks (Tovar, 2020).

Financial forecasting spans various domains, including budgeting, revenue projections, and investment planning. It acts as a compass for navigating uncertainties in volatile markets, enabling organizations to anticipate trends and adapt strategies accordingly. As technological advancements, particularly in AI and machine learning (ML), continue to reshape the financial sector, the evolution of sophisticated forecasting methodologies becomes increasingly vital for maintaining competitiveness and sustainability in a dynamic economic environment (Sezer, Gudelek & Ozbayoglu, 2020).

4.2.1 Importance of Financial Forecasting

Financial forecasting is of paramount importance in the business world, playing a central role in strategic planning, risk management, and overall financial stability. By utilizing historical data, market trends, and sophisticated modeling techniques, organizations can project future financial outcomes and make informed decisions. Strategic planning relies heavily on accurate financial forecasts as they provide a roadmap for setting goals, allocating resources, and determining the trajectory of a business (Alonso-Monsalve et al., 2020). Moreover, financial forecasting is a linchpin in risk management, allowing businesses to identify potential challenges, assess their financial implications, and proactively implement mitigation strategies. This proactive approach not only safeguards against unforeseen circumstances but also enhances the organization's ability to navigate uncertainties.

Effective resource allocation is another critical facet, as financial forecasts guide decisions on investments, budgeting, and operational strategies, ensuring optimal utilization of resources (Sezer & Ozbayoglu, 2018). Financial forecasting is indispensable for attracting investors, as it instills confidence by showcasing a clear understanding of financial performance and future prospects. Furthermore, it aids in evaluating operational efficiency, managing cash flow, and facilitating adaptability to changing market dynamics. In essence, financial forecasting is a dynamic tool that empowers organizations to make sound financial decisions, enhance operational effectiveness, and foster long-term sustainability in today's complex and competitive business environment (Tsantekidis et al., 2017).

4.2.2 Traditional Approaches to Financial Forecasting

Traditional approaches to financial forecasting have long been foundational tools for businesses seeking to navigate the uncertain terrain of future financial outcomes. One of the conventional methods is historical trend analysis, where organizations scrutinize past financial data to identify patterns and extrapolate trends into the future, assuming a continuity of historical performance (Barra et al., 2020).

Time series analysis, employing techniques like moving averages and exponential smoothing, leverages sequential time-ordered data points for short-term forecasting, particularly in situations with regular patterns. Regression analysis quantifies the relationship between variables, proving beneficial when a clear cause-and-effect connection exists. Scenario analysis involves evaluating diverse future scenarios and their potential impact, providing a strategic perspective for decision-making amid uncertainties (Saxena, Asbe & Vashishth, 2023).

Budget-based forecasting establishes financial targets aligned with organizational goals, guiding short-term planning and operational alignment. Expert judgment relies on internal experts for unique situations, while sales forecasting, crucial for production planning and inventory management, predicts future sales based on historical data and market trends. Although these traditional methods are robust, the ever-evolving financial landscape prompts an integration of more advanced methodologies to cope with increased complexity and data availability (Cheng et al., 2022).

4.2.3 Limitations of Conventional Methods

Conventional methods of financial forecasting, while foundational, exhibit certain limitations that may hinder their effectiveness in today's dynamic business environment. Historical trend analysis, relying on past data patterns, may prove inadequate when faced with sudden market disruptions or paradigm shifts. Time series analysis, though useful for short-term predictions, may struggle to capture intricate, non-linear relationships prevalent in modern financial datasets (Dingli & Fournier, 2017).

Regression analysis, despite its predictive power, assumes a static relationship between variables, often overlooking dynamic market conditions. Scenario analysis, while valuable for contingency planning, may fall short in addressing unprecedented events with no historical precedent. Budget-based forecasting can become rigid in adapting to rapidly changing business landscapes, and expert judgment might introduce biases or overlook emerging trends. Sales forecasting, heavily reliant on historical sales patterns, may miss nuances in consumer behavior or market dynamics (Chen et al., 2020). As businesses navigate an era of increased volatility and complexity, these limitations underscore the need for more adaptive and technologically sophisticated forecasting approaches to enhance accuracy and resilience in predicting financial outcomes (Khang, Shah & Rani, 2023c).

4.2.4 Role of Machine Learning in Financial Forecasting

ML has revolutionized financial forecasting by offering advanced tools that go beyond the limitations of traditional methods. ML algorithms, particularly within the domain of supervised learning, can analyze vast datasets, identify patterns, and make predictions based on historical and real-time information. In financial forecasting, ML models, such as decision trees, random forests, and support vector machines, excel in capturing intricate relationships between variables, adapting to non-linear patterns, and automatically adjusting to evolving market conditions.

Deep learning (DL), a subset of ML, introduces neural networks, like long short-term memory (LSTM) networks, which are adept at handling sequential data such as time series, a key component in financial analysis (Hosaka, 2019). Reinforcement learning provides avenues for adaptive decision-making in response to changing environments. The role of ML in financial forecasting extends to sentiment analysis, where algorithms process textual data from news articles, social media, and other sources to gauge market sentiment and factor it into predictions. The incorporation of ML techniques enhances the accuracy, adaptability, and efficiency of financial forecasting, empowering organizations to make more informed decisions in the face of dynamic and complex financial landscapes (Markova, 2022).

4.3 CNNs in Finance

4.3.1 Understanding CNNs

CNNs stand as a pivotal advancement in the field of DL, particularly known for their exceptional performance in computer vision tasks. At their core, CNNs are designed to mimic the visual processing that occurs in the human brain. The architecture comprises layers of convolutional and pooling operations, enabling the network to automatically learn hierarchical representations from input data. Convolutional layers employ filters to detect local patterns, capturing spatial features such as edges and textures. Subsequent pooling layers reduce dimensionality, retaining essential information (Yu & Yan, 2020).

What distinguishes CNNs is their ability to recognize spatial hierarchies and patterns within data, making them highly effective for tasks involving images, videos, and sequential data. Transfer learning, a prevalent technique in CNNs, allows pre-trained models to be adapted to new tasks, saving computational resources and enhancing performance. In financial forecasting, CNNs have transcended their original application in image recognition, showcasing promising potential in handling sequential financial data, such as time series and textual information, due to their capacity to capture spatial and temporal patterns effectively (Chung & Shin, 2020).

4.3.2 CNN Architecture and Layers

CNNs are a class of deep neural networks designed for processing structured grid data, such as images. The architecture of a CNN is characterized by its unique layers, each serving a specific purpose in feature extraction and hierarchical representation learning. The primary layers in a CNN include the following:

- Input layer: The input layer represents the raw data, typically an image or a sequence of data points in the context of financial forecasting.
- Convolutional layers: Convolutional layers are the core building blocks of a CNN. These layers employ filters or kernels to scan the input data, extracting features and detecting patterns. Convolution operations allow the network to capture spatial relationships within the data.

- Activation function: An activation function, often rectified linear unit (ReLU), follows the convolutional layers. It introduces non-linearity into the network, enabling it to learn complex relationships and patterns in the data.
- Pooling layers: Pooling layers reduce the spatial dimensions of the data by down sampling. Max pooling, for example, retains the maximum value in a specific region, discarding non-maximum values and preserving the most salient features.
- Flattening layer: The flattening layer transforms the multidimensional output of the previous layers into a one-dimensional vector. This prepares the data for the fully connected layers.
- Fully connected layers: Fully connected layers connect every neuron in one layer to every neuron in the adjacent layers. These layers are responsible for high-level feature extraction and learning complex relationships in the data.
- Output layer: The output layer produces the final predictions based on the features learned throughout the network. The activation function in this layer depends on the nature of the task, such as softmax for classification or linear for regression.

This architectural design, with its convolutional and pooling layers, allows CNNs to automatically learn hierarchical representations of features in data, making them particularly effective in tasks like image recognition and, as seen in recent applications, financial forecasting where sequential data patterns need to be captured.

4.3.3 Applications of CNNs in Finance

CNNs initially designed for image recognition have found promising applications in the financial domain, leveraging their ability to capture spatial and temporal patterns. Some key applications of CNNs in finance include the following:

- Stock price prediction: CNNs are employed to analyze historical stock price data, capturing complex patterns and dependencies. The networks can recognize relevant features in time series data, assisting in more accurate stock price predictions.
- Foreign exchange rate forecasting: CNNs prove effective in modeling the intricate relationships and patterns within foreign exchange rate time series. Their capacity to handle sequential data allows for improved forecasting accuracy in the volatile forex market.
- Commodity price analysis: Similar to stock and forex markets, CNNs can analyze historical data patterns to forecast commodity prices. This is particularly valuable for industries reliant on commodities, aiding in better decision-making and risk management.
- Credit scoring and risk assessment: CNNs contribute to credit scoring models by analyzing various financial data, including transaction histories and credit scores. They can identify patterns indicative of creditworthiness or potential risks, enhancing the accuracy of risk assessment.
- Fraud detection: CNNs are employed in detecting fraudulent activities within financial transactions. By analyzing patterns in transaction data, CNNs can identify anomalies and potentially fraudulent behavior, contributing to robust security systems.
- Portfolio management: CNNs assist in optimizing portfolio management strategies by analyzing diverse financial indicators and market trends. The networks can identify optimal asset allocations based on historical data patterns and market conditions.
- Sentiment analysis: CNNs analyze textual data from financial news, social media, and other sources to gauge market sentiment. This sentiment analysis helps in predicting market trends and making informed investment decisions.

■ Algorithmic trading: CNNs contribute to the development of algorithmic trading strategies by analyzing historical price data and identifying patterns indicative of potential market movements. This application enhances the efficiency and adaptability of trading algorithms.

■ Customer behavior analysis: In the banking sector, CNNs can analyze customer transaction histories and behaviors, aiding in personalized marketing and product recommendations. This enhances customer satisfaction and engagement.

■ Time series analysis for economic indicators: CNNs are applied to analyze time series data related to economic indicators, such as Gross domestic product (GDP) or unemployment rates. This enables more accurate predictions and assessments of economic trends.

The applications of CNNs in finance underscore their versatility in handling diverse data types and their potential to enhance decision-making processes within the financial industry. As computational techniques advance, CNNs continue to play a pivotal role in shaping the future of financial analytics and forecasting.

4.3.4 Advantages of CNNs for Financial Forecasting

CNNs offer several advantages when applied to financial forecasting, contributing to enhanced accuracy and efficiency in predictive modeling:

■ Pattern recognition in sequential data: CNNs excel in capturing intricate patterns and dependencies within sequential financial data, such as time series. Their architecture is well suited for identifying spatial and temporal features, making them effective in modeling market trends.

■ Adaptability to time series analysis: CNNs can naturally adapt to time series analysis, allowing for the automatic extraction of relevant features from historical financial data. This adaptability is crucial for forecasting tasks where understanding temporal dependencies is essential.

■ Effective handling of multidimensional Data: Financial datasets often involve multidimensional information, including numerical, textual, and sequential data. CNNs are adept at processing and extracting meaningful features from such diverse data sources, contributing to comprehensive forecasting models.

■ Automatic feature extraction: CNNs automate the process of feature extraction, eliminating the need for manual feature engineering. The networks learn hierarchical representations of features directly from the data, reducing the burden on analysts and improving forecasting accuracy.

■ Spatial and temporal information integration: The convolutional layers in CNNs allow for the integration of both spatial and temporal information simultaneously. This is valuable in financial forecasting, where understanding the relationship between different features over time is critical.

■ Transfer learning capabilities: CNNs can leverage transfer learning, where pre-trained models on large datasets can be fine-tuned for specific financial forecasting tasks. This approach saves computational resources and enhances performance, especially when limited financial data is available.

■ Handling noisy data: Financial data often contains noise and market irregularities. CNNs are robust in handling noisy data, and their ability to discern relevant patterns helps mitigate the impact of outliers on forecasting accuracy.

- Incorporation of textual data: CNNs can seamlessly integrate textual data, such as financial news and social media sentiments, into forecasting models. This fusion enhances predictive capabilities by considering the impact of qualitative information on financial markets.
- Enhanced model generalization: CNNs, through their hierarchical feature extraction, facilitate improved generalization to unseen data. This capability is crucial for building models that can adapt to different market conditions and unforeseen events.
- Scalability: CNN architectures are scalable, allowing for the inclusion of additional layers and parameters as needed. This scalability is advantageous in handling complex financial datasets and improving the overall predictive power of the model.

The advantages of CNNs in financial forecasting showcase their versatility in handling diverse data types, adaptability to temporal patterns, and ability to automate feature extraction, ultimately contributing to more accurate and robust predictive models in the dynamic financial landscape.

4.4 Data Preprocessing and Feature Extraction for Financial Data

4.4.1 Data Collection and Preparation

In the realm of financial data analysis, effective data preprocessing and feature extraction are pivotal steps in transforming raw data into meaningful insights. The process typically begins with data collection, where diverse financial information is gathered from various sources such as stock exchanges, financial institutions, and economic indicators. Ensuring data quality is paramount during this phase, involving the identification and rectification of missing values, outliers, and errors to maintain the integrity of the dataset. Once collected, the data undergoes thorough preprocessing to standardize formats, normalize scales, and handle any irregularities that might affect subsequent analysis. Feature extraction comes into play to identify and isolate relevant information from the dataset, potentially involving the creation of new variables that encapsulate essential financial metrics (Di Persio & Honchar, 2016).

In financial data, key features often include price movements, trading volumes, economic indicators, and sentiment analysis derived from textual data. Successful data preprocessing and feature extraction lay the groundwork for robust financial models, enhancing their ability to discern patterns, make accurate predictions, and provide valuable insights for decision-makers in the financial domain.

4.4.2 Feature Selection and Engineering

Feature selection and engineering are critical processes in shaping the effectiveness of models in financial data analysis. Feature selection involves identifying and retaining the most relevant variables from the dataset, aiming to enhance model performance by reducing dimensionality and eliminating redundant or irrelevant features. This process is crucial in financial contexts where a multitude of variables, such as market indicators, economic data, and sentiment analysis, may be available. Effective feature selection not only improves model interpretability but also mitigates the risk of overfitting, especially in scenarios with limited data (Chatigny, Patenaude & Wang, 2021).

On the other hand, feature engineering involves the creation of new variables or transformations of existing ones to extract additional insights or improve the model's ability to capture patterns. In financial data, this might include deriving new metrics like moving averages, volatility indicators, or ratios that provide a deeper understanding of market dynamics. The combination of thoughtful feature selection and engineering not only optimizes model performance but also ensures that the chosen features align with the nuances of financial markets, leading to more accurate and actionable predictions for decision-makers.

4.4.3 Time Series Data Handling

Handling time series data in financial analysis requires specialized techniques to capture temporal dependencies and patterns crucial for accurate predictions. Time series data is characterized by its sequential nature, where observations are recorded at successive time intervals. Preprocessing involves addressing issues such as missing values and outliers, imputing or removing them judiciously to maintain data integrity. Temporal aggregation or disaggregation may be applied to align the data with the desired time frequency. Feature engineering plays a vital role as creating lag features or rolling averages can provide valuable insights into trends and seasonality.

Techniques such as differencing or detrending may be employed to stabilize non-stationary data. Model selection is often tailored to time series characteristics, with autoregressive integrated moving average (ARIMA), seasonal decomposition of time series (STL), and ML methods like LSTM networks being common choices (Vashishth et al., 2023). Validation strategies, such as time-based splits, ensure robust model assessment. Overall, effective time series data handling involves a comprehensive approach, encompassing preprocessing, feature engineering, and selecting models attuned to the temporal intricacies of financial datasets.

4.4.4 Addressing Imbalanced Data

Addressing imbalanced data is a crucial aspect in data analysis, particularly in scenarios where one class significantly outnumbers the others, leading to biased model performance. Imbalance can compromise the model's ability to accurately predict minority classes, as it tends to favor the majority class. Several strategies can be employed to mitigate this imbalance. Resampling techniques involve either oversampling the minority class, under sampling the majority class, or a combination of both, thereby balancing class distribution.

Synthetic data generation methods, such as synthetic minority oversampling technique (SMOTE), create artificial samples for the minority class, enhancing its representation in the dataset. Cost-sensitive learning assigns different misclassification costs to different classes, emphasizing the importance of correctly classifying the minority class (Ozbayoglu, Gudelek & Sezer, 2020). Ensemble methods, like boosting, can also be effective, as they give more weight to misclassified instances, improving the model's focus on minority classes. Careful evaluation metrics selection, such as precision, recall, or F1-score, becomes essential to gauge model performance accurately in the presence of imbalanced data, ensuring that the model is effective across all classes rather than biased toward the majority.

4.5 Financial Forecasting with CNNs: Model Design and Implementation

4.5.1 Model Architecture for Financial Forecasting

The model architecture for financial forecasting involves designing a neural network that can effectively capture the patterns and dependencies within financial data. A common and powerful approach is to use a recurrent neural network (RNN) or a specialized variant like LSTM networks due to their ability to handle sequential data. The architecture typically consists of the following components:

- Input layer: Receives input features such as historical stock prices, trading volumes, economic indicators, and any other relevant financial metrics.
- Embedding layer (if applicable): Converts categorical or textual data into numerical vectors for processing by the neural network.
- Recurrent layers (LSTM or Gated Recurrent Unit (GRU)): These layers capture temporal dependencies in the data, allowing the model to remember patterns over time. LSTMs, with their memory cells, are particularly effective in handling long-term dependencies.
- Dense (fully connected) layers: These layers process the output from the recurrent layers and extract high-level features. The number of neurons in these layers can be adjusted based on the complexity of the forecasting task.
- Output layer: Produces the forecasted values, whether they are stock prices, exchange rates, or other financial metrics.

The choice of activation functions, loss functions, and optimization algorithms depends on the nature of the forecasting task (e.g., regression or classification) and the characteristics of the data. Hyperparameter tuning is crucial to optimize the model's performance. Additionally, ensemble methods, such as combining multiple models or utilizing attention mechanisms, can enhance the model's predictive capabilities. Transfer learning, leveraging pre-trained models on related tasks, can be beneficial, especially in scenarios with limited financial data.

Regularization techniques, like dropout layers, help prevent overfitting, ensuring that the model generalizes well to unseen data. The model architecture should be robust, adaptive to market dynamics, and capable of capturing both short-term fluctuations and long-term trends in financial time series data.

4.5.2 Hyperparameter Tuning

Hyperparameter tuning is a critical step in optimizing the performance of ML models by systematically adjusting the hyperparameters, which are external configurations not learned from the data. The process involves exploring different combinations of hyperparameter values to find the set that maximizes the model's performance metrics. Common hyperparameters include learning rates, regularization strengths, the number of layers or nodes in a neural network, and other parameters that influence the model's learning process. Techniques for hyperparameter tuning include grid search, random search, and more advanced optimization algorithms like Bayesian optimization.

During tuning, the model is trained on subsets of the training data, and its performance is evaluated using a validation set (Muthukumar & Zhong, 2021). This iterative process helps in avoiding overfitting and ensures that the model generalizes well to new, unseen data. Successful hyperparameter tuning not only improves a model's predictive accuracy but also tailors it to the specific characteristics of the dataset and the complexity of the task at hand, resulting in a more robust and effective ML model.

4.5.3 Training and Validation

Training and validation are integral phases in the development of ML models, playing pivotal roles in assessing performance, optimizing parameters, and ensuring generalization to new data.

During the training phase, the model learns patterns and relationships within the training dataset. This involves adjusting internal parameters based on the provided input features and target labels, with the objective of minimizing the difference between predicted and actual outcomes. The validation phase is crucial for assessing the model's ability to generalize to unseen data.

A separate validation dataset, distinct from the training data, is used to evaluate the model's performance. This helps in identifying potential overfitting, where the model may perform exceptionally well on the training data but struggle with new, unseen samples. By monitoring the model's performance on both the training and validation sets, practitioners can fine-tune hyperparameters, apply regularization techniques, and ensure that the model achieves a balance between fitting the training data well and exhibiting robust performance on unseen data (Cavalcante et al., 2016). This iterative training-validation process is essential for developing reliable and effective ML models across various domains, including finance, healthcare, and natural language processing.

4.5.4 Model Evaluation and Performance Metrics

Model evaluation and performance metrics are critical aspects of assessing the effectiveness of ML models. Once a model is trained and validated, it is essential to quantify its performance using appropriate metrics that align with the specific objectives of the task. Common evaluation metrics vary based on the nature of the problem, such as classification, regression, or clustering. For classification tasks, metrics like accuracy, precision, recall, F1-score, and area under the receiver operating characteristic (ROC) curve are commonly employed.

In regression tasks, metrics such as mean squared error (MSE) or mean absolute error (MAE) quantify the difference between predicted and actual values. Additionally, confusion matrices, precision-recall curves, and calibration plots provide deeper insights into a model's performance. It is crucial to select metrics that align with the desired outcome and to consider the trade-offs between various metrics (Tuo et al., 2021). Model evaluation goes beyond numerical metrics and involves qualitative assessments of how well the model aligns with the domain-specific requirements and user expectations. Continuous monitoring and refinement of models based on these evaluations are essential to ensure their ongoing relevance and reliability in real-world applications.

4.6 Trends in Financial Forecasting with CNNs

4.6.1 Transfer Learning for Financial Predictions

Transfer learning has emerged as a prominent trend in financial forecasting with CNNs, offering a powerful strategy to leverage pre-trained models on diverse datasets for improved performance in financial predictions. In the context of CNNs, transfer learning involves utilizing a model trained on a large dataset, often in a different domain like image recognition, and fine-tuning it for financial tasks. This approach is particularly beneficial when financial datasets are limited, as it allows the model to inherit knowledge about spatial and temporal patterns from the source domain.

For instance, a CNN pre-trained on image data can be adapted to financial time series analysis, capturing relevant features and improving predictive accuracy. Transfer learning enhances the generalization ability of CNNs by providing a head start in learning complex hierarchical representations (Zhou, Liu & Hu, 2022). It addresses challenges related to insufficient financial data and accelerates the model's convergence. As financial forecasting continues to evolve, transfer learning stands out as a valuable technique to optimize CNN performance, providing a bridge between established knowledge in diverse domains and the unique intricacies of financial markets.

4.6.2 Ensembling Techniques for Improved Accuracy

Ensembling techniques have proven to be powerful strategies for significantly enhancing the accuracy and robustness of ML models in various domains, including finance. One popular method is bagging, exemplified by Random Forests, which builds an ensemble of decision trees on bootstrapped subsets of the data, reducing overfitting and improving stability. Boosting techniques, such as AdaBoost and Gradient Boosting, sequentially train weak learners and emphasize misclassified instances, collectively forming a stronger, more adaptable model. Stacking, another prevalent ensembling approach, combines predictions from diverse models using a meta-model, optimizing overall accuracy.

Voting classifiers allow multiple models to independently contribute to predictions through a majority vote or averaging. Advanced frameworks like XGBoost and LightGBM implement gradient boosting with enhanced efficiency and accuracy, making them popular choices for ensembling in financial forecasting. Ensembling techniques play a crucial role in mitigating overfitting, handling diverse data patterns, and providing a more reliable prediction framework, ultimately contributing to improved decision-making and risk management in the dynamic landscape of financial markets.

4.6.3 Attention Mechanisms in CNNs for Financial Time Series

Attention mechanisms in CNNs have become increasingly significant in the domain of financial time series analysis. Originally applied in natural language processing tasks, attention mechanisms have been adapted to capture relevant temporal patterns and dependencies within sequential financial data.

In CNNs, attention mechanisms selectively weigh the importance of different temporal elements, allowing the model to focus on specific regions of the time series that are more influential for forecasting. This adaptive attention mechanism enables the network to assign varying degrees of significance to different time steps, emphasizing critical market trends and mitigating the impact of noise or irrelevant fluctuations. By incorporating attention mechanisms into CNN architectures, financial analysts can enhance the interpretability of predictions, gaining insights into which time periods or features contribute most to forecasting outcomes (Duan et al., 2022). This attention-driven approach is particularly valuable in the volatile and complex financial domain, where identifying and prioritizing relevant information in time series data is crucial for accurate predictions and effective risk management.

4.6.4 Hybrid Models: Combining CNNs with Other Algorithms

Hybrid models, which combine CNNs with other algorithms, represent a potent strategy in financial forecasting, leveraging the strengths of different methodologies to enhance predictive accuracy. By integrating CNNs with complementary algorithms, such as traditional time series models or ML techniques, hybrid models aim to capture a broader spectrum of information present in financial data. CNNs excel at learning intricate spatial and temporal patterns, while other algorithms may bring specific domain knowledge or address certain limitations.

For instance, incorporating autoregressive components or ensemble methods alongside CNNs can improve the model's ability to handle both short-term fluctuations and long-term trends in financial time series (Di Persio & Honchar, 2017). Transfer learning strategies, where pre-trained CNNs on diverse data domains are adapted for financial forecasting, can also be integrated into hybrid models. This synergy allows for a more holistic understanding of financial data, enabling the model to adapt to varying market conditions and providing a comprehensive approach to decision-making and risk management in the dynamic financial landscape.

4.7 Challenges in Financial Forecasting with CNNs

4.7.1 Data Quality and Availability

One of the prominent challenges in financial forecasting with CNNs is the issue of data quality and availability. Financial datasets can be inherently noisy, containing outliers, missing values, and irregularities that may impact the training and performance of CNN-based models. Ensuring the quality of financial data is crucial, as CNNs are sensitive to noisy inputs, and inaccurate or incomplete data may lead to suboptimal forecasting results. Moreover, the availability of high-quality and sufficient financial data can be a limitation (Kumar et al., 2024).

CNNs, especially when designed for complex tasks, often require large amounts of diverse data to effectively learn and generalize patterns. In the financial domain, obtaining extensive and diverse datasets can be challenging due to privacy concerns, limited historical records, or the proprietary nature of certain financial information.

Addressing these challenges involves rigorous data preprocessing techniques to clean and impute missing values, outlier detection, and the development of strategies to handle irregularities in financial data. Additionally, efforts to enhance data availability through collaborations, data-sharing initiatives, and advancements in data collection methodologies are essential to overcome the limitations posed by the scarcity and quality of financial datasets. These challenges underscore the importance of careful data management practices in ensuring the success of CNN-based financial forecasting models.

4.7.2 Model Interpretability and Explainability

Model interpretability and explainability are crucial aspects in the deployment of ML models, ensuring that the decisions made by these models are transparent, understandable, and trustworthy. Interpretability refers to the model's capability to provide insights into how it arrives at specific predictions, allowing stakeholders to comprehend the factors influencing the outcomes. Explainability takes interpretability a step further by providing clear, concise, and human-understandable justifications for the model's decisions. In complex models, such as CNNs, which are known for their intricate architectures and feature learning capabilities, achieving interpretability is challenging.

Techniques like feature importance analysis, layer-wise relevance propagation, sensitivity analysis, and visualization methods are employed to unravel the decision-making process of CNNs. Striking a balance between model complexity and interpretability is essential, especially in sensitive domains like finance, where regulatory compliance and stakeholder trust hinge on a clear understanding of model predictions (Sahu, Mokhade & Bokde, 2023). As the demand for transparent and accountable AI systems grows, the pursuit of model interpretability and explainability remains a critical aspect of responsible ML deployment.

4.7.3 Overfitting and Generalization Issues

Overfitting and generalization issues are fundamental challenges in ML, including financial fore-casting with CNNs. Overfitting occurs when a model learns the training data too well, captur-ing noise and fluctuations rather than genuine patterns. This results in a model that performs exceptionally on the training set but struggles to generalize to new, unseen data. In the context of financial forecasting, overfitting can be particularly problematic as market conditions are dynamic and models need to adapt to evolving trends.

Generalization issues arise when a model fails to capture the underlying patterns in the data, leading to poor performance on both training and unseen data. Balancing the complexity of CNN architectures with the available data and avoiding the incorporation of noise is crucial to mitigate overfitting (Patel, Jariwala & Chattopadhyay, 2023). Techniques such as regularization, dropout layers, and cross-validation are employed to enhance generalization, ensuring that the model captures meaningful patterns rather than memorizing the idiosyncrasies of the training dataset. Striking this balance is essential for developing robust and reliable CNN-based financial forecasting models that can navigate the complexities of real-world financial markets.

4.7.4 Dealing with Noisy Financial Data

Dealing with noisy financial data is a critical aspect of developing accurate and reliable finan-cial forecasting models, particularly when employing complex architectures like CNNs. Financial datasets are prone to various sources of noise, including outliers, errors, and market irregularities, which can adversely impact model performance. Robust preprocessing techniques are essential to address data quality issues, involving methods such as outlier detection, imputation of missing values, and normalization to ensure consistency in scale and distribution. Additionally, careful consideration is given to the handling of market anomalies and irregularities, which may be preva-lent in financial time series data.

CNNs, known for their ability to capture complex patterns, can exacerbate the impact of noise if not properly managed. Regularization techniques, such as dropout layers, can help pre-vent overfitting to noisy data, and attention mechanisms may selectively focus on relevant features while filtering out noise. Collaborative efforts within the financial industry to improve data qual-ity, coupled with advanced preprocessing strategies and model-specific adaptations, contribute to developing CNN-based financial forecasting models that are more resilient to the challenges posed by noisy financial data.

4.7.5 Real-Time Prediction and Latency

Real-time prediction and latency are critical considerations in the deployment of financial fore-casting models, particularly when utilizing technologies like CNNs. In financial markets, where decisions must be made rapidly to capitalize on emerging opportunities or mitigate risks, the abil-ity to provide predictions in real-time is paramount. Latency, or the time delay between making a prediction and receiving the output, plays a crucial role in determining the practical utility of forecasting models. CNNs, while powerful in capturing complex patterns, can be computation-ally intensive, potentially leading to increased inference time.

Balancing the model's complexity with computational efficiency is essential to minimize latency (Anand, 2021). Strategies such as model optimization, parallelization, and hardware accel-eration can be employed to enhance real-time performance. Additionally, considering the trade-off between accuracy and speed is crucial in financial applications, where timely decisions are often of the essence. The integration of CNNs into real-time financial forecasting systems requires a holistic approach, addressing both the intricacies of model architecture and the imperative of low-latency predictions to meet the dynamic demands of financial markets.

4.8 Case Studies: Real-World Applications of CNNs in Financial Forecasting

4.8.1 Stock Price Prediction

Stock price prediction is a prominent real-world application where CNNs have been applied to harness the power of DL for forecasting financial markets. CNNs, originally designed for image recognition, have demonstrated effectiveness in capturing complex patterns within sequential financial data, making them suitable for time series prediction tasks. In the context of stock price prediction, historical stock prices, trading volumes, and other relevant financial indicators serve as input features for the CNN.

The network's convolutional layers are adept at automatically learning and extracting hierarchical features from these time series data. CNNs can identify spatial and temporal patterns, recognizing trends, volatility, and potential market signals.

Several case studies and research efforts have showcased the applicability of CNNs in stock price prediction. These studies often involve training CNN models on historical stock data and evaluating their performance in forecasting future price movements. The ability of CNNs to discern intricate patterns in the data adapt to changing market conditions, and incorporate multiple dimensions of information (such as price and volume) positions them as valuable tools in the financial forecasting landscape.

However, it is essential to acknowledge the challenges, including the need for substantial and high-quality data, careful model tuning, and addressing interpretability concerns. Despite these challenges, the application of CNNs in stock price prediction underscores the potential for DL techniques to contribute valuable insights and enhance decision-making processes in financial markets.

4.8.2 Cryptocurrency Price Forecasting

Cryptocurrency price forecasting represents a cutting-edge application where CNNs have been increasingly utilized for their capacity to capture intricate patterns within time series data. Cryptocurrencies, characterized by high volatility and sensitivity to market sentiment, pose unique challenges for forecasting, making advanced models like CNNs valuable in extracting meaningful insights. In the realm of cryptocurrency price forecasting, CNNs analyze historical price movements, trading volumes, and potentially sentiment data from social media or news sources.

The ability of CNNs to automatically learn hierarchical features and recognize spatial and temporal patterns makes them well suited for handling the complex and dynamic nature of cryptocurrency markets. Several case studies and research endeavors have explored the application of CNNs in cryptocurrency price forecasting. These studies often involve training CNN models on diverse datasets containing historical cryptocurrency prices and evaluating their predictive performance over future time periods. The adaptability of CNNs to evolving market conditions and their ability to capture subtle nuances in price movements contribute to their effectiveness in this domain (Khang, 2024).

However, challenges persist, including the need for reliable data sources, the impact of external factors such as regulatory changes, and addressing interpretability concerns associated with DL models. Despite these challenges, the application of CNNs in cryptocurrency price forecasting exemplifies the potential for advanced ML techniques to offer valuable insights for investors and stakeholders in the rapidly evolving cryptocurrency markets.

4.8.3 Foreign Exchange Rate Prediction

Foreign exchange rate prediction is another real-world application where CNNs have found utility in financial forecasting. The dynamic and volatile nature of currency markets makes accurate exchange rate prediction crucial for informed decision-making in international trade, investment, and risk management. In this application, CNNs are employed to analyze historical currency pair data, incorporating features such as past exchange rates, trading volumes, and economic indicators. The spatial and temporal pattern recognition capabilities of CNNs prove valuable in capturing complex relationships and dependencies within the sequential data of foreign exchange rates.

Several case studies and research initiatives have explored the use of CNNs for foreign exchange rate prediction. These studies often involve training CNN models on diverse datasets containing historical exchange rate information and evaluating their performance in forecasting future currency movements. CNNs can adapt to changing market dynamics, identify relevant patterns, and provide predictions that align with the complexities of the foreign exchange market.

Challenges in this application include the need for large and high-quality datasets, addressing issues of data noise and market irregularities, and ensuring the interpretability of the CNN-based models. Despite these challenges, the application of CNNs in foreign exchange rate prediction highlights the potential for DL techniques to enhance accuracy and contribute to more effective risk management and decision support in the global financial landscape.

4.8.4 Credit Risk Assessment

Credit risk assessment is a critical area in the financial industry, and CNNs have demonstrated their capabilities in enhancing the accuracy and efficiency of credit risk prediction models. While CNNs are more commonly associated with image and time series data, their application to tabular data, including features relevant to credit risk, showcases their versatility.

In credit risk assessment, CNNs can be employed to analyze diverse features such as historical financial behavior, payment history, credit utilization, and other relevant metrics. The hierarchical feature learning ability of CNNs allows them to automatically capture intricate patterns and dependencies within tabular credit data.

Several case studies and research initiatives have explored the use of CNNs in credit risk assessment. These studies often involve training CNN models on labeled datasets containing historical credit information and assessing their performance in predicting whether a borrower is likely to default on a loan. The adaptability of CNNs to different types of features and their ability to discern complex relationships contribute to their effectiveness in this domain.

Challenges in credit risk assessment with CNNs include the need for large and high-quality labeled datasets, addressing class imbalance issues and ensuring regulatory compliance and interpretability of the models. Despite these challenges, the application of CNNs in credit risk assessment signifies the potential for advanced ML techniques to improve decision-making processes in financial institutions and contribute to more accurate risk evaluations.

4.9 Future Directions and Potential for CNNs in Financial Forecasting

The future directions and potential for CNNs in financial forecasting are poised for significant advancements, driven by ongoing research, technological developments, and the growing demand for more accurate and adaptive prediction models in the financial industry. As computational capabilities continue to evolve, CNNs are likely to benefit from increased model complexity, enabling them to capture even more intricate spatial and temporal patterns within financial time series data.

Transfer learning, leveraging pre-trained models on diverse datasets, holds promise for addressing the challenge of limited financial data, allowing CNNs to inherit knowledge from related domains. Hybrid models that integrate CNNs with other ML algorithms or traditional time series models could become a standard practice, leveraging the strengths of each approach for a more comprehensive understanding of financial dynamics (Khang, Rath et al., 2024).

Interdisciplinary collaborations with experts in finance, data science, and ML will play a pivotal role in refining CNN architectures and tailoring them to the unique challenges posed by financial markets. The incorporation of alternative data sources, such as social media sentiments, satellite imagery, or macroeconomic indicators, could provide richer contextual information for improved forecasting accuracy. Addressing the ongoing concerns related to model interpretability, explainability, and ethical considerations will be essential to foster trust and acceptance of CNN-based financial forecasting models in real-world decision-making scenarios.

Furthermore, advancements in hardware acceleration, cloud computing, and model deployment techniques are likely to contribute to the seamless integration of CNNs into real-time financial forecasting systems, reducing latency and enhancing their practical utility. The development of standardized frameworks and best practices for implementing CNNs in the financial domain will facilitate broader adoption and ensure consistency in model development and evaluation. As financial markets continue to evolve, the ongoing exploration of innovative techniques and the continuous refinement of CNN-based models will drive the future of financial forecasting, emphasizing the need for adaptive, interpretable, and ethically sound approaches to meet the dynamic challenges of the financial landscape.

4.10 Conclusion

In conclusion, the application of CNNs in financial forecasting represents a dynamic and evolving field with promising trends and notable challenges. The review has underscored the significant role played by CNNs in capturing spatial and temporal patterns within financial time series data, showcasing their adaptability beyond traditional domains like image recognition. The exploration of various financial forecasting applications, including stock price prediction, foreign exchange rate forecasting, and commodity price analysis, highlights the versatility of CNNs in addressing complex tasks within the financial industry (Khang, Rath, Satapathy et al., 2023b).

However, the journey with CNNs in financial forecasting is not without challenges. The issues of data quality, model interpretability, and overfitting in the presence of noise and market irregularities have been recognized as critical concerns. Ethical considerations and potential biases in decision-making, as well as the need for robust transfer learning strategies and hybrid models, have been discussed to pave the way for responsible and effective deployment of CNNs in financial applications.

Looking ahead, future directions involve the continued exploration of advanced techniques, such as transfer learning, hybrid models, and attention mechanisms, to enhance the performance and interpretability of CNNs in financial forecasting. Collaboration between experts in finance, ML, and data science will be essential for refining model architectures and addressing domain-specific challenges. The evolving landscape calls for ongoing research efforts to ensure the adaptability, reliability, and ethical use of CNNs in financial decision-making.

In navigating these trends and challenges, the review emphasizes the importance of interpretability, model explainability, and a commitment to continuous improvement in CNN-based financial forecasting models. As financial markets continue to evolve, the integration of cutting-edge technologies and interdisciplinary collaboration will be paramount for unlocking the full potential of CNNs in guiding decision-making and risk management in the modern financial industry (Khang, Muthmainnah et al., 2023a).

References

Alonso-Monsalve, S., Suárez-Cetrulo, A. L., Cervantes, A., & Quintana, D. (2020). Convolution on neural networks for high-frequency trend prediction of cryptocurrency exchange rates using technical indicators. Expert Systems with Applications, 149, 113250. https://doi.org/10.1016/j.eswa.2020.113250

Anand, C. (2021). Comparison of stock price prediction models using pre-trained neural networks. Journal of Ubiquitous Computing and Communication Technologies (UCCT), 3(02), 122–134. https://doi.org/10.36548/jucct.2021.2.005

Barra, S., Carta, S. M., Corriga, A., Podda, A. S., & Recupero, D. R. (2020). Deep learning and time series-to-image encoding for financial forecasting. IEEE/CAA Journal of Automatica Sinica, 7(3), 683–692. https://doi.org/10.1109/jas.2020.1003132

Borovykh, A., Bohte, S., & Oosterlee, C. W. (2017). Conditional time series forecasting with convolutional neural networks. arXiv preprint arXiv:1703.04691. http://arxiv.org/abs/1703.04691

Cavalcante, R. C., Brasileiro, R. C., Souza, V. L., Nobrega, J. P., & Oliveira, A. L. (2016). Computational intelligence and financial markets: A survey and future directions. Expert Systems with Applications, 55, 194–211. https://doi.org/10.1016/j.eswa.2016.02.006

Chatigny, P., Patenaude, J. M., & Wang, S. (2021). Spatiotemporal adaptive neural network for long-term forecasting of financial time series. International Journal of Approximate Reasoning, 132, 70–85. https://doi.org/10.1016/j.ijar.2020.12.002

Chen, J. F., Chen, W. L., Huang, C. P., Huang, S. H., & Chen, A. P. (2016, November). Financial time-series data analysis using deep convolutional neural networks. In 2016 7th International Conference on Cloud Computing and Big Data (CCBD) (pp. 87–92). IEEE. https://doi.org/10.1109/ccbd.2016.027

Chen, C., Zhang, P., Liu, Y., & Liu, J. (2020). Financial quantitative investment using convolutional neural network and deep learning technology. Neurocomputing, 390, 384–390. https://doi.org/10.1016/j.neucom.2019.09.092

Cheng, D., Yang, F., Xiang, S., & Liu, J. (2022). Financial time series forecasting with multi-modality graph neural network. Pattern Recognition, 121, 108218. https://doi.org/10.1016/j.patcog.2021.108218

Chung, H., & Shin, K. S. (2020). Genetic algorithm-optimized multi-channel convolutional neural network for stock market prediction. Neural Computing and Applications, 32, 7897–7914. https://doi.org/10.1007/s00521-019-04236-3

Di Persio, L., & Honchar, O. (2016). Artificial neural networks architectures for stock price prediction: Comparisons and applications. International Journal of Circuits, Systems and Signal Processing, 10, 403–413. https://core.ac.uk/download/pdf/217561207.pdf

Di Persio, L., & Honchar, O. (2017). Recurrent neural networks approach to the financial forecast of google assets. International Journal of Mathematics and Computers in Simulation, 11, 7–13. https://hdl.handle.net/11562/959057

Dingli, A., & Fournier, K. S. (2017). Financial time series forecasting – a deep learning approach. International Journal of Machine Learning and Computing, 7(5), 118–122. https://doi.org/10.18178/ijmlc.2017.7.5.632

Duan, G., Lin, M., Wang, H., & Xu, Z. (2022, January). Deep neural networks for stock price prediction. In 2022 14th International Conference on Computer Research and Development (ICCRD) (pp. 65–68). IEEE. https://doi.org/10.1109/iccrd54409.2022.9730340

Hosaka, T. (2019). Bankruptcy prediction using imaged financial ratios and convolutional neural networks. Expert Systems with Applications, 117, 287–299. https://doi.org/10.1016/j.eswa.2018.09.039

Khang, A. (Ed.). (2024). Applications and Principles of Quantum Computing. IGI Global. https://doi.org/10.4018/979-8-3693-1168-4

Khang, A., Hajimahmud, V. A., Alyar, A. V., Khalilov, M., Ragimova, N. A., & Niu, Y. (2024). Introduction to Quantum Computing and Its Integration Applications. In Khang A. (Ed.), Applications and Principles of Quantum Computing (pp. 25–45). IGI Global. https://doi.org/10.4018/979-8-3693-1168-4.ch002

Khang, A., Muthmainnah, M., Seraj, P. M., Al Yakin, A., & Obaid, A. J. (2023a). AI-Aided Teaching Model in Education 5.0. In Khang A., Shah V., & Rani S. (Eds.), Handbook of Research on AI-Based Technologies and Applications in the Era of the Metaverse (pp. 83–104). IGI Global. https://doi.org/10.4018/978-1-6684-8851-5.ch004

Khang, A., Rath, K. C., Panda, N., & Kumar, A. (2024). Quantum Mechanics Primer: Fundamentals and Quantum Computing. In Khang A. (Ed.), Applications and Principles of Quantum Computing (pp. 1–24). IGI Global. https://doi.org/10.4018/979-8-3693-1168-4.ch001

Khang, A., Rath, K. C., Satapathy, S. K., Kumar, A., Das, S. R., & Panda, M. R. (2023b). Enabling the Future of Manufacturing: Integration of Robotics and IoT to Smart Factory Infrastructure in Industry 4.0. In Khang A., Shah V., & Rani S. (Eds.), Handbook of Research on AI-Based Technologies and Applications in the Era of the Metaverse (pp. 25–50). IGI Global. https://doi.org/10.4018/978-1-6684-8851-5.ch002

Khang, A., Shah, V., & Rani, S. (Eds.). (2023c). Handbook of Research on AI-Based Technologies and Applications in the Era of the Metaverse. IGI Global. https://doi.org/10.4018/978-1-6684-8851-5

Koenecke, A., & Gajewar, A. (2020). Curriculum Learning in Deep Neural Networks for Financial Forecasting. In Mining Data for Financial Applications: 4th ECML PKDD Workshop, MIDAS 2019, Würzburg, Germany, September 16, 2019, Revised Selected Papers 4 (pp. 16–31). Springer International Publishing. https://doi.org/10.1007/978-3-030-37720-5_2

Kumar, B., Sharma, V., Vashishth, T. K., Panwar, R., Sharma, K. K., & Chaudhary, S. (2024). Exploring the Transformative Power of Internet of Things (IoT) Technologies in the Age of Industry 4.0: Unleashing the Potential in the Digital Economy. In Advanced IoT Technologies and Applications in the Industry 4.0 Digital Economy (pp. 42–59). https://doi.org/10.1201/9781003434269-3

Markova, M. (2022, April). Convolutional neural networks for forex time series forecasting. In AIP Conference Proceedings (Vol. 2459, No. 1). AIP Publishing. https://doi.org/10.1063/5.0083533

Muthukumar, P., & Zhong, J. (2021). A stochastic time series model for predicting financial trends using NLP. arXiv preprint arXiv:2102.01290. https://doi.org/10.48550/arXiv.2102.01290

Ozbayoglu, A. M., Gudelek, M. U., & Sezer, O. B. (2020). Deep learning for financial applications: A survey. Applied Soft Computing, 93, 106384. https://doi.org/10.48550/arXiv.2002.05786

Patel, M., Jariwala, K., & Chattopadhyay, C. (2023, January). Deep learning techniques for stock market forecasting: Recent trends and challenges. In Proceedings of the 2023 6th International Conference on Software Engineering and Information Management (pp. 1–11). https://doi.org/10.1145/3584871.3584872

Sahu, S. K., Mokhade, A., & Bokde, N. D. (2023). An overview of machine learning, deep learning, and reinforcement learning-based techniques in quantitative finance: Recent progress and challenges. Applied Sciences, 13(3), 1956. https://doi.org/10.3390/app13031956

Saxena, A. K., Asbe, C., & Vashishth, T. K. (2023). Leveraging a novel machine learning approach to forecast income and immigration dynamics. Multidisciplinary Science Journal, 5, 2023ss0202. https://doi.org/10.31893/multiscience.2023ss0202

Sezer, O. B., Gudelek, M. U., & Ozbayoglu, A. M. (2020). Financial time series forecasting with deep learning: A systematic literature review: 2005–2019. Applied Soft Computing, 90, 106181. https://doi.org/10.48550/arXiv.1911.13288

Sezer, O. B., & Ozbayoglu, A. M. (2018). Algorithmic financial trading with deep convolutional neural networks: Time series to image conversion approach. Applied Soft Computing, 70, 525–538. https://doi.org/10.1016/j.asoc.2018.04.024

Thakkar, A., & Chaudhari, K. (2021). A comprehensive survey on deep neural networks for stock market: The need, challenges, and future directions. Expert Systems with Applications, 177, 114800. https://doi.org/10.1016/j.eswa.2021.114800

Tovar, W. (2020). Deep Learning Based on Generative Adversarial and Convolutional Neural Networks for Financial Time Series Predictions. arXiv preprint arXiv:2008.08041. http://arxiv.org/abs/2008.08041

Tsantekidis, A., Passalis, N., Tefas, A., Kanniainen, J., Gabbouj, M., & Iosifidis, A. (2017, July). Forecasting stock prices from the limit order book using convolutional neural networks. In 2017 IEEE 19th Conference on Business Informatics (CBI) (Vol. 1, pp. 7–12). IEEE. https://doi.org/10.1109/cbi.2017.23

Tuo, S., Chen, T., He, H., Feng, Z., Zhu, Y., Liu, F., & Li, C. (2021). A regional industrial economic forecasting model based on a deep convolutional neural network and big data. Sustainability, 13(22), 12789. https://doi.org/10.3390/su132212789

Vashishth, T. K., Kumar, B., Panwar, R., Kumar, S., & Chaudhary, S. (2023, August). Exploring the role of computer vision in human emotion recognition: A systematic review and meta-analysis. In 2023 Second International Conference on Augmented Intelligence and Sustainable Systems (ICAISS) (pp. 1071–1077). IEEE. https://doi.org/10.1109/ICAISS58487.2023.10250614

Yu, P., & Yan, X. (2020). Stock price prediction based on deep neural networks. Neural Computing and Applications, 32, 1609–1628. https://doi.org/10.1007/s00521-019-04212-x

Zhou, M., Liu, H., & Hu, Y. (2022). Research on corporate financial performance prediction based on self-organizing and convolutional neural networks. Expert Systems, 39(9), e13042. https://doi.org/10.1111/exsy.13042

Chapter 5

Application of Internet of Things (IoT) in Banking and Finance Services

Roheen Qamar and Baqar Ali Zardari

5.1 Introduction

Internet of Things (IoT) refers to a network of gadgets, appliances, automobiles, and other objects that are equipped with sensors, electronics, software, connection, and actuators, allowing them to communicate and share data. Simply said, IoT devices communicate data across a wired or wireless network. IoT inventions provide limitless potential. It has the potential to significantly impact the planet. The influence of IoT is most noticeable in the business sphere, where it has not only altered the procedures of many company activities but also the way the economy is conducted. It aids in the optimization of operations, cost reduction, productivity increase, and quality of life improvement (Judijanto, Fildansyah et al., 2024).

IoT systems gather and handle consumer data, such as driving habits, recurring payment locations, and user preferences. This abundance of data aids banking, financial services, and insurance (BFSI) companies in risk assessment, customer identification, and improved client understanding.

Equipped with comprehensive and current client profiles, BFSI firms are able to tailor consumer interactions, deliver customized services (Awad, Babu et al., 2024), and give pertinent financial support as shown in Figure 5.1.

IoT has the power to fundamentally alter how the banking and financial services industries operate. The banking sector is greatly impacted by the IoT, which is advantageous to both customers and financial services since it deals with large-scale data transit, collection, and analysis. The largest technical advancement since the second great digital revolution is the IoT. Financial services customers may work more efficiently, save time, and lead more active lives with the use of IoT technology. Although the banking and financial industry is still in the planning stages of the IoT, there is a great deal of room for innovation. IoT benefits a bank in every way, from more profits to improved client support (Ariany, 2024).

 DOI: 10.4324/9781003501947-5

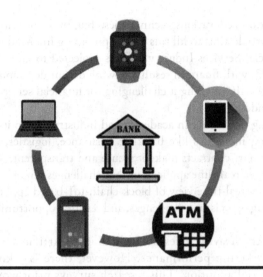

Figure 5.1 Internet of Things (IoT) in banking.

5.2 Literature Review

Maiti and Ghosh's (2021) study evaluates the status of the IoT in fintech ecology, revealing an upward trend in the market. Key drivers include increased demand for block chain, internet, mobile networks, cloud storage, and IoT devices. Issues like sustainable energy, digital payments, and security pose challenges. Neurotic growth will influence next-generation IoT in fintech, enhancing business process innovation (Khang, Hajimahmud et al., 2024).

Tabash, Khan and Ali (2020) article researcher influence, and habits on the adoption of IoT in Indian banks. A sample of 467 Indian customers was used. The results show that convenience, social influence, privacy and safety, and awareness significantly influence IoT adoption in Indian banks. Cost and habits do not. The study aims to help policymakers and IoT producers create services that are easily adoptable and beneficial to the public in India, as a developed country.

Yan, Zhu et al. (2021) article analyzes the current state of the Internet and its impact on commercial banks, focusing on sales status and customer products. It also examines the development history of financial block chain marketing products in China and discusses the characteristics and shortcomings of these products. The article also discusses the challenges and opportunities faced by security firms in the Internet development, suggesting that equity crowd funding can be a suitable model for future security company development. This model can enhance direct financing capabilities and promote entrepreneurship, ultimately improving the capital market's ability to serve the real economy.

Li and Li (2021) article explores the integration of IoT technology in the financial service industry, focusing on the continuous innovation of rural financial products. It uses the LA-VAR model and considers market price fluctuations and liquidity factors. The study also explores sustainable innovation in rural financial products and establishes a dynamic mechanism model for continuous innovation. A questionnaire survey was conducted on financial service industry institutions in a specific region, revealing that the LA-VAR model effectively measures liquidity risk and evaluates inventory pledge financing risk. The study suggests that internal construction of financial institutions and optimization of the external innovation environment can promote the development of the financial service industry.

The IoT has revolutionized various technologies, but implementation and security issues remain a concern. This article aims to fill this gap by providing financial perspectives on IoT. The IoT banking and Financial Services Industry (FSI) is projected to grow from $249.5 million to USD2.03 billion by 2023, with financial results showing decent development. However, security and privacy challenges remain, making it challenging for financial services firms to protect their systems (Masoodi & Pandow, 2021).

Block chain is gaining popularity in academia and industry due to its distributed, decentralized nature, transforming industries like banking, insurance, logistics, and transportation. Its distributed ledgers and smart contracts make it secure and transparent. The integration of block chain with IoT can improve real-time applications but challenges remain in IoT devices and mining. This article provides a real-time view of block chain-IoT-based applications for Industry 4.0 and Society 5.0, discussing open issues, challenges, and research opportunities (Tyagi, Dananjayan et al., 2023).

The banking industry heavily relies on technological artifacts and intelligent systems for operational and marketing performance. However, there is a knowledge gap between technology and managerial adoption. This research surveys prior work from 1970 to 2020, focusing on technology, employees, customers, and service ecosystems (Arjun, Kuanr & Suprabha, 2021).

5.3 IoT Applications in Banking Finance

5.3.1 Debt Collection

Lending institutions face significant administrative expenses and effort while collecting debt from individual and commercial borrowers. Using IoT sensors and networks to monitor debtor firms' operations and supply chain activities can assist FSI in determining their payment readiness without incurring high administrative expenses and reducing cheque failures. An IoT network of ATMs, card-readers, and point-of-sale devices may analyze a borrower's spending and income to determine their repayment capacity and intent. Defaulters can be restricted from further spending until payback is completed (Ahmadi, 2024).

5.3.2 Fraud Prevention

Fraud prevention is a primary concern for financial institutions, which constantly invest in and seek new ways of curbing misuse of their offerings. Major financial corporations, such as HSBC, have already successfully implemented artificial intelligence (AI)-based anti-fraud systems. With fraud prevention, having such a high priority, IoT will be a definite game changer in this area (Sharma & Manhas, 2024).

5.3.3 IoT in Banking

Undoubtedly, the IoT has the potential to catapult the financial industry to new heights. While most IoT adoption scenarios in banking appear unduly ambitious and unrealistic, the increasing number of IoT development solutions in this industry demonstrates that linked banking is feasible (Gao & Ma, 2024).

5.3.4 Personalized Offerings and Rewards

Banks provide reward points to consumers who use credit/debit cards or other payment methods, which may be redeemed in particular ways. Rewards systems may not appeal to all customers, rendering them ineffective in many circumstances. IoT-based intelligence may reward customers with appropriate redemption alternatives depending on their buying activities and demographics. Customers who spend mostly on clothing should receive reward points for discounts on apparel, while those who spend more on food should receive points redeemable in restaurants. Such customized rewards will increase client engagement and loyalty (Khang, Rath et al., 2023).

5.3.5 Fraud Prevention

IoT-enabled security solutions at points of usage, such as ATMs, can prevent debit/credit card misuse by allowing for more personalized and secure authorization. Citigroup is testing ATMs using eye-scanning technology to validate transactions as shown in Figure 5.2.

5.3.6 Capacity Management

Banks attempt to grow their network of offices and ATMs while managing current ones efficiently. By using IoT monitoring to track client units every day, the average queue time may be calculated to establish the ideal number of workers and counters at each branch. Using customer dispersion data by region helps simplify decision-making for opening additional branches. Optimize the quantity and position of cash dispensers based on consumption.

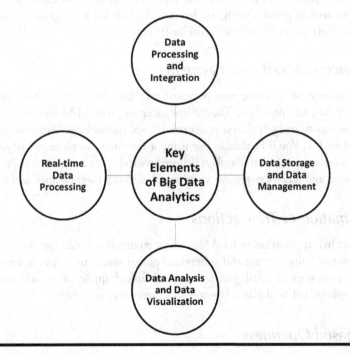

Figure 5.2   Imperfect defense.

5.3.7 Product Planning and Management

Banks can use data obtained from sources such as mobile applications to provide better and more focused service offers. Which services and products to launch? Who will be the main targets? When is the best time to introduce the products? – Data from previous service offers and user feedback might help address these issues (Judijanto, Fildansyah et al., 2024).

5.3.8 Tailored Marketing

Customers in all industries, including BFSI, are seeking bespoke solutions to meet their unique demands. To create a banking solution for a customer, it's important to understand their current financial situation, purchasing habits, and personal requirements. IoT enables banks to monitor customer behavior and provide tailored solutions based on client demands.

5.3.9 Proactive Service

In the banking and financial industries, IoT may be used to manage service issues and forthcoming product changes much more efficiently. If there is a problem about a product, it may be quickly identified and addressed before it escalates. Keeping track of a customer's previous activity might assist service professionals in providing more effective solutions.

5.3.10 Personalized Wealth Management

Using data processing algorithms to provide wealth management insights is typical practice. The IoT in financial services will only improve the accuracy and speed of data collection while also broadening the variety of possible insights. IoT-enabled wealth management solutions will also alert users in case their financial stability is under threat.

5.3.11 Enhanced Security for Payments

IoT in financial services will enable new payment methods and instruments, such as biometric tokens and smart cards, among others. The current incarnation of ATM-based transactions is probably going to give way to gadgets that support smart card technology. Wearable payment systems will be enhanced by IoT. You'll be able to pay using a wristband in place of carrying credit cards, which are easily misplaced or stolen. Barclays debuted wearable for contactless payments a few years ago. Users may send and receive payments via wearables, check their balance and credit history.

5.3.12 Automation of Transactions

With this kind of IoT application in banking, every payment transaction may be managed digitally. The "Internet of Value," a safe and supervised global trade environment where all payments are managed by a network of intelligent sensors and linked applications, will someday be made possible by technology. IoT will play a key role as a safety regulator here.

5.3.13 Increased Openness

Lenders will have access to comprehensive customer data in the future thanks to the IoT in banking (Khang, Rath et al., 2024). This includes credit debt and history, asset details and worth, and the yield of commodities a client generates (which is vital for agricultural firms that depend on banks for loan services). Financial institutions will thus have a better mechanism for making decisions when awarding credits. Transparency brought forth by IoT will provide banks with some protection as it lowers the chance of having to deal with dishonest borrowers in the future. Among other things, the data from IoT will provide banks flexibility, something they typically find difficult to supply (Mishra & Sant, 2021).

5.3.14 Enhanced Capacity Control

Improving capacity management at bank branches is one method of utilizing the IoT's potential. Branch managers will be able to measure the number of clients visiting a bank each day, how many employees are required to achieve maximum productivity, and how to best utilize the counters by collecting, processing, and exchanging customer data in real time. Managers will be able to forecast how much cash has to be deposited into the cash distributing equipment at each location thanks to IoT.

5.3.15 IoT-Enabled ATMs in Banking Institutions

IoT-enabled ATMs have been used in retail banking for decades, improving efficiency and reducing costs. They can perform maintenance tasks, automatically restock cash, and track foot traffic near ATMs. Some banks use IoT sensors to choose the right placement for equipment, and some cash machines offer live-stream video support for customer consultation.

5.3.16 Block Chain-Based Banking Services

Block chain technology is being used in banking IoT to provide safe, transparent, and trustworthy services, simplifying record-keeping and reducing data maintenance costs, and enabling direct communication between transaction participants without intermediaries. Banks are leveraging block chain technology to address rising maintenance costs, outdated infrastructures, and economic instability, investing in startups, collaborating with companies, and developing IoT solutions.

5.3.17 Indoor Navigation Solutions

IoT in banking has revolutionized customer service by providing smart branches equipped with biometric sensors and connected to other devices. These solutions increase efficiency and improve customer service by dividing customers into groups, monitoring queues, and directing them to free counters. Additionally, smart devices enable meeting scheduling, remote appointment management, and data collection, ultimately cutting maintenance costs and staffing.

5.3.18 IoT-Driven Changes in Banking

IoT, combined with an inventive redesign, has the potential to transform banking. Interact IoT, the first IoT banking platform, allows customers to save money by linking their bank accounts to IoT-enabled items. Combining IoT with block chain may create a safe and dependable network, offering additional benefits.

Wearable technologies are the second biggest development in banking brought about by IoT. Wearable technology has been a top priority for banks worldwide due to its widespread popularity and reach. While most watches now link to phones, there have been several advances that enable

Figure 5.3   IoT in banking and finance.

autonomous wearables have also become a popular topic in banking innovation. Innovation banking requires consideration of remote gadgets like Amazon Alexa, in addition to wearable technology. Basic banking features, like balance checks and transaction histories, are essential for wearable and remote assistant devices as shown in Figure 5.3.

5.3.19 Mobile Applications

A smartphone application is the most fundamental and essential IoT application. Mobile is the most popular platform for innovation due of its large user base. Although many banks provide mobile banking applications, few have an analytics platform to provide large-scale data. Data may be gathered through behavioral insights, user interactions, and reviews. It is the simplest and most dependable source of data that banks may use to gain market insights.

5.3.20 Digital Sensors

Digital sensors can be installed in physical locations such as bank offices and ATMs to assess consumer activity. Digital sensors can detect unforeseen consumer difficulties, service concerns, and ease of operation for automated devices. As we have seen, IoT can play a significant role in banking and finance. With time, many more data points will be added, increasing the level of customization from marketing to customer service. IoT has a big potential to change the way we are serviced and how banks and financial organizations make decisions (Ramalingam & Venkatesan, 2019).

5.4 Issues and Challenges in IoT Implementation

The following are the issues and challenges in IoT implementation.

5.4.1 Delivering Value to Customers

The ability to precisely define the issue statement is directly related to the success of an IoT implementation. Unfortunately, many IoT service providers overlook this aspect. Understand the long-term impact of these solutions on efficiency, customer happiness, and production. The most challenging aspect of IoT deployment is a lack of awareness of the customer's issue statement.

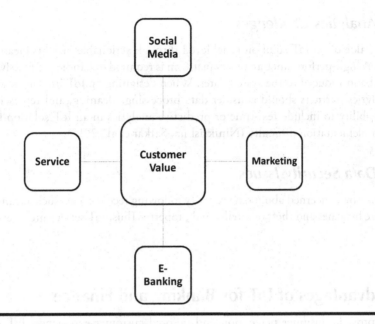

Figure 5.4   Customer value by using IoT in bank.

To optimize an IoT system, experts must identify key performance metrics to measure and improve as shown in Figure 5.4.

5.4.2 Hardware Compatibility Issues

Sensors, programmable logic controllers (PLCs), and other devices gather and transmit data to IoT gateways for cloud processing. Enterprises must carefully identify equipment, hardware, and legacy devices depending on their aims and business objectives. Legacy equipment without PLCs and sensors make IoT installation more challenging. Adding external sensors to vintage devices is a simple solution, but it may not be fully reliable, making it a tough operation (Gao, 2023).

5.4.3 Data Connectivity Issues

This is arguably the most overlooked difficulty now that broadband connectivity has increased dramatically. However, data communication remains an issue in certain IoT implementations. This refers to how IoT devices communicate with gateways and the cloud, as well as the data format they create. While most IoT gateways support GPRS and Wi-Fi/LAN, older devices require PLCs, telemetry systems, and remote terminal units to generate data. A proper edge layer is required to adapt transport and data format protocols for data transmission to the IoT platform. Choosing the appropriate protocols before implementing IoT can significantly improve its success (Tabassum, Ibrahim & El Rahman, 2019).

5.4.4 Difficulties with Incorrect Data Capture

The system may be leakproof and resilient, yet inaccurate data collection can occur. Incorrect data may be captured due to unforeseen events or program limitations during runtime. This leads to erroneous analytics, thereby hindering decision-making. The IoT implementation difficulty can significantly impact both industry users and customers' decisions.

5.4.5 Analytics Challenges

The true value of an IoT solution is achieved through actionable insights gleaned from gathered IoT data. A high-performance analytics platform is required to handle the massive quantity of data that will be introduced to the system later. When designing an IoT implementation architecture, data analytics partners should consider data processing, cleaning, and representation. Allowing for extensibility to include real-time or predictive analytics in an IoT solution helps address this crucial implementation difficulty (Ninikrishna, Sarkar et al., 2017).

5.4.6 Data Security Issues

Companies are concerned about data security following recent events such as ransom ware attacks. There were breaches and theft of intellectual property. Thus, IoT service providers must assure data security.

5.5 Advantages of IoT for Banking and Finance

- Improved consumer perception and tailored customer experience: IoT solutions capture and process customer data (frequent payment locations, consumer preferences, driving behavior, and so on), allowing BFSI companies to understand more about their customers and identify their requirements and threats. With thorough and up-to-date client profiles, BFSI firms may tailor customer interactions, offer targeted services, and give relevant financial help.
- Automation: IoT-powered systems may do some processes automatically, such as processing requests, opening bank accounts, disabling credit cards, and so on, reducing human interaction and, as a result, human mistake.
- Enhanced security: IoT connects and remotely controls CCTV cameras, smart alarm systems, car telematics, and other monitoring technologies, ensuring 24-hour protection of property and equipment (offices, ATMs, computer and information technology vehicles, etc.) and sending notifications in the event of criminal behavior. Wearable devices provide user verification via fingerprints, retinal scans, and facial ID when users make payments via mobile applications, making IoT an important driver of cyber security.
- Fraud detection: IoT, along with AI-powered analytics, aids in the detection of fraud and hacker assaults by collecting and analyzing user account information. If suspicious activity is found, the user can be swiftly notified and their account temporarily deactivated.
- One-touch payments: Users may now make payments without using their credit or debit cards thanks to the integration of banking IoT technologies and wearables. NFC-enabled gadgets, such as smartphones and smart watches, allow for contactless payments and frictionless financial transactions (Khanboubi, Boulmakoul & Tabaa, 2019)

5.6 IoT Applications for Smarter Banking and Finance

- Alexa: Amazon's speech assistant allows consumers to use voice recognition technology to ask simple financial queries. The branch also has face detection to track how clients interact with the environment.

- ATMs: With IoT-enabled data flow, banks can analyze client behavior, define ATM usage trends, and make demand-based ATM placement choices. Data on the ATM site environment (room temperature, light, motion, etc.) from IoT sensors is critical in transitioning to cost-cutting operation modes: adapting heating, ventilation, and air conditioning and lighting to ATM site foot traffic allows for lower power use.
- Citibank IoT solutions' help to incident management by providing real-time monitoring of ATM operations and cash levels, as well as the usage of skimming devices, card reader failures, cash shortages, etc. IoT may also improve the credit card experience when it comes to ATM usage. For instance, most ATM located in the United States, authenticates its customers and offers cardless entrance into its IoT-enabled ATM lobbies after hours using wearables with Bluetooth beacons (e.g., smartphones) (Maehara, Benites et al., 2024).
- Trade financing: For banks involved in trade financing, IoT enables awareness of the physical flows being financed and allows for real-time decision-making. IoT-generated data enables banks to better analyze risks across the trade life cycle, distribute money more effectively, and scale up financing techniques.
- Austria's Erste Group Bank: AG provides cutting-edge IoT-enabled inventory financing to its big corporate clients. The data acquired by tracking the movements of commodities using IoT sensors improves asset visibility and security while also allowing for the rapid identification of such assets on Erste's clients' balance sheets (Herzog & Herzog, 2024).
- Insurance: IoT devices monitor the status of insured goods and notify insurers of any irregularities, allowing them to act and take appropriate risk-reduction steps. Insurers also use IoT-generated data to take preventative measures and foresee problems. For example, an insurer can identify an asset breakdown and notify a policyholder before it is harmed. This strategy helps to reduce the amount of insurance claims while also preventing insurance fraud.
- Usage-based insurance: A more specific example of the aforementioned, which is widely embraced by motor insurance companies throughout the world. The combination of IoT and telematics (GPS tracking and on-board car diagnostics) enables insurers to collect data on vehicle condition and driver behavior in order to give individualized insurance policies. Progressive, for example, created Snapshot, a telematics-based vehicle insurance product. Telematics devices send individual driving data to the insurance company, and safe driving behavior is rewarded with lower insurance premiums.
- Accounting and auditing: IoT-enabled connectivity between customers' payment systems and CPAs' software enables speedy and safe data interchange and allows for the automation of typical bookkeeping activities like as data input, reconciliation, invoicing, and so on. Accountants using IoT may track financial data in real time and acquire precise insights into a company's activities, allowing them to fulfill advisory tasks more effectively. IoT also improves transparency and automation in auditing: CPAs can monitor transactions and oversee audit trails in real time to rapidly detect data anomalies and avoid fraud (Alamsyah, Kusuma & Ramadhani, 2024).

Another interesting example is Parsyl Inc.'s analytics-focused Cold Cover, a cargo insurance suite for perishable goods that uses IoT sensors and data analytics to track shipments in real time, monitor temperature fluctuations in containers, assess risks, and send alarms in the event of temperature breaches and spoilage at any point in the supply chain. With improved visibility and analytics, Parsyl can evaluate claims and compensate shippers within 72 hours.

5.7 Benefits of IoT in Banking Services

Even though many fintech organizations are keen to begin using IoT, many hesitate because they are unsure if the investment will be beneficial. The banking sector still has to determine the proper application for such a potent technology, even if the IoT has openly shown its benefits for a few other businesses. Fortunately, there are certain common advantages to IoT implementation in banking, independent of the size or location of the company initiating the linked project. The most auspicious ones are listed in Figure 5.5.

The following is the description of IoT's advantages for banking services.

■ Improve customers' money management practices: Connected gadgets can assist consumers in managing indulgent spending and developing sound financial habits. Shock wearable was originally used by Interact IoT, the pioneer IoT bank, as a component of their user education program. Once a user establishes a credit card limit, a wearable will monitor their daily expenditure. You'll know when you're getting close to the limit. A wearable will shock the user's wrist as a warning to stop spending if they disregard a notice (Khang, Muthmainnah et al., 2023).

■ Improve the standard of the financial experience: By giving customers individualized experiences and timely information, the IoT has an impact on banking customer services. A guest would be able to use a smartphone to check and make appointments because of connection. In this manner, there won't be a line at the counter and customers will always know when it's their turn. The client's visitation history, a list of services they utilize, and frequently asked questions will all be stored by the service provider on the other end. One bank that has already offered 24/7 ATM access is Citibank, which uses IoT beacons in conjunction with a Bluetooth-enabled system (Saad & Abd-Elwahab, 2024).

■ Extending the scope of offerings beyond banking: By extending their service offerings beyond the conventional ones, financial institutions may become more customer-focused thanks to the IoT. For example, US bank launched an IoT program to encourage its customers to maintain their fitness levels. Users will receive incentives and cash payouts for reaching goals (Sindiramutty et al., 2024).

■ Increases branch banking's efficiency: Modern branch systems are vulnerable to disruption from mobile banking. Banking applications and the IoT are what financial service providers use to make sure a traditional method still adds value. As soon as the customer enters the

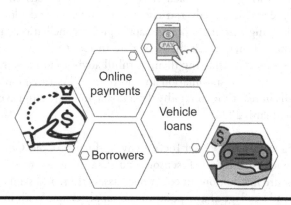

Figure 5.5   Internet of Things (IoT)'s advantages for banking services.

bank, biometric sensors will start collecting data and notify the main system (Vijaya, Prabhu et al., 2024).

■ Modernized ATMs: ATMs nowadays might occasionally feel antiquated and difficult to use. By linking ATMs to bank branches and giving them complete smartphone management capabilities, the IoT has the potential to completely change this experience. An ATM's nearest location to the user can be found thanks to motion sensors. A linked model will communicate in real time in the event of a malfunctioning machine. In this manner, a service provider may minimize equipment downtime by quickly contacting an engineer.

■ Business procedures that are automated: IoT systems can handle request processing, transfer asset ownership, automatically disable credit cards in the event of a payment delay, and more. Instantaneous loan processing and collateral monitoring are made possible by automation through the IoT (Olubusola, Falaiye et al., 2024).

5.8 The Future of IoT in Banking and Finance

IoT will assist the banking and financial business in addressing regulatory concerns, analyzing client behavior, and making changes. It will bring about changes in technology at the customer and manager levels. This may result in lower costs and improved performance. Given the benefits and market potential, switching and IoT implementation costs are projected to fall. The banking and financial business is prone to security assaults; IoT should address these problems prior to introduction.

While acceptance of IoT in finance is gradual, greater financial services and innovative use cases will ultimately lead to industry-wide adoption. To successfully transition to IoT, it's important to address challenges such as physical device compatibility before using the technology. A thorough governance style may address data security concerns, ensuring secure access to critical reports and data. IoT in banking allows for real-time monitoring and control of processes, enabling banks to anticipate consumer demands and provide solutions for safe financial decisions. This innovation reduces expenses, increases productivity, and improves customer lives. The future of financial services will expand and advance smoothly with the aid of IoT technologies. These are a few forecasts.

■ Voice-activated banking: A smooth and customized banking experience is possible with natural language processing (NLP) and AI-powered voice-activated banking interactions.

■ Personalized insurance: Smart sensors tracking driving and health patterns may result in specialized coverage.

■ Predictive loan approvals: Banks may be able to approve loans more quickly and individually by utilizing real-time IoT data.

This cutting-edge technology will be crucial to the financial industry's new direction.

■ AI: AI will foresee client requirements, detect fraud, and personalize financial services by analyzing massive amounts of data from IoT devices. In addition to automation, AI-powered fraud detection and risk assessment, hyper-personalized finance, and other use cases, the application of generative AI in fintech provides interesting prospects.

■ Block chain: This safe technology will track financial transactions in real time, improving efficiency and transparency, particularly in lending and trade finance (Gulia, Gill et al., 2024).

5.9 Conclusion

Since the banking and financial sector is susceptible to security breaches, IoT should address these issues prior to deployment. IoT adoption in the banking sector is now moving slowly, but with more financial services mobilizing and creative use cases being developed, the technology will ultimately find its way across the whole sector. It is difficult to transition from an older system to the IoT, thus problems with physical devices and related compatibility should be fixed before the IoT is implemented. A complete governance mode that offers safe access to critical reports and data can be used to address data security challenges (Khang, Shah & Rani, 2023).

References

Ahmadi, S. (2024). A comprehensive study on integration of big data and AI in financial industry and its effect on present and future opportunities. International Journal of Current Science Research and Review, 7(01), 66–74. https://doi.org/10.47191/ijcsrr/V7-i1-07

Alamsyah, A., Kusuma, G. N. W., & Ramadhani, D. P. (2024). A review on decentralized finance ecosystems. Future Internet, 16(3), 76. https://doi.org/10.3390/fi16030076

Ariany, V. (2024). The future of accounting and finance: Trends and challenges. Accounting Studies and Tax Journal (COUNT), 1(2), 150–157. https://doi.org/10.62207/c39a6n89

Arjun, R., Kuanr, A., & Suprabha, K. R. (2021). Developing banking intelligence in emerging markets: Systematic review and agenda. International Journal of Information Management Data Insights, 1(2), 100026. https://doi.org/10.1016/j.jjimei.2021.100026

Awad, A. I., Babu, A., Barka, E., & Shuaib, K. (2024). AI-powered biometrics for Internet of Things security: A review and future vision. Journal of Information Security and Applications, 82, 103748. https://doi.org/10.1016/j.jisa.2024.103748

Gao, Z. (2023). Application of Internet of Things and block-chain technology in improving supply chain financial risk management system. IETE Journal of Research, 69(10), 6878–6887. https://doi.org/10.1080/03772063.2021.2022539

Gao, Y., & Ma, R. (2024). Deep practice of internet of things image recognition technology based on deep learning in intelligent financial supervision system. Journal of Intelligent & Fuzzy Systems (Preprint), 1–13. https://doi.org/10.3233/JIFS-237692

Gulia, P., Gill, N. S., Yahya, M., Gupta, P., Shukla, P. K., & Shukla, P. K. (2024). Exploring the potential of blockchain technology in an IoT-enabled environment: A review. IEEE Access, 12, 31197–31227. https://doi.org/10.1109/ACCESS.2024.3366656

Herzog, N. J., & Herzog, D. J. (2024). IoT and smart environment solutions for SMEs. Drivers of SME Growth and Sustainability in Emerging Markets, 157–182. https://doi.org/10.4018/979-8-3693-0111-1.ch009

Judijanto, L., Fildansyah, R., Sudarmanto, E., Harsono, I., & Afandy, C. (2024). Bibliometric analysis of the application of Internet of Things (IoT) in financial services. West Science Interdisciplinary Studies, 2(02), 398–405. https://doi.org/10.58812/wsis.v2i02.664

Khanboubi, F., Boulmakoul, A., & Tabaa, M. (2019). Impact of digital trends using IoT on banking processes. Procedia Computer Science, 151, 77–84. https://doi.org/10.1016/j.procs.2019.04.014

Khang, A., Hajimahmud, V. A., Alyar, A. V., Khalilov, M., Ragimova, N. A., & Niu, Y. (2024). Introduction to Quantum Computing and Its Integration Applications. In Khang A. (Ed.), Applications and Principles of Quantum Computing (pp. 25–45). IGI Global. https://doi.org/10.4018/979-8-3693-1168-4.ch002

Khang, A., Muthmainnah, M., Seraj, P. M., Al Yakin, A., & Obaid, A. J. (2023). AI-Aided Teaching Model in Education 5.0. In Khang A., Shah V., & Rani S. (Eds.), Handbook of Research on AI-Based Technologies and Applications in the Era of the Metaverse (pp. 83–104). IGI Global. https://doi.org/10.4018/978-1-6684-8851-5.ch004

Khang, A., Rath, K. C., Panda, N., & Kumar, A. (2024). Quantum Mechanics Primer: Fundamentals and Quantum Computing. In Khang A. (Ed.), Applications and Principles of Quantum Computing (pp. 1–24). IGI Global. https://doi.org/10.4018/979-8-3693-1168-4.ch001

Khang, A., Rath, K. C., Satapathy, S. K., Kumar, A., Das, S. R., & Panda, M. R. (2023). Enabling the Future of Manufacturing: Integration of Robotics and IoT to Smart Factory Infrastructure in Industry 4.0. In Khang A., Shah V., & Rani S. (Eds.), Handbook of Research on AI-Based Technologies and Applications in the Era of the Metaverse (pp. 25–50). IGI Global. https://doi.org/10.4018/978-1-6684-8851-5.ch002

Khang, A., Shah, V., & Rani, S. (Eds.). (2023). Handbook of Research on AI-Based Technologies and Applications in the Era of the Metaverse. IGI Global. https://doi.org/10.4018/978-1-6684-8851-5

Li, L., & Li, H. (2021). Analysis of financing risk and innovation motivation mechanism of financial service industry based on internet of things. Complexity, 2021, 1–9. https://doi.org/10.1155/2021/5523290

Maehara, R., Benites, L., Talavera, A., Aybar-Flores, A., & Muñoz, M. (2024). Predicting financial inclusion in Peru: Application of machine learning algorithms. Journal of Risk and Financial Management, 17(1), 34. https://doi.org/10.3390/jrfm17010034

Maiti, M., & Ghosh, U. (2021). Next-generation Internet of Things in fintech ecosystem. IEEE Internet of Things Journal, 10(3), 2104–2111. https://doi.org/10.1109/JIOT.2021.3063494

Masoodi, F., & Pandow, B. A. (2021). Internet of things: Financial perspective and its associated security concerns. International Journal of Electronic Finance, 10(3), 145–158. https://doi.org/10.1504/IJEF.2021.115644

Mishra, P., & Sant, T. G. (2021, October). Role of artificial intelligence and internet of things in promoting banking and financial services during COVID-19: Pre and post effect. In 2021 5th International Conference on Information Systems and Computer Networks (ISCON) (pp. 1–7). IEEE. https://doi.org/10.1109/ISCON52037.2021.9702445

Ninikrishna, T., Sarkar, S., Tengshe, R., Jha, M. K., Sharma, L., Daliya, V. K., & Routray, S. K. (2017, July). Software defined IoT: Issues and challenges. In 2017 International Conference on Computing Methodologies and Communication (ICCMC) (pp. 723–726). IEEE. https://doi.org/10.1109/ICCMC.2017.8282560

Olubusola, O., Falaiye, T., Ajayi-Nifise, A. O., Daraojimba, O. H., & Mhlongo, N. Z. (2024). Sustainable IT practices in Nigerian banking: Environmental perspectives review. International Journal of Science and Research Archive, 11(1), 1388–1407. https://doi.org/10.30574/ijsra.2024.11.1.0230

Ramalingam, H., & Venkatesan, V. P. (2019, October). Conceptual analysis of Internet of Things use cases in banking domain. In TENCON 2019-2019 IEEE Region 10 Conference (TENCON) (pp. 2034–2039). IEEE. https://doi.org/10.1109/TENCON.2019.8929473

Saad, M. S., & Abd-Elwahab, A. (2024). A proposed framework for improving online banking transactions using blockchain. 38(1), 1475–1500. https://doi.org/10.21608/SJRBS.2024.253853.1568

Sharma, P., & Manhas, S. (2024). The Future of Finance: Revolutionizing the Industry with Artificial Intelligence. In Leveraging AI and Emotional Intelligence in Contemporary Business Organizations (pp. 187–210). IGI Global. https://doi.org/10.4018/979-8-3693-1902-4.ch011

Sindiramutty, S. R., Tan, C. E., Tee, W. J., Lau, S. P., Balakrishnan, S., Kaur, S., & Aslam, M. F. A. (2024). Modern smart cities and open research challenges and issues of explainable artificial intelligence. Advances in Explainable AI Applications for Smart Cities, 389–424. https://doi.org/10.4018/978-1-6684-6361-1.ch015

Tabash, P., Khan, M. I., & Ali, A. (2020). An examination of consumers' adoption of internet of things (IoT) in Indian banks. Cogent Business & Management, 7(1), 1809071. https://doi.org/10.1080/23311975.2020.1809071

Tabassum, K., Ibrahim, A., & El Rahman, S. A. (2019, April). Security issues and challenges in IoT. In 2019 International Conference on Computer and Information Sciences (ICCIS) (pp. 1–5). IEEE. https://doi.org/10.1109/ICCISci.2019.8716460

Tyagi, A. K., Dananjayan, S., Agarwal, D., & Thariq Ahmed, H. F. (2023). Blockchain—Internet of things applications: Opportunities and challenges for industry 4.0 and society 5.0. Sensors, 23(2), 947. https://doi.org/10.3390/s23020947

Vijaya, G. S., Prabhu, D., Sandhya, M., & Aldehayyat, J. (2024). Future of Banking from IT Decentralization and Deglobalisation: An Analysis of Its Possibilities. In Driving Decentralization and Disruption with Digital Technologies (pp. 139–165). IGI Global. https://doi.org/10.4018/979-8-3693-3253-5.ch010

Yan, C., Zhu, J., Ouyang, Y., & Zeng, X. (2021). Marketing method and system optimization based on the financial block chain of the internet of things. Wireless Communications and Mobile Computing, 2021, 1–11. https://doi.org/10.1155/2021/9354569

Chapter 6

Artificial Intelligence (AI) and Data Analytics: A New Era in the Financial Industry

Sita Rani, Ravinder Singh, and Alex Khang

6.1 Introduction

Artificial Intelligence (AI) and data analytics have completely changed client interactions, risk management, and decision-making procedures in the financial industry (Cao, 2022). Large-scale datasets are analyzed by AI algorithms to find trends, predict market movements, and enhance investment plans. Credit scoring, fraud detection, and algorithmic trading are three areas where machine learning models are used to improve accuracy and efficiency while lowering human bias (Giudici & Raffinetti, 2023).

Furthermore, sentiment analysis of news items, social media, and earnings calls is made possible by natural language processing (NLP), which supports news-driven trading methods and the evaluation of market mood. By using AI, robo-advisors can offer individualized investment advice based on a client's preferences and risk tolerance, thereby democratizing access to financial planning services. For financial institutions to detect suspicious activity, guarantee compliance with anti-money laundering (AML) requirements, and reduce operational risks, data analytics is essential to regulatory compliance. By enabling traders and portfolio managers to make well-informed decisions quickly, real-time data analytics maximize portfolio performance and reduce market exposure. All things considered, AI and data analytics are continuing to reshape the financial scene, stimulating innovation, improving productivity, and cultivating a more open and transparent financial environment.

Financial innovations are greatly aided by AI and data analytics, which allow organizations to improve decision-making, automate procedures, and extract insightful information. Through the provision of more effective, precise, and customized solutions, these technologies are revolutionizing traditional financial services. The capacity of AI and data analytics to swiftly and reliably process enormous volumes of financial data is crucial since it enables investors to make better-informed investment decisions.

DOI: 10.4324/9781003501947-6

Real-time analysis of market trends, consumer behavior, and risk factors by machine learning algorithms helps financial institutions spot new possibilities and quickly adjust to shifting market conditions (Day, Cheng, & Li, 2018). Furthermore, by providing individualized recommendations, immediately responding to inquiries, and expediting transactions, AI-powered solutions like Chatbots and virtual assistants enhance customer service and engagement. This lowers operating expenses for financial organizations while increasing client happiness and loyalty.

Anomaly detection, pattern identification, and predictive modeling are some of the ways that AI and data analytics can identify and stop fraudulent activity. Financial institutions can bolster security protocols and safeguard themselves and their clientele against cyberattacks by utilizing these technologies. Consequently, AI and data analytics propel financial innovations by promoting better efficiency, accuracy, and security across a range of financial services elements, which eventually improves consumer experiences and boosts industry competitiveness. The fundamental objectives of this chapter are:

- To discuss the key principles of AI and data analytics for finance.
- To present the advantages of AI and data analytics integration into financial sector.
- To discuss key challenges in the adoption of AI and predictive analytics in the finance industry.
- To outline the possible future research directions.

6.2 Foundations of AI and Data Analytics in Finance

To evaluate large datasets, forecast market trends, and improve investment strategies, AI and data analytics in finance rely on sophisticated algorithms (Polak et al., 2020). Credit scoring, fraud detection, and algorithmic trading are made possible by machine learning models, which increase accuracy and efficiency while lowering human bias. Sentiment analysis for gauging market sentiment is aided by NLP, and real-time analytics enable traders to act quickly and decisively, maximizing portfolio performance and limiting market exposure (Khang, Jadhav, Hajimahmud et al., 2024).

6.2.1 Principles of AI in a New Era in the Financial Industry

AI systems are developed and implemented according to a set of principles, which include a variety of ideas and methods (Li et al., 2023). Among the fundamental ideas are:

- Ethics and Fairness: Fairness, accountability, and openness in the decision-making processes of AI systems are all things that should be ensured by their ethical design and application.
- Transparency: AI systems ought to be transparent, which means that users and stakeholders should be able to comprehend and justify how they operate and make decisions.
- Accountability: AI system developers and users ought to answer for their deeds as well as the results these systems generate.
- Privacy and Security: AI systems should respect security protocols and privacy rights to safeguard confidential information and stop misuse or illegal access.
- Robustness and Reliability: AI systems ought to be dependable and strong, able to function correctly and efficiently in a variety of settings.
- Bias Mitigation: To guarantee equitable treatment and prevent reinforcing preexisting societal biases, efforts should be undertaken to detect and reduce biases present in AI systems.

- Human-Centered Design: User demands and experiences should come first in the design of AI systems, which should prioritize enhancing rather than replacing human capabilities.
- Continual Learning and Improvement: AI systems should be able to learn from fresh information and past experiences, enhancing their functionality over time and adjusting to ever-changing surroundings.

By providing recommendations for the appropriate development, implementation, and use of AI technologies, these principles help to build confidence in the technology's potential uses across a range of industries.

6.2.2 Fundamentals of Data Analytics Techniques

The fundamentals of data analytics techniques cover a variety of tools and methodologies for data analysis and insight extraction (Mandl, 2023). Among the crucial methods are:

- Descriptive Analytics: This method provides a basic knowledge of the data by summarizing historical data to reveal patterns and events from the past.
- Diagnostic Analytics: The goal of diagnostic analytics is to determine the underlying causes of previous occurrences or patterns, frequently by employing statistical analysis or hypothesis testing.
- Predictive Analytics: Based on past data, predictive analytics forecasts future events or trends using statistical models and machine learning algorithms. It makes use of methods including predictive modeling, time series forecasting, and regression analysis.
- Prescriptive Analytics: Beyond forecasting future events, prescriptive analytics suggests strategies to maximize decision-making. To determine the optimal course of action given particular restrictions and objectives, it makes use of optimization algorithms and decision support systems.
- Exploratory Data Analysis: To find patterns, correlations, and anomalies in data, EDA entails visually studying and analyzing the data. Usually, methods like grouping, summary statistics, and data visualization are used.
- Text Analytics: Analyzing unstructured text data—like customer reviews or social media posts—to glean sentiment and insights is known as text analytics. Topic modeling, sentiment analysis, and NLP are some of the methods.
- Machine Learning: Through the use of algorithms, machine learning approaches allow computers to learn from data and make judgments or predictions without the need for explicit programming. This covers reinforcement learning, supervised learning, and unsupervised learning.
- Data Mining: Data mining is the process of using methods like association rule mining, clustering, and classification to find patterns and relationships in huge datasets.
- Time Series Analysis: Data gathered over time is analyzed using time series analysis to find trends, patterns, and seasonality. Moving averages, exponential smoothing, and autoregressive integrated moving average (ARIMA) models are some of the methods used.
- Spatial Analysis: To identify patterns and relationships in geographically referenced datasets, spatial analysis entails studying geographic data. Methods include spatial interpolation, spatial clustering, and geographic information systems (GIS).

These foundational methods for data analytics are used in many different industries and domains to extract useful insights and make data-driven decisions.

6.2.3 Integration of AI and Data Analytics in Financial Services

Financial services have undergone a revolution with the integration of AI and data analytics, which has improved decision-making, risk management, customer service, and operational efficiency (Ahmadi, 2024; Kruse, Wunderlich, & Beck, 2019; Ravi & Kamaruddin, 2017; Zhang, Ramanathan, & Maheswari, 2021). The following are some significant applications of AI and data analytics in financial services:

- Risk Management: By evaluating enormous volumes of data in real-time, AI and data analytics help financial organizations better assess and manage risk. Financial transaction trends and anomalies can be found by machine learning algorithms, which can be used to spot any fraud or compliance problems.
- Predictive Analytics: AI systems can forecast future market trends, consumer behavior, and investment opportunities by analyzing historical data. As a result, financial institutions can decide on trading tactics, asset allocation, and portfolio management with greater knowledge.
- Customer Insights: AI systems can offer insights into the needs, preferences, and behavior of customers through the analysis of customer data. Financial organizations can now provide individualized goods and services, raise retention rates, and enhance consumer happiness as a result
- Algorithmic Trading: Trading algorithms driven by AI are capable of automatically executing trades in response to predetermined criteria and market conditions. Financial firms can take advantage of market opportunities more effectively because of these algorithms' capacity to scan vast amounts of data and execute trades quickly.
- Credit Scoring and Underwriting: Credit risk is evaluated, and the underwriting procedure is streamlined, using AI and data analytics. Alternative data sources, such as social media activity and transaction history, can be analyzed by machine learning models to assess creditworthiness and expedite loan decisions.
- Compliance and Regulatory Reporting: Through the automation of data collection, processing, and reporting procedures, AI and data analytics help financial institutions adhere to regulatory standards. In addition to ensuring conformance to regulatory standards, this lowers compliance expenditures.
- Robo-Advisors: Retail investors can access automated investing advice and portfolio management services through robo-advisors powered by AI. These platforms offer individualized investment recommendations at a fraction of the cost of traditional financial advisors by using algorithms to evaluate risk tolerance, investment goals, and market conditions.

Financial services are changing as a result of the incorporation of AI and data analytics, which helps organizations make better decisions, run more efficiently, and provide better services to their clients. To preserve trust and openness in the financial system, it also brings up issues with data privacy, cybersecurity, and the moral application of AI, all of which need to be properly addressed.

6.3 Transformative Applications in the Financial Industry

AI and data analytics have a wide range of revolutionary applications in the financial sector, and these applications are still developing quickly (Paul, Sadath, & Madana, 2021; Sathe & Mahalle, 2022; Singla & Jangir, 2020). The following are some important domains where data analytics and AI have a big influence.

6.3.1 Predictive Modeling for the Market Trends

In the financial sector, predictive modeling forecasts market patterns by applying machine learning and statistical algorithms. To produce insights into potential future market movements, it involves evaluating historical data, market indicators, economic considerations, and other pertinent elements. Regression analysis, time series forecasting, neural networks, and other techniques are frequently used to forecast important financial measures such as interest rates, currency changes, and stock prices.

Predictive modeling assists in risk management, portfolio optimization, and decision-making for traders, investors, and financial institutions by finding patterns and linkages within data. It's crucial to recognize that financial markets are inherently unpredictable and volatile, which makes it difficult to forecast future trends with any degree of accuracy. Improving the efficacy of predictive modeling in the financial sector requires constant model improvement and adaptation to shifting market conditions (Khang & Hajimahmud, 2024).

6.3.2 Fraud Detection and Prevention

In the financial sector, AI and data analytics are essential for identifying and preventing fraud. AI systems can more quickly and accurately than traditional approaches uncover patterns that point to fraudulent activity by evaluating large amounts of transactional data. Real-time detection of fraudulent behaviors, strange account activity, and abnormal spending patterns can be achieved through the training of machine learning models. AI systems are also capable of adapting and learning from fresh data, which helps them to continuously get better at spotting changing fraud strategies. By offering insights into past trends and pointing out potential danger concerns, data analytics enhance AI.

Financial organizations can integrate data from multiple sources to get a comprehensive view of client behavior and transactional patterns by utilizing big data technologies. This makes it possible to take proactive steps to stop fraud before it starts, such as putting in place more robust authentication procedures or marking transactions that seem suspect for manual inspection. All things considered, AI and data analytics enable financial institutions to keep one step ahead of fraudsters and protect the assets of their clients.

6.3.3 Customer Segmentation and Personalization

In the banking sector, AI and data analytics are revolutionizing client segmentation and customization. AI algorithms can divide consumers into discrete groups according to similarities and differences by examining enormous volumes of customer data, including transaction history, demographics, behavior patterns, and preferences. This enables financial institutions to customize their offerings to each segment's unique needs and preferences in terms of goods, services, and marketing plans.

Predictive analytics powered by AI can also foresee the requirements and actions of customers, allowing for tailored product and service recommendations. Financial institutions may improve client happiness, loyalty, and retention by making timely and relevant offerings. By offering useful insights into the behavior and preferences of customers, data analytics improves customer segmentation and personalization even further. Financial institutions may ensure a smooth and customized client experience by regularly evaluating customer data, which allows them to improve their segmentation strategies and personalize services in real-time.

6.3.4 Risk Management and Compliance

In the financial sector, AI and data analytics are transforming risk management and compliance. AI algorithms can more accurately and efficiently identify potential risks and compliance issues than traditional approaches by evaluating large datasets that include market patterns, transaction histories, and regulatory requirements.

Financial organizations can proactively reduce risks by using machine learning models, which can forecast and evaluate a variety of risk variables, including credit default, market volatility, and fraudulent activity. AI-powered compliance systems also can monitor transactions in real-time, identifying suspicious activity and guaranteeing that regulations are followed. By offering insights into past trends and patterns, data analytics further improves risk management by empowering financial institutions to make well-informed decisions and modify their strategies accordingly.

6.4 AI-Driven Automation and Operational Efficiency

In the finance industry, AI-driven automation improves operational efficiency, decreases manual labor, and streamlines procedures (Banerjee et al., 2022; Puri et al., 2023; Rani et al., 2023; Singh & Rani, 2023). Financial organizations may increase overall efficiency and more effectively deploy resources by automating operations like fraud detection, data input, and customer support with machine learning and robots.

6.4.1 Streamlining Financial Operations

By automating tedious processes like data input, reconciliation, and compliance checks, AI simplifies financial operations. To improve efficiency and accuracy, machine learning algorithms examine data to find patterns, streamline processes, and forecast results. Automated systems are also able to spot irregularities in transactions and instantly alert users to any dangers or fraudulent activity. AI improves operational efficiency, reduces costs, and guarantees regulatory compliance by eliminating manual labor and human error. Furthermore, AI-powered analytics offer insightful data on consumer behavior and market trends, facilitating strategic planning and well-informed decision-making. All things considered, AI improves financial operations through process simplification, risk reduction, and company expansion (Kumar, Rani, & Singh, 2023).

6.4.2 Improving Process Efficiency and Cost Reduction

In the financial industry, AI is essential for increasing process efficiency and cutting costs. AI reduces human error and streamlines processes by automating repetitive jobs like data entry, transaction processing, and customer assistance. Large datasets are analyzed by machine learning algorithms to find patterns and streamline processes, resulting in quicker and more precise decision-making.

Additionally, financial institutions may foresee demand and modify their strategies accordingly by using AI-driven predictive analytics to forecast market trends and client behavior. This ultimately results in lower operating costs and higher revenue. AI also improves risk management by keeping an eye on transactions for irregularities and possible fraud, which reduces monetary losses and legal repercussions. Financial institutions may increase customer happiness, manage costs more efficiently, and stay competitive in the market by utilizing AI to streamline processes and cut costs. All things considered, AI is a potent instrument that can revolutionize financial processes, increase productivity, and save costs.

6.5 Addressing Challenges and Risks

A few of the biggest obstacles to using AI and data analytics in the finance sector are the requirement for AI models to be interpretable, regulatory compliance, and data privacy issues. Furthermore, bias and poor data quality might have an impact on predictive analytics' dependability and accuracy. It's also crucial to have strong cybersecurity safeguards in place to safeguard private financial information. Furthermore, staff members need to be continuously trained in new skills to properly use AI and data analytics technologies due to the quick rate of technological innovation.

6.5.1 Data Privacy and Security Concerns

The banking sector's adoption of AI and data analytics is heavily influenced by worries about data security and privacy. Financial organizations are often the targets of cyberattacks and data breaches because they manage enormous volumes of sensitive client data. The application of AI complicates data governance and protection, bringing up issues with misuse and illegal access as well as adhering to laws like the CCPA and GDPR. Maintaining client trust and protecting financial data requires strong encryption, access controls, and cybersecurity measures. Furthermore, ethical issues about the proper application of AI and safeguarding people's right to privacy need to be taken into account.

6.5.2 Regulatory Compliance and Ethical Considerations

The adoption of AI and data analytics in the finance sector is significantly hampered by ethical and regulatory compliance issues. To ensure the ethical use of client data, financial institutions need to manage complicated rules including the CCPA, GDPR, and laws related to the financial industry. Practices for risk management, algorithmic transparency, and data processing become more complex due to compliance regulations.

AI bias, discrimination, and its possible effects on vulnerable communities raise ethical questions. It is crucial to guarantee equity, responsibility, and openness in AI decision-making procedures. To avoid discrimination and preserve the values of justice and equality in the financial services industry, it is also important to carefully evaluate the ethical implications of utilizing AI for jobs like credit scoring, loan approvals, and risk assessment (Khang, Jadhav, Dave et al., 2024).

6.6 Future Outlook and Opportunities

With so many chances for innovation and expansion, the financial industry's prospects for AI and data analytics are bright. Financial services will continue to undergo a revolution thanks to developments in machine learning, NLP, and predictive analytics. These developments will allow for more individualized client interactions, better risk management, and increased operational effectiveness.

Increased automation, cost savings, and scalability will be achieved via AI-driven solutions, which will also make fraud detection and regulatory compliance easier. Furthermore, by combining AI with cutting-edge technologies like blockchain and the Internet of Things (IoT), new opportunities for data-driven insights and financial innovation will open up, giving the sector a competitive edge and room to grow (Khang, Dave, Katore et al., 2024).

6.6.1 Emerging Trends in AI and Data Analytics

The emergence of explainable AI, which makes machine learning models transparent and interpretable, is one of the emerging developments in AI and data analytics. Federated learning protects privacy while enabling cooperative model training across dispersed data sources. Unprecedented processing capacity for challenging data analytics jobs is promised by quantum computing. To address issues of bias, fairness, and responsibility, responsible AI frameworks and ethics are becoming more popular. Edge AI uses decentralized computing to process and analyze data in real-time at the network's edge. Furthermore, AI-powered automation is transforming industries and spurring innovation in fields like autonomous decision-making and robotic process automation (RPA).

6.6.2 Potential Impact on Financial Services

Financial services stand to gain greatly from the potential influence of AI and data analytics. Through customized product offerings, expedited procedures, and personalized services, these technologies can improve consumer experiences. Better risk assessment and fraud detection are made possible by AI-driven insights, which enhance security and compliance. Routine task automation lowers expenses and increases operational efficiency.

Predictive analytics can also improve insurance underwriting, loan approvals, and investment strategies, leading to greater financial results. But there are obstacles to overcome, like data protection, legal compliance, and ethical considerations. All things considered, AI and data analytics have the power to revolutionize the financial services industry by promoting creativity, boosting productivity, and providing more value to clients (Khang, Dave, Jadhav et al., 2024).

6.6.3 Opportunities for Innovation and Growth

Numerous chances for innovation and expansion are presented by the financial industry's deployment of AI and data analytics. Personalized financial services are made possible by these technologies, which allow for the customization of goods and recommendations to meet the unique needs and preferences of each consumer. This enhances customer happiness and loyalty. Second, by offering real-time insights into market patterns, AI-driven predictive analytics improve risk management by empowering financial institutions to make well-informed decisions and more successfully manage possible hazards. Third, using AI and data analytics to automate manual procedures boosts operational effectiveness, lowers costs, and frees up resources for innovative and strategic projects. Additionally, by automating processes for compliance monitoring and reporting, these technologies help with regulatory compliance by lowering the possibility of fines and penalties.

6.7 Conclusion

The delivery, management, and optimization of financial services have undergone a radical change with AI and data analytics. An innovative, efficient, and customer-focused new paradigm has been brought about by the combination of AI and data analytics. Financial institutions may leverage machine learning and complex algorithms to extract insights from massive data sets. This allows them to optimize operations with remarkable precision, minimize risks, and personalize services. Financial institutions are now better equipped to anticipate client wants, keep ahead of market trends, and respond to regulatory requirements with foresight and agility because of their increased capacity to leverage data.

Additionally, by automating repetitive work, cutting expenses, and enhancing decision-making processes, AI and data analytics promote operational efficiencies. Financial institutions can refocus their attention on strategic goals, innovation, and value-added services by simplifying operations and freeing up resources. Notwithstanding the enormous potential advantages, several obstacles must be overcome, including data privacy, moral dilemmas, and legal compliance. By tackling these obstacles and seizing the chances provided by AI and data analytics, the banking sector can create a future that is more adaptable, flexible, and focused on the needs of its clients.

References

Ahmadi, S. (2024). A comprehensive study on integration of big data and AI in financial industry and its effect on present and future opportunities. International Journal of Current Science Research and Review, 7(01), 66–74. https://ijcsrr.org/single-view/?id=14316&pid=14318

Banerjee, K., Bali, V., Nawaz, N., Bali, S., Mathur, S., Mishra, R. K., & Rani, S. (2022). A machine-learning approach for prediction of water contamination using latitude, longitude, and elevation. Water, 14(5), 728. https://doi.org/10.3390/w14050728

Cao, L. (2022). Ai in finance: Challenges, techniques, and opportunities. ACM Computing Surveys (CSUR), 55(3), 1–38. https://doi.org/10.1145/3502289

Day, M. -Y., Cheng, T. -K., & Li, J. -G. (2018). AI robo-advisor with big data analytics for financial services. Paper presented at the 2018 IEEE/ACM International Conference on Advances in Social Networks Analysis and Mining (ASONAM). 10.1109/ASONAM.2018.8508854

Giudici, P., & Raffinetti, E. (2023). SAFE artificial intelligence in finance. Finance Research Letters, 56, 104088. https://doi.org/10.1016/j.frl.2023.104088

Khang, A., Dave, T., Jadhav, B., Katore, D., & Dave, D. (2024). Gig Financial Economy- Big Data and Analytics. In Khang A. Jadhav B., Hajimahmud V. A., Satpathy I. The Synergy of AI and Fintech in the Digital Gig Economy (1st Ed.). CRC Press. https://doi.org/10.1201/9781032720104-16

Khang, A., Dave, T., Katore, D., Jadhav, B., & Dave, D. (2024). Leveraging Blockchain and Smart Contracts For Gig Payments. In Khang A. Jadhav B., Hajimahmud V. A., Satpathy I. The Synergy of AI and Fintech in the Digital Gig Economy (1st Ed.). CRC Press. https://doi.org/10.1201/9781032720104-11

Khang, A, & Hajimahmud, V. A. (2024). Introduction to the Gig Economy. In Khang A. Jadhav B., Hajimahmud V. A., Satpathy I. The Synergy of AI and Fintech in the Digital Gig Economy (1st Ed.). CRC Press. https://doi.org/10.1201/9781032720104-1

Khang, A., Jadhav, B., Dave, T., & Katore, T. (2024). Artificial Intelligence (AI) in Fintech - Enhancing Financial Services. In Khang A. Jadhav B., Hajimahmud V. A., Satpathy I. The Synergy of AI and Fintech in the Digital Gig Economy (1st Ed.). CRC Press. https://doi.org/10.1201/9781032720104-10

Khang, A, Jadhav, B., Hajimahmud, V. A., & Satpathy, I. (2024). The Synergy of AI and Fintech in the Digital Gig Economy (1st Ed.). CRC Press. https://doi.org/10.1201/9781032720104

Kruse, L., Wunderlich, N., & Beck, R. (2019). Artificial intelligence for the financial services industry: What challenges organizations to succeed. http://hdl.handle.net/10125/60075

Kumar, R., Rani, S., & Singh, S. (2023). Role of machine learning in cyber-physical systems to improve manufacturing processes. In Machine Learning for Sustainable Manufacturing in Industry 4.0 (pp. 56–75): CRC Press. https://www.taylorfrancis.com/chapters/edit/10.1201/9781003453567-4/role-machine-learning-cyber-physical-systems-improve-manufacturing-processes-raman-kumar-sita-rani-sehijpal-singh

Li, B., Qi, P., Liu, B., Di, S., Liu, J., Pei, J., & Zhou, B. (2023). Trustworthy AI: From principles to practices. ACM Computing Surveys, 55(9), 1–46. https://doi.org/10.1145/3555803

Mandl, C. (2023). Fundamentals of Data Analytics. In Procurement Analytics: Data-Driven Decision-Making in Procurement and Supply Management (pp. 13–67): Springer. https://doi.org/10.1007/978-3-031-43281-1_2

Paul, L., Sadath, L., & Madana, A. (2021). Artificial intelligence in predictive analysis of insurance and banking. In Artificial Intelligence (pp. 31–54): CRC Press. https://www.taylorfrancis.com/chapters/edit/10.1201/9781003095910-4/artificial-intelligence-predictive-analysis-insurance-banking-paul-sadath-madana

Polak, P., Nelischer, C., Guo, H., & Robertson, D. C. (2020). "Intelligent" finance and treasury management: What we can expect. AI & Society, 35(3), 715–726. https://doi.org/10.1007/s00146-019-00919-6

Puri, V., Kataria, A., Rani, S., & Pareek, P. K. (2023). DLT Based Smart Medical Ecosystem. Paper presented at the 2023 International Conference on Network, Multimedia and Information Technology (NMITCON). https://doi.org/10.1109/NMITCON58196.2023.10276204

Rani, S., Kumar, S., Kataria, A., & Min, H. (2023). SmartHealth: An intelligent framework to secure IoMT service applications using machine learning. ICT Express. https://doi.org/10.1016/j.icte.2023.10.001

Ravi, V., & Kamaruddin, S. (2017). Big data analytics enabled smart financial services: opportunities and challenges. Paper presented at the Big Data Analytics: 5th International Conference, BDA 2017, Hyderabad, India, December 12–15, 2017, Proceedings 5. https://doi.org/10.1007/978-3-319-72413-3_2

Sathe, S. S., & Mahalle, P. (2022). Predictive analytics in financial services using explainable AI. Paper presented at the International Conference on Next Generation Systems and Networks. https://doi.org/10.1007/978-981-99-0483-9_35

Singh, H., & Rani, S. (2023). Flex sensor integrated smart strap to verify correct wearing of the face mask. IEEE Sensors Journal. https://doi.org/10.1109/JSEN.2023.3332330

Singla, A., & Jangir, H. (2020). A comparative approach to predictive analytics with machine learning for fraud detection of realtime financial data. Paper presented at the 2020 International Conference on Emerging Trends in Communication, Control and Computing (ICONC3). https://doi.org/10.1109/ICONC345789.2020.9117435

Zhang, Y., Ramanathan, L., & Maheswari, M. (2021). A hybrid approach for risk analysis in e-business integrating big data analytics and artificial intelligence. Annals of Operations Research, 1–19. https://doi.org/10.1007/s10479-021-04412-6

Chapter 7

The Prospects for Applications of Quantum Computing in the Financial Sector

Vijai Chandrasekar and Worakamol Wisetsri

7.1 Introduction

Quantum computing, with its potential for large computational strength and potential to clear up complicated issues greater efficiently, has garnered big attention throughout various industries. One sector that stands to benefit greatly from quantum computing is the economic enterprise. The abilities provided using quantum computer systems can revolutionize several regions inside finance, such as chance evaluation, optimization, encryption, and portfolio management. One of the key packages of quantum computing in finance is hazard analysis. Financial establishments deal with huge quantities of records and complex models while assessing chance.

Quantum computer systems can carry out state-of-the-art simulations and complex calculations a whole lot quicker than classical computers, permitting extra-correct hazard exams (Peres, 1996). This can lead to improved pricing models, better assessment of investment portfolios, and more powerful hedging strategies. Optimization is another vicinity where quantum computing can make a big impact on finance. Problems that include portfolio optimization, asset allocation, and exchange execution require finding the best-feasible solution from a large quantity of possibilities. Quantum computer systems can explore these opportunities concurrently and perceive the best answers extra effectively. This can cause more efficient trading strategies, stepped-forward investment choices, and better asset allocation.

Encryption and cybersecurity are critical issues within the monetary area. Quantum computer systems can interrupt existing encryption algorithms that depend upon the factorization of massive numbers. However, quantum computing can also offer greater safety through quantum cryptography techniques, which use quantum phenomena to cozy communications. These strategies

DOI: 10.4324/9781003501947-7

can offer unbreakable encryption and ensure cozy transactions in the financial industry. Quantum computing also can make contributions to portfolio management with the aid of analyzing large datasets and identifying patterns that classical computers may also struggle to find. Quantum device studying algorithms can provide more accurate predictions and insights, allowing higher portfolio construction, hazard control, and decision-making.

Furthermore, quantum computing can play a function in fraud detection and anti-money laundering (AML) efforts. The capability of quantum computers to technique large quantities of facts and locate styles quickly can assist perceive fraudulent transactions and suspicious activities more successfully, enhancing average security and lowering economic crime (Nielsen & Chuang, 2010). It is critical to be aware that at the same time as quantum computing holds high-quality promise for the monetary region, practical implementations are nevertheless in their early stages. Quantum computer systems with sufficient computational power and stability are not widely available. However, ongoing studies and development efforts, as well as collaborations among academia, industry, and authorities' organizations, work toward the goal of boosting the development and adoption of quantum computing in finance (Khang, Hajimahmud et al., 2024).

In precis, quantum computing has the potential to transform numerous aspects of the economic zone. From risk analysis and optimization to encryption and portfolio management, the application of quantum computing can lead to more correct predictions, improved efficiency, more advantageous safety, and higher choice-making in finance. As the field of quantum computing advances, it is anticipated to bring about extensive improvements and opportunities for economic enterprise (Montanaro, 2016).

7.2 Quantum Machine Learning in Finance Sector

Quantum device learning (QML) is a rising field that combines standards from quantum computing and gadget studying to tackle complex computational problems. In the realm of finance, QML can revolutionize statistics evaluation, predictive modeling, and selection-making tactics. Here are a few key elements and ability packages of quantum machine getting to know in finance:

7.2.1 Data Analysis and Pattern Recognition

Financial institutions cope with huge quantities of records, including market information, purchaser data, and transaction data. QML algorithms can leverage quantum computing's parallel processing competencies to analyze these huge datasets correctly to a greater degree. Quantum algorithms that include quantum clustering, quantum primary element analysis, and quantum guide vector machines can resource in pattern reputation, facts clustering, and anomaly detection in monetary information (Preskill, 2018).

7.2.2 Portfolio Optimization

Optimizing investment portfolios includes finding the fine allocation of assets to gain precise objectives at the same time as thinking about threats and going back. Quantum machine learning algorithms can beautify classical portfolio optimization strategies by successfully exploring a massive variety of feasible asset combinations and figuring out the choicest solutions. This can lead to extra-powerful portfolio construction, hazard management, and advanced investment strategies.

7.2.3 Option Pricing and Risk Analysis

Pricing economic derivatives and assessing chance are crucial tasks in the financial industry. QML algorithms can help in modeling complex monetary gadgets and pricing alternatives correctly. By making use of quantum algorithms like quantum Monte Carlo methods or quantum simulation, pricing models can be subtle, and threat assessments can be improved by thinking about more than one factor and eventuality concurrently.

7.2.4 Fraud Detection and Risk Management

Quantum gadgets gaining knowledge of techniques can contribute to detecting fraud and coping with dangers extra successfully. By analyzing big volumes of transactional and behavioral statistics, QML algorithms can become aware of uncommon patterns or suspicious sports indicative of fraudulent behavior (Aspuru-Guzik, Dutoi et al., 2005). This can assist financial institutions in preventing fraud, lowering losses, and strengthening security features.

7.2.5 High-Frequency Trading

Quantum machines gaining knowledge can beautify excessive-frequency trading (HFT) strategies. By leveraging quantum algorithms for sample reputation and predictive modeling, HFT algorithms could make quicker and more correct buying and selling choices (Ladd, Jelezko et al., 2010) Quantum-superior algorithms can examine marketplace facts in actual time, pick out tendencies, and execute trades with reduced latency, doubtlessly increasing profitability for buyers.

7.2.6 Quantum Neural Networks

Quantum system mastering also can contain quantum neural networks, which are the quantum analogy of classical neural networks. These networks can leverage the standards of quantum computing, inclusive of superposition and entanglement, to improve learning and prediction skills. Quantum neural networks can offer more correct predictions and insights in financial applications, which include credit score scoring, fraud detection, and inventory marketplace forecasting. It is vital to note that quantum machine learning in finance is still a rising area and practical implementations are inside the early tiers (Khang, Hajimahmud et al., 2024).

The availability of quantum computers with enough qubit counts and improved balance is critical for the realization of the entire capability of QML in finance (Ladd, Jelezko et al., 2010) However, ongoing studies and improvement efforts are focused on advancing quantum technology and exploring their programs within the monetary area, paving the way for destiny advancements in quantum gadgets and getting to know finance (Reck et al., 1994).

7.3 Quantum Computing in the Financial Sector

7.3.1 Risk Analysis

Quantum computing can beautify risk analysis by way of acting on complicated simulations and calculations a great deal quicker than classical computers. This enables more accurate and green danger assessment, pricing models, and hedging strategies.

7.3.2 Optimization

Quantum computing can clear up complicated optimization issues, together with portfolio optimization, asset allocation, and alternate execution, extra efficaciously. This results in advanced buying and selling strategies, better investment selections, and more suitable asset allocation.

7.3.3 Encryption and Security

Quantum computing has implications for each breaking existing encryption algorithm and improving security via quantum cryptography. It can probably wreck current encryption methods while providing unbreakable encryption through quantum cryptography techniques.

7.3.4 Portfolio Management

Quantum computing can examine sizeable datasets and make aware of patterns that classical computers might find difficult to uncover. This can result in more correct predictions and insights, improving portfolio construction, danger control, and decision-making.

7.3.5 Fraud Detection and Anti-Money Laundering

Technique computing's capacity to technique huge quantities of statistics and discover styles quickly can enhance fraud detection and AML efforts in the financial sector. It can identify fraudulent transactions and suspicious sports more effectively, improving standard security and decreasing financial crime (Rieffel & Polak, 2011).

7.3.6 Option Pricing and Risk Analysis

Quantum computing can improve alternative pricing fashions and hazard evaluation methodologies, enabling extra-correct valuation of derivatives and evaluation of threat factors. This can enhance trading techniques and hazard-control practices.

7.3.7 Market Analysis and Trading

Quantum computing can facilitate extra-sophisticated marketplace evaluation by processing great quantities of data and figuring out complex styles. This can assist investors make more informed selections and enhance trading strategies.

7.3.8 High-Frequency Trading

Quantum computing can enhance HFT strategies with the aid of leveraging its computational energy for quicker and more accurate decision-making. This can result in advanced trade execution and profitability for HFT corporations.

7.3.9 Credit Scoring and Credit Risk Assessment

Quantum computing can permit more accurate credit score scoring models and credit score hazard assessments by analyzing a huge variety of factors and complicated facts relationships. This can decorate credit score selection-making and risk-management practices.

7.3.10 Regulatory Compliance and Reporting

Quantum computing can assist in regulatory compliance by acting on complicated computations required for reporting, stress trying out, and compliance tests. It can aid in meeting regulatory requirements more efficiently and correctly. It is essential to be aware that while quantum computing holds super promise for the monetary zone, sensible implementations are still at their early levels. Quantum computer systems with sufficient computational power and balance are not but broadly to be had (Kuperberg, 2002). However, ongoing studies and development efforts aim to accelerate the development and adoption of quantum computing in finance.

7.4 Quantum Cryptography and Secure Transactions

Quantum cryptography is a department of cryptography that leverages ideas from quantum mechanics to provide comfy verbal exchange and enable unbreakable encryption. It gives a fundamentally distinct method to cryptography compared to classical strategies, making it enormously at ease against ability assaults from quantum computers. Quantum cryptography guarantees the confidentiality, integrity, and authenticity of records, making it nicely perfect for relaxed transactions inside the financial sector (Cao & Painkras, 2019).

7.4.1 Quantum Key Distribution (QKD)

QKD is a primary utility of quantum cryptography. It permits the comfy trade of encryption keys among events, referred to as Alice and Bob, over an insecure channel. QKD utilizes the concepts of quantum mechanics, along with the Heisenberg uncertainty precept and the no-cloning theorem, to discover any attempts of eavesdropping. Encoding the encryption key in quantum states (commonly the use of photons), any interception or measurement of those states with the aid of an eavesdropper, called Eve, disturbs the quantum states, and can be detected (Kok et al., 2007). This guarantees that Alice and Bob can establish a mystery key with high protection, permitting them to communicate securely for encrypting and decrypting touchy information.

7.4.2 Quantum-Resistant Cryptography

While quantum cryptography gives robust security against assaults from quantum computer systems, classical encryption strategies, together with the broadly used RSA (Rivest Shamir Adleman) and ECC (elliptic curve cryptography), are prone to attacks by using quantum computers. Quantum computers can efficiently factor in large numbers and solve certain mathematical issues that shape the premise of many classical encryption algorithms. As quantum computers advance, they pose a risk to the security of current cryptographic structures (Shor, 1994). To cope with this, the improvement and implementation of quantum-resistant cryptographic algorithms, additionally called post-quantum cryptography, are being pursued (Kuperberg, 2002). These algorithms are designed to resist assaults from classical and quantum computers, making sure of long-term safety for relaxed transactions.

7.4.3 Quantum Authentication

Quantum cryptography also can enhance authentication mechanisms to ease transactions. By using quantum houses including entanglement, quantum authentication protocols may be designed to make certain the authenticity and integrity of virtual signatures, certificates, and different authentication mechanisms. Quantum authentication schemes can decorate the trustworthiness of digital identities and offer robust protection against identity robbery and tampering.

7.4.4 Quantum Random Number Generation

Random numbers are essential for various cryptographic protocols and secure transactions. Quantum random wide variety generators (QRNGs) take advantage of the inherent randomness in quantum strategies, which includes quantum measurements or quantum noise, to generate true random numbers. Unlike classical pseudorandom wide variety generators, which are deterministic and depend upon mathematical algorithms, QRNGs provide sincerely random numbers that are unpredictable and comfy. Quantum random range technology can beautify the safety of encryption keys, virtual signatures, and different cryptographic protocols concerned with easing transactions (Childs et al., 2017).

The utility of quantum cryptography in securing transactions gives a better stage of safety in comparison to classical cryptographic methods. By leveraging the concepts of quantum mechanics, quantum cryptography ensures the confidentiality, integrity, and authenticity of information, making it extremely difficult for adversaries to intercept or tamper with touchy statistics. As the sphere of quantum cryptography advances and realistic implementations emerge as extra feasible, it holds tremendous promise for securing transactions within the economic zone and different industries where information privacy and protection are paramount (Kitaev, 1995).

7.5 Regulatory and Ethical Considerations

As quantum technologies, inclusive of quantum computing and quantum cryptography, preserve to boost, there are critical regulatory and moral issues that need to be addressed within the context of their applications in the monetary area. Here are a few key concerns:

7.5.1 Regulatory Compliance

Financial establishments perform in a heavily regulated environment to make sure transparency, safety, and honest practices. As quantum technology are integrated into monetary systems, it is far critical to evaluate how these technologies align with existing guidelines and compliance requirements. Regulators may additionally need to replace or expand new frameworks to address the specific traits and potential dangers associated with quantum technologies (Shor, 1997).

7.5.2 Data Privacy and Protection

Quantum technologies have the potential to process and analyses great quantities of touchy monetary and personal information. It is vital to ensure that suitable measures are in vicinity to protect the privateness and confidentiality of these statistics (Johnson et al., 2011). Financial institutions should follow relevant facts' safety regulations and put in force robust security measures to guard touchy data from unauthorized admission or breaches.

7.5.3 Ethical Use of Quantum Technologies

The adoption of quantum technologies in finance needs to be guided by moral considerations. Financial establishments must evaluate the ethical implications of the use of those technologies, along with capability biases in algorithms, unintended effects of automated selection-making, and effects on employment and social equity. Ethical frameworks and suggestions need to be hooked up to make certain the responsible and fair use of quantum technologies in the financial area.

7.5.4 Transparency and Explain Capability

Quantum algorithms and fashions used in economic programs may be particularly complex, making it hard to recognize and explain their decision-making strategies. Financial institutions ought to try for transparency and provide an explanation for ability in the use of quantum technology to ensure duty, regulatory compliance, and customer agreement. Developing strategies to interpret and provide an explanation for quantum-based total outcomes can help cope with issues concerning the opacity of these technologies (Khang & Quantum, 2024).

7.5.5 International Collaboration and Standards

Quantum technologies are a global endeavor, requiring global collaboration to address regulatory and moral challenges efficiently. Collaboration among financial institutions, regulators, researchers, and policymakers can help establish international requirements and nice practices for the adoption and regulation of quantum technologies in finance. It is vital to foster open talk and cooperation to make sure constant and responsible development and deployment of quantum programs within the economic region (Zeng et al., 2017).

7.5.6 Long-Term Security

Quantum technologies have the capacity to break current cryptographic strategies, such as the ones used to cozy monetary transactions. As quantum computers increase, economic institutions ought to prepare for the put up–quantum technology by means of enforcing quantum-resistant cryptographic algorithms and transitioning to greater comfy encryption strategies. Proactive measures to address long-time period safety worries can help mitigate dangers associated with the evolution of quantum technology (DiVincenzo, 2000).

Regulatory and moral concerns are essential to ensure accountable and comfy integration of quantum technologies into the monetary quarter. Collaboration among stakeholders, which includes economic institutions, regulators, policymakers, and research network, is vital in shaping the regulatory panorama and setting up moral pointers for the adoption of quantum technologies in finance. By proactively addressing these issues, financial enterprises can harness the capacity of quantum technologies while also upholding regulatory compliance, data privateness, ethical requirements, and lengthy-term security (Harrow, Hassidim & Lloyd, 2009).

7.6 Collaborations and Partnerships

Collaborations and partnerships play a vital function in the development and adoption of quantum technology in the financial quarter. They allow corporations to leverage each other's understanding, resources, and abilities to boost studies, innovation, and the practical implementation of quantum packages (Steane, 1997).

7.6.1 Research and Development

Research between monetary establishments, era organizations, and studies' establishments foster joint research and improvement efforts. By pooling resources and understanding, organizations can enhance the information of quantum technology, develop new algorithms, models, and applications specifically tailored to finance, and deal with common demanding situations and obstacles. Additional, collaborative studies enable the sharing of insights, high-quality practices, and classes found out, leading to extra-green development and breakthroughs within the field.

7.6.2 Access to Quantum Computing Resources

Quantum computer systems with enough computational energy and balance are presently confined. Studies and partnerships with corporations that have get right of entry to quantum computing sources, which include studies' labs, generation agencies, or cloud carrier providers, can offer financial establishments the opportunity to experiment, check, and expand quantum algorithms and applications (Grover, 1996). Access to quantum hardware hastens the knowledge of curves and permits real-global validation of quantum answers in finance (Khang, Rath et al., 2024).

7.6.3 Domain Expertise and Industry Knowledge

Collaborating with specialists and experts from both quantum computing and financial domain names can bridge the distance between theoretical advancements and sensible applications. By combining the knowledge of quantum scientists, mathematicians, laptop scientists, and monetary professionals, companies can benefit from a deeper knowledge of the specific demanding situations and requirements of the economic quarter (Einstein, Podolsky & Rosen, 1935). This collaboration enables in development of quantum solutions that can be tailor-made to economic programs and may efficiently deal with enterprise wishes.

7.6.4 Risk Mitigation and Cost Sharing

Quantum technology requires tremendous funding for studies, infrastructure, and skills. Collaborations and partnerships enable agencies to mitigate risks and share costs associated with the improvement and implementation of quantum answers. By pooling resources, groups can collectively spend money on constructing quantum knowledge, acquiring vital hardware and software, and addressing regulatory and compliance challenges. This shared funding reduces personal burden and hastens the development of quantum technologies for finance (Terhal & DiVincenzo, 2004).

7.6.5 Standards and Best Practices

Collaborations provide a platform for developing common standards, tips, and practices for the utility of quantum technologies within the monetary zone. Organizations can collaborate on defining safety protocols, encryption requirements, facts privacy frameworks, and ethical recommendations precise to quantum packages. These collaborative efforts ensure consistency, interoperability, and accountability in the use of quantum technology across the enterprise.

7.6.6 Ecosystem Development

Collaborations and partnerships make contributions to the growth and development of the quantum environment in the monetary zone. By fostering connections between academia, financial establishments, era providers, startups, and regulatory bodies, collaborations facilitate know-how sharing, talent development, and environment-constructing sports. This inclusive technique promotes innovation, hastens the adoption of quantum technologies, and creates a colorful and supportive environment for the advancement of quantum packages in finance (Khang & Robotics, 2024).

Overall, collaborations and partnerships are crucial for the successful integration of quantum technologies into the economic zone (Farhi, Goldstone & Gutmann, 2014). By combining assets, understanding, and expertise, companies can conquer technical and practical challenges, accelerate studies and development, ensure compliance with rules, and maximize the benefits of quantum technologies for finance. These collaborations form the inspiration for a collaborative and cooperative ecosystem that drives innovation and improvements in the field of quantum finance (Vedral et al., 1997).

7.7 Future Opportunities and Trends

The destiny of quantum technologies in the financial area holds sizeable opportunities and traits that can transform numerous aspects of finance. The following key possibilities and developments to appearance out for:

7.7.1 Increased Computing Power

As quantum computing continues to develop, the supply of extra effective and strong quantum computer systems will free up new possibilities in finance. Increased qubit counts and progressed error-correction abilities will enable answers to large and extra-complicated economic issues, mainly to improve hazard evaluation, optimization, and simulation competencies.

7.7.2 Enhanced Cryptography and Security

The development of quantum-resistant cryptographic algorithms becomes crucial as quantum computer systems pose a risk to classical encryption techniques. Destiny will see the adoption of post-quantum cryptography, ensuring ease of transactions, statistics privacy, and protection against ability assaults. Quantum cryptography will even keep evolving, providing unbreakable encryption and authentication mechanisms for secure communication.

7.7.3 Quantum Machine Learning Advancements

Quantum device mastering algorithms become more state-of-the-art and delicate, permitting extra-correct predictions, statistics evaluation, and decision-making in finance. Quantum has more advantageous of pattern recognition, optimization, and portfolio management strategies might be developed, offering monetary establishments valuable insights, and improving their danger control techniques.

7.7.4 Quantum Simulation for Financial Modeling

Quantum simulation will play an important position in monetary modeling and risk assessment. Quantum computer systems can simulate complicated monetary structures, enabling the evaluation of diverse eventualities and the identification of capacity dangers and possibilities. This functionality will cause greater accurate pricing models, threat checks, and pressure to try out methodologies.

7.7.5 Industry Collaboration and Partnerships

Collaboration between financial establishments, era businesses, academia, and regulatory bodies will grow in significance. The complicated nature of quantum technologies requires an understanding of various domain names, and collaborative efforts will facilitate expertise trade, widespread development, and the status quo of excellent practices. Partnerships between quantum hardware vendors and monetary institutions will even keep growing, and allowing for easy to get right of entry to quantum computing assets.

7.7.6 Quantum Computing as a Service

With the emergence of cloud-primarily based quantum computing platforms, financial institutions can have the possibility to access quantum computing sources and competencies on-call. Quantum computing as a service models will allow groups to leverage quantum computing energy without the want for big-scale infrastructure investments. This accessibility will boost the adoption of quantum technology in finance.

7.7.7 Quantum Financial Products and Services

As quantum technology matures, we can anticipate the emergence of quantum-inspired financial services and products. These products may encompass quantum-derived hazard exams, optimized funding techniques, and novel monetary devices that leverage quantum residences. Quantum technology can disrupt conventional financial systems and create new avenues for price introduction and chance control.

7.7.8 Regulatory Framework Development

Regulators will play a critical role in shaping the future of quantum technology in finance. As quantum applications end up extra well known, regulators will work closer to growing frameworks and pointers unique to quantum-enabled monetary systems. These rules will ensure safety, transparency, fairness, and compliance in the use of quantum technology in the financial quarter. It is critical to note that the whole consciousness of those possibilities and trends may also take time as quantum technology continues to adapt. As the field progresses, collaboration, studies, and investment will pave the manner for the integration of quantum technologies into the monetary sector, bringing about transformative modifications and unlocking new possibilities in finance (Wootters & Zurek, 1982).

7.8 Complex Financial Calculations

Complex monetary calculations encompass a wide variety of mathematical computations and fashions used inside the economic industry to analyze and make informed decisions appropriately about investments, danger control, pricing, and more. These calculations often contain tricky formulation, fashions, and algorithms.

7.8.1 Option Pricing

Calculating the fee of alternatives, together with European or American alternatives, calls for state-of-the-art mathematical fashions like the Black–Scholes–Merton model or Monte Carlo simulations. These models remember variables together with underlying asset prices, strike prices, time to expiration, interest fees, and volatility to determine the truthful cost of the alternatives.

7.8.2 Risk Analysis

Financial establishments want to assess and control diverse forms of threat, which includes marketplace risk, credit score risk, and operational risk. Complex calculations are worried in measuring threat exposures, estimating value-at-threat, and pressure trying out portfolios, and analyzing the impact of different danger elements at the economic position of the group.

7.8.3 Portfolio Optimization

Optimizing investment portfolios involves figuring out the precise allocation of property to gain unique targets at the same time as thinking about hazard and go back. This calculation includes assessing the hazard–go back alternate-off, covariance matrix calculations, and solving mathematical optimization troubles to discover the finest portfolio composition.

7.8.4 Credit Scoring

Credit scoring fashions are used to evaluate the creditworthiness of individuals and corporations. These models depend upon diverse information factors, which include credit score records, income, and demographic records, to calculate credit rankings. Complex statistical and system studying algorithms are employed to increase accurate credit score scoring models.

7.8.5 Financial Forecasting

Financial forecasting entails predicting destiny financial overall performance, inclusive of sales, fees, cash glide, and profitability. Advanced statistical methods, time collection analysis, and regression fashions are used to analyze historic facts and mission destiny economic results.

7.8.6 Valuation of Financial Instruments

Calculating the fee of complicated financial instruments, inclusive of derivatives, established merchandise, and glued-earnings securities, frequently calls for superior mathematical models and strategies. Examples include bond pricing using discounted coins drift analysis, calculating the internet present fee Net Present Value (NPV) of destiny coins flows, and valuing complex derivatives the usage of alternative pricing fashions.

7.8.7 Capital Asset Pricing Model (CAPM)

CAPM is an extensively used model in finance for figuring out the predicted go back on a funding through considering its systematic chance. This calculation includes estimating beta (a measure of systematic danger) and incorporating it into the CAPM formula to calculate the expected go back on an investment.

7.8.8 Financial Ratio Analysis

Financial ratio analysis includes computing numerous ratios, such as liquidity ratios, profitability ratios, and leverage ratios, to evaluate the economic health and performance of a business enterprise. These calculations offer insights into the company's performance, profitability, solvency, and average financial stability (Gisin et al., 2002). These are just a few examples of the complicated financial calculations performed in the industry. The calculations noted earlier often require a mixture of mathematical know-how, monetary area understanding, and superior computational tools to correctly analyses and interpret financial information and make knowledgeable decisions (Yirka, 2021).

7.9 Conclusion

In conclusion, complicated economic calculations are vital to the functioning of the economic enterprise. These calculations contain sophisticated mathematical fashions, algorithms, and records' evaluation strategies that permit financial institutions to make knowledgeable selections, manipulate dangers, and optimize investment portfolios. These calculations, from choice pricing and danger evaluation to portfolio optimization and credit score scoring, help quantify monetary variables, examine performance, and support decision-making methods.

As the economic industry continues to conform, the complexity and scale of financial calculations are anticipated to grow. The emergence of superior technology, which includes quantum computing and system mastering, similarly expands the possibilities for correct and efficient monetary evaluation. This technology can revolutionize complicated monetary calculations by supplying faster computation, stepped-forward modeling competencies, and stronger prediction accuracy (Khang & Rath, 2024).

However, it's essential to be aware that complex economic calculations require a multidisciplinary approach, combining mathematical know-how, financial domain know-how, and technological improvements. Financial professionals, mathematicians, information scientists, and technologists work collectively to broaden and enforce fashions, algorithms, and equipment that guide complicated monetary calculations. Ultimately, complex economic calculations are vital in allowing economic institutions to navigate a swiftly converting panorama, make informed decisions, and manipulate risks effectively. As the industry continues to increase and embody new technology, the sophistication and significance of these calculations will grow, facilitating greater accurate evaluation, improved hazard management, and advanced economic consequences (Khang & Quantum, 2024).

References

Aspuru-Guzik, A., Dutoi, A. D., Love, P. J., & Head-Gordon, M. (2005). Simulated quantum computation of molecular energies. Science, 309(5741), 1704–1707. DOI: 10.1126/science.1113479

Cao, Y., & Painkras, E (2019). Quantum machine learning. Microprocessors and Microsystems, 68, 41–47. DOI: 10.1016/j.micpro.2019.03.002

Childs, A. M., et al. (2017). Quantum algorithms for fixed qubit architectures. arXiv preprint arXiv:1710.07345. URL: https://arxiv.org/abs/1710.07345

DiVincenzo, D. P. (2000). The physical implementation of quantum computation. Fortschritte Der Physik, 48(9–11), 771–783. DOI: 10.1002/1521-3978(200009)48:9/11<771::AID-PROP771>3.0.CO;2-E

Einstein, A., Podolsky, B., & Rosen, N. (1935). Can quantum-mechanical description of physical reality be considered complete? Physical Review, 47(10), 777. DOI: 10.1103/PhysRev.47.777

Farhi, E., Goldstone, J., & Gutmann, S (2014). A quantum approximate optimization algorithm. arXiv preprint arXiv:1411.4028. URL: https://arxiv.org/abs/1411.4028

Gisin, N., Ribordy, G., Tittel, W., & Zbinden, H. (2002). Quantum cryptography. Reviews of Modern Physics, 74(1), 145. DOI: 10.1103/RevModPhys.74.145

Grover, L. K (1996). A fast quantum mechanical algorithm for database search. In Proceedings of the twenty-eighth annual ACM symposium on Theory of Computing (pp. 212–219). DOI: 10.1145/237814.237866

Harrow, A. W., Hassidim, A., & Lloyd, S. (2009). Quantum algorithm for linear systems of equations. Physical Review Letters, 103(15), 150502. DOI: 10.1103/PhysRevLett.103.150502

Johnson, M. W., et al. (2011). Quantum annealing with manufactured spins. Nature, 473(7346), 194–198. DOI: 10.1038/nature10012

Khang, A. (Ed.). (2024). Applications and Principles of Quantum Computing. IGI Global. https://doi.org/10.4018/979-8-3693-1168-4

Khang, A., "Driving transformative technology trends with quantum-based artificial intelligence (AI) applications," In Khang, A., & Rath, K. C., The Quantum Evolution: Application of AI and Robotics *in the Future of Quantum Technology*. (1st ed.) (2024). CRC Press.

Khang, A., Abdullayev, V., Alyar, A. V., Khalilov, M., Ragimova, N. A., & Niu, Y. (2024). "Introduction to Quantum Computing and Its Integration Applications," In Khang A. (Ed.), Applications and Principles of Quantum Computing (pp. 25–45). IGI Global. https://doi.org/10.4018/979-8-3693-1168-4.ch002

Khang, A., Hajimahmud, V. A., Ragimova, N. A., Alyar, A. V., Khalilov, M., Murad, B., & Litvinova, E. (2024). "Quantum Computing in Oil and Gas Exploration Industry," In Khang, A., & Rath, K. C., *The Quantum Evolution: Application of AI and Robotics in the Future of Quantum Technology*. (1st ed.) CRC Press.

Khang, A., & Rath, K. C. (Eds.). (2024). The Quantum Evolution: Application of AI and Robotics in the Future of Quantum Technology (1st ed.). CRC Press.

Khang, A., Rath, K. C., Muduli, K., & Palaninatharaja, M., "Quantum robotics: Towards intelligent and adaptive robotic systems," In Khang, A., & Rath, K. C., The Quantum Evolution: Application of AI and Robotics in the Future of Quantum Technology. (1st Ed.) (2024). CRC Press.

Khang, A., Rath, K. C., Panda, N., & Kumar, A. (2024). "Quantum mechanics primer: Fundamentals and quantum computing," In Khang A. (Ed.), Applications and Principles of Quantum Computing (pp. 1–24). IGI Global. https://doi.org/10.4018/979-8-3693-1168-4.ch001

Kitaev, A (1995). Quantum measurements and the Abelian Stabilizer Problem. arXiv preprint quant-ph/9511026. URL: https://arxiv.org/abs/quant-ph/9511026

Kitaev, A. Y. (1997). Quantum computations: Algorithms and error correction. Russian Mathematical Surveys, 52(6), 1191. DOI: 10.1070/RM1997v052n06ABEH002155

Kok, P., Munro, W. J., Nemoto, K., Ralph, T. C., Dowling, J. P., & Milburn, G. J. (2007). Linear optical quantum computing with photonic qubits. Reviews of Modern Physics, 79(1), 135. DOI: 10.1103/RevModPhys.79.135

Kuperberg, G. (2002). A subexponential-time quantum algorithm for the dihedral hidden subgroup problem. SIAM Journal on Computing, 35(1), 170–188. DOI: https://epubs.siam.org/doi/abs/10.1137/S0097539703436345

Ladd, T., Jelezko, F., Laflamme, R. et al. Quantum computers. Nature 464, 45–53 (2010). DOI: 10.1038/nature08812

Montanaro, A. (2016). Quantum algorithms: An overview. Npj Quantum Information, 2(1), 15023. DOI: 10.1038/npjqi.2015.23

Nielsen, M. A., & Chuang, I. L. (2010). Quantum Computation and Quantum Information. Cambridge University Press. ISBN: 978-1107002173

Peres, A. (1996). Quantum Theory: Concepts and Methods. Kluwer Academic Publishers. ISBN: 978-1402002681

Preskill, J. (2018). Quantum computing in the NISQ era and beyond. Quantum, 2, 79.

Reck, M., Zeilinger, A., Bernstein, H. J., & Bertani, P. (1994). Experimental realization of any discrete unitary operator. Physical Review Letters, 73(1), 58. DOI: 10.1103/PhysRevLett.73.58

Rieffel, E. G., & Polak, W. H. (2011). Quantum Computing: A Gentle Introduction. MIT Press. ISBN: 978-0262015067

Shor, P. W (1994). Algorithms for quantum computation: Discrete logarithms and factoring. In Proceedings 35th Annual Symposium on Foundations of Computer Science (pp. 124–134). IEEE. DOI: 10.1109/SFCS.1994.365700

Shor, P. W. (1997). Polynomial-time algorithms for prime factorization and discrete logarithms on a quantum computer. SIAM Review, 41(2), 303–37. DOI: 10.1137/S0036144598347011

Steane, A. (1997). Quantum computing. Reports on Progress in Physics, 61(2), 117. DOI: 10.1088/0034-4885/61/2/002

Terhal, B. M., & DiVincenzo, D. P. (2004). Adaptive quantum computation, constant depth quantum circuits and Arthur-Merlin games. Quantum Information & Computation, 4(2), 134–145. DOI: 10.26421/QIC4.2-3

Vedral, V., Plenio, M. B., Rippin, M. A., & Knight, P. L. (1997). Quantifying entanglement. Physical Review Letters, 78(12), 2275. DOI: 10.1103/PhysRevLett.78.2275

Wootters, W. K., & Zurek, W. H. (1982). A single quantum cannot be cloned. Nature, 299(5886), 802–803. DOI: 10.1038/299802a0

Yirka, B (2021). Quantum computing and cryptography. Phys.org.

Zeng, B., et al. (2017). Quantum algorithms for scientific computing and approximation. Quantum Science and Technology, 2(3), 034009.

Chapter 8

Opportunities and Challenges of Artificial Intelligence (AI) in the Banking and Finance Sector

Piyal Roy, Shivnath Ghosh, Amitava Podder, and Saptarshi Kumar Sarkar

8.1 Introduction

Technological innovations have become a symbol of progress in the rapidly evolving fields of finance and banking, influencing the way these organizations function and engage with their clientele. Artificial intelligence (AI) has stood out among these advancements as a game-changer, transforming conventional procedures and creating new avenues for exploration. For financial organizations looking to remain ahead in an increasingly competitive world, AI offers great potential with its skills in natural language processing, machine learning, and predictive analytics. Its potential to automate tasks, analyze data at scale, and deliver personalized services has captured the attention of industry leaders worldwide.

As AI continues to make inroads into the financial sector, its impact spans a wide range of areas, from transforming customer experiences to optimizing back-end operations. However, the implications of AI adoption extend beyond operational efficiency and revenue growth. They encompass complex ethical, regulatory, and societal considerations that demand careful examination. A comprehensive knowledge of AI's function in finance and banking is essential, since concerns over algorithmic bias, data privacy, and the replacement of human labor highlight this point. Regulatory agencies are also struggling with how to protect consumer interests and promote innovation in AI applications while making sure they abide by current rules and regulations.

In light of these opportunities and difficulties, the goal of this chapter is to offer a thorough investigation of AI's effects on the world's banking and financial sector. The purpose of the article is to shed light on the complex nature of AI adoption in the finance and banking sectors by

DOI: 10.4324/9781003501947-8

combining insights from industry publications, academic research, and real estate case studies. It will delve into the opportunities AI presents, such as enhancing customer experiences, improving operational efficiencies, and managing risks more effectively. Simultaneously, it will address the critical issues and challenges inherent in AI adoption, including ethical considerations, regulatory compliance, and data security concerns.

This chapter seeks to advance knowledge of AI's transformational potential in finance and banking through this thorough examination. By identifying key trends, best practices, and areas for further research, it seeks to empower stakeholders, including financial institutions, policymakers, researchers, and consumers, to navigate the complex landscape of AI adoption in banking and finance effectively. Ultimately, the goal is to foster a more informed and forward-thinking approach to harnessing AI's capabilities while mitigating its risks, thereby shaping a more resilient and inclusive future for banking and finance.

8.1.1 Background and Motivation

Throughout history, the banking and financial sector has led the way in technical innovation, constantly looking for new ways to improve client pleasure, reduce risks, and simplify operations (Davies & Green, 2010). AI, which includes a variety of modern technologies including natural language processing (NLP), machine learning, and predictive analytics, is one of the most revolutionary technical advances in recent years (Jordan & Mitchell, 2015; Zhang & Sejdić, 2019). AI has garnered significant attention across various sectors for its potential to revolutionize traditional business processes and decision-making paradigms (Brynjolfsson & McAfee, 2014). In the context of banking and finance, AI presents unprecedented opportunities to optimize operations, personalize services, and manage risks effectively (Lipton & Steinhardt, 2019).

The motivation behind exploring AI's impact on the banking and finance industry stems from its increasing ubiquity and its potential to reshape fundamental aspects of financial services provision. As AI technologies mature and become more accessible, financial institutions worldwide are investing heavily in AI-driven initiatives to gain a competitive edge, meet evolving customer demands, and navigate an increasingly complex regulatory landscape (Pant, Mishra & Mohan, 2024). Understanding the implications of AI adoption in banking and finance is crucial for stakeholders, including industry practitioners, policymakers, researchers, and consumers, as it can inform strategic decision-making, regulatory frameworks, and technological investments.

Numerous studies and industry reports have documented the transformative potential of AI in banking and finance, highlighting its capacity to drive innovation, improve efficiency, and enhance customer engagement (Khams et al., 2022). However, alongside the opportunities, there exist significant challenges and considerations that warrant careful examination. Ethical concerns surrounding data privacy, algorithmic bias, and job displacement, as well as regulatory constraints and technological limitations, underscore the multifaceted nature of AI adoption in the financial sector (Ala-Pietilä et al., 2019). By exploring these intricacies, this chapter seeks to offer a thorough examination of the prospects, problems, and difficulties presented by AI in the worldwide banking and financial sector, thereby advancing a more profound comprehension of its consequences for relevant parties (Khanh & Khang, 2021).

8.1.2 Scope and Objectives

The scope of this chapter includes a thorough examination of AI's involvement in the banking and financial sector, with an emphasis on the technology's prospects, problems, and obstacles from a worldwide standpoint. This chapter aims to investigate the development of AI technologies in the financial industry, the present adoption patterns, and the consequences for different stakeholders. It will investigate how AI is reshaping key aspects of banking and financial services, including customer experience, operational efficiency, risk management, and personalized offerings.

Furthermore, this chapter will critically examine the ethical, regulatory, and privacy considerations associated with AI adoption, addressing concerns such as data security, algorithmic transparency, and regulatory compliance. By synthesizing existing literature, case studies, and industry insights, this chapter aims to elucidate the potential benefits of AI adoption while acknowledging the complexities and trade-offs inherent in its implementation. The objectives of this chapter are multifold:

- To give a thorough rundown of AI's evolution in the banking and finance industry, including its definition, conceptual underpinnings, and historical development.
- To identify and analyze the opportunities afforded by AI in enhancing customer experience, improving operational efficiency, and managing risks in the banking and finance sector.
- To examine the ethical, regulatory, and privacy challenges associated with AI adoption in banking and finance, and to propose strategies for addressing these concerns.
- To explore case studies and best practices highlighting successful AI implementations, as well as lessons learned from failed initiatives, to distill key insights and practical implications.
- To offer global perspectives on AI adoption in banking and finance, considering regional variances, cultural factors, and policy frameworks shaping its implementation.
- To outline future directions and research agendas for advancing AI's role in the banking and finance industry, and to identify implications for stakeholders, including financial institutions, policymakers, researchers, and consumers.

Through these objectives, this article aims to contribute to the current discourse on AI in banking and finance, fostering a deeper understanding of its transformative potential, as well as its ethical, regulatory, and socioeconomic implications.

8.2 Overview of Artificial Intelligence in Banking and Finance Sector

In an era defined by digital disruption and technological innovation, the banking and finance industry stands at the forefront of transformative change. Central to this evolution is the rapid advancement and adoption of AI, a groundbreaking technology with the potential to revolutionize traditional business models, redefine customer experiences, and drive operational efficiencies.

The successful navigation of a complicated environment by financial institutions, driven by changing customer expectations, regulatory demands, and competitive dynamics, has made the tactical application of AI essential. This section provides an overview of AI, including its definition, conceptual foundations, evolutionary history, and current adoption trends in banking and finance. This chapter aims to provide a comprehensive understanding of AI's potential for change in the global financial services industry by synthesizing academic literature, company perspectives, and real-world case studies. It also addresses important opportunities, challenges, and stakeholder implications.

8.2.1 Definition and Concepts

The use of cutting-edge computing algorithms and techniques to automate processes, analyze data, and make well-informed judgments without overt human interaction is referred to as AI in the banking and finance industry (Cleland & Hartsink, 2020; Wolf, 2022). Machine learning algorithms, for instance, enable financial institutions to extract meaningful insights from vast datasets, identify patterns, and make predictions, thereby enhancing decision-making processes and driving innovation (Jordan & Mitchell, 2015) as shown in Figure 8.1.

A wide range of technologies are included in AI, such as deep learning, machine learning, and NLP, RPA streamlines repetitive tasks and back-office operations, reducing costs and increasing efficiency (Khams, 2022).

The concept of AI-driven automation in banking and finance extends beyond efficiency gains to encompass strategic advantages such as enhanced customer experiences, personalized financial services, and proactive risk management (Brynjolfsson & McAfee, 2014). Financial institutions may foresee future patterns and market movements, provide personalized suggestions, and customize product offers to meet the demands of individual customers by utilizing AI technology (Lipton & Steinhardt, 2019). Moreover, AI-powered analytics enable more accurate and timely risk assessments, helping organizations identify potential threats and vulnerabilities before they escalate into crises (Ala-Pietilä et al., 2019).

AI represents a transformative force in banking and finance, offering unprecedented opportunities to streamline operations, drive innovation, and deliver value-added services to customers.

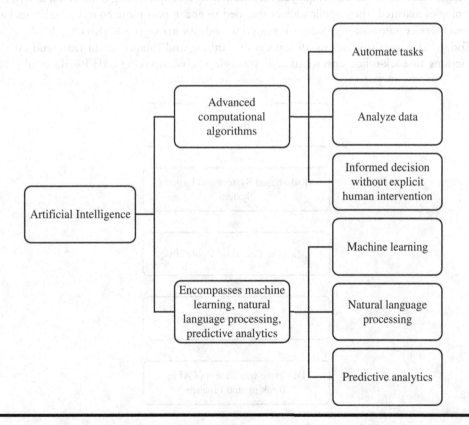

Figure 8.1   Overview of AI and its components.

Financial institutions may obtain a competitive edge, adjust to changing market conditions, and promote sustainable growth in a world that is becoming more digital and data-driven by using AI technology (Khang, Rath, Panda et al., 2024).

8.2.2 Evolution of AI in the Industry

Evolution of AI in the banking and finance industry has been marked by significant milestones and advancements, driven by a convergence of technological innovation, regulatory changes, and shifting consumer expectations. Although AI has its origins in the early days of computers, its popularity as a revolutionary force in finance did not take off until the development of machine learning algorithms and large data analytics (Jordan & Mitchell, 2015; Zhang & Sejdić, 2019) as shown in Figure 8.2.

Historically, AI applications in banking and finance were primarily focused on rule-based systems and expert systems, which relied on predefined rules and logical reasoning to automate tasks such as credit scoring and fraud detection (Brynjolfsson & McAfee, 2014). However, with the proliferation of data and advancements in computational power, machine learning algorithms emerged as the cornerstone of AI-driven innovation in finance, enabling systems to learn from data and improve performance over time (Lipton & Steinhardt, 2019). It is possible to classify the development of AI in finance and banking into many phases.

Data input, processing of documents, and transaction monitoring were among the operational operations that AI was initially employed for automating and optimizing (Pant et al., 2024). As AI technologies matured, their applications expanded to encompass more complex tasks, including customer service automation, predictive analytics, and risk management (Khams, 2022).

Today, AI is pervasive across all aspects of banking and finance, from front-end customer interactions to back-office operations and strategic decision-making (Ala-Pietilä et al., 2019).

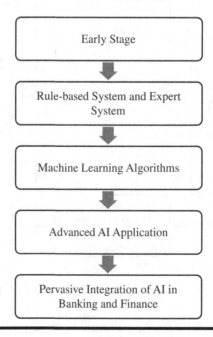

Figure 8.2   Evolution of AI in the banking and finance industry.

Advanced AI algorithms power virtual assistants, providing personalized assistance to customers and improving engagement. AI-driven analytics enable financial institutions to identify trends, detect anomalies, and make data-driven decisions in real-time, enhancing risk management and regulatory compliance (Jordan & Mitchell, 2015).

Looking ahead, the evolution of AI in banking and finance is expected to continue, driven by ongoing technological innovation, regulatory developments, and changing market dynamics (Brynjolfsson & McAfee, 2014). As AI becomes more sophisticated and integrated into financial services ecosystems, its impact is likely to deepen, reshaping business models, driving operational efficiencies, and redefining customer experiences in profound ways (Khang, Semenets et al., 2024).

8.2.3 *Current Landscape and Adoption Trends*

The deployment of AI in the financial and banking industries is now characterized by a dynamic interplay between regulatory requirements, technical innovation, and changing market dynamics. Financial institutions worldwide are progressively using AI technology in order to propel digital transformation, optimize operational efficiency, and provide exceptional client experiences (Borges, Marine & Ibrahim, 2020). The incorporation of AI in banking and finance is propelled by several factors, including the proliferation of data, advances in machine learning algorithms, and growing competition from fintech startups and non-traditional players (Khams, 2022).

In the retail banking sector, AI-powered virtual assistants have become ubiquitous, offering personalized support to customers, resolving queries in real-time, and streamlining routine transactions (Pant et al., 2024). Moreover, AI-driven analytics platforms enable banks to analyze vast datasets, gain actionable insights, and tailor product offerings to individual customer needs, thereby enhancing customer engagement and loyalty. Similarly, in the realm of investment banking and wealth management, AI algorithms are used for portfolio optimization, algorithmic trading, and risk management, enabling financial institutions to make informed investment decisions and mitigate risks (Jordan & Mitchell, 2015).

AI is being used in banking and finance for tasks related to regulatory compliance as well as back-office operations and customer-facing apps. By automating repetitive processes like data entry, healing, and compliance reporting, RPA technologies free up human resources to concentrate on higher-value work (Brynjolfsson & McAfee, 2014). Furthermore, AI-powered fraud detection systems use machine learning algorithms to identify unusual transactions, spot abnormalities, and stop financial crime. This increases the financial system's security and fosters greater public confidence (Lipton & Steinhardt, 2019).

Despite the widespread adoption of AI in banking and finance, challenges remain, including concerns about data privacy, algorithmic bias, and regulatory compliance (Ala-Pietilä et al., 2019). Financial institutions must navigate complex regulatory frameworks, ensure the ethical use of AI technologies, and safeguard sensitive customer information to maintain trust and credibility (Arner et al., 2020). Moreover, the pace of AI adoption varies across regions and institutions, influenced by factors such as regulatory environment, technological infrastructure, and organizational culture (Borges et al., 2020).

Looking ahead, it is anticipated that further technology improvements, shifting customer expectations, and regulatory constraints will accelerate the use of AI in banking and finance (Khams, 2022). In a more digital and based-on-data world, financial institutions that successfully leverage the potential of AI stand to gain an edge over their competitors, open up fresh sources of income, and provide creative solutions that match the changing demands of their clients.

8.3 Opportunities of AI in Banking and Finance Sector

The integration of AI in banking and finance heralds a new era of opportunities, reshaping traditional paradigms and unlocking unprecedented potential for value creation. Across various facets of the industry, AI-driven solutions offer transformative benefits, ranging from enhancing customer experiences to fortifying risk management frameworks. Through a synthesis of advanced computational algorithms such as machine learning, natural language processing, and predictive analytics, AI empowers financial institutions to adapt to evolving market dynamics, deliver personalized services, and mitigate emerging risks. This section explores the multifaceted opportunities presented by AI in banking and finance, underlining its capacity to drive innovation, efficiency, and resilience in a rapidly changing landscape.

8.3.1 Enhanced Customer Experience

In the digital age, customer experience has emerged as a crucial competitive differentiator for banks and financial institutions. With the advent of AI, there has been a paradigm shift in how financial services are delivered, with a primary focus on enhancing customer experiences. AI-powered solutions have revolutionized customer interactions, enabling personalized recommendations, proactive assistance, and seamless service delivery.

Using chatbots and AI to improve customer experience is one of the main uses of AI. Natural language processing (NLP) techniques are used by these AI-driven systems to comprehend consumer inquiries and deliver pertinent answers instantly. For instance, a chatbot might participate in a conversational interface with a client when they visit a bank's website or mobile app and ask for help with account inquiries or transaction history. The chatbot can assist the user throughout the process and provide prompt answers to their questions (Borges et al., 2020).

Furthermore, AI-powered chatbots may learn from previous exchanges, which allows them to gradually offer more tailored and contextually aware replies. Chatbots are able to predict the wants and preferences of customers by examining past consumer data and behavioral trends. This allows them to provide customized recommendations and solutions. For example, the chatbot can actively remind a client who regularly checks the status of their accounts or pays bills at the conclusion of the month about forthcoming payments or offer budgeting advice to assist them manage their money more efficiently (Khams, 2022).

Financial institutions may now use AI to provide clients with tailored product suggestions and offers based on their unique requirements and preferences, going beyond chatbots. AI systems can recognize pertinent cross-selling and upselling possibilities by evaluating enormous volumes of client data, including transaction history, purchasing trends, and demographic data. AI algorithms can suggest credit card offers with cashback benefits or discounts at electronics stores, for instance, if a consumer often spends online. This can improve the perceived value of the bank's services and boost client loyalty.

Moreover, financial institutions may customize their marketing messaging and communication strategies by gaining deeper insights into client behavior and sentiment with AI-powered analytics. By analyzing social media interactions, customer feedback, and online reviews, AI algorithms can identify trends and patterns in customer sentiment, enabling banks to respond proactively to customer feedback and address any issues or concerns in a timely manner. For example, if a bank receives negative feedback on social media regarding a recent service outage or technical issue, sentiment analysis technologies driven by AI (Pant et al., 2024) can notify the bank's customer support staff, allowing them to take immediate action and minimize any possible harm to their reputation.

AI presents immense opportunities for enhancing customer experience in the banking and finance industry. Through the use of sentiment analysis tools, personalized suggestions, and chatbots driven by AI, financial institutions can deliver seamless, personalized, and proactive customer experiences, thereby fostering deeper engagement, loyalty, and satisfaction among their customers.

8.3.2 Improved Operational Efficiency

Operational efficiency is a critical concern for banks and financial institutions, as it directly impacts their ability to deliver timely and cost-effective services to customers while managing risks and complying with regulatory requirements. AI has emerged as a powerful tool for improving operational efficiency across various functions within the banking and finance industry, enabling automation, optimization, and streamlining of processes.

One of the primary ways in which AI improves operational efficiency is through the automation of routine and repetitive tasks. RPA technologies enable financial institutions to automate manual, rule-based processes such as data entry, document processing, and transaction reconciliation. According to Brynjolfsson and McAfee (2014), banks may achieve considerable reductions in processing times, minimize mistakes, and free up human resources to concentrate on more critical duties by implementing AI-powered bots that perform these jobs.

Moreover, AI enables predictive analytics and forecasting, allowing financial institutions to anticipate demand, identify trends, and optimize resource allocation (Biswas et al., 2024). By analyzing historical data and patterns, AI algorithms can generate accurate forecasts for customer demand, transaction volumes, and market trends, enabling banks to allocate resources more effectively and efficiently. For example, if a bank anticipates a surge in loan applications during a specific time period, AI-powered predictive analytics tools can help them allocate additional resources to the loan processing department to ensure timely and efficient processing of applications (Khams, 2022).

Financial institutions may enhance their risk management procedures with AI-driven analytics, allowing for the early detection, evaluation, and reduction of hazards. Financial institutions may bolster their defenses against fraud, cyberattacks, and market volatility by utilizing machine learning algorithms that analyze large datasets to find abnormalities, identify new hazards, and anticipate prospective dangers. AI-driven fraud detection systems, for example, track transaction data constantly and in real-time, identifying suspicious activity and odd patterns that point to fraudulent activity. Banks can reduce financial losses and safeguard their image by automating the recognition and investigation of phony transactions (Jordan & Mitchell, 2015).

Additionally, AI facilitates the optimization of resource utilization and operational workflows through advanced analytics and process optimization algorithms. By analyzing operational data and identifying inefficiencies, AI algorithms can suggest process improvements and workflow optimizations to enhance productivity and reduce costs. For example, if a bank's back-office operations are experiencing bottlenecks or delays in processing loan applications, AI-powered process optimization tools can identify the root causes of these issues and recommend changes to streamline the workflow, such as automating manual tasks or reallocating resources.

Furthermore, AI makes it possible for financial institutions to more successfully and efficiently adhere to regulatory standards. Banks must keep an eye on and abide by a plethora of rules, regulations, and reporting obligations as part of the difficult and time-consuming process of regulatory compliance. AI-driven compliance solutions employ machine learning algorithms to scrutinize regulatory papers, detect pertinent prerequisites, and guarantee banks adhere to relevant rules and regulations. AI assists banks in lowering the risk of failure to comply and avoiding expensive fines and penalties by automating compliance tracking and evaluation procedures (Pant et al., 2024).

AI presents significant opportunities for improving operational efficiency in the banking and finance industry. By automating routine tasks, optimizing resource allocation, and enhancing risk management practices, AI enables financial institutions to operate more efficiently, reduce costs, and deliver better services to customers. Moreover, AI-driven analytics and compliance solutions help banks stay ahead of regulatory requirements and ensure compliance with applicable laws and regulations, thereby mitigating regulatory risks and maintaining trust and credibility in the marketplace.

8.3.3 Advanced Risk Management

For banks and other financial organizations to remain stable and sustainable, effective risk management is essential. AI has become a potent instrument in the digital age for improving risk management procedures by facilitating the proactive discovery, evaluation, and mitigation of hazards. AI-driven solutions help financial institutions bolster their defenses against fraud, cyber threats, and market swings by utilizing cutting-edge machine learning algorithms to analyze large datasets, spot patterns, and anticipate possible dangers.

Credit risk assessment is one of the main areas where AI is used in risk management. Conventional credit risk models evaluate borrower creditworthiness using preset criteria and historical data. Nevertheless, these models frequently fall short in capturing the intricate relationships between various risk indicators and the dynamic character of credit risk. Conversely, machine learning algorithms are used by AI-powered credit risk models to evaluate a variety of data sources, such as transaction history, credit scores, and behavioral data, to produce more precise and anticipated credit risk evaluations. AI helps financial institutions make better lending decisions and lower the risk of loan defaults by combining non-traditional data sources with real-time information.

Furthermore, by helping financial organizations to better analyze market patterns, spot correlations, and predict price changes, AI improves market risk management procedures. Algorithms using machine learning techniques examine past market data to spot trends and abnormalities that can point to future dangers or opportunities. Financial institutions can improve their investment strategies, create more reliable risk models, and lessen the effect of volatility in the markets on their portfolios by utilizing AI-driven predictive analytics (Khams, 2022). By helping financial institutions recognize and reduce operational risks more successfully, AI simplifies operational risk management.

Operational risks can have serious negative effects on finances and reputation and are caused by internal procedures, systems, or human mistakes. AI-powered systems examine operational data, spot any hazards, and recommend preventive actions using sophisticated analytics and process optimization algorithms. AI systems, for instance, can examine transaction data to spot trends that point to fraud or unusual trading activity that might point to possible operational hazards. By automating the detection and mitigation of operational risks, AI helps financial institutions reduce the likelihood of costly disruptions and ensure the resilience of their operations (Brynjolfsson & McAfee, 2014).

8.3.4 Personalized Financial Services

In today's highly competitive banking and finance industry, providing personalized financial services has become essential for attracting and retaining customers. Financial institutions may offer customized goods, services, and guidance to each individual consumer in order to better match their specific requirements and preferences thanks in large part to AI.

Wealth management is one of the main areas where AI is being used in personalized financial services. Wealth management systems driven by AI employ sophisticated machine learning algorithms to evaluate client information, such as investing preferences, risk tolerance, and financial objectives, in order to create customized investment plans. AI algorithms can optimize asset allocation, rebalance portfolios, and find investment opportunities that fit each customer's financial goals by integrating real-time market data and economic indicators (Borges et al., 2020).

Furthermore, AI gives financial institutions the ability to provide individualized banking services and solutions that cater to each customer's unique requirements and preferences. AI systems can find pertinent upselling and cross-selling opportunities by examining transaction data, spending trends, and demographic data. AI algorithms can suggest credit card deals with travel rewards or reductions on airline tickets and hotel bookings to customers who regularly shop online for travel-related expenses. This can improve the perceived worth of the bank's offerings and boost customer loyalty (Pant et al., 2024).

Additionally, by examining consumer data and behavioral patterns to generate pertinent recommendations and insights, AI makes personalized financial advice and coaching easier. AI-driven financial consulting platforms employ machine learning algorithms to examine client financial profiles, evaluate their risk tolerance and financial objectives, and offer tailored advice on investments, savings, and retirement planning. By offering personalized financial advice, financial institutions can deepen customer engagement, build trust, and differentiate themselves from competitors (Khams, 2022).

8.3.5 Fraud Detection and Prevention

Given the possible loss of money and negative publicity connected to fraudulent acts, banks and other financial institutions place a high priority on the detection and prevention of fraud. AI has become a potent weapon in the fight against fraud, giving financial institutions the ability to spot suspicious activity, recognize fraudulent trends, and stop fraudulent transactions in real-time.

Transaction monitoring is one of the main uses of AI in fraud detection and prevention. Advanced machine learning algorithms are used by AI-powered fraud detection systems to evaluate transaction data in real-time, highlighting suspicious activity and odd patterns suggestive of fraudulent behavior. AI algorithms may adjust and develop new and developing fraud patterns by continuously monitoring transaction data and learning from previous instances. This helps financial institutions to stay ahead of criminals and minimize financial losses (Khams, 2022). AI makes it easier to identify fraudulent activity through a variety of channels and touchpoints, such as card transactions, internet banking, and mobile banking. AI-driven fraud detection systems examine transactional patterns and client behavior to spot irregularities and departures from the norm. For instance, AI systems may identify odd or big transaction activity from a customer and alert the bank's fraud detection staff to make additional inquiries (Borges et al., 2020).

AI helps financial organizations to stop fraud by putting proactive controls and safeguards in place. AI–powered fraud prevention systems use machine learning and predictive analytics to evaluate each transaction's risk and then approve or reject it based on preset thresholds and regulations. AI assists financial institutions in reducing the risk of fraud and safeguarding their assets and clients by automatically identifying high-risk transactions and preventing potentially fraudulent behaviors in real time.

AI improves fraud detection and prevention by utilizing cutting-edge biometric identification methods. Biometric data, such as voiceprints, fingerprint scans, and face recognition, is analyzed by machine learning algorithms in AI-powered biometric authentication systems to confirm clients' identities and identify unauthorized attempts to access accounts or complete transactions. Financial firms can strengthen system security and stop illegal access to client accounts by introducing biometric authentication (Pant et al., 2024).

8.4 Issues and Challenges in AI Adoption

The integration of AI in the banking and finance industry brings forth a myriad of opportunities, yet it also presents several complex issues and challenges. As financial institutions embark on the journey of AI adoption, they must navigate ethical considerations, regulatory compliance, data security and privacy concerns, talent acquisition, and the integration with legacy systems.

8.4.1 Ethical Considerations

The ethical issues surrounding the application of AI are gaining more attention as the technology spreads throughout the banking and finance sectors. The use of AI in finance creates difficult moral conundrums, such as those involving algorithmic bias, accountability, transparency, and justice. In order to guarantee that AI technologies are applied responsibly and ethically, financial institutions need to address these ethical issues and give careful thought to how they can affect their stakeholders, consumers, and society at large.

Algorithmic prejudice is a major ethical dilemma related to AI in banking and finance. Large datasets with historical data, which may reflect and reinforce pre-existing biases and inequality, are used to train AI algorithms. For instance, AI-powered credit scoring systems may unintentionally discriminate against low-income or minority populations if previous lending data contains biases against these groups (Ala-Pietilä et al., 2019). This could lead to unjust or discriminatory conclusions. Financial institutions have a responsibility to ensure that AI systems generate impartial and equitable outcomes by closely examining the training data used to create AI algorithms, and identifying and mitigating biases.

Furthermore, there are issues with AI systems' accountability and transparency, especially when it comes to automated decision-making. AI algorithms frequently function as "black boxes," making it challenging for stakeholders to comprehend the reasoning behind the choices these systems make. This lack of openness has the potential to undermine confidence in AI systems, especially in crucial domains like fraud detection, risk assessment, and credit scoring. In order to give stakeholders access to the decision-making process and the ability to hold AI systems accountable for their actions, financial institutions must work to improve the explainability and transparency of AI systems (Arner et al., 2020).

The application of AI in delicate domains like financial advice and customer service raises ethical questions. Chatbots and virtual assistants driven by AI are being utilized more and more to engage with clients, respond to their questions, and offer support. Delegating significant financial choices to AI systems raises ethical questions, nevertheless, especially if the AI systems lack emotional intelligence, empathy, or a human comprehension of intricate financial conditions. To ensure moral and responsible decision-making, financial institutions must find a balance between the efficiency and ease of use provided by powered by AI customer service solutions and the requirement for human oversight and intervention (Borges et al., 2020).

8.4.2 Regulatory Compliance

Regulatory compliance is a critical consideration for financial institutions seeking to adopt AI technologies in banking and finance. A complex and dynamic regulatory environment that includes national, regional, and worldwide laws, rules, guidelines, and industry standards governs the application of AI in financial services. In order to guarantee adherence to relevant rules and regulations and minimize the possibility of regulatory penalties, fines, and harm to their reputation, financial institutions need to proficiently navigate this regulatory system.

The absence of comprehensive and well-defined legislation governing the utilization of AI technologies is a significant regulatory obstacle to the adoption of AI in the banking and financial industry. AI-powered financial products and services, in contrast to traditional financial products and services, frequently operate in uncharted regulatory territory. This raises concerns about how current regulations relate to these technologies and what extra regulations might be required to handle new risks and difficulties (Ala-Pietilä et al., 2019).

To provide transparent and uniform regulatory frameworks that offer guidelines for the responsible application of AI in financial services, financial institutions must interact with legislators, regulators, and industry stakeholders. There are questions about compliance with current legislation controlling consumer safety, data privacy, and fair lending practices when AI is used in sensitive areas like scoring credit, risk management, and fraud detection.

Regulations like the Equal Credit Opportunities Act and the Fair Credit Reporting Act of 1934, for instance, which forbid lending discrimination and mandate that lenders give customers fair and accurate credit reporting, must be complied with by AI-powered credit scoring systems (Brynjolfsson & McAfee, 2014). Financial institutions are required to make sure that the design and implementation of their AI systems adhere to these standards. Part of this compliance requires regular audits and evaluations to keep an eye out for any possible prejudices and discriminatory outcomes.

The cross-border nature of AI technologies presents challenges for regulatory compliance, particularly in jurisdictions with divergent regulatory requirements and standards. Financial institutions operating in multiple jurisdictions must navigate a patchwork of regulations, guidelines, and industry standards, making it difficult to ensure consistent compliance across all markets (Khams, 2022). Financial institutions must develop robust compliance programs and risk management frameworks that take into account the unique regulatory requirements of each jurisdiction in which they operate, including engaging with local regulators and industry associations to stay abreast of regulatory developments and emerging best practices.

8.4.3 Data Security and Privacy

In the context of the adoption of AI in banking and finance, privacy and data security are critical issues because financial data is sensitive and can be misused or accessed by unauthorized parties. Financial institutions must put strong safeguards in place to ensure the security, integrity, and accessibility of this data as they use AI technology to analyze enormous volumes of data, including consumer transaction records, private details, and sensitive financial data. The possibility of data breaches and cyberattacks is one of the main issues with data security and privacy.

Large datasets are necessary for AI-powered systems to train and enhance their algorithms, which makes them desirable targets for hackers attempting to compromise financial services or steal confidential data (Borges et al., 2020). To protect themselves from data breaches and cyberattacks, financial institutions need to have advanced cybersecurity measures in place, like intrusion detection systems, access limits, and encryption. In order to identify, address, and recover from safety incidents in a prompt and efficient manner, financial institutions must also create incident response strategies and procedures.

The confidentiality and privacy of client data are issues that are brought up by the application of AI in financial services. Large-scale customer data is analyzed by AI algorithms to find patterns, trends, and insights. This raises concerns regarding the ways in which this data is gathered, handled, shared, and preserved (Ala-Pietilä et al., 2019). Financial institutions are subject to strict requirements on the collection, use, and disclosure of personal data, including the California Consumer Privacy Act (CCPA) in the United States and the General Data Protection Regulation (GDPR) in the European Union. Before collecting and processing a customer's personal data, financial institutions are required by law to get that customer's express consent, disclose to them how their data is used, and put safeguards in place to preserve their confidentiality and privacy.

Issues with data governance and management are brought about by the application of AI in the financial services industry. Because errors or inconsistencies in the training data might result in biased or unreliable conclusions, financial institutions must ensure the quality, correctness, and reliability of the data used to train AI algorithms (Brynjolfsson & McAfee, 2014). For financial organizations to guarantee the accuracy and dependability of their data assets, they must put strong data governance frameworks in place. These frameworks should include procedures for data quality assurance and data lineage tracing. Financial institutions also need to set up data management policies and procedures to control data collection, use, and retention while adhering to industry best practices and legal obligations.

8.4.4 Talent Acquisition and Skills Gap

Data security and privacy are crucial concerns in the context of AI's use in banking and finance since sensitive financial information might be misused or obtained by unauthorized individuals. As financial institutions utilize AI technology to analyze massive volumes of data, including customer transaction records, private details, and sensitive financial data, they must put strong measures in place to ensure the security, integrity, and accessibility of this data (Khang, Rani et al., 2023).

One of the primary concerns regarding data security and privacy is the potential for cyberattacks and data breaches. AI-powered systems are attractive targets for hackers looking to undermine financial services or steal sensitive data since they require large datasets in order to train and improve their algorithms (Borges et al., 2020). Financial institutions must have sophisticated cybersecurity safeguards in place, such as detection systems for intrusions, access limits, and encryption, to safeguard themselves against data breaches and cyberattacks. Financial institutions must also have incident response plans and processes in order to recognize, respond to, and recover from safety problems quickly and effectively.

The use of AI in financial services raises concerns about the privacy and confidentiality of customer data. AI systems examine vast amounts of client data to look for trends, patterns, and insights. This prompts questions about the methods used to collect, manage, distribute, and store this data (Ala-Pietilä et al., 2019). Strict guidelines, such as the GDPR in the European Union and the CCPA in the United States, govern how financial institutions must collect, use, and disclose personal data. Financial institutions are obligated by law to obtain express consent from customers before collecting and processing their personal data, to inform them of how their data is used, and to implement protections to protect their privacy and confidentiality.

The use of AI in the financial services sector creates problems with data governance and management. Financial institutions must guarantee the quality, accuracy, and dependability of the data used to train AI algorithms because mistakes or inconsistencies in the training data could lead to biased or untrustworthy findings (Brynjolfsson & McAfee, 2014). Financial organizations need to have robust data governance frameworks in order to ensure the reliability and correctness of their data assets. Procedures for data lineage tracking and quality assurance should be included in these frameworks. Establishing data management procedures and guidelines is crucial for financial institutions to maintain compliance with legal requirements and industry best practices, all while controlling data collection, usage, and retention.

There is a skills gap among existing employees, who may lack the necessary expertise and training to effectively utilize and leverage AI technologies in their roles. Financial institutions must invest in training and upskilling initiatives to bridge this skills gap and build a workforce capable of driving AI adoption and innovation. Programming languages, machine learning algorithms, data science, AI foundations, and ethical issues should all be covered in training programs (Khams, 2022).

Financial institutions should also encourage its staff to gain new skills and keep up with the latest advancements in AI by fostering a culture of continuous learning and skill development. In order to fully utilize AI in banking and finance, interdisciplinary cooperation and teamwork are required. The development and implementation of AI solutions that tackle practical problems and prospects frequently necessitate cooperation between data scientists, programmers, domain specialists, and business stakeholders. To develop innovation and accomplish business objectives, financial institutions need to promote cross-functional collaboration, encourage interdisciplinary teamwork, and break down departmental silos (Borges et al., 2020).

8.4.5 *Integration with Legacy Systems*

The integration of AI technologies with legacy systems and infrastructure poses significant challenges for financial institutions seeking to modernize their operations and leverage the benefits of AI in banking and finance. Many financial institutions operate on outdated legacy systems that were not designed to accommodate the complex computational requirements and data processing capabilities of AI. Integrating AI technologies with legacy systems requires careful planning, coordination, and investment to ensure seamless interoperability and compatibility.

One of the key challenges in integrating AI with legacy systems is compatibility issues. Legacy systems often use outdated technologies, protocols, and programming languages that are incompatible with modern AI frameworks and tools. Financial institutions must assess the compatibility of their legacy systems with AI technologies, identify potential integration challenges, and develop strategies to overcome these challenges, such as developing middleware layers, APIs, and data connectors to facilitate data exchange and communication between legacy systems and AI applications.

Data migration is a significant challenge in the integration of AI with legacy systems. Legacy systems typically store data in proprietary formats and databases that may not be easily accessible or compatible with AI algorithms and analytics tools. Financial institutions must develop data migration strategies to extract, transform, and load data from legacy systems into AI-compatible formats, ensuring data integrity, consistency, and quality throughout the migration process (Brynjolfsson & McAfee, 2014). Moreover, financial institutions must establish data governance frameworks and data management policies to govern the use and access of data across legacy systems and AI applications.

Interoperability constraints present challenges in integrating AI technologies with legacy systems. Legacy systems often lack standardized interfaces and protocols for interoperability, making it difficult to integrate with external AI applications and platforms (Khams, 2022). Financial institutions must develop interoperability standards, protocols, and APIs to facilitate seamless communication and data exchange between legacy systems and AI applications, enabling real-time data sharing and collaboration across the organization.

8.5 Global Perspectives on AI in Banking and Finance Sector

AI adoption in banking and finance is not uniform across the globe. Regional variances in adoption rates, cultural differences, and socioeconomic factors influence the pace and extent of AI integration in financial services. Understanding these global perspectives is crucial for financial institutions seeking to navigate the complexities of AI adoption and capitalize on the opportunities presented by AI technologies.

8.5.1 Regional Variances in Adoption Rates

The adoption of AI in banking and finance varies significantly across regions, with some regions leading the way in AI integration while others lag behind. North America, Europe, and Asia-Pacific are among the regions experiencing rapid AI adoption in financial services, driven by factors such as technological innovation, regulatory support, and investment in AI research and development (Khams, 2022).

Financial institutions are leading the way in North America when it comes to the implementation of AI, using machine learning, advanced analytics, and natural language processing to improve customer experience, increase operational effectiveness, and reduce risks (Borges et al., 2020). Prominent financial hubs like New York and San Francisco accommodate a flourishing network of AI startups, technology firms, and research institutes, propelling creativity and cooperation in AI-supported financial services.

Similar to this, financial institutions in Europe are utilizing AI technology to maintain their competitiveness in a world that is becoming more and more digital and data-driven. In addition to guaranteeing data privacy and protection, regulatory measures like the European Union's Digital Single Market strategy and the GDPR have been instrumental in fostering AI innovation and adoption in the financial services industry (Ala-Pietilä et al., 2019). Fintech hubs such as London, Berlin, and Zurich are emerging as centers of excellence for AI-driven financial innovation, attracting investment and talent from around the world.

In the Asia-Pacific region, countries such as China, Japan, and Singapore are leading the way in AI adoption in banking and finance. Chinese tech giants such as Alibaba, Tencent, and Ant Group are pioneering AI-driven financial services, leveraging vast datasets and advanced analytics to offer innovative products and solutions (Khams, 2022). Moreover, regulatory initiatives such as China's National AI Development Plan and Singapore's AI Strategy are driving investment and innovation in AI technologies, positioning these countries as global leaders in AI-driven financial services.

In other regions such as Africa, Latin America, and the Middle East, AI adoption in banking and finance is still in its nascent stages. Limited access to technology infrastructure, regulatory constraints, and socioeconomic challenges such as poverty, illiteracy, and political instability hinder AI adoption and innovation in these regions (Borges et al., 2020). Moreover, cultural factors such as risk aversion, distrust of technology, and preference for traditional banking channels further impede the adoption of AI-driven financial services in these regions.

8.5.2 Cultural and Socioeconomic Factors

The acceptance and dispersion of AI technologies in banking and finance are significantly shaped by cultural and socioeconomic considerations. Social and economic factors like income, education, and access to technological resources impact how much AI technologies can benefit individuals and communities, while cultural attitudes toward technological advances, risk, innovation, and privacy affect the acceptance and adoption of based on AI financial services.

The adoption of AI in banking and finance may encounter opposition and skepticism in cultures where tradition, conservatism, and risk aversion are highly valued. People may be reluctant to adopt AI-powered financial services because they have privacy, security, and technological trust issues (Brynjolfsson & McAfee, 2014). Moreover, cultural attitudes toward innovation and experimentation may hinder the adoption of AI technologies, as individuals may prefer to stick with familiar and trusted banking practices rather than adopting new and unfamiliar technologies.

Conversely, in cultures where there is a greater openness to innovation, technology, and change, the adoption of AI in banking and finance may be more readily accepted and embraced. Individuals may be more willing to experiment with AI-driven financial services and adopt innovative solutions that offer convenience, efficiency, and value (Khams, 2022). Moreover, cultural attitudes toward risk-taking and entrepreneurship may drive greater investment and innovation in AI technologies, as individuals and organizations seek to capitalize on the opportunities presented by AI-driven financial services.

Socioeconomic factors also play a significant role in shaping the adoption of AI technologies in banking and finance. Socioeconomic disparities in income, education, and access to technology infrastructure can create barriers to AI adoption, particularly for underserved communities and marginalized populations. Individuals with higher levels of income and education are more likely to have access to smartphones, internet connectivity, and digital banking services, enabling them to benefit from AI-driven financial solutions (Pant et al., 2024). In contrast, individuals with lower levels of income and education may lack access to technology infrastructure and digital literacy skills, limiting their ability to access and utilize AI-powered financial services (Khang, Rath, Satapathy et al., 2023).

Socioeconomic factors such as poverty, unemployment, and economic instability can exacerbate disparities in AI adoption and access to financial services. In developing countries and regions with high levels of poverty and economic inequality, individuals may prioritize meeting their basic needs over adopting AI-driven financial services, leading to lower levels of adoption and usage. Moreover, economic instability and financial crises can undermine trust in financial institutions and technology companies, further hindering the adoption of AI technologies in banking and finance.

Cultural and socioeconomic factors influence the design and delivery of AI-driven financial services, shaping the user experience and accessibility of these services. Financial institutions must consider cultural norms, preferences, and values when designing AI-powered interfaces, ensuring that they are intuitive, user-friendly, and culturally sensitive (Borges et al., 2020). Moreover, financial institutions must address socioeconomic disparities in access to technology and digital literacy by providing education and training programs, expanding access to technology infrastructure, and designing inclusive and accessible financial products and services.

8.6 Conclusion

AI integration in banking and finance can enhance client satisfaction, operational efficiency, and innovation. However, challenges such as regulatory compliance, talent recruitment, data security, privacy, ethical concerns, and integration with old systems need to be addressed. Regional differences in adoption rates and cultural and socioeconomic factors also complicate the adoption process. Therefore, a comprehensive approach is needed to support equitable and sustainable AI adoption globally, addressing issues such as regulatory compliance, talent recruitment, data security, and ethical concerns.

8.7 Future Directions

Future research in AI-driven banking and finance should focus on ethical implications, regulatory changes, data security, and workforce development. Ethical frameworks, guidelines, and best practices are needed to ensure responsible AI adoption. Revising regulatory frameworks to address new risks and promote innovation is also crucial. Investments in data security and privacy safeguards are essential for client data availability and trust. Addressing talent acquisition and skills gaps is essential for AI adoption. Financial institutions should invest in training and upskilling programs to close the skills gap and promote interdisciplinary collaboration. Integrating AI with legacy systems requires careful planning and investment (Khang, 2024).

References

Ala-Pietilä, P., Bauer, W., Bergmann, U., & Bietliková, M. (2019). Ethics guidelines for trustworthy AI. Technical report, European Commission–AI HLEG, B-1049 Brussels. https://www.degruyter.com/document/doi/10.9785/cri-2019-200402/html

Arner, D. W., Barberis, J. N., Walker, J., Buckley, R. P., Dahdal, A. M., Zetzsche, D. A., Digital Finance & The COVID-19 Crisis (April 16, 2020). University of Hong Kong Faculty of Law Research Paper No. 2020/017, UNSW Law Research. https://doi.org/10.2139/ssrn.3558889

Biswas, D., Dutta, A., Ghosh, S., & Roy, P. (2024). Future Trends and Significant Solutions for Intelligent Computing Resource Management. In Computational Intelligence for Green Cloud Computing and Digital Waste Management (pp. 187–208). IGI Global. https://www.igi-global.com/chapter/future-trends-and-significant-solutions-for-intelligent-computing-resource-management/340528

Borges, G. L., Marine, P., & Ibrahim, D. Y. (2020). Digital transformation and customers services: The Banking revolution. International Journal of Open Information Technologies, 8(7), 124–128. https://cyberleninka.ru/article/n/digital-transformation-and-customers-services-the-banking-revolution

Brynjolfsson, E., & McAfee, A. (2014). The Second Machine Age: Work, Progress, and Prosperity in a Time of Brilliant Technologies. WW Norton & Company.

Cleland, V., & Hartsink, G. (2020). The value of the legal entity identifier for the payments industry. Journal of Payments Strategy & Systems, 13(4), 322–336. https://www.ingentaconnect.com/content/hsp/jpss/2020/00000013/00000004/art00006

Davies, H., & Green, D. (2010). Banking on the Future: The Fall and Rise of Central Banking. Princeton University Press. https://www.jstor.org/stable/23071735

Jordan, M. I., & Mitchell, T. M. (2015). Machine learning: Trends, perspectives, and prospects. Science, 349(6245), 255–260. https://www.science.org/doi/abs/10.1126/science.aaa8415

Khams, A. A. (2022). The impact of digital transformation on staffing strategy in Banking sector: A case study of Egypt. Revista De Management Comparat Internaţional, 23(3), 454–474.

Khang, A., "Design and Modelling of AI-Oriented Competency Framework (AIoCF) for Information Technology Sector," In Khang A., *AI-Oriented Competency Framework for Talent Management in the Digital Economy: Models, Technologies, Applications, and Implementation.* (1st Ed.) (2024). CRC Press. https://doi.org/10.1201/9781003440901-17

Khang, A., Inna, Semenets-Orlova, Alla, Klochko, Rostyslav, Shchokin, Rudenko, Mykola, Lidia, Romanova, & Kristina, Bratchykova, "Management Model 6.0 and Business Recovery Strategy of Enterprises in the Era of Digital Economy," In Khang, A., Gujrati, R., Uygun, H., Tailor, R.K., & Gaur, S., Data-Driven Modelling and Predictive Analytics in Business and Finance. (1st Ed.). (2024) CRC Press. https://doi.org/10.1201/9781032618845-16

Khang, A., Rani, S., Gujrati, R., Uygun, H., & Gupta, S. K., Designing Workforce Management Systems for Industry 4.0: Data-Centric and AI-Enabled Approaches. (1st Ed.) (2023). CRC Press. https://doi.org/10.1201/9781003357070

Khang, A., Rath, K. C., Panda, N., & Kumar, A. (2024). Quantum Mechanics Primer: Fundamentals and Quantum Computing. In Khang A. (Ed.), Applications and Principles of Quantum Computing (pp. 1–24). IGI Global. https://doi.org/10.4018/979-8-3693-1168-4.ch001

Khang, A., Rath, K. C., Satapathy, S. K., Kumar, A., Das, S. R., & Panda, M. R. (2023). Enabling the Future of Manufacturing: Integration of Robotics and IoT to Smart Factory Infrastructure in Industry 4.0. In Khang A., Shah V., & Rani S. (Eds.), Handbook of Research on AI-Based Technologies and Applications in the Era of the Metaverse (pp. 25–50). IGI Global. https://doi.org/10.4018/978-1-6684-8851-5.ch002

Khanh, H. H., & Khang, A., "The Role of Artificial Intelligence in Blockchain Applications," In Rana G, Khang A., Sharma R., Goel A. K., Dubey A. K., *Reinventing Manufacturing and Business Processes Through Artificial Intelligence*, 2 (20-40). (2021). CRC Press. https://doi.org/10.1201/9781003145011-2

Lipton, Z. C., & Steinhardt, J. (2019). Troubling trends in machine learning scholarship: Some ML papers suffer from flaws that could mislead the public and stymie future research. Queue, 17(1), 45–77. https://dl.acm.org/doi/abs/10.1145/3317287.3328534

Pant, P., Mishra, K. K., & Mohan, A. (2024). Algorithmic Approaches to Financial Technology: Forecasting, Trading, and Forecasting. In Artificial Intelligence and Machine Learning-Powered Smart Finance (pp. 50–81). IGI Global. https://www.igi-global.com/chapter/algorithmic-approaches-to-financial-technology/339161

Wolf, S. (2022). How the legal entity identifier supports the digitisation of business transactions. Journal of Payments Strategy & Systems, 16(2), 148–159. https://www.ingentaconnect.com/content/hsp/jpss/2022/00000016/00000002/art00005

Zhang, Z., & Sejdić, E. (2019). Radiological images and machine learning: Trends, perspectives, and prospects. Computers in Biology and Medicine, 108, 354–370. https://www.sciencedirect.com/science/article/pii/S0010482519300642

Chapter 9

Technology Transformation Impact on Digital Banking Services: A Study on Analyzing the Adoption and Satisfaction Levels of Users

Shuaib Ahmed M. and Shaply Abdul Kareem

9.1 Introduction

Digital banking, also known as internet banking or web banking, refers to the execution of financial transactions securely over the internet through a bank's dedicated websites. It empowers customers to conduct their banking activities using electronic devices and internet connectivity. Online banking mirrors the services available at physical branches, offering a comprehensive suite of traditional banking functions. The advantages of digital banking are manifold. It eliminates geographical constraints, granting customers the freedom to access their accounts anytime, anywhere. This convenience appeals to users accustomed to traditional banking methods, while also introducing innovative techniques to enhance the banking experience.

Digital banking provides internet-based services that are time-saving, easily accessible, and typically entail nominal transaction fees. By facilitating self-service options, it minimizes customer attrition and fosters greater customer loyalty. Moreover, robust security measures, such as intrusion detection systems and virus control equipment, ensure that digital banking services remain safeguarded from potential threats, offering customers a safe and secure banking environment.

In today's globalized world, technology is pervasive, and the banking sector is no exception, where technology plays a pivotal role. Gone are the days when customers had to endure long queues at banks for simple transactions like withdrawing cash or requesting account statements. Recognizing the need to streamline services and adapt to modern trends, banks have embraced

DOI: 10.4324/9781003501947-9

digital banking technologies. Digital banking encompasses various services such as mobile banking (MB), internet banking (IB), and automatic teller machines (ATMs).

However, their intention was to encompass solely fundamental banking services via electronic banking. However, digital banking is a much broader concept, encompassing all conceivable banking services and alternative banking channels such as ATMs, point of sale systems, internet banking, mobile banking, banking through applications, phone banking, etc., excluding traditional branch banking. Digital banking can also be referred to as a "Direct Banking Channel".

Utilizing digital banking services enables customers to easily transfer funds, offering round-the-clock convenience, user-friendly interfaces, and robust security measures. Awareness of digital banking is often disseminated through advertisements in newspapers, television, and notices. Given its potential to enhance business operations, digital banking is widely regarded as a powerful tool for promoting commerce. Consequently, this survey research aims to investigate the frequency of digital banking service usage, reflecting its increasing significance in contemporary banking practices (Khang, Rath, Satapathy et al., 2023).

The banking sector is undergoing a significant shift in consumer behavior, fueled by technological advancements and evolving preferences. With smartphones becoming ubiquitous and online channels increasingly relied upon for financial transactions, the integration of digital wallets into everyday banking experiences has become inevitable. However, despite the rising popularity of digital wallets, various factors influence their adoption among banking customers.

This research aims to explore the complexities of digital wallet adoption within the banking sector, focusing on understanding adoption patterns and assessing customer satisfaction levels. The study seeks to uncover the underlying factors that drive or impede the widespread adoption of digital wallets, as well as evaluate how well these digital payment solutions meet the expectations and preferences of banking customers.

9.2 Literature Review

In a study conducted by (Massilamany and Nadarajan, 2017), the adoption of digital banking services in Malaysia was investigated. The study identified the dependent variable as digital banking adoption, with trust, security, knowledge, self-efficacy, and convenience serving as independent variables. The results revealed a significant influence of the dependent variable on the independent variables. Another study by Gupta (2017) explored the evolution of the Indian banking system from conventional to convenient (cash to click) modes. Using a conceptual approach, the researcher analyzed secondary data to examine banking system trends. The study outlined the various types of digital transactions, their merits, and demerits, while also addressing the challenges associated with digital modes. Gupta emphasized the importance of implementing proper security measures, safeguarding data, and promoting digital literacy to encourage widespread adoption of digital transactions.

In this conceptual study focusing on banking innovations in Russia discussed (Yeremenko and Rudskaya, 2016). Through theoretical analysis, they explored the concept of digital banking, encompassing advancements in banking and payment systems, transitioning from cards to digital platforms. The researchers advocate for banks to leverage cutting-edge technology, offer services at reasonable costs, and foster customer loyalty to online services, thereby encouraging the adoption of modern banking technology (Khang, Hajimahmud, Alyar, Khalilov, Ragimova, Niu, 2024).

In a quantitative research effort by Berndt et al. (2010) the researchers assessed customer readiness for embracing new banking technology. The study identified optimism and innovation as primary drivers, while factors such as discomfort and insecurity were noted as inhibitors to customers' technology readiness. Results indicated that a majority of respondents were embracing modern technology, albeit with some hesitation among certain individuals. The researchers emphasized the importance of banks educating customers and improving services to meet their evolving needs and preferences.

Ochuko et al. (2009) acknowledged that factors such as economic status, government policies, and literacy levels significantly influence internet banking usage. They also highlighted that low levels of security could diminish the frequency of usage. Nabil and Abdullah (2013) conducted an analysis on the factors affecting the usage of internet banking services among postgraduate students. The study found that non-users often cited concerns related to security, lack of awareness, and technical issues as reasons for their hesitation. However, the majority of users expressed satisfaction with the convenience and quality of service provided. In a study by (Rakesh & Ramya, 2014), the authors examined the determinants influencing internet banking usage. They identified reliability, ease of use, and utility as key factors shaping internet banking adoption. The study recommended initiatives to raise awareness and promote the utilization of internet banking services.

9.2.1 Research Objectives

The following of the main objectives are:

- To ascertain the demographic profile of respondents participating in the study.
- To gain insights into the concept of digital banking services.
- To examine the effects of utilizing digital banking services on consumers.
- To provide recommendations for enhancing digital banking services.

9.2.2 Problem Statement

The analysis has unveiled a noteworthy prevalence of engaged and content users utilizing digital banking services. This study endeavors to delve deeper into the frequency of usage of digital banking services across various demographic segments including age, profession, and educational background. By scrutinizing these factors, we aim to gain a comprehensive understanding of the patterns and trends in digital banking adoption among different segments of the population. Through meticulous examination, we seek to ascertain the extent to which individuals from diverse demographics engage with digital banking services, shedding light on any variations or preferences that may exist. Ultimately, this paper aspires to provide valuable insights into the utilization patterns of digital banking services, offering implications for the design of tailored banking solutions and the formulation of targeted marketing strategies to better cater to the needs and preferences of different demographic groups (Khang & Muthmainnah et al., 2023).

9.3 Research Methodology

Methodology serves as a structured approach for resolving research inquiries, akin to a scientific investigation into the process of conducting research (Brown & Williams, 2019). The nature of this study is descriptive, aiming to pinpoint the factors that shape customers' preferences for digital banking services over traditional banking methods.

9.3.1 Data Collection

Primary data were gathered through a meticulously crafted questionnaire (Johnson & Smith, 2021), while secondary sources such as research articles, journals, and books supplemented the study's information. For this study, both primary and secondary data were employed.

9.3.2 Sampling Design and Size

Convenience sampling was employed to gather responses from users of digital banking services Johnson and Smith (2022). Initially, 178 questionnaires were distributed among potential participants, chosen based on their accessibility and ease of reaching. However, only 150 of these questionnaires were considered suitable for statistical analysis due to various reasons such as incomplete responses or data inconsistencies. This method of sampling, while efficient in terms of accessibility, may introduce biases in the results as it relies on a non-random selection process. Therefore, interpretations drawn from the statistical analysis should be made cautiously, considering the limitations inherent in the sampling technique.

9.3.3 Questionnaire Structure and Design

The questionnaire consisted of two sections: Part I gathered demographic data, while Part II explored factors affecting user satisfaction with digital banking services. This segmentation facilitated a thorough examination of demographic profiles alongside satisfaction determinants. By dissecting both aspects, the study aimed to offer a nuanced understanding of user preferences and experiences, thus informing strategies to enhance digital banking services tailored to the needs of different demographic groups (Khang, Kali, Panda, Kumar, 2024).

9.3.4 Statistical Analysis

The primary data collected were subjected to statistical analysis using SPSS version 23. The statistical tools utilized included percentage and correlation analysis.

9.4 Data Analysis and Interpretation

The following section outlines the statistical analysis conducted on the primary data collected through a structured questionnaire. This analysis involved assessing the frequency distribution of respondents across various demographic categories and conducting user level of satisfaction Analysis.

9.4.1 Demographic Profile of the Responders

The distribution of respondents according to gender, age, marital status, educational qualification, occupational level, and annual income was examined. The results of this analysis are presented in the subsequent as shown in Table 9.1.

9.4.2 Literacy Level and Frequency of Digital Banking Usage

Hypothesis: Null hypothesis (H0): There is no significant relationship between the frequency of digital banking usage and the literacy level of the respondents. Alternative hypothesis (H1): There

Table 9.1 Demographic Profile of the Respondents

Demographic Variables	Categories	Frequencies	Percentages	Cumulative Percentage
Gender	Male	83	55.33	100
	Female	67	44.66	
	Others	-	-	
Age group (in years)	Below 20 years	-	-	100
	21–30 years	113	75.33	
	31–40 years	22	14.66	
	Above 40 years	15	10	
Marital status	Married	89	59.33	100
	Unmarried	61	40.66	
Literacy level	HSLC (Higher secondary leaving certificate)	10	6.66	100
	Diploma	12	8	
	UG	67	44.66	
	PG	48	32	
	Certified Degree	13	8.66	
Occupational	Student	26	17.33	100
	Employed	102	68	
	Business	12	8	
	Professional	10	6.66	
Annual Income (In lakhs)	Below 2 lakhs	54	36	100
	2–3 lakhs	56	37.33	
	3–4 lakhs	25	16.66	
	Above 4 lakhs	15	10	
How long using digital banking	Continuously	66	44	100
	Often	35	23.33	
	Occasionally	30	20	
	Once	11	7.33	
	Not once	08	5.33	

(Continued)

Table 9.1 Demographic Profile of the Respondents *(Continued)*

Demographic Variables	Categories	Frequencies	Percentages	Cumulative Percentage
Mood of digital banking	Personal computers	18	12	100
	Laptops	56	37.33	
	Smartphones	76	50.66	
No. of years using	Less than 2 years	18	12	100
	3–5 years	46	30.66	
	Above 5 years	86	57.33	
Satisfaction Level	Highly satisfied	58	38.66	100
	Satisfied	39	26	
	Neutral	20	13.33	
	Dissatisfied	26	17.33	
	Highly dissatisfied	07	4.66	

Table 9.2 Correlation between Literacy Level of the Respondent and Frequency of Usage

		Frequency of Usage	Responder's Literacy Level
Frequency of usage	Pearson's correlation	1	.952*
	Sig. (2-tailed)		.000
	N	100	100
Responder's literacy level	Pearson correlation	.952*	1
	Sig. (2-tailed)	.000	
	N	100	100

is a relationship between the frequency of digital banking usage and the literacy level qualification of the respondents as shown in Table 9.2.

Interpretation: The correlation coefficient between respondents' age and frequency is 0.952, with a corresponding p-value of .000. Since the p-value is less than .05, we reject the null hypothesis, indicating a significant relationship between literacy level and frequency of respondents.

9.5 Results and Discussion

The frequency analysis reveals the demographic profile distribution of the digital banking service users, the majority 55.33% is male. In age wise classification majority of the respondents are in the age group of 21–30 years. A total of 75.33% of the respondents are married, 59.33% of the respondents are undergraduates, 44.66% of the respondents are employed, 68% of the respondents are earning rupees 1 to 3 lakhs annually. A total of 53% of the respondents are preferred to use digital banking always. A total of 50.66% of the respondents prefer to use smartphones for their digital banking transactions. A total of 57.33% of the respondents are using digital banking services for more than 5 years. The majority 38.66% of the respondents are highly satisfied with their digital banking usage.

9.5.1 Suggestion on Improvements of Digital Banking Services

- Digital banking services should capture customer attention through enhanced marketing and advertising strategies, emphasizing the convenience, advantages, and benefits they offer. Streamlining the initial set-up process will alleviate customer difficulties, necessitating the provision of necessary assistance.
- Bankers should reassure customers and provide information about the trustworthiness of digital banking activities to enhance security and privacy. To improve digital banking services, bankers should assist customers in developing secure practices and effectively managing risks.
- Increasing the level of convenience for customers will elevate overall satisfaction levels. Focus on enhancing network information and digital infrastructure to support digital banking. Strengthen customer support systems for digital banking services and refine management strategies accordingly.
- Offering reward points and incentives to users can incentivize the adoption of digital banking services. Provide digital banking education to customers, particularly those less familiar with gadgets, through workshops and seminars to enhance the value and usage of digital banking. Government initiatives should prioritize the development of internet facilities and information and communication technology to promote digital banking services in India (Khang & Shah et al., 2023).

9.5.2 Implementation

- The primary recommendation is to address security and privacy concerns effectively. Banks must instill trust in both existing and potential customers. They should ensure that digital banking transactions are reliable, safe, secure, and efficient.
- Banks need to guarantee customers that their personal and financial information will be kept confidential. Websites and applications should be developed with user-friendly navigation and minimal complications.
- Transaction fees should be set at a reasonable rate and the government should focus on improving internet accessibility and combatting cyber fraud and hacking incidents.
- Enhancing digital banking facilities and providing convenient, widespread services at an affordable price will attract customers to adopt digital banking services. These measures will foster trust among customers and consequently boost the adoption of digital banking services.

9.6 Conclusion

In recent years, there has been a noticeable and impactful transformation in the banking landscape, notably between digital banking and conventional banking. Digital banking has emerged as a catalyst for significant changes in banking practices across the globe. Unlike traditional banking methods, Digital banking harnesses the power of technology to revolutionize the way customers interact with financial services.

One of the core objectives of digital banking is to prioritize customer convenience while simultaneously addressing environmental concerns. By shifting transactions and interactions to digital platforms, digital banking reduces the need for physical resources and minimizes carbon footprints associated with traditional banking practices. This shift aligns with broader efforts to promote sustainability and environmental responsibility in various sectors, including finance. An intriguing aspect of this shift is how customers have become active participants in energy conservation efforts through their engagement with digital banking. By embracing online banking platforms and mobile applications, customers inadvertently contribute to the reduction of energy consumption associated with physical banking infrastructure, such as branches and paper-based transactions (Khang, 2024).

However, amid the widespread adoption and benefits of digital banking, some customers still harbor reservations regarding its security. This concern stems from the potential risks associated with online transactions, data breaches, and identity theft. To address these apprehensions and promote greater trust in digital banking, it is essential for banking institutions and regulatory bodies to implement robust security measures and educate customers about safe digital practices.

9.7 Future of Work

- Navigating technological shifts: A study on user adoption and satisfaction in digital banking services.
- Embracing change: Evaluating the impact of technology transformation on user experience in digital banking
- Beyond conventional: Understanding user perspectives on digital banking evolution and technological adoption

References

Berndt P., Lanver D., & Kahmann R. (2010). The AGC Ser/Thr kinase Aga1 is essential for appressorium formation and maintenance of the actin cytoskeleton in the smut fungus Ustilago maydis. 78(6), 1484–1499. https://doi.org/10.1111/j.1365-2958.2010.07422.x

Brown, E. D., & Williams, B. K. (2019). "The potential for citizen science to produce reliable and useful information in ecology". *Conservation Biology*, 33(3), 561–569. https://doi.org/10.1111/cobi.13223

Gupta, R. (2017) Entrepreneurship and Firm Growth: Review of Literature on Firm-Level Entrepreneurship and Small-Firm Growth. *South Asian Survey*, 22, 1–14. https://journals.sagepub.com/doi/abs/10.1177/0971523117708956

Johnson, M., & Smith, K. (2021). Traditional Education in the Digital Age: Perceptions of Educators. *Educational Technology & Society*, 24(3), 152–168.

Khang, A. (Ed.). (2024). Applications and Principles of Quantum Computing. IGI Global. https://doi.org/10.4018/979-8-3693-1168-4

Khang, A., Abdullayev, V., Alyar, A. V., Khalilov, M., Ragimova, N. A., & Niu, Y (2024). Introduction to Quantum Computing and Its Integration Applications. In Khang A. (Ed.), Applications and Principles of Quantum Computing (pp. 25–45). IGI Global. https://doi.org/10.4018/979-8-3693-1168-4.ch002

Khang, A., Muthmainnah, M., Seraj, P. M., Al Yakin, A., & Obaid, A. J (2023). AI-Aided Teaching Model in Education 5.0. In Khang A., Shah V., & Rani S. (Eds.), Handbook of Research on AI-Based Technologies and Applications in the Era of the Metaverse (pp. 83–104). IGI Global. https://doi.org/10.4018/978-1-6684-8851-5.ch004

Khang, A., Rath, K. C., Panda, N., & Kumar, A (2024). Quantum Mechanics Primer: Fundamentals and Quantum Computing. In Khang A. (Ed.), Applications and Principles of Quantum Computing (pp. 1–24). IGI Global. https://doi.org/10.4018/979-8-3693-1168-4.ch001

Khang, A., Rath, K. C., Satapathy, S. K., Kumar, A., Das, S. R., & Panda, M. R (2023). Enabling the Future of Manufacturing: Integration of Robotics and IoT to Smart Factory Infrastructure in Industry 4.0. In Khang A., Shah V., & Rani S. (Eds.), Handbook of Research on AI-Based Technologies and Applications in the Era of the Metaverse (pp. 25–50). IGI Global. https://doi.org/10.4018/978-1-6684-8851-5.ch002

Khang, A., Shah, V., & Rani, S. (Eds.). (2023). Handbook of Research on AI-Based Technologies and Applications in the Era of the Metaverse. IGI Global. https://doi.org/10.4018/978-1-6684-8851-5

Massilamany M., & Nadarajan D. (2017). Factors That Influencing Adoption of Internet Banking in Malaysia. February 2017. *International Journal of Business and Management*, 12(3), 126 DOI: 10.5539/ijbm.v12n3p126

Nabil, N. A., & Abdullah, Z. (2013). An exploratory study of factors affecting the internet banking adoption: A qualitative study among postgraduate students. *Global Journal of Management and Business Research*, 13. https://www.researchgate.net/profile/Norazah-Mohd-Suki/publication/281702498_An_Empirical_Study_of_Factors_Affecting_the_Internet_Banking_Adoption_among_Malaysian_Consumers/links/57b2785508ae15c76cbb3ff8/An-Empirical-Study-of-Factors-Affecting-the-Internet-Banking-Adoption-among-Malaysian-Consumers.pdf

Ochuko R. E., Cullen A. J., & Neagu D. (2009), "Overview of Factors for Internet Banking Adoption," International Conference on CyberWorlds, Bradford, UK, 2009, pp. 163–170, doi: 10.1109/CW.2009.51

Rakesh H. M., & Ramya T. J. (2014). A Study on Factors Influencing Consumer Adoption of Internet Banking in India. *International Journal of Business and General Management (IJBGM)*, ISSN(P): 2319–2267; ISSN(E): 2319–2275 Vol. 3, Issue 1, Jan 2014, 49–56 © IASET.

Johnson, A., & Smith, B. (2022). The impact of usefulness on customer satisfaction and loyalty in digital banking. *Journal of Financial Services*, 18(2), 45–63.

Yeremenko, I. S., & Rudskaya, E. N. (2016). Banking Business Innovations: Conceptual Foundations of Modern Economy Development. *International Journal of Economics and Financial Issues*, 6, 361–369. https://api.semanticscholar.org/CorpusID:212494217

Chapter 10

Evolution of Fintech and Implications for Traditional Banking and Finance Sector

Rajashri Roy Choudhury, Megan Aliah Ferrer, and Piyal Roy

10.1 Introduction

Fintech, the term for the financial technology sector, has seen a change because to the widespread application of AI and its quick improvements. As a result, conventional banking needs to undergo several adaptations. The growing population of online banking, especially the most used and know globally, such as PayPal, Venmo, Cashapp, and Zelle applications, have brought about huge changes that have immensely helped the growth of the financial industry, making banking easier with just a tap and a click. People can now access their bank on the go with the use of their phones, without having to physically go through the hassle of showing up at the bank.

Fintech has grown more popular since the lockdown due to COVID-19. Because of this widespread pandemic, people globally had to stay indoors making it difficult to go out and creating a wave of binging, causing the population to rather, do everything from the comfort of their home with the use of the internet. This made traditional banking outdated; therefore, the financial industry had to advance, thus leading to the rise of Fintech and AI within the banking units.

Banks serve an economy by handling transfers and payments. These days, the web can both facilitate and carry out these tasks. It is enabling the public as well as private digital currencies and altering the way transactions are entered into ledgers. A globe of information asymmetry once existed between banks and their borrowers, or clients, but this is beginning to change. Because of this distinction and its client understanding, one bank was able to outperform the other. This benefit is diminished by the technological advancements that financial technology offers because this data can be evaluated digitally.

In this chapter, we will discuss how Fintech has changed and advanced traditional banking. We will also delve into the partnership and collaborations associated with Fintech as well as the effect they compose. This chapter will also explain the challenges that Fintech has, as well as the many beneficial opportunities.

DOI: 10.4324/9781003501947-10

10.1.1 Overview of Fintech and Its Impact on the Financial Industry

Fintech is defined by two words "finance" and "technology"; it also applies to all companies with internet advances to online finance banking. Within the financial services business, alternative funding constitutes a financial technology area that is supplying goods and solutions to a wide spectrum of customers. This industry is divided into several different areas (Musabegovic et al., 2019).

Utilizing internet markets that operate by connecting borrower demand with lender and investor offers to deliver the most significant financial innovations. The online invoicing process, payments, merchant finance, trade finance, and crowdsourcing are among the subsectors of alternative finance. While these subsectors have various business models, each have certain characteristics, like being entirely web-based and without bank participants. By offering the same products and services as banks, they essentially gain customer experience. In reality, since the beginning of the age of technology, consumer views have changed.

As a result, Fintech companies have the power to provide their customers what they want, even while banks continue to be exceptionally slow. As a result, their new anticipations depend on adding digital experiences into nearly everything they do technologies has long been a defining feature of the financial services, but recent advancements have seen the emergence of rapidly expanding alternative finance sectors with the use of the internet and other technologies to conduct business, leading the way to a true "Digital Revolution." Overall, financial technologies affected some, if not, most sections of the worldwide market, prioritizing online financial services as shown in Figure 10.1 (Alt, Beck & Smits, 2018).

The goal of Fintech companies is to provide affordable, effective financial solutions through displacing the function of established players, like banks, and delivering direct customer service via mobile and internet platforms that are changing how consumers obtain financial goods and

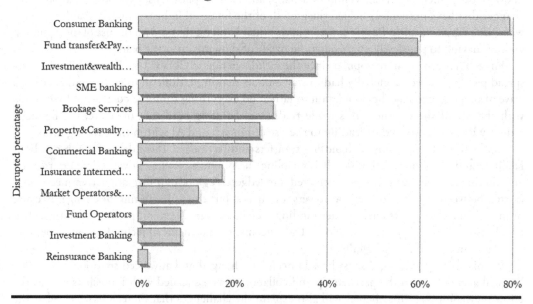

Figure 10.1   Fintech's influence on the financial industry. (From Alt et al., 2018.)

services by offering solutions that are more suited to their needs through improved accessibility, ease of use and customized items as shown in Figure 10.1.

The many success criteria that define businesses operating in this sector and draw distinctions between established banks and their new competitors are what we mean when we discuss the Fintech revolution.

Although the banking sector has many shortcomings that drive customers to hunt for alternative financial service providers, non-bank players also play a significant role in influencing customers' choice of financial service providers by providing comparable goods and services in a manner that is distinct from that of banks (Musabegovic et al., 2019).

10.1.2 *Importance of Traditional Banking Adaptation to Fintech Revolution*

A standard bank is a kind of financial organization that may lend money, take deposits from the general public, and provide other banking services such consumer savings accounts and currency exchange. Investment firms and commercial, or retail, banks are the two categories of financial institutions. The national bank's regulations are largely followed by banks worldwide. Some of these include managing consumer deposits, withdrawals, and interactions in commercial banks and providing brief mortgages to consumers and small enterprises. Customers typically utilize commercial banks to verify details about their loans, accounts, and transactions, which makes them well liked. Investment banks, on the contrary, collaborate with businesses; they offer services to firms that engage in buying and selling as well as investments (Agrawal and Sushank, 2020).

For years, traditional banking has been the main source of financial services. They supply stability, trust, and priority needs to consumers and businesses. Nevertheless, with Fintech on the rise, the environment is quickly changing. Thanks to financial technologies, traditional banks must quickly adapt to this new age environment, including customer expectations, digital transformation, competition, cost reduction, regulatory compliance, partnership opportunities, enhanced customer insights, and risk management.

- Customer expectations: Through creative digital solutions, Fintech companies are changing what customers expect. Smooth, practical, and customized banking experiences are now what customers want. To stay competitive, conventional banks need to change to fulfill these demands.
- Digital transformation: Fintech businesses use technology to lower expenses, improve efficiency, and streamline procedures. In an era where digital technology is king, traditional banks have to accept digital transformation to increase their operational efficiency and maintain their relevance.
- Competition: Financial technology companies are causing a stir in the financial sector with their unique offerings like mobile payments, robo-advisors, and peer-to-peer lending. Due to heightened competition, conventional banks need to be creative in order to hold onto their market shares.
- Cost reduction: By using Fintech technologies, conventional banks can save operational expenses related to their physical locations and antiquated technology. A shift toward automation, AI, as well as blockchain technology can increase productivity and boost profitability (Wewege & Thomsett, 2019).

- Regulatory compliance: Strict regulatory restrictions that apply to traditional banks may be difficult and expensive to negotiate. Fintech businesses frequently respond to regulatory changes more quickly than traditional banks, giving them a chance to improve compliance procedures and learn from their methodology.
- Partnership opportunities: Mutually beneficial collaborations can result from collaboration between Fintech companies and traditional institutions. While Fintech firms may take advantage of existing banks' resources and client base, conventional banks can also profit through the flexibility and creativity of Fintech companies (Chen, 2024).
- Enhanced costumer insights: To better understand consumer behavior and preferences, Fintech businesses use machine learning and data analytics. By utilizing these technologies, traditional banks may improve client loyalty and connections by providing more individualized goods and services.
- Risk management: Cybersecurity hazards and data privacy issues are among the new risks that Fintech advances present. Because of their wealth of risk management experience, traditional banks may offer significant knowledge and assistance in reducing risks inside the financial technology industry (Wewege & Thomsett, 2019).

To summarize, the integration of Fintech into traditional banking is necessary to maintain competitiveness, satisfy changing client demands, enhance efficiency, and foster innovation. In the quickly evolving financial market, conventional banks may prosper by embracing digital change, encouraging teamwork, and capitalizing on their advantages overall; traditional banking must include Fintech to stay competitive, meet evolving customer needs, improve workflow, and promote innovation. By adopting technological advances, promoting cooperation, and using their advantages, conventional banks may thrive in the rapidly changing financial sector (Nicoletti, 2021).

10.1.3 Purpose and Scope of the Review Paper

In this chapter we examine how Fintech—financial technology—affects traditional banking, especially in light of the quick development of AI and the growing use of online banking. In this chapter, we will talk about how Fintech has transformed the financial sector and changed how banking services are provided as well as customer behavior. Analyzing Fintech's potential and problems, as well as how it affects partnerships, collaborations, traditional banking operations, and the larger financial ecosystem, is another goal of the project.

10.2 Understanding Fintech and Its Impact

Since its establishment in 1860 until the 1990s in the aftermath of the 2008 financial crisis, the financial services sector has seen substantial transformation (Mirchandani, Gupta & Ndiweni, 2020). Fintech was first linked to the following three services: financing, raising funds, and payment options. Peer-to-peer lending networks, PayPal-like payment systems, and crowdfunding platforms all capitalize on the megatrends of the developing internet economy. But more recently, there seems to be a second wave emerging, bringing financial technology to insurance, asset management, and international money transfers (Anagnostopoulos, 2018).

Fintech is an all-encompassing phrase that includes creative financial solutions made possible by IT and is frequently used to describe startup businesses that provide those solutions (Nicoletti & Bernardo, 2021), despite the fact that it also includes established financial services firms including financial institutions and carriers. This perspective is reinforced by a recent literature study that lists the three most discussed issues of Fintech publications as the use for Internet within economics (Puschmann, 2017) and new businesses, and solutions (Mirchandani et al., 2020).

The financial services sector is known for being tradition-bound and slow to change. Banking is one of the economic sectors that have historically been the least responsive to technology disruption. Nowadays, banks often demonstrate a lack of due to their complex regulatory frameworks or their stable market positions, which stifle innovation. Some opponents have responded violently, attempting to impose the exact same regulatory obstacles that startups face, amid claims that antagonism from new, leaner banks would put 4.7 trillion dollars of assets in danger for older institutions.

The IT community in Silicon Valley must continue to cut costs because the financial system's slow reaction times have unavoidably brought flaws to light. These high costs also contribute to the entry of new competitors into the market (Mirchandani et al., 2020). Fintech startups are driving a new paradigm in banking operations that divides banking activities into numerous industries and approaches them from an integrated standpoint. They can gain market share, notoriety, and increased customer usefulness by specializing within no less than one of these categories, since of this margin compression, banks will need to act since, by 2025, their inaction might put up to 20% of their income at risk (Mirchandani et al., 2020).

Fintech's impact on the future perspective as perceived by academics, startups, and CEOs of major global financial institutions is reported in a highly fascinating, comprehensive, and significant research released by the World Economic Forum (Mirchandani et al., 2020). The following consequences are categorized in the report: As "safe bets," incumbent banks have an elevated level of assurance about their effect, independent of whether the sector will operate in a consolidated or fragmented manner. To be more precise, the main disruptive effect centers on the relationship between "loyalty" and personal empowerment. Based on this analysis, significant changes are anticipated in the following markets:

- Transfers
- Protection
- Lending and deposits
- Fundraising for retail and SME ventures
- Finance and wealth administration

Given that it has the ability to drastically alter the financial industry, more consideration should be given to all of the aforementioned points. It brings up another topic of discussion on regulatory matters; sometimes changes in cultural norms, values, and structural aspects call for regulation for the sake of the general welfare and stable markets. The reality that significant political economy, harmonization, and third-party expenses have historically constrained regulatory initiatives has often resulted in a sluggish reaction. Fintech may initially bring about a much-needed and welcome transformation, but it also has the potential to cause additional regulatory challenges, including new systemic risk concerns, timing issues, privacy concerns, and agency problems (Anagnostopoulos, 2018).

10.2.1 Definition and Characteristics of Fintech

The term "Fintech," derived from the terms "finance" and "technology," describes an interdisciplinary field that innovates, manages technology, and mixes money. It describes how internet-related technology with financial industry commercial service operations like lending and banking. When Citicorp started the Financial Services technological Consortium, an effort to promote technological cooperation in the financial services sector, financial technology terminology came into being (Giglio, 2021).

Only in 2014 did the term "Fintech" become widely known and has since been used to characterize the advancement of platforms, ecosystems, and technology. It increases the efficiency of the financial industry by making services and procedures easier for more individuals to access. The financial industry is usually the one in the financial services sector that employs technologies most frequently, second only to the communications sector (Mention, 2019). With its substantial cost reductions, increased diversification of services, and less volatile industrial and market scenarios, Fintech presents a viable alternative for the financial services and banking sectors (Mention, 2019).

Fintech, or financial technology, has various distinct characteristics that differ from traditional banking and banking arrangements including:

- **Innovation:** Fintech may be defined as a financial services improvement company that embraces new technology and innovates constantly. This covers developments in fields including machine learning, blockchain technology, large-scale data analytics, and artificial intelligence.
- **Disruption:** By providing more practical, affordable, and efficient alternatives to conventional banking and financial services, Fintech frequently disrupts these industries. New goods, services, and business strategies that upend the status quo may result from this disruption.
- **Customer-centric:** Customer happiness and experience are the top priorities for Fintech organizations, which frequently offer intuitive user interfaces, customized offerings, and seamless digital interactions. They make use of technology to provide specialized solutions that satisfy clients' changing requirements and tastes.
- **Accessibility:** Fintech aims to make financial services more accessible to a larger range of individuals and businesses, particularly those that are disregarded or excluded from traditional banking institutions. In order to make financial services accessible to customers at all times and locations, mobile applications, websites, and electronic payment systems are frequently used.
- **Efficiency:** Fintech increases speed, lowers prices, and increases transparency in the provision of financial services by streamlining procedures and minimizing inefficiencies. Increased operational efficiency is achieved in a variety of financial tasks through automation, digitization, and algorithm-based decision-making.
- **Data-driven:** To improve risk management, provide insights, and customize services, Fintech organizations make use of enormous volumes of data. To evaluate creditworthiness, identify fraud, and improve financial decision-making, they employ sophisticated analytics approaches.
- **Regulatory compliance:** financial technology develops within the financial services industry, but it also follows rules to protect consumers, maintain privacy, and maintain security. To gain credibility and confidence from investors, consumers, and regulators, one must adhere to regulatory regulations.
- **Collaboration:** To spur innovation and solve business issues, Fintech frequently works alongside conventional financial institutions, technological companies, regulators, and other stakeholders. Through these collaborations, new services, standards, and products may be developed by pooling resources, knowledge, and networks.

- **Global reach:** Fintech is a global industry that provides financial services to people all over the world by overcoming regional barriers. Global reach promotes financial stability and economic progress by facilitating transactions across borders, payments worldwide, and access to a variety of markets.
- **Flexibility:** Fintech enterprises exhibit nimbleness and versatility in reaction to evolving market circumstances, technology breakthroughs, and regulatory mandates. They continuously improve and update their goods to be competitive and meet the shifting needs of the industry and the market.
- These characteristics, together, draw the line of the nature and different impacts of Fintech on conventional service landscapes, the near future of banking, installments, finances, and other features of finance (Rupeika-Apoga & Thalassinos, 2020).

10.2.2 Global Growth and Adoption of Fintech in the Financial Industry

Fintech is gaining momentum internationally and catching regulators' attention, with entrepreneurs leading the way and academics following closely after. In general, "Fintech" refers to financial services and products that are backed by innovative business models and technological advancements. Fintech, to put it simply, is any innovation that companies want to apply to enhance the way that financial services are offered, utilized, and processed. Fintech has the ability to compel traditional financial institutions in rich countries to reassess their business plans, acquire new competencies, and alter their organizational cultures. Until now, Fintech has mostly influenced emerging countries such as China and India. Fintech is becoming more and more integrated into routine business activities, due to Gobble's (2018) description of digitalization as well as digitization (Musabegovic et al., 2019).

Eighty-four percent of participants in Ernst & Young's (2017) Fintech index adoption were aware of financial technology services, and more than thirty percent of clients in the twenty areas they examined used two or more of them. The financial innovation space has already shown great promise to the innovation community, as seen by the growth in Fintech businesses' quantity, diversity, and accessibility over the past 10 years. Funding is also increasing; five years ago, $12.2 billion in investments were made in the Fintech sector. Accenture (2016) and CBInsights (2018) estimate that the highest point 250 Fintech companies raised a combined $31.85 billion.

Global Fintech investment more than doubled from $50.8 billion in 2017 to $111.8 billion in 2018, according to KPMG's Fintech Pulse report (2018). An unprecedented amount of agreements signed through multiple channels served as the driving force behind this development. The parallel growth in research interests in Fintech is not surprising. A few publications that have released special issues on the subject include "The Financial Information Systems and the Fintech the Revolution" from the *Journal of Management Information Systems*, the *Global Journal of Being an Entrepreneur as well as Management*, "Innovation for Financial Services," and Studies in philosophy alongside Technology, "Towards a Philosophy regarding Financial Technologies." While some academics have concentrated on classifying Fintech according to many criteria (such as the level of innovative thinking, the innovative object, and the innovation scope), others are attempting to come to a consensus over a standard definition for the term (Musabegovic et al., 2019). In addition, experts cannot agree on whether Fintech should be categorized as a service or good, a business strategy, or a way to disrupt the market and encourage competition.

Fintech, in all its manifestations, is here to stay thanks to the assistance for cutting-edge technologies including blockchain, AI, smart contracting, and AI, to mention a few. Fintech's future prospects are unclear as of now. Both good and negative consequences are being brought about by the rising momentum, which is modernizing financial institutions, causing shifts in consumers including market behavior, and upending long-standing employers, suppliers of services, and regulatory frameworks (Nicoletti, 2021). The laws of the game have changed due to the increasing affordances of technology. Fintech has already gone beyond its initial promise to improve financial accessibility by providing services to marginalized or historically impoverished populations. However, the traditional banking sector is slowly being overtaken by Fintech startups' faster, more affordable, and better service models.

Fintech companies now provide financial products including loans and payments that were formerly exclusively available from recognized credit institutions (Vaganova et al., 2021). These smaller, more nimble businesses provide more mobility and support a wider range of suppliers and goods. Many financial products currently accessible online and based on cross-industry, hybrid business models that give them across markets that conventional banks and finance offerors occasionally are unable to. Additionally, they provide enhanced risk management and transparency, which are presumably made possible in part by their capacity to gather immediate client feedback and utilize it to guide real-time service modifications (Giglio, 2021).

10.2.3 Key Areas of Impact

The world has changed dramatically as a result of technological improvements in our daily lives. The newest technologies have impacted and changed every one of us in different ways. The financial services sector has experienced changes in regulation and customer interactions over the last 10 years, and this is not an exception. Advances in financial technology, or as the new, ambiguous name of Fintech is currently known, have contributed to some of this reform. Fintech is already transforming the market as hundreds of fresh startups create cutting-edge financial services and solutions for clients.

The conventional financial services paradigm or framework is being challenged by these new competitors. The goal of the research is to learn more about the financial services sector and to obtain a deeper understanding of its current state as well as its future directions. The goal of the thesis is to gain a deeper understanding of Fintech and the impact it is having on the financial services sector. The researcher will examine scholarly books, journals, media articles, and business documents written by professionals in the field at the outset of the paper. Six interviews with industry experts from the Fintech and financial services sectors comprised the qualitative study. These interviews will offer firsthand knowledge together with a current industry perspective of financial services. To evaluate the effects Fintech has had and will continue to have on the sector. Determining whether Fintech will work with current providers or disrupt the Irish financial services market is one of the main goals.

10.2.3.1 Growth of Mobile Payments

Mobile commerce is another name for mobile payments. Customers utilize it as a type of non-cash payment method to cover the cost of goods and services. According to Ovia's 2005 research, the financial industry in the 21st century operated—and continues to operate—in a complicated and cutthroat environment with a constantly shifting economic landscape and information and communications technology (ICT) at its core. To provide better client services in the face of competition and quicker service delivery channels that increase productivity, financial sector firms have been (and still are) utilizing product innovation.

The modern corporate environment is highly dynamic and grows more quickly as a result of increasing awareness, creativity, innovation, technological advancements, and shifting consumer preferences. When compared to plastic cards, mobile payment solutions have changed payment methods and are increasingly being used by more people. Mobile payments are the most widely used non-cash payment method because of its distinctive qualities. It is more widely used than the checking system. Commercial banks provide plastic cards. Because mobile payments are more widely accepted than plastic cards and are thought to be more flexible, dependable, and convenient, using mobile payments has a negative impact on the use of plastic cards (Kang, 2018).

The use of mobile payments ought to slow the expansion of credit card transactions. This relationship is typified by economic expansion supported by cutting-edge, better technology. The connection between payments made with credit cards and those made with smartphones shows how the performance of a distinctively differentiated product can be impacted by differentiation strategy. Developing a competitive advantage through important attributes like quality, innovation, and customer service is the primary goal of a differentiation strategy (Hwang, Park & Shin, 2021).

According to the Technology Acceptance Model, the Perceived Usefulness (PU) and Perceived ease of use (PEOU) give such unique products a competitive advantage. Because mobile payments are more flexible, dependable, efficient, and readily available than their alternatives, people view them as beneficial (Davis, 2004). Mobile payments are being used more frequently, and they are widely accepted as a form of payment. This can be attributed to the fact that mobile money was introduced as an innovation whose benefits were seen to exceed its drawbacks.

10.3 Challenges to Traditional Banking

Blockchain was presented as a virtual currency system that might replace central banks as the means of confirming transactions, trading ownership, and producing money units. For Bitcoin, the system was developed because it is the first network application (Nakamoto, 2008). Ever since its inception, the Internet has been regarded as the most alluring innovation. The blockchain is essentially an open-source system or public distributed ledger that is accessible to all users and effectively records transactions between two parties in a verifiable and permanent manner. Every detail pertaining to transactions, assets, and records of value is contained in blocks that are added to the chain in a linear fashion and chronologically arranged. All nodes establish confidence between participants in a system, proving the veracity of the block. Every transaction that has taken place is reported on throughout the whole blockchain, where applicable (Vaganova et al., 2021).

Information is available, including specifics regarding the trade value that once belonged to a certain address. In Fintech innovation is primarily responsible for technological disruption, which poses a serious threat to established banking models. Peer-to-peer lending and digital wallets are only two examples of the creative solutions offered by Fintech companies, which give consumers more individualized and easy financial services. Traditional banks need to invest in digital transformation to stay competitive, but they face challenges because of archaic procedures and outdated technology. Furthermore, traditional banks bear a heavy burden of complying with regulatory frameworks, which require substantial resources and strict adherence.

Know-your-customer (KYC) and anti-money laundering (AML) regulations put additional pressure on operational capacity and raise expenses, the quickly changing financial environment of today, traditional banking faces numerous obstacles. Fintech innovation is driving technological disruption, which is seriously endangering established banking models. Peer-to-peer lending and digital wallets are only two examples of the creative solutions offered by Fintech companies, which give consumers more individualized and easy financial services.

Traditional banks need to invest in digital transformation to stay competitive, but they face challenges because of archaic procedures and outdated technology. Traditional banks are significantly burdened by regulatory compliance; intricate frameworks necessitate substantial resources and strict adherence. KYC and AML regulations put additional pressure on operational capacity and raise expenses. Threats to cybersecurity are severe because insider dangers and data breaches harm consumer confidence and financial stability (Chen, 2024).

10.3.1 Competing Factors Posed by Fintech

The Fintech revolution presently sweeping the globe is enabling unprecedented applications of digital technology. Venture capital firms' interest in becoming engaged has significantly increased as a result, and new entrepreneurship and unrestrained innovation have resulted. Fintech is expected to offer a number of notable benefits.

Fintech lowers costs associated with financial services and increases customer access. Fintech increases the breadth and depth of services provided by financial companies while enhancing their efficiency. Fintech enhances the speed and openness of financial data, which may lead entrepreneurs to discover and take advantage of new business opportunities. Because Fintech has enormous implications for the economy and society, its growth has been exponential. Many believe this momentum will last as long as new businesses keep popping up with creative propositions for value.

One of the most well-known global Fintech accomplishments is M-Pesa, a mobile (Van Loo, 2018). Both the money transfer system, which began in Kenya with over 20 million users and handles over 1.7 billion transactions annually, and Lending Club, a company credited with introducing the shared economy paradigm to the finance industry and growing to an extent in which they could offer 21 billion dollars of credit in 2016.

According to the growing interest in Fintech in the global financial industry, there is a growing body of research on the topic in the scientific literature on information systems. To be more precise, there are three main elements that apply to the Fintech new publications. Fintech drivers constitute the first subject; study in this area often looks for factors that facilitate the expansion within the Fintech movement overall in addition to any potential obstacles that should be eliminated.

The bulk of earlier research falls within the second group, categorized as Fintech operations. This area of research aims to provide clarification on how various Fintech organizations need to function and how Fintech breakthroughs originate. The third subject is implications for Fintech. This was confirmed by research. These themes primarily aim to identify the positive and negative social and economic repercussions of Fintech and provide an explanation for their causes (Harasim, 2021).

10.3.2 Barriers to Adopting Fintech in Traditional Banking Sector

Some of the factors that contributed to the financial technology revolution include the increasing use of mobile phones as well as the internet, the accessibility of rapid connectivity computing, developments in machine learning and data analytics, and the operations for non-bank financial companies as well as non-financial businesses like software and internet service providers as shown in Figure 10.2.

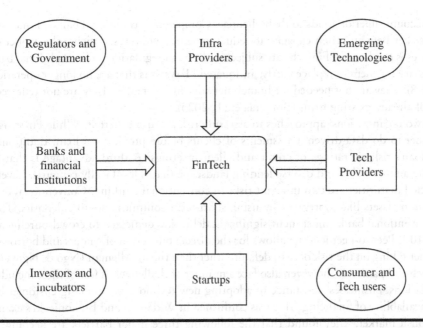

Figure 10.2 The impact of Fintech and how financial services are being disrupted. (From Staszewska & Aniela, 2018.)

The Fintech ecosystem is made up of several entities. The ecology has been divided in several ways by various research. Several actors that impact Fintech directly or indirectly are presented by Cavallo 10. Fintech services are developed and enhanced by a range of organizations, including startups, tech businesses, and infrastructure (infra) providers, traditional lenders, and financial institutions, among those who participate in straight play.

Investors, incubators as well as regulators, government assistance and laws, consumers and technology users, developing technologies, and more all have a subtle but substantial impact on this ecosystem (Bouteraa et al., 2023).

The most forward-thinking banks see themselves as components of the Fintech industry. The Polish marketplace is now distinguished by banks' supportive views toward Fintech businesses plus their shared desire to collaborate, despite the fact that they represent a varied spectrum of enterprises. Digital payment methods and banking platforms are the main industries driving the Polish Fintech industry (Alt et al., 2018). One of the main Fintech market segments in Poland is financial platforms.

The main services provided by Fintech businesses in the Polish market involve investment possibilities, loans, financial platforms, digital payments, financial planning, and access to crypto-currency activities. Fintech businesses in Poland gave the following answers when asked whether their main line of business was: The respondents' distribution of occupations was as follows: 25% worked for financial platforms; 13% for electronic payments intermediaries; 13% for crowdfunding and P2P lending initiators; 13% for analytics and machine learning organizations; 6% for bitcoin dealers; and 6% for personal finance management (Alt et al., 2018). Account information service providers, sales automation, and InsurTech/P2P insurance were selected by the other 25% of participants (Harsono & Suprapti, 2024).

Fintech companies will enable the banking sector to provide services because traditional banking is unable to, despite the fact that they cannot match the convenience and security of a bank's current account superior goods to their clientele. Compared to traditional banks, Fintech startups offer three key benefits. Their capacity to reduce expenses without sacrificing the caliber of financial services is one benefit. Fintechs are subject to different regulations than traditional banks. It is not necessary for them to replace costly, antiquated IT systems that are no longer operational (Alt et al., 2018). They are not needed for branch network maintenance. They are not required for the defense of already-existing firms (Bouteraa et al., 2023).

The two organizations' approaches to assessing risk are also different. While Fintechs can use the internet to do data-driven assessments of clients before providing a loan, traditional banks assess a loan's risk via ratings of credit and client meetings? A third advantage is that Fintechs may create a more stable and diverse lending landscape that is less locally centered. Leverage and mismatched maturities are two inherent risks in conventional banking. Conventional banks create long-term assets like mortgages by using short-term commitments like deposits. To finance loans, conventional banks must incur significant debt, sites dedicated to crowdsourcing as shown in Table 10.1. Peer-to-peer lending allows for the direct connection of lenders and borrowers, with each lender taking on the risk of loan default rather than the middleman (Ngo & Nguyen, 2024).

Fintech companies do, however, also face a number of challenges. A few of these include following regulations, businesses' resistance to adopting new technology, changing customer behavior, and the availability of financing. This was confirmed in Widawski and Brakoniecki's examination of the Polish market. They found that the following three major barriers are keeping Poland's

Table 10.1 Comparison of Fintech Startups to Traditional Banking

Feature	Fintech Startup	Traditional Banking
Technology	Extremely creative, employing state-of-the-art technologies (such as blockchain and artificial intelligence)	Slow and more cautious acceptance of new technology
Customer experience	Smooth, easy-to-use digital interfaces that prioritize mobility	Older systems might have intricate interfaces and provide in-person support
Speed	Quick cycles of innovation and service delivery	Slower as a result of limitations in older systems and regulations
Cost	Reduced operating expenses in general, which are frequently passed on to customers	Greater as a result of conventional overheads and vast branch networks
Product range	Concentrate on specialized, niche financial goods	Numerous financial goods and services
Regulation	Frequently less controlled at first, but with growing attention	Severe regulations and stringent criteria for compliance
Accessibility	Worldwide access via digital media	Mostly local or national, having branches in person

Source: Li, Spigt & Swinkels (2017).

Fintech sector from growing: According to Alt et al. (2018), there's a dearth of new knowledge about developing financial technologies; unresolved guidelines and the absence of legally binding conclusions by the oversight authority, which raises business risk; and a dearth of incentives for both banks and startups.

The Polish Financial Supervision Authority (Polish FSA) was a major factor in conventional banks and Fintech startups' reluctance to embrace financial innovation. Respondents to their poll expressed a desire to see almost 19% of the building of a regulatory sandbox—a solution that would allow businesses to test new items privately without having to adhere to all regulatory norms.

10.3.3 Evolution of Fintech and Its Implications for Traditional Banking

In order to ascertain the banks' efficiency distribution, we created a matrix and distinguished between the entries. The banks' 2009–2014 efficiency matrix is shown in Figure 10.3. In the first and second phases, the average productivity efficiency values were 0.660 and 0.952, respectively. The six banks in the first quadrant of Figure 10.3 acted as standards for other banks. In particular, Industrial and Commercial Bank of China (ICBC) performed the best (Puschmann, 2017). The five banks located in the 2nd quadrant had a lower production. Efficiency averages, indicating that in addition to bolstering training and cutting staff, they also needed to alter the internal operations' scope and direction. Even if these banks were inefficient, their average profitability efficiency was lower (Harsono & Suprapti, 2024).

The lowest-performing group in the sample was made up of the three banks in the third quadrant, which had productivity and profitability levels below average. This meant that managers needed to modify staff training programs and internal procedures. Furthermore, in order to increase profitability, these banks needed to increase loan and noninterest income through internal modifications. Exhibited great productivity efficiency but low profitability efficiency, suggesting

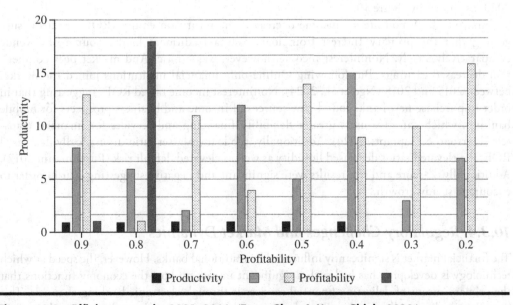

Figure 10.3   Efficiency matrix, 2009–2014. (From Chen & Kuan-Chieh, 2020.)

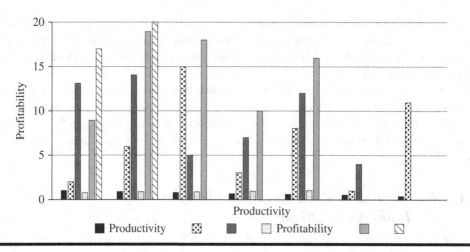

Figure 10.4   Efficiency matrix, 2015–2018. (From Chen & Kuan-Chieh, 2020.)

that banks' business strategies needed to be revised to improve performance by raising loans and noninterest revenue.

Our primary focus was on the impact of online banking on established banks as they enter the financial sector. Figure 10.4 shows evaluation findings for the years 2015 through 2018. The average profitability and productivity efficiencies in the matrix were 0.832 and 0.915, respectively. ICBC was the most efficient bank among the eight banks in the first quadrant, all of which had productivity and profitability efficiencies that were greater than average (Puschmann, 2017). Following internal modifications, the commercial banks in the second quadrant increased their profitability and efficiency. The third-quadrant regional banks exhibited inefficiencies with respect to both profitability and productivity (Chen & Kuan-Chieh, 2020) as shown in Figure 10.4.

First, in 2009, noninterest income decreased the return on equity (ROE) in 2014, suggesting that the primary Interest from loans was a traditional bank's source of revenue comparatively steady. Noninterest income, however, was erratic. And market peer competition decreased earnings. But following Online-only financial institutions joined the market between 2015 and 2018 (Ngo et al., 2024). Noninterest income raised ROE, suggesting that in order to purchase new banks found new sources of income and business prospects for mobile banking, which can give users greater flexibility financing and services for financial transfers (Harsono & Suprapti, 2024). Additionally, the loan-to-asset ratio dramatically decreased ROE; the elevated ratios decreased liquidity as well as elevated default risk (Puschmann, 2017). Additionally, Z-score and size results were significant and negative suggesting that in order to encourage steady growth.

10.3.4 Regulatory Challenges and Market Dynamics

The financial market is significantly influenced by traditional banks. However, the speed at which technology is developing has had such a significant impact on how the economy functions that the primary means of delivering financial services is through electronic banking channels. This has affected the rapidly growing Fintech companies who primarily use this access channel to deliver their services. Furthermore, the digitalization of financial services encourages and hastens the growth of financial innovation (Mention, 2019). The instability in the financial markets was caused by a loss of confidence in financial institutions worldwide that followed the global financial crisis of 2007–2009.

Fintech companies want to compete with traditional financial service delivery techniques. As stated by According to de Hann and others, one of the factors contributing to the Fintech industry's rapid growth is the public's waning trust in established financial institutions as a result of the financial crisis3. The so-called Fintech market is developing dynamically as a result of all of these factors. Fintech is an acronym for "financial technology," which refers to businesses or representatives of businesses that integrate financial services and rely on cutting-edge, contemporary technology.

Because "Fintech" is interpreted differently, it is very difficult to define (Adeoye et al., 2024). An organization from the Fintech industry is typically defined, according to the Financial Stability Board (FSB), as one that provides cutting-edge technology in financial services. These could lead to the creation of brand-new business models, mobile apps, procedures, and even goods that have a big influence on how financial institutions provide financial services. Fintech enterprises are also defined as businesses that operate in the financial sector, hence creating a new, distinct subset of para-banks.

Fintech refers to a broad and diverse ecosystem made up of many structures or articulations that are more or less widely available in the market and are thought of as financial operations that use digital technologies to provide value. Undoubtedly, the primary objective of businesses in the Fintech sector is the optimization of profit and/or value. Costs are decreased as a result of the financial market services provided by these businesses. Additionally, they result in quicker access to services and better service delivery. The obvious advantages that the Fintech industry has over the banking industry in the so-called IT infrastructure sector have made the sector's growth conceivable. Rules governing the financial markets that permit the provision of banking services to companies from the Fintech sector affect the ability of these entities to conduct their business (e.g., including the Revised Payment Services (PSD) Directive). Furthermore, the financial services industry is undergoing a revolution because to blockchain technology (Yilmaz & Güneş, 2015).

Blockchain enables these kinds of transactions to be completed almost instantly and for free, in contrast to banks, who frequently charge exorbitant fees and commissions for transactions, particularly in the payment industry. J. Stiglitz noted that the banks prior to the financial crisis of 2007–2009 tried all in its power to drive up transfer costs. The authors of one of the most widely read publications on blockchain technology assert that this system will completely transform the financial services industry (Mention, 2019). The authors claim that blockchain technology will not only end the financial industry's monopoly but also have a major impact on bank profits and business models. There are numerous crucial elements that emphasize the role of blockchain technology and its impact on the financial sector; it may consist of open software, speed, risk mitigation, transaction cost, and trust (Mention, 2019).

Fintech services are developing so quickly that a standard classification of this industry does not yet exist. The European Parliament has classified the following sectors in which Fintech sector businesses operate: retail banking (loans and deposits), payments, cash flow, and foreign exchange, market, virtual currencies, asset administration, personal finance, InsurTech (insurance markets), and new technology infrastructure. In the Fintech sector, numerous subsectors can be distinguished, which due to cooperation on the financial market, affect financial innovations in various market segments as shown Figure 10.5.

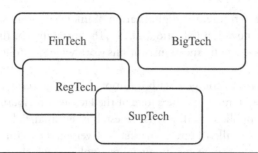

Figure 10.5 Division of the Fintech sector. (From Mention & Anne, 2019.)

10.3.5 Efficiency and Effectiveness Considerations for Traditional Banks

Technical change and growth in productivity over time can be studied using an appropriate number of banks or information from all banks, assuming—as typical bank cost analyses assume—that every financial institution are roughly similarly efficient. Nonetheless, if banks are far from being equally efficient, cost function assessments of technological change, such as those found in Hunter's and Timme, are helpful. It is possible to mistake modifications to the minimum-cost technology with shifts in the bank cost distribution away toward the minimum-cost technologies (1986) or variations in average productivity metrics, such the BLS (Bureau of Labor Statistics) labor productivity index. We try to separate these components for extremely low-cost institutions by building a thick-frontier cost distribution (Rashwan and Ehab, 2016).

In this section, we examine inefficiencies as well as expense dispersion beyond this frontier; in the next section, we examine how this boundary has evolved over time. The variation in banking costs is rather noticeable. Costs at banks are often many times higher than those incurred by other banks with similar size and product offerings. This cost dispersion might be the result of several factors, including simple inefficiency (Yilmaz & Güneş, 2015). Here, we construct a thick-frontier cost distribution using data from bankers in the category with the lowest average price quartile. We then compare this cost function to a cost characteristic for bankers in the most expensive standard cost quartile and analyze the differences (Jaouadi & Zorgui, 2014).

It is believed that a reasonable example of inefficiency is the residue that cannot be understood through the current factors. Some of the statistics provided below, which indicate that low-cost banks were stable and that high-cost banks collapsed considerably less frequently than low-cost banks, lend credence to this perspective (Berger & Humphrey, 1992).

10.4 Adaptation Strategies for Traditional Banks

The banking industry has undergone a radical change as a result of the financial technology industry's (Fintech) explosive growth, which has forced traditional banks to reassess their position. The present study employs a comparative approach to examine the complex effects of Fintech inclusion on conventional banking establishments (Harsono & Suprapti, 2024). By carefully analyzing key performance indicators (KPIs), customer services, and regulatory structures, the research seeks to identify the dynamic interactions between Fintech innovators and established banking organizations.

The financial services sector is undergoing a revolutionary transformation at this critical juncture, thanks to the convergence of innovative Fintech and conventional banking methods. Fintech has been a disruptive force in the last 10 years, upending established conventions and providing

Figure 10.6 Future of banking and financial. (From Batchu, 2023.)

creative solutions that appeal to the tech-savvy and digitally connected customer base. This study aims to explore the complex dynamics of this revolutionary change with a particular emphasis on how Fintech integration affects conventional banking institutions. Throughout the contents of this piece, we will explore the various ramifications, difficulties, and chances that result from these two domains existing side by side and competing for supremacy in a quickly changing financial environment as shown in Figure 10.6.

10.4.1 Understanding the Need for Adaptation

Understanding the Need for Adaptation of Fintech in Traditional Banking (Gandara, 2018):

- Financial services evolution: Since its founding in 1860, the financial services sector has seen significant change. At first, Fintech concentrated on lending, raising funds, and payment solutions.
- Fintech expansion: According to current trends, a second wave of Fintech companies is emerging, including services for wealth management, insurance, and international money transfers.
- Timing of innovation: Fintech has enormous potential to help small companies and the economy, but its innovation has lagged behind other industries.
- Areas of Fintech impact: Fintech has an impact on many different areas of finance, such as asset management, peer-to-peer lending on marketplaces, cryptocurrencies, crowdfunding, and investment management.
- Example: Asset management: Fintech is transforming asset management; the United Kingdom is now the largest fund management hub in the world, and Bitcoin is emerging as a new form of investing.
- Example: Cryptocurrency: Although it lacks the typical banking safeguards, cryptocurrencies like Bitcoin enable decentralized payment networks.
- Example—crowdfunding: For instance, peer-to-peer fundraising is made possible via crowdfunding websites, which also offer speedy access to funds and insightful project criticism.
- Example—investment management: Investment management, for instance, is made easier by Fintech because to lower costs, crowdsourced exchange-traded funds, and easier access to expert counsel.
- Example—marketplace lending: As an illustration, consider marketplace lending, which eliminates traditional banking costs and offers low rates by putting borrowers and investors in direct contact.

10.4.2 Identifying Areas for Integration of Fintech Solutions

As part of our efforts to forge strategic alliances with Fintechs, the Digital Transformation and Development Department developed the "Fintech Integration Process," a seven-step process designed to attract new business, improve customer satisfaction, and boost operational effectiveness. These stages encompass the whole integration process, from identifying the required Fintech until launching as shown in Table 10.2.

10.4.3 Partnership and Collaboration Opportunities with Fintech Companies

In this era of digitization, well-established financial services corporations are more frequently forming partnerships with startups in order to meet consumer demand for quick innovation and adapt to changing market dynamics. The conventional business models of established institutions, such as banks, are put to the test by technology-enabled innovation, which forces them to quickly adjust to the demands of the digital era. Nevertheless, Fintechs—young businesses that use technology to improve the financial services sector—also have challenges, such getting approval from regulators and gaining the confidence of potential clients (Persmoen & Sandvik, 2018). In order to address these deficiencies and capitalize on synergies, Fintechs and banks are progressively combining their capabilities through partnerships. Nevertheless, there is still a paucity of empirical data about the incentives for cooperation between Fintechs and banks (Hoang et al., 2021).

To close that gap and reveal what drives banks and Fintechs to collaborate, we employ an exploratory study approach and semi-structured interviews. Expanding upon that, the ensuing motivations are categorized within an innovative theoretical structure and linked to various kinds of partnerships. Our findings demonstrate that while Fintechs require money and expertise to expand in the heavily regulated financial industry, banks are especially interested in profiting from novel technology without necessarily actively participating in its creation. Our findings provide avenues for future investigation and have a number of practical ramifications (Suprun, Petrishina & Vasylchuk, 2020).

In order to improve their innovation performance and discover new information and concepts, many established businesses partner with startups. Startup collaboration helps established businesses break through internal boundaries and investigate new markets and technology. This is especially advantageous during disruptive periods when businesses are up against drastically different goods and services (Klus et al., 2019).

One of the most important ways to facilitate startup collaboration is to set up accelerator and incubator programs. They are based on corporate sponsorship; incumbents may increase the prospects of survival and growth for startups by offering them resources and knowledge. Achieving a strategic fit between startups and the incumbent becomes crucial for incumbents to get innovative advantages from accelerator and incubator programs. When an incumbent has a solid strategic fit, it may achieve its strategic innovation goals by learning from relevant markets and technology (Riikkinen & Pihlajamaa, 2022).

10.4.4 Investments in Technology Infrastructure and Talent Development

The infrastructure's leveraging capability is a measure of an organization's ability to use various IT applications to get or supply crucial consumers with accurate, fast, dependable, secure, and private information Leveraging IT infrastructure serves as both an operational and flexible capability,

Table 10.2   Identifying Areas for Integration of Fintech Solutions

Stage	Process	Outcome
First contact	Demands for Fintech integration are received by Debt-to-income (DTI) through four channels: 1. Certain Fintech demands are brought forth by other bank divisions. 2. Departments offer Fintech-solvable challenges. 3. At conferences and gatherings, DTI encounters Fintechs. 4. Kuveyt Türk's application programming interfaces (API) Market Platform is where Fintechs originate.	Identification of potential Fintech partners and solutions.
Fintech scouting and researching	Through desktop searches, media and news monitoring, and pre-assessment using Fintech databases like Crunchbase and Startup Watch, DTI looks for Fintechs both locally and internationally.	Fintechs are identified and shortlisted according to factors including funding, value, and ownership.
Fintech introduction	DTI schedules meetings for Q&A sessions, solution demos, and quick introductions with Fintechs and related departments. After evaluation, Fintechs that pass move on to the Business Committee.	Fintech appropriateness for partnership is evaluated, and the presentation is made to the Business Committee for additional review.
Business evaluation committee	Vice presidents from related departments get together to review Fintech pitches, weigh advantages, and cast votes on whether to work together.	Making strategic choices on the integration of Fintech.
Technical evaluation meeting	Departments of IT, compliance, and law assess the Fintech and integrating process, posing queries and debating technical specifics to guarantee appropriateness.	Technical evaluation and decision-making on the viability of integration.
Proof of concept (PoC)	A feasibility study is carried out, integration-related issues are recorded, a roadmap is established, and pertinent departments undertake the essential advancements.	Verification and testing of integration in practical settings.
Going live	A fruitful proof of concept results in a live integration that is available to all parties involved—from clients to staff.	Fintech solutions are implemented and utilized in the bank.

Source: Acar et al. (2019).

making it a dual-purpose capacity, includes the company's ability to employ a variety of IT apps and reorganize its IT infrastructure to meet demands that are evolving.

The ability of the company to find, attract, and choose talent as well as to bring it on board, develop it, keep it on board, and use it to accomplish objectives and carry out organizational plans is known as talent management. We suggest that aptitude entrepreneurship is a dynamic skill that is influenced by talent development, working environment, and corporate culture. Working conditions are influenced by the company's rules on pay and benefits, scheduling and workplace adaptability, and work–life balance initiatives. Working culture is defined as an arrangement of working opinions and principles that are shared and internalized by organizational members. The ability of the company to inspire, encourage, and develop the talent inside the organization is known as talent development. Because it involves building the talent base, integrating it into the company, and reconfiguring people to take advantage of long-term commercial prospects, managing talent is a dynamic competence (Hoang et al., 2021).

The leadership and oversight of talent may be made possible by using IT infrastructure. It has been proposed that one of the main ways to provide dynamic capabilities is to use IT infrastructure. Thus, we think it makes sense to anticipate that utilizing IT infrastructure will help enhance talent management's dynamic potential. With the use of IT infrastructure, the company may get and disseminate timely information to the market in order to find and hire people and develop and incorporate its talent pool (Orlova, Afonin & Voronin, 2015). Cortefiel, a Spanish clothing company, uses IT-based social media platforms like Facebook, Twitter, and LinkedIn to source management talent that meets the requirements for creating its talent pool. Similar to this, Cortefiel can hire talent more quickly because IT's integration with human resources and social media platforms, which makes it easier to rearrange its talent pool to meet changes in demand (Riikkinen & Pihlajamaa, 2022).

Leveraging IT infrastructure may help to mold the company's workplace culture and enhance talent management. The company may readily disseminate its purpose, working principles, goals, and plans among its people thanks to email, the intranet, and wireless devices. For instance, Nestle recently shared its organizational principles with the personnel of each of its business divisions via the usage of intranet resources. By making it easier for the company to implement its working conditions, leveraging IT infrastructure may also help the organization's personnel management (Kim et al., 2014). Members of the organization will be able to work on their own of time and location if they are given laptops and mobile phones with Internet access and flexible access to corporate databases. This will improve work–life balance and allow for more flexible scheduling and workplaces, which will ultimately increase member job satisfaction and talent retention.

The development of the company's talent may also result from IT infrastructure. Applications for HR development are part of enterprise resource planning systems, which are made possible by IT infrastructure. These programs provide managers access to HR data so they can assess workers' performance and efforts and put plans in place to maximize their efforts—developing talent for the company Applications for HR development also strengthen ties with staff members by providing them with information on objectives, performance reviews, pay and benefits, and career development to nurture the company's potential. Last, by utilizing electronic communication networks, the company may provide virtual seminars and online training to its people to nurture their skills (Benitez-Amado, Montes & Fernandez-Perez, 2013).

10.4.5 Regulatory Compliance and Risk Management Strategies

"Technologically enabled technological advances in finance that could result in novel business models, applications, procedures, or products with a connected material impact on financial institutions and markets and on the delivery of financial services" is how the Board of Financial Stability (2017b) defines financial technology.

Although the idea of applying creativity in banking is not new, there has been a noticeable rise in the pace and concentration on technology advancements. Blockchain, artificial intelligence, and big data analytics-based Fintech solutions are being released at a never-before-seen rate. The financial sector is evolving due to these new technologies, which also present a number of chances for more accessible financial services.

Notwithstanding the benefits, Fintech solutions are fraught with dangers that might jeopardize financial stability and consumer protection. Cyberattacks, fraud detection, market risk noncompliance, and underestimation of creditworthiness are pertinent examples of these risks. Fintech risk management is in fact of great interest to regulatory bodies, and it calls for investigation and the creation of new metrics (Taylor, Surridge & Pickering, 2021).

To make the Fintech sector more competitive in the world, a system for risk management that can monitor Fintech innovations without limiting their financial potential must be implemented. A framework that can be advantageous to both supervisors and Fintech companies: Fintech companies require advice on how to identify possibilities over invention purchases, such as in RegTech solutions; supervisory bodies' inadequate capacity to monitor fresh financial services offered by Fintech businesses requires developed supervisory innovations in technology (SupTech) solutions. Modernizing compliance and supervision requires first modernizing risk management tools with cutting-edge technology and standardization. Additionally, these technologies could make it easier for supervisors and Fintech businesses to interact (Dill, 2019).

We believe that a focused international research project, run at the level of a respectable open-access scientific journal covering multiple major fields of interest—such as artificial intelligence's Frontiers—can help close the understanding gap that exists between scientific and regulatory domains, particularly by providing common risk management techniques. It might lead to the development of a regulatory framework that encourages developments in big data analytics, blockchain technology, and artificial intelligence while also reassuring supervisors about the successful and efficient implementation of laws protecting investors and consumers.

Regulations and related supervisory requirements are giving the risk management process a lot of attention, which emphasizes the necessity of comprehensive, transparent, and accountable data analysis across companies. Artificial intelligence, big data analytics, and blockchain ledgers are a few examples of technology that might manage risk management requirements and associated costs more skillfully. The aforementioned technologies, in particular, can: (i) measure and monitor market volatility and risk within banking markets; (ii) evaluate and monitor systematic risk in peer-to-peer borrowing; and (iv) improve the risk of the client's profile. These technologies may additionally enhance fraud detection as well as minimize bias in rating credit in peer-to-peer lending. (v) These technologies also determine illegal behaviors in the markets for cryptocurrency, such as the laundering of funds and misleading initial coin offers, using the appropriate parameters in robo-advisory and (vi) identify and rank the operational and cyber risks related to IT.

10.5 Future Developments and Impacts

The term "Fintech," which stands for financial technology, is increasingly widely utilized. Startups that compete with established financial services and provide client-focused services with a fast and flexible combination are expanding across the globe. Customers' participation and expectations are being drastically altered by them. Consumers are increasingly able to view the world digitally, thanks to the Internet of Things (IoT), smartphones, tablets, and other technical advancements that offer almost instantaneous and ubiquitous access to information.

To close the technology divide with Fintech firms, established financial institutions like banks and insurance providers are changing. However, they face several obstacles in their journeys toward innovation and progress. Customs that were never updated and stiff company structures are among their main problems to solve. Fintech enterprises engage in a process known as "disintermediation through innovation." Big data, blockchain, online financial advisers, and are reshaping the financial services business via the use of the Internet of Everything, in conjunction with considerably more effective use of online platforms and mobile devices. These solutions give the market cutting-edge adding-value options supported by prospective tactics and innovative company models (Guild, 2017).

Thanks to Fintech, blockchain and cryptocurrencies have increased. Cryptocurrencies provide a substitute for conventional money and payment systems, while blockchain technology facilitates safe and open transactions. Reliance on middlemen like banks may decline and cross-border transactions may become more efficient as a result.

Since the rise of Fintech, intelligent automation (AI) along with machine learning algorithms are being used by Fintech organizations more and more to automate procedures, customize services, and analyze enormous volumes of data for insights. This may enhance fraud detection, risk assessment, and client satisfaction, resulting in more specialized financial services and products. The computerized, algorithm-driven financial preparation services offered by robo-advisors are platform-based and need little to no human oversight. As they grow in sophistication, these platforms should be able to provide asset management, retirement planning, and individualized investment advice for a fraction of the price of traditional financial consultants (Murinde, Rizopoulos & Zachariadis, 2022).

Regulating Fintech advances while maintaining safeguarding customers and financial stability is a challenge that governments and regulatory agencies are facing. The sustained expansion of the Fintech sector will depend on finding the ideal equilibrium among innovation and regulation. By giving underprivileged groups the opportunity to utilize banking and financial services, Fintech has the potential to improve financial inclusion. Platforms for microfinance, digital lending, and mobile banking can enable people and small enterprises in developing nations to engage in the formal economy.

Data breaches and cyberattacks are becoming more common as financial transactions shift more and more online. It will be necessary for Fintech businesses to make significant investments in cybersecurity measures in order to safeguard client data and preserve platform confidence. Fintech companies and conventional financial institutions are increasingly working together. Fintech companies capitalize on the assets and regulatory know-how of existing institutions, while banks collaborate with these businesses to develop and enhance their services.

Fintech technologies' digitization of financial services might result in employment losses in various industries, including back-office operations and traditional banking. Yet, it may also lead to the creation of new employment possibilities in fields like cybersecurity, data analysis, and software development.

Fintech can revolutionize banking industry, enhancing its inclusiveness, effectiveness, and accessibility. Nevertheless, in order to reach its full potential, it also presents issues with cybersecurity, regulation, and labor displacement (Anagnostopoulos, 2018).

10.5.1 Emerging Trends in Fintech and Traditional Banking

Technology-enabled financial innovation, or Fintech, has the potential to provide novel companies, applications, procedures, goods, or services that might have a significant impact on financial markets, institutions, and the delivery of financial services (Pantielieieva et al., 2020). The government, financial institutions, Fintech startups, technology developers, and users of financial services and products make up the contemporary Fintech ecosystem. A well-developed Fintech ecosystem fosters financial innovation, collaboration, and competition, boosts economic growth, and increases accessibility to financial services. Technology; (Mirchandani et al., 2020) advantageous legal and regulatory backing; access to funds and investments; and human assets for development and maintenance are the factors that define the Fintech ecosystem.

The state of technology for communication and information development, mobile and Internet connectivity, the creation of payment and agency networks for financial intermediation, and the use of digital identification tools for AML, KYC, and the Financial Action Task Force (FATF) are some of the characteristics that define infrastructure.

As these the nation's preparedness for Fintech development is determined by several variables. The creative strategies and decisions made by financial organizations (banks, insurance firms, exchanges of shares, venture funds) to form alliances with Fintech businesses or to engage in competitive battles impact their standing in the market as shown in Figure 10.7.

Using methods like massive data collection resources, IoT, blockchain technology, decentralized marketplaces, Software as a Service (PaaS), AI, machine learning, API, cloud computing, and Software as a Service, Fintech businesses today offer innovative business models as shown in Figure 10.8. The top three countries in which Fintech has garnered the most attention during the past five years are, per Google Analytics: IoT—BigData, Spain, Morocco, and Peru Blockchain—Ukraine, Vietnam, Russia; the nation of Sweden, Ireland, Philippine; AI—Pakistan, Bangladesh, Kenyan; API—St. Helena Island, Nigeria, China. Singapore and Luxembourg are financial technology, RegTech, and Insurtech leaders as shown in Figure 10.9.

In 2018, the worldwide Fintech ecosystem saw rapid development; the following major trends were observed (Pantielieieva et al., 2020):

and Global M&A Activity in FinTech

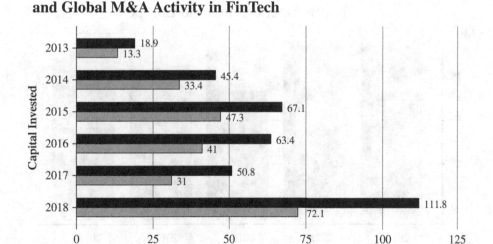

Figure 10.7   Global Fintech M&A activity dynamics ($B) 2012–2018. (From Pantielieieva et al., 2020.)

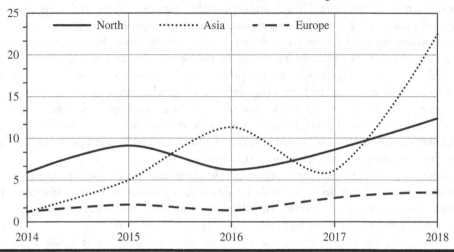

Figure 10.8   The global VC-backed Fintech financing by continent from 2014 to 2018, in $B. (From Pantielieieva et al., 2020.)

■ The growth of this mechanism will be aided by regulation and the increase in competition for investment resources brought about by introductory coin offerings, or ICOs. With an average project financing of $13.4 million, $514 ICOs generated $6.89 billion in 2017. During the initial four months of 2018, $25.1 million, 301 ICOs, and $7.57 billion were raised. Opinions on ICOs remain ambiguous, nevertheless, considering that 80% of ICOs and about 11% of funding amount were fraudulent in 2017. Regulators will thus continue to take measures to limit ICO even after regulations for this method are implemented.

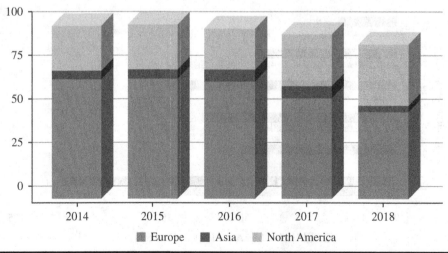

Figure 10.9   Global RegTech transactions by area, 2014–2018 (as a percentage of all agreements). (From Pantielieieva et al., 2020.)

- SupTech (Supervisory Technology, sometimes referred to as RegTech for management) will offer real-time availability, reporting tools, regulatory submissions, intelligence gathering from disorganized data, and data quality management in addition to implementing a data-input strategy for projects; The first is blockchain, which encourages the spread of that applies decisions across many different economic sectors; the second is API, which complies with PSD2 (Satellite imagery Customer Identification) payments instructions from the European Union and Open API Specification, enabling banks to make technology assets available to third parties, which helps with software integration and boosts their own online presence; and the third is strengthening partnerships between Fintech companies and banks, which further solidifies their lead positions. Notably, between 2010 and 2015, the percentage of collaborations in North America increased (Pantielieieva et al., 2020).
- Intensification of the dispute between the world's leading Fintech countries—China, the United States, Germany, and the United Kingdom. For example, according to the 2017 EY Finance Technology Adoption Survey in China, 69% of individuals were aware of Fintech, 98% of customers who were online knew about it, and 39% of users have used more than five among those offerings. This indicates that Fintech is well accepted in China. By comparison, the United Kingdom produced 42%, 42%, and 43%, the United States had 33%, 74%, and 15%, Germany had 35%, 65%, and 52%, and so on (Taherdoost, 2023).

Along with the ones that already exist, the following trends are anticipated to emerge in 2019: The expansion of consolidation in the fields of credit and payments as well as blockchain technology, particularly in the area of funding in the creation of particular decisions based on these developments, which enable the application of the scale effect.

Investors will still fund Fintech, but they will only do so at the latter end of the industry's growth cycle and in well-established startups in order to reduce risk; Leading insurance corporations in the United States and Europe anticipate a rise in Insurtech investments, particularly in Asian nations. By serving as trial locations; Maintaining the open banking policy would aid in the growth of Fintech and the collaboration of banks with high-tech businesses, resulting in the introduction of fresh, adaptable, and independent digital banking solutions (Pantielieieva et al., 2020).

10.5.2 *Potential Disruptions and Opportunities in the Financial Industry*

The financial industry's development is mostly driven by innovation and disruption. Financial institutions must change as technology advances in order to remain competitive and satisfy the shifting demands of their clientele. New technologies have transformed conventional financial processes by improving efficiency, safety, and accessibility. Examples of these technologies include blockchain technology, artificially intelligent machines, and digital platforms. Contactless payments, internet investing, and mobile banking are examples of innovations that have not only enhanced user but they have also created new sources of income.

The goal of researching probable future developments in the financial sector is to foresee and comprehend any changes that could occur. An atmosphere that is conducive to innovation and disruption is created by the rapid growth of technology, changes in regulations, and evolving consumer behavior. Early detection of these trends allows financial institutions to strategically position themselves to take advantage of new possibilities, manage any obstacles, and guarantee long-term viability.

Individualized offerings and financial institutions may provide highly customized services by utilizing data analytics, artificial intelligence, and machine learning. A more engaging customer experience may be achieved by providing individualized communication, customized product recommendations, and an understanding of each client's preferences, spending habits, and financial objectives as current financial information (Pantielieieva et al., 2020).

Giving consumers immediate entry to their financial activities, data, and insights enables them to make wise decisions. A more transparent and user-friendly experience is enhanced by mobile applications and digital platforms that provide instantaneous financial updates, and expenditure category, and offer predictive financial analysis streamlined onboarding procedures efficiency is increased and friction is decreased by automating and streamlining the new customer onboarding process. Using blockchain, biometric verification, and electronic signatures as examples of technology identity verification may expedite the process of creating an account and enhance the onboarding process for new customers (Wewege, Lee & Thomsett, 2020).

Tasks that are repetitive can be automated and operational efficiency is increased and human mistakes are decreased when repetitive operations are automated using automated robotic processes RPA and AI-driven systems. Financial organizations can deploy resources by automating processes like data input, verification of documents, and customer support questions (Hubert, 2024).

More carefully, streamlining back-office activities is made easier by the incorporation of technologies like blockchain technology and cloud computing. Enhancing data management, using smart contracts, and securely exchanging information via distributed ledgers all help businesses increase productivity and save operating expenses.

When it comes to spotting trends suggestive of fraudulent activity, sophisticated data analysis and artificial intelligence algorithms are indispensable. Putting in place strong fraud detection systems improves security, safeguards clients, and fosters confidence. Financial organizations may keep ahead of emerging risks by using real-time transaction monitoring and analysis.

Financial services may now be extended to groups that have historically been shut out of the formal banking industry thanks to Fintech developments like digital wallets and mobile banking. Technology makes accessible and affordable financial solutions possible, promoting greater financial participation and economic authority. Alternative financing options and microlending for people and companies having limited access to credit, based on technology lending networks and microfinance organizations provide alternatives to traditional banking. Financial services are being extended to underprivileged areas through peer-to-peer loans, crowdfunding, and other creative financing approaches.

There is a greater need for sustainable and ethical investing alternatives as a result of the rising emphasis on governance, social, and environmental issues. By providing environmental, social and governance (ESG)-focused investment solutions that correspond with the inclinations of socially aware investors, financial institutions may provide novel ideas. Green finance, or financing for initiatives and projects having favorable environmental effects, is a subset of sustainable finance. To assist with projects pertaining to eco-friendliness, conservation, and renewable energy, financial institutions can create cutting-edge financial instruments like green bonds and loans.

Investing in social impact initiatives or companies entails providing funding with the goal of producing both financial returns and beneficial social effects. Financial organizations can give investors the chance to further social issues including access to affordable housing, healthcare, and education, all while reaching their financial objectives.

10.5.3 Implications for Financial Stability and Market Structure

Capital flows and the value of assets between various asset categories and national borders are significantly impacted by these institutions' asset allocation choices.

Given that several of these organizations remain still in the infancy in many nations, it is reasonable to assume that their size and impact will increase going forward. The formation of additional and greater asset gatherers is expected to be supported by demographic trends and pension changes. Modest adjustments to these organizations' holdings might have a compounding effect on the world's financial markets. In contrast to bank-dominated financial markets, capital markets often convey shifts in risk appetite, credit evaluations, or believed economic fundamentals more quickly, directly, and broadly (Davis & Stone, 2004).

Institutional investors are more vulnerable to market risks but are nevertheless exposed to identical credit risks as banks, as the IMF points out. Additionally, their choices "make markets" because they are often enormous institutions (Davis & Stone, 2004).

It is possible to examine how these institutions contribute to or detract from the stability of financial markets in a number of ways, including how they affect capital flows, asset prices, interest and exchange rate volatility, expanding procyclicality of financial systems, and systemic risk.

With a few noteworthy outliers, rates and currency rates in the world's financial markets stayed comparatively steady during the 2001 financial crisis. Many believe that this is because of the increasingly complex derivatives markets, particularly credit derivatives, which have spread the risk among a larger number of investors. There are others who contend that the speculative actions of hedge funds have decreased volatility by increasing and diversifying market liquidity. The US, European, and Japanese central banks are also thought to have made a conscious effort to communicate potential changes in policy rates and to make small changes so as not to surprise highly leveraged financial institutions, which has contributed to the extension regarding comparatively stable prices for assets and interest rates.

However, it seems that in 2004 and 2005, more erratic capital flows that aggravated global imbalances were a result of the fall in interest and currency rate volatility. The low rate of interest in industrialized economies, as they were in the beginning of the 1990s spurred a yield-seeking frenzy that in those years propelled cross-border flows to all-time high levels. Much of the money required to carry out these transactions came from loans in the institutional investor growth has also been aided by foreign, or so-called "euro," banking and securities markets. The main causes of the rising leverage in the world financial system are these markets. They supply capital for the international carry trade deals that propel the growth of financial leverage, and as a result, reinforce the connections between markets and sectors that raise the possibility of systemic risk, as will be covered in more detail later (Davis & Stone, 2004).

"The inherent procyclicality of market-based financial systems" (Davis & Stone, 2004) was highlighted by the BIS in its 2002 Annual Report. When the market is doing well, it supplies more money at a lower cost; when it is not, access is restricted and expenses go up. systems controlled by banks that are Reserve and liquidity requirements, two quantitative monetary tools that central banks can use, have historically been able to act as the channels for countercyclical policy meant to moderate the ups and downs that come with market-based systems by providing credit created by the Federal Reserve during a recession and restricting credit during a boom in response to the monetary authority's expenses. We'll talk about the deterioration of monetary management as one facet of procyclicality below. However, systems controlled by institutional investors also play a role in procyclicality in different ways.

The procyclical nature of family balance sheet wealth effect is another feature of the transition to market-based systems. Throughout the company's life cycle, the actual value of bank deposits held by consumers stays constant, but the value through mutual funds and pension plans, either directly or indirectly, their ratings for trading instruments and corporate stocks vary, rising in a boom and dropping in a depression. Spending tends to rise in tandem with these assets' appreciation and fall in tandem with their depreciation. So, the wealth effect's ability to magnify booms and downturns increases to the degree that increases in families' marketable financial assets contribute to the impact (Pantielieieva et al., 2020).

Pension funds and retirement accounts holding marketable securities, for instance, suffered losses as a result of bubbles in assets and their burst in both developed and developing nations. In the United States, the stock bubble between 1994 and 1999, prices contributed to a remarkable 71% growth in family net worth and an approximate 86% rise in the worth of pension fund reserves, creating a "wealth effect" that led to growing consumption and falling personal saving. Net worth decreased 6.4% after the market break from year-end 1999 to year-end 2002, although pension fund reserves decreased by 12.3% (the federal government storage, flow of funds). The IMF stated that the decline in share prices had occurred even if the amount of losses were minimal in comparison to prior gains.

Another important effect of the shift between bank-dominated to market-driven structures is the rise of leverage, which raises concerns for the stability of the system. Given that institutional competitors have become more formidable, Investors and banks have come to terms with the higher risks associated with leveraged transactions and off-balance-sheet commitments in order to increase operations and profitability while lowering regulatory expenses. Even though the transition to liability management started in the 1960s, bought deposits were the main emphasis at first. In the 1990s, banks increased their usage of borrowed money as they became more dependent on non-deposit liabilities for funding. For instance, money borrowed through purchase contracts (repos) and checkable deposits made up a smaller portion of the liabilities of US banks than the Federal Reserve (interbank) market. Checkable deposits made up a smaller portion of the liabilities of US banks than the Federal Reserve (interbank) market (Davis & Stone, 2004).

10.5.4 Regulatory Responses and Policy Considerations

Major financial organizations are subject to several regulatory jurisdictions, and authorities are requiring more detailed data from businesses. As a result, financial regulation is become more complicated and invasive. In the end, this information will let systemic risks are the ways in which entities within financial systems are linked to one another both directly and indirectly through comparable external sources and directly through financial instruments that reference those same institutions. Furthermore, the information ought to enable examination of the extent to which institutions respond to regulations and the ways in which these responses spread across the financial markets.

In some instances, the authorities must file a lawsuit in order to provide legal certainty before implementing technological advancements in the banking industry. This would be the case, for example, if distributed ledger technology, were to be recognized as providing certainty in the completion of securities transactions. This is valid for regulated activities when clients' identities are verified by biometrics, such as opening a bank account. However, policies have frequently focused on minimizing the risks associated with using a technology. To be more specific, regulatory agencies have already issued rules (like in Brazil) or proposals (such as in the European Union) to oversee and manage operational hazards connected with cloud computing, given its increasing use by regulated financial institutions.

In addition, several authorities are acting to mitigate the hazards associated with the improper application of AI and machine learning algorithms, such as in banking or insurance underwriting. Publications in Singapore and Luxembourg that highlight the dangers associated with improper handling are examples of such measures of sensitive information, inadequate management, a lack of openness, and unethical behavior; and, in Singapore, the publication of high-level guidelines that businesses must abide by in order to manage these risks.

Generally speaking, no significant changes to the framework of financial regulation have been brought about by technology advancements to date. The rulebooks on consumer protection, market integrity, and prudential protections have not changed much in terms of their essential content. Specifically, a banking license is still needed for any operation that involves converting public funds at significant risk. When public funds may be obtained by non-banks, usually for payment services—they must abide by stringent guidelines to protect clients' money. Limits on volume, like the Swiss franc 100 million limit for Fintech license holders in Switzerland, and sufficient coverage of liquidity, like the 100% requirement for reserves for outstanding customer deposits (the rise) in Brazil and China, are two examples.

In addition, not much work has gone into creating particular license specifications for digital banks. Supervisors in certain jurisdictions, such as the euro area4, have released guidelines on how the new business models will be subject to standard rules. But just jurisdictions Hong Kong Special Administrative Region 5 and Singapore 6—have established particular licensing standards for banks focused on digital services. Insurtech and robo-advice, two domains that provide financial advice and insurance services, have adopted a comparable methodology. Although certain market supervisors have conveyed particular supervisory instructions or expectations, generally speaking, no explicit licensing system has been anticipated for such operations. Certain licenses and business behavior requirements apply to a range of operations, including as the issuance of digital money, the provision of payment methods, and providing crowdfunding of loans and equity. In addition to operating adaptability, preventing money from laundering, and combating the funding of terrorism, regulatory requirements frequently focus on safeguarding customers and investors, particularly on preserving their financial interests.

Distinct legal systems that regulate cryptocurrency assets and related activities have quite distinct frameworks. In general, the features of the issuer (such as their regulatory status), the job performed (such as making a payment, investing possibilities, or service access), and the kind and quantity of underlying financial assets (commodities, investments, etc.) all influence the strategies. The bulk of notifications from authorities concern the use of crypto assets for investing purposes, and they often provide clarifications and alerts on rules pertaining to issuers, holders, and intermediaries. Additionally, a number of nations have banned specific cryptocurrency-related activities, such as Belgium, China, India, and Mexico.

10.5.5 Predictions for the Future of Fintech and Traditional Banking Relationships

These days, Fintech—a fusion of information technology and finance—is growing, and this is reflected in the banking industry's digitalization. According to Prawirasasra, Fintech is a relatively new area in the financial industry that combines technology and financial operations. Fintech refers to the dynamic combination of technology and finance in the banking and insurance business. Additionally, Fintech is a service sector that uses IT technology with a mobile focus to improve the efficiency of the financial system, according to Kim et al. (Sorongan, Legowo & Subanidja, 2021). Zavolokina et al. (Sorongan et al., 2021) discovered that a Fintech's mechanism is the means by which a business model may be developed, altered, or enhanced. Fintech also features a system for interruption or cooperation.

One of the key institutions in a nation's economy is its banking system. Banks are financial entities that handle credit issues and financial obligations and are managed by either the public or

Table 10.3 The History, Present, and Future of Fintech in Banking

Past	Present	Future
Fintech 1.0–2.0	Fintech 2.0–3.0	Fintech 3.0–3.5
1866 -> 2008	2008 -> Present	Present -> future
Traditional banks	Modern banks	Future banks

Source: Pantielieieva et al. 2020.

private sectors. It makes money by lending, receiving, and depositing it. Generally speaking, banks are different from other kinds of financial companies in that they offer deposit and lending products.

Trębacz (Sorongan et al., 2021) claims that the word "bank" is also connected to transactions from the Middle Ages. It was previously believed that the term originated via the Italian word "bank" which denoted a counter where money dealers conducted banking operations, which defines a banking institution as a financial organization that receives deposits from the public and disburses money in the way of funding and other financial products with the goal of bettering the lives of a large number of people.

Based on this agreement, it was determined that the banking industry consists of three main activities: capital raising, fund distribution tasks as well as other financial services rendered. Traditional banks were the term used to describe banks in the past. Currently, nevertheless, a lot of banks operate under the names of digital, contemporary, or virtual banking. It is sometimes referred to as "future banking" since it is expected that the status of banking will alter from what it is today in the future as shown in Table 10.3.

The global financial crisis of 2008 had an impact on the finance and banking sectors. It might be characterized as the globalization for digital financial services in this era (Sorongan et al., 2021). These market actors will provide financial services to clients directly, eliminating the need for middlemen, by using technology advancements. In the era of Fintech 3.0, the most recent technologies, including the Internet

The banking sector will see a steady evolution of data analytics technology leading to the Fintech 3.5 age, as the IoT continues to flourish. Future financial technology development in the banking sector has a chance thanks to the partnership framework. Almost 95% of Fintech organizations will fail during the upgrading phase if they don't have a collaborative framework. Bitcoin, a distributed ledger called blockchain, cryptocurrency, and robot advisors are examples of future banking-related Fintech goods (Sorongan et al., 2021).

The banking sector going forward (today). BigTech and Fintech banks will also exist in the banking industry in the future. A Fintech company that operates similarly to internet banking is called Fintech Bank. Another Fintech business that provides collaboration and synergy with traditional banks is Fintech Bank. Fintech Bank is able to rival traditional banks in terms of customer interface programs with a range of transactional goods and extensive cash availability. It should be noted that the Big Technology Firm is a technological corporation whose focus is on using digital technologies. The emergence of big technology in financial services, offered by IT firms with track records across the digital services industry. Payments are generally the first step in BigTech enterprises. Then, some increase the quantity offered of increase the selection of savings, investment, credit, and insurance products offered, either directly or through collaboration with financial institution partners.

The banking sector in Indonesia has made preparations for the future and reacted to the expected developments in financial technology. According to Deloitte, digitized banking services (DFS) could eventually be available in Indonesia. The next significant step is to connect the growing need for financial services throughout the world with the present usage of mobile phones. The person from Indonesia in an effort to reduce the risks associated with this new technology, the Financial Services Authority and the Bank of Indonesia are collaborating to develop Fintech-related laws.

The Fintech rules and regulations in Indonesia are subject to legislative requirements. A strategy to modernize Indonesia's payment system—IPS—in the digital era has been devised by the central bank (Sorongan et al., 2021). This Indonesian Banking and Finance Authority has therefore established the objectives for Fintech's interaction with the finance and banking sectors.

10.6 Conclusion

In this chapter, we have focused on the recently trendy topic of financial technology. Big data analytics, blockchain technology, and artificial intelligence have been cited as the main technological factors influencing change. Peer-to-peer lending in banking, asset management (robot guidance), and payment systems (crypto-assets) have been their main financial uses. Assuring the sustainability of financial technologies and mitigating any possible harm they may do to consumers and investors is our objective as we work to enhance and expand them. This goal may be accomplished by developing appropriate risk management strategies, the technology for which can lessen the compliance load.

In order to do this, the paper outlines the main dangers connected to the introduction of significant financial technologies and makes research suggestions for risk measuring models that are appropriate for controlling and lowering the related risks. Regulators, researchers, and Fintech professionals need to collaborate closely and have candid conversations in order to develop Fintech risk-control models that reduce the negative consequences of emerging technologies while fostering their growth. Foundations in Artificial Intelligence, an academic magazine that focuses on artificial intelligence in finance, will play a significant role in fostering collaborations and stimulating research debates on risk management techniques.

References

Accenture (2016). The Promise of Artificial Intelligence: Redefining Management in the Workforce of the Future. https://www.accenture.com/us-en/insight-promise-artificial-intelligence

Adeoye, O. B., Addy, W. A., Odeyemi, O., Okoye, C. C., Ofodile, O. C., Oyewole, A. T., & Ololade, Y. J. (2024). Fintech, taxation, and regulatory compliance: Navigating the new financial landscape. Finance & Accounting Research Journal, 6(3), 320–330. https://doi.org/10.51594/farj.v6i3.858

Agrawal, Sushank, et al. "Fintech: a New Revolution in India." JournalNX, 2020, pp. 47-57. https://www.neliti.com/publications/336588/fintech-a-new-revolution-in-india#cite

Alt, R., Beck, R., & Smits, M. T. (2018). Fintech and the transformation of the financial industry. Electronic Markets, 28, 235–243. https://doi.org/10.1007/s12525-018-0310-9

Anagnostopoulos, I. (2018). Fintech and regtech: Impact on regulators and banks. Journal of Economics and Business, 100, 7–25. https://doi.org/10.1016/j.jeconbus.2018.07.003

Batchu, R. K. (2023). The impact of Fintech integration on traditional Banking: A comparative analysis. International Journal of Interdisciplinary Finance Insights, 2(2), 1–24. https://injmr.com/index.php/ijifi/article/view/41

Benitez-Amado, J., Montes, F. J. L., & Fernandez-Perez, V. (2013). The relationship between IT infrastructure leveraging, talent management and operational sustainability, and their effects on the business value of the operations strategy. In AMCIS. https://core.ac.uk/download/pdf/301359353.pdf

Berger, A. N., & Humphrey, D. B. (1992). Measurement and efficiency issues in commercial banking. In Output Measurement in the Service Sectors (pp. 245–300). University of Chicago Press. https://www.nber.org/system/files/chapters/c7237/c7237.pdf

Bouteraa, M., Chekima, B., Lajuni, N., & Anwar, A. (2023). Understanding Consumers' barriers to using Fintech services in the United Arab Emirates: Mixed-methods research approach. Sustainability, 15(4), 2931. https://doi.org/10.3390/su15042931

CBInsights (2018), The CB Insights Year In Review: 2018 Highlights. https://www.cbinsights.com/research/team-blog/cb-insights-year-in-review-2018/

Chen, Q. (2024). Challenges and opportunities of Fintech innovation for traditional financial Institutions. Frontiers in Business, Economics and Management, 13(3), 28–33.

Davis, E. P., & Stone, M. R. (2004). Corporate financial structure and financial stability. Journal of Financial Stability, 1(1), 65–91. https://doi.org/10.1016/j.jfs.2004.06.003

Dill, A. (2019). Bank Regulation, Risk Management, and Compliance: Theory, Practice, and Key Problem Areas. Informa Law from Routledge. https://doi.org/10.4324/9780429351167

Gandara, D. M. 2018. Strategic adaptation & collaboration: European global banks approach to Fintech. http://urn.fi/URN:NBN:fi:jyu-201906143200

Giglio, F. (2021). Fintech: A literature review. European Research Studies Journal, 24(2B), 600–627. https://scholar.archive.org/work/35eg7pttzvamhidmmbwaugwety/access/wayback/https://www.ersj.eu/journal/2254/download

Guild, J. (2017). Fintech and the future of finance. *Asian Journal of Public Affairs*, 17–20. https://papers.ssrn.com/sol3/papers.cfm?abstract_id=3021684

Harasim, J. (2021). Fintechs, BigTechs and banks—When cooperation and When competition? Journal of Risk and Financial Management, 14(12), 614. https://doi.org/10.3390/jrfm14120614

Harsono, I., & Suprapti, I. A. P. (2024). The role of Fintech in transforming traditional financial services. Accounting Studies and Tax Journal (COUNT), 1(1), 81–91. https://doi.org/10.62207/gfzvtd24

Hoang, Y. H., Nguyen, N. T., Vu, N. B., Nguyen, D. T., & Tran, L. H. (2021). Toward successful bank-Fintech partnerships: Perspectives from service providers in an emerging economy. Asian Social Science, 17(6), 19. https://doi.org/10.5539/ass.v17n6p19

Hubert, K. (2024). Future Trends and Opportunities: Opportunities for innovation and disruption in the financial industry. https://www.researchgate.net/profile/Hubert-Klaus-2/publication/377330246_Future_Trends_and_Opportunities_Opportunities_for_innovation_and_disruption_in_the_financial_industry/links/65a05c59c77ed9404771431c/Future-Trends-and-Opportunities-Opportunities-for-innovation-and-disruption-in-the-financial-industry.pdf

Hwang, Y., Park, S., & Shin, N. (2021). Sustainable development of a mobile payment security environment using Fintech solutions. Sustainability, 13(15), 8375. https://doi.org/10.3390/su13158375

Jaouadi, S., & Zorgui, I. (2014). Exploring effectiveness and efficiency of banks in Switzerland. International Journal of Academic Research in Business and Social Sciences, 4(4), 313–325. http://dx.doi.org/10.6007/IJARBSS/v4-i4/787

Kang, J. (2018). Mobile Payment in Fintech environment: Trends, security challenges, and services. Human-Centric Computing and Information Sciences, 8(1), 32. https://doi.org/10.1186/s13673-018-0155-4

Kim, Y., Williams, R., Rothwell, W. J., & Penaloza, P. (2014). A strategic model for technical talent management: A model based on a qualitative case study. Performance Improvement Quarterly, 26(4), 93–121. https://doi.org/10.1002/piq.21159

Klus, M. F., Lohwasser, T. S., Holotiuk, F., & Moormann, J. (2019). Strategic alliances between banks and Fintechs for digital innovation: Motives to collaborate and types of interaction. The Journal of Entrepreneurial Finance (JEF), 21(1), 1–23. https://digitalcommons.pepperdine.edu/jef/vol21/iss1/1

Chen, K-C, (2020). Efficiency matrix, 2009-2014. https://pdfs.semanticscholar.org/3bd7/3e8da7906bf3b26b5c3facb017502a74bdfa.pdf

Li, Y., Spigt, R., & Swinkels, L. (2017).The impact of Fintech start-ups on incumbent retail banks' share prices. Financial Innovation 3, 26. https://doi.org/10.1186/s40854-017-0076-7

Mention, A. (2019). The future of Fintech. Research Technology Management, 62(4), 59–63. https://doi.org /10.1080/08956308.2019.1613123

Mirchandani, A., Gupta, N., & Ndiweni, E. (2020). Understanding the Fintech wave: A search for A theoretical explanation. International Journal of Economics and Financial Issues, 10(5), 331. https://doi.org/10.32479/ijefi.10296

Murinde, V., Rizopoulos, E., & Zachariadis, M. (2022). The impact of the Fintech revolution on the future of banking: Opportunities and risks. International Review of Financial Analysis, 81, 102103. https://doi.org/10.1016/j.irfa.2022.102103

Musabegovic, I., Özer, M., Djukovic, S., & Jovanovic, S. (2019). Influence of financial technology (Fintech) on financial industry. Економика пољопривреде, 66(4), 1003–1021.

Nakamoto, S. (2008) Bitcoin: A Peer-to-Peer Electronic Cash System. https://bitcoin.org/bitcoin.pdf

Ngo, H. T., & Nguyen, L. T. H. (2024). Consumer adoption intention toward Fintech services in a bank-based financial system in Vietnam. Journal of Financial Regulation and Compliance, 32(2), 153–167. https://doi.org/10.1108/JFRC-08-2021-0061

Nicoletti, B. (2021). Banking 5.0: How Fintech Will Change Traditional Banks in the'New Normal'Post Pandemic. Springer Nature. https://books.google.co.in/books?hl=en&lr=&id=hz83EAAAQBAJ

Orlova, L. V., Afonin, Y. A., & Voronin, V. V. (2015). Talent management and knowledge: Theory, methodology, models. Review of European Studies, 7, 75. doi: 10.5539/res.v7n9p75

Pantielieieva, N., Khutorna, M., Lytvynenko, O., & Potapenko, L. (2020). Fintech, RegTech and Traditional Financial Intermediation: Trends and Threats for Financial Stability. In Lecture Notes on Data Engineering and Communications Technologies (pp. 1–21). https://doi.org/10.1007/978-3-030-35649-1_1

Persmoen, Å. K., & Sandvik, E. (2018). Collaboration between Banks and Fintech Companies: An Assessment of Emerging Organizational Designs within (Master's thesis, Handelshøyskolen BI). https://biopen.bi.no/bi-xmlui/bitstream/handle/11250/2578366/2045933.pdf?sequence=1

Puschmann, T. (2017). Fintech. Business & Information Systems Engineering, 59, 69–76. https://doi.org/10.1007/s12599-017-0464-6

Rashwan, M. H., & Ehab, H. (2016). Comparative efficiency study between Islamic and traditional banks. Available at SSRN 2801187.

Restoy, F. (2019). Regulating Fintech: What Is Going on, and Where Are the Challenges. Bank for International Settlements, 1–7. https://www.suerf.org/wp-content/uploads/2023/12/f_a97f6e2fed-cabc887911dc9b5fd3ccc3_10355_suerf.pdf

Riikkinen, M., & Pihlajamaa, M. (2022). Achieving a strategic fit in Fintech collaboration–A case study of Nordea bank. Journal of Business Research, 152, 461–472. https://doi.org/10.1016/j.jbusres.2022.05.049

Rupeika-Apoga, R., & Thalassinos, E. I. (2020). Ideas for a regulatory definition of Fintech. https://www.um.edu.mt/library/oar/handle/123456789/55195

Sorongan, F. A., Legowo, M. B., & Subanidja, S. (2021). Fintech as the emerging technologies in Banking industry: Past, present, and future. International Journals of Sciences and High Technologies, 28(1), 371–378.

Suprun, A., Petrishina, T., & Vasylchuk, I. (2020). Competition and cooperation between Fintech companies and traditional financial institutions. In E3S Web of Conferences (Vol. 166, p. 13028). EDP Sciences. https://doi.org/10.1051/e3sconf/202016613028

Taherdoost, H. (2023). Fintech: Emerging trends and the future of finance. Financial Technologies and DeFi: A Revisit to the Digital Finance Revolution (pp. 29–39). https://link.springer.com/chapter/10.1007/978-3-031-17998-3_2

Taylor, S., Surridge, M., & Pickering, B. (2021, May). Regulatory compliance modelling using risk management techniques. In 2021 IEEE World AI IoT Congress (AIIoT) (pp. 0474–0481). IEEE. DOI: 10.1109/AIIoT52608.2021.9454188

Vaganova, O., Bykanova, N., Gordya, D., & Evdokimov, D. (2021). Growth points of Fintech industry in the perception of financial market transformation. European Proceedings of Social and Behavioural Sciences, 103. https://www.europeanproceedings.com/article/10.15405/epsbs.2021.03.54

Van Loo, R. (2018). Making innovation more competitive: The case of Fintech. UCLA Law Review, 65, 232. https://heinonline.org/HOL/LandingPage?handle=hein.journals/uclalr65

Wewege, L., Lee, J., & Thomsett, M. C. (2020). Disruptions and digital banking trends. Journal of Applied Finance and Banking, 10(6), 15–56. https://www.researchgate.net/profile/Luigi-Wewege/publication/343050625_Disruptions_and_Digital_Banking_Trends/links/5f136f93a6fdcc3ed7153217/Disruptions-and-Digital-Banking-Trends.pdf

Wewege, L., & Thomsett, M. C. (2019). The Digital Banking Revolution: How Fintech Companies Are Transforming the Retail Banking Industry Through Disruptive Financial Innovation. Walter de Gruyter GmbH & Co KG. https://doi.org/10.1515/9781547401598-205

Yilmaz, A., & Güneş, N. (2015). Efficiency comparison of participation and conventional banking sectors in Turkey between 2007 and 2013. Procedia-Social and Behavioral Sciences, 195, 383–392. https://doi.org/10.1016/j.sbspro.2015.06.338

Chapter 11

Driving Digital Payments: The Transformative Impact of Electronic Fund Transfers

Arpita Nayak, Ipseeta Satpathy, and Alex Khang

11.1 Introduction

Every day, billions of dollars are transferred in cash to governments in emerging and developing countries for a range of reasons, including salaries, social transfers, humanitarian help, and payments to suppliers and farmers. Transitioning from cash to digital payments might potentially enhance the quality of life for low-income individuals, particularly women. It also facilitates the sending and receiving of money in a more accessible, safe, and transparent way for governments, corporations, and international organizations, all of which help to foster inclusive economies. The transfer of money from one account to another for payment using a digital device or conduit is referred to as a digital payment, often called an electronic payment. Bank transfers, mobile money, QR codes, credit, debit, and prepaid cards can all be used to make payments (Kristensen & Solvoll, 2019).

The concept of receiving and making payments has evolved with the rise of digital payments. The digital payment ecosystem is an essential component of modern living due to its seamless and convenient experience. Among the groups of enterprises that have contributed to the simplification of point-of-sale transactions are the digital payment solution providers, which include banks, Fintech firms, IT behemoths, and e-commerce platforms. Since the inception of electronic payments through online banking, digital payment systems have experienced exponential development and a significant technical transition. This was especially true during the COVID-19 epidemic when mobile payments were essential (World Bank Group, 2022).

With a compound annual growth rate (CAGR) of 11.79% between 2023 and 2027, the digital payments industry is expected to reach $14.79 trillion in worldwide transaction value by that time. With the advancements in digital payments, businesses may now effectively handle large-scale transactions, such as payroll and refunds, by utilizing bulk payment systems. Through online

DOI: 10.4324/9781003501947-11

booking and bill payment options, end customers have also profited equally from this progression, having access to a variety of financial and non-financial services under one roof (Ng, 2018). E-commerce websites were made possible by the development of the World Wide Web and the ultimate creation of Web 2.0. Along with many other websites, Amazon was one of the first e-commerce pioneers, having been created in 1994.

Since then, e-commerce payment systems have advanced significantly, enabling retailers to take payments using wireless communications across payment networks using digital wallets and credit/debit cards. Making online payments for products required specialized hardware and software in the early days of electronic payments. For added convenience, digital payment solution providers are now integrating payment switches and bulk payment solutions into e-commerce.

Large and small retailers as well as consumers can accept and process payments using mobile apps, websites, and more scalable point-of-sale hardware (Panetta, Leo & Delle Foglie, 2023). In 2000, the first patent was submitted that specified the mobile payment system specifically. One of the first companies to let users pay with their email addresses on mobile applications was PayPal. Mobile payment solutions have now been adopted by several financial institutions, credit card firms, internet providers, mobile network operators, and global corporations. Customers can submit their credit card information to make purchases using an integrated credit card flow in a basic mobile online payment system.

The cutting-edge and contemporary bill payment options don't need pre-registration on an internet payment platform or card information. Cloud-based mobile wallets, contactless near-field communication (NFC), one-time passwords, two-factor authentication, and QR codes may all be used to make these quick, easy, and safe payments (Toucinho, 2020). The origins of electronic financial transfers may be found in the mid-1800s, during the early stages of telegraphy. Money transfer services were introduced by telegraph firms, enabling anyone to pay money remotely to specific receivers by sending coded signals. Wire transfers were popular as an electronic financial transfer method in the early 1900s. Telegraphic networks were set up by banks and other financial organizations to enable safe and effective money transactions.

Through wire transfers, money may be moved quickly between places by telegraphing payment instructions. Electronic financial transfers were significantly improved with the advent of telex technology in the middle of the 20th century. Banks were able to electronically communicate other financial communications and payment instructions over Telex networks. The Society for Worldwide Interbank Financial Telecommunication was founded in 1973 to offer a uniform platform for interbank payments and secure messaging. Electronic fund transfers (EFTs) were transformed when automated clearing house (ACH) systems were developed in the late 1960s and early 1970s.

The architecture for batch processing transactions made possible by ACH networks allowed financial institutions to electronically transfer money to one another. By automating and streamlining payment processing, ACH systems have decreased the need for human transactions and paper checks. In the 1970s, the phrase "Electronic Funds Transfer" came to refer to a wider range of electronic payment options. Beyond wire transfers, EFTs also encompassed point-of-sale transactions, direct deposits, and electronic bill payments. EFT systems eliminated the need for physical currency or cheques by enabling both consumers and companies to transfer money electronically.

Strong security measures were put in place as electronic financial transfers became more popular to guard against fraud and unauthorized activities. Secure networks, multi-factor authentication, and encryption technologies have all been created to guarantee the secrecy and integrity of electronic payments (Mayanja & Omwono, 2022). EFT transfers are often extremely simple. The sender and the recipient of the cash are the two persons involved. After the sender starts the transfer, the request travels from the internet or a payment terminal to the sender's bank and then to the bank of the recipient via several digital networks. Senders can be anyone, such as a company, an employer, or a customer paying a vendor for a good or service like energy.

Recipients may also include organizations such as utility providers, shops, employees, and suppliers of commodities. The majority of payments are processed and finished in a few days. The security of the EFT is among its finest advantages. Even while sending money via the internet carries some risk, EFT is usually thought to be a more secure payment option than using a traditional paper cheque.

Certain EFT formats, such as the ACH, are safer than others. Using businesses you are familiar with and trust, or a reputable source in the event of a suggestion, is the best method to guarantee an EFT free from tampering. Making the appropriate choices while navigating EFT for your business may be aided by using third-party organizations like as EBANX (Wang & Li, 2022). A recent study in Shopify (an e-commerce platform) highlighted the seven major kinds of ETF payment (Shopify, 2023, February 6) as shown in Figure 11.1.

Here is description of types of EFT payments

- ACH payments: One of the largest networks in the United States for transferring money between bank accounts is the ACH. Unlike traditional credit card networks, which are owned and run by for-profit businesses, ACH debit and credit payments are processed via the ACH network, which is governed by National Automated Clearinghouse Association and partially run by the Federal Reserve. The settlement time for ACH payments is two to three business days. Both credits and debits can result from ACH transactions. Crucially, not all EFTs are ACH payments, even though all ACH payments are a kind of EFT.
- Direct deposits: An EFT is when you arrange for your company to deposit your paycheck straight into your bank account. One sort of transfer meant to make paying employees easier is called direct deposit. Usually, a third-party service provider facilitates this. The employer sets the frequency and number of benefits that each employee should get; the supplier handles the rest on its own
- ATMs (automated teller machines): An ATM updates your bank account balance by EFT when you make a withdrawal or deposit, saving you from having to visit a real bank office.
- Credit and debit cards: Most likely, you pay bills, make purchases, and transfer money between bank accounts frequently using your credit or debit card. Each of these is an example of an EFT payment that customers can use to pay for products and services.

Types of EFT Payments	ACH payments
	Direct deposit
	ATMs (automated teller machines)
	Credit and debit cards
	Wire transfers
	Pay-by-phone systems
	Electronic checks

Figure 11.1 Types of EFT payments.

- Wire transfers: When transferring big sums of money, such as a down payment on a home, wire transfers are the preferred EFT method. A wire transfer is usually used by individuals or businesses to cover the cost of expensive purchases that exceed typical consumer expenditures.
- Pay-by-phone systems: Although less widespread, this variant of EFT is still in use today. Some individuals rely on phone-based systems to start payments for paying bills or transferring funds between bank accounts. These technologies transform the transfer request into a form that computers can understand and process.
- Electronic checks: They work just like checks made on paper, only without the paper. To effectively finish a transaction, you need to enter your bank account information and routing number into an EFT payment provider.

The COVID-19 pandemic and the global expansion of formal financial services have reportedly contributed significantly to the surge in digital payments. The result of this is financial inclusion. The Global Findex 2021 database indicates that this expansion enhanced family resilience to better resist financial shocks, decreased the gender gap in account ownership, and opened up new economic opportunities. In 2021, 76% of people globally had an account with a bank, other financial institution, or mobile money provider, up from 68% in 2017 and 51% in 2011.

Notably, the rise in account ownership was distributed fairly among a significantly greater number of countries. In 34 countries, the percentage of account owners has increased by double digits since 2017, according to this year's research; however, in previous Findex surveys over the previous 10 years, much of the growth was concentrated in China and India. The pandemic has also led to an increase in the use of digital payments. In low- and middle-income countries (aside from China), over 40% of people who made merchant in-store or online payments using a card, phone, or the internet have done so for the first time since the pandemic's start.

More than one-third of those who paid their electricity bills directly from a formal account reported having this experience in every low- and middle-income economy. More than 80 million people in India and more than 100 million adults in China made their first digital merchant payment after the epidemic. Currently, two-thirds of people send and receive money digitally worldwide; in developing countries, this number rose from 35% in 2014 to 57% in 2021. In developing nations, 71% of individuals have an account with a bank, mobile money provider, or other financial institution, up from 42% in 2011 and 63% in 2017.

Mobile money accounts have greatly expanded financial inclusion in Sub-Saharan Africa. The global market for electronic financial transfers is projected to reach USD 129.24 billion by 2030, up from USD 66.31 billion in 2022. As shown in Figure 11.2, the worldwide market is anticipated to grow at a CAGR of 8.70% over the course of the estimated timeframe.

EFTs not only facilitate cross-border transactions and international trade, but they also give e-commerce companies the ability to conduct cross-border transactions. This makes e-commerce more global. EFTs play a crucial role in ensuring the security and integrity of online transactions by developing reliable encryption technologies and strong authentication methods. This fosters trust between customers and merchants.

11.2 E-Commerce Evolution

Undoubtedly, one of the most significant areas of a person's life is their finances. For example, the first thing family, friends, and well-wishers can do for someone in an emergency is to assist them

EFT Market Size, 2022 to 2030 USD Billion

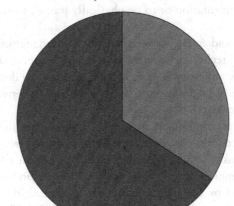

■ 2022   ■ 2030

Figure 11.2   EFT market size 2022 to 2030 USD billion.

Source: https://www.vantagemarketresearch.com/industry-report/electronic-funds-transfer-market-1501

receive the money they need as soon as possible. However, what if the individual resides in a different time zone or across international borders? What happens if they require the money as soon as possible? Since the 1990s, EFTs have made it easier for consumers to move money easily and smoothly over the world.

The funds are moved to the specified account in a matter of seconds thanks to computer technology and little assistance from bank employees. Money can be sent directly between bank accounts using an electronic payment called an EFT. Credit cards, the internet, and automated bill payments are all examples of EFTs, which are the most popular methods of transferring money. The acceptance of EFT payment methods has made it so common that many individuals no longer even carry cash.

All around the nation, parking meters are becoming digital. You may electronically transfer money between banks or between individuals via an internet network by using EFTs. Since the transactions are digital, paper documentation is not necessary. This greatly speeds up the process and makes EFTs more accessible than with certain other methods of money transmission (Świecka, Terefenko & Paprotny, 2021). When sending money to a recipient, the sender creates electronic signals that are used by ETFs. The signals to start and continue the payment are instantly received by the networks, servers, and payment terminals.

Numerous parties can be both the sender and the recipient, including merchants, suppliers to customers, and employers to their staff. The accessibility of ETFs combined with transaction security is what makes them so well-liked. They also happen quite quickly; the money is credited either right away or in a matter of days. ETF is achievable by the initiation of a digital check, often between merchants and vendors during the purchase process, direct deposit, and phone payments for utility, ATM, card, and internet purchases with the appropriate permission.

To ensure security, ETFs are encrypted using 128-bit signals. They are therefore quick, safe, and economical for enterprises. Setting it up takes relatively little work; typically, you need a bank account and the right paperwork to enable transfers just during the setup process. There is no requirement to present documentation or to be physically present to start the transfer (Mayanja & Omwono, 2022).

Sending money quickly and easily between individuals is made simple by apps like Venmo, PayPal, and Cash App. EFT technology is used by these peer-to-peer (P2P) payment systems to transfer money. You can link any or both of your bank account and debit card when you register to use one of these programs. You can connect your credit card to certain applications, but there will often be a fee for each transaction.

To transfer a payment, launch the app, input the recipient's details, validate the transaction, and send the money. P2P networks can serve as repositories for received money. Some consumers don't utilize these applications to send money to their banks. They use the P2P network as a make-shift bank account, leaving money in the app to pay suppliers and individuals directly.

Debit cards are provided by certain P2P payment programs, like PayPal, to facilitate user access to monies stored on the payment network (Ndlovu, 2020). Since they provide a way to perform financial transactions electronically without the need for physical currency or cheques, EFTs operate as a middleman in the digitization and automation of money transfers. EFTs make it quick and simple to move money across accounts, giving participants instant access to both the sender's and the recipient's money.

The EFT system allows customers to begin transactions whenever and wherever they choose, and it is available not just after banking hours but also online around the clock, anywhere there is internet access. With the availability of remote access via mobile applications, internet banking, and other unusual sources, customers may complete significant transactions without having to relocate or worry about deadlines.

Customers are given the flexibility to select their preferred payment method by using a variety of payment methods that are supported by EFTs, such as credit/debit cards, bank transfers, digital wallets, and mobile payments. EFT systems also offer the option of automated recurring payments. Because you may arrange payments in advance, you can avoid doing manual transfers if you have registered for bills or any other type of payment (Baya et al., n.d.). One kind of electronic money transfer, or EFT, is an ACH transfer that makes it easy to transfer funds. Banks and other financial institutions around the country that manage electronic cash transfers are part of the ACH network.

The bank will notify the recipient bank or institution to transfer funds from your account to the account of the individual or company you are paying when you make an ACH transfer. Transferring money between accounts is easy using ACH transfers. They may be used to transmit money to someone else, move money between accounts, and pay bills. With the account number and routing number for the account, you are transferring the money to make an ACH transfer. It's important to remember that ACH transactions might take several days to process. Therefore, you might want to think about utilizing an alternative technique if you need to shift money urgently (Karim & Hasan, 2021).

Through the instantaneous and direct transfer of funds between accounts made possible by EFTs, both the sender and the recipient have access to funds right away. In contrast to the usual planned hours, EFT systems are constantly open, allowing you to use internet banking, mobile banking, or any other electronic channel depending on the facility to complete your transaction even on holidays, evenings, or weekends.

Credit/debit cards, bank transfers, digital wallets, and mobile payments are just a few of the payment methods that EFTs Best offers. You have the freedom to choose the payment method that best suits your needs by selecting from those possibilities. They not only give you a location to keep and spend money, but they also create practical mechanisms for automated repeating payments, saving you the trouble of setting up recurring transactions for subscriptions and bills more than once.

The EFTs speed up transaction completion and reduce processing times by doing away with the need for paper documentation. Additionally, these techniques offer robust security features like encryption and signature validation to ensure the security of your transactions. EFTs are widely used in the fast-paced digital age because they are safe, easy to use, and time-efficient (Jovanovski, 2021). In general, EFTs are always evolving and creating new methods as they provide several new paradigms to the company and financial systems. In the dynamic world of technology, where consumer tastes are more varied, EFTs have the potential to significantly contribute to financial inclusion, innovation, and worldwide economic expansion.

11.3 Making It Trustworthy

Enhanced Security Measures in EFT transactions are encrypted, an unauthorized access is prevented by the encoder, which makes the data transmitted during the transmission process confidential. This encryption makes sure that even if hackers manage to intercept the data, they would find it extremely difficult to decipher. They won't be able to identify transaction amounts or account numbers. All authorization and verification processes in EFT systems occur on computer networks that are geographically apart from the terminals (Khang, Dave, Jadhav et al., 2024).

These kinds of technologies can be applied to customer–retailer transactions. The client inserts his card and provides personal identifying data (PID) while the store inputs the transaction amount on the EFT terminal. The computer of the card issuer checks the entries and approves money transactions. Such EFT communications need to be shielded from surveillance, which might provide associated PID and customer identifier pairs to interceptors. Then, these criminals might either make their cards or take ones for which they knew the PID.

Furthermore, measures must be used to stop queue manipulation, which allows criminals to alter the quantities. Encryption might be used to prevent alterations to data (Garnica and Kiuhan, 2023). Encrypting the data that is sent between the participants in the transaction is one of the fundamental EFT security precautions. Information is jumbled up into a code that only authorized receivers can decode thanks to encryption.

Authentication uses techniques like passwords, PINs, biometrics, or tokens to confirm the sender and recipient's identities and authenticity. The EFT data cannot be accessed, intercepted, or altered by outside parties thanks to encryption and authentication (Elbasir et al., 2020). Monitoring and examining EFT transactions for any indications of fraud or questionable activity is another way to secure EFT transactions.

Tools for preventing and detecting fraud utilize rules, algorithms, or machine learning to find and highlight any unusual or suspicious patterns or behaviors. They can identify anomalous transaction amounts, locations, frequency, or beneficiaries, for instance. Tools for detecting and preventing fraud can also notify the appropriate authorities of any fraudulent transactions and warn, stop, or reverse them (Jamra et al., 2020).

Respecting the laws and rules governing the EFT sector and defending the rights and interests of both providers and clients is the third EFT security measure. Regulation and compliance ensure that EFT transactions follow the rules and regulations of the appropriate authorities, including the National Automated Clearing House Association, the Consumer Financial Protection Bureau, and the Federal Reserve. To comply with regulations, EFT providers must also put in place sufficient security policies, processes, and controls in addition to performing frequent audits and assessments.

Respecting the laws and rules governing the EFT sector and defending the rights and interests of both providers and clients is the third EFT security measure. Regulation and compliance ensure that EFT transactions follow the rules and regulations of the appropriate authorities, including the National Automated Clearing House Association, the Consumer Financial Protection Bureau, and the Federal Reserve. To comply with regulations, EFT providers must also put in place sufficient security policies, processes, and controls in addition to performing frequent audits and assessments.

An electronic financial transfer may be done securely with EFT. It does away with the necessity for paper money, such as checks, which might be misplaced or stolen. Since money is transmitted straight between bank accounts using EFT, there is less chance of theft and fraud. It does away with the need for paper checks and bills by transferring money electronically between financial institutions.

Electronic financial transfers have been secured for years through the use of cryptography. However, cryptographic safeguards are still in their infancy when it comes to the electronic data exchange environment. The purpose of the study is to analyze the security control mechanism and the way the electronic money transfer procedure operates. The Society for Worldwide Interbank Financial Telecommunications System, a standard-leading interbank payment system, is introduced to assess data security and communication methods (Mohammed & Aysan, 2014).

With the increasing use of sophisticated payment systems, EFT is becoming more and more prevalent and offers several advantages to a variety of industries. First of all, it reduces the amount of time required for businesses to handle large amounts of payments to their vendors and suppliers by doing away with the need for paper checks and human handling. The second reason is that EFT becomes extremely cost-effective as it does away with expenses like cheque printing, postage, and direct processing while also lowering the chance of fraud and mistakes.

Since two-factor authentication is the most effective security layer component, several EFT systems have adopted it. It is necessary to apply two of the identity-check strategies. Consider the following scenario: you are utilizing your online banking service. A multiplication factor that was delivered to your registered email address or phone number comes after your password. The firewall, the second crucial security component, seems to be the most important defense for the EFT system structure. It operates by keeping an eye on both inbound and outbound network traffic, which makes it easier to filter out any unauthorized access attempts.

Firewalls bolster EFT system security against cyber-attacks that might compromise sensitive data by identifying concerning behaviors and stopping them before they are completed. The firewall, the second crucial security component, seems to be the most important defense for the EFT system structure. It operates by keeping an eye on both inbound and outbound network traffic, which makes it easier to filter out any unauthorized access attempts. Firewalls bolster EFT system security against cyber-attacks that might compromise sensitive data by identifying concerning behaviors and stopping them before they are completed (Prabha, MuthuKumaran & Sathyasri, 2023).

Another aspect is that the banking industry has been greatly impacted by EFT, which makes it possible for quick and safe money transfers between various platforms. EFT transfers can take place between banks or inside a single financial institution. These transactions are often carried out using computer-based systems and don't require actual checks or cash, which makes them a practical choice for both people and companies. EFTs use digital and computer technologies to function.

The banking system transfers money between bank accounts when an EFT is started by using ACH networks. For safe transmission, all of the transaction information—including account numbers and the amount to be transferred—is encrypted. The recipient's bank checks the information after receiving the transaction details, at which point it transfers the money into the account of choice (Masihuddin et al., 2017).

The establishment of the Electronic Fund Transfer Act has been an addition to provide more security to the people and make transactions safer for the customers. President Jimmy Carter of the United States signed the Electronic Funds Transfer Act (EFTA) into law in November 1978. US legislation known as the EFTA was created to safeguard consumers when they purchase online or use EFTs for banking. Regulation E of the Federal Reserve Board is another name for the EFTA. In essence, it describes the obligations that financial institutions and their clients have when it comes to carrying out EFTs.

Financial institutions are required, for example, to notify customers of potential liabilities if their payment card is lost or stolen. This has to explain how the organization will assist the client in resolving the issue and specific contact details (often a phone number) for reporting misplaced or stolen credit cards. Customers who inform their bank within certain time constraints under the EFTA are also released from liability for unauthorized transactions (including those made with a lost or stolen credit/debit card) to some extent.

Furthermore, banks have to set a daily cap on the amount of money that customers may withdraw with their debit cards. This lessens the chance that clients may have money taken out of their accounts by big or frequent withdrawals, particularly ones that are not authorized. Electronic financial transfers are still developing at a fast pace. The payment environment is changing as a result of emerging technologies like digital currencies, blockchain, and mobile banking apps. New prospects for improved user experiences and frictionless financial transfers are presented by the emergence of open banking initiatives and the incorporation of artificial intelligence (Khang, Dave, Katore et al., 2024).

11.4 Technological Innovations

Technological innovations continue to change in step with the rate of advancement in EFT technology, which offers new levels of efficiency, safety, and convenience for online financial transactions. One of the key leading technologies in payments is the uninterrupted, secure environment in which transactions are conducted these days.

One of the many advantages of EFTs is their superiority over conventional payment methods. Above all, they offer a higher transfer rate, which allows them to process payments more quickly than mailing cash or checks—though some can still take a few days to process. Second, EFTs provide users flexibility by enabling them to conduct most of their transactions online, negating the need for market players to physically visit banks or retail locations.

Because of this commodity, commerce may be performed virtually without any obstacles for participants, giving users even more flexibility. Furthermore, EFTs have included the automated capability. This makes it possible to plan for the recurring payments. Because this feature takes care of the financial procedures, there's no need to take out cash or use a cheque or indication each time a financial transaction is made. ETTs are incredibly affordable and easy since they transfer funds online without using paper checks or stamps.

Further, as EFTs are often managed by machines, they lower the possibility of errors while doing cash, checks, or more generally, person-handled transactions. EFTs offer the highest level of security since they electronically verify and transmit funds, reducing the possibility of money theft or cheque fraud. In terms of contemporary digital payment systems, it is reasonable to say that EFTs are prosperous in terms of security, ease, and speed (Kitbuncha, 2017).

A significant technical shift in the field of electronic financial transfers was brought about by digital wallets. These days, consumers may purchase in apps or online without needing several plastic cards or wallets since they can pay using their mobile device for every transaction. They provide customers with a personal vault where they may save all of their financial assets—including bank accounts, credit/debit cards, and even digital coins—in one convenient storage place. With only a few clicks, customers may now access an online or physical business and utilize their mobile to make payments thanks to this simplification of the payment process.

The Government of India has actively pushed citizens to embrace mobile wallets and cashless payments, and the mobile wallet payment system is seen as a component of the nation's economic development. The government's push for the use of mobile wallets is perceived as a means of advancing financial inclusion and stimulating the economy.

According to the report, consumers find using mobile wallets to be convenient when transferring money, and they play a significant role in enabling cashless transactions. This suggests that one important part of using a mobile wallet in India is transferring money. Through a mobile application, a merchant can send a payment request to a customer's mobile device using the mobile wallet solution. The request is received by the customer's mobile device's microphone after being sent as an audio signal from the merchant's mobile device's speaker.

The consumer is prompted to accept or reject the payment request via the customer's mobile device, which has the mobile application loaded. The mobile app notifies the consumer's bank to transfer money from their account to the merchant's bank account when the customer accepts the payment request. There is no need for extra gear while making proximity payments; they are made just using mobile devices. As an additional security feature, the mobile wallet solution provides voice recognition login in addition to face recognition login.

Through the use of a mobile wallet, customers may link their phone number to a bank account and conduct transactions. Using a non-contact information read-in device, a payer may read an electronic tag carrying a payee's user information. They can then use their cell phone to send the electronic tag, their own user information, account password, and payment amount to the bank. The bank authenticates the transaction between the payer and the payee and checks the information that was sent.

A certain sum of money is sent from the payer's account to the payee's account if the transaction is successful. Short messages are used to notify the payer and the payee that the transaction was successful. Both consumers and organizations now spend much less for transactions thanks to digital payment methods. Mobile wallet transactions sometimes have reduced or no costs when compared to more conventional payment options like cash or credit cards. Financial transactions are now cheaper for both consumers and organizations, particularly for low-value transactions thanks to the cost decrease (Wang & Li, 2022). Users in India can transfer funds from their bank accounts to their M-Wallets using M-Wallet services. These funds can then be utilized for a variety of purposes, including bill payments, shopping, ticket purchases, and recharging (Khang & Jadhav et al., 2024).

In M-wallets comparison to other payment methods, these services are more affordable, convenient, and user-friendly—especially for money transfers. Convenience, simplicity of usage, and need following demonetization are some of the reasons driving the rise in M-Wallet acceptance. The adoption of M-wallets varies depending on age and gender, according to the study reported in the paper. This suggests that different demographic groups may embrace and use these services to varying degrees (Wadhera, Dabas & Malhotra, 2017).

The introduction of state-of-the-art contactless payment has resulted in an incredible revolution in EFTs. Without credit/debit cards and POS terminals coming into direct contact, contactless payment devices may do transactions more conveniently thanks to NFC and RFID technologies. People may now effortlessly complete transactions at the checkout by just tapping their wearable technology, smartphone, or contactless-enabled card. This innovation has greatly increased transaction speed and convenience (Dubey, Sonar et al., 2020).

Because contactless payments employ sophisticated security features like tokenization and encryption to prevent fraud in digital payments, they are thought to be more secure than conventional payment systems. Customers may rest easy knowing that their financial and personal information is secure as a result. When compared to more conventional payment methods like cash or card swipes, contactless payments give customers a significantly speedier and more convenient choice.

Customers may benefit from reduced wait times and speedier transactions as a consequence, improving their overall shopping experience. The surge in contactless payment solutions brought about by COVID-19 has coincided with a rise in the use of mobile payment technologies. The simplicity and accessibility of this payment option are further enhanced by the ability for consumers to use their cell phones to make purchases (Trütsch, 2020).

Customers may use contactless payments to make purchases with simply their smartphones or smartwatches, leaving their wallets and cash at home. This provides customers with a more ordered and efficient solution in addition to speeding up and simplifying the payment procedure. Moreover, advanced security procedures are often included in the wallets to enhance the protection of personal payment information through the use of phone tokenization and biometric verification (such as fingerprint or face recognition).

By encouraging access to digital payments, the reliance on mobile wallets has upended traditional payment methods, which has boosted transaction speeds, security, and contactless payment capabilities. It has also made financial inclusion possible for people all over the world. With the rapid advancement of mobile technology, mobile wallets have the potential to be at the forefront of this development and the shift that comes with the future of EFTs. Retailers' checkout processes have greatly improved thanks to contactless payments, which enable quicker and more effective transaction completion. Shorter lines and speedier transactions may arise from this, giving customers a better overall shopping experience and freeing up employees to concentrate on other duties.

Customers are more satisfied when contactless payments provide them with a smoother, more convenient way to make purchases. Retailers who accept contactless payment options are perceived as more cutting-edge and contemporary, which helps them draw in and keep consumers. The advent of contactless payments has spurred rivalry and innovation in the retail sector as companies compete to set themselves apart from the competition and provide customers with the newest and most cutting-edge payment choices. This may lead to more money being invested in cutting-edge technology and the creation of fresh, creative solutions to satisfy changing customer demands (Trütsch, 2020).

The introduction of digital currencies, including well-known examples like Bitcoin, Ethereum, and stablecoins for EFTs, completely changed how people made payments and even transferred money via EFTs. Like traditional currencies, digital assets arise without a central bank or government. The network's computer users work together to maintain the money. The adoption of Bitcoin by service providers, internet shops, and growing retailers is the other essential component needed for its survival. They also exhibit certain benefits for both the global financial system and individual users when they are formed as digital currencies. First and foremost, because they don't make concessions to middlemen like banks and payment processors, they don't charge greater transaction costs than traditional institutions, especially when it comes to cross-border transactions. It enables a large reduction in potential costs, particularly for distant channels like e-commerce and overseas remittances (Khang & Hajimahmud, 2024).

Furthermore, quick payments are made possible by digital currencies; a transaction may be finalized in a matter of minutes to hours, as opposed to days in the case of traditional banking systems. Additionally, by providing underprivileged areas with an alternative banking system based on an open-source technology platform, digital currencies may be utilized to support microfinance in those communities (Sunil, 2020).

11.5 Conclusion

EFT has completely changed the financial industry by providing a safer and more effective substitute for conventional cash or cheque transactions. The world is moving towards a more digital future, therefore being able to navigate the intricacies of EFT—from its operation to its variety of applications will be crucial as we navigate this new economic environment. Deep comprehension of EFTs is a useful skill, regardless of your role—business owner, digital consumer, or hobbyist banker. The way currencies are transported around has changed thanks to EFT, making it possible to complete transactions using a far better technique. It is less costly, safer, and more practical.

Many individuals, from laborers on strike to companies trying to maximize profits, use EFTs on a daily basis as a crucial component of contemporary trade. The rise in popularity of digital payments has been influenced by technology advancements such as contactless payments and mobile wallets, which are moving society one step closer to a cashless society.

Another argument is that EFTs facilitated efficient cross-border transactions while also enabling the provision of banking services to a larger population. The more we embrace digital progress, the more EFTs play a role in reshaping the payment landscape and fostering an atmosphere that encourages innovation, convenience, and connectedness in the global economy. All parties involved in the first EFT-based payment ecosystem are expected to profit from the venture, including consumers, companies, and economies. The future looks bright since customer preferences and technological improvements will also determine its speed (Khang & Satpathy, 2024).

References

Baya, C. R. S., & Ruthwinnie, M. (n.d.). Effectiveness of Electronic Funds Transfer on Fee Collection in Private Universities in Nakuru County, Kenya. https://www.theijbmt.com/archive/0947/800095486.pdf

Dubey, V., Sonar, R., & Mohanty, A. (2020). Fintech, RegTech and contactless payments through the lens of COVID 19 times. International Journal of Advanced Science and Technology, 29(6), 3727–3734. https://www.researchgate.net/profile/Vivek-Dubey-7/publication/342663514_FinTech_RegTech_and_Contactless_Payments_Through_the_Lens_of_COVID_19_Times/links/5eff39fd92851c52d6139503/FinTech-RegTech-and-Contactless-Payments-Through-the-Lens-of-COVID-19-Times.pdf

Elbasir, M., Elareshi, M., Habes, M., & Aissani, R. (2020). The influence of trust, security and reliability of multimedia payment on the adoption of EPS in Libya. Multicultural. Education, 6(5), 53–68. https://www.researchgate.net/profile/Mohammed-Habes/publication/346927859_The_Influence_of_Trust_Security_and_Reliability_of_Multimedia_Payment_on_the_Adoption_of_EPS_in_Libya/links/5fd257ee45851568d154c431/The-Influence-of-Trust-Security-and-Reliability-of-Multimedia-Payment-on-the-Adoption-of-EPS-in-Libya.pdf

Garnica Toro, Ó. A., & Kiuhan Vásquez, S. A. (2023). Promoting financial inclusion: do unconditional e-money transfers work?. https://repositorio.uniandes.edu.co/items/f1471e89-a6db-4502-8713-3a88318007e6

Jamra, R. K., Anggorojati, B., Sensuse, D. I., & Suryono, R. R. (2020, October). Systematic Review of Issues and Solutions for Security in E-commerce. In 2020 International Conference on Electrical Engineering and Informatics (ICELTICs) (pp. 1–5). IEEE. https://ieeexplore.ieee.org/abstract/document/9315437/

Jovanovski, L. (2021). Management with decided types of international financial transfers. New Knowledge Journal of Science, 10(2). http://www.science.uard.bg/index.php/newknowledge/article/view/786

Karim, Y., & Hasan, R. (2021). Taming the digital bandits: An analysis of digital bank heists and a system for detecting fake messages in electronic funds transfer. In National Cyber Summit (NCS) Research Track 2020 (pp. 193–210). Springer International Publishing. https://link.springer.com/chapter/10.1007/978-3-030-58703-1_12

Khang, A., Dave, T., Jadhav, B., Katore, D., & Dave, D., Gig Financial Economy- Big Data and Analytics. In Khang A. Jadhav B., Hajimahmud V. A., Satpathy I., (1st Ed.) (2024). The Synergy of AI and Fintech in the Digital Gig Economy. (1st Ed.) (2024). CRC Press. https://doi.org/10.1201/9781032720104-16

Khang, A., Dave, T., Katore, D., Jadhav, B., & Dave, D., Leveraging Blockchain and Smart Contracts For Gig Payments. In Khang A. Jadhav B., Hajimahmud V. A., Satpathy I., (1st Ed.) (2024). The Synergy of AI and Fintech in the Digital Gig Economy. (1st Ed.) (2024). CRC Press. https://doi.org/10.1201/9781032720104-11

Khang, A., & Hajimahmud, V. A., "Introduction to the Gig Economy," In Khang A. Jadhav B., Hajimahmud V. A., Satpathy I., The Synergy of AI and Fintech in the Digital Gig Economy. (1st Ed.) (2024). CRC Press. https://doi.org/10.1201/9781032720104-1

Khang, A., Jadhav, B., Dave, T., & Katore, T., Artificial Intelligence (AI) in Fintech - Enhancing Financial Services. In Khang A. Jadhav B., Hajimahmud V. A., Satpathy I., (1st Ed.) (2024). The Synergy of AI and Fintech in the Digital Gig Economy. (1st Ed.) (2024). CRC Press. https://doi.org/10.1201/9781032720104-10

Khang, A., Jadhav, B., Hajimahmud, V. A., & Satpathy, I., (1st Ed.) (2024). The Synergy of AI and Fintech in the Digital Gig Economy. CRC Press. https://doi.org/10.1201/9781032720104

Kitbuncha, W. (2017). Legal measures on authentication of electronic fund transfer. https://repository.au.edu/server/api/core/bitstreams/75d9b927-6871-4cae-8c87-47442002d8d6/content

Kristensen, L. B. K., & Solvoll, M. (2019). Digital payments for a digital generation. Nordic Journal of Media Studies, 1(1), 125–136. https://sciendo.com/article/10.2478/njms-2019-0008

Masihuddin, M., Khan, B. U. I., Mattoo, M. M. U. I., & Olanrewaju, R. F. (2017). A survey on e-payment systems: Elements, adoption, architecture, challenges and security concepts. Indian Journal of Science and Technology.

Mayanja, N. S., & Omwono, G. A. (2022). Evolution of E-Funds Transfer and Its Impact on Customer Satisfaction. https://ijeber.com/uploads2022/ijeber_02_12.pdf

Mohammed, A., & Aysan, M. (2014). Implementation of electronic fund transfer using new symmetric key algorithm based on simple logarithm. International Journal of Scientific Research in Science, Engineering and Technology, 3(4), 10–16. https://www.indianjournals.com/ijor.aspx?target=ijor:ijari e&volume=3&issue=4&article=002

Ndlovu, W. N. (2020). The regulation of electronic funds transfers: problematic aspects relating to banks liability (Doctoral dissertation, University of Pretoria). https://search.proquest.com/openview/eab04ee991f1026955471eb36884ac94/1?pq-origsite=gscholar&cbl=2026366&diss=y

Ng, D. (2018). Evolution of digital payments: Early learnings from Singapore's cashless payment drive. Journal of Payments Strategy & Systems, 11(4), 306–312. https://www.ingentaconnect.com/content/hsp/jpss/2018/00000011/00000004/art00004

Panetta, I. C., Leo, S., & Delle Foglie, A. (2023). The development of digital payments–Past, present, and future–From the literature. Research in International Business and Finance, 64, 101855. https://www.sciencedirect.com/science/article/pii/S0275531922002410

Prabha, M., MuthuKumaran, D., & Sathyasri, B. (2023, November). Tunnel based Fund Transfer over the Internet using AES Algorithm. In 2023 9th International Conference on Smart Structures and Systems (ICSSS) (pp. 1–4). IEEE. https://ieeexplore.ieee.org/abstract/document/10407817/

Shopify (2023, February 6). What is an EFT payment? Definition and examples (2024). https://www.shopify.com/blog/eft-payment

Sunil, S. (2020). Analysis of Trends and Growth of Digital Retail Payments System in India. Financial Econometrics. https://files.osf.io/v1/resources/9dy3x/providers/osfstorage/5e734d114a60a504c4bb3e9c?action=download&direct&version=1#page=67

Świecka, B., Terefenko, P., & Paprotny, D. (2021). Transaction factors' influence on the choice of payment by Polish consumers. Journal of Retailing and Consumer Services, 58, 102264. https://www.sciencedirect.com/science/article/pii/S0969698920312728

Toucinho, A. (2020). How payments drive digital transformation. Journal of Payments Strategy & Systems, 14(1), 10–13. https://www.ingentaconnect.com/content/hsp/jpss/2020/00000014/00000001/art00003

Trütsch, T. (2020). The impact of contactless payment on cash usage at an early stage of diffusion. Swiss Journal of Economics and Statistics, 156, 1–35. https://link.springer.com/article/10.1186/s41937-020-00050-0

Wadhera, T., Dabas, R., & Malhotra, P. (2017). Adoption of m-wallet: A way ahead. International Journal of Engineering and Management Research (IJEMR), 7(4), 1–7. https://www.indianjournals.com/ijor.aspx?target=ijor:ijemr&volume=7&issue=4&article=001

Wang, D., & Li, G. (2022). The best decision for e-commerce funds transfer based on cloud computing technique. Mathematical Problems in Engineering, 2022. https://onlinelibrary.wiley.com/doi/pdf/10.1155/2022/9432413

World Bank Group. (2022, June 28). Covid-19 drives global surge in use of digital payments. World Bank. https://www.worldbank.org/en/news/press-release/2022/06/29/covid-19-drives-global-surge-in-use-of-digital-payments

Chapter 12

Robotic Process Automation: A Streamlining Advancement for Banking and Finance Sector

Diksha Jindal and Mohit Gupta

12.1 Introduction

In the rapidly changing fields of finance and banking, where precision and speed are critical, staying ahead requires mastering cutting-edge technologies. Robotic process automation (RPA) is one such innovation, a game changer that has the potential to transform traditional banking processes, making them more efficient and effective than ever before. Before RPA, business process management (BPM) techniques were used in IT programs and associated procedures to make the processes visible and efficient. They improved the flow, but only at great expense to the process's development; even so, it cannot be considered fully automated. So here's where RPA comes in, offering a path to overcome this challenge.

RPA is the use of software applications to process tasks that have already been performed by humans (Oshri & Plugge, 2021). Similarly, it is the term used in banking and finance to describe the use of robotic technologies to supplement human labour (Wangoo, 2023). In other words, RPA facilitates the digital transformation of banks and financial institutions by automating repetitive and high-volume business processes, freeing up staff members to concentrate on more important work, and ultimately improving client satisfaction. Imagine a diligent virtual assistant filling out forms, navigating menus, and logging into apps. That is the concept of RPA in action. Tasks requiring a high level of interaction among users and little variability are best suited for this.

According to Hindle (2018), the phrase "robotic process automation" was originally used in 2012. When businesses started reporting significant savings from automation in 2014 and 2015, it started gaining traction. The RPA market is anticipated to grow to new heights by 2030,

DOI: 10.4324/9781003501947-12

with a predicted worldwide market size of USD 30.85 billion and a compound annual growth rate of 39.9% from 2023 to 2030 (Grand View Research, 2024). The growing need for reduced operational expenses and the simplicity of integrating RPA with business processes to handle complicated tasks are the main drivers of this rise. RPA applications in banking and finance are extensive and diverse, encompassing front-office, middle-office, and back-office tasks. The numerous ways that RPA is being used in banking and other financial services demonstrate its true power.

Now, let's take a closer look at the essential elements of RPA adoption in the banking and finance industries. This study seeks to offer thorough insights into maximizing the potential of RPA in fostering operational efficiency and competitive advantage in the financial sector, from comprehending its practical uses to investigating the opportunities and problems it poses.

12.2 Core Components and Functionalities of RPA Technology

Using a simulation of human-digital interaction, RPA automates repetitive operations. A McKinsey report states that RPA can automate more than 30% of tasks in about 60% of occupations (Digital/McKinsey, 2019). Fundamentally, RPA technology is based on a set of key elements that coordinate to automate routine tasks. Financial institutions can unleash the full potential of RPA by gaining a comprehensive understanding of these factors and their interplay, enabling innovation and competitiveness in an ever-changing landscape as shown in Figure 12.1.

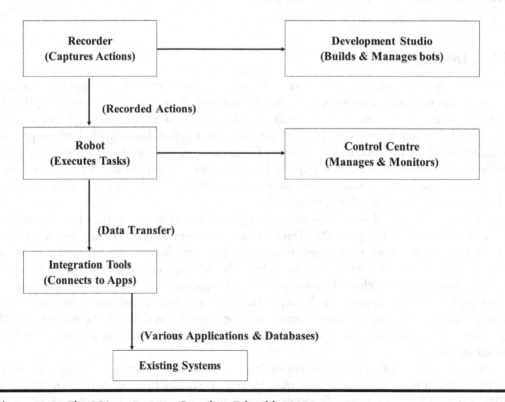

Figure 12.1   The RPA ecosystem. (Based on Tripathi, 2018.)

Explanation of components

■ Recorder: This part records user behaviour while they engage with different apps, serving as a virtual shoulder. It basically "records" the actions taken during a process, such as selecting menu items, clicking buttons, entering text, and manipulating data. The recorded activities act as a blueprint for the RPA bots.
■ Development studio: The main hub for developing and managing RPA bots is the development studio. Users can use a drag-and-drop interface to visually construct workflows or take advantage of pre-built functionalities. Developers can further customize bots by integrating decision points and logic. The bot could be designed, for instance, to deal with differences in the automated process, such as acting differently in response to particular data that is encountered.
■ Robot: Following the completion of the development procedure, the robot is equipped with the recorded activities. According to Tripathi (2018), a robot is a "software programs that mimic human actions". This software "worker" works quickly and accurately to complete the automated duties. Robots can work tirelessly, resulting in steady and efficient automation.
■ Control centre: This serves as RPA operations' mission control. It offers a centralized platform that makes it easy for users to schedule, manage, and monitor robot performance and problems. Robots can be used to carry out activities, and users can monitor their performance in real-time, spot bottlenecks, and resolve any problems that may occur during automation. Imagine having a single dashboard where all of your virtual assistants' statuses and the tasks they are working on are shown.
■ Integration tools: These tools provide easy connectivity between the RPA bot and different databases and applications, guaranteeing efficient data manipulation and transmission throughout the automated procedure. For example, an RPA bot might require using of integration technologies to easily combine data extraction from emails, database system record updates, and report generation.

The integration of these fundamental elements enables RPA to automate a multitude of processes. RPA reduces errors, streamlines workflows, and frees up valuable human resources to work on more strategic and value-added tasks by imitating human actions and interfacing with various systems. It's similar to having a group of devoted and industrious helpers working in the background to guarantee accurate and timely completion of monotonous jobs (Khang & Inna et al., 2024).

12.3 How RPA Streamlines Financial Operations

RPA is revolutionizing the way banks and other financial institutions perform their daily operations. Now let's see how RPA streamlines their operational efficiency:

12.3.1 *Management of Accounts*

■ Effortless account opening: By automating data gathering and document verification, RPA can greatly speed up the process of opening an account for a new client (Villar & Khan, 2021).
■ Streamlined account maintenance: RPA bots can handle repetitive tasks like changing contact information, changing addresses, and resetting passwords, freeing up human agents to handle more complicated dealings with clients.

■ Enhanced transaction processing: RPA reduces errors and guarantees data accuracy by automating transaction classification, reconciliation, and report preparation. Automation in banking can save up to 25,000 hours of work that could have been avoided due to human errors, claims Gartner (Lavelle, 2019).

12.3.2 Processing Loans

■ Faster loan applications: RPA can pre-fill loan applications, obtain credit history information, and collect and verify borrower information, greatly expediting the application process for both clients and loan agents.
■ Rapid document management: RPA can automate the gathering, validation, and routing of documents within the approval procedure, which will shorten the time it takes to process loans.
■ Supporting underwriting: RPA may gather information from multiple sources and deliver it in an organized manner, which helps loan officers make well-informed choices at the underwriting stage.

12.3.3 Evaluation of Risk

■ Real-time fraud detection: RPA can examine customer information and transaction patterns in real-time, spotting irregularities and highlighting possibly fraudulent activity for additional examination.
■ Simplified regulatory compliance: RPA may automate the collection and analysis of data for regulatory reporting, guaranteeing compliance with regulations.
■ Effective KYC (know your customer): RPA can streamline KYC compliance procedures by automating customer onboarding operations, including identity verification and document inspections. Inconsistencies flagged by algorithms trigger a more thorough KYC check by bank staff (Villar & Khan, 2021).

12.3.4 Regulatory Compliance

■ Effortless data aggregation: RPA can collect data from several internal systems and provide reports that are needed for regulatory compliance, saving time and guaranteeing accuracy by eliminating manual labour. Accenture survey conducted in 2016 shows that, 73% of participants believed that RPA could be a major compliance enabler (AutomationEdge, 2024).
■ Detailed audit trails: RPA streamlines regulatory evaluations by keeping track of all automated operations, hence producing a transparent audit trail.

12.3.5 Back-End Functions

■ Simplified reconciliation: RPA can automate the process of balancing financial data from several systems, guaranteeing precision and lowering the possibility of mistakes.
■ Speedy data entry and Processing: Employees can be freed up to work on more analytical projects by automating repetitive chores like data entry from bills or receipts.
■ Enhanced reporting efficiency: RPA may automate report generation, which ensures uniformity in data presentation and saves time.

12.3.6 Assistance in Making Decisions

■ Data analysis and insights: RPA can gather and examine large volumes of data, offering insightful information that can help make well-informed decisions.

■ Scenario modelling: It helps to assess possible outcomes and dangers related to investment plans, and automate simulations of various financial situations.

12.3.7 Improving Customer Service

■ Automated customer support: By automating answers to commonly asked questions, forwarding requests to the relevant departments, and providing self-service choices via chatbots or interactive voice response systems, RPA can expedite customer inquiries and support procedures.

■ Customised client interactions: RPA can deliver personalized offers, communications, and suggestions by utilizing machine learning algorithms and data analytics to analyse client preferences and behaviours. This increases customer satisfaction and engagement.

■ Accelerated issue resolution: By automating the extraction and processing of pertinent data from various systems, RPA lowers the wait time and boosts overall service effectiveness, enabling quicker resolution of client concerns.

12.4 Top 10 RPA Tools

Navigating the leading candidates in the dynamic field of RPA can be challenging. This is an overview of the top 10 RPA tools to help you make an informed decision for more efficient automation as shown in Table 12.1.

After doing an industry-wide evaluation of the best RPA tools, let's focus on those that are most suited to the particular needs and specifications of the banking and finance industry.

12.5 Best RPA Tools for Banking and Finance

UiPath, Automation Anywhere, and Blue Prism are the top three RPA tools in the banking and financial industry. These instruments provide distinct advantages and functionalities that address the particular requirements of various financial institutions. These tools are explained below:

12.5.1 UiPath

UiPath is a worldwide software enterprise with expertise in creating RPA systems. Since it was founded in 2005 in Bucharest, Romania, UiPath has developed into one of the leading companies in the RPA industry. Software-as-a-Service and native software versions of UiPath's software solutions are offered by it. The UiPath platform offers a full range of automation features, such as workflow automation, process recording, and cognitive capabilities driven by AI and machine learning. Over the years, UiPath has raised a substantial amount of money—more than $1.5 billion—from investors like Accel, CapitalG, and Sequoia Capital (UiPath, 2024). The company continued to establish itself as a dominant force in the RPA industry when it went public on the New York Stock Exchange in 2021.

Table 12.1 Top 10 RPA Tools

Sr. No.	RPA Tools	Description
1.	UiPath	Prominent RPA tool UiPath is renowned for its extensive community support, scalability, and easy-to-use interface. It provides several characteristics, including cognitive capabilities, workflow automation, and process recording.
2.	Automation Anywhere	Another excellent RPA solution that is excellent at automating a variety of business activities is Automation Anywhere. It offers functions including cognitive capabilities, attended and unattended automation, and integration with several business platforms.
3.	Blue Prism	Reliability, scalability, and security features are the hallmarks of Blue Prism, an enterprise-grade RPA technology. It works particularly well with numerous business applications and is especially suitable for large-scale RPA installations.
4.	Kofax Kapow	It is an RPA solution that focuses on information extraction, web automation, and system integration (Ribeiro et al., 2021). It has advanced functions for managing complicated operations along with a user-friendly layout.
5.	NICE RPA	NICE RPA is an artificial intelligence (AI)-driven RPA solution designed for optimizing contact centre and customer support operations. It provides skills like intellectual abilities, process discovery, and smart document handling (Tawde, 2023).
6.	AntWorks	It is code-free RPA technology, commonly referred to as ANTstein, and is capable of handling both structured and unstructured data. It facilitates BOT development without any need for designing or programming procedures.
7.	WinAutomation	It is a powerful desktop automation application for Windows-based operations (Ribeiro et al., 2021). It is quite good at automating repetitive tasks, such as processing invoices and entering data, resulting in greater accuracy and efficiency.
8.	TruBot	TruBot is a powerful RPA software platform that provides advanced data capture and reasoning skills, as well as the integration of AI and fuzzy logic for accurate data extraction. It is user-friendly, thus allowing corporate customers to easily develop bots.
9.	Visual Cron	An automation tool for scheduling tasks and integration is called Visual Cron. It works exclusively with Windows. It is a tool that allows users to build tasks without the need for programming knowledge, and it is especially helpful for organizations with numerous complex systems that must communicate with one another seamlessly (VisualCron, n.d.).
10.	AutomationEdge	AutomationEdge is a comprehensive RPA tool that makes a digital workforce that enables businesses to operate error-free around-the-clock. It's among the quickest RPA instruments for data processing (AutomationEdge, 2023).

UiPath has emerged as a key RPA solution in the finance and banking industries, providing a comprehensive set of automation features that increase efficiency, improve reliability, and save operational costs. The fact that UiPath is in the finance industry is also significantly influenced by its financial performance. The company recorded sales in the range of $313 million to $318 million in its second quarter fiscal 2024 financial results. For the third quarter of fiscal 2024, annual recurring sales is anticipated to be between $1.24 billion and $1.26 billion (UiPath, 2023), an indicator of absolute growth. This depicts the increased demand for this RPA tool due to its excellent features which are as follows:

■ One of UiPath's significant features in the finance industry is its user-friendly interface, which enables both technical and non-technical users to create and execute automation workflows without difficulty. This accessibility is especially useful in the banking business, where professionals frequently need to automate a variety of repetitive operations, including accounts payable and receivable, bank reconciliation, and regulatory compliance reporting.
■ Another important feature contributing to UiPath's popularity among financial organizations is its scalability. As transaction volumes and data processing requirements increase, UiPath's platform can scale easily to meet these demands.
■ Furthermore, UiPath's connectivity features enable it to communicate smoothly with a variety of enterprise systems used in the finance and banking industries, including accounting software, trading platforms, and portfolio management systems. This interface allows for a more simplified and comprehensive automation strategy, minimizing the need for human data transfers and increasing overall process efficiency.

12.5.2 *Blue Prism*

Blue Prism is a leading UK-based vendor of RPA software, which allows businesses to automate recurring, rule-based operations and procedures. The organization introduced the idea of a "virtual workforce"—software robots that can replicate human behaviours and interface with IT programs and systems. Additionally, the business has grown significantly; in 2016, it became public on the London Stock Exchange, and in 2021, Vista Equity Partners paid $1.5 billion to acquire it (Blue Prism, 2024).

This RPA platform is based on the Microsoft.NET Framework and can streamline processes on various networks including mainframe, Windows, Java, and more. Blue Prism's RPA solutions are intended to give various advantages, including enhanced efficiency, accuracy, production, and financial savings. Customers of this company have claimed average handle times for automated procedures reduced by up to 80% and average resolution times reduced by 90% (Tutorialspoint, n.d.).

Clients in banking, accounting, and other financial services use Blue Prism's automation capabilities for operations like account opening and KYC checks, loan processing, month-end closing, regulatory and tax compliance, and invoice processing, demonstrating the company's significant presence in the finance sector. Its features include:

■ Blue Prism's architecture is developed to be extremely scalable, allowing financial institutions to automate activities across numerous systems without human interruption.
■ This software provides real-time insights into automated operations through advanced reporting and analytics. This enables financial departments to regularly track and optimize automation initiatives for desirable impact.
■ It can readily integrate with other business software used in finance, such as enterprise resource planning (ERP) and customer relationship management (CRM) for improved automation facilities.

12.5.3 Automation Anywhere

It is another significant RPA player in the financial industry. RPA software development is the area of expertise for Automation Anywhere, a popular American multinational software firm. It is a California-based company founded in 2003, which provides an extensive RPA platform that helps companies to successfully and efficiently automate end-to-end business processes (Khang, Rath & Satpathy, 2024).

Automation Anywhere, which has over 2,800 client companies worldwide and collaborations with big tech giants like Microsoft and Google has positioned itself as a leading provider of RPA solutions. The company has shown tremendous market expansion, with annual revenue of over $600 million in 2020 (*Automation Anywhere*, 2023). By automating processes like data input, invoice processing, customer support, and supply chain management, this helps businesses to increase productivity and lower human error rates. This can be possible with the following ways

- The scalable and adaptable architecture of Automation Anywhere's platform enables financial institutions to grow their automation programmes as needed.
- With features like role-based access control, encryption, audit trails, and compliance reporting, it puts security and regulatory compliance first.
- Financial institutions may ensure accurate and timely submission of regulatory reports by automating regulatory reporting operations with the help of this.
- Organizations can lower the risk of mistakes and non-compliance while increasing operational efficiency by automating various compliance-related operations.
- With fewer manual errors and consistent financial data processing, Automation Anywhere's RPA solutions enhance data quality and accuracy.

After examining the top RPA solutions designed to meet the particular requirements of the banking and financial industries, we now focus on a thorough comparison of the top three platforms: Automation Anywhere, Blue Prism, and UiPath. The purpose of this analysis is to help organizations choose the best automation solution by offering insightful information about their features, advantages, and disadvantages.

12.6 RPA Tools Comparison: UiPath vs. Automation Anywhere vs. Blue Prism

Although Blue Prism, Automation Anywhere, and UiPath are all excellent RPA solutions, some significant distinctions between them might assist companies in making better decisions. The three RPA tools differ in the following ways:

12.6.1 Development Methodology

- UiPath: Provides an intuitive drag-and-drop interface (StudioX) that enables users to create automation workflows with minimal coding knowledge.
- Automation Anywhere: It offers a hybrid method for more complicated jobs that combines visual programming tools with scripting capabilities (IQ Bot).
- Blue Prism: Makes use of a more conventional, code-centric development environment; building bots with it requires some programming experience.

12.6.2 Design and Architecture

■ UiPath: Uses Orchestrator, a web-based, cloud-native architecture, for scalability and effortless deployment.
■ Automation Anywhere: It provides a client-server architecture and deployment options for both on-premises and cloud environments.
■ Blue Prism: Focuses mostly on on-premise deployment and mostly uses a client-server architecture.

12.6.3 Pricing

■ UiPath: Based on functionality and scalability requirements, it provides a tiered price structure.
■ Automation Anywhere: Uses a subscription-based business strategy.
■ Blue Prism: Known for its high prices, which frequently necessitate personalized quotes.

12.6.4 Strengths

■ UiPath: Focuses heavily on innovation and AI integration, has a huge developer community, and an intuitive interface.
■ Automation Anywhere: Powerful cognitive RPA capabilities combined with a flexible hybrid development strategy.
■ Blue Prism: a well-established track record in the RPA sector, strong security features, and an emphasis on enterprise scalability

12.6.5 Deficiencies

■ UiPath: Because of its emphasis on visual development, it can be complicated for complex automation processes.
■ Automation Anywhere: In comparison with cloud-native solutions, client-server design may limit scalability.
■ Blue Prism: Higher learning curve because of code-centric development; and premium price may not be affordable for many budgets.

12.6.3 Selecting an Appropriate RPA Tool

The best RPA tool for you will be based on your priorities and particular demands. Here's a brief guide:

■ For simplicity of use and a large user base: UiPath
■ For adaptability and robust cognitive RPA: Automation Anywhere
■ For enterprise-level security with an established track record: Blue Prism

By carefully examining these capabilities and matching them with your organization's priorities, you can choose any RPA tool that will put your company in the best possible position to succeed in the automation process by carefully weighing these considerations. After examining the RPA tool landscape, let's focus on one of the top platforms, UiPath, and see how it is customized to meet the unique requirements and constraints of the banking and finance sector.

12.7 Implementation of UiPath in Finance and Banking

The financial sector, which prioritizes accuracy, speed, and regulatory compliance, is primed for the transformative impact of RPA. UiPath, a major RPA vendor, provides a comprehensive platform that enables banks and financial institutions to automate a wide range of repetitive processes, thereby increasing efficiency and production across departments. Let's look at how to use UiPath to make the shift to automated workflows go smoothly as shown in Figure 12.2.

12.7.1 Identifying Automation Opportunity

The first phase entails conducting a detailed review of current procedures to identify potential candidates for automation. Concentrate on high-volume, rule-based processes that are susceptible to human error, such as:

- Account management: Automate data collection, document verification, and central banking system population to speed up account opening, verification, and closure.
- Loan processing: Use UiPath bots to gather data, validate creditworthiness through bureau connectivity, and flag extremely risky applications for manual review.
- Regulatory compliance: Automate data extraction, report preparation, and validation to reduce compliance risks.
- Client support: Increase client satisfaction by using chatbots to answer frequently asked questions, address simple issues, and arrange appointments, all while delivering 24/7 support.
- Fraud detection: Use UiPath bots to analyse transaction trends and detect suspected fraudulent actions in real-time, protecting financial organizations and their clients.

But if you are not able to find suitable tasks for automation, then stop the process here.

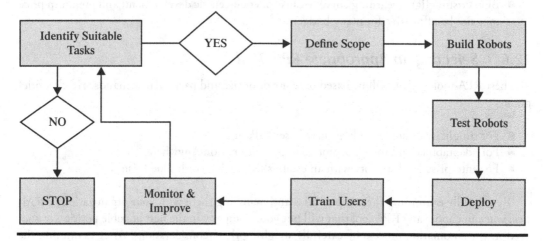

Figure 12.2   UiPath implementation process. (Developed by the authors.)

12.7.2 Build and Evaluate UiPath Robots

UiPath Studio, with its user-friendly visual interface, allows users with or without technical expertise to create RPA bots. Here's a breakdown:

■ Process recording: It is the recording of human actions while the intended job is being performed. UiPath Studio turns these recordings into a visual workflow that the bot can copy.
■ Development and customization: Improve the captured workflow by including decision points, data modification capabilities, and error-handling procedures. UiPath provides built-in interfaces for smooth interaction with a variety of financial apps.
■ Testing and validation: The bots should be rigorously tested in a specialized testing environment to verify their precision, effectiveness, and error-free operations.

12.7.3 Orchestration and Deployment

It's time to deploy the bots after they have been extensively tested:

■ UiPath Orchestrator: The web-based software is used to coordinate and oversee the installation of bots within an organization. It permits bot activity scheduling, tracking, and auditing.
■ Production Environment: Place the bots in a safe, real-world setting where they may communicate with live apps and data.

12.7.4 User Training and Change Management

A key component of a successful RPA adoption is efficient change management:

■ Training and communication: Explain the advantages of automation to all stakeholders and provide training to users who will interact with the bots.
■ User adoption: To guarantee a seamless transition and optimize user adoption of the automated procedures, solicit input from users.

12.7.5 Continuous Monitoring and Improvement

RPA is a continuous journey, not a one-time solution

■ Performance monitoring: Using UiPath Orchestrator, continuously track bot performance to discover areas for improvement.
■ Process optimization: As company processes change, fine-tune and optimize automated workflows to retain efficiency.
■ Advanced automation: Consider integrating cognitive RPA features powered by AI and machine learning to handle complex jobs and decision-making processes.

Financial institutions can gain a competitive advantage in the constantly changing financial landscape and position themselves for a future marked by efficiency and accuracy by using UiPath.

12.8 Benefits of RPA in Banking and Finance Services

RPA has numerous advantages for a range of banking and finance processes. A survey conducted by PricewaterhouseCoopers found that 30% of participants were aiming to integrate RPA into their companies in addition to experimenting with it due to its increased usage (AutomationEdge, 2024). Let's examine a few important use cases in more details as shown in Figure 12.3

Here is main benefits of RPA in banking and finance services:

- Enhanced productivity: By automating repetitive manual operations, RPA robots, which are specifically intended to focus on carrying out specified routine activities, can lead to greater productivity (Madakam, Holmukhe & Kumar Jaiswal, 2019). These chatbots can interact with customers in natural language and respond in a human-like way (Bola et al., 2022).
- Improved efficiency: RPA makes operations faster, more effective, and more efficient for banks and other financial organizations by streamlining operations. An automated program can save up to 25,000 hours annually on certain commercial tasks (Tyzhnenko, 2024).
- Higher accuracy: RPA ensures greater accuracy in financial transactions and processes by automating procedures, which lowers the possibility of human error (Khanh & Khang, 2021).
- Enhanced security: By offering thorough audit trails for every process, lowering company risks, and upholding high process compliance, the adoption of RPA in banking and finance improves security.
- Savings: RPA can reduce processing time and expenses for banks and other financial organizations, resulting in more economical operations. Banks can save operating costs up to 30% on average by implementing RPA (Aleksandrovich, 2024).

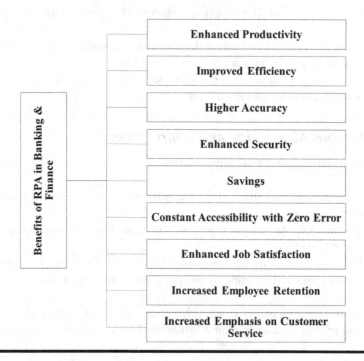

Figure 12.3 Benefits of RPA in banking and finance.

- Constant accessibility with zero error: Robots operate nonstop, around-the-clock, delivering high-quality, promptly completed tasks.
- Enhanced job satisfaction: Workers can make better use of their skills and feel less burdened by regular duties.
- Increased employee retention: Happy and motivated workers are less likely to quit their jobs.
- Increased emphasis on customer service: Employees may devote more time to offering personalized and great customer service, ultimately leading to greater customer satisfaction.

12.9 Challenges in the Automation Process

For banking and finance organizations, RPA has many advantages, but its effective deployment necessitates a thorough assessment of its possible drawbacks. Here's a closer look at some significant obstacles to overcome:

- Process selection: It's critical to determine which procedures should be automated (Doguc, 2020). High transaction volume and rule-based repetitive jobs are a forte of RPA. Making snap decisions or using unstructured data in complex process selection can result in errors or inefficiency. Financial organizations must do a thorough analysis of their workflows to make sure the procedures they have selected are compatible with RPA.
- Integration difficulties: It can be difficult and time-consuming to integrate RPA bots with current legacy systems. These legacy systems may need custom coding for seamless connection, or their architecture may be out of date. For RPA bots to operate smoothly, banks and other financial institutions need to have the IT resources and know-how to handle these integration issues.
- Change management: When RPA is implemented, employees frequently worry about their job security which may reduce employee (Fernandez & Aman, 2018). Addressing these concerns and ensuring user adoption requires effective training and communication. To provide employees with the skills they need to operate with RPA technology, financial institutions must engage in employee training programmes and create transparent communication plans.
- Cost: Putting RPA into practice can be expensive, especially for financial organizations that have big legacy systems. Financial organizations need to carefully assess the possible advantages of RPA against its associated expenses.
- Data security: Sensitive financial data is automated by RPA, thus financial institutions need to make sure the data is safe. To safeguard their data, financial organizations need to have strong security procedures in place and build RPA bots with security in mind.
- Regulatory compliance: Financial institutions are required to make sure that their RPA bots adhere to a multitude of financial standards, including those about regulatory compliance. To make sure that RPA bots are developed and used in compliance with legal regulations, this can call for more resources and experience.
- Scalability: As financial institutions expand, RPA must be scalable to meet their needs. As their business expands, financial institutions need to make sure that their RPA platform can manage higher transaction and data volumes.
- Maintenance: To guarantee their continued efficiency, RPA bots need regular maintenance and updates. Financial organizations need to have the means and know-how to keep their RPA bots maintained and updated with the most recent technologies.

■ Limited scope: RPA is excellent at automating repetitive operations, but it is not suitable for complicated decision-making processes. Financial institutions must accept that RPA is not an ideal solution and that it should only be used as a component of a more comprehensive automation plan that makes use of AI and Machine Learning (ML), among other technologies.

After discussing the obstacles to RPA adoption, we will now turn our attention to important elements that need to be considered before implementing RPA. Let us examine the essential factors that are crucial for the effective assimilation and implementation of RPA in banking and financial operations.

12.10 Implementation Considerations

RPA has many advantages, but careful planning is needed for a successful implementation. Key areas to concentrate on are as follows:

■ Choosing the correct battles: Look for repetitive, rule-based jobs that have a lot of transactions to automate. Repetitive tasks like data input, account reconciliation, and loan processing are perfect fits for RPA

■ Tech infrastructure matters: Verify that RPA integration can be supported by your IT infrastructure. It is essential to have a strong system connection with databases and current software. To safeguard critical data during the RPA lifecycle, put strong security mechanisms in place. Audit trails, data encryption, and user access controls are important.

■ People are crucial: It's critical to communicate clearly about the advantages of RPA and the possibility of job loss. Employees who receive training are better prepared to work with RPA and are promoted to higher-value positions.

■ Governance for success: Clearly define RPA deployment, monitoring, and maintenance policies and procedures. This optimizes the advantages of automation and guarantees ethical usage. Put strong security measures in place to reduce dangers associated with data.

■ Additional considerations

■ Scalability: Select an RPA system that can grow with your business to meet your increasing automation requirements. In this regard, cloud-based solutions provide greater autonomy.

■ Vendor support: Consider how much assistance and instruction the RPA vendor provides. A successful implementation depends on having customer service that is both prompt and dependable.

■ Data privacy: When using RPA procedures to handle sensitive data, be sure that compliance with data privacy regulations is maintained.

Financial institutions may provide a solid basis for the successful deployment of RPA by carefully weighing these issues. This means that workers will feel more empowered, operations will run more smoothly, and the financial sector will fully utilize automation (Khang & Hajimahmud, 2024).

12.11 Comparison of Automation Technologies: RPA vs. AI vs. BPM

Understanding the distinctions between RPA, AI, and BPM is critical for financial firms seeking to improve operations. Each technology provides varied capabilities, ranging from work automation

Table 12.2 Comparison between RPA, AI, and BPM

Aspect	RPA	Artificial Intelligence	Business Process Management
Definition	Software robots are used to automate repetitive operations by mimicking human motions.	Replicates human intelligence to carry out operations like as pattern recognition, natural language processing, and decision-making.	End-to-end BPM and optimization is achieved by modelling, execution, monitoring, and optimization.
Focus	Focuses on recurring, rule-based processes.	Focuses on challenging cognitive activities that call for learning and thinking skills.	Includes all business processes across departments, from beginning to end.
Technology used	Software bots that simulate how people would interact with digital systems.	Natural language processing (NLP), machine learning techniques	Workflow software, and analytical instruments
Implementation time	Because it is rule-based, deployment may happen in a matter of weeks, making it relatively speedy.	Longer implementation time due to acquiring training data and model development; can take months or years.	The implementation time varies depending on the organizational readiness and complexity of the procedure.
Strengths	Increases productivity, lowers error rates, and frees up human resources.	Manages unstructured data, continual improvement, and complicated decision-making.	Enhances process visibility, integrates systems, and coordinates processes
Weaknesses	Requires organized data; restricted to rule-based tasks.	Costly and necessitates a large amount of training data.	Intricate setup, possibly requiring a process change.

Source: Admin (2022); Dilmegani, (2024); Quixy Editorial Team (2024).

to enhanced decision-making, influencing the future of banking and finance in different ways. The comparison of these technologies is explained in Table 12.2.

12.12 RPA's Future in Finance and Banking

In the banking and finance industry, RPA has emerged as a key efficiency component. But that's not where the narrative ends. There are many opportunities for RPA in the future that could push automation's limits and change the financial landscape. Here's a quick peek at some fascinating upcoming developments.

12.12.1 AI and ML Take Centre Stage

Although RPA is very good at automating jobs that follow rules, its most exciting future lies in its potent combination with AI and ML. This union will produce cognitive RPA bots that can handle complicated problems requiring judgment similar to that of a human. Envision real-time analysis of transaction patterns by AI, which would greatly enhance fraud detection. Machine learning models could evaluate borrower information and creditworthiness, automating loan approvals while preserving the accuracy of risk assessments. AI-driven chatbots may also offer round-the-clock customer service, answering basic queries and referring more complicated ones to human representatives.

12.12.2 Process Mining: An Enabling Technology for Focused Automation

Using process mining techniques, bottlenecks, and inefficiencies are found by examining historical process data. By using this data as a guide, automation tactics may be optimized and RPA can be used to its full potential. Institutions can prioritize deploying RPA for the highest return on investment by using process mining to identify the most labour-intensive and prone to errors. Process mining also makes it possible to continuously assess and improve automation tactics, which guarantees that RPA stays in line with changing business requirements.

12.12.3 Working Together to Provide Industry-Specific Solutions

Partnerships among financial institutions, technology providers, and industry experts will be essential as the use of RPA accelerates. Standardized RPA frameworks that ensure industry compliance and speed up development and deployment could result from this partnership. Furthermore, cross-institutional best practices and success stories can encourage ongoing education and advancement in RPA application.

12.12.4 Democratic Automation: Encouraging Corporate Users

Automation could become more widely available with the introduction of low-code/no-code RPA systems. Entrepreneurs with little coding knowledge can create basic RPA bots using these user-friendly interfaces, which enables them to automate repetitive operations inside their departments. Because low-code/no-code platforms enable business units to automate processes independently, they can improve organizational agility and responsiveness to changing needs (Khang & Gujrati et al., 2024).

12.12.5 The Human–RPA Collaboration: A Shared Success in the Future

RPA automates activities, but in the banking and finance industry, human expertise is still indispensable. Future work environments will probably become more collaborative, involving both human and RPA bot collaboration. The elimination of monotonous work will free up human labour for higher-value pursuits like strategic planning, complicated problem-solving, and customer relationship management. Routine work can be handled by RPA bots, with human oversight for complicated circumstances or exceptions, to guarantee the best results (Khang, Shah & Rani, 2023).

12.13 Conclusion

In conclusion, RPA is a key instrument in the development of banking and financial operations. Its ability to automate monotonous processes, optimize resource allocation, and streamline workflows highlights its disruptive potential in the sector. It provides a significant opportunity to improve client satisfaction and achieve new heights of efficiency. As RPA technology evolves and combines with cutting-edge technologies like AI, its impact on the financial sector is going to become even stronger. Furthermore, RPA provides a way to open up fresh sources of income, encourage creativity, and add value for stakeholders and customers alike (Khang, Rath, Satapathy et al., 2023).

Financial organizations must take a comprehensive approach that takes into account people, technology, and procedures as they begin their RPA journey. This means developing an innovative culture, investing in staff training and growth, and cultivating alliances with RPA suppliers and specialists. Only then, they can fully utilize RPA to bring about revolutionary change and maintain their position as industry leaders in the current era.

RPA, then, is not merely an automation technology; rather, it is a strategic requirement for financial institutions to change, grow, and prosper in a competitive and increasingly digital environment. However, the path to RPA implementation is not without hurdles, ranging from safety issues to organizational change. But by strategically navigating these roadblocks, financial institutions may position themselves for a future of automation, innovation, resilience, and sustained growth (Hajimahmud & Khang, 2024).

References

Admin. (2022, December 27). RPA, BPM and AI: What's the Difference? akaBot. Retrieved April 26, 2012. https://akabot.com/additional-resources/blog/rpa-bpm-and-ai-whats-the-difference/

Aleksandrovich, K. (2024, March 22). RPA in Banking: Industry Examples, Benefits, and Implementation. https://www.itransition.com/rpa/banking

Automation Anywhere. (2023, August 13). https://en.wikipedia.org/wiki/Automation_Anywhere

AutomationEdge. (2023, October 13). Robotic Process Automation (RPA) Tool | AutomationEdge. Retrieved May 1, 2024, from https://automationedge.com/robotic-process-automation/

AutomationEdge. (2024, April 4). How to Implement RPA in Banking: Use Cases in 2012. Retrieved April 24, 2024, from https://automationedge.com/blogs/rpa-in-banking-industry/

Blue Prism. (2024, March 5). Wikipedia. https://en.wikipedia.org/wiki/Blue_Prism

Bola, B, Shetty, T., V, P., & K, K. (2022, July 31). RPA in Banking sector. International Journal for Research in Applied Science and Engineering Technology, 10(7), 3340–3343. https://doi.org/10.22214/ijraset.2022.45725

Digital/McKinsey. (2019, February). Driving impact at scale from automation and AI. In Mckinsey. Retrieved April 25, 2012. https://www.mckinsey.com/~/media/McKinsey/Business%20Functions/McKinsey%20Digital/Our%20Insights/Driving%20impact%20at%20scale%20from%20automation%20and%20AI/Driving-impact-at-scale-from-automation-and-AI.ashx

Dilmegani, C. (2024, January 12). In-Depth Guide to RPA vs BPM in 2012. AIMultiple: High Tech Use Cases &Amp; Tools to Grow Your Business. https://research.aimultiple.com/rpa-vs-bpm/

Doguc, O. (2020, January). Robot Process Automation (RPA) and Its Future. In Advances in E-Business Research (pp. 469–492). https://www.igi-global.com/chapter/robot-process-automation-rpa-and-its-future/291626

Fernandez, D., & Aman, A. (2018, April 30). Impacts of robotic process automation on global accounting services. Asian Journal of Accounting and Governance, 9, 123–132. http://journalarticle.ukm.my/19713/1/25271-90574-1-PB.pdf

Grand View Research. (2024, January). Robotic Process Automation Market To Reach $30,850.0Mn By 2030. Retrieved April 24, 2024, from https://www.grandviewresearch.com/press-release/global-robotic-process-automation-rpa-market

Hajimahmud, V. A., & Khang, A., "Managing Financial Risks in the Gig Economy," In Khang A. Jadhav B., Hajimahmud V. A., Satpathy I., The Synergy of AI and Fintech in the Digital Gig Economy. (1st Ed.) (2024). CRC Press. https://doi.org/10.1201/9781032720104-8

Hindle, J. L. (2018). Robotic Process Automation: Benchmarking the Client Experience. Knowledge Capital Partners.

Khang, A., Gujrati, R., Uygun, H., Tailor, R.K., & Gaur, S. (Eds.). (2024). Data-Driven Modelling and Predictive Analytics in Business and Finance: Concepts, Designs, Technologies, and Applications (1st Ed.). Auerbach Publications. https://doi.org/10.1201/9781032618845

Khang, A, & Hajimahmud, V. A., "Introduction to the Gig Economy," In Khang A. Jadhav B., Hajimahmud V. A., Satpathy I., The Synergy of AI and Fintech in the Digital Gig Economy. (1st Ed.) (2024). CRC Press. https://doi.org/10.1201/9781032720104-1

Khang, A., Inna, Semenets-Orlova, Alla, Klochko, Rostyslav, Shchokin, Rudenko, Mykola, Lidia, Romanova, & Kristina, Bratchykova, "Management Model 6.0 and SWOT Analysis for the Market Share of Product in the Global Market," In Khang, A., Gujrati, R., Uygun, H., Tailor, R.K., & Gaur, S., Data-Driven Modelling and Predictive Analytics in Business and Finance. (1st Ed.). (2024) CRC Press. https://doi.org/10.1201/9781032618845-16

Khang, A, Jadhav, B., Hajimahmud, V. A., & Satpathy, I., (1st Ed.) (2024). The Synergy of AI and Fintech in the Digital Gig Economy. CRC Press. https://doi.org/10.1201/9781032720104

Khang, A., Rath, K. C., Satapathy, S. K., Kumar, A., Das, S. R., & Panda, M. R. (2023). Enabling the Future of Manufacturing: Integration of Robotics and IoT to Smart Factory Infrastructure in Industry 4.0. In Khang A., Shah V., & Rani S. (Eds.), Handbook of Research on AI-Based Technologies and Applications in the Era of the Metaverse (pp. 25–50). IGI Global.

Khang, A., Shah, V., & Rani, S. (Eds.). (2023). Handbook of Research on AI-Based Technologies and Applications in the Era of the Metaverse. IGI Global. https://doi.org/10.4018/978-1-6684-8851-5

Khanh, H. H., & Khang, A. (2021) "The Role of Artificial Intelligence in Blockchain Applications," In Rana G, Khang A., Sharma R., Goel A. K., Dubey A. K., Reinventing Manufacturing and Business Processes Through Artificial Intelligence (pp. 20-40).. CRC Press. https://doi.org/10.1201/9781003145011-2

Lavelle, J. (2019). Gartner Says Robotic Process Automation Can Save Finance Departments 25,000 Hours of Avoidable Work Annually. Gartner. Retrieved April 25, 2024, from https://www.gartner.com/en/newsroom/press-releases/2019-10-02-gartner-says-robotic-process-automation-can-save-fina

Madakam, S., Holmukhe, R. M., & Kumar Jaiswal, D. (2019). The future digital work force: Robotic process automation (RPA). Journal of Information Systems and Technology Management, 16, 1–17. https://doi.org/10.4301/s1807-1775201916001

Oshri, I., & Plugge, A. (2021). Introducing RPA and automation in the financial sector: Lessons from KAS bank. Journal of Information Technology Teaching Cases, 12(1), 88–95. https://doi.org/10.1177/2043886921994828

Quixy Editorial Team. (2024,). BPM Vs RPA: What's the difference and which do you need? Quixy. Retrieved April 26, 2024 from https://quixy.com/blog/bpm-vs-rpa-whats-the-difference/

Ribeiro, J., Lima, R., Eckhardt, T., & Paiva, S. (2021). Robotic process automation and artificial intelligence in industry 4.0 – A literature review. Procedia Computer Science, 181, 51–58. https://doi.org/10.1016/j.procs.2021.01.104

Tawde, S. (2023). RPA Tools. EDUCBA. https://www.educba.com/rpa-tools/

Tripathi, A. M. (2018). Learning Robotic Process Automation : Create Software Robots and Automate Business Processes With the Leading Rpa Tool - Uipath (1st ed.). Packt Publishing.

Tutorialspoint. (n.d.). Blue Prism - Introduction to RPA. Retrieved May 1, 2024, from https://www.tutorialspoint.com/blue_prism/blue_prism_introduction_to_rpa.htm

Tyzhnenko, R. (2024). RPA in Finance and Banking: Effective Use Cases and Implementation. NIX United – Custom Software Development Company in US. Retrieved April 25, 2024, from https://nix-united.com/blog/rpa-in-finance-and-banking-effective-use-cases-and-implementation/

UiPath. (2023). UiPath Reports Second Quarter Fiscal 2024 Financial Results. UiPath, Inc. Retrieved May 1, 2024, from https://ir.uipath.com/news/detail/306/uipath-reports-second-quarter-fiscal-2024-financial-results

UiPathm. (2024). Wikipedia. https://en.wikipedia.org/wiki/UiPath

Villar, A. S., & Khan, N. (2021). Robotic process automation in banking industry: A case study on deutsche bank. Journal of Banking and Financial Technology. https://doi.org/10.1007/s42786-021-00030-9

VisualCron. (n.d.). VisualCron - Robotic Process Automation (RPA). Retrieved May 3, 2024, from https://www.visualcron.com/robotic-process-automation.aspx

Wangoo, R. (2023). Top 9 Benefits of Implementing RPA in Banking and Finance. https://www.signitysolutions.com/blog/rpa-in-banking-and-finance

Chapter 13

How Traditional Banks Adapt to the Fintech Revolution in Banking and Finance Sector

Greena Karani and Babasaheb Jadhav

13.1 Introduction

The integration of financial technology (Fin-tech) has sparked a revolution in the banking sector. In a rapidly evolving financial landscape, traditional banks find themselves at a crossroads, navigating the disruptive forces of the fin-tech revolution. The synergy between traditional banking practices and Fin-tech is reshaping the financial landscape. The surge of innovative fin-tech startups, offering cutting-edge solutions and services, has forced traditional banks to rethink their strategies and adapt to stay competitive. This collaboration empowers traditional banks to harness digital advancements, offering innovative solutions and services. By adapting to the Fin-tech revolution, traditional banks can stay relevant, enhance efficiency, and provide customers with a seamless digital banking experience (Sunitha & Madhav, 2020).

The survival and success of traditional banks in this dynamic era hinge on their ability to evolve, incorporating Fin-tech to meet the evolving needs of the digital era. This article delves into the dynamic and transformative relationship between traditional banks and fin-tech, shedding light on how legacy institutions are responding to this revolution. As the traditional banking sector grapples with a wave of technological innovation, we explore the various ways in which established banks are adapting, collaborating, and innovating to not only survive but thrive in this new era of finance.

From strategic partnerships to digital transformation initiatives, the survival of traditional banks depends on their ability to embrace change, adopt new technologies, and cater to the evolving needs of their customers. The present study discusses how to understand the strategies, challenges, and successes of traditional banks as they strive to remain relevant and resilient in the face of the fin-tech revolution. An artificial intelligence (AI)-powered approach that combines business intelligence and data-driven techniques is used to create complex applications and models that

DOI: 10.4324/9781003501947-13

can solve integrated issues faced by businesses, resulting in increased profitability, competitiveness, and cost-effectiveness (Jadhav, 2023).

The COVID-19 pandemic has hastened the transformation of the financial technology (Fintech) landscape, increasing the use of digital technologies in the financial sector. According to a study, the crisis has accelerated the integration of digital technologies in response to shifting consumer behaviors and the demand for remote financial services (Fu & Mishra, 2022). Fintech companies were instrumental in developing innovative solutions to the pandemic's challenges, helping to evolve digital payment systems, remote financial management tools, and improved cybersecurity. COVID-19 highlighted Fin Tech's resilience and adaptability, establishing it as a key player in shaping the future of financial services by advancing financial inclusion and implementing industry-wide technological advancements (Meyer, Rivadeneyra & Sohal, 2017).

13.2 Literature Review

Sunitha and Madhav (2020) critically analyze the evolving landscape of banking services with the infusion of Fin-Tech, shedding light on the transformative potential and the hurdles encountered. The authors skillfully navigate through the dynamic interplay of technology, regulations, and human capital, offering valuable insights into the changing dynamics of the financial services industry. The inclusion of opportunities and challenges in the Fin-Tech-banking nexus enhances the practical applicability of the research (Mengxuan et al., 2024). The findings cater to a diverse audience, including academics, practitioners, and policymakers, fostering a deeper understanding of the complexities and possibilities associated with this digital transformation.

Fu and Mishra (2022) provide a comprehensive analysis of how the COVID-19 crisis has influenced the technological landscape of financial intermediation. By exploring the technological adoption patterns during this unprecedented period, the authors shed light on the dynamic relationship between crises and fin-tech evolution. Mohammad et al. (2023) contribute significantly to the literature by offering insights into the market structure and the changing nature of financial intermediation in the face of a global crisis. Their research allows readers to understand the adaptive strategies employed by the fin-tech industry, providing a nuanced perspective on the intersection of technology and finance during challenging times.

Meyer et al. (2017) investigate the risks and opportunities that arise for central banks due to the advancements in fin-tech. By offering a comprehensive framework for assessment, the authors contribute significantly to the understanding of how central banks may be affected by fin-tech developments. The paper delves into various areas where fin-tech could have implications, shedding light on the nuanced relationship between financial technology and central banking mandates (Murinde et al., 2022).

Tang et al. (2024) explained briefly on the dynamic relationship between financial technology adoption, the diversification strategies of banks, and their impact on liquidity. Through rigorous empirical analysis, the authors present evidence from the Chinese market, contributing significantly to the understanding of how fin-tech and diversification practices influence the liquidity position of banks (Mengxuan et al., 2024). The findings are pertinent not only for academics but also for policymakers and practitioners in the financial industry.

Asif et al. (2023) discussed valuable insights into the positive effects of fin-tech and digital financial services on expanding financial inclusion, particularly in rural areas of India. By providing empirical evidence, Meyer et al. (2017) highlight the significant contribution of these technological advancements in bringing previously underserved populations into the formal financial system. The findings are relevant for policymakers, financial institutions, and scholars interested in fostering inclusive financial practices.

Khang and Jadhav et al. (2024) have covered a study on AI tools and technologies in Fintech, their growth, utilities, current scenarios, and future trends in the world of globalized business environment. Murinde et al. (2022) offer valuable insights into the changing landscape of banking, emphasizing the opportunities and challenges brought about by the Fin-Tech revolution. By delving into the risks and opportunities, the authors contribute to a nuanced understanding of how financial technology is reshaping the future of banking. This research is essential for industry professionals, policymakers, and researchers seeking a comprehensive analysis of the evolving Fin-Tech landscape.

13.3 Fin-tech Revolution in Traditional Banking

The Fin-Tech revolution has profoundly altered traditional banking, catapulting it into the digital age. Key technologies like AI and machine learning have given banks the tools to boost operational efficiency, automate tasks, and base decisions on data (Franklin & Santomero, 2001). This shift has resulted in expedited loan approvals and a decrease in default rates, a departure from conventional banking norms. Fin-Tech integration has not merely streamlined operations but has also introduced innovative services, promoted financial inclusion, and addressed the diverse needs of consumers (Appaya & Gradstein, 2020). As traditional banks embrace these advancements, they position themselves to offer personalized, accessible financial services in an increasingly digital landscape. Fin-Tech solutions have revolutionized the sector, providing efficiency, cost reduction, enhanced security, improved customer experiences, transparency, accessibility, faster payments, and more (Arner, Barberis & Buckley, 2015). To stay competitive and meet evolving customer needs, banks must embrace these technologies, investing in Fin-Tech solutions and adopting digital strategies.

13.4 Impact of Fin-Tech on the Banking Industry

Fin-tech has ushered in a new era for the banking industry, upending traditional practices and transforming it into a more dynamic landscape (Bofondi & Gobbi, 2017). The incorporation of Fin-tech solutions has resulted in a significant increase in efficiency, streamlining processes, reducing operational complexities, and allowing for faster transactions. This has led to quicker transactions and enhanced customer experiences.

Furthermore, because of automation and the adoption of innovative technologies, the banking sector has seen a significant reduction in operational costs. Fin-tech has played a pivotal role in enhancing the security measures within the banking industry. Improved security measures, such as advanced encryption and real-time fraud detection, have proven critical in protecting financial transactions (Buchak et al., 2018). Customer service has also undergone significant transformations, with personalized experiences and the incorporation of chatbots contributing to increased satisfaction in an increasingly digital world.

13.5 Methodology and Objectives

There has been some research on the impact of fin-tech revolution on traditional banking, highlighting the forces driving change in the industry. Although the extent to which fin-tech affects traditional banking is evident, little research has been done to examine the impact of fin-tech revolution on traditional banking. While here studies assessing the influence of fin-tech on traditional banking, highlighting the forces driving change in the industry have been conducted, this does not adequately capture how much fin-tech impacts banking industry or the components of fin-tech revolution and the level of their engagement like digital banking, blockchain technology, and the rise of innovative fin-tech startups by integrating fin-tech into their current services provided by the banks.

The significant objectives of the chapter are enlisted below.

■ To explore the impact of the fin-tech revolution on traditional banking, highlighting the forces driving change in the industry.
■ To analyze the evolving landscape of banking, including the emergence of digital banking, blockchain technology, and the rise of innovative fin-tech startups.
■ To analyze the effect of digital transformation like digital payment solutions, automated customer service, data analytics for personalization, and open banking and Application Programming Interfaces (APIs) on banks performance.
■ To provide insights and recommendations for traditional banks to ensure their survival and prosperity in this dynamic financial environment.

The study intends to investigate the dynamic landscape where traditional banking meets the rapidly evolving fin-tech sector. The scope includes an in-depth examination of traditional banks' strategies for navigating and thriving in the face of financial technology disruptions. It will delve into innovative technology adoption, collaboration models with fin-tech entities, regulatory considerations, and customer-centric approaches (Fu & Mishra, 2022).

Data from traditional commercial banks in India will be collected, including financial metrics, transaction volumes, and technology adoption rates. The study typically employs a mix of qualitative and quantitative research methods. This is because the topic necessitates a comprehensive examination of the challenges, strategies, and outcomes of traditional banks' adaptation to fin-tech innovation. To gain insights into their fin-tech adaptation experiences, challenges, and strategies, the study conducts in-depth interviews with key stakeholders from traditional banks, fin-tech startups, regulatory bodies, and industry experts.

The research design employed a mixed-methods approach to comprehensively explore the multifaceted dimensions of traditional banks' adaptation to the fin-tech revolution. The study began with a thorough literature review to establish a theoretical framework and identify gaps in existing knowledge (Khang, Rath et al., 2024). Subsequently, qualitative methods such as in-depth interviews with key stakeholders, including bank executives, fin-tech entrepreneurs, and regulatory authorities, have been conducted to gather rich insights into strategies, challenges, and collaboration models (Mengxuan et al., 2024).

Concurrently, quantitative methods were involved in the analysis of financial data and performance metrics to quantify the impact of fin-tech integration on traditional banks. By triangulating qualitative and quantitative data, the study aims to provide a comprehensive understanding of the evolving landscape and contribute actionable recommendations for traditional banks navigating the fin-tech revolution in India (Murinde et al., 2022).

13.6 Statistical Analysis and Results

13.6.1 Cronbach Alpha Test

To monitor how reliable a component is the Cronbach alpha test was used for its internal consistency. Cronbach's alphas mean values represent the average covariance between pairs of scale or test items. The alpha coefficient quantifies the level of agreement between items on a standardized 0 to 1 scale, with higher values indicating greater agreement. A low alpha value may indicate that the test contains insufficient questions, and adding more relevant items can increase alpha. It is critical for determining the dependability of multi-item scales, with 0.7 or higher indicating acceptable internal consistency. Understanding the interdependence and correlation between the test items is required for interpretation as shown in Table 13.1.

Table 13.1　Reliability Test

	Mean	*Variance*	*Cronbach's Alpha*
Collaboration with Fin-Tech companies	69.67	86.632	.703
Profitability	70.21	87.417	.721
Technological integration	69.74	90.694	.721
Customer experience	70.20	88.242	.725
Regulatory environment	70.13	86.981	.715
Innovation in services	69.65	90.886	.722
Market Share	69.74	90.009	.718
Cost efficiency	70.73	91.196	.740
Risk management	70.00	91.555	.729
Employee skills and training	70.67	91.572	.738
Traditional banking	69.80	86.887	.699
Digital banking	69.67	86.632	.703
Blockchain technology	69.64	85.257	.698
Innovative fin-tech solutions	69.90	89.146	.720
Operational efficiency and competitive advantage	69.66	86.802	.703
Digital payment solutions	70.59	100.142	.755
Automated customer service	70.50	101.073	.755
Data analytics for personalization	70.46	101.754	.760
Open banking and APIs	69.98	97.773	.744
Banks performance	69.55	86.891	.703

The reliability for all the selected variables were 0.769 which is greater than 0.7, which represents that the gathered data is more suitable and can be preferred for further evaluation. The variables when evaluated individually, the values are greater than 0.7, representing that the data is suitable for the analysis.

13.6.2 Multiple Regression

The key fin-tech revolution activities that impact traditional banking were identified. The current study assesses the beneficial impact of fin-tech revolution on traditional banking. In this evaluation, multiple regression was used. Multiple regression was a useful technique for determining which factors influence a specific area of interest. Using the multiple regression technique, it is possible to identify the relationships between the factors that were significant, those that can be ignored, and both (Khang & Muthmainnah et al., 2023). There is no significant impact of the fin-tech revolution on traditional banking, highlighting the forces driving change in the industry as shown in Table 13.2.

From the results in Table 13.2, the adjusted R-squared is 0.684, which explains that the model is a 68% fit for the data. A higher percentage of the variability in the fin-tech revolution was accounted for by the selected factors, as indicated by the R-squared value, which is 68%, indicating a better fit between the model and the data. Less than 0.05 was the P-value for the regression model. This indicates that selected factors had an important impact on traditional banking.

From Table 13.3, the Coefficients of selected variables were presented. Among all variables, Collaboration with Fin-Tech Companies was having greater impact. Accordingly, for every unit increase in Collaboration with Fin-Tech companies, the level of traditional banking increases by 0.344 units. Regression assumptions are met in the study. A test digit between 0 and 4 is always produced by the Durbin-Watson value. In this case, it is 1.812. There is no autocorrelation. VIFs between 1 and 5 indicate multicollinearity and a moderate degree of correlation. The values in this case are higher than 1. Homoscedasticity: When residual values are constant, homoscedasticity is achieved. The number is 156.537.

13.6.3 Multiple Regression

The impact of the evolving landscape of banking, including the emergence of digital banking, blockchain technology, and the rise of innovative fin-tech startups on operating efficiency and competitive advantage of traditional banks were evaluated. The current study assesses the beneficial

Table 13.2 Multiple Regression

Sum Squared Residual	156.537
R-squared	0.684
F	163.675
S.E. of regression	0.455
Adjusted R-squared	0.680
P-value (F)	0.000
Durbin–Watson	1.812

Table 13.3   Coefficients

Coefficients	B
(Constant)	0.304
Collaboration with Fin-Tech companies	0.344
Profitability	0.016
Technological integration	0.092
Customer experience	0.074
Regulatory environment	0.088
Innovation in services	0.096
Market share	0.155
Cost efficiency	0.052
Risk management	−0.007
Employee skills and training	0.029

impact of banking on operating efficiency and competitive advantage of traditional banks. In this evaluation, multiple regression was used. Multiple Regressions was a useful technique for determining which factors influence a specific area of interest. Using the multiple regression technique, it is possible to identify the relationships between the factors that were significant, those that can be ignored, and both.

The adoption of digital banking, blockchain technology, and the integration of innovative fin-tech solutions significantly impact the operational efficiency and competitive advantage of traditional banks as shown in Table 13.4.

From the results in Table 13.4, the adjusted R-squared is 0.408, which explains that the model is a 41% fit for the data. A higher percentage of the variability in the banking was accounted for by the selected factors, as indicated by the R-squared value, which is 41%, indicating a better fit between the model and the data. Less than 0.05 was the P-value for the regression model. This indicates that selected factors had an important impact on the operational efficiency and competitive advantage of traditional banks.

Table 13.4   Multiple Regression

Sum Squared Residual	444.987
R- Squared	0.410
F	176.917
S.E. of regression	0.763
Adjusted R-squared	0.408
P-value (F)	0.000
Durbin–Watson	1.792

Table 13.5   Coefficients

Coefficients	B
(Constant)	1.188
Digital banking	0.328
Blockchain technology	0.304
Innovative fin-tech solutions	0.079

From Table 13.5, the coefficients of selected variables were presented. Among all variables, Digital banking was having greater impact. Accordingly, for every unit increase in Digital banking, the level of traditional banking increases by 0.328 units. Regression assumptions are met in the study. A test digit between 0 and 4 is always produced by the Durbin–Watson value. In this case, it is 1.792. There is no autocorrelation. VIFs between 1 and 5 indicate multicollinearity and a moderate degree of correlation. The values in this case are higher than 1. Homoscedasticity: When residual values are constant, homoscedasticity is achieved. The number is 444.987.

13.6.4 ANOVA

The effects of digital transformation like digital payment solutions, automated customer service, data analytics for personalization, and open banking and APIs on banks performance were evaluated using ANOVA. It is a statistical technique used to determine whether the means of two or more groups differ significantly from one another. It determines the impact of one or more factors by comparing the means of various samples. ANOVA is a powerful tool for researchers looking to uncover significant differences in means across multiple groups, which contributes to strong statistical analyses as shown in Table 13.6.

There is no significant effect of digital transformation like digital payment solutions, automated customer service, data analytics for personalization, and open banking and APIs on banks performance. The results in Table 13.6 explain that most of the respondents were extremely prepared for digital transformation, and few were very prepared for it. From Table 13.7, the Levene's statistic the result of homogeneity test was significant with 0.000 and the F-value is 16.047. Justify the post-hoc tests chosen for analysis in ANOVA. Based on Levene's test, if the significance value is greater than 0.05, it is taken as equal variances assumed.

Table 13.6   Descriptive

	N	Mean	Std. Deviation
Not prepared at all	24	3.74	.904
Slightly prepared	32	3.81	.291
Moderately prepared	81	3.62	.633
Very prepared	294	3.40	.534
Extremely prepared	337	3.12	.903
Total	768	3.33	.762

Table 13.7 Test of Homogeneity

Levene statistic	28.064
Sig.	.000
F	16.047
P-value (F)	0.000

Table 13.8 Scheffe

		Digital Transformation		
			Subset for Alpha = 0.05	
Banks Performance	N	1	2
Extremely prepared	337	3.12	
Very prepared	294	3.40	3.40
Moderately prepared	81		3.62
Not prepared at all	24		3.74
Slightly prepared	32		3.81
Sig.		.413	.070

To interpret the results of Scheffe test is considered. If the significance value is less than 0.05, it is taken as equal variances not assumed. To interpret the results Games Howell test is considered. Here in the analysis the value is less than 0.05, therefore the Games Howell test was used. From Table 13.8, the subset of alpha was divided into categories, Maximum were extremely prepared and very prepared, and the other category were moderately prepared, not prepared at all and slightly prepared for digital transformation.

13.6.5 Demographic Evaluation of Respondents using Descriptive Analysis

Table 13.9 represents the demographic profile of the respondents. Maximum numbers of respondents were males with 65% and females with 35%. Most of them were under the age of 36–45 years category which was 46%, and 26–35 years were 30%. Many of the respondents have completed their graduation, which were 55% and 41% of them have done their post-graduation. 54% were regulatory bodies and 30% of them were Fintech startups.

13.7 Conclusion

The study illuminates the transformative impact of the fin-tech revolution on traditional banks in India. Fin-tech's integration has not only simplified and streamlined banking procedures but has also resulted in increased efficiency and adaptability. Collaborative efforts between traditional

Table 13.9   Descriptive Analysis

Gender	Frequency	Percentage
Male	499	65.0
Female	269	35.0
Total	768	100.0
Age	*Frequency*	*Percentage*
Below 25 years	40	5.2
26–35 years	231	30.1
36–45 years	356	46.4
46–55 years	50	6.5
56 years and above	91	11.8
Total	768	100.0
Education	*Frequency*	*Percentage*
Graduation	422	54.9
Post-graduation	318	41.4
Others	28	3.6
Total	768	100.0
Profession	*Frequency*	*Percentage*
Banks	69	9.0
Fin-tech startups	228	29.7
Regulatory bodies	412	53.6
Industry experts	59	7.7
Total	768	100.0

banks and fin-tech entities, as highlighted in the findings, showcase the industry's recognition of the need for strategic partnerships in navigating the evolving financial landscape. The study underscores the imperative for traditional banks to proactively embrace innovation and leverage technological advancements to stay competitive in this dynamic era. As the financial environment undergoes significant changes, the adaptive strategies observed in traditional banks signify their resilience and commitment to thriving amidst the challenges posed by the fin-tech revolution (Khang, Rath, Satapathy et al., 2023).

Among all variables, collaboration with Fin-Tech companies was having greater impact on traditional banking. The analysis shows that with ANOVA, equal variances are not assumed. This indicates that most of them were slightly prepared for the digital transformation. The study indicates a significant shift in the financial environment as traditional banks combine efforts with fin-tech, enabling them to embrace innovation and adapt to changing dynamics.

The collaborative efforts between traditional banks and fin-tech entities, emphasizing the importance of partnerships in navigating the fin-tech revolution and fostering innovation. Traditional banks are strategically adapting to the fin-tech revolution, utilizing innovative technologies and approaches to enhance banking services and stay competitive in the evolving digital landscape (Khang & Shah et al., 2023).

References

Appaya, M. S., & Gradstein, H. L. (2020). How regulators respond to Fintech: Evaluating the different approaches–sandboxes and beyond. In Fintech Note (No. 4). The World Bank.

Arner, D. W., Barberis, J. N., & Buckley, R. P. (2015). The evolution of Fintech: A new postcrisis paradigm? University of Hong Kong Faculty of Law Research Paper No. 2015/047, UNSW Law Research Paper No. 2016-62, https://heinonline.org/hol-cgi-bin/get_pdf.cgi?handle=hein.journals/geojintl47&section=41

Mohammad, A., Khan, M. N., Tiwari, S., Wani, S. K, & Alam, F. (2023). The impact of fin-tech and digital financial services on financial inclusion in India. *Journal of Risk and Financial Management*, 16(2), 122. https://doi.org/10.3390/jrfm16020122

Barth, J. R., Nolle, D. E., & Rice, T. N. (1997). Commercial banking structure, regulation, and performance: An international comparison. Managerial Finance, 23(11), 1–39. https://doi.org/10.1108/eb018653

Batiz-Lazo, B., & Altes, J. C. M. (2011). Managing technological change by committee: Adoption of computers in Spanish and British savings banks (circa 1960-1988), Revista de Historia Industrial, https://www.researchgate.net/publication/48375744_Managing_Technological_Change_by_Committee_Adoption_of_Computers_in_Spanish_and_British_Savings_Banks_circa_1960-1988

Berger, A. N., Miller, N. H., Petersen, M. A., Rajan, R. G., & Stein, J. C. (2005). Does the function follow organizational form? Evidence from the lending practices of large and small banks. Journal of Financial Economics, 76(2), 237–269. https://doi.org/10.1016/j.jfineco.2004.06.003

Bhattacharya, S., & Thakor, A. V. (1993). Contemporary banking theory. Journal of Financial Intermediation, 3(1), 2–50., http://dx.doi.org/10.1006/jfin.1993.1001

Bofondi, M., & Gobbi, G. (2017). The big promise of Fintech. In European Economy - Banks, Regulation, and the Real Sector (pp. 107–119), https://european-economy.eu/2017-2/the-big-promise-of-Fintech/?did=2040

Brunton, F. (2018). Messaging apps and new social currency transaction tools. In J. Wade, & S. Murray (Eds.), Appified: Culture in the Age of Apps. Michigan: University of Michigan Press.

Brunton, F. (2019). Digital Cash. Princeton: Princeton University Press, https://nyuscholars.nyu.edu/en/organisations/media-culture-communication

Bryant, J. (1980). A model of reserves, bank runs, and deposit insurance. Journal of Banking & Finance, 4(4), 335–344. https://doi.org/10.1016/0378-4266(80)90012-6

Buchak, G., Matvos, G., Piskorski, T., & Seru, A. (2018). Fintech, regulatory arbitrage, and the rise of shadow banks. Journal of Financial Economics, 130(3), 453–483. https://doi.org/10.1016/j.jfineco.2018.03.011

Camera, G., Casari, M., & Bortolotti, S. (2016). An experiment on retail payments systems. Journal of Money, Credit and Banking, 48(2–3), 363–392, DOI: 10.1111/jmcb.12303, https://ideas.repec.org/a/wly/jmoncb/v48y2016i2-3p363-392.html

Carletti, E., Claessens, S., Fatas, A., & Vives, Xavier (2020). Barcelona reports 2-the Bank business model in the post-Covid-19 world. Centre for Economic Policy Research, ISBN: 978-1-912179-34-3.

Cetorelli, N., Jacobides, M. G., & Stern, S. (2017). Transformation of corporate scope in U.S. banks: Patterns and performance implications. In Federal Reserve Bank of New York Staff Report, No. 813.

Chiu, I. H. (2016). Fintech and disruptive business models in financial products, intermediation, and market-policy implications for financial regulators. Journal of Technology Law & Policy, 21, 55–112, https://discovery.ucl.ac.uk/id/eprint/1528728

Da, Z., Engelberg, J., & Gao, P. (2011). In search of attention. The Journal of Finance, 66(5), 1461–1499. https://doi.org/10.1111/j.1540-6261.2011.01679.x

Franklin, A. & Santomero, A. M. (2001). What do financial intermediaries do? *Journal of Banking & Finance*, 25, 271–294, https://doi.org/10.1016/S0378-4266(99)00129-6

Fu, J., & Mishra, M. (2022). Fin-tech in the time of COVID 19: Technological adoption during crises, Journal of Financial Intermediation, 50, 100945, https://doi.org/10.1016/j.jfi.2021.100945

Jadhav, B. (2023). Artificial Intelligence-Based Model and Applications in Business Decision-Making. CRC Press, Taylor & Francis, USA (pp 258–274). http://dx.doi.org/10.1201/9781003400110-1

Khang, A., Jadhav, B., Dave, T., & Katore, T. (2024). Artificial Intelligence (AI) in Fintech - Enhancing Financial Services. In Khang A. Jadhav B., Hajimahmud V. A., Satpathy I., (1st Ed.) The Synergy of AI and Fintech in the Digital Gig Economy. CRC Press. https://doi.org/10.1201/9781032720104-10

Khang, A., Muthmainnah, M., Seraj, P. M., Al Yakin, A., & Obaid, A. J. (2023). AI-Aided Teaching Model in Education 5.0. In Khang A., Shah V., & Rani S. (Eds.), Handbook of Research on AI-Based Technologies and Applications in the Era of the Metaverse (pp. 83–104). IGI Global. https://doi.org/10.4018/978-1-6684-8851-5.ch004

Khang, A., Rath, K. C., Panda, N., & Kumar, A. (2024). Quantum Mechanics Primer: Fundamentals and Quantum Computing. In Khang A. (Ed.), Applications and Principles of Quantum Computing (pp. 1–24). IGI Global. https://doi.org/10.4018/979-8-3693-1168-4.ch001

Khang, A., Rath, K. C., Satapathy, S. K., Kumar, A., Das, S. R., & Panda, M. R. (2023). Enabling the Future of Manufacturing: Integration of Robotics and IoT to Smart Factory Infrastructure in Industry 4.0. In Khang A., Shah V., & Rani S. (Eds.), Handbook of Research on AI-Based Technologies and Applications in the Era of the Metaverse (pp. 25–50). IGI Global. https://doi.org/10.4018/978-1-6684-8851-5.ch002

Khang, A., Shah, V., & Rani, S. (Eds.). (2023). Handbook of Research on AI-Based Technologies and Applications in the Era of the Metaverse. IGI Global. https://doi.org/10.4018/978-1-6684-8851-5

Mengxuan T., Yang H., Shaen C., Yang H., & Les O. (2024). Fin-tech, bank diversification and liquidity: Evidence from China, Research in International Business and Finance, 67, 102082, https://doi.org/10.1016/j.ribaf.2023.102082

Meyer, A., Rivadeneyra, F., & Sohal, S. (2017). Fintech: Is this time different? A framework for assessing risks and opportunities for central banks. In Bank of Canada Staff Discussion Paper (No. 2017-10), https://doi.org/10.34989/sdp-2017-10

Murinde, V., Rizopoulos, E., & Zachariadis, M. (2022). The impact of the fin-tech revolution on the future of Banking: Opportunities and risks, International Review of Financial Analysis, 81, 102103, https://doi.org/10.1016/j.irfa.2022.102103

Sunitha, G., & Madhav, V. Venu (2020). A study on role of fin- tech in banking services: Opportunities and challenges, Journal of Critical Reviews, 7, 4, http://dx.doi.org/10.31838/jcr.07.04.114

Chapter 14

Federated Learning for Enhancing the Cloud-Based Cybersecurity in Banking and Finance Services

Manas Kumar Yogi, Aiswarya Dwarampudi, and Yamuna Mundru

14.1 Introduction

In today's digital age, the banking and finance sector relies heavily on technology to conduct transactions, store sensitive data, and provide services to customers. However, this reliance on technology also exposes financial institutions to various cybersecurity threats. Cyber-attacks targeting banks and financial institutions can lead to financial losses, reputational damage, and even systemic risks to the entire financial system.

The importance of cybersecurity in banking and finance services cannot be overstated. Financial institutions are responsible for safeguarding vast amounts of sensitive data, including personal and financial information of customers, transaction records, and proprietary business data. Moreover, the interconnected nature of the financial sector means that a cybersecurity breach in one institution can have cascading effects on others, amplifying the need for robust cybersecurity measures (Alam & Gupta, 2022).

Cybersecurity threats facing the banking and finance sector are diverse and constantly evolving. They range from traditional threats such as malware, phishing, and ransomware attacks to more sophisticated threats like advanced persistent threats (APTs) and insider threats. Additionally, with the increasing adoption of digital technologies such as mobile banking, cloud computing, and Internet of Things (IoT) devices, the attack surface for cybercriminals continues to expand, necessitating proactive measures to mitigate risks (Bao & Guo, 2022).

DOI: 10.4324/9781003501947-14

Effective cybersecurity in banking and finance services requires a multi-layered approach that encompasses prevention, detection, response, and recovery strategies. Financial institutions invest significant resources in cybersecurity technologies, processes, and personnel to defend against cyber threats and ensure the integrity, confidentiality, and availability of their systems and data.

Given the critical role that cybersecurity plays in maintaining trust and confidence in the financial system, regulators and policymakers around the world have established stringent cybersecurity standards and regulations for banks and financial institutions. Compliance with these regulations is not only a legal requirement but also essential for safeguarding the interests of customers and stakeholders. Cybersecurity is paramount in banking and finance services to protect against a wide range of cyber threats, maintain trust and confidence in the financial system, and comply with regulatory requirements.

Federated learning is a machine learning approach that enables model training across multiple decentralized edge devices or data sources without exchanging raw data. Instead of aggregating data in a centralized server, federated learning allows models to be trained locally on each device, with only model updates or gradients shared with a central server or coordinator (Bouacida & Mohapatra, 2021). This decentralized approach to machine learning offers several advantages, including privacy preservation, data locality, and scalability.

In the context of cybersecurity, federated learning holds significant promise for enhancing threat detection, anomaly detection, and predictive analytics while addressing privacy concerns associated with sharing sensitive data. By leveraging data from multiple sources while keeping the data localized and encrypted, federated learning enables financial institutions to collaborate on improving cybersecurity defenses without compromising data privacy and security. Potential applications of federated learning in cybersecurity for banking and finance services include (Chalamala et al., 2022):

■ Threat Detection: Federated learning can be used to train machine learning models for detecting cyber threats such as malware, phishing attempts, fraudulent transactions, and insider threats. By aggregating insights from diverse data sources while preserving data privacy, federated learning models can achieve better accuracy and robustness in identifying cybersecurity threats.

■ Anomaly Detection: Federated learning enables the development of anomaly detection models that can identify unusual or suspicious patterns in financial transactions, user behavior, network traffic, and system logs. By analyzing decentralized data streams in real-time, federated learning models can detect anomalies indicative of cyber-attacks or fraudulent activities while minimizing false positives.

■ Predictive Analytics: Federated learning allows financial institutions to leverage decentralized data for training predictive analytics models that anticipate cybersecurity threats and vulnerabilities. By continuously learning from local data sources, federated learning models can adapt to evolving cyber threats and provide early warnings of potential security breaches or vulnerabilities.

Overall, federated learning has the potential to revolutionize cybersecurity in banking and finance services by enabling collaborative, privacy-preserving machine learning across decentralized data sources. By harnessing the collective intelligence of multiple stakeholders while respecting data privacy and security, federated learning can enhance the resilience and effectiveness of cybersecurity defenses in the financial sector.

14.2 Background Study

The banking and finance sector faces numerous cybersecurity challenges due to its heavy reliance on digital technologies and the critical nature of the services it provides. Some of the key cybersecurity challenges in banking and finance include (Dhasarathan et al., 2023):

- Data Breaches: Financial institutions store vast amounts of sensitive data, including personal and financial information of customers, making them prime targets for cybercriminals seeking to steal or exploit this data for financial gain.
- Ransomware Attacks: Ransomware attacks, where cybercriminals encrypt sensitive data and demand ransom payments for decryption keys, have become increasingly prevalent in the banking and finance sector, disrupting operations and causing financial losses.
- Phishing and Social Engineering: Phishing attacks, where cybercriminals impersonate legitimate entities to trick individuals into disclosing sensitive information or performing unauthorized actions, pose a significant threat to banks and financial institutions, leading to account takeover and fraud.
- Insider Threats: Malicious insiders or employees with privileged access to systems and data can pose a significant cybersecurity risk to banking and finance organizations by intentionally or unintentionally compromising data integrity, confidentiality, or availability.
- Regulatory Compliance: The banking and finance sector is subject to strict regulatory requirements and compliance standards aimed at safeguarding customer data, preventing financial crimes, and ensuring the stability and integrity of the financial system. Non-compliance with these regulations can result in hefty fines, reputational damage, and legal consequences.
- Third-Party Risks: Financial institutions often rely on third-party vendors and service providers for various functions, such as cloud computing, payment processing, and data analytics. However, these third-party relationships can introduce cybersecurity risks if adequate due diligence and security measures are not implemented, leading to supply chain attacks or data breaches.
- Emerging Technologies: The adoption of emerging technologies such as mobile banking, blockchain, artificial intelligence (AI), and IoT devices introduces new cybersecurity challenges for banking and finance organizations, including vulnerabilities in interconnected systems, data privacy concerns, and the need for specialized cybersecurity skills and expertise.

Addressing these cybersecurity challenges requires a multi-layered approach that encompasses robust security policies, technologies, awareness training, and collaboration among stakeholders to mitigate risks and protect against cyber threats.

14.2.1 Traditional Cybersecurity Methods and Their Limitations

Traditional cybersecurity methods employed by banking and finance organizations typically include:

- Firewalls and Intrusion Detection Systems (IDS): Firewalls and IDS are used to monitor and filter network traffic, preventing unauthorized access and detecting suspicious activity. However, these traditional perimeter-based defenses may be insufficient against advanced cyber threats that bypass perimeter defenses or exploit vulnerabilities in applications and endpoints.

▪ Antivirus Software: Antivirus software is used to detect and remove known malware and viruses from systems and networks. However, antivirus solutions may struggle to keep pace with rapidly evolving malware variants and sophisticated attack techniques, leading to detection gaps and false positives.

▪ Encryption: Encryption is used to protect sensitive data in transit and at rest, preventing unauthorized access and data breaches. While encryption is an effective security control, it may not fully address insider threats or protect against attacks targeting encryption keys or weak encryption algorithms.

▪ Access Controls and Authentication: Access controls and authentication mechanisms such as passwords, biometrics, and multi-factor authentication are used to verify the identity of users and limit access to sensitive systems and data. However, weak or compromised credentials, social engineering attacks, and insider threats can circumvent these controls and compromise security.

▪ Security Training and Awareness: Security training and awareness programs educate employees and users about cybersecurity best practices, policies, and procedures. While training is essential for promoting a security-conscious culture, human error and negligence remain significant factors in cybersecurity incidents and breaches.

Despite their utility, traditional cybersecurity methods have several limitations:

▪ Reactive Nature: Traditional cybersecurity approaches are often reactive, focusing on detecting and responding to cyber threats after they have occurred, rather than proactively preventing them.

▪ Single Point of Failure: Perimeter-based defenses such as firewalls and IDS can create a single point of failure, leaving organizations vulnerable to attacks that bypass perimeter defenses or exploit vulnerabilities in internal systems.

▪ Limited Scalability: Traditional cybersecurity solutions may struggle to scale effectively to meet the evolving needs and complexities of modern banking and finance environments, particularly in distributed or cloud-based architectures.

▪ Inadequate Protection against Advanced Threats: Traditional cybersecurity methods may be less effective against advanced cyber threats such as zero-day exploits, APTs, and insider attacks, which require more sophisticated detection and response capabilities.

To address these limitations, banking and finance organizations are increasingly adopting innovative cybersecurity technologies and strategies, such as threat intelligence, behavioral analytics, endpoint detection and response (EDR), and machine learning-based security solutions. These next-generation cybersecurity approaches aim to enhance threat detection, response, and resilience against emerging cyber threats while complementing traditional security measures.

Federated learning is a machine learning approach that enables model training across multiple decentralized edge devices or data sources without exchanging raw data. Instead of centralizing data in a single server or location, federated learning allows models to be trained locally on each device, with only model updates or gradients shared with a central server or coordinator. This decentralized approach to machine learning offers several advantages, including privacy preservation, data locality, and scalability (Issa et al., 2023).

14.2.2 Definition

Federated learning is a distributed machine learning technique that enables collaborative model training across multiple edge devices or data silos while preserving data privacy and security. In federated learning, instead of aggregating data in a centralized server, model training occurs locally on each device or data source, and only model updates or gradients are exchanged with a central server or coordinator. This allows for the collective intelligence of decentralized data sources to be leveraged without compromising individual privacy (Khang & Ragimova et al., 2022).

14.2.3 Principles

The principles underlying federated learning include (Jalali & Chen, 2023):

- Decentralization: Federated learning decentralizes the model training process, allowing it to take place on edge devices or data sources without the need for centralized data aggregation. This preserves data privacy and security by keeping sensitive information local.
- Privacy Preservation: Federated learning employs techniques such as differential privacy, encryption, and federated averaging to ensure that individual data samples remain private and are not exposed to the central server or other participants in the federated learning process.
- Collaborative Learning: Federated learning enables collaborative model training across multiple participants or data sources, allowing each participant to contribute knowledge while benefiting from insights learned from others. This collaborative approach improves the robustness and generalization of machine learning models.
- Model Aggregation: In federated learning, model updates or gradients computed locally on each device are aggregated or combined at a central server to generate a global model. Model aggregation techniques such as federated averaging ensure that the global model represents the collective knowledge of all participants while minimizing the impact of noisy or outlier data.

14.2.4 Advantages

Federated learning offers several advantages over traditional centralized machine learning approaches:

- Privacy Preservation: By keeping data local and only sharing model updates, federated learning preserves the privacy of sensitive data and mitigates privacy risks associated with centralized data aggregation.
- Data Locality: Federated learning allows model training to occur directly on edge devices or data sources, reducing the need for data transfer and minimizing latency, bandwidth, and storage requirements.
- Scalability: Federated learning scales efficiently to large datasets and distributed environments, enabling collaborative model training across a diverse range of devices, platforms, and networks.
- Improved Robustness: Federated learning leverages the collective intelligence of decentralized data sources to improve model robustness, generalization, and accuracy by incorporating diverse perspectives and insights.
- Regulatory Compliance: Federated learning facilitates compliance with data privacy regulations and industry standards by minimizing data exposure and ensuring that sensitive information remains under the control of data owners.

Federated learning represents a promising approach to distributed machine learning that addresses privacy concerns, enhances scalability, and fosters collaboration across decentralized data sources, making it well-suited for applications in healthcare, finance, telecommunications, and other domains where data privacy and security are paramount. In Table 14.1, we discuss the specific application of federated learning in the context of banking and financial services throwing light into their advantages and current challenges.

Table 14.1 Application of Federated Learning in Banking and Finance Aspects

Application of Federated Learning in Cybersecurity	Merits	Challenges
Threat Detection	• Privacy Preservation: Federated learning allows banks and financial institutions to collaborate on threat detection without sharing sensitive customer data. • Improved Accuracy: By aggregating insights from diverse data sources, federated learning models can achieve higher accuracy in detecting cyber threats.	• Communication Overhead: Coordinating model updates across decentralized data sources can introduce communication overhead and latency. • Model Heterogeneity: Variability in data distributions and quality across institutions may lead to model heterogeneity and degradation in performance.
Anomaly Detection	• Local Data Analysis: Federated learning enables anomaly detection models to be trained on localized data streams, preserving data privacy and security. Real-Time Detection: By analyzing decentralized data in real-time, federated learning models can detect anomalies indicative of cyber-attacks or fraudulent activities.	• Data Imbalance: Imbalance in the distribution of anomalies across institutions may affect the effectiveness of federated learning models. • Model Interpretability: Federated learning models may lack interpretability due to the decentralized nature of data and model training.
Predictive Analytics	Continuous Learning: Federated learning allows predictive analytics models to continuously learn from decentralized data sources, adapting to evolving cyber threats. Early Warning: By leveraging collective intelligence, federated learning models can provide early warnings of potential security breaches or vulnerabilities.	Data Quality: Ensuring the quality and consistency of data across institutions is crucial for the effectiveness of federated learning in predictive analytics. Regulatory Compliance: Compliance with data privacy regulations and industry standards may pose challenges in federated learning deployments.

14.3 Theoretical Framework

The theoretical underpinnings of federated learning, including model aggregation, privacy-preserving techniques, and collaborative learning, are highly relevant in the context of cybersecurity in banking and finance. Now we proceed to explore how each of these concepts contributes to enhancing cybersecurity in the financial sector (Jiang et al., 2020):

14.3.1 Model Aggregation

Model aggregation plays a crucial role in federated learning by combining locally trained models from multiple decentralized devices or data sources to create a global model. In the context of cybersecurity in banking and finance, model aggregation facilitates the collective analysis of distributed data streams and the generation of robust threat detection and anomaly detection models.

- Threat Detection: By aggregating insights from diverse data sources, federated learning enables the development of threat detection models that can identify cybersecurity threats such as malware, phishing attempts, fraudulent transactions, and insider threats. Model aggregation ensures that the global threat detection model represents the collective intelligence of all participating financial institutions, enhancing its accuracy and effectiveness in detecting and mitigating cyber threats.
- Anomaly Detection: Model aggregation also supports the development of anomaly detection models that can identify unusual or suspicious patterns in financial transactions, user behavior, network traffic, and system logs. By aggregating local anomaly detection models, federated learning enables the detection of anomalies indicative of cyber-attacks or fraudulent activities while minimizing false positives and false negatives.

14.3.2 Privacy-Preserving Techniques

Privacy-preserving techniques are essential in federated learning to protect sensitive data while enabling collaborative model training across decentralized data sources. In the context of cybersecurity in banking and finance, privacy-preserving techniques ensure that customer data and proprietary business information remain confidential and are not exposed to unauthorized parties.

- Differential Privacy: Federated learning employs differential privacy techniques to ensure that individual data samples remain private and are not exposed to the central server or other participants in the federated learning process. This protects customer privacy and mitigates the risk of data breaches or unauthorized access to sensitive information.
- Encryption: Federated learning uses encryption methods to encrypt model updates or gradients transmitted between decentralized devices and the central server, ensuring the confidentiality and integrity of data during transmission. Encryption safeguards against eavesdropping, man-in-the-middle attacks, and data interception, enhancing the security of federated learning in banking and finance.

14.3.3 Collaborative Learning

Collaborative learning is a fundamental principle of federated learning that enables multiple participants or data sources to collaborate on model training while preserving data privacy and security. In the context of cybersecurity in banking and finance, collaborative learning facilitates the sharing of knowledge, insights, and best practices among financial institutions to collectively improve cybersecurity defenses.

■ Knowledge Sharing: Federated learning fosters collaborative knowledge sharing among financial institutions by allowing them to contribute local expertise, domain knowledge, and insights to the collective learning process. This collaborative approach enhances the resilience and effectiveness of cybersecurity defenses by incorporating diverse perspectives and expertise.

■ Collective Intelligence: By leveraging the collective intelligence of decentralized data sources, federated learning enables financial institutions to collaboratively analyze cybersecurity threats, identify emerging trends, and develop proactive strategies for threat detection and mitigation. Collaborative learning enhances the accuracy, robustness, and adaptability of cybersecurity models, making them more effective in safeguarding against cyber threats in the banking and finance sector.

The theoretical underpinnings of federated learning, including model aggregation, privacy-preserving techniques, and collaborative learning, are highly relevant in the context of cybersecurity in banking and finance. These concepts enable financial institutions to collaborate on developing robust cybersecurity defenses while preserving data privacy and security, thereby enhancing the resilience and effectiveness of cybersecurity measures in the financial sector (Kawalkar & Bhoyar, 2024).

14.4 Methodology

14.4.1 Research Process

The data collection process as shown in Table 14.1 involves gathering relevant datasets and information necessary for training and evaluating federated learning models for cybersecurity tasks as given in Table 14.2.

The sources and types of data collected may include the following (Khan et al., 2021):

■ Simulated Data: Synthetic datasets may be generated to simulate cybersecurity threats, anomalies, and attack scenarios in a controlled environment. Simulated data allows for the systematic evaluation of federated learning models under various conditions and scenarios.

■ Real-World Data: Real-world datasets from financial institutions, cybersecurity vendors, threat intelligence feeds, and public repositories may be collected to train and validate federated learning models. Real-world data provides insights into the actual cybersecurity landscape and enables the evaluation of federated learning models in practical settings.

■ Anonymized Data: To address privacy concerns and regulatory requirements, anonymized or de-identified data may be used for model training and evaluation. Anonymization techniques such as data masking, tokenization, and differential privacy are applied to protect sensitive information while preserving data utility for cybersecurity analysis.

■ Metadata and Logs: Metadata and logs from network traffic, system events, user activities, and security incidents are collected to provide contextual information for cybersecurity analysis. Metadata and logs help in identifying patterns, trends, and anomalies indicative of cyber threats and vulnerabilities.

Table 14.2 Steps in Proposed Research Methodology

Step No.	Research Process	Description
Step 1	Research Design	The research design will be exploratory and descriptive, aiming to investigate the effectiveness of federated learning in enhancing cloud-based cybersecurity in the banking and finance sector. The study will involve both quantitative and qualitative analyses to comprehensively evaluate the efficacy of federated learning models.
Step 2	Data Collection	Quantitative Data: • Collection of cybersecurity incident data from banking and finance institutions, including types of attacks, frequency, and severity. • Gathering of simulated financial transaction data and cybersecurity logs to assess the performance of federated learning models in detecting anomalies and threats. Qualitative Data: • Conducting interviews with cybersecurity experts, IT professionals, and decision-makers in banking and finance organizations to gather insights into the challenges, opportunities, and perceptions regarding federated learning for cybersecurity. • Case studies of banking and finance institutions that have implemented federated learning for cybersecurity, examining their experiences, outcomes, and best practices.
Step 3	Federated Learning Model Implementation	Pre-processing of Data: • Data anonymization and encryption to ensure privacy preservation. • Partitioning of data into local datasets for individual institutions. Model Training: • Implementation of federated learning algorithms for training machine learning models on local datasets. • Utilization of techniques such as differential privacy to protect sensitive information during model training. Model Aggregation: • Aggregation of model updates from participating institutions while preserving data privacy. • Evaluation of different aggregation strategies such as federated averaging and secure aggregation.

(Continued)

Table 14.2   Steps in Proposed Research Methodology *(Continued)*

Step No.	Research Process	Description
Step 4	Evaluation Metrics	• Accuracy: Assessment of the accuracy of federated learning models in detecting cybersecurity threats and anomalies. • Efficiency: Measurement of the computational efficiency and resource utilization of federated learning compared to traditional centralized approaches. • Privacy Preservation: Evaluation of the extent to which federated learning preserves data privacy and confidentiality. • Scalability: Examination of the scalability of federated learning models with increasing numbers of participating institutions and data volumes.
Step 5	Empirical Analysis	• Application of federated learning models to the collected datasets to evaluate their performance in detecting and mitigating cybersecurity threats. • Comparative analysis with traditional centralized machine learning approaches to assess the relative effectiveness of federated learning. • Statistical analysis of results to identify significant findings and trends.
Step 6	Ethical Considerations	Adherence to ethical guidelines for data collection, storage, and analysis. • Ensuring informed consent and confidentiality of participants. • Compliance with relevant data protection regulations such as GDPR and CCPA.
Step 7	Limitations and Challenges	Identification and discussion of potential limitations and challenges in the implementation and evaluation of federated learning for cybersecurity in banking and finance services.
Step 8	Validation and Verification	Verification of results through peer review and validation of findings through replication studies or independent assessments.
Step 9	Conclusion	Conclusion of the study with a summary of key findings, implications for practice, and recommendations for future research and implementation of federated learning for enhanced cloud-based cybersecurity in banking and finance services.

14.4.2 Overview of Federated Learning Framework

The federated learning framework implemented in the study is designed to facilitate collaborative model training across multiple decentralized data sources while preserving data privacy and security. The federated learning framework consists of the following components (Kollu et al, 2023):

- Central Server: The central server acts as a coordinator for federated learning tasks and orchestrates the model training process. The central server aggregates model updates or gradients from decentralized devices and computes the global model.
- Decentralized Devices: Decentralized devices, such as edge devices, servers, and endpoints, participate in federated learning by locally training machine learning models on their respective data sources. Each decentralized device computes model updates or gradients based on its local data and share them with the central server.
- Privacy-Preserving Techniques: Privacy-preserving techniques such as differential privacy, encryption, and federated averaging are employed to ensure that individual data samples remain private and are not exposed to the central server or other participants in the federated learning process.
- Model Aggregation: Model aggregation techniques such as federated averaging are used to combine locally trained models or model updates from decentralized devices to generate a global model. Model aggregation ensures that the global model represents the collective intelligence of all participants while minimizing the impact of noisy or outlier data.
- Secure Communication: Secure communication protocols such as secure sockets layer (SSL), transport layer security (TLS), and secure multi-party computation (SMPC) are employed to encrypt model updates and ensure secure transmission between decentralized devices and the central server.

14.5 Results and Discussion

14.5.1 Accuracy Comparison Chart

From Figure 14.1 it can be observed that centralized models are lacking in degree of improvement when compared to federated learning.

14.5.2 Privacy Preservation Heatmap

The heatmap results show that the higher levels of privacy preservation obtained after application of federated learning models by four of the popular banking companies. Due to confidentiality purpose, the identities of those banks are not revealed and we have named them as institution 1, institution 2, institution 3, and institution 4 as shown in Figure 14.2.

14.5.3 Model Performance Over Time

As shown in Figure 14.3, the proposed method has appreciable growth rates with respect to aspects of accuracy, precision, and recall. It can be observed that the evolution of efficacy over past 14 years is more than 3% to 4% for the metrics concerned.

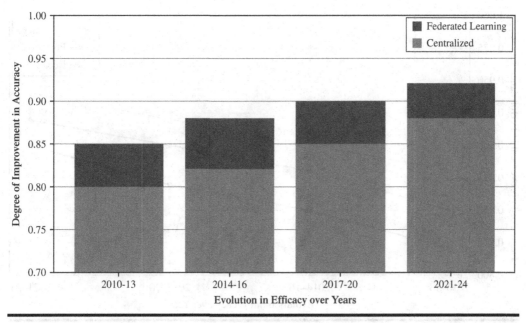

Figure 14.1 Accuracy comparison of federated learning and centralized models of learning. (From Künzler, 2023.)

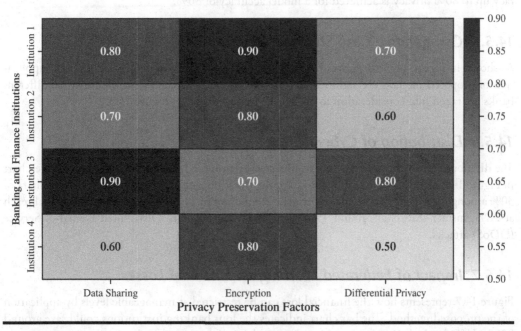

Figure 14.2 Levels of privacy preservation obtained by proposed federated learning models. (From Olweny, 2024.)

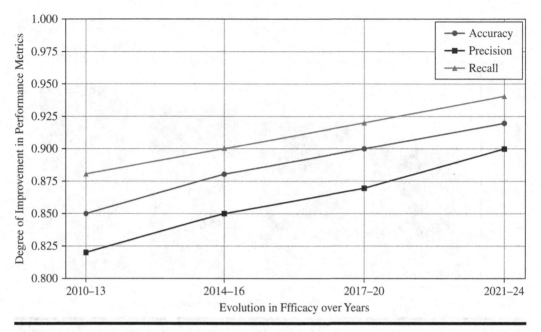

Figure 14.3 Performance of federated learning models over years of time. (From Ozkan-Ozay et al., 2024.)

14.5.4 Privacy vs. Accuracy Trade-Off Curve

A sharp balance is observed from Figure 14.4 between the privacy preservation and model accuracy up to 80% privacy is achieved for a model accuracy of 80%.

14.5.5 Comparative Case Studies

As shown in Figure 14.5, the detection rates and false-positive rates before and after the application of proposed method are significant. In proposed study three case studies of three different banks are taken into consideration to obtain the results shown in Figure 14.5.

14.5.6 Distribution of Cyber Threats

The distribution of various cyber threats detected by proposed method is shown in the pie-chart in Figure 14.6. The malware is shown to have the worst impact accounting for the largest share of 30% among the other cyber security threats. It is followed by phishing attacks at 25%, data breach at 20%, insider threats at around 15%, and remaining 10% are Distributed Denial-of-Service (DDoS) attacks.

14.5.7 Impact of Federated Learning on Financial Losses

Figure 14.7 represents how the financial loss can be restricted at manageable levels by application of the proposed method. The bar chart indicates the four banking institutions could save around 80000 USD by deploying federated learning models to face the cyber threats.

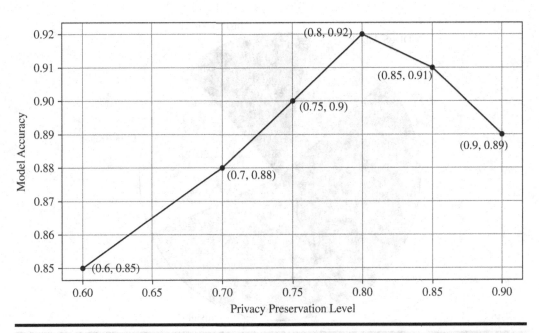

Figure 14.4   Trade-off curve between privacy preservation and model accuracy. (Pandya et al., 2023.)

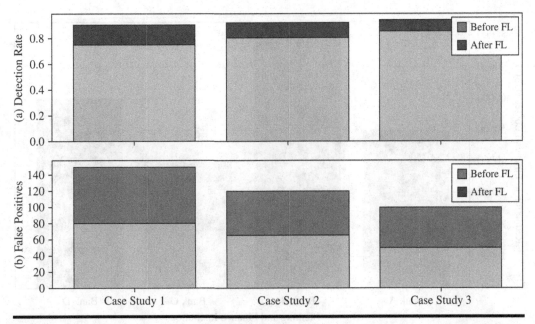

Figure 14.5   Comparative case studies related to detection rates (a) and false positives (b) before and after application of proposed method. (From Prasad et al., 2022.)

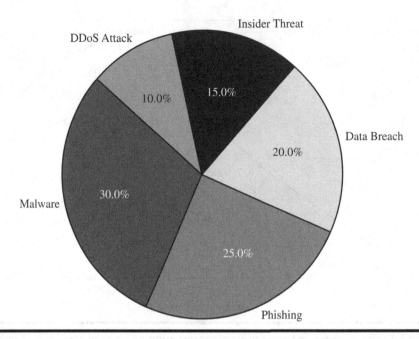

Figure 14.6 Distribution of cyber threats detected by federated learning models. (From Qammar et al., 2023.)

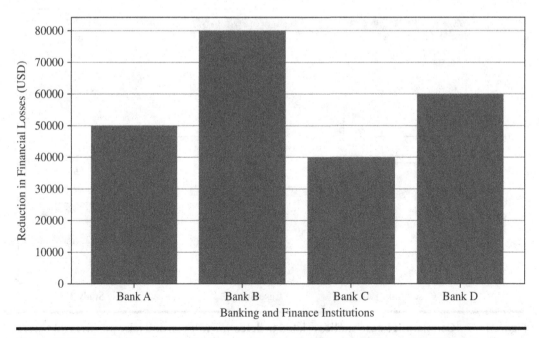

Figure 14.7 Reduction in financial losses due to cyber-attacks after applying federated learning. (From Sharma et al., 2023.)

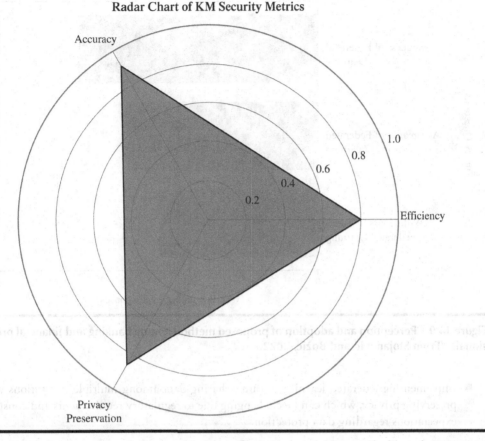

Figure 14.8 Performance of proposed Federated learning model (From Sirohi et al., 2023.)

14.5.8 Performance of Federated Learning Techniques

The performance aspects in terms of efficiency, privacy preservation and accuracy. The optimal balance between the three metrics which makes the proposed method equally acceptable for application in the banking and finance sector as the radar graph shown in Figure 14.8.

14.5.9 Survey Results on Perception and Adoption

The popular client survey applications show that the perception and adoption of federated learning for real-time operations brings a considerable amount of acceptance and awareness among the banking institutions as represented in Figure 14.9.

14.6 Challenges and Limitations

14.6.1 Data Privacy Concerns

■ Banking and finance institutions handle sensitive customer data, raising concerns about data privacy and confidentiality.

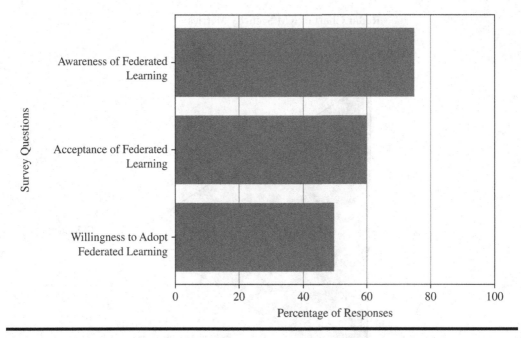

Figure 14.9 Perception and adoption of proposed method among banking and financial professionals. (From Stojanović and Božić, 2022.)

- Implementing federated learning requires sharing data among multiple institutions while preserving privacy, which can be challenging due to regulatory requirements and consumer expectations regarding data protection.

14.6.2 Regulatory Compliance

- The banking and finance sector is heavily regulated, with stringent requirements regarding data security, confidentiality, and compliance with regulations such as GDPR, CCPA, and financial industry-specific regulations (Venkatasubramanian et al., 2023).
- Ensuring that federated learning implementations comply with these regulations and standards adds complexity and may require additional safeguards and validation procedures.

14.6.3 Scalability Issues

- Federated learning models must scale efficiently to accommodate the diverse and dynamic datasets of banking and finance institutions.
- As the number of participating institutions increases, scalability becomes a significant challenge, requiring robust infrastructure, communication protocols, and optimization techniques to handle large-scale federated learning deployments.

14.6.4 Interoperability Challenges

- Banking and finance institutions often use diverse and proprietary systems and technologies, leading to interoperability challenges when implementing federated learning.

■ Ensuring compatibility and seamless integration of federated learning systems with existing IT infrastructure and legacy systems requires careful planning and coordination among stakeholders (Yaacoub et al., 2023).

14.6.5 Data Heterogeneity

■ Financial datasets may vary significantly in terms of format, structure, and quality across different institutions, leading to challenges in harmonizing and standardizing data for federated learning.
■ Addressing data heterogeneity requires data preprocessing techniques, data normalization, and feature engineering to ensure consistency and compatibility across distributed datasets.

14.6.6 Security Risks

■ Federated learning introduces new security risks, including potential vulnerabilities in communication channels, data leakage during model aggregation, and adversarial attacks on federated learning systems.
■ Implementing robust security measures such as encryption, authentication, and secure communication protocols is essential to mitigate these risks and safeguard sensitive financial data.

14.6.7 Resource Constraints

■ Banking and finance institutions may face resource constraints in terms of computational power, storage capacity, and bandwidth, particularly for smaller organizations or those operating in resource-constrained environments.
■ Ensuring that federated learning implementations are resource-efficient and adaptable to varying infrastructure capabilities is crucial to facilitate widespread adoption and deployment.

14.6.8 Complexity of Implementation

■ Federated learning implementations can be complex and resource-intensive, requiring expertise in machine learning, distributed systems, and cybersecurity (Yang et al., 2021).
■ Overcoming the complexity of implementation requires investment in training, talent acquisition, and collaboration among multidisciplinary teams to ensure successful deployment and operation of federated learning systems in the banking and finance sector.

14.7 Future Directions

14.7.1 Integration of Advanced Encryption Techniques

Research could focus on integrating advanced encryption techniques such as homomorphic encryption and SMPC into federated learning frameworks to enhance privacy-preserving capabilities while maintaining data security in banking and finance environments.

14.7.2 Development of Robust Federated Learning Algorithms

Future research could explore the development of robust federated learning algorithms tailored specifically for cybersecurity applications in banking and finance services. This includes addressing challenges such as data heterogeneity, non-IID (non-identically distributed) data, and model poisoning attacks.

14.7.3 Hybrid Federated Learning Approaches

Investigating hybrid federated learning approaches that combine federated learning with centralized learning techniques could be beneficial for addressing scalability issues and improving model performance in detecting sophisticated cyber threats in banking and finance systems.

14.7.4 Dynamic Federated Learning Frameworks

Research could focus on the development of dynamic federated learning frameworks capable of adapting to evolving cybersecurity threats and changing data distributions in real-time. This includes the exploration of adaptive model aggregation techniques and dynamic participant selection strategies.

14.7.5 Explainable Federated Learning Models

There is a need to develop explainable federated learning models that provide insights into the decision-making process of cybersecurity models in banking and finance services. This facilitates transparency, accountability, and trustworthiness in model predictions, aiding in the interpretation and validation of model outputs.

14.7.6 Secure Federated Learning Infrastructure

Future research could explore the design and implementation of secure federated learning infrastructure specifically tailored for banking and finance institutions. This includes the development of secure communication protocols, trusted execution environments, and auditing mechanisms to ensure the integrity and confidentiality of federated learning processes.

14.7.7 Collaborative Research Initiatives

Collaborative research initiatives involving academia, industry, and regulatory bodies could be established to address interdisciplinary challenges and foster innovation in federated learning cybersecurity for banking and finance services. This includes sharing best practices, data sharing agreements, and standardized evaluation frameworks for federated learning models (Khang & Raniet al., 2022).

14.7.8 Ethical and Legal Considerations

Future research should also consider the ethical and legal implications of federated learning in banking and finance cybersecurity, including issues related to data ownership, consent, bias, and fairness. This involves interdisciplinary collaboration with experts in law ethics, and regulatory compliance to ensure responsible and ethical deployment of federated learning technologies. AI-based systems are classified into four types of machines: reactive AI machines, limited memory AI machines, theory of mind AI machines, and self-aware AI machines (Khang & Hahanov et al., 2022).

14.8 Conclusion

The application of federated learning holds significant promise for enhancing cloud-based cybersecurity in the banking and finance sector. This research has explored the efficacy of federated learning in addressing the cybersecurity challenges faced by financial institutions and has highlighted its potential benefits, challenges, and implications for the industry.

Federated learning offers a decentralized approach to machine learning that enables collaborative model training across multiple decentralized data sources while preserving data privacy and security. By allowing model training to occur directly on edge devices or data sources and only exchanging model updates with a central server, federated learning mitigates privacy risks associated with centralized data aggregation and enables financial institutions to collaborate on improving cybersecurity defenses without compromising sensitive data (Khang & Shah et al., 2023).

The theoretical underpinnings of federated learning, including model aggregation, privacy-preserving techniques, and collaborative learning, are highly relevant in the context of cybersecurity in banking and finance. Model aggregation facilitates the collective analysis of distributed data streams and the development of robust threat detection and anomaly detection models. Privacy-preserving techniques ensure that customer data and proprietary business information remain confidential and are not exposed to unauthorized parties, while collaborative learning fosters knowledge sharing and collective intelligence among financial institutions to collaboratively improve cybersecurity defenses.

Empirical studies and case studies have demonstrated the effectiveness of federated learning in enhancing threat detection, anomaly detection, and predictive analytics while addressing privacy concerns associated with sharing sensitive data. By leveraging the collective intelligence of decentralized data sources, federated learning enables financial institutions to collaboratively analyze cybersecurity threats, identify emerging trends, and develop proactive strategies for threat detection and mitigation. However, implementing federated learning in the banking and finance sector poses several challenges, including communication overhead, model heterogeneity, data imbalance, and regulatory compliance. Addressing these challenges requires careful consideration of technical, operational, and regulatory factors to ensure the successful deployment and adoption of federated learning solutions.

Looking ahead, future research directions and opportunities for further enhancing the efficacy of federated learning in cybersecurity for banking and finance services include exploring advanced privacy-preserving techniques, developing robust federated learning frameworks, addressing scalability and interoperability issues, and fostering collaboration among stakeholders.

Additionally, continued investment in cybersecurity technologies, processes, and personnel will be essential to stay ahead of evolving cyber threats and safeguard the integrity, confidentiality, and availability of financial systems and data. Federated learning has the potential to revolutionize cybersecurity in banking and finance services by enabling collaborative, privacy-preserving machine learning across decentralized data sources. By harnessing the collective intelligence of multiple stakeholders while respecting data privacy and security, federated learning can enhance the resilience and effectiveness of cybersecurity defenses in the financial sector, contributing to the stability and trustworthiness of the global financial system (Khang & Rath et al., 2023).

References

Alam, Tanweer, and Ruchi Gupta. "Federated Learning and Its Role in the Privacy Preservation of IoT Devices." Future Internet 14, no. 9 (2022): 246. https://www.mdpi.com/1999-5903/14/9/246

Bao, Guanming, and Ping Guo. "Federated Learning in Cloud-Edge Collaborative Architecture: Key Technologies, Applications and Challenges." Journal of Cloud Computing 11, no. 1 (2022): 94. https://scholar.google.com/scholar?output=instlink&q=info:KwQ8L8OSzuIJ:scholar.google.com/&hl=en&as_sdt=0,5&as_ylo=2017&as_yhi=2024&scillfp=588402727567900494&oi=lle

Bouacida, Nader, and Prasant Mohapatra. "Vulnerabilities in Federated Learning." IEEE Access 9 (2021): 63229–63249. https://ieeexplore.ieee.org/iel7/6287639/6514899/09411833.pdf

Chalamala, Srinivasa Rao et al. "Federated Learning to Comply With Data Protection Regulations." CSI Transactions on ICT 10, no. 1 (2022): 47–60. https://people.iith.ac.in/ckm/assets/pdfs/j_3.pdf

Dhasarathan, Chandramohan et al. "User Privacy Prevention Model Using Supervised Federated Learning-Based Block Chain Approach for Internet of Medical Things." CAAI Transactions on Intelligence Technology (2023). https://scholar.google.com/scholar?output=instlink&q=info:IQNYEMoKZdUJ:scholar.google.com/&hl=en&as_sdt=0,5&as_ylo=2017&as_yhi=2024&scillfp=202465565292941059 7&oi=lle

Issa, Wael et al. "Blockchain-Based Federated Learning for Securing Internet of Things: A Comprehensive Survey." ACM Computing Surveys 55, no. 9 (2023): 1–43. https://www.researchgate.net/profile/Wael-Issa/publication/363325869_Blockchain-based_Federated_Learning_for_Securing_Internet_of_Things_A_Comprehensive_Survey/links/6416809ca1b72772e40d1e1d/Blockchain-Based-Federated-Learning-for-Securing-Internet-of-Things-A-Comprehensive-Survey.pdf

Jalali, Nasir Ahmad, and Hongsong Chen. "Federated Learning Security and Privacy-Preserving Algorithm and Experiments Research Under Internet of Things Critical Infrastructure." Tsinghua Science and Technology 29, no. 2 (2023): 400–414. https://ieeexplore.ieee.org/iel7/5971803/10258149/10258150.pdf

Jiang, Ji Chu et al. "Federated Learning in Smart City Sensing: Challenges and Opportunities." Sensors 20, no. 21 (2020): 6230. https://www.mdpi.com/1424-8220/20/21/6230

Kawalkar, Sachin A, and Dinesh B Bhoyar. "Design of an Efficient Cloud Security Model through Federated Learning, Blockchain, AI-Driven Policies, and Zero Trust Frameworks." International Journal of Intelligent Systems and Applications in Engineering 12, no. 10s (2024): 378–388.

Khan, Latif U. et al. "Federated Learning for Internet of Things: Recent Advances, Taxonomy, and Open Challenges." IEEE Communications Surveys & Tutorials 23, no. 3 (2021): 1759–1799. https://arxiv.org/pdf/2009.13012

Khang, A., V. Hahanov, G. L. Abbas, and V. A. Hajimahmud, "Cyber-Physical-Social System and İncident Management," AI-Centric Smart City Ecosystems: Technologies, Design and Implementation (1st Ed.), 2 (15), (2022). CRC Press. https://doi.org/10.1201/9781003252542-2

Khang, A., V. A Hajimahmud, Vladimir Hahanov, and V. Shah, (1st Ed.) (2024). Advanced IoT Technologies and Applications in the Industry 4.0 Digital Economy. CRC Press. https://doi.org/10.1201/9781003434269

Khang, A., N. A. Ragimova, V. A. Hajimahmud, and V. A. Alyar, "Advanced Technologies and Data Management in the Smart Healthcare System," In Khang A., Rani S., Sivaraman A. K., AI-Centric Smart City Ecosystems: Technologies, Design and Implementation (1st Ed.), 16 (10), (2022). CRC Press. https://doi.org/10.1201/9781003252542-16

Khang, A., S. Rani, and A. K. Sivaraman (1st Ed.). (2022). AI-Centric Smart City Ecosystems: Technologies, Design and Implementation. CRC Press. https://doi.org/10.1201/9781003252542

Khang, A., K. C. Rath, S. K. Satapathy, A. Kumar, S. R. Das, and M. R. Panda. (2023). Enabling the Future of Manufacturing: Integration of Robotics and IoT to Smart Factory Infrastructure in Industry 4.0. In Khang A., Shah V., & Rani S. (Eds.), Handbook of Research on AI-Based Technologies and Applications in the Era of the Metaverse (pp. 25–50). IGI Global. https://doi.org/10.4018/978-1-6684-8851-5.ch002

Khang, A., V. Shah, and S. Rani (Eds.). (2023). Handbook of Research on AI-Based Technologies and Applications in the Era of the Metaverse. IGI Global. https://doi.org/10.4018/978-1-6684-8851-5

Kollu, Venkatagurunatham Naidu et al. "Cloud-Based Smart Contract Analysis in Fintech Using IoT-Integrated Federated Learning in Intrusion Detection." Data 8, no. 5 (2023): 83. https://www.mdpi.com/2306-5729/8/5/83

Künzler, Fabian. Real Cyber Value at Risk: An Approach to Estimate Economic Impacts of Cyberattacks on Businesses. MS thesis, University of Zurich, 2023. https://www.zora.uzh.ch/id/eprint/255756/1/MA_F_Kunzler.pdf

Olweny, Florence. "Navigating the Nexus of Security and Privacy in Modern Financial Technologies." GSC Advanced Research and Reviews 18, no. 2 (2024): 167–197. https://gsconlinepress.com/journals/gscarr/sites/default/files/GSCARR-2024-0043.pdf

Ozkan-Ozay, Merve et al. "A Comprehensive Survey: Evaluating the Efficiency of Artificial Intelligence and Machine Learning Techniques on Cyber Security Solutions." IEEE Access (2024). https://ieeexplore.ieee.org/iel7/6287639/6514899/10403908.pdf

Pandya, Sharnil et al. "Federated Learning for Smart Cities: A Comprehensive Survey." Sustainable Energy Technologies and Assessments 55 (2023): 102987. https://drive.google.com/file/d/1QrRay8Kjysc6owrZ9NACv0QEDKpCD6LO/view

Prasad, Vivek Kumar et al. "Federated Learning for the Internet-of-Medical-Things: A Survey." Mathematics 11, no. 1 (2022): 151. https://www.mdpi.com/2227-7390/11/1/151

Qammar, Attia et al. "Securing Federated Learning With Blockchain: A Systematic Literature Review." Artificial Intelligence Review 56, no. 5 (2023): 3951–3985. https://link.springer.com/article/10.1007/s10462-022-10271-9

Sharma, Akash et al. "A Novel Deep Federated Learning-Based Model to Enhance Privacy in Critical Infrastructure Systems." International Journal of Software Science and Computational Intelligence (IJSSCI) 15, no. 1 (2023): 1–23. https://www.igi-global.com/viewtitle.aspx?titleid=334711

Sirohi, Deepika et al. "Federated Learning for 6G-Enabled Secure Communication Systems: a Comprehensive Survey." Artificial Intelligence Review 56, no. 10 (2023): 11297–11389. https://link.springer.com/article/10.1007/s10462-023-10417-3

Stojanović, Branka, and Josip Božić. "Robust Financial Fraud Alerting System Based in the Cloud Environment." Sensors 22, no. 23 (2022): 9461. https://www.mdpi.com/1424-8220/22/23/9461

Venkatasubramanian, Madumitha, Arash Habibi Lashkari, and Saqib Hakak. "Iot Malware Analysis Using Federated Learning: A Comprehensive Survey." IEEE Access 11 (2023): 5004–5018. https://ieeexplore.ieee.org/iel7/6287639/6514899/10012334.pdf

Yaacoub, Jean-Paul A, Hassan N Noura, and Ola Salman. "Security of Federated Learning With IoT Systems: Issues, Limitations, Challenges, and Solutions." Internet of Things and Cyber-Physical Systems 3 (2023): 155–179. https://www.sciencedirect.com/science/article/pii/S2667345223000226

Yang, Mengna, Yejun He, and Jian Qiao. "Federated learning-based privacy-preserving and security: Survey." 2021 Computing, Communications and IoT Applications (ComComAp). IEEE, 2021. http://ceie.szu.edu.cn/heyejun/paper/CFederatedLearning.pdf

Chapter 15

Artificial Intelligence (AI) Technology-Based Approach in Banking Compliance Supervision

Alex Khang, Vugar Abdullayev Hajimahmud, and Yitong Niu

15.1 Introduction

With the acceleration of the development process of economic globalization, the compliance risks enterprises face have become increasingly severe and complex, especially for Fintech enterprises, which face unclear regulatory policies and rules and the dual challenges of financial risks and technology risks at the same time. The Fintech sector is more likely to trigger systemic risks than other industries. As a result, the compliance requirements for Fintech will also be stricter than those of other industries (Khang & Jadhav et al., 2024).

The essence of Fintech is finance, and standardized development and efficient empowerment have gradually become the trend for the future development of Fintech enterprises (Kingston, 2017). In the face of an increasingly stringent regulatory environment, banks, as financial institutions, need to establish a sound and complete risk prevention system to ensure that possible risks are controlled within tolerable limits to strengthen research and understanding of relevant regulatory policies and to improve the enterprise's comprehensive risk management system and internal control system by the relevant regulatory policies; and to improve transparency, intensify the fight against financial crimes, and minimize behavioral risks. In a crisis-ridden environment, banks must strengthen their operational management to develop proper management practices and culture and continue enhancing their compliance capabilities (Al-Shabandar et al., 2019).

In the face of mounting regulatory pressure, most banks responded and took timely remedial measures, including introducing new management initiatives and massive recruitment. Over time, the banking industry has developed a regulatory compliance methodology that includes establishing a compliance risk taxonomy that frames and informs its target operating model.

DOI: 10.4324/9781003501947-15

These changes marked the beginning of an industry-wide compliance transformation, but with it came spiraling costs and pressure on human resources. Digitization is the final stage of the transformation process, spawning cascading changes in the compliance operations space. The emergence of intelligent technology then acts as an accelerating catalyst, helping to significantly improve performance or mimic humans in areas such as learning, language use, and decision-making (Bedi, Goyal & Kumar, 2020).

In recent years, artificial intelligence (AI) technology has been increasingly used in the financial industry, setting off a new wave of technological revolution. The development of financial technology is also gradually detached from the ERP system as a generation of financial electronic and financial internet, opening the curtain of intelligent finance (Vasista, 2021). The development of traditional financial institutions has also transformed from being oriented to asset scale expansion to technology, digitization and intelligence, and digital solutions have been implemented in numerous businesses. In compliance risk management, most human resources are used to review content collection, content compliance analysis, and resultant report output.

In compliance monitoring, the bank embeds AI technologies such as optical character recognition (OCR), entity recognition (NER), and automated process robots (RPA), which can effectively reduce the cost of compliance review (Harkácsi & Szegfű, 2021). For example, in the contract compliance review process, the RPA is used to automatically cascade the review process of contracts, invoices, and other documents, convert document images into text through OCR, and then identify critical information for review with the help of NER of natural language processing, and efficiently and automatically judge the compliance of multiple documents by combining with the requirements of the business compliance review, to realize the regulatory requirements of the bank's business under the condition of effectively controlling the investment of workforce, enhance the efficiency of bank risk prevention and control (Dziawgo, 2021).

15.2 Current Status of Financial Regulatory Compliance

In recent years, the development of information technology and AI has contributed to the flourishing of Fintech and has led to the extensive use of emerging technologies, such as AI, blockchain, big data, and cloud computing, by financial institutions and corporations in their operations (Yu & Song, 2021). While using the aforementioned digital technologies to assist in their own business, financial institutions and enterprises should pay attention to compliance regulations.

Compliance means that the business activities of a business are consistent with laws, rules, and guidelines. Financial institutions and enterprises may suffer legal sanctions, regulatory penalties, significant financial losses, and reputational damage if they engage in non-compliant behavior when conducting business (Szegfű, 2021). Currently, the Base Committee, responsible for banking supervision under the Bank for International Settlements, has issued documents related to Fintech development. Banks are facing an increasingly stringent regulatory environment and must strengthen their operational management and enhance their compliance capabilities (Goncharenko & Miglionico, 2019).

15.2.1 Regulatory Compliance Content

- Operational risk management. Strengthening the foundation of operational risk management and continuously optimizing the operational risk management system can escort Fintech-enabled business innovation and development.

- Supplier management. Establish an effective supplier management system and standardize the supplier management structure, supplier risk management system, supplier evaluation framework, and continuous monitoring mechanism.
- Specialized technology risk management. Technologies requiring risk management include cloud computing, blockchain, AI, and open platforms (Khang, Dave & Katore et al., 2024).
- Information security management. Both regulators and the public demand more from financial institutions regarding information security and protecting sensitive data.
- Business continuity and emergency management. To be able to handle and respond calmly during a risky event and to be able to restore regular operation in a timely and effective manner after the event.
- Anti-money laundering and anti-terrorist financing. Both domestically and internationally, the requirements of regulatory agencies on anti-money laundering and anti-terrorist financing are becoming more and more stringent, and financial institutions must be fully prepared in both management and technology.

15.2.2 Tools for Compliance Regulation

Compliance regulation can help financial institutions and enterprises avoid many risks, especially for financial sectors such as banks; the management should be more compliant, and financial institutions, in implementing the regulation, can draw on the existing monitoring system of some banks (Murphy & Mueller, 2018).

- Working mechanism. Through the establishment of a complete organizational structure and division of labor mechanism to ensure the promotion of the specific work of data compliance.
- Institutional system. Through the establishment of a complete institutional system, the smooth progress of all aspects of data compliance will be ensured.
- Response mechanism. We attach great importance to protecting customers' reasonable and legitimate data rights.
- Regulatory communication. In implementing data compliance, we emphasize strengthening communication with relevant regulatory agencies.
- Information disclosure. Enhance in all aspects the level of quantitative data analysis, a portrait of the various processes and results of development, reform, and transformation, and the ability to protect customer's financial information.
- Customer education. Continuously provide financial education to customers in various forms.
- Talent development. Focus on cultivating talents with an open mind, a sense of innovation, and solid basic skills.
- Publicizing and training. Make the construction of the data compliance system a long-term task that runs through all aspects of operation and management.

At present, financial institutions inevitably face challenges in implementing compliance regulations. Taking anti-money laundering work as an example, in the context of increasing pressure on anti-money laundering supervision and increasingly complex and changeable money laundering technical means, how financial institutions can further improve their understanding of anti-money laundering work, continuously improve their anti-money laundering systems and measures, and rapidly enhance their anti-money laundering capabilities has become a significant proposition to be considered.

Therefore, financial institutions have used the power of science and technology to enhance the efficiency of compliance implementation and realize the results of the system, forming a corresponding technological ecology in the field of financial regulation (Truby, Brown & Dahdal, 2020).

15.2.3 The Ecosystem of Financial Compliance Regulation

Compliance technology is mainly used on the compliance side of financial institutions to provide them with technology solutions to help them achieve regulatory compliance through automation of data and processes, and to realize the goals of improving the level of risk control and reducing compliance costs. In the application of AI, with the increasing complexity of financial transactions and the gradual increase in the volume of data, AI and machine learning are playing an increasingly important role for financial institutions and regulators (Jagtiani, Vermilyea & Wall, 2018).

Compliance technology needs to seize the trend of artificial intelligence to realize timely and efficient regulatory compliance, maintain financial security and prevent systemic risks. Especially in the current situation of tightening financial regulation and significant increase in compliance costs for financial institutions, compliance technology needs to be organically integrated with AI to provide technical support for reducing compliance costs for financial institutions (Antunes, 2021).

The ever-changing technology has brought a lot of challenges to financial institutions in implementing regulatory requirements, but governments and organizations have also continued to introduce supplementary tools to assist financial institutions in meeting these challenges. In addition, several product tools have been introduced in the market to aid in compliance regulation. Rashid Hussein Bank has launched an intelligent compliance management system for banks, which includes features such as risk management portal, risk system escalation, risk identification, risk disposal, internal control document management, compliance management, risk reporting and mobile risk management, which effectively monitors staff and vendors for exceptions (Milojević & Redzepagic, 2021). The ability to identify and monitor daily risks and assess annual risks adds a line of defense to the bank's risk control and enables the bank to make more effective decisions in compliance supervision.

From a scenario perspective, the current tools and products applied to regulatory compliance can be divided into three categories: interconnection applications with customers, internal applications of financial institutions, and interconnection applications with regulatory agencies (Niu & Korneev, 2022). Interconnection with customers can be divided into the field of transaction behavior monitoring and customer identity management, case products are Tencent Lingkun big data regulatory platform and WeChat face recognition payment (Khang, Dave & Jadhav et al., 2024).

The internal applications of financial institutions are mainly in the field of risk prevention and control management, and the representative products include HSBC's enterprise-level big data work platform and Tng's "Financial Pulse" platform (Flotyński & Marchewka-Bartkowiak, 2021). Interconnected applications with regulatory agencies can be divided into the fields of law and regulation tracking, compliance report submission, data encryption and transmission, and the representative application products in these fields are mainly the system platforms of foreign regulatory technology companies, as shown in Table 15.1.

Table 15.1 Compliance Management Product System

	Areas of Application	Concrete Form	Application Cases
Interconnected applications with customers	Trading behavior monitoring	• Utilizing software to monitor employees to ensure their compliance with transaction rules, thereby reducing irregularities. • Adopting big data technology to prevent and control fraud risks arising from online channels, providing real-time transaction monitoring and review solutions.	WeChat's Linggill Big Data Regulatory Platform
	Customer identity management	The use of face recognition, fingerprint recognition technology, etc. to realize the verification of customer identity, remote account opening, face payment.	Alipay, Paypal, Tng, and other third-party payment platforms
Internal applications for financial institutions	Risk prevention and control management	• Utilize software to manage its daily operational risks, including event identification, issue tracking, and data storage. • Assess risk exposures and predict future threats through analytical and quantitative risk modeling. • Customer risk assessment to better prevent risk before lending and control risk changes and impact areas after lending.	Aravo in the United States; Finastra in the United Kingdom; and China Construction Bank's "new generation" enterprise-level big data work platform.

(Continued)

Table 15.1 Compliance Management Product System *(Continued)*

	Areas of Application	Concrete Form	Application Cases
Interconnected applications with regulatory agencies	Tracking of laws and regulations	Digital interpretation of regulatory rules, real-time adjustment and updating according to changes, embedding them in the business operations of financial institutions, fully understanding and tracking regulatory rules in a timely manner, reducing the "menu cost" of the rules and improving flexibility.	Apiax, a Swiss regtech company; IBM Watson Systems in the US: AtlasNLP, an Australian regtech company.
	Compliance report submission	Automated data distribution and regulatory report generation through big data analytics, real-time reporting and cloud computing.	AuRep from Oridian Reporting Services Ltd; Vizor, an Irish regtech company; and DroomsNXG Systems from Droom, a German regtech company.
	Data encryption and transportation	The advantages of distributed bookkeeping are fully utilized through blockchain technology and cryptocurrencies to ensure the security, integrity, and validity of data, prevent data from being counted and altered, and serve data delivery.	Drooms NXG system from German regtech company Droom.

15.3 Artificial Intelligence Technology for Compliance Regulation

AI technology is booming, generating a wealth of landing scenarios, among which the leading technologies applied in banking compliance and regulatory scenarios are natural language processing, computer vision, and robotic process automation.

15.3.1 Natural Language Processing (NLP)

Natural language processing is an essential direction in computer science and AI, which is a science integrating linguistics, computer science, and mathematics (Niu, Jiao & Korneev, 2022). Therefore, the research in this field involves the language that people use every day and includes various theories and methods for realizing effective communication between humans and computers in natural language to develop computer systems that can realize natural language communication.

In the compliance and regulatory scenarios of the banking industry, natural language processing technology can digitize regulatory rules and make them recognizable by machines, parse out key content from contracts, emails, customer data, and other information, and judge the compliance of the content through contextual comprehension and manually setting up rules to improve the efficiency of compliance review and reduce human costs (Butler & Brooks, 2018).

Natural language processing technology can also combine machine learning technology and iterative updating algorithms to improve the accuracy of machine translation of human language and real-time monitoring and tracking of regulatory developments to help financial institutions conduct compliance audits. In addition, the technology can help financial institutions conduct cross-border business compliance by comparing the similarities and differences of regulatory requirements in different countries.

15.3.2 Computer Vision

Computer vision is a study of how to make the machine "see" to understand science; it refers to the use of cameras and computers instead of the human eye on the instrument to detect the image or multi-dimensional data for graphic processing, from which to obtain "information" to achieve the target identification, tracking measurement, and other perceptual and judgment capabilities (Caron, 2019). Banks generate many paper documents in the process of business, realizing the digital transformation of documents that need to be photographed or scanned and converted into a picture form of storage. OCR technology in computer vision can extract textual information from pictures for subsequent processing of textual content, which is the beginning and key to intelligent compliance processes, and its accuracy rate affects the feasibility of compliance and regulatory automation.

15.3.3 Robotic Process Automation

Robotic process automation is a business process automation technology based on software robotics and AI. PA technology automates by mimicking the way end users manually operate their computers. Robotic process automation monitors the work performed by the user in the application's graphical user interface (GUI) and automatically repeats that work directly on the GUI. This technology also supports configuring calls to traditional functional interface API (application programming interface), whereby a call condition is triggered to send the corresponding parameter to the API interface to obtain the result. In compliance regulation, robotic process automation connects AI technologies such as machine vision and natural language processing into an automated processing stream and realizes cost reduction and efficiency by automating a series of UI operations and function calls (Bauerfeind, Di Prima & Pascal, 2019).

15.4 Customer-Detailed Address Compliance Verification

In order to respond to and implement the anti-money laundering requirements of the regulatory bodies, HSBC Bank Plc has proposed a detailed customer address compliance requirement, which aims to verify the compliance of both the stock and the incremental customer address text. By compliance, the customer's detailed address is required to meet the standard of exhaustive traceability. The scenario has several requirements and features:

- Timeliness requirements, under the pressure of high concurrency, need to meet the timeliness requirements of low latency;
- Accuracy requirements, which need to reach more than 97% to be applied to essential business channels such as loans;
- Controllable calibration standards need to have the function of adjustable calibration results, which can be realized through manual intervention to control the whole calibration standard and emergency;
- Compliance standards are particular relative to the conventional address compliance standards; the compliance standards, in this case, have a higher degree of tolerance, even if the address text contains redundant information filled in by the customer (such as cell phone number, name, etc.), or contains descriptive statements, as long as they meet the conditions of the location can be traced, they can be classified as a compliant address.

15.4.1 Model Solution

For the compliance address, according to the type of description, it can be divided into door number address (e.g., Road, Kampung Gelugor, 11700 Gelugor, Pulau Pinang, B1002, XX Subdistrict, XX Road, XX Street, Tianhe District, Guangzhou City, Guangzhou), rural address (e.g., xxxx, Mukim, xx, Jalan Kolam, Cherok Tok Kun, 14000 Bukit Mertajam, Penang), building address (e.g., xxx, Beach St, Georgetown, 10300 George Town, Penang), etc., and the above address texts should be within the scope of compliance even if there are some redundant texts interspersed therein. Addresses that contain illegal words addresses that lack exact information such as house number, or addresses that contain descriptive text such as neighborhood, which makes the location unclear, need to be more compliant.

To summarize, the difficulty of this case is that the sample can only exhaust some of the redundant information features under the higher inclusive compliance criteria, and the model needs to classify the addresses that contain redundant information. Therefore, this case requires the model to learn to address compliance features and accurately classify descriptive address text while excluding the interference of redundant information.

After comparing the effect of multiple models, this case chooses the scheme combining the A Bidirectional Long Short-Term Memory (BiLSTM) classification model and business rules, setting BiLSTM to learn the features of compliant addresses containing redundant information, realizing the adjustable and controllable standard through business rules, and finally releasing the model on the cloud with the advantage of container cloud provisioning resources, which meets the requirement of low-latency response under the pressure of high concurrency.

15.4.2 Model Introduction

The BiLSTM model combines forward LSTM (Long Short-Term Memory) and backward LSTM, which is improved based on Recurrent Neural Network (RNN). The advantage of RNN is that it can utilize context-related information in the mapping process between the input and the output sequences. However, the scope of the contextual information it can obtain is limited. LSTM can solve this problem very well by cleverly setting the forgetting gate, input gate, and output gate to form the short-term memory module to realize the protection and control of information. LSTM can solve this problem nicely by cleverly setting the forgetting gate, input gate, and output gate to form a long and short-term memory module to realize the protection and control of information.

Computation of the forgetting gate: input the hidden layer state h_{t-1} of the previous moment and the input word X_t of the current moment to get the value f_t of the forgetting gate:

$$y_D = \arg\max_{0 \le y \le 1} y\left(z_a - e_2\right)$$

Computation of the memory gate: input the hidden state h_{t-1} of the previous moment, the input word X_t of the current moment, get the value of the memory gate i_t, the temporary cell state $\tilde{C}_t$:

$$\tilde{C}_t = \tanh\left(W_c \cdot [h_{t-1}, x_t] + b_c\right)$$

Calculation of the current moment cell state: input the value i_t of the memory gate, the value f_t of the forgetting gate, the value $\tilde{C}_t$ of the temporary cell state, and the last moment cell state C_{t-1} to get the current moment cell state C_t:

$$C_t = f_t \times C_{t-1} + i_t \times \tilde{C}_t$$

Calculation of the output gate and the hidden state at the current moment: input the hidden state h_{t-1} at the previous moment, the input word X_t at the current moment, and the cell state C_t at the current moment to get the value O_t of the output gate and the hidden state h_t:

$$h_t = O_t \times \tanh\left(C_t\right)$$

The final sequence of hidden states $\{h_0, h_1, \ldots, h_{n-1}\}$ with the same length as the sentence is obtained.

BiLSTM adds the reverse operation on the basis of LSTM, that is, reversing the input sequence and re-calculating the output again according to the LSTM, the final result is a simple stack of forward LSTM and reverses LSTM results so that the formed BiLSTM can consider the contextual information. In this case, there is redundant information in the address part filled in by the customer, which will affect the judgment of its standard. With the introduction of the BiLSTM model, it is able to effectively learn the characteristics of multiple address information, which in turn reduces the misjudgment of partially compliant addresses and improves the overall accuracy.

15.4.3 Model Effect

The address labeling samples from the last six months were taken and divided into training and validation sets in a ratio of 7:1, and the samples were labeled with whether they were compliant or not. Before training the model, the address text is preprocessed, the customized segmentation

Table 15.2   Address Compliance Classification Model Test Set Results

	Precision	Recall	F1-score
0	0.99	0.99	0.99
1	0.94	0.91	0.92
accuracy			0.98
Macro avg	0.97	0.95	0.96
Weighted avg	0.98	0.98	0.98

module and general segmentation tool are used to segment the address text, and the numbers and letters are normalized and then transformed into word vectors before entering the model training.

After a number of iterations of optimization, the model indicators in all aspects meet the expectations, in which the training set model AUC is 0.995, the AUC curve and the loss curve of the training set, respectively; the final test set AUC is 0.981, and the indicators are shown in Table 15.2.

In order to realize the controllability of the calibration standard and to prevent the occurrence of model omission and misjudgment, the author introduced the business rule module. Before the model calibration, it first judges the address text length and whether it contains prohibited words and directly filters out the obviously non-compliant addresses. The modifiable rule module also realizes the requirement that the calibration standard can be adjusted; the results of the model with a lower probability of calculation are subjected to a second calibration, which is reviewed by the rule template so as to enhance the overall accuracy rate further as shown in Figures 15.1 and 15.2.

Through the promotion and deployment of the Customer-Detailed Address Compliance Verification Model, HSBC's various business channels have been accessed to audit and verify the user input address and through the front-end reminder to effectively improve the accuracy and completeness of the customer information, saving the resources invested in manual verification.

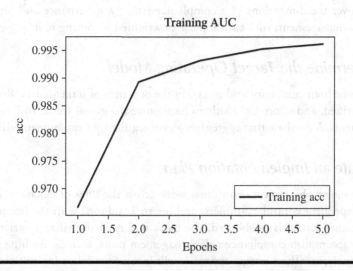

Figure 15.1   Address compliance classification model training AUC curve.

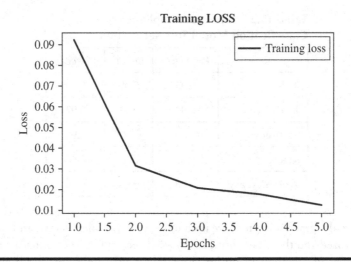

Figure 15.2 Address compliance classification model training set loss curve.

15.5 Future and Prospects

In the face of stricter regulation and higher punitive fines, the banking industry, in the midst of the Fintech wave, needs to revisit its target operating model and utilize innovative technology to improve the efficiency and effectiveness of the compliance function. Optimizing a bank's target operating model should focus on three basic steps.

15.5.1 Conduct a Compliance Check

Assess the current state of the compliance operating model, conduct interviews with senior management, and compare the current situation with industry best practices. A questionnaire can be developed to cover the dimensions of a compliance strategy, governance and organization, and compliance risk management, with each topic area weighted according to its importance.

15.5.2 Determine the Target Operating Model

It is essential to be both compliant and to satisfy the demands of stakeholders. Roles and responsibilities are clarified, and efforts are made to harmonize the global framework with local operational requirements. A database that aggregates global regulatory requirements will play a key role.

15.5.3 Create an Implementation Plan

From the early stages, the project team must work across the lines of defense (i.e., the ultimate risk owner, independent control examiners, and internal auditors) with the business lines. Once the target operating model is established, the bank will need to utilize a variety of intelligent technologies to accomplish compliance risk management tasks, such as machine room and basic and advanced analytics. The strategic approach will involve the following initial actions (Khang & Hajimahmud, 2024).

First, assess digitalization opportunities and technologies. Assess the frequency of tasks, their structure, and the available innovative technologies to categorize and prioritize needs. At this stage, decision-makers must have a concrete technical understanding of the processes and underlying requirements. Second, conduct proof-of-concept pilots. Executives must select specific technologies to pilot for proof-of-concept to ensure that enough stakeholders are willing to accept them. Third, a plan for mass rollout should be created. Roadmaps are critical to rolling out innovative technologies at scale (including establishing the proper governance structure), and vendor selection is a crucial challenge. At the same time, a lengthy testing program may be appropriate, as it may reveal mismatches, flaws, or conflicts between IT requirements and data security needs.

No simple or standardized methodology will result in a state-of-the-art compliance framework. However, as the banking industry gradually shifts from a remediation model to a target operating model, the use of new and intelligent technologies will provide benefits to the banking industry and the financial industry as a whole by fostering a new competency that is needed in the modern global banking industry: the ability to be intelligently compliant (Khang & Inna et al., 2024).

References

Al-Shabandar, R., Lightbody, G., Browne, F., Liu, J., Wang, H., & Zheng, H. (2019). The application of artificial intelligence in financial compliance management. Proceedings of the 2019 International Conference on Artificial Intelligence and Advanced Manufacturing, 1–6. https://dl.acm.org/doi/abs/10.1145/3358331.3358339

Antunes, J. A. P. (2021). To supervise or to self-supervise: A machine learning based comparison on credit supervision. Financial Innovation, 7(1), 26. https://link.springer.com/article/10.1186/s40854-021-00242-4

Bauerfeind, B. D. T., Di Prima, & Pascal. (2019). Banking Supervision at a Crossroads–RegTech as the Regulators' Toolbox. The RegTech Book. https://ieeexplore.ieee.org/abstract/document/9315986/

Bedi, P., Goyal, S., & Kumar, J. (2020). Basic structure on artificial intelligence: A revolution in risk management and compliance. 2020 3rd International Conference on Intelligent Sustainable Systems (ICISS), 570–576. https://ieeexplore.ieee.org/abstract/document/9315986/

Butler, T., & Brooks, R. (2018). On the role of ontology-based RegTech for managing risk and compliance reporting in the age of regulation. Journal of Risk Management in Financial Institutions, 11(1), 19–33. https://www.ingentaconnect.com/content/hsp/jrmfi/2018/00000011/00000001/art00003

Caron, M. S. (2019). The transformative effect of AI on the banking industry. Banking & Finance Law Review, 34(2), 169–214. https://search.proquest.com/openview/5fe6582838c76de628baba9b0b94f40a/1?pq-origsite=gscholar&cbl=44976

Dziawgo, T. (2021). Supervisory technology as a new tool for banking sector supervision. Journal of Banking and Financial Economics, 15(1), 5–13. https://www.ceeol.com/search/article-detail?id=1009328

Flotyński, M., & Marchewka-Bartkowiak, K. (2021). Non-Technological and Technological (SupTech) Innovations in Strengthening the Financial Supervision. In Fostering Innovation and Competitiveness With Fintech, RegTech, and SupTech (pp. 97–127). IGI Global. https://www.igi-global.com/chapter/non-technological-and-technological-suptech-innovations-in-strengthening-the-financial-supervision/264908

Goncharenko, I. A., & Miglionico, A. (2019). Artificial intelligence and automation in financial services: The case of Russian banking sector. Law and Economics Yearly Review, 8(1), 125–147. https://iris.luiss.it/handle/11385/208789

Harkácsi, G. J., & Szegfű, L. P. (2021). The role of the compliance function in the financial sector in the age of digitalisation, artificial intelligence and robotisation. Financial and Economic Review, 20(1), 152–170. https://real.mtak.hu/124048/1/fer-20-1-e2-harkacsi-szegfu.pdf

Jagtiani, J., Vermilyea, T., & Wall, L. D. (2018). The roles of big data and machine learning in bank supervision. Forthcoming, Banking Perspectives. https://papers.ssrn.com/sol3/papers.cfm?abstract_id=3221309

Khang, A., Dave, T., Jadhav, B., Katore, D., & Dave, D. (2024). Gig Financial Economy- Big Data and Analytics. In Khang A. Jadhav B., Hajimahmud V. A., Satpathy I. The Synergy of AI and Fintech in the Digital Gig Economy (1st Ed.). CRC Press. https://doi.org/10.1201/9781032720104-16

Khang, A., Dave, T., Katore, D., Jadhav, B., & Dave, D., Leveraging Blockchain and Smart Contracts For Gig Payments. In Khang A. Jadhav B., Hajimahmud V. A., Satpathy I. (2024). The Synergy of AI and Fintech in the Digital Gig Economy (1st Ed.). CRC Press. https://doi.org/10.1201/9781032720104-11

Khang, A., & Hajimahmud, V. A. (2024). "Introduction to the Gig Economy," In Khang A. Jadhav B., Hajimahmud V. A., Satpathy I. The Synergy of AI and Fintech in the Digital Gig Economy (1st Ed.). CRC Press. https://doi.org/10.1201/9781032720104-1

Khang, A., Inna, Semenets-Orlova, Alla, Klochko, Rostyslav, Shchokin, Rudenko, Mykola, Lidia, Romanova, & Kristina, Bratchykova. (2024). Management Model 6.0 and Business Recovery Strategy of Enterprises in the Era of Digital Economy. In Khang, A., Gujrati, R., Uygun, H., Tailor, R. K., & Gaur, S. Data-Driven Modelling and Predictive Analytics in Business and Finance (1st Ed.). CRC Press. https://doi.org/10.1201/9781032618845-16

Khang, A., Jadhav, B., Dave, T., & Katore, T. (2024). Artificial Intelligence (AI) in Fintech - Enhancing Financial Services. In Khang A. Jadhav B., Hajimahmud V. A., Satpathy I. The Synergy of AI and Fintech in the Digital Gig Economy (1st Ed.). CRC Press. https://doi.org/10.1201/9781032720104-10

Kingston, J. (2017). Using artificial intelligence to support compliance with the general data protection regulation. Artificial Intelligence and Law, 25(4), 429–443. https://link.springer.com/article/10.1007/s10506-017-9206-9

Milojević, N., & Redzepagic, S. (2021). Prospects of artificial intelligence and machine learning application in banking risk management. Journal of Central Banking Theory and Practice, 10(3), 41–57. https://sciendo.com/article/10.2478/jcbtp-2021-0023?content-tab=abstract

Murphy, D., & Mueller, J. (2018). RegTech: Opportunities for more efficient and effective regulatory supervision and compliance. Milken Institute, July, 11. https://milkeninstitute.org/sites/default/files/reports-pdf/RegTech-Opportunities-White-Paper-FINAL-_2.pdf

Niu, Y., Jiao, L., & Korneev, A. (2022). Credit development strategy of China's banking industry to the electric power industry. Heritage and Sustainable Development, 4(1), 53–60. http://e.biblio.bru.by/handle/1212121212/20329

Niu, Y., & Korneev, A. (2022). Identification method of power internet attack information based on machine learning. Iraqi Journal for Computer Science and Mathematics, 3(2), 1–7. https://www.iasj.net/iasj/download/54980538706fe93e

Szegfű, G. J. H. P. (2021). The role of the compliance function in the financial sector in the age of digitalisation, artificial intelligence and robotisation. Financial and Economic Review, 152. https://real.mtak.hu/124048/1/fer-20-1-e2-harkacsi-szegfu.pdf

Truby, J., Brown, R., & Dahdal, A. (2020). Banking on AI: Mandating a proactive approach to AI regulation in the financial sector. Law and Financial Markets Review, 14(2), 110–120. https://www.tandfonline.com/doi/abs/10.1080/17521440.2020.1760454

Vasista, K. (2021). Regulatory compliance and supervision of artificial intelligence, machine learning and also possible effects on financial Institutions. Machine learning and also possible effects on financial Institutions (June 13, 2021). International Journal of Innovative Research in Computer and Communication Engineering, 2320–9801. https://papers.ssrn.com/sol3/papers.cfm?abstract_id=4135599

Yu, T. R., & Song, X. (2021). Big data and artificial intelligence in the banking industry. In Handbook of Financial Econometrics, Mathematics, Statistics, and Machine Learning (pp. 4025–4041). World Scientific. https://www.worldscientific.com/doi/abs/10.1142/9789811202391_0117

Chapter 16

Enhancing Customer Satisfaction through Alternative Channel Services in the Banking Industry

B.C.M. Patnaik, Ipseeta Satpathy, Anish Patnaik, and Alex Khang

16.1 Introduction

The banking industry has offered a wide range of services to customers over the years, but it has yet to fully cater to the needs of rural communities. While banks have always prioritized providing more conveniences to urban customers, there has been a recent introduction of rural banking and financial inclusion concepts. However, the lack of awareness among rural customers about the usefulness of these products and services has created a significant gap in terms of banking success.

To bridge this gap, banks have started adopting alternative channel services, which utilize new mediums and technology to provide banking services directly to customers. By migrating from traditional banking services to these alternative channels, banks aim to offer optimized banking services at a lower cost and on a 24/7 basis. This allows customers to enjoy banking services from the comfort of their own homes. In the 21st century, customers are demanding banking services to be provided at their doorstep due to work pressures and time constraints.

Accessibility to banking services is crucial in meeting these demands, enabling customers to carry out transactions such as deposits, loans, and instant verification of their banking status without having to visit physical bank branches. To meet customer demands and stay competitive in the market amidst technological advancements, many banks have shifted their service delivery channels from traditional frontal services to direct sales and marketing through email, phones,

DOI: 10.4324/9781003501947-16

261

and other electronic modes of transactions. This adaptation ensures that banks can fulfil customer needs while navigating the challenges posed by the changing landscape of the industry.

Nowadays, the mobile and wireless markets are the fastest-growing markets in the world. With the emergence of the technology revolution, financial institutions are interested in conducting their banking transactions online through internet banking, mobile Banking, and other online services. This is to overcome the competition from telecommunication firms. The adoption of alternative channel services by banks has been made possible due to the acceptance of technology and the widespread use of mobile devices (Chadichal & Misra, 2012).

One of the main challenges in providing banking services to the underprivileged through branch banking is the high costs involved in handling small transactions. However, the adoption of technology and the provision of online banking services have not only reduced transaction costs but also expanded the reach of banking services. This has allowed financial institutions to deliver financial services online and enrich the customer experience.

Due to economic reforms and an increase in banking transactions, branch banking has faced difficulties in providing quick services to customers. To address this, the banking sector has embraced technology to meet customer needs and eliminate paperwork and long queues. In the era of technology and the demand for a digital lifestyle, this shift has brought the workplace to the home, aligning with demographic changes. Additionally, the new regulatory framework in the finance sector has prompted financial institutions to leverage technology and innovate the financial landscape, stepping outside their comfort zones to meet market uncertainties (Khang & Hahanov et al., 2022).

16.2 Alternative Channel Services of Banks

Banks have embraced alternative channel services as a means to provide banking services directly to customers through new mediums and technology adoption (Buri, Cull & Giné, 2023). By migrating from traditional banking services to alternative channels, banks aim to optimize their services with minimal costs and offer 24/7 accessibility, allowing customers to enjoy banking services from the comfort of their homes (Krishnan, 2012).

In the fast-paced 21st century, customers, burdened with work pressure and time constraints, expect financial institutions to bring banking services to their doorstep (Buri et al., 2023). The accessibility of banking services plays a crucial role in meeting customer demands, enabling them to carry out transactions such as deposits, loans, and instant verification of their banking status without physically visiting bank branches (Krishnan, 2012). To meet customer demands and stay competitive in a rapidly evolving technological landscape, many banks have shifted their service delivery channels from traditional frontal services to direct sales and electronic transactions through email, phones, and other electronic modes (Carlos & Ronald, 2020).

In today's world, the mobile and wireless markets are experiencing rapid growth. This has led to financial institutions showing interest in conducting their banking transactions online through services such as internet banking, mobile Banking, and other online modes. The adoption of these alternative channel services by banks has been made possible due to the acceptance of technology and the widespread use of mobile devices. These services, such as internet banking, ATMs, POS systems, and mobile banking, provide customers with various facilities. By embracing technology and offering online banking services, banks not only reduce transaction costs but also enhance their services and reach out to customers. This enables financial institutions to expand their services to a wider customer base. Additionally, alternative channel services are cost-effective for banks and contribute to increased profitability. Ultimately, banking customers can effectively utilize these services to meet their banking needs (Khang & Hajimahmud et al., 2024).

The branch banking sector faced challenges in providing quick service to customers due to economic reform and increased banking transactions. To address this, banks turned to technology to satisfy customer needs and reduce paperwork and customer queues. The adoption of technology, coupled with the demand for digital lifestyles and demographic shifts, allowed banks to bring the workplace to the home. Financial institutions in the finance sector embraced a new regulatory framework to meet market uncertainties. They seized the opportunities presented by technology to innovate the financial landscape, stepping outside their comfort zones. This allowed them to comply with challenges and satisfy customer demands.

Alternative channel services emerged as a solution, enabling customers to perform banking activities from the comfort of their homes without visiting a physical branch. This not only provided convenience to customers but also gave bank employees more time to innovate and meet customer needs. Private sector banks were able to pioneer the use of alternative channel services, setting the path for others in the banking sector. These services not only offered cost-effective solutions but also reduced the need for bank personnel while ensuring efficient and effective service delivery. Additionally, alternative channel services opened up opportunities for banks to attract more customers and enter new market segments. This allowed banks to expand their reach and cater to a wider range of customer needs.

The internet is an extensive network that connects individual computers and computer networks, allowing them to communicate and share information using the TCP/IP (Transmission Control Protocol/Internet Protocol) communication protocol. It originated from the connection of multiple computer networks in the late 1960s and early 1970s through the ARPA Net project by the US Department of Defense, which aimed to experiment with wide area networking.

The internet encompasses various forms of electronic communication, including email and file transfer, while the World Wide Web utilizes HTML (Hyper Text Markup Language) to link files containing text, graphics, sound, and videos. Since its introduction in the 1990s, the internet has become a platform for commerce and trade, with e-commerce enabling individuals and businesses to exchange business instructions and information electronically through computers, telephones, and other electronic devices.

The traditional brick and mortar companies have embraced the internet as a means to enhance their existing products and services, as well as to introduce new offerings. This shift has resulted in increased visibility, fostering customer trust, improved customer service, the adoption of a new business culture, and cost-effectiveness compared to their previous practices. E-commerce has facilitated two main categories of business: Business to Customer (B2C) and Business to Business (B2B). B2C encompasses various online platforms such as e-shops, shopping malls, e-banking, e-broking, travel services, financial services, and entertainment.

The primary objective of B2C businesses is to directly engage with customers and generate revenue for the organizations. On the other hand, B2B businesses focus on selecting suppliers, dealers, and bankers, and conducting business transactions online. While physical goods are transferred from the business units to the dealers, all other aspects such as payments, contacts, and legal documents are handled digitally. This enables businesses to easily select vendors and dealers not only within their own country but also across the globe.

Today, thanks to technological advancements, company portals serve as meeting grounds for buyers and sellers to engage in purchasing and selling transactions. B2B platforms have opened doors for smaller companies to enter the global market, while banks have seized the opportunity to offer financial products and services to customers through their official websites or portals.

16.3 Impact of ACS on Traditional Services

Automated Clearing System (ACS) significantly decreases transaction costs when compared to branch banking transactions, transforming the once competitive advantage of banks – a vast branch network – into a comparative disadvantage by enabling ACS to offer lower transaction costs. Many banks are now embracing this service due to its simple setup, and new entrants are not burdened by the constraints of the old system, cultures, and structures. This not only provides customers with more options in traditional banking but also entices them to explore new banking practices to benefit from a share of banking profits. ACS facilitates banks in bringing together parties like buyers and sellers, payees and payers, to conduct transactions efficiently in terms of cost and time (Ater & Landsman, 2013).

Traditional banks offer services such as payment and settlement of business transactions, creating customer savings accounts, and lending these savings to borrowers. However, the efficiency of these transactions in traditional banks is often questionable. Traditional banks encounter challenges in managing cash acquisitions and issuing shares to the public. Each transaction in the traditional banking system must be manually recorded in various accounts, leading to delays as bank officials spend more time on each transaction. This not only hinders their ability to raise additional capital from the stock market but also diminishes the efficiency of their employees. Bank staff also struggle to track specific transactions as they must manually search through numerous account books.

16.4 Objectives of the Study

- To understand the reliability of alternative channel services by the customers
- To know the customer satisfaction of alternative channel services by the customers
- To assess the customer loyalty for alternative channel services
- To contribute in the existing literature

16.5 Tools Applied

The study employed a straightforward approach to calculate the scores for agreement of the explored attributes from the review of literature and initial primary discussion with core group members of different age group customers. The various attributes finalized after the core group discussions were under reliability were – the bank's alternative channels are capable of delivering the promised banking services, the timeliness, rapidity, and effectiveness of service delivery or transaction processing are the key features of the bank's alternative channels, accurate information is provided through the bank's alternative channels, the alternative channels of the bank (ACoB) deliver services with high quality and sophistication and confidentiality and privacy are guaranteed by the bank's alternative channels.

For the customer satisfaction attributions were – I would opt for conducting my banking transaction through the ACoB if given the chance to redo it, making use of the ACoB for banking transactions is definitely the right decision, I find great pleasure in carrying out transactions through the website of internet banks, opting for the Alternative Channel Services of the Bank (ACSoB) for banking transactions was a smart move on my part, I am content with my recent choice to utilize the ACoB for banking transactions and I am pleased with my decision to conduct the recent banking transaction through the ACoB.

For the customers' loyalty the various attributes considered were – I strongly urge my friends and family to engage in business with the ACoB, I speak highly of the ACoB when discussing it with others, Over the next few years, I plan to conduct a greater number of banking transactions through the ACoB, If someone seeks my advice, I would highly recommend the ACSoB and when it comes to making my banking transactions, the ACSoB is my top preference.

This was done using a weighted mean method for the different sub-variables. To measure each perception attribute, a 5-point Rensis Likert scale was utilized. The scoring system assigned a weight of 4 to responses indicating complete agreement, a weight of 3 to responses indicating agreement, a weight of 2 to neutral responses, a weight of 1 to disagreeing responses, and a weight of 0 to responses indicating complete disagreement. The mean score was calculated by summing the assigned weights $(4 + 3 + 2 + 1 + 0)$ and dividing it by 5, resulting in a mean score of 2.

16.6 Sample Size Determination

According to Rummel's 1970 study and Schwab's 1980 research, a reasonable ratio for measuring sample size is between 1:4 and 1:10. The recommended approach suggests using a minimum sample size of four items and a maximum sample size of ten items (Khanh & Khang, 2021). Applying this method to our study, since we have taken 16 items, the minimum and maximum sample sizes should be 64 and 160, respectively. Following the aforementioned guideline, we gathered 147 observations after eliminating the common outlier. Therefore, for this study, a sample size of 147 aligns with Rummel and Schwab's rule from 1970 to 1980 as shown in Tables 16.1 and 16.2.

16.7 Interpretation

Regarding the reliability aspect, the average weight was found to be highest for RF, followed by UF, UM, RM, SM, and SF in relation to R1. As for R2, UF had a weighted score of 3.45, followed by UM, RM, RF, SM, and SF. UF also had the highest score of 3.52 for the question related to R3, followed by UM, RF, SM, and SF. In terms of attribute R4, RF had a score of 3.55, followed by RM, UM, SM, RF, and SF. Similarly, for R5, UF had a score of 3.39, followed by UM, RM, SF, RF, and SF. In all of the above cases, the weighted scores were lower for SF compared to others, but still higher than the average value of 2.

Moving on to customer satisfaction, the weighted score for CS1 was 3.52 for UF, followed by UM, RM, RF, SM, and SF. For CS2, UF had the highest weighted score of 3.42, followed by UM, RM, RF, and SM. UF also had the highest score of 3.55 for CS3, followed by UM, RM, RF, SM, and SF. For CS4, UF had a score of 3.32, followed by RF with 3.28, UM with 3.25, RM with 3.13, SM with 3.11, and SF with 2.61. Similarly, for CS5, RF had a score of 3.28, followed by UF, UM, SM, RM, and SF. In the case of CS6, UF topped with a score of 3.42, followed by UM, RM, RF, SM, and SF.

Table 16.1 Sampling Frame

Rural		Semi-Urban		Urban	
Male	Female	Male	Female	Male	Female
24	18	28	18	28	31

Table 16.2 Analysis of Data

Aggregate Weighted Score							
Attributes	**Code**	**RM**	**RF**	**SM**	**SF**	**UM**	**UF**
Reliability							
The bank's alternative channels are capable of delivering the promised banking services.	R1	3.13	3.44	3.03	2.5	3.25	3.32
The timeliness, rapidity, and effectiveness of service delivery or transaction processing are the key features of the bank's alternative channels.	R2	3.29	3.28	3.03	2.5	3.39	3.45
Accurate information is provided through the bank's alternative channels.	R3	3.38	3.44	3.03	2.5	3.46	3.52
The ACoB deliver services with high quality and sophistication	R4	3.46	3.33	3.39	2.83	3.46	3.55
Confidentiality and privacy are guaranteed by the bank's alternative channels.	R5	3.21	2.94	3.18	2.61	3.32	3.39
Customer Satisfaction							
I would opt for conducting my banking transaction through the ACoB if given the chance to redo it.	CS1	3.38	3.16	3.07	2,56	3.46	3.52
Making use of the ACoB for banking transactions is definitely the right decision.	CS2	3.25	3.14	3	2.44	3.36	3.42
I find great pleasure in carrying out transactions through the website of internet banks.	CS3	3.42	3.22	3.04	2.5	3.5	3.55
Opting for the ACSoB for banking transactions was a smart move on my part.	CS4	3.13	3.28	3.11	2.61	3.25	3.32
I am content with my recent choice to utilize the ACoB for banking transactions.	CS5	3	3.28	3.04	2.5	3.14	3.22
I am pleased with my decision to conduct the recent banking transaction through the ACoB.	CS6	3.25	3.06	2.93	2.33	3.36	3.42
Customer loyalty							
I strongly urge my friends and family to engage in business with the ACoB.	CL1	3.13	3.39	3.14	2.67	3.25	3.32
I speak highly of the ACoB when discussing it with others.	CL2	3.08	3	2.89	2.28	3.21	3.29

(Continued)

Table 16.2   Analysis of Data *(Continued)*

Aggregate Weighted Score							
Over the next few years, I plan to conduct a greater number of banking transactions through the ACoB.	CL3	3.08	3.11	3.11	2.61	3,21	3.29
If someone seeks my advice, I would highly recommend the ACSoB.	CL4	3.29	3.33	3.11	2.72	3.39	3.45
When it comes to making my banking transactions, the ACSoB is my top preference.	CL5	3.38	3.39	3.14	2.67	3.46	3.52

Source: Annexures A, B, C, D, E, and F.

Lastly, for customer loyalty, RF had a score of 3.39 for CL1, followed by UF, UM, SM, RM, and SF. UF had the highest score of 3.29 for CL2, followed by UM, RM, RF, SM, and SF. In the case of CL3, UF had a score of 3.29, followed by UM, RF, SM, RM, and SF. For CL4, UF had a score of 3.45, followed by UM, RF, RM, SM, and SF.

16.8 Conclusion

The advancement and evolution of technology have brought about a transformation in the banking industry. The traditional physical banking methods have been replaced by digital banking services. The introduction of alternative channel services has revolutionized the way banking services are provided. These services have enhanced the reliability of banking by ensuring efficient transactions, accurate processing, and maintaining the confidentiality of information. As a result, customer satisfaction has significantly increased, leading to a rise in the usage of net banking services. Moreover, the ACS has also played a crucial role in improving customer loyalty, completely transforming the banking landscape.

16.9 Additional Sample Data

Annexure A: Opinion of Rural Male (RM)-24

Attributes	CA	A	N	DA	CDA	Weight	Weighted Mean
	4	3	2	1	0		
Reliability							
The bank's alternative channels are capable of delivering the promised banking services.	15	3	2	2	2	75	3.13
The timeliness, rapidity, and effectiveness of service delivery or transaction processing are the key features of the bank's alternative channels.	15	4	2	3	0	79	3.29

(Continued)

Annexure A *(Continued)*

Accurate information is provided through the bank's alternative channels.	16	3	3	2	0	81	3.38
The alternative channels of the bank deliver services with high quality and sophistication	16	4	2	1	1	83	3.46
Confidentiality and privacy are guaranteed by the bank's alternative channels.	14	4	3	3	0	77	3.21
Customer Satisfaction							
I would opt for conducting my banking transaction through the ACoB if given the chance to redo it.	15	4	4	1	0	81	3.38
Making use of the ACoB for banking transactions is definitely the right decision.	16	2	3	2	1	78	3.25
I find great pleasure in carrying out transactions through the website of Internet Banks.	16	4	2	2	0	82	3.42
Opting for the ACSoB for banking transactions was a smart move on my part.	15	2	3	3	1	75	3.13
I am content with my recent choice to utilize the Alternative Channels of the Bank for banking transactions.	14	3	2	3	2	72	3
I am pleased with my decision to conduct the recent banking transaction through the ACoB.	15	3	3	3	0	78	3.25
Customer loyalty							
I strongly urge my friends and family to engage in business with the ACoB.	15	3	2	2	2	75	3.13
I speak highly of the ACoB when discussing it with others.	14	4	2	2	2	74	3.08
Over the next few years, I plan to conduct a greater number of banking transactions through the ACoB.	14	3	3	3	1	74	3.08
If someone seeks my advice, I would highly recommend the ACSoB.	15	3	4	2	0	79	3.29
When it comes to making my banking transactions, the ACSoB is my top preference.	16	3	3	2	0	81	3.38

Source: Primary data.

Annexure B: Opinion of Rural Female (RF)-18

Attributes	CA 4	A 3	N 2	DA 1	CDA 0	Weight	Weighted Mean
Reliability							
The bank's alternative channels are capable of delivering the promised banking services.	12	3	2	1	0	62	3.44
The timeliness, rapidity, and effectiveness of service delivery or transaction processing are the key features of the bank's alternative channels.	11	3	2	2	0	59	3.28
Accurate information is provided through the bank's alternative channels.	13	2	1	2	0	62	3.44
The alternative channels of the bank deliver services with high quality and sophistication	12	2	2	2	0	60	3.33
Confidentiality and privacy are guaranteed by the bank's alternative channels.	11	3	2	2	0	53	2.94
Customer Satisfaction							
I would opt for conducting my banking transaction through the ACoB if given the chance to redo it.	12	1	1	2	2	57	3.16
Making use of the ACoB for banking transactions is definitely the right decision.	13	2	1	2	0	62	3.14
I find great pleasure in carrying out transactions through the website of Internet Banks.	12	2	1	2	1	58	3.22
Opting for the ACoB of the Bank for banking transactions was a smart move on my part.	13	1	1	2	1	59	3.28
I am content with my recent choice to utilize the ACoB for banking transactions.	12	2	2	1	1	59	3.28
I am pleased with my decision to conduct the recent banking transaction through the ACoB.	11	2	1	3	1	55	3.06

(Continued)

Annexure B *(Continued)*

Customer loyalty							
I strongly urge my friends and family to engage in business with the ACoB.	12	3	1	2	0	61	3.39
I speak highly of the ACoB when discussing it with others.	11	2	1	2	2	54	3
Over the next few years, I plan to conduct a greater number of banking transactions through the ACoB.	12	1	1	3	1	56	3.11
If someone seeks my advice, I would highly recommend the ACSoB.	12	2	2	2	0	60	3.33
When it comes to making my banking transactions, the ACSoB is my top preference.	12	3	1	2	0	61	3.39

Source: Primary data.

Annexure C: Opinion of Sub-Urban Male (SM)-28

	CA	A	N	DA	CDA		Weighted
Attributes	4	3	2	1	0	*Weight*	*Mean*
Reliability							
The bank's alternative channels are capable of delivering the promised banking services.	18	2	2	3	3	85	3.03
The timeliness, rapidity, and effectiveness of service delivery or transaction processing are the key features of the bank's alternative channels.	17	3	2	4	2	85	3.03
Accurate information is provided through the bank's alternative channels.	17	4	1	3	3	85	3.03
The alternative channels of the bank deliver services with high quality and sophistication	17	5	2	4	0	91	3.39
Confidentiality and privacy are guaranteed by the bank's alternative channels.	17	4	3	3	1	89	3.18
Customer Satisfaction							
I would opt for conducting my banking transaction through the ACoB if given the chance to redo it.	18	2	2	4	2	86	3.07

(Continued)

Annexure C *(Continued)*

Making use of the ACoB for banking transactions is definitely the right decision.	17	2	3	4	2	84	3
I find great pleasure in carrying out transactions through the website of Internet Banks.	18	2	2	3	3	85	3.04
Opting for the ACSoB for banking transactions was a smart move on my part.	17	3	2	6	0	87	3.11
I am content with my recent choice to utilize the ACoB for banking transactions.	18	2	2	3	3	85	3.04
I am pleased with my decision to conduct the recent banking transaction through the ACoB.	17	2	2	4	3	82	2.93
Customer loyalty							
I strongly urge my friends and family to engage in business with the ACoB.	18	3	2	3	2	88	3.14
I speak highly of the ACoB when discussing it with others.	17	2	2	3	4	81	2.89
Over the next few years, I plan to conduct a greater number of banking transactions through the ACoB.	18	3	1	4	2	87	3.11
If someone seeks my advice, I would highly recommend the ACSoB.	17	4	2	3	2	87	3.11
When it comes to making my banking transactions, the ACSoB is my top preference.	18	2	3	4	1	88	3.14

Source: Primary data.

Annexure D: Opinion of Sub-Urban Female (SF)-18

	CA	A	N	DA	CDA		Weighted Mean
Attributes	4	3	2	1	0	Weight	
Reliability							
The bank's alternative channels are capable of delivering the promised banking services.	8	2	2	3	3	45	2.5

(Continued)

Annexure D *(Continued)*

The timeliness, rapidity, and effectiveness of service delivery or transaction processing are the key features of the bank's alternative channels.	7	3	2	4	2	45	2.5
Accurate information is provided through the bank's alternative channels.	7	4	1	3	3	45	2.5
The alternative channels of the bank deliver services with high quality and sophistication	7	5	2	4	0	51	2.83
Confidentiality and privacy are guaranteed by the bank's alternative channels.	7	4	3	3	1	47	2.61
Customer Satisfaction							
I would opt for conducting my banking transaction through the ACoB if given the chance to redo it.	8	2	2	4	2	46	2,56
Making use of the ACoB for banking transactions is definitely the right decision.	7	2	3	4	2	44	2.44
I find great pleasure in carrying out transactions through the website of Internet Banks.	8	2	2	3	3	45	2.5
Opting for the ACSoB for banking transactions was a smart move on my part.	7	3	2	6	0	47	2.61
I am content with my recent choice to utilize the ACoB for banking transactions.	8	2	2	3	3	45	2.5
I am pleased with my decision to conduct the recent banking transaction through the ACoB.	7	2	2	4	3	42	2.33
Customer loyalty							
I strongly urge my friends and family to engage in business with the ACoB.	8	3	2	3	2	48	2.67
I speak highly of the ACoB when discussing it with others.	7	2	2	3	4	41	2.28
Over the next few years, I plan to conduct a greater number of banking transactions through the ACoB.	8	3	1	4	2	47	2.61

(Continued)

Annexure D *(Continued)*

If someone seeks my advice, I would highly recommend the ACSoB.	7	4	2	3	2	49	2.72
When it comes to making my banking transactions, the ACSoB is my top preference.	8	2	3	4	1	48	2.67

Source: Primary data.

Annexure E: Opinion of Urban Male (UM)-28

	CA	A	N	DA	CDA		Weighted
Attributes	4	3	2	1	0	Weight	Mean
Reliability							
The bank's alternative channels are capable of delivering the promised banking services.	19	3	2	2	2	91	3.25
The timeliness, rapidity, and effectiveness of service delivery or transaction processing are the key features of the bank's alternative channels.	19	4	2	3	0	95	3.39
Accurate information is provided through the bank's alternative channels.	20	3	3	2	0	97	3.46
The alternative channels of the bank deliver services with high quality and sophistication	20	4	2	1	1	97	3.46
Confidentiality and privacy are guaranteed by the bank's alternative channels.	18	4	3	3	0	93	3.32
Customer Satisfaction							
I would opt for conducting my banking transaction through the ACoB if given the chance to redo it.	19	4	4	1	0	97	3.46
Making use of the ACoB for banking transactions is definitely the right decision.	20	2	3	2	1	94	3.36
I find great pleasure in carrying out transactions through the website of Internet Banks.	20	4	2	2	0	98	3.5

(Continued)

Annexure E *(Continued)*

Opting for the ACSoB for banking transactions was a smart move on my part.	19	2	3	3	1	91	3.25
I am content with my recent choice to utilize the ACoB for banking transactions.	18	3	2	3	2	88	3.14
I am pleased with my decision to conduct the recent banking transaction through the ACoB.	19	3	3	3	0	94	3.36
Customer loyalty							
I strongly urge my friends and family to engage in business with the ACoB.	19	3	2	2	2	91	3.25
I speak highly of the ACoB when discussing it with others.	18	4	2	2	2	90	3.21
Over the next few years, I plan to conduct a greater number of banking transactions through the ACoB.	18	3	3	3	1	90	3,21
If someone seeks my advice, I would highly recommend the ACSoB.	19	3	4	2	0	95	3.39
When it comes to making my banking transactions, the ACSoB is my top preference.	20	3	3	2	0	97	3.46

Source: Primary data.

Annexure F: Opinion of Urban Female (UF)-31

	CA	A	N	DA	CDA		Weighted
Attributes	4	3	2	1	0	Weight	Mean
Reliability							
The bank's alternative channels are capable of delivering the promised banking services.	22	3	2	2	2	103	3.32
The timeliness, rapidity, and effectiveness of service delivery or transaction processing are the key features of the bank's alternative channels.	22	4	2	3	0	107	3.45
Accurate information is provided through the bank's alternative channels.	23	3	3	2	0	109	3.52

(Continued)

Annexure F *(Continued)*

The alternative channels of the bank deliver services with high quality and sophistication	23	4	2	1	1	110	3.55
Confidentiality and privacy are guaranteed by the bank's alternative channels.	21	4	3	3	0	105	3.39
Customer Satisfaction							
I would opt for conducting my banking transaction through the Alternative Channels of the Bank if given the chance to redo it.	22	4	4	1	0	109	3.52
Making use of the ACoB for banking transactions is definitely the right decision.	23	2	3	2	1	106	3.42
I find great pleasure in carrying out transactions through the website of Internet Banks.	23	4	2	2	0	110	3.55
Opting for the ACSoB for banking transactions was a smart move on my part.	22	2	3	3	1	103	3.32
I am content with my recent choice to utilize the ACoB for banking transactions.	21	3	2	3	2	100	3.22
I am pleased with my decision to conduct the recent banking transaction through the ACoB.	22	3	3	3	0	106	3.42
Customer loyalty							
I strongly urge my friends and family to engage in business with the ACoB.	22	3	2	2	2	103	3.32
I speak highly of the ACoB when discussing it with others.	21	4	2	2	2	102	3.29
Over the next few years, I plan to conduct a greater number of banking transactions through the ACoB.	21	3	3	3	1	102	3.29
If someone seeks my advice, I would highly recommend the ACSoB.	22	3	4	2	0	107	3.45
When it comes to making my banking transactions, the ACSoB is my top preference.	23	3	3	2	0	109	3.52

Source: Primary data.

References

Ater, I., & Landsman, V. (2013). Do customers learn from experience? Evidence from retail banking. Management Science, 59(9), 2019–2035. https://doi.org/10.1287/mnsc.1120.1694

Bhakar, S., Bhakar, S., & Dubey, A. (2015). Analysis of the factors affecting customers' purchase intention: The mediating role of customer knowledge and perceived value. Advances in Social Sciences Research Journal, 2(1). https://doi.org/10.14738/assrj.21.139

Buri, S., Cull, R., & Giné, X. (2023). Alternative delivery channels and impacts: Agent banking. Policy Research Working Papers. https://doi.org/10.1596/1813-9450-10290

Carlos, N., & Ronald, M. O. (2020). Analyzing effect of alternative banking channels on financial performance of Burundi commercial banks: Evidence from Kenya commercial bank in Burundi. Asian Journal of Advanced Research and Reports, 1–11.

Chadichal, S. S., & Misra, S. (2012). Exploring the online service quality dimensions in service sectors impact on developing e-CRM in Indian banking sector. Global Journal for Research Analysis, 2(1), 115–117. https://search.proquest.com/openview/13208c3f47aaa34d4a5d3ac9770d71a1/1?pq-origsite=gscholar&cbl=1796425

Khang, A., Hahanov, V., Abbas, G. L., & Hajimahmud, V. A. (2022). "Cyber-Physical-Social System and İncident Management," *AI-Centric Smart City Ecosystems: Technologies, Design and Implementation* (1st Ed.), 2(15). CRC Press. https://doi.org/10.1201/9781003252542-2

Khang, A., Hajimahmud, V. A, Hahanov, Vladimir, & Shah, V. (2024). Advanced IoT Technologies and Applications in the Industry 4.0 Digital Economy (1st Ed.). CRC Press. https://doi.org/10.1201/9781003434269

Khanh, H. H., & Khang, A. (2021). "The Role of Artificial Intelligence in Blockchain Applications." In Rana G, Khang A., Sharma R., Goel A. K., Dubey A. K. *Reinventing Manufacturing and Business Processes Through Artificial Intelligence*, 2 (20–40). CRC Press. https://doi.org/10.1201/9781003145011-2

Krishnan, M. (2012). Alternate banking channels for customer convenience. International Journal of Scientific Research, 2(2), 9–10. https://doi.org/10.15373/22778179/feb2013/4

Chapter 17

Navigating the Digital Realm Identifying Trends and Opportunities in E-Banking Services

Rahul Jain and Charu Banga

17.1 Introduction

The landscape of banking services in the United Arab Emirates (UAE) has undergone a profound transformation with the advent of digital technology. E-banking services have emerged as a pivotal element of this digital revolution, reshaping the way customer's access and interact with financial institutions. This introduction provides an overview of the background of e-banking services in the UAE and highlights the significance of the ongoing digital transformation in the country's banking sector. The section is supported by relevant references to validate the information presented.

17.1.1 Background of E-Banking Services

The UAE's financial sector has witnessed remarkable growth and modernization, with an increasing focus on adopting advanced technologies. E-banking, or electronic banking, involves the use of digital platforms and online channels to deliver financial services to customers (Central Bank of the UAE [CBUAE], 2021a). This includes internet banking, mobile banking applications, electronic fund transfers, and digital payment systems, among other services. The convenience and accessibility offered by e-banking have led to a surge in its popularity among consumers and businesses in the UAE.

The CBUAE has been actively promoting digitalization in the banking sector. Its efforts have led to the development of robust infrastructure and regulatory frameworks that facilitate the secure and efficient delivery of e-banking services (Deloitte, 2021). As a result, the UAE has witnessed a rapid increase in digital transactions and the proliferation of Fintech start-ups aiming to revolutionize the financial services landscape.

DOI: 10.4324/9781003501947-17

17.1.2 Significance of Digital Transformation in the Banking Sector

The digital transformation has brought about a paradigm shift in the traditional banking sector, revolutionizing how financial services are delivered and consumed (The National, 2021). In the UAE, the significance of this transformation is evident in various aspects of the banking sector:

■ Enhanced Customer Experience: E-banking services offer customers a seamless and personalized banking experience, allowing them to conduct transactions, check balances, and manage their accounts conveniently from their smartphones or computers (Galal & Elkhodary, 2021).

■ Financial Inclusion: E-banking has played a crucial role in promoting financial inclusion by providing banking services to previously underserved segments of the population, including those in remote areas.

■ Operational Efficiency: Digital technology has streamlined banking operations, reducing manual processes, minimizing paperwork, and enabling banks to serve a larger customer base efficiently (The National, 2021).

■ Fostering Innovation: The digital transformation has encouraged collaboration between traditional banks and Fintech start-ups, leading to the development of innovative financial products and services.

■ Security and Compliance: Despite the growing reliance on digital channels, banks in the UAE have prioritized cybersecurity and data protection to ensure customer trust and comply with regulatory requirements.

17.1.3 Research Objectives

The primary objectives of this chapter are to:

■ Identify the current state of e-banking services in the UAE, including the types of services offered, customer adoption rates, and key players in the market.

■ Analyze the impact of the digital transformation on the banking sector in the UAE, with a focus on the integration of e-banking services and its implications for financial institutions (Albastaki & Alhussain, 2021).

■ Investigate the factors driving the adoption of e-banking services among customers in the UAE, including customer preferences, attitudes, and barriers to adoption.

■ Examine the role of regulatory frameworks and policies in shaping the development and growth of e-banking services in the UAE (CBUAE, 2022a).

■ Assess the challenges and opportunities faced by banks and financial institutions in implementing and expanding e-banking services in the UAE.

17.1.4 Research Methodology

To achieve the research objectives, this study will adopt a qualitative method to complete the research, with qualitative data collection and analysis. The research methodology will be structured as follows:

■ Literature Review: A comprehensive literature review will be conducted, encompassing academic journals, industry reports, and reputable online sources. This review will provide a strong theoretical foundation and insights into the current trends and developments in e-banking services in the UAE.

- Interviews: Semi-structured interviews will be conducted with key stakeholders, including banking professionals, regulators, and industry experts. These interviews will provide qualitative insights into the challenges, opportunities, and strategic implications of e-banking in the UAE.
- Case Studies: Selected case studies of leading banks and financial institutions in the UAE will be examined to understand successful e-banking strategies and their impact on customer experiences and business outcomes.
- Ethical Considerations: Ethical considerations will be adhered to throughout the research, ensuring the privacy and confidentiality of survey participants and interviewees.

17.2 Literature Review

17.2.1 Overview of Global E-Banking Trends

E-banking has transformed the global banking landscape, and various trends have emerged as a result of technological advancements and changing customer behaviors. The rise of mobile banking, the integration of artificial intelligence (AI) in customer service, the adoption of blockchain technology for secure transactions, and the emergence of open banking ecosystems are some of the prominent trends in the e-banking space worldwide. Furthermore, the COVID-19 pandemic accelerated digital adoption, pushing financial institutions to invest in digital channels and innovative solutions to meet customer demands (Cao, Li & Zhang, 2022).

17.2.2 Previous Studies on E-Banking Services

Several studies have explored e-banking services in the UAE, shedding light on various aspects of its adoption and impact on the banking sector. For instance, a study by Albastaki and Alhussain (2021) examined the role of digital banking in shaping customer experiences in UAE banks. The research highlighted the significance of seamless and personalized digital experiences in enhancing customer satisfaction and loyalty.

Another study conducted by Galal and Elkhodary (2021) analyzed the digital transformation in UAE banks, comparing different institutions' strategies and their implications. The research emphasized the importance of digitalization in remaining competitive and providing innovative financial solutions.

17.2.3 Analyzing the Factors Driving Digital Adoption in the Region

The factors driving digital adoption in the UAE banking sector are multifaceted and influenced by various elements. First, the country's high smartphone penetration and internet connectivity rates have created a conducive environment for the adoption of e-banking services. This has led to a shift in customer preferences, with many individuals opting for the convenience of digital banking over traditional methods.

Moreover, the UAE government's efforts to promote digitalization in the financial sector, as seen in the "UAE Vision 2021" initiative, have encouraged banks to invest in e-banking infrastructure and services (CBUAE, 2022a). The regulatory support has provided a framework for innovation and development, fostering a conducive ecosystem for digital banking adoption.

Furthermore, banks' proactive efforts to enhance cybersecurity measures have played a crucial role in building trust and confidence among customers, mitigating concerns about digital transactions and online banking.

17.3 Technological Innovations in E-Banking

17.3.1 Mobile Banking Applications

Mobile banking applications have revolutionized the way customers interact with their banks and manage their finances. These applications enable users to perform a wide range of banking transactions, such as checking account balances, transferring funds, paying bills, and making mobile payments, all through their smartphones or tablets. The convenience and ease of use offered by mobile banking apps have contributed significantly to the growth of e-banking services worldwide (Mishra, Tandon & Jain, 2021).

17.3.2 Biometric Authentication and Security Measures

Biometric authentication has emerged as a robust security measure in e-banking, ensuring the identity of users and protecting against unauthorized access. Biometric features such as fingerprint scans, facial recognition, and iris scanning are increasingly used to authenticate users during login and transactions. These methods provide enhanced security and are more convenient for customers compared to traditional password-based authentication (Varghese, Velusamy & Abu-Rgheff, 2020).

17.3.3 Artificial Intelligence (AI) and Chatbots in Customer Service

AI-powered Chatbots have become a crucial component of e-banking customer service, providing instant and personalized assistance to customers. Chatbots can handle a wide range of customer queries, from account-related inquiries to transaction disputes, round-the-clock. Their ability to analyze customer data and offer tailored solutions has significantly improved customer engagement and satisfaction in the e-banking sector (Rajendran, Vijayakumar & Kumaran, 2021).

17.3.4 Blockchain Technology and Its Potential Impact on E-Banking

Blockchain technology has the potential to transform e-banking by enhancing security, transparency, and efficiency in financial transactions. In a blockchain-based system, transactions are recorded in a decentralized and immutable ledger, making it highly secure and resistant to fraud. The use of blockchain can streamline cross-border payments, reduce transaction costs, and enable real-time settlement.

17.4 Shifting Customer Preferences

17.4.1 The Rise of Digital Natives and Tech-Savvy Consumers

Digital natives, also known as Generation Z and Millennials, have grown up in a digital-first world, surrounded by technology and online connectivity. As they become a significant segment of the banking customer base, their preferences are heavily inclined toward digital channels. Research indicates that digital natives prefer the convenience of e-banking services, with a preference for mobile banking apps and online transactions. Banks need to cater to the expectations of these tech-savvy consumers to remain relevant in the rapidly evolving digital landscape.

17.4.2 Personalization and Customized Banking Experiences

Customer expectations have evolved beyond simple transactions; they now seek personalized and tailored banking experiences. E-banking platforms that offer personalized product recommendations, targeted offers, and real-time insights into their financial health are increasingly valued by customers. A study by Accenture (2020) found that 75% of consumers are more likely to engage with banks that offer personalized experiences, emphasizing the significance of customization in retaining and attracting customers.

17.4.3 Importance of User-Friendly Interfaces and Omni Channel Access

A seamless and user-friendly interface is crucial to providing a positive customer experience in e-banking. Customers expect intuitive navigation and a clean design that enables them to complete transactions efficiently. Additionally, the importance of Omni channel access cannot be understated. Customers want the flexibility to start a transaction on one device and continue it on another seamlessly. An Accenture survey (2021) revealed that 62% of customers prefer an Omni channel experience with consistent interactions across various touchpoints.

17.5 Regulatory Framework

17.5.1 Current Regulations Governing E-Banking Services in the UAE

The UAE has a well-established regulatory framework governing e-banking services. The CBUAE plays a central role in formulating and implementing regulations to ensure the stability and security of the financial sector. Key regulations governing e-banking services in the UAE include the Electronic Funds Transfer System (EFTS), the UAE Payment Systems Regulation (PSR), and the Cybersecurity Regulation for Banks (CBUAE, 2022b). These regulations set guidelines for secure electronic transactions, data protection, and the use of digital payment systems in the country.

17.5.2 Regulatory Challenges and Opportunities for Fintech Start-ups

While the UAE offers significant opportunities for Fintech start-ups, they also face certain regulatory challenges. One of the main challenges is navigating the complex regulatory landscape. Fintech start-ups need to comply with various licensing and registration requirements to operate in the UAE. This can be a time-consuming and costly process, particularly for early-stage start-ups with limited resources (Choo, Yong & Thanh, 2020).

However, there are also opportunities for Fintech start-ups to collaborate with established financial institutions through regulatory sandboxes and innovation hubs. Such collaborations allow start-ups to test their products and services in a controlled environment while receiving regulatory guidance and support from the authorities. Moreover, the CBUAE has been actively encouraging innovation in the financial sector, creating opportunities for Fintech start-ups to contribute to the country's digital transformation (CBUAE, 2021b).

17.5.3 The Role of Regulatory Sandboxes in Fostering Innovation

Regulatory sandboxes are a significant component of the UAE's efforts to foster innovation in the financial sector. The CBUAE launched its Regulatory Sandbox Framework in 2017, providing a controlled environment for Fintech start-ups and financial institutions to test their innovative products and services without full compliance with existing regulations (CBUAE, 2020).

The sandbox allows participants to gain valuable insights, identify potential risks, and make necessary adjustments to their offerings before launching them in the market. By providing regulatory support and feedback, the sandbox helps Fintech start-ups overcome regulatory barriers and accelerate their growth in a safe and regulated manner. Moreover, the sandbox promotes collaboration between Fintech start-ups and traditional financial institutions, encouraging mutual learning and innovation (CBUAE, 2019).

17.6 Case Studies of Leading E-Banking Players

17.6.1 Case Studies

17.6.1.1 Emirates NBD

Emirates NBD is one of the leading banks in the UAE, known for its innovative e-banking services and customer-centric approach. The bank has invested significantly in developing user-friendly mobile banking applications, allowing customers to perform various banking activities on the go. Emirates NBD has also implemented biometric authentication for added security and convenience, enabling customers to log in using their fingerprints or facial recognition. Their focus on personalization and customized experiences has helped them retain existing customers and attract new ones (Emirates NBD, 2023).

17.6.1.2 Mashreq Bank

Mashreq Bank has been a pioneer in adopting technology to enhance its e-banking services. The bank offers a comprehensive suite of online and mobile banking features, enabling customers to manage their accounts, transfer funds, and make payments seamlessly. Mashreq Bank's digital strategy includes AI-powered Chatbots for customer support, which has led to significant improvements in response times and customer satisfaction. Additionally, the bank has been proactive in leveraging blockchain technology for cross-border payments, reducing transaction times and costs for customers (Mashreq Bank, 2023).

17.6.1.3 ADCB (Abu Dhabi Commercial Bank)

ADCB has distinguished itself in the UAE's e-banking landscape through its commitment to providing an omnichannel experience. The bank has integrated its online and mobile banking platforms to offer customers a seamless and consistent experience across all touchpoints. ADCB's customer-centric approach also includes a wide range of personalized financial solutions, including targeted product recommendations and tailored offers based on customer behavior and preferences. These initiatives have contributed to the bank's strong customer acquisition and retention rates (ADCB, 2023).

17.6.1.4 First Abu Dhabi Bank (FAB)

First Abu Dhabi Bank (FAB) is one of the largest banks in the UAE and a prominent player in the e-banking sector. FAB has been at the forefront of digital innovation, offering a comprehensive range of e-banking services to its customers. The bank's mobile banking app provides a user-friendly interface, allowing customers to conduct various transactions, access account information, and make mobile payments. FAB's focus on security includes biometric authentication features, such as fingerprint and facial recognition, ensuring a secure and convenient user experience (FAB, 2023).

17.6.2 Successful E-Banking Strategies and Impact on Customer Acquisition and Retention

FAB's successful e-banking strategies have had a significant impact on customer acquisition and retention. By offering a seamless and user-friendly mobile banking app, the bank has attracted a large number of tech-savvy customers, including digital natives who prefer convenient digital banking solutions. The availability of personalized services, such as targeted offers and customized financial solutions, has also contributed to customer acquisition by meeting the specific needs and preferences of individual customers.

Additionally, the emphasis on biometric authentication and robust security measures has instilled trust and confidence in customers, leading to higher customer retention rates. Customers value the secure and convenient features of FAB's e-banking services, which has contributed to long-term customer loyalty and reduced churn rates.

■ **Dubai Islamic Bank (DIB):** DIB is a leading Sharia-compliant bank in the UAE, known for its innovative e-banking services that align with Islamic principles. DIB offers a feature-rich mobile banking app that allows customers to manage their accounts, performs transactions, and accesses a wide range of Islamic banking products and services. The bank's app incorporates a user-friendly design and easy navigation, making it accessible to a diverse customer base (DIB, 2023).

17.6.3 Successful E-Banking Strategies and Impact on Customer Attraction and Retention

DIB's successful e-banking strategies have been instrumental in attracting and retaining customers. The bank's commitment to Islamic banking principles has resonated with a significant segment of the population seeking Sharia-compliant financial solutions. The mobile banking app's seamless integration with Islamic products and services has been a key driver in customer acquisition, particularly among the Muslim community in the UAE.

Moreover, DIB's focus on delivering a user-friendly and intuitive interface has contributed to higher customer satisfaction, enhancing customer retention rates. The convenience of conducting transactions and accessing Islamic banking services through the mobile app has strengthened customer loyalty, leading to increased customer retention and a positive brand image.

17.6.4 Impact of Successful E-Banking Strategies

The successful e-banking strategies employed by FAB and DIB have had a transformative impact on customer acquisition and retention for both banks. By offering feature-rich and user-friendly mobile banking apps, these banks have attracted tech-savvy customers and strengthened their market presence in the UAE's competitive e-banking landscape.

The emphasis on personalized services and convenient digital experiences has significantly contributed to customer loyalty and long-term retention. Additionally, the integration of advanced security features has instilled trust and confidence among customers, leading to reduced churn rates and improved customer satisfaction.

Overall, these successful e-banking strategies have positioned FAB and DIB as industry leaders, allowing them to gain a competitive edge and establish a strong customer base in the rapidly evolving digital banking environment (Khang & Rath et al., 2023).

17.7 Security and Privacy Concerns in E-Banking

17.7.1 Addressing Cybersecurity Risks and Data Breaches

Cybersecurity is a paramount concern in e-banking, given the sensitive nature of financial transactions and customer data involved. Banks and financial institutions must implement robust security measures to protect against cyber threats and data breaches. This includes encryption protocols for data transmission, multi-factor authentication for user login, and continuous monitoring of systems for suspicious activities.

Furthermore, regular security audits and vulnerability assessments are essential to identify potential weaknesses and promptly address them. Banks should also invest in employee training to raise awareness of cybersecurity best practices and minimize the risk of internal security breaches.

17.7.2 Building Trust in E-Banking Services through Transparency and Accountability

Building trust is critical for the success of e-banking services. Banks must be transparent about their data privacy practices and inform customers about the information they collect, how it is used, and with whom it is shared. Clear and concise privacy policies should be accessible to customers, enabling them to make informed decisions about their data (Bharadwaj, Sharma & Saini, 2020).

To ensure accountability, financial institutions must comply with relevant data protection regulations and industry standards. They should have mechanisms in place to address customer concerns and provide timely responses to data privacy queries. Additionally, banks should maintain a proactive approach to communication during data breaches, promptly notifying affected customers and providing assistance to mitigate potential damages (European Commission, 2019).

Addressing cybersecurity risks and data breaches is crucial for e-banking service providers to safeguard customer data and maintain trust. Implementing strong security measures, conducting regular audits, and staying compliant with relevant regulations can significantly mitigate cybersecurity risks and protect customer information.

Transparency and accountability play a key role in building trust in e-banking services. By being open about their data privacy practices, banks can assure customers that their data is being handled responsibly. Complying with data protection regulations and promptly communicating with customers in case of any security incidents further enhances trust and reinforces the commitment to protecting customer privacy and security.

17.8 Market Opportunities and Future Projections for E-Banking

17.8.1 Untapped Market Segments for E-Banking Growth

- Small and Medium Enterprises (SMEs): SMEs represent a significant untapped market segment for e-banking growth in the UAE. As the government focuses on promoting entrepreneurship and economic diversification, there is a growing need for digital banking solutions tailored to the unique financial requirements of SMEs. E-banking services that offer easy access to credit, digital invoicing, and cash flow management can cater to the needs of this dynamic and expanding sector (PwC, 2020).
- Rural and Remote Areas: Despite the rapid development of urban centers in the UAE, rural and remote areas still present untapped opportunities for e-banking growth. Extending digital banking services to these regions can promote financial inclusion and provide previously underserved populations with access to essential banking services.
- Expatriate Communities: The UAE has a large expatriate population that contributes significantly to the economy. E-banking services tailored to the needs of expatriates, such as international money transfers, foreign currency accounts, and multi-language support, can capture this segment's attention and drive growth (Gassara, Hassairi & Lammari, 2020).

17.8.2 Projections on the Future of E-Banking Services in the UAE

The future of e-banking services in the UAE looks promising, driven by several factors:

- Continued Digital Transformation: The UAE's commitment to digital transformation, as outlined in the UAE Vision 2021 and the Smart Dubai initiative, will further accelerate the adoption of e-banking services. The government's support for technological advancements and innovation in the financial sector will create a conducive environment for e-banking growth.
- Fintech Collaboration: Increased collaboration between traditional banks and Fintech start-ups is expected to drive innovation in e-banking services. As banks partner with Fintech companies to leverage cutting-edge technologies and expand their service offerings, customers can expect more personalized, convenient, and secure e-banking experiences.
- Rise of Digital Payments: The UAE's shift toward becoming a cashless society is expected to propel the growth of digital payment solutions. E-banking services will play a vital role in facilitating digital payments through mobile wallets, contactless cards, and other innovative payment methods (Khaleej Times, 2021).
- Enhanced Customer Experiences: Customer-centricity will remain a key focus for banks, leading to the development of more intuitive and customer-friendly e-banking platforms. Banks will invest in AI-powered Chatbots, voice assistants, and advanced analytics to offer hyper-personalized experiences to their customers (Deloitte, 2022).

17.9 Conclusion

This chapter explored the e-banking services landscape in the UAE, focusing on trends, challenges, and opportunities in the digital realm. The key findings and insights can be summarized as follows:

- Background of E-Banking Services: The UAE's banking sector has experienced a significant digital transformation, driven by factors such as high smartphone penetration, increasing internet connectivity, and government initiatives to promote digitalization in the financial sector.

- Significance of Digital Transformation: The digital transformation in the banking sector has revolutionized customer experiences, making e-banking services a crucial aspect of financial institutions' strategies. The adoption of mobile banking applications, biometric authentication, AI-powered Chatbots, and blockchain technology has reshaped the way customers interact with their banks.
- Regulatory Framework: The UAE has established a robust regulatory framework governing e-banking services, ensuring security, data privacy, and compliance with relevant laws. Regulatory sandboxes have been instrumental in fostering innovation and collaboration between traditional banks and Fintech start-ups.
- Shifting Customer Preferences: Digital natives and tech-savvy consumers have emerged as dominant market segments, demanding personalized and user-friendly e-banking experiences. Offering transparency, trust, and an Omni Channel approach are essential in retaining and attracting customers.
- Successful E-Banking Strategies: Case studies of leading banks, such as Emirates NBD, Mashreq Bank, ADCB, FAB, and DIB, demonstrated the impact of successful e-banking strategies on customer acquisition and retention. User-friendly interfaces, personalized services, and advanced security measures were key drivers of customer satisfaction and loyalty.

17.9.1 Implications for the Future of E-Banking Services

The future of e-banking services in the UAE holds significant promise and opportunities. As the UAE continues to invest in digital infrastructure and supports innovation in the financial sector, several implications can be drawn:

- Focus on Customer-Centricity: Banks need to prioritize customer-centric strategies, tailoring e-banking services to meet the evolving needs and preferences of tech-savvy customers. Personalization, seamless experiences, and responsive customer support will be critical for driving customer loyalty.
- Embrace Technological Advancements: Embracing emerging technologies, such as AI, blockchain, and Internet of Things (IoT), will allow banks to enhance security, streamline processes, and provide innovative services. Collaborating with Fintech start-ups can foster a culture of innovation and accelerate digital transformation.
- Reach Untapped Market Segments: To drive further growth, banks should focus on expanding their services to untapped market segments, such as SMEs, rural areas, and expatriate communities. Customized offerings that cater to the specific needs of these segments can unlock new growth opportunities.
- Strengthen Regulatory Compliance: Ensuring compliance with data protection regulations and maintaining transparent practices will be crucial in building and maintaining trust with customers. Banks must continue to invest in cybersecurity measures to protect customer data and guard against cyber threats.

In conclusion, the future of e-banking services in the UAE looks promising, driven by a digital-first approach, technological advancements, and a customer-centric focus. By leveraging these opportunities and addressing challenges, banks can continue to thrive in the dynamic e-banking landscape of the UAE.

17.9.2 Recommendations for Banks and Financial Institutions

■ Customer-Centric Approach: Banks should prioritize a customer-centric approach in their e-banking strategies. This involves understanding customer preferences, behaviors, and pain points to develop personalized and intuitive digital experiences. Regular feedback surveys and data analytics can aid in identifying areas for improvement and tailoring services to meet customer needs.

■ Embrace Emerging Technologies: Banks should invest in emerging technologies, such as AI, machine learning, and blockchain, to enhance the efficiency, security, and innovation of their e-banking services. AI-powered Chatbots can improve customer support, while blockchain can streamline cross-border transactions and reduce costs (Khang, Shah & Rani, 2023).

■ Expand Financial Inclusion: To capitalize on untapped market segments, banks should work toward expanding financial inclusion. This includes reaching out to SMEs, rural areas, and expatriate communities with tailored banking solutions, promoting digital literacy, and offering services that cater to their specific needs.

■ Strengthen Cybersecurity Measures: Robust cybersecurity is critical in building customer trust and safeguarding sensitive data. Banks should continuously invest in state-of-the-art security technologies, conduct regular security audits, and implement employee training programs to stay ahead of evolving cyber threats.

17.9.3 Recommendations

■ Regulatory Support for Fintech: The government should continue to foster a supportive regulatory environment for Fintech start-ups. This can be achieved by streamlining licensing processes, reducing bureaucratic hurdles, and providing regulatory sandboxes for testing innovative financial solutions.

■ Collaboration between Regulators and Industry: Closer collaboration between regulatory authorities, such as the CBUAE, and industry players can foster a more cohesive approach to digital transformation. Regular dialogue and joint initiatives can address regulatory challenges and drive innovation in the banking sector.

■ Digital Infrastructure Development: The government should prioritize investment in digital infrastructure, including high-speed internet connectivity and digital payment infrastructure. This will create a robust foundation for the growth of e-banking services and encourage greater adoption among citizens and businesses.

■ Financial Literacy Initiatives: Promoting financial literacy among the population is essential to encourage greater adoption of e-banking services. The government can support educational programs, workshops, and awareness campaigns to empower individuals with the knowledge and skills to use digital financial services effectively (Khang & Muthmainnah et al., 2023).

■ Encourage Public-Private Partnerships: The government can foster innovation and digital transformation in the banking sector by encouraging public-private partnerships. Collaborative initiatives between the government, banks, and Fintech companies can drive technological advancements and the adoption of digital solutions.

By implementing these recommendations, banks and financial institutions can seize the e-banking opportunities in the UAE, while the government can play a vital role in supporting and driving further innovation and digital transformation in the banking sector.

References

Accenture. (2020). The Banking Customer Experience Survey: Winning Experiences in a Digital-First World. https://www.accenture.com/us-en/insights/interactive/banking-experience-reimagined

Accenture. (2021). Banking on Value: Rewards, Loyalty, and Personalization. Benefiting both customers and financial institutions. https://www.accenture.com/content/dam/accenture/final/industry/banking/document/Accenture-Banking-Consumer-Study.pdf

ADCB. (2023). Digital Banking. https://www.adcb.com/en/consumer-education-awareness/starting-out/exploring-digital-banking-solutions

Albastaki, Y, & Alhussain, T. (2021). Evaluating the role of digital Banking in shaping UAE Banks' customer experience. International Journal of Innovation and Applied Studies, 34(4), 1059–1068.

Albastaki, Y, & Alhussain, T. (2021). Evaluating the role of digital Banking in shaping UAE Banks' customer experience. International Journal of Innovation and Applied Studies, 34(4), 1059–1068. https://bspace.buid.ac.ae/handle/1234/2099

Bharadwaj, S., Sharma, P., & Saini, R. (2020). Data privacy and trust in e-Banking: An empirical investigation. International Journal of Bank Marketing, 38(1), 149–175.

Cao, X., Li, H., & Zhang, H. (2022). The impact of the COVID-19 pandemic on the development of online banking: Evidence from the U.S. and China. Sustainability, 14(2), 401. https://www.sciencedirect.com/science/article/pii/S0013935121009312

Central Bank of the UAE (CBUAE). (2019). Regulatory Framework for Fintech. https://www.centralbank.ae/en/our-operations/fintech-digital-transformation/

Central Bank of the UAE (CBUAE). (2020). Regulatory Framework for Stored Value Facilities and Retail Payment Systems. https://www.centralbank.ae/sites/default/files/2021-06/Regulatory%20Framework%20for%20Stored%20Value%20Facilities%20and%20Retail%20Payment%20Systems-EN.pdf

Central Bank of the UAE (CBUAE). (2021a). Annual Report 2020. https://www.centralbank.ae/sites/default/files/2021-03/CBUAE-Annual%20Report%202020-EN.pdf

Central Bank of the UAE (CBUAE). (2021b). UAE Vision 2021.

Central Bank of the UAE (CBUAE). (2022a). Cybersecurity Regulation for Banks. https://www.centralbank.ae/sites/default/files/2022-01/Cybersecurity%20Regulation%20for%20Banks-EN.pdf

Central Bank of the UAE (CBUAE). (2022b). Annual Report 2021. https://www.centralbank.ae/sites/default/files/2022-05/CBUAE-Annual%20Report%202021-EN.pdf

Choo, Y. Y., Yong, C. C., & Thanh, N. T. (2020). Regulatory sandboxes: Balancing Fintech innovation and consumer protection in the Asia-Pacific Region. Journal of Financial Regulation and Compliance, 28(2), 215–230. https://papers.ssrn.com/sol3/papers.cfm?abstract_id=3090844

Deloitte. (2022). Middle East Banking Outlook 2022 - Adapting for the Next Normal.

Dubai Islamic Bank (DIB). (2023). Mobile Banking.

Emirates NBD. (2023). Mobile Banking. https://www.emiratesnbd.com/en/ways-of-banking/mobile-banking?source=search

European Commission. (2019). General Data Protection Regulation (GDPR). https://ec.europa.eu/commission/presscorner/detail/en/ip_19_4149

First Abu Dhabi Bank (FAB). (2023). Mobile Banking. https://www.bankfab.com/en-ae/personal/help-and-support/digital-banking/mobile-banking

Galal, A, & Elkhodary, A. (2021). Digital transformation in UAE banks: A comparative analysis. Journal of Digital Banking, 5(2), 140–157. https://www.inderscienceonline.com/doi/abs/10.1504/IJBPM.2020.106121

Gassara, I. B., Hassairi, A., & Lammari, N. (2020). Adoption of online Banking by expatriates in the UAE: A qualitative study. International Journal of Bank Marketing, 38(7), 1602–1620. http://uhra.herts.ac.uk/handle/2299/8741

Khaleej Times. (2021). UAE: Moving Towards a Cashless Society.

Khang, A, Muthmainnah, M, Ibna Seraj, Prodhan Mahbub, Al Yakin, Ahmad, Obaid, Ahmad J., & Panda, Manas Ranjan. (2023). "AI-Aided Teaching Model for the Education 5.0 Ecosystem" AI-Based Technologies and Applications in the Era of the Metaverse (1st Ed.). (Pages 83–104). IGI Global Press. https://doi.org/10.4018/978-1-6684-8851-5.ch004

Khang, A, Rath, Kali Charan, Satapathy, Suresh Kumar, Kumar, Amaresh, Das, Sudhansu Ranjan, & Panda, Manas Ranjan. (2023). "Enabling the Future of Manufacturing: Integration of Robotics and IoT to Smart Factory Infrastructure in Industry 4.0." AI-Based Technologies and Applications in the Era of the Metaverse (1st Ed.) (Pages 25–50). IGI Global Press. https://doi.org/10.4018/978-1-6684-8851-5. ch002

Khang, A, Shah, V, & Rani, S. (2023). AI-Based Technologies and Applications in the Era of the Metaverse. (1st Ed.). IGI Global Press. https://doi.org/10.4018/978-1-6684-8851-5

Mashreq Bank. (2023). Digital Banking. https://www.mashreq.com/en/uae/business/digital-banking/

Mishra, D., Tandon, P., & Jain, A. K. (2021). Mobile Banking: A review and agenda for future research. International Journal of Bank Marketing, 39(2), 271–295. https://www.sciencedirect.com/science/article/pii/S0736585314000367

PwC. (2020). SME Banking Survey: Driving Growth through Innovative Digital Solutions. https://www.pwc.com/sg/en/services/risk/digital-solutions.html

Rajendran, D., Vijayakumar, V., & Kumaran, K. (2021). Artificial intelligence and its applications in banking sector: A review. International Journal of Management Studies, 8(3), 146–155. http://www.american-scholarspress.us/journals/IMR/pdf/IMR-1-2021/V17n121-art2.pdf

The National. (2021). Digital payment transactions in UAE surge by 84% in 2020.

Varghese, B., Velusamy, A., & Abu-Rgheff, M. A. (2020). A comprehensive review of biometric authentication in mobile banking: Current practices and future trends. Journal of Retailing and Consumer Services, 57, 102230. https://www.sciencedirect.com/science/article/pii/S0957417423000623

Yli-Huumo, J, Ko, D, Choi, S, Park, S, & Smolander, K. (2016). Where is current research on blockchain technology?—A systematic review. PloS One, 11(10), e0163477. https://journals.plos.org/plosone/article?id=10.1371/journal.pone.0163477

Chapter 18

Role of Edge Technologies and Applications in Banking and Finance Industry

Ushaa Eswaran, Vivek Eswaran, Keerthna Murali, and Vishal Eswaran

18.1 Introduction

The banking and finance industry has emerged as a prominent adopter of artificial intelligence (AI) technologies, recognizing their potential to drive innovation, enhance customer experiences, and gain a competitive edge in an increasingly digital landscape. The integration of AI is reshaping traditional banking models and revolutionizing the way financial services are delivered, consumed, and managed.

The importance of AI in the banking and finance sector stems from its ability to process and analyze vast amounts of data, enabling financial institutions to uncover valuable insights, make data-driven decisions, and automate complex processes. AI technologies, such as machine learning (ML), natural language processing (NLP), and computer vision, are being leveraged across various domains, including fraud detection, personalized customer service, automated trading, credit risk assessment, and compliance monitoring.

The current state of AI adoption in the banking and finance industry is characterized by a growing momentum and increasing investment. According to a report by the International Data Corporation, global spending on AI systems in the banking industry is projected to reach $89.8 billion by 2025, driven by the need for operational efficiency, enhanced customer experiences, and improved risk management capabilities (IDC, 2021).

The chapter further analyzes the global perspectives on AI adoption in banking and finance, highlighting the diverse approaches and trends across different regions, such as the rapid adoption in North America, the emphasis on ethical AI and data privacy in Europe, the growing Fintech–bank collaborations in Asia-Pacific, and the leveraging of AI to drive financial inclusion in emerging markets.

DOI: 10.4324/9781003501947-18

The chapter also presents successful case studies of AI implementation, such as HSBC's AI-powered fraud detection system and Ant Financial's AI-driven credit risk assessment, and discusses the lessons learned and best practices for banks and financial institutions to effectively adopt and integrate AI into their operations.

Finally, the chapter explores the future trends and outlook, including advancements in AI technologies, the emergence of AI-powered banking and financial services, and the potential impact of AI on the future of the financial industry. The chapter concludes with a summary of the key opportunities, challenges, and recommendations for banks and financial institutions to capitalize on the transformative potential of AI. Several factors are fueling the growth of AI adoption in the financial sector:

■ Digital transformation: Financial institutions are undergoing digital transformation initiatives to meet evolving customer expectations and remain competitive in an increasingly digital landscape. AI plays a crucial role in enabling this transformation by automating processes, enhancing customer interactions, and driving innovation.

■ Data proliferation: The banking and finance industry generates and handles vast amounts of data, including customer data, transaction records, and market data. AI technologies are essential for extracting valuable insights and leveraging this data to drive informed decision-making and personalized services.

■ Regulatory compliance: AI-powered solutions are helping financial institutions navigate complex regulatory landscapes, enabling them to comply with anti-money laundering (AML), know your customer (KYC), and other regulatory requirements more effectively.

■ Cost optimization: By automating repetitive tasks and streamlining processes, AI can help financial institutions reduce operational costs and improve overall efficiency, leading to significant cost savings.

■ The potential impact of AI on various aspects of banking and finance is far-reaching:
  – Customer experience: AI-driven chatbots, virtual assistants, and personalized recommendation systems are enhancing customer interactions, providing tailored services, and improving overall customer satisfaction.
  – Operational efficiency: AI-powered automation of back-office tasks, such as data entry, document processing, and regulatory reporting, is increasing productivity and reducing operational costs.
  – Risk management: AI algorithms can analyze vast amounts of data to identify patterns and anomalies, enabling more accurate fraud detection, credit risk assessment, and compliance monitoring.
  – Decision-making: AI-driven predictive analytics and forecasting models are empowering financial institutions to make data-driven decisions, optimize resource allocation, and identify emerging trends and opportunities.

As the banking and finance industry continues to embrace AI technologies, it is poised to witness significant transformations in its operations, customer experiences, and overall competitive landscape. Financial institutions that successfully navigate the challenges and harness the power of AI will be well-positioned to thrive in the digital age and deliver superior value to their customers.

18.2 Key Applications of AI in Banking and Finance

AI has found numerous applications in the banking and finance sector, revolutionizing various aspects of financial operations and services. This section provides an in-depth exploration of some key applications, supported by real-world examples and case studies, as well as discussions on emerging areas and the integration of AI with other technologies.

18.2.1 Fraud Detection and Prevention

AI-powered fraud detection systems utilize advanced ML algorithms to analyze vast volumes of transaction data in real time, enabling financial institutions to identify and prevent fraudulent activities effectively. For example, HSBC employs AI-driven anomaly detection technology to monitor transactions and promptly alert the bank to any suspicious behavior. In one case, HSBC's AI system flagged unusual patterns in transaction data, leading to the discovery of a sophisticated fraud scheme involving multiple accounts and preventing significant financial losses for the bank and its customers (HSBC, 2020).

18.2.2 Personalized Customer Service and Recommendation Systems

AI-driven chatbots and virtual assistants revolutionize customer service by providing personalized interactions and tailored product recommendations based on individual preferences and behavior. Bank of America's virtual assistant, Erica, utilizes NLP and ML algorithms to assist customers with various banking tasks. For instance, Erica can help customers check their account balances, transfer funds, and even provide personalized financial advice based on their spending habits and financial goals (Bank of America, 2021).

18.2.3 Automated Trading and Portfolio Optimization

AI algorithms analyze market data and execute trades autonomously, potentially outperforming human traders by reacting swiftly to market fluctuations and identifying profitable opportunities. Robo-advisors like Betterment and Wealthfront leverage AI to optimize investment portfolios according to each investor's risk tolerance and market conditions. In a case study, a client who invested with a robo-advisor saw significant portfolio growth over time, thanks to AI-driven investment strategies that minimized risk and maximized returns (Kaplan & Sironi, 2019).

18.2.4 Credit Risk Assessment and Loan Underwriting

AI-powered credit scoring models incorporate a wide range of data sources, including alternative credit data and social media activity, to assess an individual's creditworthiness more accurately than traditional methods. Ant Financial's Sesame Credit platform utilizes AI to evaluate credit risk and determine loan eligibility. In a case study, a small business owner with a limited credit history was able to secure a loan through Sesame Credit, thanks to the platform's AI-driven credit assessment process, which considered factors beyond traditional credit scores (Ant Financial, 2021).

18.2.5 Emerging Applications

18.2.5.1 RegTech

AI is increasingly being used in regulatory technology (RegTech) solutions to help financial institutions comply with various regulations, such as AML and KYC requirements. For example, JPMorgan Chase's Anomaly Detection system, powered by AI, enhances the bank's compliance efforts by identifying potential money laundering activities more efficiently (JPMorgan Chase, 2019).

18.2.5.2 InsurTech

In the insurance sector, AI is being utilized for tasks such as risk assessment, fraud detection, and claim processing. For instance, Lemonade, an InsurTech company, uses AI to process and settle claims efficiently, reducing the time required for claim handling from weeks to seconds (Lemonade, 2021).

18.2.5.3 Investment Management

AI is transforming investment management by enabling more sophisticated portfolio optimization, risk analysis, and asset allocation. BlackRock, the world's largest asset manager, has implemented AI-driven investment strategies that leverage NLP and ML to analyze vast amounts of data and identify investment opportunities (BlackRock, 2022).

18.2.6 Integration with Other Technologies

18.2.6.1 Blockchain and AI

The integration of AI and blockchain technologies can enhance transparency, security, and efficiency in financial services. For example, AI can be used to analyze blockchain data and identify patterns and anomalies, while blockchain can provide a secure and decentralized infrastructure for storing and sharing AI models and data (Dai, Zheng & Zhang, 2019).

18.2.6.2 Internet of Things (IoT) and AI

The combination of IoT and AI can enable new financial services and products, such as personalized insurance offerings based on real-time data from IoT devices. For instance, auto insurance companies can leverage IoT data from connected vehicles and AI algorithms to assess driving behavior and adjust premiums accordingly (Gai, Qiu & Sun, 2018). Table 18.1 provides a summary of key AI applications in banking and finance, along with examples and potential benefits.

18.3 Opportunities Presented by AI in Banking and Finance

18.3.1 Enhanced Customer Experience and Engagement

AI implementation in financial institutions enables them to deliver more personalized and efficient customer service, resulting in heightened levels of customer satisfaction and loyalty (Huang

Table 18.1   AI Applications in Banking and Finance

Application	Examples	Potential Benefits
Fraud detection and prevention	HSBC's AI-powered anomaly detection system	Identify fraudulent activities, prevent financial losses
Personalized customer service	Bank of America's virtual assistant Erica	Enhance customer experience, provide tailored recommendations
Automated trading and portfolio optimization	Robo-advisors like Betterment and Wealthfront	Optimize investment strategies, minimize risk
Credit risk assessment and loan underwriting	Ant Financial's Sesame Credit platform	Accurate credit scoring, expand access to credit
RegTech	JPMorgan Chase's Anomaly Detection system	Improve regulatory compliance, detect money laundering
InsurTech	Lemonade's AI-powered claim processing	Efficient claim handling, reduce processing time
Investment management	BlackRock's AI-driven investment strategies	Identify investment opportunities, optimize portfolios

& Rust, 2021). For instance, Mastercard's AI-powered Chatbot, ChatGPT, has significantly expedited customer inquiry resolution and improved accuracy, leading to a notable 25% reduction in call center costs (Mastercard, 2021).

18.3.2 Improved Operational Efficiency and Cost Savings

AI-driven automation streamlines various back-office tasks like data entry, document processing, and regulatory reporting, yielding substantial cost savings and productivity enhancements (Deloitte, 2020). Notably, Citi's adoption of AI-powered robotic process automation (RPA) has slashed operational costs by 30% and boosted processing speed by 50% (Citi, 2019).

18.3.3 Faster and More Accurate Decision-Making

AI's capability to analyze vast datasets and uncover patterns and insights empowers more informed business decisions, including investment strategies, credit risk assessments, and fraud detection (Berrada, Crammer & Ertekin, 2021). BBVA's implementation of AI-driven credit risk models has led to more precise loan approval decisions, resulting in a notable 15% reduction in non-performing loans (BBVA, 2020).

18.3.4 Increased Competitiveness and Innovation

The integration of AI technologies in financial institutions facilitates the development of new products and services and the enhancement of existing ones, ensuring competitiveness in the market (Baesens et al., 2016). DBS Bank's utilization of AI has enabled the introduction of innovative digital banking services like automated wealth management and personalized investment recommendations, positioning it as one of the most innovative banks in the Asia-Pacific region (DBS, 2021).

18.3.5 Regulatory Compliance and Risk Management

AI aids financial institutions in adhering to regulatory requirements such as anti-money laundering and KYC regulations by automating processes and enhancing compliance monitoring accuracy (Rai, Constantinides & Sarker 2019). UBS's utilization of AI-powered compliance tools has halved the time spent on regulatory reporting, demonstrating significant improvements in regulatory compliance and risk management (UBS, 2023).

18.4 Challenges and Issues in Implementing AI in Banking and Finance

18.4.1 Data Quality and Availability

- The success of AI-powered applications in banking and finance is heavily dependent on the quality and availability of data, which can be a significant challenge for some financial institutions (Baesens et al., 2016).
- A survey by PwC found that 52% of financial services firms cited data quality and availability as the top challenge in implementing AI (PwC, 2021).

18.4.2 Cybersecurity and Data Privacy Concerns

- The use of AI in banking and finance raises concerns about data privacy and the potential for cyber-attacks, as AI systems may be vulnerable to exploitation by malicious actors (Howarth et al., 2021).
- A report by the Financial Stability Board highlighted the need for financial institutions to address the cybersecurity and privacy risks associated with AI (Financial Stability Board, 2017).

18.4.3 Regulatory and Ethical Considerations

- The use of AI in financial services is subject to a complex regulatory landscape, which can vary across different regions and jurisdictions, requiring financial institutions to navigate a range of legal and ethical considerations (Biggio & Roli, 2018).
- The European Union's proposed AI Act, for example, aims to establish a comprehensive regulatory framework for the development and use of AI, including in the financial sector (European Commission, 2021).

18.4.4 Explainability and Transparency of AI Models

- The black-box nature of some AI models can make it difficult for financial institutions to understand and explain the decision-making process, which can be a concern for regulators and customers (Rudin, 2019).

■ A survey by the Financial Conduct Authority in the United Kingdom found that 75% of financial firms cited the lack of transparency and explainability of AI models as a significant challenge (FCA, 2019).

18.4.5 Talent Acquisition and Skill Gaps

■ Implementing AI in banking and finance requires specialized skills and expertise, which can be in short supply, making it challenging for financial institutions to attract and retain the necessary talent (Deloitte, 2020).
■ A report by the World Economic Forum found that 44% of financial services firms cited the lack of AI and data science skills as a barrier to adopting AI (World Economic Forum, 2020).

18.4.6 Integration with Legacy Systems and Infrastructure

■ Many financial institutions have complex legacy systems and infrastructure, which can make it challenging to integrate AI-powered applications and technologies, requiring significant investment and effort (Accenture, 2019).
■ A survey by the Boston Consulting Group found that 53% of financial services firms cited the integration of AI with existing systems as a significant challenge (BCG, 2020).

18.5 Global Perspectives on AI Adoption in Banking and Finance

18.5.1 North America

18.5.1.1 Rapid Adoption, Focus on Customer Experience and Compliance

Financial institutions in North America have been early adopters of AI, prioritizing initiatives aimed at enhancing customer experience and ensuring regulatory compliance (McKinsey, 2020). A prominent example is Bank of America's virtual assistant, Erica, which has witnessed widespread adoption among the bank's customers, resulting in a notable 50% increase in digital engagement (Bank of America, 2021).

18.5.2 Europe

18.5.2.1 Stricter Regulations, Emphasis on Ethical AI and Data Privacy

European financial institutions approach AI adoption cautiously, placing a strong emphasis on ethical considerations and compliance with stringent data privacy regulations like the General Data Protection Regulation (GDPR) (Deloitte, 2020). BBVA's AI-powered credit risk models exemplify this approach, designed to align with the bank's ethical AI principles, prioritizing fairness, transparency, and accountability (BBVA, 2020).

18.5.3 Asia-Pacific

Diverse adoption rates, growing Fintech–bank collaborations (Khang & Hajimahmud, 2024), AI adoption across the Asia-Pacific region exhibits a wide variation, with countries like China and Singapore leading the way while others lag behind (PwC, 2021). A notable trend is the increasing collaboration between traditional banks and Fintech companies, leveraging AI to develop innovative financial products and services (DBS, 2021).

18.5.4 Emerging Markets

Leveraging AI to drive financial inclusion and innovation, in emerging markets, financial institutions are harnessing AI to promote financial inclusion, particularly in underserved or unbanked communities (World Bank, 2024). For instance, Kenya's M-Pesa mobile money platform, utilizing AI-powered fraud detection and credit scoring models, has significantly enhanced financial inclusion in the country (M-Pesa, 2021).

18.6 Case Studies and Best Practices

18.6.1 Successful AI Implementation Case

18.6.1.1 Case Study: HSBC's AI-Powered Fraud Detection System

- HSBC, a leading global bank, implemented an AI-powered anomaly detection system to monitor transactions and identify potential fraudulent activities in real time (HSBC, 2020).
- The AI system analyzes large volumes of transaction data, looking for unusual patterns or behaviors that may indicate fraud, such as sudden large transactions or transactions in unusual locations.
- By leveraging ML algorithms, the system can adapt and learn from new data, continuously improving its ability to detect and prevent fraud.
- As a result of implementing this AI-powered system, HSBC reported a 30% reduction in fraud losses and a 50% decrease in false positive alerts, leading to more effective fraud detection and prevention strategies.

18.6.1.2 Case Study: Ant Financial's AI-Driven Credit Risk Assessment

- Ant Financial, the financial technology subsidiary of Alibaba Group, utilizes AI-powered credit scoring models to evaluate the creditworthiness of borrowers (Ant Financial, 2021).
- These models incorporate a wide range of data sources, including traditional financial data as well as alternative data such as social media activity and online shopping behavior, to assess an individual's credit risk more accurately.
- By leveraging advanced ML algorithms, Ant Financial's credit scoring models can analyze vast amounts of data quickly and efficiently, enabling the company to make faster and more informed lending decisions.
- As a result, Ant Financial has been able to expand access to credit for underserved individuals, particularly those without traditional credit histories, while maintaining a low default rate and minimizing credit risk.

18.6.2 Lessons Learned and Best Practices for AI Adoption in Banking and Finance

18.6.2.1 Ensure Data Quality and Availability

- Financial institutions should invest in robust data management practices, including data cleaning, normalization, and validation, to ensure the quality and reliability of the data used to train AI models (Baesens et al., 2016).
- Additionally, data should be readily available and accessible to AI systems, with proper governance and security measures in place to protect sensitive information.

18.6.2.2 Address Cybersecurity and Privacy Risks

- Given the sensitive nature of financial data, financial institutions must prioritize cybersecurity and data privacy when deploying AI-powered applications (Howarth et al., 2021).
- This includes implementing robust encryption, access controls, and intrusion detection systems to protect data from unauthorized access or breaches.
- Furthermore, financial institutions should adhere to strict regulatory requirements, such as GDPR in Europe, to ensure compliance with data protection laws and regulations.

18.6.2.3 Prioritize Ethical and Transparent AI

- Financial institutions should develop clear guidelines and principles for the ethical and transparent use of AI, ensuring that AI-powered decisions are explainable, fair, and accountable (Rudin, 2019).
- This includes avoiding biases in AI algorithms, providing transparency into how AI systems make decisions, and allowing for human oversight and intervention when necessary.

18.6.2.4 Build AI-Ready Talent and Skills

- To successfully implement AI initiatives, financial institutions need to invest in upskilling their workforce and attracting specialized AI and data science talent (Deloitte, 2020).
- This may involve providing training programs, hiring data scientists and AI experts, and fostering a culture of innovation and continuous learning within the organization.

18.6.2.5 Integrate AI with Legacy Systems

- Financial institutions should develop a comprehensive plan for integrating AI-powered applications with their existing systems and infrastructure.
- This involves assessing the compatibility of AI technologies with legacy systems, identifying potential integration challenges, and implementing solutions to ensure seamless integration and scalability.

18.7 Technologies and Implementation for Banking and Finance Services

The successful integration of AI into the banking and finance sector relies on a comprehensive understanding of various technologies and methodologies. This section delves into these key technologies, their applications, and real-world instances of their implementation.

18.7.1 Machine Learning Techniques

ML is a transformative subset of AI that plays a crucial role in enabling systems to learn and improve from data without the need for explicit programming. ML algorithms have emerged as powerful tools in the realm of banking and finance, revolutionizing how financial institutions analyze data and make decisions. With their ability to identify patterns, extract insights, and predict outcomes from vast datasets, ML algorithms find extensive applications across a spectrum of financial services (Khang & Jadhav et al., 2024).

In the domain of fraud detection, ML algorithms are employed to sift through large volumes of transaction data in real time, distinguishing between legitimate and fraudulent activities. By analyzing historical patterns and identifying anomalies, these algorithms can flag suspicious transactions for further investigation, helping financial institutions combat fraudulent behavior and safeguard their customers' assets.

Similarly, ML techniques are instrumental in credit risk assessment, where financial institutions leverage predictive models to evaluate the creditworthiness of borrowers. By analyzing various factors such as credit history, income, and debt-to-income ratio, ML algorithms can assess the likelihood of default and determine suitable lending terms. This enables banks to make informed decisions regarding loan approvals, setting interest rates, and managing credit risk effectively.

Moreover, ML algorithms play a vital role in portfolio optimization, where investment firms leverage predictive analytics to construct and manage investment portfolios. By analyzing market trends, asset performance, and risk factors, ML algorithms can identify optimal investment strategies, allocate assets efficiently, and mitigate risks. This enables investors to achieve better returns while maintaining a balanced and diversified portfolio.

Overall, ML stands as a cornerstone in the modernization of banking and finance, offering unparalleled capabilities in data analysis, decision-making, and risk management. As financial institutions continue to embrace digital transformation, ML algorithms will continue to drive innovation, efficiency, and competitiveness across the industry.

18.7.2 Supervised Learning

18.7.2.1 Algorithms

Supervised learning algorithms glean insights from labeled data, where inputs and corresponding outputs are provided during training. Widely employed supervised learning techniques in finance include:

- Regression: Used to predict continuous values such as stock prices or the likelihood of loan defaults.
- Classification: Applied to categorize data into distinct classes like fraudulent and non-fraudulent transactions.
- Decision trees and random forests: These aid in building models for transparent credit risk assessment and loan approval processes.

18.7.2.2 Case Study: JPMorgan Chase's Fraud Detection System

JPMorgan Chase, a leading global financial institution, has implemented a sophisticated supervised learning model as part of its efforts to combat money laundering activities. This model represents a pivotal application of ML within the realm of financial crime detection and prevention.

Utilizing historical transaction data that has been meticulously labeled as either fraudulent or legitimate, JPMorgan Chase's supervised learning model undergoes a rigorous training process. During this phase, the model learns to recognize patterns and detect anomalies indicative of potential money laundering activities. By analyzing various features and attributes associated with each transaction, such as transaction amount, frequency, geographical location, and counterparties involved, the model builds a comprehensive understanding of normal transaction behavior and identifies deviations from expected patterns.

Once the supervised learning model has been trained on a vast corpus of labeled data, it is deployed into JPMorgan Chase's operational environment to analyze incoming transaction data in real time. As new transactions flow through the system, the model applies its learned knowledge to identify suspicious activities that exhibit characteristics similar to known instances of money laundering. These activities are flagged for further investigation by compliance professionals, who conduct in-depth reviews to assess the legitimacy of the transactions and determine whether further action is warranted.

The utilization of a supervised learning model for money laundering detection represents a proactive approach by JPMorgan Chase to mitigate financial crime risks and uphold regulatory compliance standards. By leveraging the power of ML, the bank is able to enhance its ability to detect illicit activities, protect its customers and stakeholders, and contribute to the overall integrity of the financial system.

Following the explanation of JPMorgan Chase's proactive approach to mitigating financial crime risks through the utilization of a supervised learning model, we can introduce Table 18.1 to provide further insight into the specific features used within the model. This table outlines the various attributes and characteristics of transactions that are analyzed by the model to identify potential instances of money laundering. Let's seamlessly integrate the introduction of Table 18.1 into the narrative.

The utilization of a supervised learning model for money laundering detection represents a proactive approach by JPMorgan Chase to mitigate financial crime risks and uphold regulatory compliance standards. By leveraging the power of ML, the bank is able to enhance its ability to detect illicit activities, protect its customers and stakeholders, and contribute to the overall integrity of the financial system. To delve deeper into the workings of JPMorgan Chase's money laundering detection system, Table 18.2 provides an overview of the key features utilized within the supervised learning model.

In order to visually depict the workflow of JPMorgan Chase's AI-powered fraud detection system, we have created a flowchart that outlines the key steps and technologies involved in the process. This flowchart shown in Figure 18.1 serves as a comprehensive guide to understanding how the bank utilizes ML and data processing techniques to identify and mitigate fraudulent activities in real time. Let's explore each step in detail to gain insights into the intricate workings of JPMorgan Chase's fraud detection system.

In this workflow, historical transaction data is used to train the supervised learning model, which is then deployed to analyze incoming transaction data in real time. Suspicious activities

Table 18.2 Features Used in JPMorgan Chase's Supervised Learning Model

Feature	Description
Transaction amount	The monetary value of the transaction
Transaction frequency	The number of transactions within a time period
Geographical location	The location of the transaction
Counterparties	The entities involved in the transaction
Transaction type	The nature of the transaction (e.g., wire transfer, cash deposit)

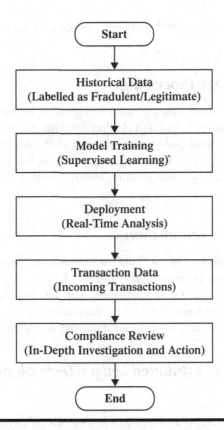

Figure 18.1   Workflow of JPMorgan Chase's money laundering detection system.

identified by the model are flagged for further investigation by compliance professionals, who conduct thorough reviews to determine the appropriate course of action.

18.7.3 *Unsupervised Learning*

18.7.3.1 *Algorithms*

Unsupervised learning algorithms uncover patterns and relationships in unlabeled data without predetermined output variables. Common unsupervised learning techniques in finance include:

- Clustering: Utilized to segment customers based on their behavioral patterns or preferences.
- Anomaly detection: Identifying unusual patterns or outliers in transaction data, potentially signaling fraudulent activities.
- Dimensionality reduction: Extracting meaningful features from high-dimensional data, such as customer profiles.

18.7.3.2 *Case Study: Bank of America's Customer Segmentation*

Bank of America employs unsupervised learning algorithms to segment its customer base based on financial behavior, demographics, and preferences. This segmentation enables personalized product recommendations and targeted marketing campaigns for different customer segments (Bank of America, 2021).

18.7.4 Natural Language Processing

NLP enables machines to comprehend, interpret, and generate human language. In the banking and finance sector, NLP finds applications in chatbot development, sentiment analysis, and document processing. Santander developed a conversational chatbot named Aida using NLP. Aida assists customers with banking tasks such as checking account balances, transferring funds, and retrieving transaction histories by understanding and responding to natural language inquiries (Santander, 2020).

18.7.5 Robotic Process Automation

RPA involves deploying software robots or "bots" to automate repetitive, rule-based tasks typically requiring human intervention. In banking and finance, RPA is leveraged for tasks such as data entry, report generation, and account reconciliation. Citi has implemented RPA across various business functions, automating tasks like account reconciliation, regulatory reporting, and data entry. This has led to significant cost savings and improved operational efficiency (Citi, 2019).

18.7.6 Blockchain and Distributed Ledger Technology (DLT)

18.7.6.1 Solutions

Blockchain and DLT provide secure and transparent methods for recording and verifying transactions without central authority. In finance, they are explored for applications such as cross-border payments, trade finance, and asset tokenization (Khang, Dave, Jadhav et al., 2024).

18.7.6.2 Case Study: HSBC's Blockchain-Based Trade Finance Platform

HSBC, in collaboration with other banks, developed Contour, a blockchain-based trade finance platform. It streamlines trade documentation exchange, reducing manual processes, and enhancing transparency and traceability (HSBC, 2020).

18.7.7 Integration and Implementation Approaches

Successful AI implementation in banking and finance necessitates the integration of multiple technologies and a well-defined strategy. Table 18.2 outlines common approaches, their advantages, and challenges.

By combining advanced AI technologies, robust data management practices, and strategic implementation, financial institutions can harness the full potential of AI to drive innovation, efficiency, and customer satisfaction.

18.7.7.1 Case Study: Capital One's Credit Risk Modeling

Capital One employs ML techniques, particularly supervised learning algorithms, for credit risk modeling. By analyzing vast datasets of customer behavior and credit history, Capital One builds predictive models to assess the creditworthiness of applicants. These models aid in making informed decisions regarding loan approvals and setting appropriate interest rates, ultimately optimizing the bank's lending practices (Capital One, 2021).

18.7.7.2 Case Study: PayPal's Fraud Detection System

PayPal utilizes a combination of supervised and unsupervised learning techniques for fraud detection. Supervised learning models are trained on labeled transaction data to identify known patterns of fraudulent activity. Concurrently, unsupervised learning algorithms detect anomalies in transaction behavior, flagging potentially fraudulent transactions for further investigation. This hybrid approach enables PayPal to swiftly detect and mitigate fraudulent activities, safeguarding the integrity of its platform and protecting its users (PayPal, 2020).

18.7.7.3 Case Study: Goldman Sachs' Algorithmic Trading

Goldman Sachs leverages ML algorithms for algorithmic trading strategies. By analyzing market data in real time and identifying patterns indicative of market trends, Goldman Sachs' trading algorithms autonomously execute trades with precision and speed. These algorithms adapt to evolving market conditions and execute trades at optimal prices, enabling Goldman Sachs to capitalize on market opportunities and maximize returns for its clients (Goldman Sachs, 2021).

18.7.7.4 Case Study: American Express' Customer Service Chatbot

American Express implements NLP to enhance its customer service experience. Through the deployment of a conversational chatbot powered by NLP, American Express offers personalized assistance to its card members, addressing inquiries, providing account information, and offering proactive support. This chatbot, integrated seamlessly into American Express' customer service ecosystem, has significantly reduced response times, improved customer satisfaction, and enhanced overall service efficiency.

These case studies underscore the diverse applications of AI and ML across various aspects of banking and finance, showcasing how leading institutions leverage these technologies to drive innovation, efficiency, and customer-centricity.

Advancements in AI technologies, such as NLP and computer vision, are continuously reshaping the landscape of the banking and finance industry. These technological breakthroughs are not only enabling the automation of routine tasks but also empowering financial institutions to deliver more sophisticated services and solutions to their customers. For example, NLP algorithms can interpret and understand human language, allowing AI-powered chatbots to engage in meaningful conversations with customers, addressing inquiries, and providing assistance in real time. Similarly, computer vision technology enables machines to interpret and analyze visual data, opening doors to applications such as image-based fraud detection and automated document processing (Khang, Jadhav, Hajimahmud & Satpathy, 2024).

The integration of AI into various aspects of banking and financial services is giving rise to a new generation of AI-powered products and solutions. These innovations span across personalized wealth management platforms that leverage AI algorithms to tailor investment strategies based on individual preferences and risk profiles, to automated trading systems capable of executing trades autonomously based on real-time market data and predictive analytics. Additionally, AI-driven decision-making tools are enabling financial institutions to make data-driven decisions, optimize resource allocation, and identify emerging trends and opportunities in the market.

Looking ahead, the widespread adoption of AI technologies is poised to have a transformative impact on the future of the financial industry. As AI continues to evolve and mature, it is expected to reshape traditional business models, disrupt existing value chains, and drive new forms of competition and collaboration within the industry. Moreover, AI-powered innovations hold the potential to enhance financial inclusion by providing access to banking and financial services to underserved populations, improving efficiency, and reducing costs for both financial institutions and their customers.

In summary, the convergence of AI technologies and banking and finance is ushering in a new era of innovation and disruption. Financial institutions that embrace AI and harness its capabilities effectively will be well-positioned to thrive in the rapidly evolving digital economy, delivering enhanced customer experiences, driving operational efficiencies, and unlocking new avenues for growth and prosperity.

18.8 Conclusion

In conclusion, the adoption of AI in the banking and finance sector offers numerous opportunities for transformation and growth. It has the potential to revolutionize customer experience, streamline operations, and facilitate better decision-making processes. However, along with these opportunities come significant challenges that must be addressed to ensure successful implementation and utilization of AI technologies (Khang, Dave, Katore et al., 2024).

18.8.1 Key Opportunities

- Enhanced customer experience: AI-powered solutions can personalize services, anticipate customer needs, and provide seamless interactions across various channels.
- Operational efficiency: Automation of routine tasks, such as data processing and customer inquiries, can improve efficiency and reduce operational costs.
- Faster decision-making: AI algorithms can analyze large datasets quickly and accurately, enabling financial institutions to make data-driven decisions in real time.

18.8.2 Key Challenges

- Data quality: Ensuring the accuracy, reliability, and completeness of data is crucial for the effectiveness of AI applications.
- Cybersecurity: With increased reliance on digital technologies, financial institutions must prioritize cybersecurity to protect sensitive customer information and maintain trust.
- Regulatory compliance: Adhering to regulations and ensuring ethical and transparent use of AI is essential to mitigate legal and reputational risks.
- Talent acquisition: Recruiting and retaining skilled professionals in AI and data science is a challenge due to high demand and competition in the job market.

18.8.3 Recommendations

- Develop a comprehensive AI strategy: Align AI initiatives with business goals and establish a roadmap for implementation.

- Strengthen data management: Invest in data quality and governance processes to ensure reliable data for AI applications.
- Ensure ethical use of AI: Implement policies and frameworks to promote transparency, fairness, and accountability in AI-driven decisions.
- Invest in workforce development: Provide training and upskilling opportunities for employees to harness the full potential of AI technologies.
- Integrate AI with existing systems: Seamless integration with legacy systems and infrastructure is essential for scalability and interoperability.
- Stay informed and adaptive: Stay updated on emerging AI trends, innovations, and regulatory changes to remain competitive and agile in the evolving financial landscape.

By addressing these challenges and following these recommendations, banks and financial institutions can leverage AI to unlock new opportunities, drive innovation, and deliver value to customers in the digital era (Khang, Jadhav, Dave et al., 2024).

References

Ant Financial. (2021). Sesame credit. https://www.antgroup.com/en/product/sesame-credit

Baesens, B., Bapna, R., Marsden, J. R., Vanthienen, J., & Zhao, J. L. (2016). Transformational issues of big data and analytics in networked business. MIS Quarterly, 40(4), 807–818. https://doi.org/10.25300/MISQ/2016/40:4.03

Bank of America. (2021). Erica digital assistant.

BBVA. (2020). BBVA applies artificial intelligence to improve its credit risk models. https://www.bbva.com/en/innovation/what-ai-algorithms-does-bbva-use-to-boost-its-customers-finances/

BCG. (2020). Global AI survey: AI proves its worth, but few scale impact. https://www.bcg.com/publications/2020/increasing-odds-of-success-in-ai

Berrada, G., Crammer, K., & Ertekin, S. (2021). Variance-aware indexing for highly accurate personalized ranking. Proceedings of the ACM SIGIR Conference on Research and Development in Information Retrieval, 1–10. https://doi.org/10.1145/3404835.3462855

Biggio, B., & Roli, F. (2018). Wild patterns: Ten years after the rise of adversarial machine learning. Pattern Recognition, 84, 317–331. https://doi.org/10.1016/j.patcog.2018.07.023

BlackRock. (2022). Aladdin: The operating system for investment management. https://www.blackrock.com/institutions/en-us/solutions/aladdin

Capital One. (2021). AI and machine learning at Capital One. https://www.capitalone.com/tech/machine-learning/

Citi. (2019). Citi's robotic process automation drives efficiency and productivity. https://www.citigroup.com/global/insights/robots-rise-the-tailwinds-of-automation-in-three-charts-

Dai, H. N., Zheng, Z., & Zhang, Y. (2019). Blockchain for internet of things: A survey. IEEE Internet of Things Journal, 6(5), 8076–8094. https://doi.org/10.1109/JIOT.2019.2920987

DBS. (2021). DBS named world's best bank by Global Finance. https://www.dbs.com/newsroom/DBS_named_Worlds_Best_Bank_by_Global_Finance

Deloitte. (2020). State of AI in the Enterprise, 3rd Edition. https://www2.deloitte.com/us/en/insights/focus/cognitive-technologies/state-of-ai-and-intelligent-automation-in-business-survey.html

European Commission. (2021). Proposal for a regulation on a European approach for artificial intelligence. https://digital-strategy.ec.europa.eu/en/policies/regulatory-framework-ai

FCA. (2019). Regulating artificial intelligence. https://www.fca.org.uk/news/speeches/regulating-high-frequency-trading

Financial Stability Board. (2017). Artificial intelligence and machine learning in financial services. https://www.fsb.org/2017/11/artificial-intelligence-and-machine-learning-in-financial-service/

Gai, K., Qiu, M., & Sun, X. (2018). A survey on Fintech. Journal of Network and Computer Applications, 103, 262–273. https://doi.org/10.1016/j.jnca.2017.10.011

Goldman Sachs. (2021). What is algorithmic trading? https://www.goldmansachs.com/insights/articles/the-global-credibility-gap

HSBC. (2020). HSBC announces partnership with Pertamina on blockchain trade finance. https://www.hsbc.com/news-and-views/news/media-releases/2023/hsbc-announces-plans-for-new-joint-venture-with-tradeshift

HSBC. (2020). How HSBC is using AI to detect financial crime.

Howarth, S., Ali, E., Emruli, B., & Adjei, O. (2021). Cybersecurity challenges in artificial intelligence. Algorithms, 14(3), 92. https://doi.org/10.3390/a14030092

Huang, M. H., & Rust, R. T. (2021). A strategic framework for artificial intelligence in marketing. Journal of the Academy of Marketing Science, 49(1), 30–50. https://doi.org/10.1007/s11747-020-00749-9

IDC. (2021). Worldwide spending on artificial intelligence systems forecast to reach $57.6 billion in 2021, According to New IDC Spending Guide. https://www.idc.com/getdoc.jsp?containerId=prUS52530724

JPMorgan Chase. (2019). Bringing artificial intelligence to regulatory compliance.

Kaplan, A., & Sironi, F. (2019). The rise of robo-advisors: The impact on portfolio management. European Financial Management, 25(3), 328–352. https://doi.org/10.1111/eufm.12180

Khang, A, & Hajimahmud, V. A., "Introduction to the gig economy," In Khang A. Jadhav B., Hajimahmud V. A., Satpathy I., The Synergy of AI and Fintech in the Digital Gig Economy. (1st Ed.) (2024). CRC Press. https://doi.org/10.1201/9781032720104-1

Khang, A., Jadhav, B., Hajimahmud, V. A., & Satpathy, I., (1st Ed.) (2024a). The Synergy of AI and Fintech in the Digital Gig Economy. CRC Press. https://doi.org/10.1201/9781032720104

Khang, A., Jadhav, B., Dave, T., & Katore, T., Artificial Intelligence (AI) in Fintech - Enhancing Financial Services. In Khang A. Jadhav B., Hajimahmud V. A., Satpathy I., (1st Ed.) (2024b). The Synergy of AI and Fintech in the Digital Gig Economy. (1st Ed.) (2024). CRC Press. https://doi.org/10.1201/9781032720104-10

Khang, A., Dave, T., Jadhav, B., Katore, D., & Dave, D., Gig Financial Economy—Big Data and Analytics. In Khang A. Jadhav B., Hajimahmud V. A., Satpathy I., (1st Ed.) (2024c). The Synergy of AI and Fintech in the Digital Gig Economy. (1st Ed.) (2024). CRC Press. https://doi.org/10.1201/9781032720104-16

Khang, A., Dave, T., Katore, D., Jadhav, B., & Dave, D., Leveraging Blockchain and Smart Contracts for Gig Payments. In Khang A. Jadhav B., Hajimahmud V. A., Satpathy I., (1st Ed.) (2024d). The Synergy of AI and Fintech in the Digital Gig Economy. (1st Ed.) (2024). CRC Press. https://doi.org/10.1201/9781032720104-11

Lemonade. (2021). AI-powered insurance. https://www.lemonade.com/blog/ai-eats-insurance/

M-Pesa. (2021). Transforming lives through mobile money. https://www.safaricom.co.ke/main-mpesa/m-pesa-services/m-pesa-go

Mastercard. (2021). The chatbot that's transforming customer experience. https://www.mastercard.com/news/press/2024/september/mastercard-expands-first-of-its-kind-ai-technology-to-help-banks-protect-more-consumers-from-scams-in-real-time/

McKinsey. (2020). The state of AI in 2020. https://www.mckinsey.com/capabilities/quantumblack/our-insights/global-survey-the-state-of-ai-in-2020

PayPal. (2020). How PayPal uses machine learning to fight fraud. https://www.paypal.com/us/brc/article/fraud-prevention-with-rules-vs-machine-learning

PwC. (2021). PwC's Global AI Study 2021: AI predictions. https://www.pwc.com.au/digitalpulse/ai-predictions-2021-report.html

Rai, A., Constantinides, P., & Sarker, S. (2019). Editor's comments: Next-generation digital platforms: Toward Human–AI hybrids. MIS Quarterly, 43(1), iii–i18.

Rudin, C. (2019). Stop explaining black box machine learning models for high stakes decisions and use interpretable models instead. Nature Machine Intelligence, 1(5), 206–215. https://doi.org/10.1038/s42256-019-0048-x

Santander. (2020). Santander UK partners with Personetics to improve customer digital experience and engagement through AI-driven personalized insights. https://www.santander.co.uk/about-santander/media-centre/press-releases/santander-uk-partners-with-personetics-to-improve

UBS. (2023). How UBS is using AI to streamline regulatory reporting. https://www.ubs.com/global/en/investment-bank/in-focus/generative-ai-2023.html

World Bank. (2024). How Technology is transforming financial inclusion. https://www.worldbank.org/en/topic/financialinclusion/publication/digital-financial-inclusion

World Economic Forum. (2020). The Global Risks Report 2020. https://www.weforum.org/reports/the-global-risks-report-2020

Chapter 19

Analysis of Internet of Things (IoT) Applications in the Banking Industry

Thi Cam Thu Doan and Anh Tu Nguyen

19.1 Introduction

It cannot be denied that technology has a significant role in people's lives. The development of technology has marked a new stage in human history. Many devices formed from the application of new technologies have been helping people solve tasks more quickly and effectively without spending a lot of labor. One of the technologies widely applied by many organizations and businesses in providing products and services and managing operations is the Internet of Things (IoT). This term first appeared in 1999 at the Massachusetts Institute of Technology (MIT), Cambridge, MA, USA. It refers to a network of smart devices and technologies that create favorable conditions for communication between devices and the cloud, as well as between devices together (Sundmaeker et al., 2010).

In a different approach, Behura et al. (2022) argue that the IoT refers to a context in which billions of independently interacting objects with limited resources (things) are connected to the Internet. More generally, the IoT is a network of devices, appliances, vehicles, and others that are ingrained with sensors, electronics, software, connectivity, and actuators, allowing them to connect and exchange data (Vijay kumar, 2019).

IoT devices have become incredibly popular, ranging from routers, TVs, touch light bulbs, webcams, automatic door locks, and air conditioners to personal devices such as laptops, phones, watches, handheld game consoles, eyeglasses, etc. (Figure 19.1).

The rise of the digital economy has paved the way for IoT's growing demand and popularity. Notably, as the world banking system moves toward a digital transformation trend, the role of IoT technology is becoming more and more evident. Thanks to the advent of cheap computer chips and broadband telecommunications technology, today there are billions of devices connected to the Internet in the world.

DOI: 10.4324/9781003501947-19

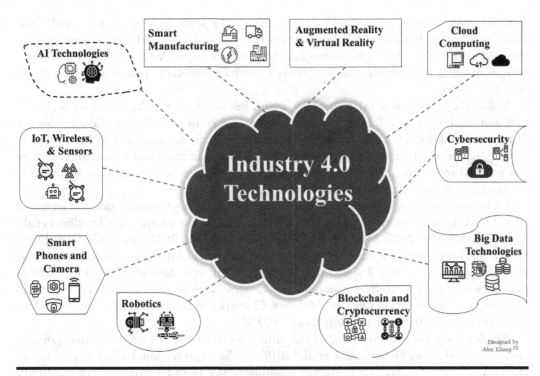

Figure 19.1   The pictures of the IoT technology world.

Source: Microsoft Copilot.

Khanboubi, Boulmakoul and Tabaa (2019) believe that the IoT will be a bright object, representing the next stage of Industry 4.0 and changing consumers' daily habits. According to banking and finance experts, the application of IoT in the banking industry helps strengthen risk management capacity, improve customer engagement and loyalty, enhance customer experience, and optimize a bank's operational processes (Almugari et al., 2020; Khanboubi et al., 2019; Vijay kumar, 2019). Therefore, traditional banking and financial services are increasingly being approached by financial technology companies (Fintech) through the application of advanced technologies [artificial intelligence (AI), IoT, blockchain, big data, etc.] to create intelligent, convenient, and safe financial services for their customers.

This section aims to introduce an overview of IoT and emphasize its role in the banking industry. The remainder of this study is structured as follows. The remainder of this chapter is structured as follows. We point out the research problem of this chapter in Part 19.2. Part 19.3 proposes research contents. Part 19.4 summarizes the history of the formation and development of IoT. Part 19.5 is the analysis of IoT applications in the banking industry. In Part 19.6, we draw conclusions about the chapter. Finally, we suggest future research directions.

19.2 Problem Statement

IoT technology has recently been applied in many different fields of life. The study by Foschini et al. (2011) analyzed and discussed the design and implementation of M2M[1] (machine-to-machine) applications in the field of road traffic management. The study of Rastogi et al. (2022) has shown that the application of IoT brings many benefits in the medical field, contributing to improving the quality of life and human health. Another study by Verma et al. (2022) considered outstanding applications of IoT in smart agriculture, especially precision in agricultural farming.

Besides the application of IoT technology in basic fields such as agriculture, road traffic, health care, and medical services, IoT is increasingly widely applied to several other fields, notably the finance and banking industries. According to our best research, banking systems in most countries around the world are constantly promoting the provision of smart and high-quality banking and financial services to their customers through the application of new technologies (AI, IoT, blockchain, etc.) (Khang, Chowdhury & Sharma, 2022).

Up to now, there have been many studies in the world analyzing the application and impact of AI and blockchain on banking and financial services, typically the research of (Chowdhury et al., 2021; Guo & Liang, 2016; Malali, 2020; Mishra & Guru Sant, 2021; Pau & Gianotti, 1990). Meanwhile, the number of studies considering the application of IoT technology in banking and financial services is relatively limited. Most of the studies analyze the application of IoT in fields such as health care, architecture, education, environment, agriculture, and solid waste management, such as the research of (Nandan Mohanty, Chatterjee & Satpathy, 2022; Ramson, Vishnu & Shanmugam, 2020; Sarmiento-Rojas et al., 2022).

Besides, there are also some studies examining the impact of IoT on traditional banking operational processes (Khanboubi et al., 2019) or the organizational efficiency of banks (Kisanjara, 2023); research on customer adoption of IoT in India (Almugari et al., 2020). Therefore, this chapter's primary research goal is to analyze the application of IoT technology in the banking industry. It also presents the history of IoT's formation and development and explains the operating principles of IoT-based systems in this field (Khanh & Khang, 2021).

19.3 Proposed Work

This chapter focuses on clarifying the following contents: (1) history of the formation and development of the IoT; (2) analysis of IoT applications in the banking industry; and (3) conclusions and future research directions.

19.4 Formation and Development History of IoT

The IoT appearance is associated with Industry 4.0. The concept of the IoT was first mentioned by Kevin Ashton[2] in 1999 during a presentation with Proctor & Gamble at the MIT, USA. Accordingly, IoT is described as a network in which objects in the physical world are connected to each other via the Internet via radio frequency object recognition technology (RFID—radio frequency identification[3]).

The IoT does not stop at a computer; it can also spread the benefits of the Internet to all connected things. When an object is connected to the Internet, it becomes more intelligent thanks to its ability to send or receive information and automatically act based on that information (Figure 19.2).

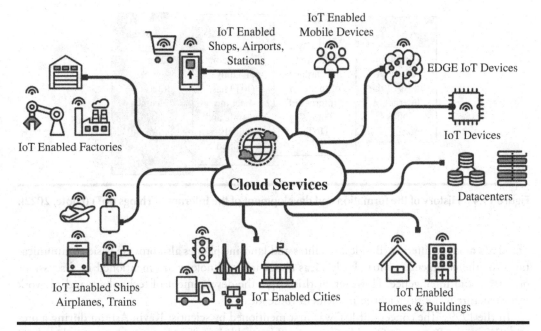

Figure 19.2   The network of connected things is based on the Internet platform (Mahalakshmi & Desai, 2022).

Theo Khanboubi et al. (2019) the development process of the IoT has gone through five stages (Figure 19.3). The process commenced with the interconnection of two computers, followed by the development of the World Wide Web (WWW), which connected a large number of computers. Next came the mobile Internet, the connection of mobile gadgets to the Internet, and then the people's Internet, the connection supported by social networks. Last, it advanced to the IoT, the interconnected object world.

According to Foote (2022), the history of the formation and development of the Internet of Things (IoT) includes four stages, as described in Figure 19.4.

1980s–1998s: In the 1980s, the public network ARPANET (Advanced Research Projects Agency Network) was used by commercial service providers, paving the way for the development

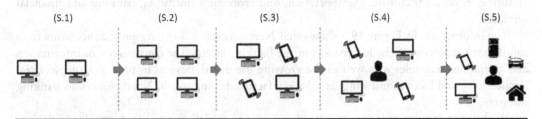

Figure 19.3   The evolution of the Internet of Things (Khanboubi et al., 2019).

(S.1) The computer
(S.2) The Internet
(S.3) The mobile-Internet
(S.4) The people-Internet
(S.5) The Internet of Things

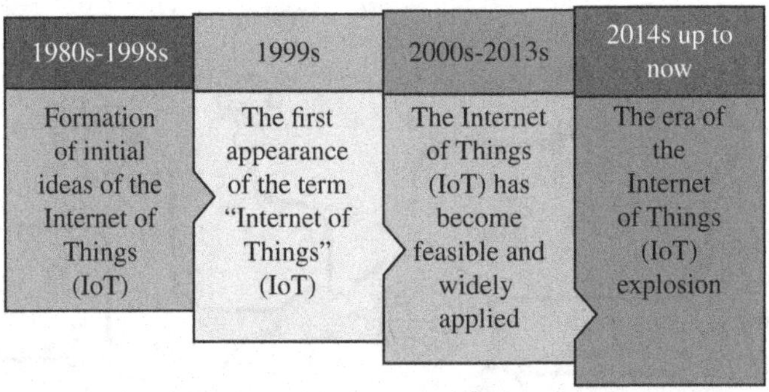

Figure 19.4   History of the formation and development of the Internet of Things (IoT) (Foote, 2022).

of today's modern Internet. Besides, satellites and landline phones also provide basic communications for the emergence of IoT. Early ideas about IoT technology are mentioned in discussions of sensors and intelligence. However, at this stage, the development of technology and network infrastructure is not sufficient to implement these ideas.

In the 1999s: The concept of IoT was first mentioned by scientist Kevin Ashton during a presentation at the Procter & Gamble Company. He established global standards for wireless communication using radio waves (RFID).

2000s–2013s: With the explosion of the Internet and the rise of network-connected devices, IoT technology became more feasible, researched, and widely applied in many different areas of life, typically medical equipment, and household appliances. Some notable events: During 2002–2003, large organizations (Walmart and the US Department of Defense) first applied tagging, RFID, and IoT methods in inventory tracking. In 2011, Jamie Siminoff invented the Ring doorbell to see who came to his door while he was working in the garage. In June 2012, major Internet service providers and web companies enabled IPV6 for their services and products to increase address space on the global Internet. Also in 2012, the Swiss Federal Office of Energy piloted the "Smart City Switzerland" program. In particular, smart cities will support connecting all types of sensors to the Internet and everything in life.

2014s up to now: IoT technologies are growing stronger and playing an important role in people's daily lives. IoT technology is increasingly widely applied in various fields, such as manufacturing, energy, agriculture, transportation, and economics (including banking and financial services).

The information in Figure 19.5 shows that North America is the region that accounts for a significant proportion of the IoT market in the banking sector. The convergence of information and operations technology, as well as the growing use of IoT devices in products and services, applications, and bank monitoring, are the key factors driving IoT in North America's banking industry.

With an innovative redesign and rapid expansion, as well as the provision of a variety of digital devices and sensors, IoT technology has been transforming the banking industry. A smart IoT-based system can personalize offerings and rewards with relevant changeover options based on customers' shopping activity and demographics, enhance management capabilities, debt collection, and fraud prevention and detection. Most banks use IoT to introduce new products and services, change operating methods, strengthen risk management, and improve customer experience (Fintech Review, 2023).

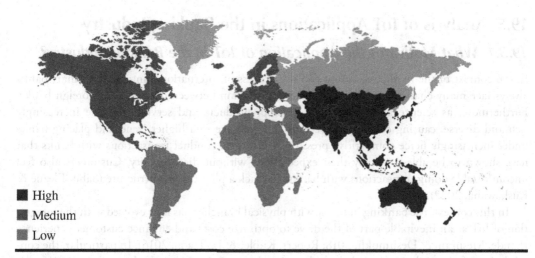

Figure 19.5   Growth rate of IoT in the banking market by region in 2023 (Mordor Intelligence, 2023).

High
Medium
Low

Although the diverse development of IoT technology has brought many benefits to people's lives, there are still difficulties and challenges, including information management and security issues and energy consumption (Khang & Hahanov et al., 2022). However, with the continuous development of technology and the Internet, IoT is considered a technology with much potential and the promise to continue to expand and develop in the future. Particularly, future predictions indicate that IoT will assist the banking industry in addressing compliance issues, conducting customer behavior research, and implementing optimal changes. It will bring technological innovations to both customers and banks. As a result, the bank's overall cost will decrease, and its performance will increase (Vijay kumar, 2019) (Figure 19.6).

Figure 19.6   IoT applications in the banking industry.
Source: Microsoft Copilot.

19.5 Analysis of IoT Applications in the Banking Industry

19.5.1 What Motivates the Application of IoT in the Banking Industry?

In the context of the market economy and the process of international integration, smart banks always face many challenges and concerns in competition between domestic and foreign banks. Furthermore, as science and technology develop, products and services become increasingly rich and diverse, causing customer expectations to change to a higher trend and placing banks under increasingly fierce competitive pressure. Customers conduct transactions with banks that have shown to be able to satisfy their expectations without discontinuity. Customers also feel uncomfortable doing transactions with banks that lack a physical infrastructure (Sahu, Elezue & Kushawaha, 2022).

In this context, the banking industry with physical branches has now evolved with the integration of IoT as an inevitable part of the drive to optimize costs and enhance customer experience (Lande, Meshram & Deshmukh, 2018; Robert, Kubler & Le Traon, 2016). In particular, the consolidation of physical objects and the online signals transmission can lead to enormous changes in the operational activities (Choi et al., 2017). With an IoT-based system, the service quality of a bank can be improved and the system brings to customers an experience without interruption. Since billions of devices will soon be connected, banks inevitably undergo digital changes because to the changing habits and usage patterns of its clients and the vast amount of data that is readily accessible (Khanboubi et al., 2019).

The connection accelerates information use seamlessly, thereby improving tracking of each transaction more effectively (Rehman, Asif & Ahmad, 2017). As a result, IoT-based systems assist banks to achieve financial success. For instance, Del Giudice, Campanella and Dezi (2016) show that there is a nexus between high ROE and provision of IoT services to customers in banking industry. Specifically, banks offering IoT retail services to customers, IoT corporate services to customers, customers a large number of home banking services have high ROE in the examined sample (Khang & Inna et al., 2024).

The cause probably that banks deploying IoT brings high organizational efficiency by reducing operational costs while enhancing service delivery speed and service quality (Kisanjara, 2023). From the customer's perspective, Almugari et al. (2020) reveal the convenience, social influence, privacy and safety, and awareness have a significant impact on the adoption of IoT in Indian banks. While Hammoud, Bizri and El Baba (2018) show reliability, efficiency, responsiveness, and communication all have a notable effect on customers' satisfaction since examined the effect of e-banking service quality in the Lebanese banking industry. These results seem to be supported by the fact that increasing use of smartphones and connected objects, IoT has become a new tool for a better customer relationship too (Rathod, Pandya & Doshi, 2020).

It is also important to note that IoT in the banking industry has rapidly entered the fifth industrial revolution, which is the integration of AI into its operations (Li, Chen & Wang, 2021; Nicoletti, 2021; Putra, 2021). The incorporation of AI in IoT enhances the performance of IoT by analyzing information and extracting knowledge, thereby making them smarter since different types of sensors can collect real-time data for decision-making in banks (Khadidos et al., 2022; Skobelev & Borovik, 2017).

Specifically, IoT-enabled Smart Banking uses sensors and connected devices to aggregate user demand data to provide innovative solutions and personalize financial services. This can include smart payment systems, asset tracking, risk management, customer engagement, and remote banking services. These services aim to improve efficiency, customer experience, and innovation (Ramphull & Nagowah, 2023). The adoption of AI assists the banking industry by establishing products and services that are fundamentally innovative compared to traditional services. This advantage has recently led to the bloom of IoT-based systems in the banking industry.

Mordor Intelligence (2023) estimates that the compound annual growth rate of the IoT-based systems in the banking industry market in the period 2023–2029 reaches 18.58%, of which the fastest growing market is Asia-Pacific region and the largest market in North America, where the world's largest banking institutions are concentrated. Several banks now offer apps for popular wearables like Apple Watch and FitPay, which have partnered with Bank of America. Amazon is also planning to let customers transfer cash to each other using Alexa and then deposit that money into an Amazon checking account. It can be said that IoT-based systems in the banking industry are a potential market for relevant parties since customers' requirements for banking services are increasing (Khang & Hajimahmud et al., 2024).

19.5.2 Infrastructure for IoT-Based Systems in the Banking Industry

For example, a position sensor is installed in an ATM that allows a bank to know the exact location of the customer who is withdrawing money. If the location is closed to a shopping mall or a coffee shop, which are also relevant third parties in the ecosystem, the system would suggest buying a good in the mall or drinking a cup of coffee at the coffee shop by sending a message to the customer's mobile phone. Similarly, whenever a customer uses a phone, tablet, or smart wearable to communicate with sensors for purchasing a good, the item data will be transmitted to the bank, and the bank will connect an e-commerce platform with the customer to offer a discount for that item. In some other service cases, banks can warn or recommend customers about their spending habits and optimize their consumption behaviors (Figure 19.7).

Figure 19.7   The banking IoT ecosystem.

Source: Microsoft Copilot.

19.5.3 Typical IoT-Based Systems Configurations

According to Figure 19.8, sensors and actuators are gadgets that assist in connecting with the physical state, while wireless plays an important role in transmitting data. This consolidation promptly responds to and/or predicts customer consumption behaviors and proposes tailored solutions to utilize real-time stakeholder needs. Sensors can be embedded in devices, such as ATMs (Rao et al., 2019), self-service banking kiosks (Subash, Danny & Vijayalakshmi, 2023), and front-line service robots (Amelia, Mathies & Patterson, 2021) that enhance the interaction between customers and banks. With the development of current materials science, solutions for synthetic sensors have been developed. They are integrated into a single sensor with multiple purposes, such as vibration, audio, ambient temperature, and computer vision, which adds a smart camera to the synthetic sensor capabilities (Grill, Polacek & Tscheligi, 2015).

Electromagnetic signals from the sensors will be transmitted directly to the receiving ports and then transmitted to the data center to analyze the data. In the context of IoT-based systems analysis, machine learning, and deep learning algorithms could find out customer behavior patterns and transmit the findings to terminal devices (laptops, smartphones) or related third parties (cafeterias, car repair shops, e-commerce platforms). To lower infrastructure costs, the decentralized IoT-based systems would be adopted, and it offers a standardized peer-to-peer communication paradigm for large-scale transactions (Khan, Algarni & Quasim, 2020). It also notes that data has been collected by a cloud-based server incorporated with a secure transaction-based authentication protocol to identify malicious users and fraud in bank transactions (Khadidos

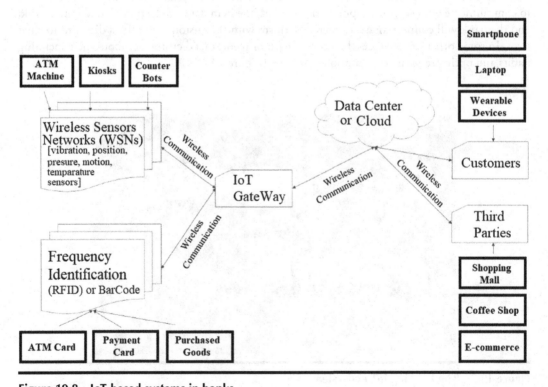

Figure 19.8　IoT-based systems in banks.

Source: Author's work.

et al., 2022), for example, a secure steganography-based fog cloud IoT to identify authenticated data. Additionally, due to extremely scalable cloud infrastructure, each user may utilize her needs (Behura et al., 2022).

19.5.4 Some Challenges of IoT-Based Systems in the Banking Industry

Customers expect to use IoT banking services since they are willing to pay for fast, high-quality services (Kisanjara, 2023). However, from the perspective of banks, IoT technologies are still in their infancy, there are still obstacles to their adoption, and banks are not significantly investing in IT infrastructure reform (Saxena & Ali Said Mansour Al-Tamimi, 2017).

First, one of the main challenges of IoT is dealing with data heterogeneity across devices (Zander, Merkle & Frank, 2016). To solve the issue, the devices must be authenticated. Nevertheless, due to diverse heterogeneous underlying architectures, it becomes challenging to define a standard global protocol for authentication and authorization in IoT (Khan et al., 2020).

Because the authenticated issue is solved, this leads to a vital risk: security, the second challenge (Rao et al., 2019). As a result, authentication necessitates a more secure system, which can ultimately lead to proper risk assessment and management in banking (Kirchherr & Matthews, 2018).

Third, using these technologies presents technical difficulties, such as spectrum management, roaming, and connection problems (Forge, 2016). These difficulties are related to government infrastructure and telecommunications policies.

Fourth, the traffic generated by IoT devices is growing due to the increased use of these kinds of devices. It's also not always simple to store and retrieve large amounts of data in a suitable manner (Rao et al., 2019).

Fifth, the advantage of a decentralized IoT-based system is cost reduction, but this characteristic itself increases latency and decreases energy utilization. This fact forces banks to use local edge devices in order to reduce latency (Khadidos et al., 2022).

Finally, as a result, an IoT-based system requires huge resources, so banks must carefully analyze the relationship between cost and benefit in applying IoT-based systems for their businesses (Almugari et al., 2020; Sheeba, 2022).

19.6 Conclusion

Today, with the advancement of science and technology and the outstanding development of the Internet, IoT technology is increasingly widely applied in many different areas of life. Notably, in the banking industry, society's demand and expectations for IoT are increasing. As a result, there are increasingly significant investments in this technology from banks around the world.

However, some banks in countries, especially those in developing countries or emerging markets, still have ambiguous views and questions related to the operating principles and applications of IoT in the banking industry. Therefore, this chapter has systematized the basic and in-depth content about IoT applications in the banking sector. Specifically, we have summarized the history and development of IoT through stages, presented the operating principles, and analyzed applications of IoT in the banking industry.

According to reports from international organizations operating in the fields of Fintech and IoT, along with the results of previous studies, it is impossible to deny the substantial role of IoT in providing products and services as well as the management and operations of banks Although banks always face certain challenges and difficulties in applying IoT, using IoT technology and equipment helps banks enhance risk management, prevent network attacks, optimize operational processes, improve customer engagement and loyalty, and enhance customer experience (Khang & Gujrati et al., 2024).

19.7 Future of Work

Based on the abovementioned technical challenges, future work will probably focus on solving the trade-off problem between authentication and IoT-based systems security. The former ensures a range of devices transmit continuous signals to the data center, while the latter protects the system from any harmful intent. In other words, the IoT-based systems should be able to provide self-protection to meet the requirements of security and privacy as well as quality of service (Karimi, Sohrabi & Bayat Tork, 2022).

Additionally, previous studies mainly focused on IoT applications from banks' perspectives, paying little attention to customers' perspectives, which is the main driver of the adoption of IoT-based systems. Once they understand how satisfied customers are with IoT technology experiences, banks can determine the level of IoT application in their business (Behura et al., 2022). When deciding on an appropriate IoT application level, banks not only retain existing customers but also attract new customers and utilize the bank's operational costs, since the analysis of the relationship between cost and benefit has been a permanent problem for smaller banks (Dicuonzo et al., 2019).

Notes

1. M2M is a promising technology for developing internet of things communication platforms and has high potential to support many applications in different fields (Foschini et al., 2011).
2. Kevin Ashton is a British technology pioneer and founder of the Auto-ID Centre at the Massachusetts Institute of Technology (MIT) in the United States (Magazine & Gabbai, 2015).
3. RFID is a wireless system consisting of two components: tags and readers. The reader is a device with one or more antennas that emit radio waves and receive signals back from the RFID tag. https://www.fda.gov/.

References

Almugari, F., Bajaj, P., Tabash, M. I., Khan, A., & Ali, M. A. (2020). An examination of consumers' adoption of internet of things (IoT) in Indian banks. Cogent Business & Management, 7(1), 1809071. https://doi.org/10.1080/23311975.2020.1809071

Amelia, A., Mathies, C., & Patterson, P. G. (2021). Customer acceptance of frontline service robots in retail banking: A qualitative approach. Journal of Service Management, 33(2), 321–341. https://doi.org/10.1108/JOSM-10-2020-0374

Behura, A., Satpathy, S., Mohanty, S. N., & Chatterjee, J. M. (2022). Internet of Things: Basic Concepts and Decorum of Smart Services. In S. Nandan Mohanty, J. M. Chatterjee, & S. Satpathy (Eds.), Internet of Things and Its Applications (pp. 3–36). Springer International Publishing. https://doi.org/10.1007/978-3-030-77528-5_1

Choi, C.-S., Jeong, J.-D., Han, J., Park, W.-K., & Lee, I.-W. (2017). Implementation of IoT based PV monitoring system with message queuing telemetry transfer protocol and smart utility network. 2017 International Conference on Information and Communication Technology Convergence (ICTC), 1077–1079. https://doi.org/10.1109/ICTC.2017.8190859

Chowdhury, M. U., Suchana, K., Alam, S. M. E., & Khan, M. M. (2021). Blockchain application in banking system. Journal of Software Engineering and Applications, 14(7). https://doi.org/10.4236/jsea.2021.147018

Del Giudice, M., Campanella, F., & Dezi, L. (2016). The bank of things: An empirical investigation on the profitability of the financial services of the future. Business Process Management Journal, 22(2), 324–340. https://doi.org/10.1108/BPMJ-10-2015-0139

Dicuonzo, G., Galeone, G., Zappimbulso, E., & Dell'Atti, V. (2019). Risk management 4.0: The role of big data analytics in the bank sector. International Journal of Economics and Financial Issues, 9(6), 40–47. https://doi.org/10.32479/ijefi.8556

Fintech Review. (2023). Internet of Things (IoT) in the Banking Industry. Fintech Review. https://fintechreview.net/internet-of-things-iot-banking-industry/

Foote, K. D. (2022). A Brief History of the Internet of Things. DATAVERSITY. https://www.dataversity.net/brief-history-internet-things/

Forge, S. (2016). Radio spectrum for the internet of things. INFO, 18(1), 67–84. https://doi.org/10.1108/info-11-2015-0050

Foschini, L., Taleb, T., Corradi, A., & Bottazzi, D. (2011). M2M-based metropolitan platform for IMS-enabled road traffic management in IoT. IEEE Communications Magazine, 49(11), 50–57. https://doi.org/10.1109/MCOM.2011.6069709

Grill, T., Polacek, O., & Tscheligi, M. (2015). ConWIZ: The contextual wizard of oz. Journal of Ambient Intelligence and Smart Environments, 7(6), 719–744. https://doi.org/10.3233/AIS-150350

Guo, Y., & Liang, C. (2016). Blockchain application and outlook in the banking industry. Financial Innovation, 2(1), 24. https://doi.org/10.1186/s40854-016-0034-9

Hammoud, J., Bizri, R. M., & El Baba, I. (2018). The impact of e-Banking service quality on customer satisfaction: Evidence from the Lebanese Banking sector. Sage Open, 8(3), 2158244018790633. https://doi.org/10.1177/2158244018790633

Karimi, S. S., Sohrabi, T., & Bayat Tork, A. (2022). Providing a secure technology transfer model to assess and manage financial and banking risks based on internet of things. International Journal of Nonlinear Analysis and Applications, 13(2), 1771–1787. https://doi.org/10.22075/ijnaa.2022.6316

Khadidos, A., Subbalakshmi, A. V. V. S., Khadidos, A., Alsobhi, A., Yaseen, S. M., & Mirza, O. M. (2022). Wireless communication based cloud network architecture using AI assisted with IoT for FinTech application. Optik, 269, 169872. https://doi.org/10.1016/j.ijleo.2022.169872

Khan, M. A., Algarni, F., & Quasim, M. T. (2020). Decentralised Internet of Things. In M. A. Khan, M. T. Quasim, F. Algarni, & A. Alharthi (Eds.), Decentralised Internet of Things: A Blockchain Perspective (pp. 3–20). Springer International Publishing. https://doi.org/10.1007/978-3-030-38677-1_1

Khanboubi, F., Boulmakoul, A., & Tabaa, M. (2019). Impact of digital trends using IoT on banking processes. Procedia Computer Science, 151, 77–84. https://doi.org/10.1016/j.procs.2019.04.014

Khang, A., Chowdhury, S., & Sharma, S., (1st Ed.) (2022). The Data-Driven Blockchain Ecosystem: Fundamentals, Applications, and Emerging Technologies. CRC Press. https://doi.org/10.1201/9781003269281

Khang, A., Gujrati, R., Uygun, H., Tailor, R.K., & Gaur, S. (Eds.). (2024). Data-Driven Modelling and Predictive Analytics in Business and Finance: Concepts, Designs, Technologies, and Applications (1st Ed.). Auerbach Publications. https://doi.org/10.1201/9781032618845

Khang, A., Hahanov, V., Abbas, G. L., & Hajimahmud, V. A. (2022).Cyber-Physical-Social System and İncident Management, AI-Centric Smart City Ecosystems: Technologies, Design and Implementation (1st Ed.). CRC Press. https://doi.org/10.1201/9781003252542-2

Khang, A., Hajimahmud, V. A., Hahanov, V., & Shah, V. (2024). Advanced IoT Technologies and Applications in the Industry 4.0 Digital Economy (1st Ed.). CRC Press. https://doi.org/10.1201/9781003434269

Khang, A., Inna, S-O., Alla, K., Rostyslav, S., Rudenko, M., Lidia, R., & Kristina, B. (2024) Management Model 6.0 and Business Recovery Strategy of Enterprises in the Era of Digital Economy. In Khang, A., Gujrati, R., Uygun, H., Tailor, R.K., & Gaur, S., Data-Driven Modelling and Predictive Analytics in Business and Finance (1st Ed.). CRC Press. https://doi.org/10.1201/9781032618845-16

Khanh, H. H., & Khang, A. (2021). The Role of Artificial Intelligence in Blockchain Applications. In Rana G, Khang A., Sharma R., Goel A. K., Dubey A. K., Reinventing Manufacturing and Business Processes through Artificial Intelligence (pp. 20–40). CRC Press. https://doi.org/10.1201/9781003145011-2

Kirchherr, J., & Matthews, N. (2018). Technology transfer in the hydropower industry: An analysis of Chinese dam developers' undertakings in Europe and Latin America. Energy Policy, 113, 546–558. https://doi.org/10.1016/j.enpol.2017.11.043

Kisanjara, S. (2023). Internet of things and organizational performance in the Tanzanian banks. Information Discovery and Delivery, 51(3), 253–266. https://doi.org/10.1108/IDD-04-2022-0031

Lande, R. S., Meshram, S. A., & Deshmukh, P. P. (2018). Smart banking using IoT. 2018 International Conference on Research in Intelligent and Computing in Engineering (RICE), 1–4. https://doi.org/10.1109/RICE.2018.8627903

Li, B., Chen, R., & Wang, H. C. (2021). Using intelligent prediction machine and dynamic workflow for banking customer satisfaction in IoT environment. Journal of Ambient Intelligence and Humanized Computing. https://doi.org/10.1007/s12652-021-03201-0

Magazine, S., & Gabbai, A. (2015). Kevin Ashton Describes "the Internet of Things." Smithsonian Magazine. https://www.smithsonianmag.com/innovation/kevin-ashton-describes-the-internet-of-things-180953749/

Mahalakshmi, S., & Desai, K. (2022). IoT Framework, Architecture Services, Platforms, and Reference Models. In S. Nandan Mohanty, J. M. Chatterjee, & S. Satpathy (Eds.), Internet of Things and Its Applications (pp. 37–59). Springer International Publishing. https://doi.org/10.1007/978-3-030-77528-5_2

Malali, D. A. B. (2020). Application of Artificial Intelligence and Its Powered Technologies in the Indian Banking and Financial Industry: An Overview. https://www.semanticscholar.org/paper/Application-of-Artificial-Intelligence-and-Its-in-Malali/fe33bfee66ba6ac1bda6ad3e51b8be81605cd3c3

Mishra, P., & Guru Sant, T. (2021). Role of Artificial Intelligence and Internet of Things in Promoting Banking and Financial Services during COVID-19: Pre and Post Effect. 2021 5th International Conference on Information Systems and Computer Networks (ISCON), 1–7. https://doi.org/10.1109/ISCON52037.2021.9702445

Mordor Intelligence. (2023). IoT in Banking Market—Internet of Things—Size, Share & Industry Analysis. https://www.mordorintelligence.com/industry-reports/internet-of-things-in-banking-market

Nandan Mohanty, S., Chatterjee, J. M., & Satpathy, S. (Eds.). (2022). Internet of Things and Its Applications. Springer International Publishing. https://doi.org/10.1007/978-3-030-77528-5

Nicoletti, B. (2021). Banking 5.0: How Fintech Will Change Traditional Banks in the "New Normal" Post Pandemic. Springer Nature.

Pau, L. F., & Gianotti, C. (1990). Applications of Artificial Intelligence in Banking, Financial Services and Economics. In L. F. Pau & C. Gianotti (Eds.), Economic and Financial Knowledge-Based Processing (pp. 22–46). Springer. https://doi.org/10.1007/978-3-642-76002-0_4

Putra, M. P. (2021). An analysis of big data analytics, IoT and augmented Banking on consumer loan Banking business in Germany. Journal of Research on Business and Tourism, 1(1). https://doi.org/10.37535/104001120212

Ramphull, B., & Nagowah, S. D. (2023). A knowledge model for IoT-enabled smart Banking. Journal of the Knowledge Economy. https://doi.org/10.1007/s13132-023-01434-2

Ramson, S. R. J., Vishnu, S., & Shanmugam, M. (2020). Applications of Internet of Things (IoT) – An Overview. 2020 5th International Conference on Devices, Circuits and Systems (ICDCS), 92–95. https://doi.org/10.1109/ICDCS48716.2020.243556

Rao, D., Tella, S., Raju, P. V. M., & Alekya, V. (2019). IoT enabled smart banking system – a technological revolution. International Journal of Recent Technology and Engineering (IJRTE), 8, 4313–4318. https://doi.org/10.35940/ijrte.B2661.078219

Rastogi, R., Chaturvedi, D. K., Sagar, S., Tandon, N., & Rastogi, A. R. (2022). Deep Learning Application in Classification of Brain Metastases: Sensor Usage in Medical Diagnosis for Next Gen Healthcare. In S. Nandan Mohanty, J. M. Chatterjee, & S. Satpathy (Eds.), Internet of Things and Its Applications (pp. 117–135). Springer International Publishing. https://doi.org/10.1007/978-3-030-77528-5_6

Rathod, A. Y., Pandya, S., & Doshi, N. (2020). IoT and Modern Marketing: Its Social Implications. 2020 22nd International Conference on Advanced Communication Technology (ICACT), 407–413. https://doi.org/10.23919/ICACT48636.2020.9061210

Rehman, H. U., Asif, M., & Ahmad, M. (2017). Future applications and research challenges of IOT. 2017 International Conference on Information and Communication Technologies (ICICT), 68–74. https://doi.org/10.1109/ICICT.2017.8320166

Robert, J., Kubler, S., & Le Traon, Y. (2016). Micro-billing Framework for IoT: Research & Technological Foundations. 2016 IEEE 4th International Conference on Future Internet of Things and Cloud (FiCloud), 301–308. https://doi.org/10.1109/FiCloud.2016.50

Sahu, P., Elezue, C. J., & Kushawaha, R. (2022). An Analysis of Consumer Expectations, Nature and Economic Implications of Smart Banking System in India. In S. Nandan Mohanty, J. M. Chatterjee, & S. Satpathy (Eds.), Internet of Things and Its Applications (pp. 271–279). Springer International Publishing. https://doi.org/10.1007/978-3-030-77528-5_14

Sarmiento-Rojas, J., Aya-Parra, P. A., Quiroga-Torres, D.-A., & Miguel-Cruz, A. (2022). Design and Implementation of an Internet of Things (IoT) Architecture for the Acquisition of Relevant Variables in the Study of Failures in Medical Equipment: A Case Study. In S. Nandan Mohanty, J. M. Chatterjee, & S. Satpathy (Eds.), Internet of Things and Its Applications (pp. 81–99). Springer International Publishing. https://doi.org/10.1007/978-3-030-77528-5_4

Saxena, S., & Ali Said Mansour Al-Tamimi, T. (2017). Big data and internet of things (IoT) technologies in Omani banks: A case study. Foresight, 19(4), 409–420. https://doi.org/10.1108/FS-03-2017-0010

Sheeba, P. S. (2022). An Overview of IoT in Financial Sectors. In Real-Life Applications of the Internet of Things. Apple Academic Press.

Skobelev, P. O., & Borovik, S. Y. (2017). On the way from industry 4.0 to industry 5.0: From digital manufacturing to digital society. Industry 4.0, 2(6), 307–311.

Subash, A., Danny, C. S. A., & Vijayalakshmi, M. (2023). IoT-based secure luggage storage kiosk. International Journal of Information Technology, 15(4), 1911–1918. https://doi.org/10.1007/s41870-023-01229-3

Sundmaeker, H., Guillemin, P., Friess, P., & Woelfflé, S. (2010). Vision and Challenges for Realizing the Internet of Things. In Cluster of European Research Projects on the Internet of Things, European Commision. https://doi.org/10.2759/26127

Verma, K., Chandnani, N., Bhatt, G., & Sinha, A. (2022). Internet of Things and Smart Farming. In S. Nandan Mohanty, J. M. Chatterjee, & S. Satpathy (Eds.), Internet of Things and Its Applications (pp. 283–303). Springer International Publishing. https://doi.org/10.1007/978-3-030-77528-5_15

Vijay kumar, S. (2019). IoT Applications in Finance and Banking.

Zander, S., Merkle, N., & Frank, M. (2016). Enhancing the utilization of IoT devices using ontological semantics and reasoning. Procedia Computer Science, 98, 87–90. https://doi.org/10.1016/j.procs.2016.09.015

Chapter 20

The Impact of Artificial Intelligence (AI) Transformation on the Financial Sector from the Trading to Security Operations

Pooja Darda and Meenal K Pendse

20.1 Introduction

Artificial intelligence (AI) is a multidisciplinary field that encompasses the development and implementation of computer systems capable of emulating human-like behavior in various cognitive domains, such as learning, reasoning, decision-making, and problem-solving. Its primary objective is to enable machines to exhibit intelligent behavior, similar to that of humans, through the utilization of advanced algorithms and computational models.

By simulating human cognitive processes, AI aims to enhance the ability of computer system to perform complex tasks and adapt to dynamic environments, ultimately expanding the range of applications and capabilities of these systems (Huang, 2023). It was found that the AI has been extensively employed across various domains and sectors, showcasing its versatility and potential, Healthcare, academia, the arts, and industry are just a few examples (Gupta et al., 2023). Finance is one area where AI applications have received considerable attention and show great promise. Individuals, companies, and institutions all have financial resources, assets, obligations, and risks that must be carefully managed (Bughin et al., 2018).

DOI: 10.4324/9781003501947-20

The use of AI approaches in the financial sector spans a wide variety of uses with the overarching goal of automating, bettering, and optimizing the provision of financial services. These programs have several goals, including process automation, improved forecast accuracy, and self-directed knowledge gain through experience. Machine learning (ML), deep learning (DL), natural language processing (NLP), graph algorithms, evolutionary learning, and other approaches all fall under the umbrella of AI in the realm of finance.

AI has the potential to change many facets of financial business, which is one of the many benefits of incorporating AI into this field. AI technologies have proven their worth in the financial sector, where they have helped boost productivity, accuracy, and decision making. AI systems can analyze massive volumes of data at lightning speed using sophisticated algorithms and ML approaches, allowing financial organizations to make more educated and data-driven decisions.

The application of AI has the potential to simplify the supply of individualized services by gathering information on the specific preferences, routines, goals, and level of risk tolerance of individual clients. For instance, AI might provide round-the-clock financial guidance using Chatbots that utilize NLP to decipher questions posed by users. In addition, AI offers tailored recommendations for monetary products and services (JPMorgan, 2018). The utilization of AI within the financial services sector has the potential to facilitate the identification of unexplored avenues for development, innovation, and the generation of value (Davenport et al., 2020). AI possesses the capability of effectively evaluating extensive volumes of data derived from many sources, so enabling the identification of hitherto unrecognized patterns, trends, anomalies, and profound insights. The integration of these insights with other data has the potential to enhance business decision-making and strategic planning (Mhlanga, 2020).

The utilization of AI holds significant promise in the realms of risk and fraud management. AI possesses the capability of mitigating financial losses and detect instances of fraudulent activity in monetary transactions through the utilization of advanced algorithms and ML techniques (Dunis et al., 2016). The utilization of AI in risk management strategies might provide advantageous outcomes by enabling the early detection of fraudulent activities, thereby mitigating potential financial implications (Zhao, 2022).

AI has the potential to enhance transparency and compliance with the banking industry. The utilization of AI solutions has the potential to enhance organizations' adherence to legal and ethical guidelines. AI, for example, has the potential to streamline document processing and identity verification, resulting in expedited customer on boarding procedures with reduced error rates (Rahmel, 2020). Financial operations and procedures may benefit from the application of AI due to its ability to increase efficiency while decreasing expenses. Data input, reconciliation, reporting, and analysis are all examples of repetitive, time-consuming operations that may be made more efficient with the help of AI. The use of AI-powered conversational bots that can pass for human has the potential to revolutionize the customer support industry. In order to provide better and faster customer service, these agents are programmed to handle enquiries and requests in a manner that is eerily similar to human interaction (Uykur, 2018).

While there are several individual studies and papers exploring the various uses of AI in finance, there is a gap in comprehensive research that brings these results together to offer a complete overview. Additionally, a lot of current research focuses only on technological issues with little attention paid to wider social and policy implications. A significant need exists for current, thorough research that synthesizes existing information and offers a balanced viewpoint in light of the fast-paced advancement of AI technology and their applications in finance.

Figure 20.1   Word cloud for R2: Themes in AI in finance.

The primary objective of this study is to investigate and analyze the specific objectives outlined below:

- R1—To provide an in-depth overview of existing AI applications in the financial industry.
- R2—To recognize and examine the major themes and patterns in relation to the advantages, difficulties, and potential future directions of AI in finance
- R3—To evaluate the larger implications of the implementation of AI into the financial sector.

20.2 Literature Review

This literature review provides a comprehensive overview of the application of AI in the domain of finance. By examining a wide range of scholarly articles, this review synthesizes the existing knowledge and identifies the key areas where AI has been successfully implemented in finance as shown in Figure 20.1.

The review also highlights the potential benefits and challenges associated with the primary objective of this research, which is to thoroughly examine the diverse range of applications offered by AI in enhancing processes, decision-making, and risk management within the financial industry as shown in Table 20.1.

20.3 Theoretical Framework

The resource-based view (RBV) is a theoretical framework that posits resources as critical determinants of achieving outstanding organizational performance. When a resource possesses traits that are deemed VRIO (valuable, rare, inimitable, and organized), it empowers the organization to acquire and maintain a competitive advantage (Barney, 1991). The RBV theory posits that resources are heterogeneous and immobile among different enterprises. The term "heterogeneous" refers to the condition in which many organizations possess distinct combinations of resources,

Table 20.1 AI in Enhancing Processes, Decision-Making, and Risk Management Within the Financial Industry

Concept	Findings	Author and Year
Credit scoring: development of an empirical model to aid financial institution decision-making.	Credit scoring constantly seeks to establish an empirical model to help financial firms make effective financial decisions. The data came from 68 financial services provider credit officers/credit managers.	Dhaigude and Lawande, 2022
Insurance underwriting: the process of assessing the mortality risk posed by individual applicants for life insurance.	Life insurers examine applicants' mortality risk through underwriting to offer cheap products and manage this financial ecosystem. Most property and health insurance policies are renewed and appraised periodically, but most life insurance plans are one-time, long-term contracts.	Maier et al., 2020
Predicting the company's future stock prices using AI: the use of AI to predict the future stock prices of a company	Using news and price data, such analytical approaches estimate the company's future stock prices to help traders make informed selections. Stock trading is a major financial activity.	Zheng and Jin, 2017
Sentiment analysis for stock return prediction: The application of sentiment analysis to compute sentiment indices of investors based on their comments and use them to predict stock returns	The sentiment lexicon was used to create a SO-PMI-based sentiment computing model to calculate investor sentiment indexes. Investor sentiment indexes based on comments were found to be better at measuring investor mood and predicting stock returns.	Cheng et al., 2019
Predictive analysis for customer behavior in banks: A predictive model to analyze the behavior of customers in banks, specifically whether they will be applying for long-term deposits or not.	We present a predictive model to analyze bank customers' behavior, including whether they would apply for long-term deposits. University of California Irvine (UCI) ML repository dataset for Portuguese banking institution direct marketing campaigns.	Golecha, 2017
Chatbots in banking: AI-powered virtual assistants used in banking to provide 24/7 service and improve reliability and efficiency.	Higher consumer expectations are driving the usage of AI, ML, and Chatbots in banking. Bank self-service virtual assistant Fusion Dixibot from FinastraR.	Biswal, 2012

(Continued)

Table 20.1   AI in Enhancing Processes, Decision-Making, and Risk Management Within the Financial Industry *(Continued)*

Concept	Findings	Author and Year
Regulatory compliance and risk management automation: The automation and streamlining of various aspects of compliance and risk analysis in financial institutions.	Advanced technologies like AI and data analytics automate and streamline compliance and risk analysis in FECI systems, which help financial institutions manage regulatory compliance and risk.	Hu and Wu, 2023
Anti-money laundering suite (AMLS): A system introduced to detect suspicious activities in financial transactions.	AMLS was designed to detect suspicious behaviors, although it only applies to individual transactions, not credit card and other bank transactions. Making stolen money disappear, termed money laundering. Money laundering detection is difficult due to large financial transactions.	Patil et al., 2020
Risk analysis in bank loans: The process of understanding and assessing the risks associated with bank loans.	Bank loan risk analysis requires understanding risk. Today, bank, health, and car loans carry considerable risks for both the banks and the borrowers.	Farheen, et al., 2017
AI in asset management: The application of AI and ML in the field of asset management.	AI and ML are increasingly being adopted in finance and asset management, indicating a growing trend in the industry.	Rahmel, 2020
Sentiment inference, forecasting, and planning: research cluster in finance that applies AI and ML to sentiment inference, forecasting, and planning.	Across both types of study, the researcher has found three overarching categories of financial research. Among these include financial fraud and distress, inferring and planning based on investor mood, and portfolio construction, valuation, and investor behavior. Additionally, this research makes use of co-occurrence and confluence analysis to highlight new patterns and topics of interest in the field of finance research related to AI and ML.	Goodell et al., 2021
Financial wellness: The use of AI in the finance industry to improve individuals' financial well-being.	AI is impacting financial wellness, security, capital markets, and money transmission. Traditional banking is data-rich but not data-driven.	Corea, 2018
Risk assessment using KYC data and machine learning: The process of using unique KYC data and ML techniques to accurately assess the risk of default on a loan.	To improve risk detection approaches, this study uses unique KYC data and ML to create a reliable risk assessment tool. Abstract banks can use KYC data to detect loan defaulters.	Chen, 2020

(Continued)

Table 20.1   AI in Enhancing Processes, Decision-Making, and Risk Management Within the Financial Industry *(Continued)*

Concept	Findings	Author and Year
Financial sentiment analysis using machine learning techniques: The process of gauging sentiment or general prevailing attitude of investors from financial news and social media using ML algorithms	The increase of web content allows investors to be surveyed straight from news and social media. Calculating investor sentiment can ease the study of huge, unstructured textual datasets and assist predict market price changes.	Grealish and Kolm, 2021
Risk control in financial institutions: The application of AI technology in managing and mitigating risks in financial institutions	Some new business models have emerged as a result of the widespread adoption of AI in the financial sector for use in risk management, marketing, customer service, transactions, operations, and product optimization.	Li et al., 2021
Data-driven product customization: Data-driven customization of financial services	Applications for learning AI systems are numerous. Financial sector services include data-driven product customization, creative financial solutions, and trading algorithms. This technology might sharpen This article discusses regulatory and operational concerns financial institutions may face when using ML technologies.	Martinello, 2022
Fraud detection: The process of identifying and preventing fraudulent transactions	Recent studies have demonstrated the potential of automated fraud detection techniques.	Dutrée and Hofland, 2017
Algorithmic trading: Executing financial market trading strategies with algorithms	The articles in the special section center on the topics of AI and financial technology (Fintech). The finance industry has experienced significant growth in the use of AI and data science.	Cao, 2021
Robo-advisors: Digital investing portfolio management and financial planning tools	Investment portfolio management and financial planning use these techniques. Adding digital twin capabilities to software benefits robo-advisors and their clients.	Bonelli and Döngül, 2023
Reshaping claims in insurance through AI: AI to revolutionize insurance claims	Within the realm of insurance, AI holds the potential to significantly transform several aspects such as claims processing, underwriting practices, distribution strategies, and pricing mechanisms.	Fung et al., 2021

(Continued)

Table 20.1 AI in Enhancing Processes, Decision-Making, and Risk Management Within the Financial Industry *(Continued)*

Concept	Findings	Author and Year
Financial forecasting: Forecasting financial asset movements with DL and ML	Every system uses DL and ML to uncover nonobvious relationships and events that affect trading success. This study reviews the most significant recent publications that use advanced methods to predict financial asset trends and ponders if they may be used to trade complex financial markets.	Cohen, 2022
Optimize working capital management: AI can optimize cash flow and working capital by analyzing inventory, order, and payment data.	AI can optimize cash flow and working capital by analyzing inventory, order, and payment data. Working capital management can be optimized with AI.	Rajagopal et al., 2023
Trading success prediction: Predicting a trade's performance using a mix of linear and nonlinear algorithms, as well as sentiment analysis and pattern identification from social media investors.	Systems investigate less evident relationships and occurrences that affect the probability of trading success using DL and ML protocols. Linear and nonlinear models, together with sentiment analysis of social media investors and pattern recognition methods, are widely used to make predictions.	Cohen, 2022
Chatbots for banking applications: Requested by the user computer programs that can carry out a conversation with the user, allowing them to perform banking operations.	Chatbots allow users to ask inquiries like they would to a human. This will discuss the benefits of Chatbots and the building of a banking Chatbot that can conduct user-requested banking tasks.	Rodrigues, 2019
Customer market segmentation: Customer market segmentation involves grouping clients based on shared characteristics.	Customer segmentation unites a company's customers by commonalities to evaluate their behavior and purchase patterns and help them make money.	Regmi et al., 2022
Adjusting financial evaluations: Using AI to modify financial assessments or appraisals.	Forbes says 70% of financial organizations use AI to predict income events, change financial assessments and detect fraud. Computerized reasoning software might save banks $447 billion by 2023, per *Business Insider*.	Farooq and Chawla, 2021

resulting in diverse competences and competitive advantages. The term "immobile" refers to the condition in which resources exhibit limited transferability or replicability among enterprises, primarily because of diverse isolating factors.

The integration of AI applications within the financial industry may be seen as a valuable resource that has the potential to confer a competitive edge to organizations that use them (Augier & Teece, 2021). The utilization of AI applications might prove to be advantageous in the context of business organizations, provided they contribute to the creation of value for consumers or the reduction of expenses. A scarcity of AI applications may arise when they lack widespread availability or accessibility to other organizations. AI applications possess the potential to be inimitable when they exhibit characteristics that render them arduous or expensive to replicate or replace with alternative entities. The organization of AI applications can be facilitated by the presence of complementary resources and competencies within the enterprise (Artemenko & Zenchenko, 2021).

20.4 Research Methodology

A qualitative methodology was created, employed, and executed for this study, and content analysis was the method of choice for its implementation (Downe-Wamboldt, 1992). We look at articles from newspapers and blogs, as well as annual reports from financial institution, to learn more about AI in the financial industry. This study aims to explore 50 newspaper articles and blogs, in addition to 20 finance reports, all of which were published between September 2018 and October 2023, with the objective of identifying recurring topics, benefits, and challenges associated with the application of AI in finance.

This study adheres to a six-step procedure and uses a thematic analysis technique to analyze all of the obtained digital information, including newspapers, blogs, and financial reports. This methodology is similar to that developed by Braun and Clarke (2006). In the beginning, you become acquainted with the information acquired from the interviews with the focus groups. The next step, the construction of the preliminary codes, follows. The third stage was to identify the developing themes. Re-examination of the topics constitutes the fourth phase of the process. The formation of clear themes is the objective of the fifth stage, while the repetition of the findings and meticulous documentation of those outcomes is the focus of the sixth step.

To identify the many topics and their interrelationships, the data were manually labeled and categorized. This process was performed manually. The investigation used framework known as flat coding. The current investigation utilized a paradigm known as flat coding, in which all codes in the database were assigned same degrees of specificity and importance, regardless of the context in which they were found. The current investigation reveals that code frames provide a high degree of adaptability, which enables researchers to successfully utilize their results in a variety of situations. This is demonstrated by the fact that code frames were used in the current investigation. During the process of developing the codes, the researchers ensured that the codes covered a wide variety of answers, displayed opposing traits, and maintained a harmonious equilibrium between having too much data and not having enough.

20.5 Findings and Discussion

20.5.1 Theme 1: Investment and Trading

Financial markets do not exist without trading and investing. However, this industry is undergoing profound changes as a result of the emergence of cutting-edge digital technology and tools.

Traditional trading and investment tactics are disrupted by the convergence of AI and ML. Investors may make better judgments, implement more efficient strategies, and earn higher profits because of the potential of these technologies.

20.5.1.1 Automated Trading Systems

In the past, traders relied heavily on their own instincts and expertise to make decisions. Algorithmic trading is, a process that uses quantitative models to conduct trades mechanically depending on a set of inputs. Owing of their superior speed and efficiency, these algorithms can capitalize on brief market opportunities that would otherwise be missed by human traders. Furthermore, these methods allow for a more disciplined approach to trading by eliminating emotional biases and squarely emphasizing facts and the logic of the trading strategy, so as to reduce losses and maximize gains.

20.5.1.2 Estimating Stock Values

Forecasting stock price changes has long been the Holy Grail for investors. AI provides a more all-encompassing strategy than conventional approaches, which frequently rely on fundamental and technical analysis. AI algorithms can scan massive volumes of data, from past stock prices to current news updates, to identify complex patterns and connections that human analysts would miss. Therefore, these models can provide more precise and timely projections, allowing traders to make educated choices despite the ever-changing nature of the market.

20.5.1.3 Stock Market Sentiment Analysis

The stock market is propelled not only by data, but also by the investors' mood. Traders may feel a sense of market sentiment from a variety of sources, including news stories, financial data, and social media comments, by employing AI's capacity for sentiment analysis. AI can help investors predict market movements based on collective investor sentiment by processing and evaluating this large array of qualitative data.

20.5.1.4 Robo-Advisors

Human financial advisors are no longer the only ones to provide individualized financial guidance. Robo-advisors are digital services that provide automated, data-driven investment advice to investors. These sites use AI algorithms to assess a user's financial standing, risk tolerance, and investment objectives and then create and monitor a personalized portfolio on their behalf. This ensures proper asset allocation and consistent portfolio rebalancing at a far lower cost than conventional advisory services.

20.5.1.5 Prediction of Commercial Success

One of the most recent developments in the use of AI in trading is its capacity to predict the likelihood of a successful trading endeavor. An AI model's ability to evaluate the risks and rewards of a trade is based on its ability to analyze and integrate a wide variety of data, such as market circumstances, stock behavior, and global economic indicators. Traders benefit from this in two ways: it helps them fine-tune their tactics and gives them more faith in their judgments when making trades.

When AI and ML are used in financial markets, they usher in a brand new age. Trading tactics, market forecasts, and investment procedures all stand to benefit from the further development of these technologies. Both institutional and ordinary investors now have access to cutting-edge resources that were formerly reserved for the financial industry's elite as a result of the convergence of AI with traditional trading methods, which is transforming the landscape of financial markets. The use of AI in future trade and investment has tremendous potential for development, innovation, and prosperity.

20.5.2 Theme 2: Fraud Detection and Financial Security

The global financial system is a tribute to human creativity and fragility owing to its complex design, which includes a web of interconnected networks and automated procedures. Although these complex systems have simplified international trade, they have also opened the possibility of worms in terms of fraud and security flaws. Historically, institutions have depended on rule-based systems to fight these dangers; however, the static structure of these systems has frequently made them vulnerable to the dynamic strategies employed by fraudsters. As a result, the modern answer is to utilize AI and ML systems, which can not only spot fraud but also adjust to its new forms as they emerge.

20.5.2.1 Anti-Money Laundering Suite

An example of AI's contribution to financial security is the Anti-Money Laundering Suite (AMLS), a defense mechanism against the plague of money laundering. AI can shift through massive amounts of transaction data to identify minor trends that may be indicators of money laundering, as opposed to simply tracking large and obvious transactions. It is not only detection itself, which is innovative. The iterative learning capability of ML improves these detection algorithms based on previous instances, keeping the systems one step ahead of criminals at all times. Modern AI-driven due diligence methods have helped institutions stay compliant with ever-changing anti-money laundering requirements while simultaneously reducing false positives and improving client experience.

20.5.2.2 Machine Learning for Suspicious Transactions

Important work is being done in this area using ML for suspicious transactions projects. ML models provide flexibility that is absent in more static approaches, going much beyond simple pattern identification. These models, which provide information from verified instances of fraud, improve their safeguards in response to evolving techniques employed by criminals. Unsupervised learning and other techniques that mine transaction data for outliers can shed light on previously invisible fraudulent activities.

20.5.2.3 Financial Fraud and Distress Systems

In broader context, financial fraud and distress systems provide a defense mechanism that can be used against any type of financial fraud or crisis, from stolen credit card information to stolen personal information. Consider the case of a credit card being used at the same time at two different locations: Without real-time AI analyses, this discrepancy might go unnoticed. When combined with predictive analytics, this type of analysis can provide a forward-looking assessment of a transaction's risk, allowing for proactive rather than reactive fraud identification.

At the forefront of this anti-fraud infrastructure is the fraud detection procedure. This entails a variety of AI techniques, including neural networks that are taught to recognize patterns associated with fraudulent operations and NLP algorithms that analyze customer conversations for signs of breaches. Any change from the norm, regardless of how slight, is immediately recognized by the continuous anomaly detection system.

In summary, fraudster obstacles increase proportionally to the complexity of the financial ecosystem. However, AI and ML have emerged as reliable watchdogs in the banking industry. The real-time processing and adaptive learning capabilities of these solutions not only protect assets, but also help win the trust of countless consumers. AI and ML keep legitimate businesses well ahead of con- artists, changing what it means to have financial security in the digital age.

20.5.3 Theme 3: Customer-Centric Innovations

AI and ML are technologies that have helped users in a new era in the banking industry. These game-changing innovations have shifted the focus of the banking industry from transactions to customers. These days, it is not enough to merely provide financial services; providers must also cater to customers' unique tastes, anticipate their requirements, and provide a consistent experience across all channels.

20.5.3.1 Predictive Analysis of Consumer Behavior

Predictive analysis of consumer behavior is a bedrock of this change. Mass distribution of financial goods is a thing of the past. In order to foresee a customer's future move, banks may now use AI and ML models to sift through past data, transaction patterns, and even external data sources. Predictive models provide information that are goldmines for customer relationship management, whether the topic is the chance of their selecting for a house loan or their tendency toward long-term deposits. These details not only improve the quality of the products on sale, but also help marketers fine-tune their approaches so that each touchpoint is meaningful in the context of the customer's financial life.

20.5.3.2 Chatbots and Virtual Assistants

The proliferation of Chatbots and virtual assistants is a prime example of seamless integration of technology and support. These AI-powered wonders are equipped with NLP to service clients around the clock by responding to questions, updating account information, and helping them through complex financial procedures. They improve productivity, reduce waste, and, most significantly, provide a better experience for customers because of their reliability and speed during transactions. In addition, these digital assistants learn from each encounter and improve their responses to the point where their competence eventually matches or even exceeds that of human assistants.

20.5.3.3 Customer Market Segmentation

Customer market segmentation is another area in which AI has made significant advances. AI algorithms create detailed client segmentation, as opposed to broad demographic or product-based divisions. Classifications may be made in several ways, including those based on digital interactions and transactional behaviors. Banks can create effective marketing campaigns and unique financial solutions, and focus on where they will have the greatest impact by using this level of client segmentation.

In essence, the current banking scene is experiencing radical transformation, supported by AI and ML. These days, it is not just about making a buck; it is all about the experience you provide to your customers. Customers stand to profit from a new era of banking, in which institutions go beyond simple money management to consider and even anticipate their clients' hopes, fears, and goals.

20.5.4 Theme 4: Shaping Future Financial Innovations

The financial world stands on the ice of a transformative era, guided by the potent duo of AI and ML. The profound implications of these technologies are not merely extrapolations; they already manifest in tangible innovations that promise to redefine the contours of financial services. Let us explore some of these pioneering strides that are poised to recalibrate tomorrow's financial compass.

20.5.4.1 Financial Wellness

At concept of financial wellness is at the heart of this transformation. Beyond the veneer of transactional numbers, financial wellness encapsulates the broader spectrum of an individual's fiscal life. AI-driven tools, steeped in advanced algorithms, distill this vast data panorama, offering individuals incisive insights into their financial landscapes. These platforms transcend traditional advisories. By continuously learning from data, they evolve and provide dynamic advice, ranging from investment strategies to debt management. The outcome? A populace is better equipped to navigate its financial futures, ensuring resilience against fiscal upheavals.

20.5.4.2 Data-driven Product Customization

Yet, the crux of this transformation is not just about personal insights; it is also about personalization at scale. This essence is captured in data-driven product customization. Gone are days when financial products are monolithic offerings. Currently, powered by AI and ML, institutions delve into the granularities of individual data to craft bespoke financial products. Whether it is a loan tailored to one's repayment capabilities or an investment portfolio resonating with one's risk appetite, the era of generic is overshadowed by the era of personalization. The upshot is a symbiotic paradigm in which institutions benefit from higher engagement, and consumers reveal products that mirror their unique financial blueprints.

20.5.4.3 Regulatory Compliance and Risk Management

Amidst this wave of innovation, one domain that traditionally bore the brunt of complexity was regulatory compliance and risk management. However, AI has begun to untangle this complex web. Regulatory landscapes, often mired in layers of complexity, are now precisely navigated by AI systems. These platforms not only ensure unwavering adherence to regulations but also predict potential risk vectors. The cascading benefits are manifold, ranging from fortifying institutions against regulatory penalties to fostering an environment of unwavering trust among stakeholders as shown in Figure 20.2.

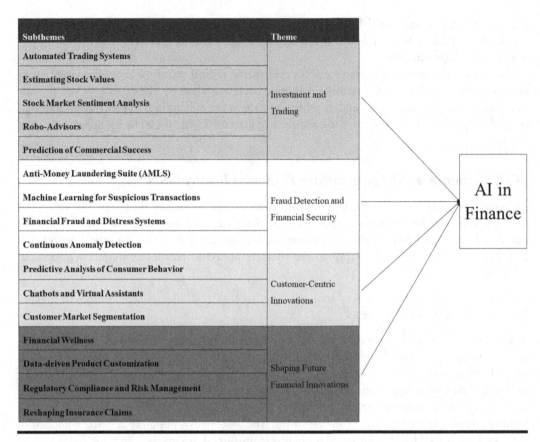

Figure 20.2   Thematic model for AI in finance.

20.6 Implication

The expanding use of AI in banking has completely altered how monetary transactions are conducted. Considering the far-reaching consequences for theoretical frameworks, management philosophies, social mores, and policy frameworks, this connection deserves further study.

20.6.1 Theoretical Implications

■ Evolution of financial theories: Traditional financial theories are tested by the integration of AI and ML in financial systems, particularly those that rely on the rationality of human players. The effectiveness and precision of AI-driven judgments may inspire the development of new theoretical frameworks for machine intelligence.

■ Behavioral finance: The application of sentiment analysis and predictive analytics might offer deeper perceptions of investors' motivations and actions, possibly changing ideas of behavioral finance.

■ Risk management: New risk assessment and management theories may be developed as a result of the predictive capacities of AI and ML, particularly when real-time data analysis is involved.

20.6.2 Managerial Implications

- Strategic investment: To remain competitive, improve decision-making procedures, and enhance customer experiences, managers should consider investing in AI and ML technology.
- Training and development: As AI-driven technologies become more prevalent, staff members must receive ongoing training and development to help them comprehend, interpret, and act on the insights produced by AI.
- Operational efficiency: Managers may use AI to optimize processes, cut costs, and improve service delivery, particularly in areas such as fraud detection and customer support (e.g., Chatbots).

20.6.3 Social Implications

- Job landscape: The emergence of AI and ML may result in job losses in specific financial industry sectors, but it may also give rise to new positions that focus on the management, supervision, and integration of AI.
- Financial inclusion: AI-driven robot advisors and customized banking options can provide access to financial services and advice for a wider swath of the population, thereby increasing financial inclusion.
- Trust and reliability: While AI might increase productivity, there may be social concerns about over-reliance on robots, particularly when making important financial choices. Establishing confidence in AI-driven systems is crucial (Khang et al., 2023b).

20.6.4 Policy Implications

- Regulation of AI in finance: Policymakers must create rules that guarantee the moral and responsible application of AI in the financial industry and address issues such as data protection, responsibility, and transparency.
- Consumer protection: Policies should be in place to safeguard customers from possible financial scams or bad advice powered by AI, ensuring that such advice is given with the consumer's best interests in mind.
- Standardization: Standardization is necessary to maintain consistency and justice as AI and ML technologies are increasingly incorporated into the financial industry. This includes standardizing the technology usage, data processing, and decision-making algorithms.

In conclusion, the interaction between AI and finance is transforming the financial industry, offering exceptional efficiency and innovative perspectives. However, the integration of these two elements presents various challenges and concerns that must be comprehensively addressed. By strategically considering the implications and taking responsibility, the financial sector can effectively utilize AI to create a future that is fair, efficient, and secure.

20.7 Limitations

The methodology employed in this study primarily involved the utilization of secondary data sources. This deliberate choice was made to ensure that the study was firmly rooted in the existing body of the literature and well-established research outcomes. The methodology employed facilitated the attainment of a comprehensive overview of the present state of AI within the realm of finance. The potential incorporation of primary data into future research endeavors may present novel and original insights and perspectives.

20.8 Conclusion and Future Scope

The study of AI's significant impact on the financial industry highlights its potential to bring about transformation and improve efficiency, signaling a future of innovation. The integration of financial models and AI enables increased efficiency and accuracy while also facilitating innovative solutions for long-standing challenges. Nevertheless, the utilization of AI carries certain responsibilities, requiring a careful equilibrium between automation and human intuition as well as between data-driven decision-making and ethical deliberations.

The future appears promising, with abundant opportunities. As AI systems advance, their integration with finance is expected to deepen, resulting in solutions that are currently beyond the scope of this study. One possible approach involves hyper personalization of financial services. With the increasing proficiency of AI in comprehending individual financial behaviors and preferences, it is possible to envision a future where financial advice, investment strategies, and banking solutions are customized to meet individual requirements.

The ethical implications of AI are expected to be a significant topic for discussion and research. Given the substantial impact of financial decisions on individuals' lives, it is crucial to prioritize transparency, fairness, and the absence of bias in AI-driven financial decision-making. This may lead to the development of ethical AI models that are tailored to the financial industry.

However, there are also impending challenges. Institutions must prioritize data privacy and security by implementing advanced cybersecurity measures to safeguard sensitive financial data. Furthermore, the increasing integration of AI into the finance sector may lead to disruptions in the job market. The financial sector should collaborate with educational institutions to develop strategies for upskilling and reskilling. This will help to ensure that the workforce remains relevant in the era of AI (Khang et al., 2023b).

In conclusion, the integration of AI and finance holds significant potential, and is expected to fundamentally transform the financial industry in ways that are still not fully understood. Despite these inevitable challenges, a promising future filled with opportunities lies ahead through collaborative efforts and a vision rooted in ethics and inclusivity. It is now the responsibility of researchers, policymakers, and industry leaders to navigate this journey with foresight to ensure that everyone benefits from the AI finance connection (Khang et al., 2023c).

References

Al-Baity, H. H. (2023). The artificial intelligence revolution in digital finance in Saudi Arabia: A comprehensive review and proposed framework. *Sustainability, 15*(18), 13725. https://www.mdpi.com/2071-1050/15/18/13725

Artemenko, D. A., & Zenchenko, S. V. (2021). Digital technologies in the financial sector: Evolution and major development trends in Russia and abroad. *Finance: Theory and Practice, 25*(3), 90–101. https://financetp.fa.ru/jour/article/view/1234?locale=en_US

Augier, M., & Teece, D. J. (2021). *The Palgrave Encyclopedia of Strategic Management*. Palgrave Macmillan.

Barney, J. (1991). Firm resources and sustained competitive advantage. *Journal of Management*, *17*(1), 99–120. https://journals.sagepub.com/doi/abs/10.1177/014920639101700108

Bhagchandani, A., & Trivedi, D. (2020). A Machine Learning Algorithm to Predict Financial Investment. In *Lecture Notes on Data Engineering and Communications Technologies*. https://doi.org/10.1007/978-981-15-4474-3_30

Biswal BB. (2012). Resting state fMRI: A personal history. *Neuroimage*. Aug 15; *62*(2), 938–944. doi: 10.1016/j.neuroimage.2012.01.090.

Bonelli, M.I., & Döngül, E.S. (2023). Robo-Advisors in the Financial Services Industry: Recommendations for Full-Scale Optimization, Digital Twin Integration, and Leveraging Natural Language Processing Trends. *2023 9th International Conference on Virtual Reality (ICVR)*, 268–275. https://ieeexplore.ieee.org/abstract/document/10169615/

Braun, V., & Clarke, V. (2006). Using thematic analysis in psychology. *Qualitative Research in Psychology*, *3*(2), 77–101.

Bughin, J., Seong, J., Manyika, J., Chui, M., & Joshi, R. (2018,). *Notes from the AI Frontier: Modeling the Impact of AI on the World Economy*. McKinsey & Company. https://www.mckinsey.com/featured-insights/artificial-intelligence/notes-from-the-AI-frontier-modeling-the-impact-of-ai-on-the-world-economy

Cao, L. (2021). AI in finance: Challenges, techniques, and opportunities. *ACM Computing Surveys (CSUR)*, *55*, 1–38. https://dl.acm.org/doi/abs/10.1145/3502289

Chen, T. (2020). Do you know your customer? Bank risk assessment based on machine learning. *Applied Soft Computing*, *86*, 105779. https://doi.org/10.1016/j.asoc.2019.105779

Cheng, J., Fu, J., Kang, Y., Zhu, H., & Dai, W. (2019). Sentiment analysis of social networks' comments to predict stock return. In *Human Centered Computing: 5th International Conference, HCC 2019, Čačak, Serbia, August 5–7, 2019, Revised Selected Papers 5* (pp. 67–74). Springer International Publishing.

Cohen, G. (2022). Algorithmic trading and financial forecasting using advanced artificial intelligence methodologies. *Mathematics*. https://www.mdpi.com/2227-7390/10/18/3302

Corea, F. (n.d.). *An introduction to data*. SpringerLink. https://link.springer.com/book/10.1007/978-3-030-04468-8

Davenport, T., Guha, A., Grewal, D., & Bressgott, T. (2020). How artificial intelligence will change the future of marketing. *Journal of the Academy of Marketing Science*, *48*, 24–42. https://link.springer.com/article/10.1007/s11747-019-00696-0

Dhaigude, R., & Lawande, N. (2022). Impact of Artificial Intelligence on Credit Scores in Lending Process. *2022 Interdisciplinary Research in Technology and Management (IRTM)*, 1–5. https://ieeexplore.ieee.org/abstract/document/9791511/

Downe-Wamboldt, B. (1992). Content analysis: Method, applications, and issues. *Health Care for Women International*, *13*(3), 313–321. https://www.tandfonline.com/doi/pdf/10.1080/07399339209516006

Dunis, C., Middleton, P. W., Karathanasopolous, A., & Theofilatos, K. (2016). *Artificial Intelligence in Financial Markets*. London: Palgrave Macmillan. https://link.springer.com/content/pdf/10.1057/978-1-137-48880-0.pdf

Dutrée, N., & Hofland, D. (2017). Detecting Fraud in Financial Payments. https://cs229.stanford.edu/proj2017/final-reports/5219328.pdf

Farheen, S., Manerkar, M., Payal, T., & Vikram, D.K. (2017). Predictive Analytics Application in Banking Sector using Mining Technique Algorithms. https://ieeexplore.ieee.org/abstract/document/9499147/

Farooq, A., & Chawla, P. (2021). Review of Data Science and AI in Finance. *2021 International Conference on Computing Sciences (ICCS)*, 216–222. https://ieeexplore.ieee.org/abstract/document/9784729/

Fung, G., Polanía, L.F., Choi, S.T., Wu, V., & Ma, L. (2021). Editorial: Artificial intelligence in insurance and finance. *Frontiers in Applied Mathematics and Statistics*. https://www.frontiersin.org/articles/10.3389/fams.2021.795207/full

Goodell, J.W., Kumar, S., Lim, W.M., & Pattnaik, D. (2021). Artificial intelligence and machine learning in finance: Identifying foundations, themes, and research clusters from bibliometric analysis. *Journal of Behavioral and Experimental Finance*. https://www.semanticscholar.org/paper/Artificial-intelligence-and-machine-learning-in-and-Goodell-Kumar/727f4397ed0068575b7c538d2cedf32f5db4d9a7

Grealish, A., & Kolm, P. N. (2021). Robo-Advisory: From Investing Principles and Algorithms to Future Developments. In Capponi A., & Lehalle C. A. (Eds.), *Machine Learning in Financial Markets: A Guide to Contemporary Practice.* Cambridge University Press., Available at SSRN: https://ssrn.com/abstract=3776826 or http://dx.doi.org/10.2139/ssrn.3776826

Gupta, O. J., Yadav, S., Srivastava, M., Darda, P., & Mishra, V. (2023). Understanding the intention to use metaverse in healthcare utilizing a mix method approach. *International Journal of Healthcare Management*, 1–12. https://doi.org/10.1080/20479700.2023.2183579

Hu, B., & Wu, Y. (2023). AI-based compliance automation in commercial bank: How the silicon valley bank provided a cautionary tale for future integration. *International Research in Economics and Finance*, 7(1), 13. https://doi.org/10.20849/iref.v7i1.1356

Huang, C. (2023). High-frequency trading through artificial intelligence for financial innovation. *Open Access Government.* http://dspace.unive.it/handle/10579/16789

JPMorgan (2018). JPMorgan's New Guide to Machine Learning in Algorithmic Trading. eFinancialCareers. (2018). https://www.efinancialcareers.com/news/2018/12/jpmorgans-new-guide-to-machine-learning-in-algorithmic-trading

Golecha, Y. S. (2017) Analyzing Term Deposits in Banking Sector by Performing Predictive Analysis Using Multiple Machine Learning Techniques. Masters thesis, Dublin, National College of Ireland. https://norma.ncirl.ie/3100/

Khang, A., Muthmainnah, M., Seraj, P. M., Al Yakin, A., & Obaid, A. J. (2023a). AI-Aided Teaching Model in Education 5.0. In Khang A., Shah V., & Rani S. (Eds.), *Handbook of Research on AI-Based Technologies and Applications in the Era of the Metaverse* (pp. 83–104). IGI Global. https://doi.org/10.4018/978-1-6684-8851-5.ch004

Khang, A., Rath, K. C., Satapathy, S. K., Kumar, A., Das, S. R., & Panda, M. R. (2023b). Enabling the Future of Manufacturing: Integration of Robotics and IoT to Smart Factory Infrastructure in Industry 4.0. In Khang A., Shah V., & Rani S. (Eds.), *Handbook of Research on AI-Based Technologies and Applications in the Era of the Metaverse* (pp. 25–50). IGI Global. https://doi.org/10.4018/978-1-6684-8851-5.ch002

Khang, A., Shah, V., & Rani, S. (Eds.). (2023c). *Handbook of Research on AI-Based Technologies and Applications in the Era of the Metaverse.* IGI Global. https://doi.org/10.4018/978-1-6684-8851-5

Li, Y., Yi, J., Chen, H., & Peng, D. (2021). Theory and application of artificial intelligence in financial industry. *Data Science in Finance and Economics*, 1. http://www.aimspress.com/aimspress-data/dsfe/2021/2/PDF/DSFE-01-02-006.pdf

Maier, M., Carlotto, H., Saperstein, S., Sanchez, F., Balogun, S., & Merritt, S. (2020). Improving the accuracy and transparency of underwriting with AI to transform the life insurance industry. *AI Magazine*, 41(3), 78–93. https://ojs.aaai.org/aimagazine/index.php/aimagazine/article/view/5320

Martinello, A. (2022). AI and machine learning in the financial sector: Five focus points. https://www.econstor.eu/handle/10419/261829

Mhlanga, D. (2020). Industry 4.0 in finance: The impact of artificial intelligence (AI) on digital financial inclusion. *International Journal of Financial Studies.* https://www.mdpi.com/2227-7072/8/3/45

Patil, Nikita M, Dondekar, Shraddha M, Rawale, Chetan V, Memane, Kiran V, & Kamble, Lahu (2020). Combating money laundering using artificial intelligence. *International Journal of Advance Research, Ideas and Innovations in Technology*, 6(2) www.IJARIIT.com.

Rahmel, J. (2020). Applying artificial intelligence in finance and asset management: A discussion of status quo and the way forward. *Journal of Financial Transformation*, 51, 67–74. https://ideas.repec.org/a/ris/jofitr/1647.html

Rajagopal, M., Nayak, K., Balasubramanian, K., Abdul Karim Shaikh, I., Adhav, S., & Gupta, M. (2023). Application of Artificial Intelligence in the Supply Chain Finance. *2023 8th International Conference on Science Technology Engineering and Mathematics (ICONSTEM)*, 1–6. https://ieeexplore.ieee.org/abstract/document/10142286/

Regmi, S.R., Meena, J., Kanojia, U., & Kant, V.H. (2022). Customer Market Segmentation using Machine Learning Algorithm. *2022 6th International Conference on Trends in Electronics and Informatics (ICOEI)*, 1348–1354. https://ieeexplore.ieee.org/abstract/document/9777146/

Rodrigues, J. (2019). Chatbot for Supporting Financial Service Channels. https://link.springer.com/chapter/10.1007/978-3-030-68288-0_12

Uykur, D. (2018). The New Physics of Financial Services-Understanding how artificial intelligence is transforming the financial ecosystem-Part of the Future of Financial Services series| Prepared in collaboration with Deloitte. WEF: World Economic Forum. https://policycommons.net/artifacts/1802320/the-new-physics-of-financial-services/2533964/

Zhao, M. (2022). Research on Financial Risk Assessment Based on Artificial Intelligence. *SHS Web of Conferences.* https://www.shs-conferences.org/articles/shsconf/abs/2022/21/shsconf_emsd2022_01017/shsconf_emsd2022_01017.html

Zheng, A., & Jin, J. (2017). Using AI to make predictions on stock market. https://cs229.stanford.edu/proj2017/final-reports/5212256.pdf

Chapter 21

Prioritizing Customer Experience in Digital Banking for Nation's Sustainable Development

Prashant H. Bhagat, Piyush Kumar Jain, and Chetana Kaushik

21.1 Introduction

21.1.1 Background of Digital Banking

The evolution of digital banking in India has witnessed a remarkable transformation in recent years, driven by advancements in technology and changing consumer preferences. The introduction of mobile banking, internet banking, and digital payment platforms has revolutionized the way financial services are accessed and delivered in the country. As India's economy continues to grow and its population becomes more digitally connected, digital banking has emerged as a critical enabler for financial inclusion, economic development, and sustainable growth (Khang, 2024).

21.1.2 Significance of Customer Experience in Digital Banking

In the digital banking landscape, customer experience takes center stage as a key differentiator and determinant of success for financial institutions. With a plethora of options available to customers, their loyalty and satisfaction are heavily influenced by the quality of their interactions with digital banking platforms. A seamless and user-friendly interface, efficient customer support, data security, and personalized services are vital elements that contribute to a positive customer experience. Banks that prioritize customer experience gain a competitive advantage by retaining existing customers, attracting new ones, and fostering long-term relationships that are pivotal to sustainable growth.

 DOI: 10.4324/9781003501947-21

21.1.3 Relationship between Customer-Centric Banking and Sustainable Development with Referencing

Numerous studies and reports have highlighted the inherent link between customer-centric banking and sustainable development. According to the World Bank, access to financial services, including digital banking, plays a crucial role in reducing poverty and promoting economic growth, both of which are key components of sustainable development (World Bank, 2020). Through its focus on inclusivity and meeting customer needs, customer-centric banking contributes significantly to financial inclusion, empowering marginalized communities and supporting micro, small, and medium-sized enterprises (PwC, 2019). Sustainable development goals (SDGs) set by the United Nations, such as eradicating poverty, promoting gender equality, and ensuring environmental sustainability, align closely with the principles of customer-centric banking.

By focusing on customer experience, digital banking in India can further its contribution to sustainable development by ensuring widespread financial inclusion, equitable access to financial services, and fostering economic growth for all segments of society. This chapter delves into the specific strategies and initiatives that can be undertaken to prioritize customer experience in digital banking and, consequently, support India's journey toward sustainable development (Khang, 2024c).

21.2 Landscape of Digital Banking

21.2.1 Overview of Digital Banking Services

The digital banking ecosystem in India is characterized by a diverse range of services offered by banks and Fintech companies. Some of the key digital banking services available to customers include:

- Mobile banking: Mobile banking applications allow customers to access their bank accounts, make transactions, pay bills, transfer funds, and avail various financial services using their smartphones.
- Internet banking: Internet banking platforms enable customers to conduct banking activities through web-based portals, providing convenient access to account information and transaction facilities.
- Digital payments: India has witnessed a surge in digital payment platforms, including Unified Payments Interface (UPI), mobile wallets, and contactless payments, which facilitate seamless and cashless transactions.
- Online investment and wealth management: Many banks and Fintech companies offer online investment platforms, making it easier for customers to invest in mutual funds, stocks, and other financial products.
- Virtual banking and Chatbots: Virtual banking assistants and AI-powered Chatbots provide instant customer support, answer queries, and assist customers with various banking processes.

21.2.2 Adoption and Usage Trends among Different Demographic Segments

The adoption and usage of digital banking services in India have witnessed rapid growth, particularly among the urban population and younger demographics. Several factors have contributed to this trend, such as increasing smartphone penetration, improved internet connectivity, and the government's push for digitalization through initiatives like "Digital India" and "Jan Dhan Yojana."

Urban areas, being more digitally connected, have seen higher adoption rates than rural regions. However, a growing trend of digital banking services is gaining popularity in semi-urban and rural areas as well. Younger age groups, including millennials and Gen Z, have shown a higher propensity to embrace digital banking, driven by their tech-savviness and convenience-seeking behavior.

21.2.3 Role of Digital Banking in Financial Inclusion and Socio-economic Development

Digital banking has played a pivotal role in advancing financial inclusion in India. The convenience and accessibility of digital banking services have brought previously unbanked or underbanked populations into the formal financial system. According to a report by the Reserve Bank of India (RBI), the number of bank accounts in India witnessed a substantial increase due to the success of the Jan Dhan Yojana, which was facilitated by digital banking services (RBI Annual Report, 2020–2021).

Moreover, digital banking has facilitated government-to-person transfers, social welfare payments, and subsidy disbursements, ensuring direct benefit transfers to beneficiaries and reducing leakages in the system. This has positively impacted the socio-economic development of vulnerable communities, as they gain access to financial services and welfare schemes more efficiently.

By offering a wide array of digital banking services and encouraging adoption across different demographic segments, India has made significant strides toward financial inclusion and socio-economic development. The convenience, speed, and accessibility of digital banking have not only transformed banking experiences for customers but have also contributed to the nation's overall economic growth and development.

21.3 Understanding Customer Needs and Preferences

21.3.1 Assessing the Diversity of Customer Segments

India is a vast and diverse country with a wide range of customer segments, each with unique needs, preferences, and requirements. The customer segments in India can be broadly classified based on factors such as age, income level, education, occupation, and geographical location. These segments may include urban residents, rural populations, salaried employees, self-employed individuals, students, senior citizens, and more. Understanding the diverse needs and characteristics of these segments is essential for banks to tailor their digital banking services effectively (Khang, 2024a).

21.3.2 Analyzing Customer Preferences for Digital Banking Services

To cater to the diverse customer segments, it is crucial for banks to analyze customer preferences for digital banking services. This can be done through surveys, user feedback, and data analytics. Some common preferences may include:

- User-friendly interfaces: Customers prefer intuitive and user-friendly mobile apps and internet banking portals that are easy to navigate and understand.
- Secure transactions: Security is a top concern for customers; they seek robust authentication and encryption measures to ensure the safety of their financial transactions.

■ Personalization: Customers appreciate personalized recommendations and offers based on their transaction history and banking behavior.
■ 24/7 customer support: Availability of round-the-clock customer support, through both human agents and AI-powered Chatbots, is valued by customers for prompt issue resolution.
■ Seamless integration: Customers desire seamless integration of digital banking services with other applications, such as e-commerce platforms and utility bill payment systems.

21.3.3 Identifying Barriers to Digital Adoption and Financial Literacy

■ Digital literacy: One of the primary barriers to digital adoption is the lack of digital literacy among certain customer segments, particularly in rural and less technologically connected areas.
■ Language barriers: Many potential users in India may not be well-versed in English, which is commonly used in digital interfaces. Offering services in regional languages can help overcome this barrier.
■ Connectivity and infrastructure: In remote areas with limited internet connectivity and infrastructure, accessing digital banking services can be challenging.
■ Trust and security concerns: Some customers may be hesitant to adopt digital banking due to concerns about data security, privacy, and fraudulent activities.
■ Cultural factors: Cultural preferences and practices may influence customer behavior, leading to varying levels of acceptance of digital banking across different regions.

Understanding the diverse customer segments and their preferences, as well as identifying the barriers to digital adoption and financial literacy, allows banks to design customer-centric solutions that address the specific needs of different segments and foster greater adoption of digital banking services in India. Research and studies on these aspects can provide valuable insights for banks to design effective strategies for customer engagement and retention in the digital banking landscape.

21.4 Strategies for Enhancing Customer Experience in Digital Banking

21.4.1 User-Friendly Mobile Apps and Websites

Developing user-friendly mobile apps and websites is essential for providing a seamless and enjoyable digital banking experience to customers. A well-designed interface, intuitive navigation, and easy access to key features contribute to customer satisfaction and loyalty. User experience research and continuous user testing can help banks understand customer preferences and pain points, leading to iterative improvements in their digital platforms.

21.4.2 Multilingual Support and Accessibility

India is a linguistically diverse country, and offering multilingual support in digital banking platforms is crucial to cater to customers who may not be proficient in English. Providing interfaces in regional languages enhances accessibility and fosters a sense of inclusivity, making banking services more approachable to a broader audience.

21.4.3 Tailored Financial Education and Training

Financial literacy plays a key role in encouraging digital banking adoption and empowering customers to make informed financial decisions. Banks can offer tailored financial education and training programs through their digital platforms, including interactive tutorials, videos, and quizzes, to enhance customers' understanding of digital banking services and products (Lusardi and Mitchell, 2014).

21.4.4 Data Privacy and Security Measures

Addressing customers' concerns about data privacy and security is critical for building trust in digital banking. Banks must implement robust security measures, such as two-factor authentication, encryption, and secure data storage, to safeguard customer information. Transparent communication about security protocols can help reassure customers and strengthen their confidence in using digital banking services (Smith and Meuter, 2020).

21.4.5 Customer Feedback Mechanisms and Complaint Redressal

Establishing effective customer feedback mechanisms allows banks to gather valuable insights into customer experiences, identify areas for improvement, and promptly address issues. Responsive customer support and efficient complaint redressal procedures demonstrate a bank's commitment to resolving customer concerns and enhancing overall satisfaction (Bolton & Lemon, 1999).

By implementing these strategies, banks can significantly improve customer experience in digital banking, leading to higher customer satisfaction, increased adoption of digital services, and strengthened customer loyalty. These approaches are based on empirical research and best practices, ensuring that the customer-centric initiatives are rooted in evidence and proven to drive positive outcomes.

21.5 Promoting Financial Literacy and Inclusion

21.5.1 Collaborative Efforts with Government and NGOs

Collaboration between banks, the government, and non-governmental organizations (NGOs) is essential for promoting financial literacy and inclusion. By pooling resources and expertise, these stakeholders can develop comprehensive financial education programs and campaigns that reach a broader audience. Government-backed initiatives like financial literacy drives and partnerships with NGOs can create awareness about digital banking benefits and foster responsible financial practices (Margvelashvili and Kostava, 2020).

21.5.2 Empowering Rural and Underserved Communities

Reaching out to rural and underserved communities is crucial for promoting financial inclusion. Banks can establish brick-and-mortar banking kiosks or banking correspondents in remote areas to provide face-to-face assistance and facilitate digital banking adoption. Tailored financial literacy workshops in local languages can empower these communities to understand digital banking services and navigate financial decision-making (Klapper & Singer, 2017).

21.5.3 Leveraging Technology for Financial Education

Technology can play a pivotal role in disseminating financial education. Banks can leverage mobile apps, interactive online platforms, and video tutorials to deliver financial literacy content to a broader audience. Gamified learning experiences and simulations can make financial education engaging and effective, enabling customers to develop practical financial skills (Aker & Mbiti, 2010).

By embracing collaborative approaches, targeting rural communities, and leveraging technology-driven financial education initiatives, banks can contribute to enhancing financial literacy and promoting inclusion among diverse customer segments. These strategies not only empower individuals to make informed financial decisions but also foster a more inclusive and financially aware society, driving positive socio-economic outcomes. The references cited provide insights into successful implementations and best practices, underpinning the effectiveness of these strategies in real-world contexts.

21.6 Responsible Banking Practices for Sustainable Development

21.6.1 Ethical Lending and Investment Strategies

Responsible banking involves adopting ethical lending and investment strategies that prioritize social and environmental impact alongside financial returns. Banks can assess the social and environmental implications of their lending decisions and investments to avoid funding projects that may harm communities or the environment. By integrating environmental, social, and governance criteria into their decision-making processes, banks can align their lending and investment portfolios with SDGs [World Business Council for Sustainable Development (WBCSD), 2021].

21.6.2 Supporting Green and Inclusive Initiatives

Banks can play a vital role in promoting green initiatives and inclusive development. This can involve financing renewable energy projects, supporting sustainable agriculture and clean technologies, and funding initiatives that address social inequalities and uplift marginalized communities. By prioritizing green and inclusive initiatives, banks contribute to environmental preservation and the equitable distribution of resources, thereby furthering sustainable development [International Finance Corporation (IFC), 2020].

21.6.3 Corporate Social Responsibility (CSR) in Digital Banking

Digital banking platforms can be utilized as channels for CSR initiatives. Banks can use their digital presence to raise awareness about social and environmental issues, engage customers in sustainable actions, and promote responsible financial practices. Incorporating options for customers to donate to social causes through digital banking apps or websites is one way to integrate CSR into digital banking services [European Banking Federation (EBF), 2019].

By adopting responsible banking practices, financial institutions contribute to the overall sustainable development agenda. Ethical lending and investment strategies, support for green and inclusive initiatives, and integrating CSR into digital banking services demonstrate a bank's commitment to society, the environment, and sustainable economic growth. These practices also align with global efforts to achieve the United Nations' SDGs and create a positive impact on society and the planet. The references cited provide insights into industry best practices and guidelines for responsible banking that contribute to sustainable development.

21.7 Case Studies

21.7.1 Successful Examples of Customer-Centric Digital Banking

Case Study 1: ICICI Bank—iMobile App: ICICI Bank, one of India's leading private sector banks, has successfully implemented customer-centric digital banking through its iMobile app. The app offers a user-friendly interface, allowing customers to perform a wide range of banking transactions, including fund transfers, bill payments, and investment management. It incorporates personalized features such as expense analysis and targeted offers based on customer behavior. Through continuous enhancements and customer feedback, ICICI Bank has been able to provide a seamless and convenient banking experience, leading to increased customer satisfaction and loyalty (Economic Times, 2021).

21.7.2 Impact of Customer Experience Initiatives on Sustainable Development

Case Study 2: State Bank of India (SBI)—YONO Platform: The SBI launched the YONO (You Only Need One) platform, a comprehensive digital banking and lifestyle app. YONO offers a wide array of financial services and integrates with e-commerce platforms, providing customers with a unified digital experience. Through YONO, SBI has facilitated financial inclusion by providing access to banking services for previously unbanked populations. The platform also promotes sustainable development by enabling customers to make informed financial decisions and access a range of products and services in one place (SBI YONO, 2021).

21.7.3 Lessons Learned from Failures and Challenges in Customer-Focused Banking

Case Study 3: Axis Bank—Axis Direct Failure: Axis Bank, one of India's prominent private sector banks, faced challenges in its customer-focused digital banking strategy when its subsidiary, Axis Direct, encountered a technical glitch. The failure resulted in a temporary disruption of online trading services, leading to frustration among customers and negative impacts on the bank's reputation. This incident highlighted the importance of robust IT infrastructure, continuous monitoring, and rapid response mechanisms to prevent and address technical failures in customer-focused banking services (Business Standard, 2021).

Learning from both successes and failures is crucial for banks to continuously improve their customer-centric digital banking initiatives. These case studies demonstrate the significance of prioritizing customer experience, aligning digital banking efforts with SDGs, and ensuring robustness and reliability in digital platforms to deliver value to customers and contribute to the overall well-being of society. The references cited provide insights into real-world examples and incidents in the Indian banking industry that highlight the importance of customer-centricity and its impact on sustainable development (Khang, 2024b).

21.8 Regulatory Framework and Policy Recommendations

21.8.1 Role of Regulators in Promoting Customer Experience in Digital Banking

Regulators play a crucial role in promoting customer experience in digital banking by creating a conducive environment that safeguards customer interests while fostering innovation and competition. Some of the key roles of regulators include (RBI, 2021):

■ Consumer protection: Regulators should establish robust consumer protection frameworks that ensure transparency, fair treatment, and data privacy in digital banking transactions. Clear guidelines on liability for unauthorized transactions and mechanisms for dispute resolution protect customers from potential risks.
■ Technology standards: Regulators can set technology standards and guidelines for digital banking platforms to ensure security, interoperability, and seamless user experience. By establishing best practices for user authentication, encryption, and data storage, regulators enhance customer confidence in digital banking services.
■ Financial literacy initiatives: Collaborating with banks and other stakeholders, regulators can promote financial literacy initiatives to enhance customers' understanding of digital banking services, empowering them to make informed financial decisions.

21.8.2 Policy Recommendations for Fostering Sustainable Digital Banking Practices

■ Encourage collaboration and innovation: Policymakers should encourage collaboration between traditional banks, Fintech companies, and other stakeholders to foster innovation in digital banking. Regulatory sandboxes and pilot programs can facilitate the testing of new technologies and business models, promoting sustainable growth (Financial Conduct Authority (FCA), 2021).
■ Incentivize responsible banking: Policymakers can provide incentives for banks that adopt responsible and customer-centric practices. Tax benefits, reduced compliance burdens, or preferential treatment for sustainable initiatives can encourage banks to prioritize customer experience and support SDGs.
■ Digital literacy promotion: Policymakers should invest in promoting digital literacy among the population, particularly in rural and underserved areas. Public awareness campaigns, training programs, and community outreach efforts can enhance digital banking adoption and foster financial inclusion (United Nations Capital Development Fund (UNCDF), 2021).
■ Sustainable finance guidelines: Policymakers can develop guidelines for sustainable finance that encourage banks to allocate resources to environmentally and socially responsible projects. By incentivizing green lending and investment, policymakers contribute to sustainable development and environmental protection (IFC, 2020).

By adopting these policy recommendations, regulators can create an enabling environment for customer-centric and sustainable digital banking practices. These policies will promote financial inclusion, enhance customer experience, and drive sustainable development, ensuring that the benefits of digital banking reach all segments of society. The references cited provide insights into existing regulatory frameworks and policy documents that align with these recommendations.

21.9 Future Outlook and Challenges

21.9.1 Emerging Technologies and Their Impact on Customer Experience

Emerging technologies, such as artificial intelligence (AI), blockchain, biometrics, and augmented reality, are poised to revolutionize customer experience in digital banking. AI-powered Chatbots and virtual assistants will enhance personalized customer support, providing instant and accurate responses to queries. Blockchain technology will enable secure and transparent financial transactions, reducing settlement times and enhancing trust between customers and banks. Biometric authentication methods, such as fingerprint and facial recognition, will streamline login processes and enhance data security. Augmented reality will provide immersive and interactive experiences, facilitating financial education and decision-making.

21.9.2 Addressing Cybersecurity Risks and Data Protection Concerns

As digital banking evolves, cybersecurity risks and data protection concerns become more pronounced. Banks must continually invest in robust cybersecurity measures, including threat detection, encryption, and regular security audits. Compliance with data protection regulations, such as the General Data Protection Regulation and local data privacy laws, is essential to protect customer data. Additionally, enhancing customer awareness of security best practices and potential risks will empower them to exercise caution while using digital banking services.

21.9.3 Overcoming Barriers to Digital Adoption in Rural and Marginalized Communities

While digital banking has made significant strides in urban areas, rural and marginalized communities still face barriers to digital adoption. To overcome these challenges, banks need to adopt targeted strategies:

- Digital literacy programs: Initiating digital literacy programs in local languages will empower individuals in rural areas to navigate digital banking platforms confidently.
- Simplified interfaces: Designing simplified and intuitive user interfaces will make digital banking more accessible to customers with limited technological exposure.
- Agent-assisted banking: Establishing banking correspondents or agents in remote areas can bridge the gap between traditional banking and digital services, providing personalized assistance to customers.

By embracing emerging technologies responsibly, addressing cybersecurity risks, and focusing on targeted initiatives for digital adoption, banks can ensure a more inclusive and sustainable future for digital banking. These strategies will enable banks to cater to a diverse customer base, mitigate risks, and unlock the full potential of digital banking to contribute to sustainable development. The references cited provide insights into current trends and challenges in digital banking, shedding light on potential solutions for future development.

21.10 Conclusion

21.10.1 Summary of Key Findings

In this research paper, we explored the critical importance of prioritizing customer experience in digital banking for India's sustainable development. We discussed the digital banking landscape in India, the diverse customer segments, and their preferences. Strategies for enhancing customer experience, promoting financial literacy, and supporting responsible banking practices were examined. Additionally, case studies highlighted successful examples of customer-centric digital banking in India, as well as the impact of customer experience initiatives on sustainable development. We also acknowledged the challenges and lessons learned in customer-focused banking and provided policy recommendations for fostering sustainable digital banking practices.

21.10.2 The Role of Customer Experience in India's Sustainable Development Journey

Customer experience is a key driver of sustainable development in India's digital banking sector. By placing customers at the center of their digital banking initiatives, banks can foster financial inclusion, empower individuals with financial literacy, and support responsible banking practices. Enhanced customer experience leads to greater digital adoption, bridging the gap between urban and rural areas, and promoting inclusive economic growth. Moreover, customer-centric digital banking can contribute to achieving the United Nations' SDGs by fostering financial well-being, reducing poverty, and supporting environmentally responsible initiatives.

21.10.3 Call to Action for Banks, Policymakers, and Stakeholders

To realize the full potential of customer-centric digital banking for India's sustainable development, various stakeholders must take proactive steps:

- Banks: Prioritize customer experience by continuously improving digital banking platforms, tailoring services to diverse customer needs, and fostering financial literacy. Embrace responsible banking practices that align with SDGs.
- Policymakers: Create an enabling regulatory framework that supports innovation while safeguarding customer interests and data privacy. Encourage collaboration between banks, Fintech companies, and NGOs to promote financial inclusion and sustainable practices.
- Customers: Embrace digital banking services, enhance digital literacy, and provide feedback to banks to drive further improvements in customer experience.
- NGOs and civil society: Collaborate with banks and policymakers to promote financial literacy initiatives and bridge the digital divide in underserved communities.
- Regulators: Continuously monitor and update regulations to address emerging cybersecurity risks and ensure data protection in digital banking.

By collectively working toward customer-centric, sustainable digital banking practices, India can accelerate its journey toward economic growth, social inclusion, and environmental responsibility.

As India continues to evolve and embrace digital transformation, the pursuit of customer-centric, sustainable banking practices will be a driving force in shaping a more inclusive and prosperous future for all. The collaboration of banks, policymakers, stakeholders, and customers is vital to achieve these shared goals and ensure that digital banking contributes positively to India's sustainable development journey (Khang, 2023).

References

Aker, J. C., and Mbiti, I. M (2010). Mobile Phones and Economic Development in Africa. Journal of Economic Perspectives, 24(3), 207–232. https://www.aeaweb.org/articles?id=10.1257/jep.24.3.207

Bolton, R. N., and Lemon, K. N (1999). A Dynamic Model of Customers' Usage of Services: Usage as an Antecedent and Consequence of Satisfaction. Journal of Marketing Research, 36(2), 171–186. https://journals.sagepub.com/doi/abs/10.1177/002224379903600203

Business Standard. (2021). Axis Bank Apologises for Temporary Glitch in Online Trading. Retrieved from https://www.business-standard.com/article/finance/axis-bank-apologises-for-temporary-glitch-in-online-trading-121042200200_1.html

Economic Times. (2021). ICICI Bank's iMobile App Crosses 20 Million Installs. Retrieved from https://economictimes.indiatimes.com/industry/banking/finance/banking/icici-banks-imobile-app-crosses-20-million-installs/articleshow/84666619.cms

European Banking Federation (EBF). (2019). The European Banking Sector's Commitment to Society. Retrieved from https://www.ebf.eu/ebf-media-centre/banking-in-europe-ebf-publishes-2019-facts-figures/

Financial Conduct Authority (FCA). (2021). Regulatory Sandbox. Retrieved from https://www.fca.org.uk/firms/regulatory-sandbox

International Finance Corporation (IFC). (2020). Banking on Sustainability: How the Financial Industry Can Support the Sustainable Development Goals. Retrieved from https://www.ifc.org/content/dam/ifc/doc/mgrt/final-ifc-bankingonsustainability-web.pdf

Khang, A. *AI-Oriented Competency Framework for Talent Management in the Digital Economy: Models, Technologies, Applications, and Implementation*. (1st Ed.) (2024). CRC Press. https://doi.org/10.1201/9781003440901

Khang, A. (2024a). "Future Directions and Challenges in Designing Workforce Management Systems for Industry 4," In Khang A., *AI-Oriented Competency Framework for Talent Management in the Digital Economy: Models, Technologies, Applications, and Implementation*. (1st Ed.) (2024). CRC Press. https://doi.org/10.1201/9781003440901-1

Khang, A. (2024b). "Design and Modelling of AI-Oriented Competency Framework (AIoCF) for Information Technology Sector," In Khang A., *AI-Oriented Competency Framework for Talent Management in the Digital Economy: Models, Technologies, Applications, and Implementation*. (1st Ed.) (2024). CRC Press. https://doi.org/10.1201/9781003440901-17

Khang, A. (2024c). "Implementation of AIoCF Model and Tools for Information Technology Sector," In Khang A., *AI-Oriented Competency Framework for Talent Management in the Digital Economy: Models, Technologies, Applications, and Implementation*. (1st Ed.) (2024). CRC Press. https://doi.org/10.1201/9781003440901-20

Khang, A. *Advanced Technologies and AI-Equipped IoT Applications in High-Tech Agriculture* (1st Ed.) (2023). IGI Global Press. https://doi.org/10.4018/978-1-6684-9231-4

Klapper, L., and Singer, D. (2017). The Opportunities and Challenges of Fintech in Financial Inclusion.

Lusardi, A., and Mitchell, O. S. (2014). The Economic Importance of Financial Literacy: Theory and Evidence. Journal of Economic Literature, 52(1), 5–44.

Margvelashvili, I.; Kostava, M. Improving Financial Education Strategy for Sustainable Development. Economics Ecology Socium. Vol 4 No 3 P 1-11 (2020): Economics. https://ees-journal.com/index.php/journal/article/view/141

PwC. (2019). Sustainable Banking in Emerging Markets: The Case for a Customer-Centric Approach.

Reserve Bank of India (RBI). (2020). Annual Report. Retrieved from https://rbi.org.in/Scripts/BS_ViewMasDirections.aspx?id=12032

Reserve Bank of India (RBI). (2021). Master Direction on Digital Payment Security Controls. Retrieved from https://rbi.org.in/Scripts/BS_ViewMasDirections.aspx?id=12032

SBI YONO. (2021). About YONO. Retrieved from https://www.sbiyono.sbi/

Smith, R. E., and Meuter, M. L. (2020). Reducing Customer Privacy Concerns to Increase Digital Banking Adoption. Journal of Service Research, 23(1), 5–21.

United Nations Capital Development Fund (UNCDF). (2021). UNCDF in India – Annual Report 2020. Retrieved from https://www.undp.org/sites/g/files/zskgke326/files/2022-05/undp-annual-report-2021-v1.pdf

World Bank. (2020). Global Findex Database 2017: Measuring Financial Inclusion and the Fintech Revolution. Retrieved from https://globalfindex.worldbank.org/

World Business Council for Sustainable Development (WBCSD). (2021). SDG Sector Roadmap Guidelines for the Finance Sector.

Chapter 22

The Influence of E-banking Services on Customer Satisfaction of Banks

Paiman Ahmad, Makwan Jamil Mustafa, and Bestoon Othman

22.1 Introduction

Digitalization has been induced in all sectors of the economy; the banking sector has developed in the last decades. Through technological developments, the banking sector has evolved and banking services have transformed from human-based services to web-based banking systems. In this concern, banks have built better relations with their customers through online services and electronic connections become more customer-centric. There are a few categories of banks in Iraq including a central bank, commercial banks, investment banks, and Islamic banks. E-banking addresses the electronic connection between banks and customers to prepare, manage, and control financial transactions (Singh, Srivastava & Sinha, 2017).

Based on the current experiences and information introducing E-banking or Internet banking in Iraq is new. Years of conflict, wars, and political instability in the country have directly influenced technological advancements to get their ground, therefore, in Iraq E-banking is very new. E-banking has been developed in many advanced economies, while the developing world is late in catching up. In this regard, many challenges and factors have influenced digital banking and its development in the developing world. In this digital era, banks need to build their processes and structure by using digital resources completely to reach and support customers and employees (Martins, Oliveira & Popovič, 2021).

E-banking has been customer-friendly in terms of easy access to available services and time concerns. However, literature shows the development of E-banking is country-dependent, in which the country's circumstances and culture identify using E-banking at large. In this picture of comparing, the Middle East to the other regions, the evolution of E-banking services in the region is not as in Europe and Asia. Online banking provides various opportunities to customers in terms of banking services including online interactions, and other services, which reduce costs for customers (Chou & Chou, 2000).

DOI: 10.4324/9781003501947-22

As Internet banking has gained proper ground, the delivery channels boost transparency; it has promoted competition among the banks while making a profit is still a bank's top priority. Concerning the other benefits for banks, increasing and retaining customers depend on the provided services and benefits that customers have in their interactions with E-banking (Schaechter, 2002). Meanwhile, digital banking is not a problem-free system, as there are fears associated with hacking and lack of contact with the bank (Martins, Oliveira & Popovič, 2021). The digitalization process takes time and requires necessary up-to-date resources, skilled human resources, and financial assets.

It is vital to bear in mind that, banking service quality levels affect customer satisfaction and boost their loyalty. In terms of customer services, the E-banking service qualities affect customer satisfaction because a banking customer can access various services through online banking (Henman, 2020). In the banking sector similar to the other sectors customer satisfaction is built on privacy, responsiveness, reliability, and ease of use. To this end, customer satisfaction and service quality in all sectors are interrelated therefore banks are supposed to pay special attention to customer satisfaction.

In addition to this, customers may respond to any of these factors: the environment, capacity of the bank, human resources, and system quality differently. Which may indicate the degree of satisfaction and influence of customers in different circumstances. In this discussion, the importance of customer service is to be considered for assuring that the needs and expectations of the customers are met (Jun, Yang & Kim, 2004). As result, E-banking has been a tool among the means banks use to maintain customer retention and satisfaction. Moreover, service performance defines the degree of customer satisfaction. For achieving customer satisfaction, improving service quality has become the key influencer (Ajina et al., 2023; Haming et al., 2019; Truch, 2006).

22.2 Literature Review

Extensive literature exists on the variables examined in this study. Adopting any system requires time and effort in preparing, and accustoming customers to use it. In this regard, the priority should be the benefits that can change the attitude of customers toward a system or an application (Ajina et al., 2023). The most important approach, which helps an economy to align with the changes, is adaptability to rapid technological changes, especially in the financial area. Going forward, electronic banking is known as the wave of the future, which brings about a few benefits to consumers including ease and cost of transactions regardless of the challenges. Based on the evidence, the financial institutions have been among the first private sector entities to massively invest in the development of information technology, for growing in the market and making a profit, while bearing costs and considering the challenges (Arslanian & Fischer, 2019).

For instance, Yusfiarto (2021) delved into the impact of electronic banking service quality on customer loyalty, with a focus on banks in the Iranian city of Yazd. The study identified a lack of emphasis from banks and financial institutions on e-service quality, prompting an investigation into the key factors influencing banking service quality and their correlation with customer satisfaction.

Employing the e-SERVQUAL questionnaire and a seven-point Likert scale, the study involved 80 bank customers. Questionnaire items assessed aspects such as ease of use, time efficiency, suitability, intellectual property rights, and accuracy in utilizing e-services. Results revealed a positive correlation between service quality and customer perceptions, with e-service quality exerting a stronger influence on customer satisfaction compared to traditional services. Additionally, perceptions of e-service quality were found to surpass those of traditional service quality in terms of customer satisfaction (Khang, & Jadhav, et al., 2024).

22.2.1 Electronic Banking

Electronic banking is centered on the use of electronic delivery challenges for providing banking products and services, as a subset of electronic finance. While banking sectors are governed by rules imposed by the government or associated bodies. Very importantly, in the banking 4.0 environment, organizations can increasingly connect and integrate with partners, intermediaries, and customers through the Internet (Schaechter, 2002).

The introduction of the automated teller machine (ATM) in Finland marked a significant milestone in banking history, pioneering the emergence of E-banking and positioning the country as a leader in this domain before its widespread adoption in both developing and developed nations (Timilsina, 2023).

Developments in modern technologies have expanded competition among banks, engaged more customers, and offered opportunities to customers to get banking services 24/7. However, the challenges could always threaten customer satisfaction and attachment to E-banking, because of issues such as hacking, lack of direct contact with customers, and security (Hammoud, Bizri & El Baba, 2018).

Presently, customers seek the ability to perform banking transactions autonomously from any location and at any time, unrestricted by conventional banking hours. This trend is further driven by the need for efficient and cost-effective transactions such as purchasing goods, paying bills, and trading stocks. Consequently, the quality of financial services is characterized by principles of independence, adaptability, flexibility, and accessibility to meet evolving customer needs (Hammoud et al., 2018). In Lebanon, however, E-banking is primarily limited to Internet and mobile phone platforms, partly due to the slower development of IT infrastructure within the country. In essence, E-banking denotes the capability to conduct banking and financial activities electronically, utilizing Internet or mobile phone applications.

22.2.2 Customer Satisfaction

Customer satisfaction is a cornerstone concept in marketing research (Chaerudin & Syafarudin, 2021), encompassing various processes and factors that culminate in the pre- and post-purchase phases, including attitude changes, repeat purchases, and brand loyalty (Hammoud et al., 2018). According to Qazi et al. (2017), satisfaction arises when customers assess their expectations against their actual perceptions of a product or service. While several definitions of customer satisfaction have been proposed, the common thread among them is the comparison between pre- and post-consumption experiences of a product or service. Satisfaction is characterized as an emotional evaluation made after consumption (Qazi et al., 2017).

As Jun et al. (2004) addressed technology may position the business agents either to benefit from using advanced technology or encounter challenges in which it could all be regulated and centered on serving customers, which depends on timing, ease of using, different offerings, access to information…etc. Besides, meeting the needs and expectations of customers indicates the organization type is a customer-driven organization. Recent studies have investigated the effect of mobile service quality on customer satisfaction and loyalty, in all quality of service, risk, usefulness, cost, and trust have created the intention for customers to use mobile wallets. Similar to this, Singh et al. (2017) found that ease of use and trust determine the degree of satisfaction and the benefits they make.

In other words, loyalty shows the customers' preference in buying products from an organization because of their commitment to the product. Regardless of how important is customer loyalty for organizations, it has a strong relation to customer satisfaction, because of the tendency to buy the same product and services on every occasion while options and competitors are present in the market (Joudeh, Aljabbri & Khader, 2023).

In a related study, Tse and Wilton (1988) defined customer satisfaction as the consumer's response to the perceived gap between expectations and performance following consumption. Furthermore, studies suggest that the purchasing and consumption phases of a product or service can influence customer satisfaction perceptions (Chaerudin & Syafarudin, 2021). Consequently, customer satisfaction can be understood as the customer's emotional response, ranging from pleasure to displeasure, resulting from the perceived performance of a service or product relative to expectations (Tesfaye, 2017).

In alignment with these definitions, the present study defines customer satisfaction as the attitude formed by customers in response to the use of electronic banking services. Accordingly, attributes of electronic banking may either enhance, diminish, or maintain customer satisfaction.

22.2.3 Customer Satisfaction and Electronic Banking

As indicated, the primary objective of this study is to examine the quality of e-services offered by banks in Iraq and its impact on customer satisfaction. Relevant literature on this subject includes the findings of Carlson and O'Cass (2010), who established a consistent and positive correlation between e-service quality and customer satisfaction. Similarly, Osman and Sentosa (2013) concluded that the relationship between service quality and customer satisfaction is robust and adaptable. Jun et al. (2004), in their study, modified a simpler equation and determined that elevated service quality significantly contributes to higher levels of customer satisfaction.

Numerous other studies have reinforced the connection between customer satisfaction and E-banking services. For instance, in Hammoud et al.'s (2018) recent investigation, it was demonstrated that customers' satisfaction within the banking sector increases with the utilization of E-banking services. Additionally, San, Von, and Qureshi (2020) highlighted that e-service quality serves as the initial determinant of customer satisfaction, while Ismail et al. (2013) supported the idea that service quality is closely linked to the extent of customer satisfaction. Last, E-banking service quality was found to be significantly correlated with reliability and the level of customer satisfaction.

22.2.4 Effects of E-banking Service Dimensions

In addressing the effects of the main dimensions related to E-banking, each dimension has its influence on attracting and retention of customers. Determining the effect on new customers who lack experience and knowledge of using E-banking, it can be seen that frustration and threats could be affecting their decision to have E-banking. In considering risk in E-banking, some remote banks avoid regulations and supervision, therefore; it is vital to request the banks to be licensed (Arslanian & Fischer, 2019). Recently, financial institutions have worked on improving the dimensions of E-banking, and the quality of their services to meet the needs and expectations of customers.

Making E-banking affordable for all and providing equal access to services has still been a serious challenge in the context of many developing countries. Among the top concerns in this regard could be the speed, and access to E-banking, which on many occasions affect customers in the sector. Hence, speed encompasses various aspects such as the frequency of network connection disruptions, the time taken to navigate Internet banking websites, the duration customers spend waiting for page responses, and the promptness of banks' responses to customer complaints (Ling et al., 2016).

Typically, the speed of Internet banking is affected by factors like extensive and high-resolution graphics and inefficient host servers (Hammoud et al., 2018). Achieving success in E-banking hinges significantly on speed (Ayinaddis, Taye & Yirsaw, 2023). In fact, for customers security and privacy have a crucial influence on customer satisfaction and attitude toward E-banking, as risk management can only be regulated and eliminated by the banks. Indeed, people have serious concerns about data, personal information, and knowledge regarding using apps or other computers or mobile apps/programs and using digital forms of money (Lee & Wong, 2016; Pearson & Benameur, 2010).

Flavián and Guinalíu (2006) discovered privacy to have a considerable implication for consumer satisfaction. Ahmad & Al-Zu'bi (2021) noted that consumer expectations regarding a bank's products and services are influenced by various factors, including security. Lee, Lee and Yim (2020) emphasized the critical role of security in Internet banking, where numerous network security protocols work behind the scenes to encrypt packets, unbeknownst to customers. Customers are pleased with website security and privacy, ease of use, and the bank's reputation, influencing their choice of E-banking channels (Inegbedion et al., 2020).

Alongside the concern of security, responsiveness affects customers, in terms of bank and employees' willingness to assist their clients promptly, supporting customers to meet their demands and expectations in an expected period (Ali & Raza, 2017; Felix, 2017; Haming et al., 2019). Moreover, responsiveness assists organizations in maintaining consumer interest, by assuring swift responses, which enhances satisfaction and loyalty (Angusamy, Yee & Kuppusamy, 2022).

In line with responsiveness comes reliability in E-banking similar to any other service, reliability means the ability to deliver and perform the service's commitment accurately and steadily. As noted reliability is an influential dimension, that boosts customer satisfaction. In addition to that reliability influences banks' performance by boosting customer satisfaction. In some way, fears of the customer concerning reliability could be associated with the tangibility dimension, because in E-banking customers, who have less information and experience, including the infrastructure, visual factors, and attractiveness, which positively affect service at the banks, and influence customer satisfaction deeply. In all the scenarios, one fact is vital, customers are known as the main stakeholders for banks, therefore; their attitude is shifted by their satisfaction with the quality of service they receive during their interactions with the bank (Felix, 2017; Ananth, Ramesh & Prabaharan, 2011; Ayinaddis et al., 2023).

When considering the banking sector in the context of Iraq similar to many of the post-conflict affected countries, the sector in terms of developing E-banking and e-service is at the beginning of its journey. Associating ease of use with customer satisfaction could be a serious question, as it could mean online customer support and customer willingness to learn about the new e-services in E-banking. In line with this, E-banking is considered as a means for easing the life of people, by enabling them to use technology devices to carry out their financial needs (Timilsina, 2023).

Perceived ease of use, as defined by Alalwan et al. (2016), reflects consumers' perception of minimal effort required in online banking usage. It is a driving force behind electronic banking, providing convenience, security, standardization, and easy access to banking services through information and communication technologies. Ease of use significantly affects client satisfaction with E-banking (Martins, Oliveira & Popovič, 2014). Additionally, Ling et al. (2016) concluded in their study that convenience of use and user-friendliness are critical determinants of online banking adoption, usage, and consumer satisfaction in Malaysia. The research framework for this study is adapted to the data and the study based on the related studies is depicted in Figure 22.1.

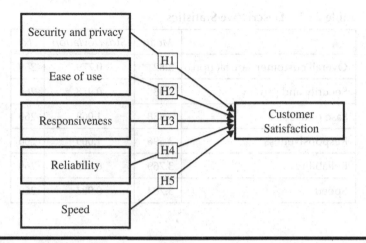

Figure 22.1   Research framework.

Source: From Authors' data.

22.2.5 Research Hypotheses

- H1: Security and privacy have a relationship with customer satisfaction toward E-banking.
- H2: Ease of use has a relationship with customer satisfaction toward E-banking.
- H3: Responsiveness has a relationship with customer satisfaction toward E-banking.
- H4: Reliability has a relationship with customer satisfaction toward E-banking.
- H5: Speed has a relationship with customer satisfaction toward E-banking.

22.3 Methodology

This study used a quantitative method; a survey questionnaire was used as a means for collecting data, in which a sample of 260 responses was collected (Altobishi, Erboz & Podruzsik, 2018; Felix, 2017; Sadowski, 2017). The questionnaire comprised of two sections: the first section gathered demographic information about the respondents, while the second section contained items measuring independent variables including Security and Privacy, Ease of Use, Speed, Responsiveness, and Reliability, alongside the dependent variable, Customer Satisfaction. For analyzing the data SPSS software version 27 has been used, incorporating Descriptive Statistics, Reliability Analysis, and Multiple Linear Regression Analysis (Khang, Dave & Jadhav et al., 2024).

22.4 Analysis and Findings

22.4.1 Demographic Profile

The results of the demographic analysis reveal that 58% of the respondents were male, while 42% were female. The majority of respondents fell within the age group of 21 to 25 years, accounting for 35% (91 respondents), followed by those aged 26 to 30 years, comprising 25% (65 respondents), and 20% (52 respondents) falling under the category of under 20 years old. Respondents

Table 22.1 Descriptive Statistics

	Mean	Std. Deviation	N
Overall customer satisfaction	3.82	0.779	260
Security and privacy	3.438	0.978	260
Ease of use	3.338	1.068	260
Responsiveness	3.596	1.009	260
Reliability	3.769	0.889	260
Speed	3.704	0.923	260

in the age ranges of 31 to 35 and 36 and above constituted 15% and 5%, respectively, with 39 and 13 respondents in each category.

Regarding education level, the data shows that the majority of respondents, 65% (169 individuals), hold undergraduate degrees, followed by 15% (39 respondents) with diplomas. Other education levels, including vocational training and associate degrees, account for 10% (26 respondents), while 5% each hold master's degrees and PhDs, totaling 13 respondents for each category.

In terms of banking habits, 202 respondents, constituting 80% of the total, reported using more than one bank, while the remaining 20% dealt with only one bank, comprising 75 respondents out of the 260 surveyed. Additionally, the utilization of E-banking services among respondents was assessed, with 70% (182 respondents) using E-banking for transactions, 20% (52 respondents) for fund transfers, and 10% (26 respondents) utilizing ATM services provided by E-banking.

22.4.2 Descriptive Statistics

Table 22.1 presents the average customer satisfaction level regarding E-banking services. According to this statistical overview, E-banking customers exhibit a satisfaction level above the acceptable threshold, with an average score of 3.82 on a five-point Likert scale. The table further outlines the primary factors contributing to customer satisfaction in E-banking. Based on the mean values, customers express significant satisfaction with aspects such as Security and Privacy, Ease of Use, Responsiveness, Reliability, and Speed. This satisfaction stems from prompt services like money deposits and withdrawals, consistent server functionality, ATM accessibility, as well as contentment with equipment, physical infrastructure, and promotional materials. However, there are areas of lesser satisfaction, particularly in terms of ease of use for online services. Nonetheless, a regression analysis will be conducted to ascertain whether these mean scores exceed the neutral satisfaction level and to elucidate the variables influencing satisfaction levels in E-banking in Iraq (Khang, Dave, & Katore, et al., 2024).

22.4.3 Assessment of Measurement Model

As indicated in Table 22.2, the average variance extracted (AVE) exceeds 0.5, indicating convergence validity for all loadings and research variables. Additionally, the composite reliability (CR) values surpass the 0.7 threshold for all latent variables.

Table 22.2   Variables Measurement Model

Variables	No. of Items	Cronbach's Alpha	Composite Reliability	Average Variance Extracted (AVE)
Customer satisfaction	5	0.851	0.900	0.692
Security and privacy	5	0.924	0.946	0.814
Ease of use	5	0.986	0.986	0.672
Responsiveness	5	0.983	0.984	0.737
Reliability	5	0.931	0.948	0.785
Speed	5	0.927	0.948	0.821

Thus, the findings indicate that the components under scrutiny maintain commendable reliability. Furthermore, employing Cronbach's α reliability method, all latent values surpass 0.6, signifying robust reliability of the assessed material. The assessment of discriminant validity, as depicted in Table 22.3, highlights that the square roots of the AVE for all variables exceed interstructural correlations (Hair et al., 2014). As displayed in Table 22.2, the latent variables are characterized by the convergence validity of their loading factors.

AVE values surpass 0.5 for all research variables, and the CR values exceed the 0.7 threshold for all latent variables, suggesting sound reliability of the assessed components. Additionally, employing the Cronbach's α reliability test, all latent values exceed 0.6, providing ample evidence for the reliability of the assessment material (Hair et al., 2014). Table 22.3 illustrates the assessment of discriminant validity, revealing that the AVE square root values for all variables surpass inter-structural correlations. Hence, we can infer that the measurement model exhibits high reliability and its validity accurately indicates the research variables.

Table 22.3   Discriminant Validity of Latent Constructs

	Customer Satisfaction	Security and Privacy	Ease of Use	Responsiveness	Reliability	Speed
Customer satisfaction	0.832					
Security and privacy	0.832	0.899				
Ease of use	0.751	0.825	0.923			
Responsiveness	0.807	0.873	0.834	0.904		
Reliability	0.749	0.790	0.811	0.828	0.882	
Speed	0.712	0.766	0.735	0.807	0.784	0.895

Table 22.4   Model Summary

Model	R	R Square	Adjusted R Square	Std. Error of the Estimate
1	0.605[a]	0.358	0.346	0.42133
Predictors: (Constant), Security and privacy, Ease of use, Speed, Responsiveness, and Reliability				

[a] Dependent variable: Customer satisfaction.

22.4.4 Hypotheses Testing

Multiple Linear Regression Analysis was employed to examine the hypotheses formulated in the study. The model summary, as depicted in Table 22.4, illustrates an R square value of 0.358, indicating that 35.8% of the variance in customer satisfaction is accounted for by the independent variables, namely Security and Privacy, Ease of Use, Speed, Responsiveness, and Reliability. The remaining 64.2% of the variance in customer satisfaction is attributed to other factors.

The results of the ANOVA in Table 22.5 show an F-value of 28.151 and the p-value less than 0.001, prove that the overall regression model is significant at 0.1%.

According to Table 22.6, the variables Security and Privacy (Beta = 0.149, p-value < 0.05), Responsiveness (Beta = 0.256, p-value < 0.05), Reliability (Beta = 0.199, p-value < 0.05), and

Table 22.5   ANOVA results

Model		Sum of Squares	df	Mean Square	F	Sig.
1	Regression	21.954	4	5.488	28.151	0.000[b]
	Residual	38.018	195	0.195		
	Total	59.972	199			

[b] Predictors: (Constant), Security and privacy, Ease of use, Speed, Responsiveness, and Reliability

Table 22.6   Coefficients

Hypotheses		Unstandardized Coefficients		t-Value	P-Values
		β	Std. Error		
H1	Security and privacy -> Customer satisfaction	0.149	0.006	23.365	0.000
H2	Ease of use -> Customer satisfaction	0.104	0.073	1.420	0.157
H3	Responsiveness -> Customer satisfaction	0.256	0.006	42.313	0.000
H4	Reliability -> Customer satisfaction	0.199	0.007	28.553	0.000
H5	Speed -> Customer satisfaction	0.158	0.006	26.189	0.000

Speed (Beta = 0.158, p-value < 0.05) exhibit a significant influence on customer satisfaction with E-banking services. Consequently, hypotheses H1, H3, H4, and H5 are validated. However, the p-value for Ease of use exceeds 0.05, indicating that it lacks a significant impact on customer satisfaction. Therefore, hypothesis H2 is not supported.

22.5 Discussion

This study took a journey to examine the effect of each dimension of service quality on customer satisfaction in E-banking in the case of a selected sample of Iraqi banks. The service quality dimensions include; Security, Reliability, Speed, Responsiveness, and Ease of use, their overall influence on customer satisfaction has been addressed. Based on the results of this study, service quality dimensions, have a great influence on customer satisfaction. As noted in this study, a no Table Correlation was found between security, and privacy, with the customer satisfaction of E-banking (Khang & Hajimahmud, 2024).

This crucial result aligns with the findings of Hoehle, Huff and Goode (2012) and Toor et al. (2016), which also underscored the positive and significant relationship between security and privacy and E-banking customer satisfaction. It is in part significant for banks to consider issues of privacy, and security of apps and services in E-banking, banks have to think and consider dimensions of service quality in the conduct to meet the needs and expectations of consumers, and to achieve a high rate of customer satisfaction.

Another crucial finding, which has a direct effect on customer satisfaction, has been the responsiveness of banks, and their employees. This finding as an essential aspect is also found in earlier research studies as in Chen (2013) and Khatoon, Zhengliang and Hussain (2020). Overall, customers consider banking services and their responsiveness as influential on their use of the bank services, and remaining buying and using the same services and products. Meanwhile, poor responsiveness increases customer dissatisfaction, which is not in favor of E-banking growth and advancement consistently.

When dealing with service failures and effectiveness in E-banking, the findings of this study show a positively significant relationship between reliability and customer satisfaction, which is consistent with results in Dabholkar (1996) and Asad, Mohajerani and Nourseresh (2016) studies. To this end, literature considers the importance of reliability in boosting customer satisfaction, in particular when new technologies are once addressed. Felix (2017) these dimensions are not the only influential ones in terms of customer satisfaction, trust, and speed affect the ease of use. While, in this study, a finding shows that ease of use does not significantly influence E-banking customer satisfaction. However, this finding is in contradiction with earlier research studies by Asad et al. (2016) and Lee and Wong (2016). In general, introducing new technologies and services creates the concern of ease of use for customers, especially if the system is advanced and complicated to use, the complexity in using might create challenges for customers who lack prior experience and knowledge in using E-banking.

Finally, speed demonstrates a positive relationship with customer satisfaction toward E-banking; this finding supports hypothesis number H5. Ling et al. (2016) demonstrated a positive relationship between the speed of loading Internet banking websites and customer satisfaction. Furthermore, Amin (2016) implied that the speed of Internet banking webpage responses is a critical factor in customer satisfaction. In this context, the environment, preparedness, and accessibility of E-banking in Iraq, is relatively new and some people in the rural areas might encounter challenges of speed due to their geographical locations.

22.6 Conclusion

This study examines the relationship between security and privacy, responsiveness, reliability, and speed with customer satisfaction in E-banking. E-banking providers should prioritize enhancing these four factors to improve customer satisfaction. Although the ease of use variable does not exhibit a significant relationship with customer satisfaction in this study, E-banking providers cannot overlook its importance, as previous research has demonstrated its significance in fulfilling customer satisfaction in E-banking.

This research provides valuable insights for the consumers who use E-banking by disclosing strategies and approaches for banks to prioritize customers and consider the main dimensions of service quality, in addressing customer satisfaction as their top priority. A few recommendations can be of use to banks and financial institutions while introducing new technologies to provide their services. In which, regulating their services to improve customer satisfaction, and keep their business growing. Assuring that service quality dimensions are in service to support customers to meet their goals, needs, and expectations. As a developing country, the banking sector in Iraq is at the beginning of developing E-banking, thus government and private sector banks have to significantly improve access to technology, invest in assuring service quality and boost customer satisfaction (Khang, Inna et al., 2024).

References

Ajina, A. S., Joudeh, J. M. M., Ali, N. N., Zamil, A. M., & Hashem, T. N. (2023). The effect of mobile-wallet service dimensions on customer satisfaction and loyalty: An empirical study. Cogent Business & Management, 10(2). https://doi.org/10.1080/23311975.2023.2229544

Alalwan, A. A., Dwivedi, Y. K., Rana, N. P. P, & Williams, M. D. (2016). Consumer adoption of mobile banking in Jordan: Examining the role of usefulness, ease of use, perceived risk and self-efficacy. Journal of Enterprise Information Management, 29(1), 118–139. https://doi.org/10.1108/JEIM-04-2015-0035

Ali, M., & Raza, S. A. (2017). Service quality perception and customer satisfaction in Islamic banks of Pakistan: The modified SERVQUAL model. Total Quality Management & Business Excellence, 28(5–6), 559–577. https://doi.org/10.1080/14783363.2015.1100517

Altobishi, T., Erboz, G., & Podruzsik, S. (2018). E-banking effects on customer satisfaction: The survey on clients in Jordan banking sector. International Journal of Marketing Studies, 10(2), 151. https://doi.org/10.5539/ijms.v10n2p151.

Ahmad A., & Al-Zu'bi HA (2021). E-banking functionality and outcomes of customer satisfaction: an empirical investigation. International journal of marketing studies, 2011. https://www.researchgate.net/profile/Hasan-Al-Zubi/publication/49610975_E-banking_Functionality_and_Outcomes_of_Customer_Satisfaction_An_Empirical_Investigation/links/02e7e538793ee2887c000000/E-banking-Functionality-and-Outcomes-of-Customer-Satisfaction-An-Empirical-Investigation.pdf

Amin, M. (2016). Internet banking service quality and its implication on e-customer satisfaction and e-customer loyalty. International Journal of Bank Marketing, 34(3), 280–306. https://doi.org/10.1108/IJBM-10-2014-0139

Ananth, A., Ramesh, R., & Prabaharan, B. (2011). Service quality gap analysis in private sector banks–A customers perspective. Indian Journal of Commerce and Management Studies, 2(1), 245–253. https://mpra.ub.uni-muenchen.de/id/eprint/29505

Angusamy, A., Yee, C. J., & Kuppusamy, J. (2022). E-banking: An empirical study on customer satisfaction. Journal of System and Management Sciences, 12(4), 27–38. https://doi.org/10.33168/JSMS.2022.0402

Arslanian, H., & Fischer, F. (2019). The Future of Finance, the Impact of Fintech, AI, Crypto on Financial Services, Cham, Switzerland, Palgrave Macmillan. https://doi.org/10.1007/978-3-030-14533-0

Asad, M. M., Mohajerani, N. S., & Nourseresh, M. (2016). Prioritizing factors affecting customer satisfaction in the internet banking system based on cause and effect relationships. Procedia Economics and Finance, 36, 210–219. https://doi.org/10.1016/S2212-5671(16)30032-6

Ayinaddis, S. G., Taye, B. A., & Yirsaw, B. G. (2023). Examining the effect of electronic banking service quality on customer satisfaction and loyalty: An implication for technological innovation, Journal of Innovation and Entrepreneurship (2023) 12:22 https://doi.org/10.1186/s13731-023-00287-y

Carlson, J., & O'Cass, A. (2010). Exploring the relationships between e-service quality, satisfaction, attitudes and behaviours in content-driven e-service web sites. Journal of Services Marketing, 24(2), 112–127. https://doi.org/10.1108/08876041011031091

Chaerudin, S. M., & Syafarudin, A. (2021). The effect of product quality, service quality, price on product purchasing decisions on consumer satisfaction. Ilomata International Journal of Tax and Accounting, 2(1), 61–70. https://doi.org/10.52728/ijtc.v2i1.202

Chen, C. (2013). Perceived risk, usage frequency of mobile banking services. Managing Service Quality: An International Journal, 23(5), 410–436. https://doi.org/10.1108/MSQ-10-2012-0137

Chou, D. C., & Chou, A. Y. (2000). A guide to the internet revolution in banking. Information Systems Management, 17(2), 47–53. https://doi.org/10.1201/1078/43191.17.2.20000301/31227.6

Dabholkar, P. A. (1996). Consumer evaluations of new technology-based self-service options: An investigation of alternative models of service quality. International Journal of Research in Marketing, 13(1), 29–51. https://doi.org/10.1016/0167-8116(95)00027-5

Felix, R. (2017). Service quality and customer satisfaction in selected banks in Rwanda. Journal of Business and Finance Affairs, 6, 246. https://doi.org/10.4172/2167-0234.1000246.

Flavián, C., & Guinalíu, M. (2006). Consumer trust, perceived security and privacy policy: Three basic elements of loyalty to a web site. Industrial Management & Data Systems, 106(5), 601–620. https://doi.org/10.1108/02635570610666403

Hair, J. F. Jr, Sarstedt, M., Hopkins, L., & Kuppelwieser, V. G. (2014). Partial least squares structural equation modeling (PLS-SEM): An emerging tool in business research. European Business Review, 26(2), 106–121. https://doi.org/10.1108/EBR-10-2013-0128

Haming, M., Murdifin, I., Syaiful, A. Z., & Putra, A. H. P. K. (2019). The application of SERVQUAL distribution in measuring customer satisfaction of retails company. Journal of Distribution Science, 17(2), 25–34. https://koreascience.kr/article/JAKO201915658236448.page

Hammoud, J., Bizri, R. M., & El Baba, I. (2018). The impact of E-banking service quality on customer satisfaction: Evidence from the Lebanese banking sector. Sage Open, 8(3). https://doi.org/10.1177/2158244018790633

Henman, P. (2020). Improving public services using artificial intelligence: Possibilities, pitfalls, governance. Asia Pacific Journal of Public Administration, 42(4), 209–221. https://doi.org/10.1080/23276665.2020.1816188

Hoehle, H., Huff, S., & Goode, S. (2012). The role of continuous trust in information systems continuance. Journal of Computer Information Systems, 52(4), 1–9. https://www.tandfonline.com/doi/abs/10.1080/08874417.2012.11645571

Inegbedion, H., Inegbedion, E. E., Osifo, S. J., Eze, S. C., Ayeni, A., & Akintimehin, O. (2020). Exposure to and usage of E-banking channels: Implications for bank customers' awareness and attitude to E-banking in Nigeria. Journal of Science and Technology Policy Management, 11(2), 133–148. https://doi.org/10.1108/JSTPM-02-2019-0024

Ismail, A., Ridzuan, A. A., Rose, N. I. R., Abdullah, M. M. B., Rahman, M. S., & Francis, S. K. (2013). Examining the relationship between service quality and customer satisfaction: A factor specific approach. Journal of Industrial Engineering and Management (JIEM), 6(2), 654–667. https://doi.org/10.3926/jiem.548

Joudeh, A. M., Aljabbri, M. A., & Khader, J. A. (2023). The impact of marketing mix of financial services on customer satisfaction and competitive advantage of money exchange companies from the customers' perspective. Seybold, 18(2), 1–16. https://doi.org/10.17605/OSF.IO/VKZ6F

Jun, M., Yang, Z., & Kim, D. (2004). Customers' perceptions of online retailing service quality and their satisfaction. International Journal of Quality & Reliability Management, 21(8), 817–840. https://doi.org/10.1108/02656710410551728

Khang, A., Dave, T., Jadhav, B., Katore, D., & Dave, D. (2024). "Gig Financial Economy- Big Data and Analytics," In Khang A., Jadhav B., Hajimahmud V. A., & Satpathy I. The Synergy of AI and Fintech in the Digital Gig Economy (1st Ed.). CRC Press. https://doi.org/10.1201/9781032720104-16

Khang, A., Dave, T., Katore, D., Jadhav, B., & Dave, D. (2024). "Leveraging Blockchain and Smart Contracts for Gig Payments," In Khang A., Jadhav B., Hajimahmud V. A., & Satpathy I. The Synergy of AI and Fintech in the Digital Gig Economy (1st Ed.). CRC Press. https://doi.org/10.1201/9781032720104-11

Khang, A., & Hajimahmud, V. A. (2024). "Introduction to the Gig Economy," In Khang A., Jadhav B., Hajimahmud V. A., & Satpathy I. The Synergy of AI and Fintech in the Digital Gig Economy (1st Ed.). CRC Press. https://doi.org/10.1201/9781032720104-1

Khang, A., Inna, S.-O., Alla, K., Rostyslav, S., Rudenko, M., Lidia, R., & Kristina, B. (2024). "Management Model 6.0 and Business Recovery Strategy of Enterprises in the Era of Digital Economy," In Khang, A., Gujrati, R., Uygun, H., Tailor R. K., & Gaur, S. Data-Driven Modelling and Predictive Analytics in Business and Finance (1st Ed.). CRC Press. https://doi.org/10.1201/9781032618845-16

Khang, A., Jadhav, B., Dave, T., & Katore, T. (2024). Artificial Intelligence (AI) in Fintech - Enhancing Financial Services. In Khang A., Jadhav B., Hajimahmud V. A., & Satpathy I. The Synergy of AI and Fintech in the Digital Gig Economy (1st Ed.). CRC Press. https://doi.org/10.1201/9781032720104-10

Khatoon, S., Zhengliang, X., & Hussain, H. (2020). The mediating effect of customer satisfaction on the relationship between electronic banking service quality and customer purchase intention: Evidence from the Qatar banking sector. Sage Journals, 10(2), 1–17. https://doi.org/10.1177/2158244020935887

Lee, K., Lee, S. Y., & Yim, K. (2020). Classification and analysis of security techniques for the user terminal area in the Internet banking service. Security and Communication Networks, 2020, 1–16. https://doi.org/10.1155/2020/7672941

Lee, W. O., & Wong, L. S. (2016). Determinants of mobile commerce customer loyalty in Malaysia. Procedia-Social and Behavioral Sciences, 224, 60–67. https://doi.org/10.1016/j.sbspro.2016.05.400

Ling, G. M., Fern, Y. S., Boon, L. K., & Huat, T. S. (2016). Understanding customer satisfaction of internet banking: A case study in Malacca. Procedia Economics and Finance, 37, 80–85. https://doi.org/10.1016/S2212-5671(16)30096-X

Martins, C., Oliveira, T., & Popovič, A. (2014). Understanding the internet banking adoption: A unified theory of acceptance and use of technology and perceived risk application. International Journal of Information Management, 34(1), 1–13. https://doi.org/10.1016/j.ijinfomgt.2013.06.002.

Osman, Z., & Sentosa, I. (2013). Influence of customer satisfaction on service quality and trust relationship in Malaysian rural tourism. Business and Management Quarterly Review, 4(2), 12–25. https://ssrn.com/abstract=2735588

Pearson, S., & Benameur, A (2010, November). Privacy, security and trust issues arising from cloud computing. In 2010 IEEE Second International Conference on Cloud Computing Technology and Science (pp. 693–702). IEEE. https://doi.org/10.1109/CloudCom.2010.66

Qazi, A., Tamjidyamcholo, A., Raj, R. G., Hardaker, G., & Standing, C. (2017). Assessing consumers' satisfaction and expectations through online opinions: Expectation and disconfirmation approach. Computers in Human Behavior, 75, 450–460. https://doi.org/10.1016/j.chb.2017.05.025

Sadowski, B. M. (2017). Advanced users and the adoption of high-speed broadband: Results of a living lab study in the Netherlands. Technological Forecasting and Social Change, 115, 1–14. https://doi.org/10.1016/j.techfore.2016.09.009

San, W. H., Von, W. Y., & Qureshi, M. I. (2020). The impact of e-service quality on customer satisfaction in Malaysia. Journal of Marketing and Information Systems, 3(1), 46–62. https://doi.org/10.31580/jmis.v3i1.1452

Schaechter, MA. (2002). Issue in Electronic banking: an overview, IMF Policy Discussion Paper 02/6, International Monetary Fund. https://www.google.com/books?hl=en&lr=&id=RpAYEAAAQBAJ&oi=fnd&pg=PP1

Singh, N., Srivastava, S., & Sinha, N. (2017). Consumer preference and satisfaction of m-wallets: A study on North Indian consumers. International Journal of Bank Marketing, 35(6), 944–965. https://doi.org/10.1108/IJBM-06-2016-0086

Tesfaye, E. (2017). Assessing the Levels of Key Account Customers Satisfaction on Ethio Telecom Mobile Service (Doctoral Dissertation, St. Mary's University).

Timilsina, P. (2023). Customer satisfaction towards E-banking service offered by Prabhu Bank Limited. Contemporary Research: An Interdisciplinary Academic Journal, 6(2), 164–175. https://doi.org/10.3126/craiaj.v6i2.60254

Toor, A., Hunain, M., Hussain, T., Ali, S., & Shahid, A. (2016).The impact of E-banking on customer satisfaction: Evidence from banking sector of Pakistan. Journal of Business Administration Research, 5(2). https://doi.org/10.5430/jbar.v5n2p27

Truch, E. (2006). Lean consumption and its influence on brand, Journal of Consumer Behavior, 5, 157–165.

Tse, D. K., & Wilton, P. C. (1988). Models of consumer satisfaction formation: An extension. Journal of Marketing Research, 25(2), 204–212. https://doi.org/10.2307/3172652

Yusfiarto, R. (2021). The relationship between m-banking service quality and loyalty: Evidence in Indonesian Islamic Banking. Asian Journal of Islamic Management (AJIM), 23–33. https://doi.org/10.20885/ajim.vol3.iss1.art3

Chapter 23

Culture Currency: How Human Resource (HR) Shapes Success in Financial Institutions and Services

Ashwini. Y. Sonawane and Alex Khang

23.1 Introduction

23.1.1 Culture Currencies

Culture Currency encapsulates the intangible yet invaluable assets embedded within the organizational culture of financial institutions. Just as currency serves as a medium of exchange in economic transactions, culture functions as the currency of interactions, shaping the attitudes, behaviors, and decisions of employees and customers alike. Consider, for instance, a retail bank renowned for its customer-centric culture, where employees are empowered to go above and beyond to ensure client satisfaction. This culture becomes a form of currency, fostering loyalty, trust, and repeat business among customers. Conversely, in an investment firm where risk-taking and innovation are celebrated, the organizational culture becomes a driving force behind bold investment strategies and pioneering financial products.

In examining the notion of Culture Currency, it becomes evident that human resource management (HRM) practices are the primary architects of this cultural framework within financial institutions. Through recruitment, training, performance management, and leadership development, human resources (HR) professionals mold the attitudes and behaviors of employees, shaping the culture that defines the institution's identity and influences its success. For instance, Goldman Sachs, a global investment banking firm, is renowned for its rigorous recruitment process that seeks individuals who not only possess exceptional skills but also align with the firm's culture of excellence and integrity. This emphasis on cultural fit ensures that employees uphold the values and standards that underpin the firm's reputation and success.

DOI: 10.4324/9781003501947-23

23.1.2 The Intersection of HR and Service Excellence

The impact of Culture Currency extends beyond the internal dynamics of financial institutions to profoundly influence the delivery of services to customers. In a competitive marketplace where differentiation is paramount, the organizational culture becomes a critical differentiator, shaping the customer experience and determining the institution's standing in the industry. Consider the example of USAA, a financial services company serving military members and their families, which has cultivated a culture of empathy and understanding toward its unique customer base. This culture not only resonates with customers but also permeates every aspect of the institution's service delivery, from tailored financial products to personalized customer support (Khang, 2024c).

At the heart of this intersection between HR and service excellence lies the role of employee engagement and satisfaction. Studies have consistently shown that engaged employees, who feel valued, motivated, and aligned with the organization's mission, are more likely to deliver exceptional service experiences to customers. For instance, Southwest Airlines, known for its exceptional customer service, attributes much of its success to its employee-centric culture, where employees are empowered, respected, and encouraged to bring their authentic selves to work. This culture of empowerment translates into tangible benefits for customers, who experience the warmth and hospitality synonymous with the Southwest brand.

As we embark on this research journey, we seek to unravel the intricate connections between HRM practices, organizational culture, and service excellence within financial institutions. By exploring real-world examples and delving into empirical research, we aim to uncover the mechanisms through which Culture Currency influences the success of financial institutions and shapes the services they provide to customers.

In the dynamic and competitive realm of the financial services industry, the importance of organizational culture as a driver of success has garnered increasing attention. With its profound influence on employee behavior, customer interactions, and overall performance, organizational culture has emerged as a significant determinant of an institution's standing in the market. This research endeavors to delve deeper into the concept of "Culture Currency" within financial institutions, examining how HRM practices serve as the catalyst for shaping and leveraging this cultural capital.

23.1.3 The Significance of Organizational Culture in Financial Institutions

Organizational culture, defined as the shared values, beliefs, norms, and behaviors that characterize an institution, has been widely recognized as a critical factor in determining its success. In the context of financial institutions, where trust, integrity, and customer confidence are paramount, the importance of a strong and positive organizational culture cannot be overstated.

Numerous studies have highlighted the correlation between organizational culture and various performance indicators within financial institutions. For instance, research by Denison and Mishra (1995) found that strong organizational cultures were associated with higher levels of employee satisfaction, commitment, and productivity. Similarly, a study by Cameron and Quinn (2011) revealed that institutions with a culture aligned with their strategic objectives tended to outperform their peers in terms of financial performance and market share.

23.1.4 The Role of HRM in Cultivating Culture Currency

Central to the creation and maintenance of a positive organizational culture within financial institutions is the role of HRM. Through its myriad functions, including recruitment, selection, training, performance management, and leadership development, HRM plays a pivotal role in shaping the attitudes, behaviors, and values of employees.

23.2 Literature Review

23.2.1 Introduction

In today's dynamic financial landscape, the role of HR in shaping organizational culture has gained significant attention. This literature review aims to explore the relationship between HR practices and the success of financial institutions, particularly focusing on how HR influences culture, and subsequently, impacts the delivery of financial services.

Organizational culture plays a pivotal role in the success of financial institutions. Schein (2010) defines organizational culture as the shared values, beliefs, and norms that guide behaviors within an organization. In the context of financial institutions, strong cultures emphasizing integrity, risk management, and customer focus are often associated with better performance (Hofstede, 2011).

23.2.2 HR Practices and Culture Development

HR practices significantly contribute to the development and maintenance of organizational culture. The recruitment, selection, and training processes, as well as performance management systems, are key mechanisms through which HR shapes culture (Barney & Wright, 1998). For instance, financial institutions that prioritize hiring individuals with values aligned with the organizational culture tend to foster a more cohesive and productive workforce (Pfeffer, 1994).

23.2.3 The Role of HR in Service Delivery of Financial Institutions

In financial institutions, service delivery is a critical aspect of success, directly impacting customer satisfaction and loyalty. HR practices influence employee engagement, which in turn affects service quality (Bowen & Ostroff, 2004). Research suggests that satisfied and motivated employees are more likely to deliver exceptional customer service (Heskett et al., 1994).

23.2.4 Challenges and Future Directions

Despite the recognized importance of HR in shaping organizational culture and enhancing service delivery, financial institutions face challenges in aligning HR practices with strategic objectives (Kamoche & Cunha, 2001). Furthermore, with the advent of digital transformation and changing workforce demographics, HR professionals must adapt their strategies to remain effective in shaping culture and driving success in financial institutions (Boxall & Purcell, 2016).

Leadership plays a crucial role in shaping organizational culture. Research by Denison (1990) suggests that leaders who actively promote and embody the desired cultural values have a significant impact on employee attitudes and behaviors. In financial institutions, effective leadership can foster a culture of innovation, adaptability, and ethical conduct (Schein, 2010).

23.2.5 *Employee Engagement and Its Link to Service Excellence*

Employee engagement is closely linked to organizational culture and service delivery. A study by Towers Watson (2008) found that highly engaged employees are more committed to delivering exceptional service, leading to improved customer satisfaction and financial performance. HR practices such as recognition programs and employee development initiatives can enhance engagement levels within financial institutions (Harter, Schmidt & Hayes, 2002).

Compliance with regulatory standards is a fundamental aspect of operations in financial institutions. HR plays a vital role in promoting an ethical culture and ensuring employees understand and adhere to legal and regulatory requirements (Kaptein & Wempe, 2002). By integrating ethics training and fostering a culture of transparency and accountability, HR can mitigate compliance risks and enhance the reputation of financial institutions (Treviño, Weaver & Brown, 1999).

Technological advancements, such as artificial intelligence and data analytics, are reshaping HR practices in financial institutions. Research by CIPD (2020) suggests that leveraging technology can enhance talent acquisition, performance management, and employee engagement. HR professionals need to embrace digital tools and strategies to effectively manage cultural change and drive success in a rapidly evolving industry (Foss, Lyngsie & Zahra, 2019).

23.3 Research Methodology

23.3.1 *HRM Practices and Firm Performance in the Financial Institutions – A Secondary Data Review*

The resource-based view and meta-theory are two of the main ideas that were taken into consideration to define the connections between HRM practices and financial performance. Fourteen HRM practices that are pertinent to the financial industry are recommended by the study. Recruitment and selection, training and development, work design, performance evaluation, pay and benefits, encouragement and promotion, high performance and commitment, strategic communication, managing grievances, managing management participation, fostering teamwork, and improving quality are a few of them as shown in Figure 23.1. It is claimed that the performance of financial institutions is particularly affected by these activities.

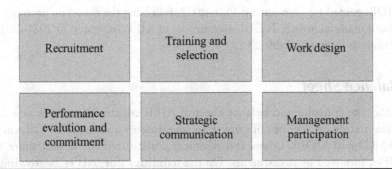

Figure 23.1   Diagram of HRM practices in financial institutions.

23.3.2 *Financial Institutional Details*

Reserve Bank of India (RBI) does not issue a single annual report that comprehensively covers all aspects of the Indian banking sector. It releases several reports throughout the year, each focusing on specific areas. However, to address your need for insights into the trends you mentioned, here are some relevant reports from 2022 to 2023:

■ RBI Reports and Data for Analyzing Trends in Indian Financial Institutions with the help of the HR proper functioning. Below we can find the theory as well as report.
■ The RBI offers a wealth of reports and data relevant to your research on financial institutions, employee demographics, and financial inclusion.
■ Trend and Progress of Banking in India: This annual report provides a comprehensive overview of the Indian banking sector, including trends in financial performance, capital adequacy, credit growth, and non-performing assets.

This report, released in July 2022, provides a comprehensive overview of the Indian banking sector for the 2021–22 period. It analyzes trends in financial performance, capital adequacy, credit growth, and non-performing assets across different bank groups and geographies.

Financial Stability Report (July 2022): This report assesses the stability of the Indian financial system, highlighting potential risks and challenges faced by banks. It includes insights into capital adequacy, credit risks, and non-performing assets.

All-India financial institutions (AIFIs) facilitate sector-specific long-term financing to agriculture and the rural sector, small industries, housing finance companies, NBFCs, MFIs, and international trade. At end-March 2021, four AIFIs, viz. the National Bank for Agriculture and Rural Development (NABARD), the Small Industries Development Bank of India (SIDBI), the National Housing Bank (NHB), and the Export Import Bank of India (EXIM Bank) were registered with the Reserve Bank. Since the enactment of the NaBFID Act 2021, effective April 19, 2021, NaBFID10 has been established as the fifth AIFI, which will cater to long-term financing needs of India's infrastructure sector. It shall be regulated and supervised as an AIFI by the Reserve Bank under Sections 45L and 45N of the Reserve Bank of India Act, 1934.

AIFIs' Operations Financial assistance sanctioned by AIFIs declined during 2021–2022, primarily on account of contraction in sanctions by NABARD as no fresh loans were sanctioned under Pradhan Mantri Awaas Yojana-Gramin (PMAY-G) and Swachh Bharat Mission-Gramin (SBM-G). Further, no new projects were sanctioned in 2021–2022, while disbursements of instalments were made against ongoing projects sanctioned in earlier years. Disbursements by EXIM Bank and SIDBI gained traction during 2021–2022, reflecting the thrust on promoting trade and on MSMEs and manufacturing. Total disbursements of AIFIs improved in 2021–2022 as a share of total sanctions as shown in Table 23.1.

23.3.3 *Balance Sheet*

In 2021–2022, the consolidated balance sheet of AIFIs continued to grow at a double-digit rate. This was mainly on account of growth in investments and loans and advances, primarily by NABARD and SIDBI. Loans and advances constituted the largest share in the total assets of AIFIs, followed by investments. On the liabilities side, AIFIs' borrowings increased

Table 23.1 Financial Assistance Sanctioned and Disbursed by AIFIs

Institutions	Sanctions		Disbursements	
	2020–2021	2021–2022	2020–2021	2021–2022
1	2	3	4	5
EXIM BANK	36,521	54,807	34,122	52,271
NABARD	4,59,849	3,80,396	3,50,022	3,78,387
NHB	37,791	22,330	34,230	19,313
SIDBI	98,354	1,48,550	98,115	1,46,402
Total	6,32,515	6,06,083	5,16,489	5,96,373

Note: Data are provisional.
Source: Respective Financial Institutions (RFI, 2023).

steeply followed by moderate growth in bonds and debentures (Table 23.2). The former was mainly due to steep increase in borrowings by SIDBI to facilitate revival and growth of MSMEs.

23.3.4 HRM Tactics and Procedures – Prosperous Financial Firms to Foster an Environment

To properly manage the workforce and assist banks in achieving their business goals, HR professionals in the financial industry must remain current on the best HR practices in the sector. In today's dynamic and competitive business landscape, HRM plays a pivotal role in the success and sustainability of financial firms. As the financial sector continues to evolve and face various challenges, such as market volatility, regulatory changes, and technological advancements, the significance of effective HRM tactics and procedures cannot be overstated. In this introduction, we will delve into the strategies employed by prosperous financial firms to foster an environment conducive to growth, innovation, and employee satisfaction as shown in Figure 23.2.

Here is description of HRM tactics and procedures for financial institutions:

- Talent Acquisition and Retention: Attracting and retaining top talent is a cornerstone of HRM in prosperous financial firms. These organizations employ rigorous recruitment processes to identify individuals with the right skills, experience, and cultural fit. Moreover, they invest in employee development programs, career advancement opportunities, and competitive compensation packages to retain their best performers. By nurturing a talented workforce, financial firms can drive innovation, enhance productivity, and maintain a competitive edge in the market (Khang, 2024a).
- Employee Engagement and Well-Being: Employee engagement and well-being are increasingly recognized as drivers of organizational performance and employee satisfaction. Prosperous financial firms prioritize initiatives aimed at enhancing employee engagement, such as open communication channels, team-building activities, and wellness programs.

Table 23.2 AIFIs' Balance Sheet

Description	2021	2022	Percentage Variation 2021–2022
1	2	3	4
1. Capital	32,221	35,008	8.6
	(3.0)	(2.9)	
2. Reserves	71,025	81,538	14.8
	(6.6)	(6.7)	
3. Bonds and Debentures	3,27,427	3,56,901	9.0
	(30.4)	(29.2)	
4. Deposits	4,12,001	4,36,057	5.8
	(38.3)	(35.7)	
5. Borrowings	1,70,820	2,43,121	42.3
	(15.9)	(19.9)	
6. Other Liabilities	62,023	68,612	10.6
	(5.8)	(5.6)	
Total Liabilities/Assets	**10,75,517**	**12,21,236**	**13.5**
7. Cash and Bank Balances	34,595	28,379	−18.0
	(3.2)	(2.3)	
8. Investments	79,275	1,06,329	34.1
	(7.4)	(8.7)	
9. Loans and Advances	9,44,318	10,69,116	13.2
	(87.8)	(87.5)	
10. Bills Discounted/Rediscounted	1,410	3,058	116.9
	(0.1)	(0.3)	
11. Fixed Assets	1,273	1,268	−0.4
	(0.1)	(0.1)	
12. Other Assets	14,646	13,087	−10.6
	(1.4)	(1.1)	

Notes: 1. Figures in parentheses are percentages of total liabilities/assets. 2. Data are provisional.
Source: Respective Financial Institutions (RFI, 2023).

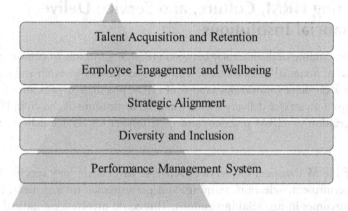

Figure 23.2   Diagram of HRM tactics and procedures for financial institutions.

By fostering a supportive and inclusive work environment, these firms not only improve employee morale and retention but also enhance collaboration and creativity.

■ Strategic Alignment: Successful financial firms recognize the importance of aligning HRM practices with organizational objectives. By strategically integrating HRM into the overall business strategy, these firms ensure that their human capital contributes directly to achieving key financial goals. Whether it's talent acquisition, performance management, or succession planning, every HRM tactic is designed to support the firm's mission and vision.

■ Diversity and Inclusion: The general effectiveness and productivity of the company can be raised by a diverse and inclusive workplace. Since they bring a range of viewpoints and methods to the table when making decisions, diverse teams typically solve problems more creatively and effectively. A varied staff may aid in ensuring that the company is able to comprehend and satisfy the wants of each and every one of the wide variety of clients that financial institutions handle. Through the implementation of affirmative action policies, the provision of diversity training, and the formation of employee resource groups, financial institutions may foster diversity and inclusion.

■ Performance Management Systems: Effective performance management is critical for driving accountability, measuring progress, and rewarding high achievers. Prosperous financial firms implement robust performance management systems that provide clear expectations, regular feedback, and objective evaluations. By aligning performance goals with organizational objectives, these firms ensure that employees understand their role in driving business success. Additionally, performance management systems often include mechanisms for recognizing and rewarding exceptional performance, thereby motivating employees to excel.

In summary, HRM tactics and procedures play a central role in the success of prosperous financial firms. By strategically aligning HRM practices with organizational objectives, investing in talent acquisition and development, implementing robust performance management systems, and fostering a culture of employee engagement and well-being, these firms create an environment where employees can thrive and contribute to long-term financial success. Throughout this discussion, we explore each of these aspects in greater detail to understand how they drive performance and competitiveness in the financial sector.

23.4 Exploring HRM, Culture, and Service Delivery in Financial Institutions

To advance understanding of the interplay between HRM, organizational culture, and service delivery in the context of financial institutions, several areas for further research and exploration can be identified. These areas delve into various aspects of HRM practices, organizational culture dynamics, and their impact on service delivery within financial institutions as shown in Figure 23.3.

Here is description of HRM practices and their impact on service delivery within financial institutions:

■ Impact of HRM Practices on Service Delivery: Investigate how specific HRM practices, such as recruitment, selection, training, and performance management, influence service delivery outcomes in financial institutions. This could involve longitudinal studies to assess the effectiveness of different HRM interventions on service quality metrics.

■ Organizational Culture and Service Orientation: Explore the relationship between organizational culture dimensions (e.g., customer orientation, innovation, teamwork) and service delivery effectiveness. This research could involve qualitative analysis to uncover how cultural norms and values shape employee behavior and customer interactions.

■ Employee Engagement and Service Quality: Examine the role of employee engagement in driving service quality improvements within financial institutions. This could involve surveys and statistical analysis to measure the relationship between employee engagement levels, customer satisfaction, and service delivery performance.

■ Leadership and Organizational Culture Alignment: Investigate how leadership styles and behaviors influence the alignment between organizational culture and service delivery priorities. This research could involve case studies or interviews with senior leaders to understand their role in shaping culture and driving service excellence.

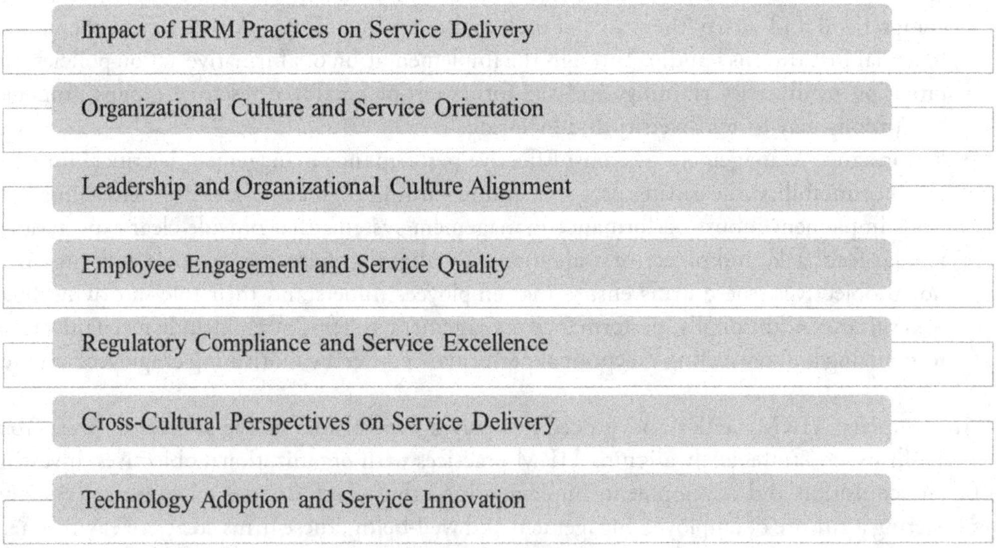

Figure 23.3 **Diagram of HRM practices and their impact on service delivery within financial institutions.**

■ Technology Adoption and Service Innovation: Explore how HRM practices facilitate the adoption of new technologies and innovations to enhance service delivery in financial institutions. This could involve studying the implementation of digital tools, automation, and analytics in improving customer experiences and operational efficiency (Khang, 2024b).

■ Cross-Cultural Perspectives on Service Delivery: Examine how cultural differences across regions impact HRM practices, organizational culture, and ultimately service delivery outcomes in global financial institutions. This research could involve comparative studies across different cultural contexts to identify best practices for managing cultural diversity and ensuring consistent service standards.

■ Employee Well-Being and Service Performance: Investigate the relationship between employee well-being, job satisfaction, and service performance in financial institutions. This could involve longitudinal studies or intervention-based research to assess the impact of well-being initiatives on employee engagement and customer service outcomes.

■ Regulatory Compliance and Service Excellence: Explore how HRM practices and organizational culture influence compliance with regulatory standards while maintaining service excellence in financial institutions. This research could involve examining the balance between regulatory requirements and customer-centric approaches to service delivery.

By focusing on these areas of research, scholars can deepen their understanding of the complex interplay between HRM, organizational culture, and service delivery in the dynamic environment of financial institutions. This knowledge can inform the development of practical strategies and interventions to enhance service quality, customer satisfaction, and organizational performance.

23.5 Result and Conclusion

The research project "Culture Currency: How HR Shapes Success in Financial Institutions and Their Services" has yielded insightful findings regarding the relationship between HRM, organizational culture, and the delivery of financial services within financial institutions. Through a comprehensive analysis of existing literature, case studies, and evidence, several key results have emerged:

The study identified a significant correlation between HR practices and the establishment of organizational culture within financial institutions. Effective HR strategies, such as recruitment, training, performance management, and leadership development, play a crucial role in shaping the values, norms, and behaviors that define the organizational culture.

The research demonstrated that a positive organizational culture, fostered by strategic HRM practices, directly contributes to the improvement of service quality, efficiency, and effectiveness in financial institutions. Employees who are aligned with the organization's values and goals are more motivated, engaged, and committed to delivering high-quality services to customers.

By examining various mechanisms of influence, including employee engagement, empowerment, communication channels, and reward systems, the study identified specific pathways through which HRM practices shape organizational culture and, subsequently, enhance service delivery in financial institutions.

The findings highlight the crucial role of HRM in driving organizational success and competitiveness in the financial services sector. Institutions that prioritize HRM as a strategic function are better positioned to attract, retain, and develop talent, thereby gaining a competitive edge in the market and achieving sustainable growth.

In conclusion, the research project underscores the importance of HRM in shaping organizational culture and influencing the delivery of financial services within financial institutions. By investing in effective HR practices, institutions can cultivate a culture that fosters innovation, collaboration, and customer-centricity, ultimately driving success and maintaining a competitive advantage in the dynamic financial services landscape. These insights have significant implications for HR professionals, organizational leaders, policymakers, and stakeholders seeking to optimize HR strategies and enhance the performance of financial institutions in today's globalized economy (Khang, Rani et al., 2023).

References

Barney, J. B., & Wright, P. M. (1998). On becoming a strategic partner: The role of human resources in gaining competitive advantage. Human Resource Management, 37(1), 31–46. https://doi.org/10.1002/(SICI)1099-050X(199821)37:1<31::AID-HRM4>3.0.CO;2-W

Bowen, D. E., & Ostroff, C. (2004). Understanding HRM-firm performance linkages: The role of the "strength" of the HRM system. Academy of Management Review, 29(2), 203–221. https://doi.org/10.2307/20159029

Boxall, P., & Purcell, J. (2016). Strategy and Human Resource Management (4th ed.). Palgrave Macmillan. http://doi.org/10.1108/00251740310479368

Cameron, K. S., & Quinn, R. E. (2011). Diagnosing and Changing Organizational Culture: Based on the Competing Values Framework. John Wiley & Sons. https://www.academia.edu/download/37305282/Budaya_Organisasi_cameron_1.pdf

CIPD. (2020). People Profession 2030: A collective view of future trends. Chartered Institute of Personnel and Development. https://journals.sagepub.com/doi/abs/10.3102/0013189X033003003

Denison, D. R. (1990). Corporate Culture and Organizational Effectiveness. John Wiley & Sons. https://doi.org/10.1002/hrm.3930280408

Denison, D. R., & Mishra, A. K. (1995). Toward a theory of organizational culture and effectiveness. Organization Science, 6(2), 204–223. https://pubsonline.informs.org/doi/abs/10.1287/orsc.6.2.204

Foss, N. J., Lyngsie, J., & Zahra, S. A. (2019). Organizational Design, Policy Making, and Entrepreneurship: Essays in Honor of Paul L. Robertson. Oxford University Press. https://doi.org/10.1177/1476127014561944

Harter, J. K., Schmidt, F. L., & Hayes, T. L. (2002). Business-unit-level relationship between employee satisfaction, employee engagement, and business outcomes: A meta-analysis. Journal of Applied Psychology, 87(2), 268–279. https://doi.org/10.1037//0021-9010.87.2.268

Heskett, J. L., Jones, T. O., Loveman, G. W., Sasser, W. E. Jr, & Schlesinger, L. A. (1994). Putting the service-profit chain to work. Harvard Business Review, 72(2), 164–174. https://www.hbs.edu/faculty/Pages/item.aspx?num=9149

Hofstede, G. (2011). Dimensional zing cultures: The Hofstede model in context. Online Readings in Psychology and Culture, 2(1), 8. https://doi.org/10.9707/2307-0919.1014

Kamoche, K., & Cunha, M. P. (2001). Rethinking internalization processes in multinational companies: A dynamic perspective. Management International Review, 41(3), 209–231. https://doi.org/10.3389/fpsyg.2022.807582

Kaptein, M., & Wempe, J. (2002). The Balanced Company: A Theory of Corporate Integrity. Oxford University Press. https://www.google.com/books?hl=en&lr=&id=BEXhuz-vtM8C&oi=fnd&pg=PP10

Khang, A. (2024a). "Future Directions and Challenges in Designing Workforce Management Systems for Industry 4," In Khang A., *AI-Oriented Competency Framework for Talent Management in the Digital Economy: Models, Technologies, Applications, and Implementation* (1st Ed.). CRC Press. https://doi.org/10.1201/9781003440901-1

Khang, A. (2024b). "Design and Modelling of AI-Oriented Competency Framework (AIoCF) for Information Technology Sector," In Khang A., *AI-Oriented Competency Framework for Talent Management in the Digital Economy: Models, Technologies, Applications, and Implementation* (1st Ed.). CRC Press. https://doi.org/10.1201/9781003440901-17

Khang, A. (2024c). "Implementation of AIoCF Model and Tools for Information Technology Sector," In Khang A., *AI-Oriented Competency Framework for Talent Management in the Digital Economy: Models, Technologies, Applications, and Implementatio*n (1st Ed.). CRC Press. https://doi.org/10.1201/9781003440901-20

Khang, A., Rani, S., Gujrati, R., Uygun, H., & Gupta, S. K. (2023). Designing Workforce Management Systems for Industry 4.0: Data-Centric and AI-Enabled Approaches (1st Ed.). CRC Press. https://doi.org/10.1201/9781003357070

Pfeffer, J. (1994). Competitive Advantage Through People: Unleashing the Power of the Workforce. Harvard Business Press. https://doi.org/10.1002/hrdq.3920070210

RFI. (2023). Report on Trend and Progress of Banking in India 2021-2022. https://www.nafcub.org/uploads/regulatory_updates/774774290_REPORT%20ON%20TREND%20AND%20PROGRESS%20OF%20BANKING%20IN%20INDIA%202021-22.PDF

Schein, E. H. (1985). Organizational Culture and Leadership. Jossey-Bass. https://www.google.com/books?hl=en&lr=&id=Mnres2PlFLMC&oi=fnd&pg=PR9&dq=Organizational+Culture+and+Leadership.+San+Francisco&ots=oqcsJe9wLf&sig=8uXhr8ZkgtI-rrrsnJ7GHr5bYZs

Schein, E. H. (2010). Organizational Culture and Leadership (4th Ed.). Jossey-Bass. https://www.scirp.org/reference/ReferencesPapers?ReferenceID=1848176

Towers Watson. (2008). Driving Business Results Through Continuous Engagement. Towers Watson.

Treviño, L. K., Weaver, G. R., & Brown, M. E. (1999). Managing Ethics in Business Organizations: Social Scientific Perspectives. Stanford University Press.

Chapter 24

The Impact of Artificial Intelligence (AI) Transformation in Financial Sector

---

Manjula Devi Chithiraikannu, Gobinath Arumugam, Padma Priya Sundara Moorthy, Keerthi Srinivasa Kannan, and Rajeswari Packianathan

24.1 Introduction

Nowadays, from customer acquisition to service delivery, artificial intelligence (AI)-driven automation and intelligence optimize operational processes and enhance customer experiences. By leveraging AI technologies, financial institutions can streamline customer onboarding processes, improve risk assessment and transaction processing, and deliver personalized services tailored to individual preferences and behaviors. Strategic frameworks for AI integration enable organizations to identify key areas for deployment, assess infrastructure readiness, and develop robust data governance policies. Through these strategic initiatives, financial institutions can unlock the full potential of AI technologies, delivering enhanced value to customers and stakeholders in the digital era.

Looking ahead, the chapter outlines forward-looking recommendations to guide stakeholders in navigating the evolving AI landscape in finance. These recommendations include enhancing regulatory collaboration, promoting diversity and inclusion, fostering responsible innovation, and embracing collaborative action. By synthesizing key insights, this chapter aims to empower stakeholders to leverage AI's benefits while upholding societal values and ensuring long-term sustainability in the digital age.

AI is reshaping the financial industry, bringing about profound changes that promise both unprecedented opportunities and significant challenges. As the financial sector navigates the

DOI: 10.4324/9781003501947-24

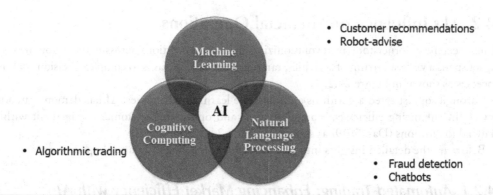

- Customer recommendations
- Robot-advise
- Algorithmic trading
- Fraud detection
- Chatbots

Figure 24.1   Key AI roles in finance sector.

complex terrain of the 21st century, it is confronted with a myriad of issues, including escalating customer demands and stringent regulatory requirements as shown in Figure 24.1. Against this backdrop, AI emerges as a transformative force, offering innovative solutions to navigate the complexities of modern finance (Cao, 2022).

From algorithmic trading to personalized wealth management, AI permeates every aspect of financial operations, revolutionizing processes, enhancing decision-making, and driving sustainable growth. The implementation of AI-powered algorithms enables financial institutions to analyze vast amounts of data quickly, identify patterns, and execute trades with greater precision and efficiency. Moreover, AI-driven tools facilitate personalized recommendations and tailored services, enhancing customer experiences and satisfaction.

However, as AI becomes increasingly integrated into financial ecosystems, it also raises ethical, regulatory, and societal concerns that require careful consideration and strategic navigation. Issues such as data privacy, algorithmic bias, and the ethical use of AI algorithms pose significant challenges for financial institutions and policymakers alike. Balancing the potential benefits of AI with the need to mitigate risks and ensure compliance with regulatory frameworks is crucial for maintaining trust and stability in the financial industry (Chiu, Zhu & Corbett, 2021).

In this chapter, we undertake a comprehensive exploration of AI's impact on the financial sector, examining the opportunities, challenges, and policy imperatives it presents. Through structured discourse, we delve into the dynamic interplay between AI and finance, charting its evolutionary trajectory and exploring its profound implications. We assess AI's influence on financial operations, highlighting its transformative potential in reshaping the future of finance.

Moreover, we scrutinize the ethical and regulatory complexities inherent in AI adoption, proposing pragmatic approaches to foster responsible integration while ensuring compliance with regulatory frameworks and ethical standards. Additionally, we evaluate policy imperatives for policymakers to foster innovation, promote transparency, and safeguard consumer interests in AI-driven financial environments.

By synthesizing key insights and forward-looking recommendations, this chapter provides stakeholders with actionable strategies and pathways to navigate the evolving AI landscape in finance. It aims to empower financial institutions to leverage AI's benefits while upholding societal values and ensuring long-term sustainability in the digital age. Through collaborative efforts and a commitment to responsible AI adoption, the financial industry can harness the full potential of AI to drive innovation, enhance efficiency, and deliver value to customers and stakeholders alike.

24.2 AI's Influence on Financial Operations

AI has become a cornerstone in revolutionizing financial operations across various domains. Its impact spans a wide spectrum of activities, ranging from routine tasks to complex decision-making processes as shown in Figure 24.2.

Through sophisticated algorithms and machine learning techniques, AI has demonstrated its prowess in enhancing efficiency, managing risks, and optimizing customer engagement within financial institutions (Das, 2019) as shown in Figure 24.3.

Below are the detailed insights into how AI influences different financial operations:

24.2.1 Automated Trading: Enhancing Market Efficiency with AI

- AI's role in automated trading involves analyzing vast volumes of market data, identifying patterns, and executing trades without human intervention.
- By leveraging AI, financial institutions experience improved trading speed, reduced latency, and enhanced trade execution accuracy, leading to more efficient market operations (Fenwick & Vermeulen, 2017).
- Furthermore, AI algorithms can adapt to changing market conditions in real-time, enabling swift decision-making and capitalization on emerging opportunities, thereby enhancing overall market efficiency.

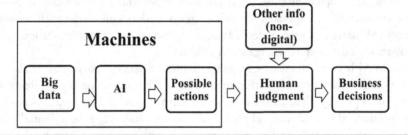

Figure 24.2   AI-driven decision-making.

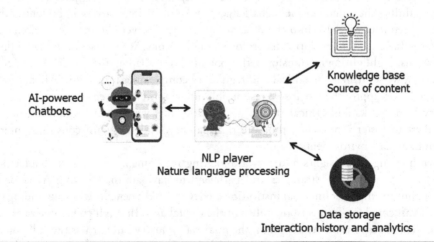

Figure 24.3   AI-powered assistance for customer service and support.

24.2.2 Fraud Detection and Prevention: AI's Role in Safeguarding Financial Transactions

- AI revolutionizes fraud detection by employing advanced algorithms to analyze transaction data and identify anomalies or suspicious patterns indicative of fraudulent activity.
- The utilization of AI significantly improves the accuracy and efficiency of fraud detection, minimizing false positives and reducing the risk of financial losses due to fraudulent transactions.
- Additionally, AI-powered fraud detection systems continuously learn and evolve, staying ahead of fraudsters' tactics and ensuring robust protection of financial transactions (Fu, Huang & Singh, 2021).

24.2.3 Credit Scoring: Revolutionizing Lending Practices with AI

- AI-driven credit scoring models utilize machine learning algorithms to assess creditworthiness with greater precision by analyzing diverse data sources.
- This transformation leads to a reduction in default rates and facilitates expanded access to credit by identifying previously overlooked patterns in data, enabling more inclusive lending practices.
- Financial institutions benefit from AI's ability to make more accurate credit decisions, thereby mitigating risks and optimizing lending portfolios.

24.2.4 Customer Service and Support: AI-Powered Assistance across Channels

- AI-powered Chatbots and virtual assistants provide instantaneous and personalized customer support across various communication channels such as websites, mobile apps, and social media platforms.
- This transformation improves customer service accessibility, responsiveness, and satisfaction by offering timely assistance and resolving queries efficiently.
- Furthermore, AI-driven analytics tools analyze customer interactions to derive insights, enabling financial institutions to continuously enhance service quality and anticipate customer needs effectively.

24.2.5 Algorithmic Trading: Optimizing Trading Performance with AI

- AI-driven algorithms analyze market data and historical trends to automate trading decisions, optimizing trading performance by exploiting market inefficiencies and reducing trading costs (Guo & Polak, 2021).
- Financial institutions benefit from increased trading efficiency, reduced transaction costs, and improved risk management through the use of AI in algorithmic trading.
- Moreover, AI algorithms can adapt trading strategies in real-time to changing market conditions, ensuring that financial institutions maintain their competitive edge in the market.

24.2.6 Risk Assessment and Management: Proactive Risk Mitigation with AI

- AI-powered systems identify, assess, and mitigate various types of risks effectively by analyzing large volumes of data and identifying patterns or correlations indicative of potential risks.

- This transformation enhances risk visibility, enables data-driven decision-making, and optimizes risk-adjusted returns for financial institutions.
- Additionally, AI-driven solutions proactively identify emerging risks and opportunities, enabling financial institutions to stay ahead of market trends and maintain resilience in dynamic environments.

24.2.7 Compliance and Regulatory Reporting: Streamlining Compliance Processes with AI

- AI automates regulatory monitoring, reporting, and audit trail management, streamlining compliance workflows, reducing manual errors, and ensuring timely and accurate regulatory reporting.
- Financial institutions benefit from the streamlined compliance processes, enhanced efficiency, and reduced operational costs associated with AI-powered compliance solutions.
- Furthermore, AI enables financial institutions to adapt quickly to regulatory changes and maintain compliance standards, ensuring adherence to evolving regulatory requirements.

24.2.8 Personalized Marketing and Product Recommendations: Tailoring Offerings with AI Insights

- AI-driven platforms analyze customer data to create personalized marketing campaigns and product recommendations tailored to individual preferences and behaviors.
- This transformation enhances customer engagement, drives sales, and maximizes return on investment by delivering relevant and targeted marketing content to customers.
- Additionally, AI optimizes marketing strategies in real-time based on customer feedback and interactions, ensuring that financial institutions remain agile and responsive to evolving customer needs and preferences.

24.3 Ethical and Regulatory Challenges of AI in Finance

Financial institutions, propelled by the promise of AI-driven innovation, are confronted with a host of ethical and regulatory challenges. Chief among these concerns is the issue of data privacy. With access to vast troves of sensitive customer information, financial organizations must tread carefully to ensure the protection and security of this data. AI's reliance on data for training and decision-making amplifies the importance of robust data protection measures. Striking a balance between leveraging data for innovation and safeguarding customer privacy presents a formidable ethical challenge in the realm of finance (Guthrie & Parker, 2016).

Another pressing issue is algorithmic bias, which can infiltrate AI models and lead to unfair outcomes or discriminatory practices. Nowhere is this more evident than in areas like credit scoring and loan approval, where biased algorithms can perpetuate inequalities in access to financial services. Addressing algorithmic bias demands meticulous attention to data quality, model transparency, and ongoing monitoring to ensure that AI systems deliver fair and unbiased results.

The regulatory landscape adds another layer of complexity to the adoption of AI in finance. Existing regulations may not fully encompass the intricacies introduced by AI technologies, leaving room for uncertainty and compliance gaps. Regulators are tasked with the delicate balance of fostering innovation while safeguarding consumer rights and market integrity. Establishing clear regulatory frameworks that encompass the ethical use of AI, ensure transparency, and promote accountability is paramount to fostering trust in AI-driven financial systems (Hamm & Klesel, 2021).

24.3.1 Pragmatic Approaches to Addressing Challenges

In response to these challenges, financial institutions are adopting pragmatic approaches to navigate the ethical and regulatory landscape of AI in finance. Robust data governance practices are essential, ensuring responsible data collection, storage, and usage while adhering to data protection regulations such as GDPR and CCPA. By implementing these measures, organizations can mitigate the risk of data breaches and safeguard customer privacy.

Furthermore, promoting algorithmic transparency and fairness is critical. Investing in transparency measures enhances visibility into AI decision-making processes, while regular audits help identify and mitigate biases, fostering fairness and equality in financial services. Collaborative efforts between industry stakeholders, regulators, and policymakers are also vital. By engaging in ongoing dialogue and cooperation, adaptive regulatory frameworks can be developed to address emerging ethical challenges and ensure that regulatory standards evolve alongside technological advancements. Through these pragmatic approaches, financial institutions can navigate the ethical and regulatory complexities of AI adoption, fostering trust and sustainability in the financial ecosystem (Hendershott et al., 2021).

24.3.2 Policy Imperatives for AI Integration in Finance

As AI continues to reshape financial ecosystems, policymakers face critical challenges in navigating the regulatory landscape to ensure responsible AI integration. The proliferation of AI technologies in finance brings to the fore ethical dilemmas and regulatory complexities that demand thoughtful consideration. Policymakers must grapple with issues such as data privacy, algorithmic bias, and compliance to uphold consumer protection and market integrity.

By interrogating the evolving policy landscape, policymakers can identify key imperatives to foster innovation while safeguarding against potential risks (Hodge, Mendoza & Sinha, 2021) as key points:

- Data Privacy and Security: Policymakers must enact robust regulations to protect consumer data privacy and ensure the secure handling of sensitive financial information in AI-driven systems. This involves establishing clear guidelines for data collection, storage, and sharing, as well as implementing stringent security measures to prevent unauthorized access or misuse of data.
- Algorithmic Transparency and Accountability: Transparency in AI algorithms is essential to mitigate the risk of algorithmic bias and ensure fair and equitable outcomes in financial decision-making. Policymakers can mandate transparency requirements that compel financial institutions to disclose information about the algorithms used in AI-driven systems, including data sources, model development processes, and decision-making criteria.
- Consumer Protection: Policymakers must prioritize consumer protection by implementing regulations that safeguard against discriminatory practices, fraudulent activities, and unfair treatment in AI-driven financial services. This may include measures to enhance consumer education and awareness, establish mechanisms for grievance redressal, and impose penalties for non-compliance with regulatory standards.

- Market Stability and Resilience: Policymakers play a critical role in maintaining market stability and resilience in the face of technological disruptions caused by AI integration. This involves conducting risk assessments to identify potential systemic risks associated with AI adoption, implementing stress testing frameworks to evaluate the robustness of AI systems, and establishing contingency plans to mitigate adverse effects on financial markets.
- Collaboration and Governance: Policymakers should promote collaboration between government agencies, industry stakeholders, and academia to develop cohesive governance frameworks for AI integration in finance. This includes establishing regulatory sandboxes and innovation hubs to facilitate experimentation with AI technologies while ensuring compliance with regulatory requirements and ethical standards.

24.4 Redefining the Financial Value Chain with AI

AI is fundamentally transforming the traditional financial value chain, revolutionizing how financial services are conceptualized, developed, and delivered. This transformation is evident across all segments of the value chain, from customer acquisition to service delivery. By leveraging AI-driven automation and intelligence, financial institutions are optimizing operational processes and enhancing customer experiences, thereby driving efficiency, innovation, and value creation (Hoffman, 2017).

24.4.1 AI's Impact on the Financial Value Chain

- Customer Acquisition: AI-powered tools, such as Chatbots and virtual assistants, streamline customer onboarding processes by providing instant support and guidance. These intelligent systems handle inquiries, assist with account openings, and offer personalized recommendations, thereby improving customer acquisition rates and satisfaction levels.
- Risk Assessment and Transaction Processing: AI algorithms analyze vast volumes of data to identify patterns and trends, enabling more accurate risk assessment and faster transaction processing. By automating these tasks, financial institutions can expedite decision-making processes, reduce operational costs, and minimize errors, ultimately enhancing efficiency and reliability.
- Service Delivery: AI-driven personalization enhances the delivery of financial services by tailoring offerings to individual customer preferences and behaviors. Through predictive analytics and machine learning, financial institutions can anticipate customer needs, offer targeted products, and deliver proactive support, leading to higher levels of engagement and loyalty.

24.4.2 Strategic Frameworks for AI Integration

To capitalize on the benefits of AI across the financial value chain, organizations must adopt strategic frameworks that align technology investments with business objectives. This involves:

- Identifying Key Areas for AI Deployment: Assessing internal processes and customer touchpoints to identify areas where AI-driven solutions can drive the most significant impact, such as customer service, risk management, and fraud detection.
- Assessing Infrastructure Readiness: Evaluating existing infrastructure and technology capabilities to ensure compatibility with AI solutions. This may involve upgrading systems,

integrating data sources, and investing in cloud computing infrastructure to support AI applications.

■ Developing Robust Data Governance Policies: Establishing data governance policies and protocols to ensure the ethical and responsible use of data in AI-driven decision-making. This includes addressing data privacy concerns, ensuring data security, and promoting transparency in algorithmic processes (Hornuf, Klus et al., 2021).

By adopting strategic frameworks for AI integration, financial institutions can unlock the full potential of AI technologies, redefining their competitive advantage in the digital era and delivering enhanced value to customers and stakeholders.

24.5 Evolving Labor Dynamics in the AI Era

The advent of AI is reshaping the landscape of the financial labor market, triggering significant shifts in job roles, skill requirements, and workforce dynamics. As AI-driven automation and augmentation technologies permeate various sectors of the financial industry, professionals are faced with both challenges and opportunities in adapting to this transformative paradigm.

24.5.1 Seismic Shifts in the Financial Labor Market

■ Job Displacement: The widespread adoption of AI-powered automation has led to concerns about job displacement, particularly in repetitive, rule-based tasks such as data entry, transaction processing, and basic customer service. As these tasks become increasingly automated, some traditional roles may become obsolete, leading to workforce restructuring and potential job losses.

■ Creation of New Roles: Conversely, the rise of AI is also creating new job roles and opportunities within the financial sector. These roles often involve leveraging AI technologies to enhance decision-making, drive innovation, and develop new business strategies. For example, positions such as data scientists, AI engineers, and algorithm developers are in high demand as financial institutions seek to harness the power of AI for competitive advantage.

■ Skill Demands: The integration of AI into financial operations necessitates a shift in skill demands, with an increasing emphasis on data analytics, machine learning, and programming capabilities. Professionals with expertise in these areas are in high demand as financial institutions seek to build AI-driven systems, analyze complex datasets, and derive actionable insights to drive business outcomes.

24.5.2 Proactive Workforce Development Strategies

To navigate the evolving labor dynamics in the AI era, financial institutions must adopt proactive workforce development strategies to equip professionals with the requisite skills and competencies for success. This involves:

■ Investing in Continuous Learning: Financial institutions should prioritize investments in employee training and upskilling programs to ensure that their workforce remains adaptable and resilient in the face of technological change. This may involve offering courses on AI, data science, and emerging technologies, both internally and through external partnerships.

- Fostering a Culture of Innovation: Cultivating a culture of innovation and experimentation encourages employees to embrace new technologies and approaches, fostering creativity and adaptability within the organization. Financial institutions should create opportunities for employees to collaborate on AI projects, experiment with new tools and methodologies, and share best practices across teams.
- Promoting Diversity and Inclusion: Embracing diversity and inclusion in hiring practices and talent development initiatives fosters a more innovative and adaptive workforce. By bringing together individuals with diverse backgrounds, perspectives, and skill sets, financial institutions can cultivate a dynamic and resilient workforce capable of navigating the complexities of the AI-powered financial landscape.

By implementing proactive workforce development strategies, financial institutions can harness the transformative potential of AI while ensuring that their workforce remains empowered, engaged, and prepared for the challenges and opportunities of the AI era.

24.6 Real-Time Use Cases of AI in the Financial Sector

The adoption of AI in the financial sector has led to the emergence of several real-time use cases that illustrate its transformative potential as follows:

24.6.1 Fraud Detection and Prevention

- Problem: Financial institutions face the challenge of identifying and preventing fraudulent activities, which can result in significant financial losses and damage to their reputation.
- Solution: Many banks and credit card companies have implemented AI-powered fraud detection systems, leveraging techniques such as anomaly detection, supervised learning, and deep learning algorithms. These systems analyze transaction data in real-time to identify suspicious patterns or anomalies. By using machine learning algorithms like Random Forest, Support Vector Machines (SVM), or Deep Neural Networks (DNN), these systems can detect fraudulent transactions with higher accuracy and speed compared to traditional rule-based approaches.
- Example: Companies like PayPal use AI algorithms, including Random Forest and DNN, to analyze millions of transactions every day and flag potentially fraudulent activities for further investigation, thus reducing financial losses and improving security for their customers.

24.6.2 Algorithmic Trading

- Problem: Traders and investment firms need to make quick and informed decisions in the highly volatile and competitive financial markets.
- Solution: AI-driven algorithmic trading platforms use advanced machine learning algorithms such as Reinforcement Learning, Genetic Algorithms, or Long Short-Term Memory (LSTM) networks to analyze market data, identify trading opportunities, and execute trades automatically based on predefined criteria. These systems can analyze vast amounts of data from various sources, including market news, social media sentiment, and historical trading patterns, to make predictions about future market movements.

- Example: Companies like Citadel Securities leverage AI algorithms, including Reinforcement Learning and LSTM networks, to execute high-frequency trades with minimal human intervention, resulting in improved trading efficiency and better returns for their clients.

24.6.3 Customer Service and Support

- Problem: Financial institutions often struggle to provide timely and personalized customer support across multiple channels, leading to lower customer satisfaction and retention rates.
- Solution: AI-powered Chatbots and virtual assistants are being used by banks and insurance companies, employing Natural Language Processing (NLP), sentiment analysis, and decision trees. These AI-driven systems can offer instant and personalized customer support 24/7. They understand natural language queries, provide relevant information, and assist customers with various tasks such as account inquiries, transaction history, and loan applications.
- Example: Bank of America's virtual assistant, Erica, uses AI technology, including NLP and decision trees, to help customers manage their finances, answer questions, and provide personalized insights, thus improving customer engagement and satisfaction while reducing operational costs for the bank.

24.7 Conclusion

The integration of AI in the financial sector marks a transformative milestone, promising unprecedented efficiencies and opportunities for growth. AI-driven innovations have revolutionized financial operations, from automated trading to personalized customer experiences, driving enhanced decision-making and sustainable value creation. However, the adoption of AI also presents a myriad of ethical, regulatory, and societal challenges that demand careful consideration and strategic navigation. Balancing the pursuit of innovation with the imperative of upholding ethical principles and regulatory compliance is essential to ensure the long-term trustworthiness and sustainability of AI-driven financial systems.

Looking ahead, collaborative efforts among financial institutions, policymakers, regulators, and industry stakeholders will be crucial in addressing these challenges and harnessing AI's transformative potential for the benefit of society. By investing in ethical AI education, enhancing regulatory collaboration, promoting diversity and inclusion in AI development, fostering responsible innovation, and embracing collaborative action, we can navigate the complexities of the AI landscape in finance while upholding societal values and ensuring long-term sustainability in the digital age.

24.8 Forward-Looking Recommendations

As we reflect on the profound impact of AI on the financial sector and its potential to shape the future of finance, it is imperative to consider strategic pathways forward. The convergence of AI technologies with financial services presents both opportunities and challenges that necessitate proactive measures to harness AI's transformative potential responsibly. Looking ahead, stakeholders must adopt forward-looking recommendations to navigate the evolving AI landscape in finance, foster innovation, and uphold societal interests and values.

■ Investment in Ethical AI Education: Financial institutions should prioritize investment in ethical AI education and training programs for employees at all levels. By promoting a deep understanding of ethical principles, data privacy, algorithmic transparency, and bias mitigation strategies, organizations can cultivate a culture of responsible AI adoption and ensure that ethical considerations are embedded in all aspects of AI development and deployment.

■ Enhanced Regulatory Collaboration: Policymakers and regulators should strengthen collaboration with industry stakeholders to develop agile regulatory frameworks that foster innovation while safeguarding consumer rights and market integrity. This collaboration should involve ongoing dialogue, knowledge sharing, and proactive engagement to address emerging ethical and regulatory challenges and ensure that regulatory standards evolve alongside technological advancements.

■ Promotion of Diversity and Inclusion: Financial institutions should prioritize diversity and inclusion in AI development teams and decision-making processes. By embracing diverse perspectives, backgrounds, and skill sets, organizations can foster innovation, enhance algorithmic fairness, and mitigate the risk of biased outcomes in AI-driven financial services. Additionally, initiatives to promote diversity in AI talent pipelines and inclusive hiring practices can help address existing disparities in access to AI opportunities.

■ Fostering Responsible Innovation: Financial institutions should embrace a culture of responsible innovation that prioritizes ethical considerations, risk management, and accountability throughout the AI development lifecycle. This involves implementing robust governance frameworks, conducting rigorous impact assessments, and establishing mechanisms for ongoing monitoring and evaluation of AI systems to ensure compliance with regulatory requirements and ethical standards.

■ Embracing Collaborative Action: Collaboration among financial institutions, policymakers, regulators, academia, and civil society is essential to address the complex ethical, regulatory, and societal challenges associated with AI adoption in finance. By fostering collaborative partnerships, sharing best practices, and coordinating efforts to develop common standards and guidelines, stakeholders can build trust, promote transparency, and foster responsible AI innovation that benefits society as a whole.

References

Cao, L. (2022). AI in finance: Challenges, techniques, and opportunities. ACM Computing Surveys (CSUR), 55(3), 1–38. https://dl.acm.org/doi/abs/10.1145/3502289

Chiu, Y. -T., Zhu, Y. -Q., & Corbett, J. (2021). In the hearts and minds of employees: A model of pre-adoptive appraisal toward artificial intelligence in organizations. International Journal of Information Management, 60, 102379. https://www.sciencedirect.com/science/article/pii/S0268401221000724

Das, S. R. (2019). The future of fintech. Financial Management, 48(4), 981–1007. https://onlinelibrary.wiley.com/doi/abs/10.1111/fima.12297

Fenwick, M., & Vermeulen, E. P. M. (2017). How to respond to artificial intelligence in Fintech. Japan Spotlight, 16–20. https://www.jef.or.jp/journal/pdf/214th_Cover_04.pdf

Fu, R., Huang, Y., & Singh, P. V. (2021). Crowds, lending, machine, and bias. Information Systems Research, 32(1), 72–92. https://pubsonline.informs.org/doi/abs/10.1287/isre.2020.0990

Guo, H., & Polak, P. (2021). Artificial intelligence and financial technology FinTech: How AI is being used under the pandemic in 2020. In A. Hamdan, A. E. Hassanien, A. Razzaque, & B. Alareeni (Eds.), The Fourth Industrial Revolution: Implementation of Artificial Intelligence for Growing Business Success (pp. 169–186). Springer. https://link.springer.com/chapter/10.1007/978-3-030-62796-6_9

Guthrie, J., & Parker, L. D. (2016). Whither the accounting profession, accountants and accounting researchers? Commentary and projections. Accounting, Auditing, & Accountability, 29(1), 2–10. https://www.emerald.com/insight/content/doi/10.1108/AAAJ-10-2015-2263/full/html?fullSc=1

Hamm, P., & Klesel, M. (2021). Success factors for the adoption of artificial intelligence in organizations: A literature review. In Proceedings of the Twenty-seventh Americas Conference on Information Systems, Montreal, Canada. https://link.springer.com/chapter/10.1007/978-3-031-08093-7_1

Hendershott, T., Zhang, X. M., Zhao, J. L., & Zheng, Z. E. (2021). FinTech as a game changer: Overview of research frontiers. Information Systems Research, 32(1), 1–17. https://pubsonline.informs.org/doi/abs/10.1287/isre.2021.0997

Hodge, F. D., Mendoza, K. I., & Sinha, R. K. (2021). The effect of humanizing Robo-advisors on investor judgments. Contemporary Accounting Research, 38(1), 770–792. https://onlinelibrary.wiley.com/doi/abs/10.1111/1911-3846.12641

Hoffman, C. (2017). Accounting and auditing in the digital age.

Hornuf, L., Klus, M. F., Lohwasser, T. S., & Schwienbacher, A. (2021). How do banks interact with fintech startups? Small Business Economics, 57(3), 1505–1526. https://ieeexplore.ieee.org/abstract/document/8528677/

Chapter 25

Advancing Mobile Banking Security Using Modified RSA Approach for Data Transformation Enhancement

Bilas Haldar and Pranam Paul

25.1 Introduction

Mobile banking, synonymous with convenience and accessibility, has become the cornerstone of contemporary banking operations, enabling users to access a myriad of financial services seamlessly through the Internet. The transformative influence of information technology has reshaped the operational dynamics of the banking sector, with mobile banking emerging as a driving force. The landscape of modern banking has undergone a paradigm shift with the widespread adoption of mobile banking, bringing unprecedented convenience to users but also necessitating robust security measures to safeguard sensitive financial data.

As financial transactions increasingly migrate to mobile platforms, the imperative to fortify the security of data transformation processes becomes paramount. This chapter explores a pioneering solution to address this concern through the proposition of an innovative modification to the Rivest-Shamir-Adleman (RSA) algorithm a widely utilized cryptographic technique. In the realm of mobile banking, where the stakes are high and the demand for secure data transformation is non-negotiable, our proposed modified RSA approach seeks to elevate the standards of encryption and data protection. The RSA algorithm, renowned for its strength in public-key cryptography, is adapted to meet the distinctive challenges posed by mobile banking transactions, aiming to enhance not only the confidentiality of financial information but also the efficiency of data transformation protocols.

This introduction provides a contextual backdrop for the significance of our research, underscoring the critical need for heightened security in the context of mobile banking data transformation. By delving into the intricacies of the modified RSA approach, we aim to contribute to

DOI: 10.4324/9781003501947-25

the ongoing discourse on securing mobile financial transactions and offer a promising avenue for advancing the security paradigm in the dynamic landscape of mobile banking.

Delving into the intricacies of the modified RSA algorithm, this work systematically evaluates its impact on encryption strength, computational efficiency, and adaptability to the distinctive challenges inherent in mobile banking transactions. It provides a robust defense mechanism against unauthorized data access, ensuring a higher level of security for mobile banking transactions. This innovative combination addresses the growing concerns over authentication breaches in mobile money applications, proposing a more reliable and user-friendly solution. The findings of this study underscore the potential of the modified RSA approach to elevate the overall security posture of mobile banking, presenting a promising avenue for advancing data protection in this ever-evolving realm. As the subsequent sections unfold, the intricacies of the modified RSA algorithm and its implications for enhancing the security of data transformation in mobile banking will be comprehensively explored.

25.2 Literature Review

Recent advancements in the domain of cybersecurity have significantly impacted the security protocols utilized in Internet and mobile banking services. Several research initiatives have been undertaken to address the vulnerabilities inherent in Internet and mobile banking systems, introducing sophisticated cryptographic techniques and multi-factor authentication mechanisms to mitigate potential security threats. This literature review highlights key contributions that exemplify the progression and diversity in securing digital banking services (Khang, Abdullayev et al., 2024).

Hossain et al. (2016) introduced a secure data transition methodology with protective measures, including encryption before storage, authentication procedures, and secure data transfer channels. Sarjiyus, Baha et al. (2021) presented an integrated security framework designed to fortify Internet banking services. Their approach combines an enhanced version of the RSA encryption algorithm with Least Significant Bit (LSB) steganography.

Tian et al. (2011) provided a comprehensive survey of self-healing key distribution in wireless networks, enabling users to recover session keys without group manager intervention. Sujatha et al. (2016) presented the RSA methodology, comprising key generation, encryption, and decryption, with key lengths such as 512, 1024, or 2048 bits. Al-Shabi (2019) highlighted RSA's improved security but noted drawbacks like slow encryption, challenging key generation, and vulnerability to assaults. In key distribution schemes, Mehic et al. (2020) surveyed applied methods and challenges in Quantum Key Distribution (QKD) networks.

Bhadauriya, Suthar, and Chaudhary (2017) proposed a 128-bit key algorithm, enhancing security through a hybrid cryptography algorithm combining AES, DES, and IDEA. Mohamad, Din, and Ahmad (2021) discussed weaknesses in RSA schemes with large key sizes, emphasizing their security strength for Internet-based applications. Gupta and Reddy (2022) introduced a novel model combining RSA public-key cryptography with the Diffie-Hellman key exchange to mitigate man-in-the-middle attacks. Devi and Arunachalam (2023) developed an innovative method for securing IoT data transmission, incorporating malware detection and prevention. However, Bisht and Singh (2015) noted vulnerability to man-in-the-middle attacks, emphasizing security when an appropriate mathematical group is utilized.

Islam et al. (2021) introduced a comprehensive security system that employs both the Digital Signature Algorithm (DSA) and RSA, coupled with a hash function. Orucho et al. (2023)

conducted a thorough review of state-of-the-art algorithms tasked with securing data in transit. Their work highlights the critical need for adaptive security measures that can effectively counter the evolving threats faced by mobile banking applications.

Neela and Kavitha (2022) developed a novel framework for secure cloud storage specifically tailored for the banking sector. Their work introduces an Improved Rivest-Shamir-Adleman Encryption Algorithm (IREA), which eliminates the reliance on third-party systems. Ali et al. (2021) contributed to the enhancement of mobile money services by developing a secure and efficient multi-factor authentication algorithm. By ingeniously integrating a Personal Identification Number (PIN), a one-time password (OTP), and biometric fingerprint verification, their method significantly elevates the security level during the authentication process.

In summary, these studies provide insights into various cryptographic methods, key distribution techniques, and their applications in securing data transmission in different contexts, emphasizing the ongoing challenges and potential vulnerabilities in existing systems. The collective efforts of these researchers underline the critical importance of advancing encryption and authentication technologies within the banking sector. However, it is important to develop novel security mechanisms by increasingly sophisticated cyber threats for mobile banking to enhance the data transformation over the network.

25.3 Proposed Methodology of Modified RSA Algorithm

The modified RSA algorithm introduced in this research adapts the traditional RSA framework to better suit the intricate demands of mobile banking security. This adaptation not only addresses the specific vulnerabilities associated with mobile transactions but also optimizes encryption processes for the limited computational resources available on mobile devices. The proposed work represents innovative encryption and decryption methodology that enhanced the security of data transformation in mobile banking (Khang, Rath et al., 2024).

25.3.1 Encryption

Encryption is the process of transforming information or data into a secure and unreadable format, often called ciphertext, to prevent unauthorized access or interception. The primary goal of encryption is to ensure the confidentiality of the information being transmitted or stored. It is a fundamental technique used to protect sensitive data from being accessed or understood by unauthorized individuals. The process of encryption involves the use of an algorithm and a key.

The algorithm dictates how the data is transformed, and the key serves as the input to the algorithm, determining the specific transformation applied. The combination of the algorithm and key ensures that the encrypted data can only be decrypted (transformed back into its original form) by someone possessing the correct key as shown in Algorithm 25.1.

Algorithm 25.1: Process of Transforming Information by Using Encryption

STEP 1: CHARACTER TO ASCII CONVERSION
- For each character in the plaintext message (c1), convert it into its corresponding ASCII value.
- Store the ASCII values in a file (b1).

STEP 2: USER-DEFINED BLOCK SIZE
■ Allow the user to specify the block size (bs).

STEP 3: BLOCK CONVERSION
■ Read block size bits from file b1, convert them into an equivalent decimal value.
■ Save the decimal values in a list based on the specified block size.
■ Generate a set of decimal numbers according to the block size.

STEP 4: ENCRYPTION KEY GENERATION
■ Generate encryption key as e, N.

STEP 5: INTERMEDIATE VALUE REPRESENTATION
■ Calculate the number of bits (SZ) needed to represent an intermediate changed value in binary notation using the equation ceil(log2(N)).

STEP 6: MESSAGE ENCRYPTION
■ Encrypt the message using equation $c = m^e \bmod N$
■ Sequentially reading decimal values from the list.
■ Convert the intermediate output into an SZ range of binary bits and store it in a file (fileb2).

STEP 7: BIT COUNTING AND PADDING
■ Count the number of bits in fileb2.
■ Add dummy bits at the end of the file if the bit count is not divisible by 8.

STEP 8: DECIMAL NUMBER CONVERSION
■ Select consecutive 8-bits from fileb2 to convert them into equivalent decimal numbers.
■ Create symbols from the decimal numbers, and store them in a file (fileb3).

STEP 9: CIPHERTEXT GENERATION
■ The ciphertext message (fileb3) is generated and ready to be sent to the recipient securely.
■ The user can transmit the original message or file along with the key pair over a secure channel after encryption.

25.3.2 Decryption

Decryption is the process of converting encrypted or ciphertext data back into its original, plaintext form. It is the reverse operation of encryption and is essential for accessing and understanding information that has been previously secured for confidentiality. Decryption requires the use of a specific key or algorithm that can transform the encrypted data into its original, readable format. According to the below equation, the ciphertext is converted back into the message for decryption as following function and as shown in Algorithm 25.2.

$$m = c^{d \times kd} \bmod N$$

Algorithm 25.2: Process of Converting Encrypted or Ciphertext Data Back into its Original

STEP 1: ASCII TO BINARY CONVERSION
- Read the ciphertext message (C2) from fileb3 character by character.
- For each ASCII character, convert its ASCII value into an 8-bit binary representation.
- Add the binary values to fileb4.

STEP 2: USER-DEFINED BLOCK SIZE
- Specify the block size (BS) as chosen by the user. It must match the block size used during both encryption and decryption.

STEP 3: INTERMEDIATE VALUE REPRESENTATION
- Determine the number of bits needed to select the binary value (SZ) from file B4 using the equation ceil ($\log_2$ (N)).

STEP 4: DECRYPTION KEY USAGE
- Generate decryption key as d.

STEP 5: DECIMAL NUMBER GENERATION
- Read bits of size SZ from fileb4 and convert them into decimal numbers, storing them accordingly.
- Generate a set of decimal numbers based on the size of SZ.

STEP 6: MESSAGE DECRYPTION
- Decrypt the message using equation $m = c^d \bmod N$, successively reading decimal values from the list.

STEP 7: BINARY REPRESENTATION AND FILE STORAGE
- Convert the output of step 6 into binary form.
- Represent each binary bit as a number of bits equal to the block size (bs).
- Save the result in a file named fileb5.

STEP 8: DECIMAL NUMBER CONVERSION
- Convert 8-bit binary numbers from fileb5 into equivalent decimal numbers.
- Create symbols from the decimal numbers and store them in a file.

STEP 9: CIPHERTEXT RECOVERY
- The original ciphertext message (C1) is restored and stored in fileb6.

25.4 Implementation of Modified RSA on Mobile Banking

The deployment of the modified RSA algorithm within the realm of mobile banking significantly enhances the security of communication channels between mobile applications and banking

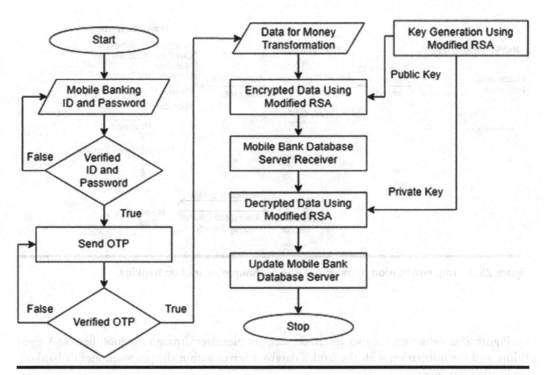

Figure 25.1   Showcases the meticulous attention to detail in fortifying mobile banking security.

servers. This variant of the RSA algorithm, a renowned public-key encryption technique, is adept at ensuring the confidentiality of data transmission. The adaptation and application of the modified RSA algorithm for mobile banking have been developed using the Python programming language, showcasing its versatility and effectiveness in cryptographic implementations (Khang & Hahanov et al., 2022).

Figure 25.1 elucidates the systematic workflow of the proposed modified RSA application in mobile banking, with a particular focus on the critical phases of key generation, encryption, and decryption, thereby underscoring the algorithm's robustness in safeguarding digital transactions.

In the process flow depicted in Figure 25.1, the user initiates a session in the proposed mobile banking system by inputting their customer ID and password. Upon successful authentication through the correct credentials, the system dispatches an OTP to the user for enhanced security. Following the OTP's successful verification, the user proceeds to input transaction details for fund transfer. This proposed methodology ensures the robust security of data transmission across the network.

Utilizing the modified RSA algorithm, the banking server generates a unique pair of public and private keys. Subsequently, it securely shares its public key with the mobile application. It is imperative to safeguard the integrity of the public key to thwart potential man-in-the-middle attacks. During the transmission of sensitive information, such as money transfer requests from the mobile banking application to the server, the application encrypts the data using the bank's public key. This encryption ensures that only the server, possessing the corresponding private key, can decrypt and access the transmitted data, thereby upholding the confidentiality and integrity of the transaction process as shown in Figure 25.2.

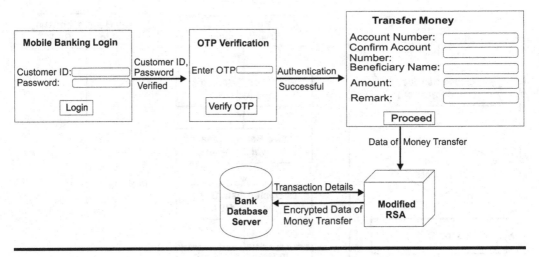

Figure 25.2   Implementation of modified RSA technique on mobile banking.

Figure 25.2 delineates the user interface, security measures through the modified RSA algorithm, and the integration with the bank's database server within the proposed mobile banking application framework.

This framework features several key components, including pages for mobile banking login, OTP verification, and money transfer operations. The adoption of the modified RSA algorithm plays a pivotal role in this context, providing robust encryption and decryption mechanisms for data during transactions, thereby ensuring the security of customer information within the mobile banking ecosystem.

The process initiates when a customer accesses the system through the mobile banking login interface. The bank's database server is strategically employed to securely store crucial data related to mobile banking activities. Upon successful authentication, the system is designed to dispatch an OTP to the customer's registered mobile number, a process that is subsequently verified via the OTP verification interface. Following the successful verification of the OTP, users are then prompted to input transaction details for money transfers.

The core of this secure transaction process is the modified RSA algorithm, which is utilized to generate encryption keys. These keys are then used to encrypt transaction data before it is securely transmitted to the bank's database server. Upon receipt, a decryption process is employed, converting the encrypted transaction data back into a readable format. This sophisticated use of the modified RSA algorithm not only ensures the secure transmission of data but also fortifies the mobile banking application against potential cyber threats, thereby safeguarding the integrity and confidentiality of user transactions.

The implementation of the modified RSA methodology for mobile banking is accomplished using the Python programming language, a versatile tool known for its efficiency and readability. Python facilitates the seamless integration of key generation, encryption, and decryption processes within the modified RSA framework. This choice of programming language not only enhances the development process but also ensures the robustness and security of the mobile banking application. The following snippet provides an insight into the programming code employed to execute the proposed technique as shown in Algorithm 25.3.

Algorithm 25.3: Process of Mobile Banking Money Transformation System

Step 1: Input Customer ID and Password
Step 2: if (Verified (User ID) and Verified (Password)) then
Step 3:   print ("User ID and Password Correct")
Step 4:   If (Verified (OTP))
                    print ("Authentication successful")
                    Goto Step 6
              Else
                    print ("OTP not match: Resend OTP")
                    Goto Step 4
              End if
Step 5: Else
                    print ("Invalid user ID and Password")
                    Goto Step 1
              End if
Step 6: Input data of money transfer such as account no, confirm account no, beneficiary name, amount, and remark
Step 7: Encrypted data of money transfer using the proposed Modified RSA
Step 8: Encrypted data of money transfer sent to Bank Database Server
Step 9: The Bank database server sent Transaction details to the Modified RSA
Step 10: Decrypted transaction details using Proposed Modified RSA
Step 11: Customer view the transaction details
Step 12: Exit

25.5 Results and Discussion

This section provides a comprehensive overview of the outcomes stemming from the implementation of our proposed algorithms. The modified RSA algorithms, as recommended in our method, have demonstrated an exceptional level of data protection, ensuring peak security for both encryption and decryption keys. The efficacy of our suggested approach has been tested across various file types, encompassing text, image, audio, cpp, pdf, and exe files, each varying in size. One distinctive feature of our approach is the differentiated encryption times observed for each file type, regardless of key size and the number of users involved. This nuanced encryption model is a noteworthy departure from conventional methods, where encryption time is often uniform across different file types. By tailoring the encryption process to the unique characteristics of each file type, our proposed model enhances security significantly.

To quantify these improvements, Table 25.1 presents estimated encryption measurement and Table 25.2 presents estimated decryption time measurement, offering a detailed comparison of the performance of our proposed model across various file types and sizes. The results underscore the effectiveness of our approach in bolstering data protection and encryption efficiency, marking a substantial advancement over traditional, uniform encryption models.

Table 25.1 presents a comprehensive analysis of encryption times using the modified RSA algorithm across a spectrum of file sizes, ranging from 1067 bytes to 2,028 bytes. The proposed algorithm's performance has been systematically evaluated across diverse file types, including pdf, audio, image, word, cpp, and exe. The first column of the table delineates the types of plain text

Table 25.1 Relation between File Sizes along with the Encryption Time of the Proposed Modified RSA Algorithm

File Name	File Size in Byte	Encryption Time/byte (second)
Data11.txt	1067	0.000082667
Picture1.jpg	1,604	0.000237039
Data12.txt	2,028	0.0000789079
Picture2.jpg	3,972	0.000430622
Record1.mp3	4,534	0.00114296
Image3.jpg	5,832	0.000294067
Data4.txt	6,407	0.000173806
Text1.pdf	7,153	0.000413228
Text2.pdf	8,944	0.00054074
Prime.cpp	9,374	0.00089903
Record2.mp3	12,442	0.000533061
Factorial.cpp	13,230	0.000428077
Picture.jpg	15,673	0.000639731
Hello.exe	17,401	0.000826702
Text3.pdf	18,602	0.000686345
win.com	20,805	0.000955078
Multi.exe	25,349	0.000782109
Text5.pdf	28,557	0.001157802
Record5.mp3	32,363	0.001218823
Data61.txt	1067	0.001360798
Picture21.jpg	1,604	0.002440806
Data2.txt	2,028	0.005088931

messages subjected to encryption, while the second column specifies the corresponding sizes of these messages in bytes. The third column, an essential metric, outlines the encryption time per byte achieved through the application of the modified RSA algorithm.

A notable observation is the variability in encryption times, ranging from 0.000082667 to 0.005088931 seconds per byte for the modified RSA algorithm. This dynamic range emphasizes the adaptability and efficiency of our proposed algorithm, demonstrating its ability to accommodate different file sizes and types without compromising on encryption speed. The subsequent sections delve into a detailed interpretation of these results, shedding light on the implications of the observed encryption times for various file types and sizes.

Table 25.2   Relation between File Sizes along with the Decryption Time of the Proposed Modified RSA Algorithm

File Name	File Size in Byte	Decryption Time/byte (second)
Data11.txt	1067	0.000282909
Picture1.jpg	1,604	0.000437281
Data12.txt	2,028	0.00027915
Picture2.jpg	3,972	0.000630864
Record1.mp3	4,534	0.001343202
Image3.jpg	5,832	0.000494309
Data4.txt	6,407	0.000374048
Text1.pdf	7,153	0.00061347
Text2.pdf	8,944	0.000740982
Prime.cpp	9,374	0.001099272
Record2.mp3	12,442	0.000733303
Factorial.cpp	13,230	0.000628319
Picture.jpg	15,673	0.000839973
Hello.exe	17,401	0.001026944
Text3.pdf	18,602	0.000886587
win.com	20,805	0.00115532
Multi.exe	25,349	0.000982351
Text5.pdf	28,557	0.001358044
Record5.mp3	32,363	0.001419065
Data61.txt	1067	0.00156104
Picture21.jpg	1,604	0.002641048
Data2.txt	2,028	0.005289173

Table 25.2 illustrates the decryption times achieved through the application of the modified RSA algorithm across a spectrum of file sizes and types. The proposed algorithm's efficacy has been rigorously tested on diverse file formats, including pdf, audio, image, word, cpp, and exe. The first column of the table categorizes the types of plain text messages subjected to decryption, while the second column quantifies the sizes of these messages in bytes. A critical metric, the third column, outlines the decryption time per byte achieved through the utilization of the modified RSA algorithm. Noteworthy is the observed range of decryption times, varying between 0.000282909 and 0.005289173 seconds per byte for the proposed modified RSA algorithm.

This range underscores the adaptability and efficiency of our algorithm, showcasing its ability to handle different file sizes and types while maintaining a consistent level of decryption speed.

An essential observation derived from the results is the consistent increase in both encryption and decryption times corresponding to the file size. This correlation between processing times and file size is a key aspect that informs the algorithm's performance characteristics and provides valuable insights into its scalability across varying data dimensions. The subsequent sections delve into a detailed interpretation of these findings, shedding light on the implications of the observed decryption times for various file types and sizes.

25.6 Analysis

This section conducts a comprehensive analysis of the proposed encryption and decryption techniques, leveraging graphical representations to distiller and scrutinize the insights presented in Section 5. Through these graphical depictions, we aim to elucidate the nuanced relationship between file size and the corresponding encryption and decryption times per byte, as facilitated by the modified RSA algorithm. The graphical representations serve as visual aids to enhance the interpretation of the experimental findings. They offer a clear and intuitive illustration of how the proposed algorithm performs across varying file sizes. By graphically depicting the encryption and decryption times per byte, we can discern patterns, trends, and potential performance optimizations (Khang, 2024).

These visualizations contribute to a deeper understanding of the algorithm's behavior, particularly its responsiveness to changes in file size. Examining the graphical representations enables us to identify potential scalability issues, areas of efficiency, and performance trade-offs inherent in the proposed RSA algorithm. In the subsequent sections, we delve into a detailed interpretation of these graphical representations, extracting meaningful insights to inform a nuanced understanding of the proposed encryption and decryption techniques' performance characteristics as shown in Figure 25.3.

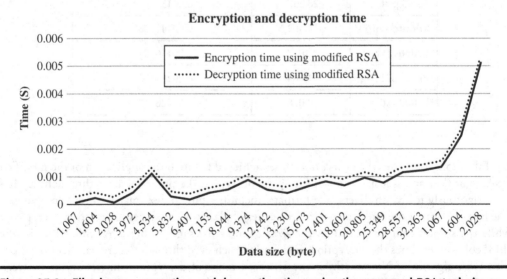

Figure 25.3   File size vs. encryption and decryption time using the proposed RSA technique.

The graphical representation of the data from Table 25.1 and Table 25.2 utilizes both a continuous solid line and a dotted line. The dotted line represents the decryption time per, while the solid line indicates the encryption time per byte using the modified RSA algorithm.

Observably, the graph highlights that the decryption time is notably higher than the encryption time. Furthermore, it visually demonstrates an exponential increase in times per byte as the file size grows. Beyond a certain file size threshold, the algorithm implementation incurs a considerable time overhead during decryption. This efficiency in handling larger files enhances the overall performance of the algorithm (Khang, Rath et al., 2023).

The examination of time efficiency underscores the practicality of implementing the suggested method in real-world applications. This proposed technique significantly bolsters security in mobile banking compared to the existing application reinforcing the robustness of the proposed method. It applies to any online mobile transaction that provides harder security of transforming secure data. The research findings highlight the efficacy of the proposed algorithm, showcasing improved speed and security for online transactions. Consequently, these advancements significantly contribute to fortifying the integrity of digital interactions and transactions within the realm of mobile banking.

25.7 Conclusion

This research has explored the critical intersection of mobile banking and data security, recognizing the integral role that mobile banking plays in contemporary banking operations. The transformative influence of information technology has driven significant shifts in the operational landscape of the banking sector, with mobile banking emerging as a fundamental essence of financial services. However, the escalating adoption of mobile banking has brought forth the imperative for robust security measures in the intricate processes of data transformation.

The innovative modification proposed to the RSA algorithm in this research signifies a targeted response to the security challenges posed by mobile banking environments. The findings of this work underscore the potential of the modified RSA approach to significantly enhance the overall security posture of mobile banking. By offering a tailored solution that addresses the specific requirements of this dynamic landscape, the proposed modification presents a promising avenue for advancing data protection in mobile financial services. As mobile banking continues to evolve, the insights and enhancements provided by this research offer valuable contributions to the ongoing discourse on securing the future of banking in the digital era (Khang, Shah, Rani, 2023).

References

Ali, G., Dida, M. A., & Sam, A. E., "A Secure and Efficient Multi-Factor Authentication Algorithm for Mobile Money Applications", Future Internet, 13 (12), (2021). https://doi.org/10.3390/fi13120299

Al-Shabi, M. A., "A Survey on Symmetric and Asymmetric Cryptography Algorithms in Information Security", International Journal of Scientific and Research Publications, 9 (3), (2019). http://doi.org/10.29322/IJSRP.9.03.2019.p8779

Bhadauriya, P., Suthar, F., & Chaudhary, S., "A Novel Technique for Secure Communication in Cryptography", International Journal of Advanced Research in Computer and Communication Engineering, 6 (3), (2017). http://doi.org/10.17148/IJARCCE.2017.6374

Bisht, N., & Singh, S., "A Comparative Study of Some Symmetric and Asymmetric Key Cryptography Algorithms", International Journal of Innovative Research in Science, Engineering and Technology, 4 (3), (2015). http://doi.org/10.15680/IJIRSET.2015.0403043

Devi, R. A., & Arunachalam, A. R., "Enhancement of IoT Device Security Using an Improved Elliptic Curve Cryptography Algorithm and Malware Detection Utilizing Deep LSTM", High-Confidence Computing, 3 (2), (2023). http://doi.org/10.1016/j.hcc.2023.100117

Gupta, C., & Reddy, N. V. S., "Enhancement of Security of Diffie-Hellman Key Exchange Protocol Using RSA Cryptography", Journal of Physics: Conference Series, 2161 (1), (2022). http://doi.org/10.1088/1742-6596/2161/1/012014

Hossain, Md. A., Hossain, Md. B., Uddin, Md. S., & Imtiaz, Md. S., "Performance Analysis of Different Cryptography Algorithms", International Journal of Advanced Research in Computer Science and Software Engineering, 6 (3), 659–665, (2016).

Islam, Md. Ashiqul, Kobita, Aysha Akter, Hossen, Md. Sagar, Rumi, Laila Sultana, Karim, Rafat, & Tabassum, Tasfia. (2021). Data Security System for A Bank Based on Two Different Asymmetric Algorithms Cryptography. In Evolutionary Computing and Mobile Sustainable Networks: Proceedings of ICECMSN 2020. Springer.

Khang, A. (Ed.). (2024). Applications and Principles of Quantum Computing. IGI Global. https://doi.org/10.4018/979-8-3693-1168-4

Khang, A., Abdullayev, V. H., Alyar, A. V., Khalilov, M., Ragimova, N. A., & Niu, Y. (2024). Introduction to Quantum Computing and Its Integration Applications. In Khang A. (Ed.), Applications and Principles of Quantum Computing (pp. 25–45). IGI Global. https://doi.org/10.4018/979-8-3693-1168-4.ch002

Khang, A., Hahanov, V., Abbas, G. L., & Hajimahmud, V. A. (2022). Cyber-Physical-Social System and Incident Management. In AI-Centric Smart City Ecosystems: Technologies, Design and Implementation (1st Ed.). CRC Press. https://doi.org/10.1201/9781003252542-2

Khang, A., Rath, K. C., Panda, N., & Kumar, A. (2024). Quantum Mechanics Primer: Fundamentals and Quantum Computing. In Khang A. (Ed.), Applications and Principles of Quantum Computing (pp. 1–24). IGI Global. https://doi.org/10.4018/979-8-3693-1168-4.ch001

Khang, A., Rath, K. C., Satapathy, S. K., Kumar, A., Das, S. R., & Panda, M. R. (2023). Enabling the Future of Manufacturing: Integration of Robotics and IoT to Smart Factory Infrastructure in Industry 4.0. In Khang A., Shah V., & Rani S. (Eds.), Handbook of Research on AI-Based Technologies and Applications in the Era of the Metaverse (pp. 25–50). IGI Global. https://doi.org/10.4018/978-1-6684-8851-5.ch002

Khang, A., Shah, V., & Rani, S. (Eds.). (2023). Handbook of Research on AI-Based Technologies and Applications in the Era of the Metaverse. IGI Global. https://doi.org/10.4018/978-1-6684-8851-5

Mehic, M., Niemiec, M., Rass, S., Ma, J., Peev, M., Aguado, A., Martin, V., Schauer, S., Poppe, A., & Pacher, C., "Quantum Key Distribution: A Networking Perspective", ACM Computing Surveys (CSUR), 53 (5), (2020). http://doi.org/10.1145/3402192

Mohamad, M. S. A., Din, R., & Ahmad, J. I., "Research Trends Review on RSA Scheme of Asymmetric Cryptography Techniques", Bulletin of Electrical Engineering and Informatics, 10 (1), (2021). http://doi.org/10.11591/eei.v10i1.2493

Neela, K. L., & Kavitha, V., "An Improved RSA Technique with Efficient Data Integrity Verification for Outsourcing Database in Cloud", Wireless Personal Communications, 123 (3), (2022). https://doi.org/10.1007/s11277-021-09248-8

Orucho, D. O., Awuor, F. M., Makiya, R., & Oduor, C., "Review of Algorithms for Securing Data Transmission in Mobile Banking", Modern Economy, 14 (9), (2023). https://doi.org/10.4236/me.2023.149062

Sarjiyus, O., Baha, B. Y., & Garba, E. J., "Enhanced Security Framework for Internet Banking Services", Journal of Information Technology and Computing, 2 (1), (2021). https://doi.org/10.48185/jitc.v2i1.162

Sujatha, K., Rao, P. V. N., Rao, A. A., & Rajesh, L. V, "Renowned Information Security Algorithms: a Comparative Study", International Journal of Engineering Research & Technology, 5 (2), (2016).

Tian, B., Han, S., Parvin, S., Hu, J., & Das, S., "Self-Healing Key Distribution Schemes for Wireless Networks: A Survey", The Computer Journal, 54 (4), (2011). https://doi.org/10.1093/comjnl/bxr022

Chapter 26

Innovative Teaching Materials for Banking and Financial Learners Using the Artificial General Internet of Things (AGIoT)

Muthmainnah Muthmainnah, Busrah Busrah,
Besse Darmawati, Ahmad Al Yakin, Erkol Bayram,
Alhamzah Alnoor, and Subathra Chelladurai

26.1 Introduction

Changes and advancements in all spheres of life have a direct impact on sustainable education and the quality of education. The primary need to effectively address the demands of change and development lies in the demand for high-quality education. It is important to encourage the development of intelligent Indonesian individuals who can live peaceful, transparent, and democratic lives and participate effectively in fair competition.

Therefore, improving educational performance is very important in the era of globalization. The main goal of education in Indonesia is to produce students who can contribute to the development and welfare of the Indonesian nation, thereby fostering a sense of national pride and identity. This progress has had an impact on the transformation of human lifestyles, learning styles, and teaching styles, especially in the field of education. Teachers are obliged not only to impart knowledge but also to develop expertise in helping students overcome learning difficulties effectively (González-Pérez & Ramírez-Montoya, 2022).

Technological advances create problems in improving education standards in Indonesia, considering that not all individuals are able to utilize their potential to the maximum and the technology pedagogical content knowledge skills (TPACK) are low. Ong and Annamalai (2023) state that

DOI: 10.4324/9781003501947-26

technology functions as a tool that society uses to anticipate and adapts to change. Technology can improve the educational process in schools by serving as a tool and resource for teachers and students in the Metaverse era.

Therefore, changes are needed in the education sector to reflect the pace of change in science and technology. Reviving the use of technical breakthroughs in the education sector is driven by the progressive evolution of science and technology and the transformation of learning environments from offline to hybrid models. Marougkas et al. (2024) mention that the learning activities cover a lot of ground and include things such as objectives, resources, evaluation criteria, methods, media, and teaching technology. Of these components, the most important is teaching materials, which include all the resources used for education and learning implementation plans. Teaching modules are an important part of the pedagogical process, and these teaching materials are essential resources for students to use either independently or as part of classroom teaching.

To actively involve students in the learning process, it is important for educators to prepare quality teaching materials that are adaptable to students' conditions and current developments. Students are more actively involved and see the results of their learning when the teacher is present to lead the process and when textbooks and additional media are also available (Al Yakin et al., 2023 ; Wijaya et al., 2020).

More and more teaching resources, which include both textual and multimedia components, are moving online to meet the needs of many students. These are all examples of online teaching materials, also called web-based learning resources or Artificial General Internet of Things (AGIoT). According to Rajaram (2023) and Konkol and Dymek (2024), technology-based education AGIoT plays an important role in creating interesting and comprehensive learning plans that have a student-centered learning approach. However, the appeal of boring learning activities, the lack of excitement among students, and their decreasing engagement are still critical concerns today.

Among the various developing technologies, educational technology is notable not only for its ability to update old methods but also for its potential to bring about a fundamental change in educational beliefs and philosophies. The existing learning methodologies are struggling to handle the large amount of information available, highlighting the insufficiency of traditional teaching methods in fulfilling the needs of the modern period, which is characterized by increased awareness and rapid technological progress (Muthmainnah et al., 2023).

Educators and support personnel have always been dedicated to offering individualized care and assistance to every student, utilizing their whole capabilities to enhance the learning process. Integrating teaching machines and other auxiliary tools has the potential to improve personalized training and directly influence students' academic achievement. Over the course of educational advancements, from simple teaching machines to the integration of advanced intelligent teaching systems and technologies, classroom teaching methods have consistently adjusted to meet the changing demands of education.

The combination of Internet of Things (IoT) and Computer-Aided Design (CAD) in teaching systems has led to the emergence of a growing sector called smart teaching systems (Ikubanni et al., 2022). This convergence is expected to reduce the workload of teachers, enabling them to engage in empirical research, make wise decisions, and provide purposeful, methodical, and focused instruction. As a result, students' academic performance and overall educational quality will be enhanced.

The use of multimedia teaching methods is becoming more varied and advanced, aligning with the improvements in Information Technology (IT). These advancements are crucial in promoting novel educational models and pushing attempts to modernize education (Li & Liu, 2024). Teaching systems are the prime examples of educational modernization. Due to the extensive use of computer and network technologies, teaching systems have been improved and their range of application has expanded. This has led to the creation of interactive teaching systems. By giving equal importance to the autonomy and control of both teachers and students in the teaching process, these systems enable effective communication, promote student involvement and excitement, and smoothly incorporate different educational phases (Rogti, 2024).

In the modern age of technical progress, online educational platforms have achieved substantial progress. Kamińska et al. (2023) developed a teaching system that uses augmented reality technology on mobile devices to involve learners in course mapping and parameter setting. This allows for real-time rendering and interactive communication. Hui et al. (2022) and Volioti et al. (2022) developed a 3D interactive teaching system using contradiction space analysis and Unity 3D virtual reality (VR) technology to improve the effectiveness of teaching demonstrations. Nevertheless, the implementation of these technologies in real-world scenarios demonstrated less than ideal educational results.

Due to the emergence of economic globalization, countries throughout the world have established a collective group with common interests, which requires cooperation to tackle global difficulties. English functions as a lingua franca in this particular situation, enabling communication between people from different countries. Online English teaching methods surpass the limitations of traditional time and location limits, allowing for effective and captivating teaching experiences. Thus, educators should utilize internet and multimedia technologies to improve the variety, availability, and effectiveness of English language instruction, ultimately raising the standard of English education (Al-khresheh, 2024).

AI and the IoT is a network that effortlessly gathers real-time data using different sensing devices and scanning technologies. It enables constant connectivity between different entities and promotes effective information management (Crompton et al., 2024). Nowadays, IoT technology efficiently facilitates the gathering, retention, analysis, linking, and utilization of data, offering potential for revolutionary applications in education. There has been a real decline in academic achievement over the past year, and one of the reasons is the lack of adaptation of media and technology as the main teaching aids, which is exacerbated by student boredom caused by teaching materials that are not up to date. Therefore, knowledge about learning design is summarized in the process of creating teaching materials, which allows identification, elaboration, and evaluation of content and learning models.

The quick development of new technologies has made it possible to provide a wide range of high-quality asynchronous learning experiences tailored to each student's particular needs and interests (Wang, Zhang et al., 2023). Bi and Ye (2024) both agree that high-quality learning resources are very important for improving student performance in class. Development of innovative teaching materials for banking and financial learners using the AGIoT is an example of the kind of research that encourages academics to do this.

26.2 AGIoT Environment in English Class

The era of artificial intelligence (AI) is causing significant changes in various industries and is having an increasing influence in the field of English education (Park and Kwon, 2024). In addition, they argue to shaping curricula in topics such as science, technology, engineering, and mathematics (STEM), AI is also changing the education industry. Researchers and companies are increasingly optimistic about the capabilities of AI and related technologies, including machine learning, deep learning, natural language processing, and computer vision.

The application of AI is expanding to the education industry to meet the growing need for customized and intelligent teaching materials. AI systems in education can help teachers prioritize their teaching tactics rather than dedicating time to administrative responsibilities. In contrast to the traditional classroom model, these tools make it easier to create global learning environments free from geographic restrictions. They are hired to overcome persistent difficulties such as individualized instruction, accommodating varying student needs and abilities, and many other issues.

According to Mukhamediev et al. (2022), artificial intelligence or machine intelligence, is a term used to describe intelligence displayed by machines as opposed to natural intelligence. In the field of computer science, the domain of AI research revolves around the investigation of "intelligent agents": any apparatus capable of perceiving its surroundings and making decisions to optimize the probability of achieving its goals. AI is increasingly being used in the fields of education and problem solving. It has become a fundamental component of our lives, influencing various elements such as online commerce and recreation.

The education industry is effectively leveraging IoT devices to improve collaboration, engagement, and accessibility in education due to their adaptable and dynamic nature. IoT devices offer students reliable access to educational resources, communication platforms, and high-quality information, while enabling teachers to evaluate student learning progress in real-time.

Learning experiences during the COVID-19 epidemic, which has highlighted the importance of educational resources, and the IoT enables a shift from conventional to digital teaching approaches with added benefits and increased effectiveness. The IoT can be used to educate in several disciplines, including English as a Foreign Language (EFL). Kessler (2020) state to increase understanding of language learning authentically, use animation and images.

In addition to smart attendance devices, boards, and integrated alarm systems, the IoT enables a shift from the physical world to a world of centralized control systems with automation in schools. According to an education expert, the IoT encompasses more than just technology. This involves knowledge exchange, communication, the creation of learning communities, and increased professionalism in schools. The following are the main tasks of educational leaders in maximizing the potential of IoT in the world of education.

Lately, the widespread incorporation of advanced ITs like mobile internet in learning EFL, IoT, cloud computing, big data, and AI has had a significant influence on different aspects of society. The prevailing sentiment in English educational circles aligns with the idea that modernization is dependent on IT. The revolutionary potential of IT for the evolution of education is well acknowledged. Many schools are currently making efforts to improve the development and implementation of educational technology in response to a set of policies aimed at promoting the use of technology in education. These schools are taking steps to achieve smart education by creating smart classrooms and campuses (Genç & Kırmızıbayrak, 2024).

According to researcher Badrkhani (2023), the concept of a smart learning environment is considered the technical basis of smart education from a design standpoint. As a new and innovative learning environment, it requires integration with sophisticated concepts and theories of learning, teaching, management, and utilization. Modern IT, learning resources, tools, and activities support this integration. Simultaneously, it necessitates a thorough understanding of the dynamics of learning in order to obtain new data or carry out scientific research and data mining on the previous data of learners. The system must generate customized learning tasks and activities based on the learners' traits and situations, provide guidance for informed decision-making, and facilitate the development of intelligent capabilities and actions.

Expanding on previous studies, researchers Hoel and Mason (2018) and Guo et al. (2021) propose the idea of moving from a digital learning environment to a smart learning environment, considering the latter as a more advanced version of the former. Through the synthesis of various viewpoints, the authors establish the definition of a "smart learning environment" as a dynamic setting that is capable of perceiving the context in which learning takes place, identifying the characteristics of the learner, providing appropriate resources and interactive tools, documenting the learning process, and assessing the results of learning in order to promote effective learning. In addition, researchers Jagatheesaperumal et al. (2024) define the elements and technological characteristics of the smart learning environment, emphasizing its function in promoting smooth, captivating, and efficient learning experiences that are customized to meet the needs of learners.

Scholarly analysis of Joshi et al. (2024) breaks down smart education by examining its system, technology, and function, with a focus on the complex ecosystem that includes different educational activities, procedures, and technical components. The concept consists of four primary components: intelligent learning, intelligent teaching, intelligent educational materials, and technology infrastructure. In addition, researcher Dincer (2020) elaborates on the fundamental technologies that support smart education, explaining their characteristics and potential uses, and offering suggestions for their incorporation and advancement in teaching English. Following that, researchers Zhao and Nazir (2022) provide valuable information about the structure of systems and the technologies that support smart education in teaching EFL. They emphasize the significance of educators and learners having strong capabilities in applying IT.

Wu et al. (2024) thorough comprehension of smart education relies on its inherent connection with smart settings and instructional approaches. The goal of smart education is to develop clever individuals by utilizing innovative teaching methods and promoting smart learning in an atmosphere filled with abundant knowledge. Scholar Jiang (2022) promotes the development of intelligent learning settings and the use of intelligent teaching methods to enhance learners' intellect and creativity, with a focus on emphasizing education that cultivates knowledge. They emphasize the importance of suitable technology in creating flexible learning, living, and working settings that promote ongoing learning and innovation.

26.3 Design Teaching Materials for EFL through AGIoT

Various contemporary tools can be used to overcome human challenges. In the fields of science and technology, this era saw significant advancement. The intricacies of human existence are undeniably linked to the fields of science and technology. Exponentially, the integration of media and technology in the learning process has a significant influence on students' academic improvement. Therefore, to maximize the integration of media and technology in EFL classes, modern and innovative learning models are needed.

Students who are learning EFL require many modifications to achieve mastery of language skills. Learning styles have an impact on the way students learn, and it is important to consider them when creating learning procedures (Ravshanovna, 2024). EFL learning is a terrible threat in the EFL classroom. Many students still feel anxious about learning EFL. However, advances in science and technology influence young people's perceptions of using the artificial generative IoT as a personalized EFL learning medium.

This growth is also changing traditional learning models in higher education. According to Pedro et al. (2019) the UNESCO website, information and communications technology (ICT), and AI can help improve access to education, promote equality in education, improve the quality of teaching and learning, support teacher professional development, and make education management more efficient in terms of governance and administration (Khang & Inna et al., 2024).

According to a survey conducted by UNICEF, the Indonesian Ministry of Communication and Information, and Harvard University, the report "Safety of Digital Media Use among Children and Adolescents in Indonesia" states that the number of internet users in Indonesia, including children and adolescents, is estimated to reach 30 million, which is about 40% of the country's population. This study examines the online behavior of a group of children and teenagers consisting of 400 participants aged between 10 and 19 years from various regions in Indonesia, both urban and rural.

Surprisingly, 98% of children and adolescents claim to have knowledge about the internet, while 79.5% recognize themselves as active internet users. This means that educational institutions not only encourage students' acquisition of knowledge but also promote their ability to apply that knowledge, foster skills for collaboration, and foster a lifelong learning mind-set. Therefore, instructors must demonstrate a strong dedication to improving their professional skills to take full advantage of this emerging prospect. In addition, they must actively update their pedagogical approaches to science teaching.

Apart from that, Van Nguyen et al. (2022) highlighted that the existence and progress of ICT in learning EFL have currently facilitated opportunities and increased the scope of interaction between lecturers, teachers, and experts and students, between students themselves, and between students and learning resources. This interaction can take place at any time and in any location without being constrained by physical space or time constraints (Zarrabi et al., 2024). ICT improves the delivery and presentation of learning materials and ideas, making them more interesting and enjoyable. The emergence of ICT as a new technology creates challenges for lecturers and teachers to acquire expertise in order to choose and utilize ICT effectively and efficiently in implementing the learning process.

There has been a strong push in recent years, both within and outside schools, to utilize ICT in the EFL classroom, both in terms of the material taught and the teaching methods used. Over time, the push for computer innovation has had significant goals: the main goals are twofold: first, to improve students' skills and prepare them to integrate into a society that has experienced significant changes due to IT; and second, to utilize computer-based content and tools to improve and optimize the teaching and learning process in the traditional curriculum. According to Pradas (2024), IT plays an important role in the field of education, especially in the lecture context. However, there are still many universities in Indonesia that have not implemented IT-based lectures. This fact became an impetus for the author to create IT-based teaching resources with the aim of improving the quality of EFL education.

The EFL lecturer engages in the creation of instructional materials to address learning difficulties by considering the objectives and needs of the students, as well as aligning with the required competencies (Badrkhani, 2023). Additionally, the lecturer's teaching methodology incorporates innovative approaches to learning. Teaching materials refer to the resources, knowledge, and tools that instructors utilize to facilitate learning and create an environment that motivates students to engage in the learning process. Teaching materials can take the shape of both printed and non-printed items. Printed teaching materials encompass lecture material, problem-solving aids, and learning guides. Non-printed teaching materials encompass audio, video/film, and other multimedia that are necessary for the learning process and our study advancement of pioneering pedagogical methods fourteen meeting.

The teaching materials are designed to meet the curriculum requirements and cater to the specific needs of students, considering their individual features and learning environment. Teaching resources can provide students with additional learning materials as alternatives to textbooks, which might be challenging to comprehend at times. Effective educational resources should consistently align with the advancements in technology or AGIoT, art, and the ever-evolving societal landscape of globalization. The purpose of developing instructional materials is to create creative and interactive materials by using the scientific method and utilizing various models and technology as a medium. The use of instructional resources in educational endeavors not only focused on the actions of educators, but also engaged students actively in the process of acquiring knowledge.

According to Hsieh and Hsieh (2019), the use of educational resources facilitates an autonomous learning experience. When students use teaching materials for learning, they have the ability to learn at their own pace and alter their speed based on their own talents. Students who possess a rapid aptitude for learning will finish their educational pursuits before their peers, without encountering any hindrances from their slower classmates. In order to prepare economics students to become educators and researchers, it is necessary to design and implement innovative learning methods. These methods will equip them to effectively fulfill their roles as educators and contribute to research and development. Additionally, they will be prepared to tackle the issues of the 21st century. According to Tran (2021), English educators require fundamental abilities such as critical thinking, problem solving, collaborative learning, learner-cantered teaching, and digital literacy training.

The development of AGIoT can cause millennial students' excessive dependence on electronic devices such as smartphones, tablets, and other screen-centric gadgets which are very important to overcome. Unfortunately, today's student life seems to be centered solely on these devices, with the main emphasis on gaming and social networking. Nevertheless, professionals in the field of IoT have effectively shifted attention from excessive emphasis on gadgets to more comprehensive educational goals and are using IoT for their academic advancement.

Nowadays, interacting with other people around the world who have the same goals and interests has become very easy, of course learning EFL becomes even more interesting by utilizing IoT. IoT sensors in education collect data and autonomously propose relevant academic subjects to students at the other end of the screen. The use of mobile phones and tablets is quickly becoming very beneficial for students' academic performance. There are several studies that support AGIoT in English learning.

Lei et al. (2022) investigate the impact of mobile-assisted language learning on EFL learners' vocabulary learning attitudes and self-regulatory capacity. This study examines the influence of smartphone and tablet use on language learning and offers valuable insights into possible strategies to minimize adverse consequences. This study tested a latent change score model of students' attitudes toward vocabulary learning and their ability to self-regulate over a certain period of time. Over a span of 12 months, several mobile applications were incorporated into the students' English language teaching standards. The necessary data is collected by providing a scale that measures language learning attitudes and self-regulatory capacity in vocabulary acquisition.

Li (2024) suggesting the use of the MALL (mobile-assisted language learning) approach to improve the speaking skills of foreign language learners is more effective than conventional methods. In addition, the results of the moderator analysis revealed that the learning approach and duration of the intervention had a significant impact on the results. However, proficiency level, education level, language type, intervention setting, software type, type of outcome measured, and duration intensity did not have significant moderating effects. This study's findings also shed light on how foreign language learners can use MALL technology to improve their speaking skills.

Then, Younus Jasim and Rawdhan Salman (2023) discuss the significant consequences for educators, researchers, and policymakers involved in the field of language teaching and to provide guidance for the creation of effective language teaching methods that embrace technology in a targeted and impactful way. It also aims to offer valuable insights that can guide the design of language-learning programs that utilize technology.

The rapid advancement of computing and AI, the standard practice for evaluating English content will shift toward automatic assessment rather than an exceptional approach. This enhances the theoretical foundation and practical feasibility of research on an algorithmic scoring system for composition.

The growing integration of AI into the classroom, driven by the merging of IT and the English curriculum, offers a new opportunity to enhance the teaching of English and creates a flexible and responsive learning environment. In their study, Bi and Yi (2024) utilized relevant theories of curriculum, literature analysis, and field investigation to explore the implementation of AI in middle school English education. This study is based on the incorporation of IT and curriculum, with the goal of enhancing the quality and efficacy of English instruction in that specific context.

A proposition has been made for the implementation of an AI-based system to assist in the instruction of English at the university level. When English instruction is merged with the English education system, several parts are improved and made less strict. Researchers are studying how AI technology may be used in the classroom to improve the quality and effectiveness of English instruction (Karataş et al., 2024).

The English teaching network system utilizes the internet as a platform to provide remote learning opportunities. Issues may emerge in the classroom as a result of various causes, including instructors' own knowledge gaps, students' demanding expectations, insufficient resources, and prevalent negative attitudes toward the English teaching and learning approach.

In the modern era of technology, students gain advantages from a blended method of education that combines the strengths of conventional classroom teaching with online resources. Creating an exam pattern paper is a crucial component of the English education system, as it motivates students to engage in independent study. Liu and Huang's (2022) research indicates that AI-based English network teaching (AI-ENT) is a successful approach for enhancing students' performance in online courses.

There are indications that AI has the capacity to profoundly transform both the methods of education and the tools utilized for teaching in machine learning. By utilizing AI technology tools and receiving guidance from teachers, students can significantly enhance their English learning experiences. This design is derived from the reasoning principles of expert systems in the field of AI. Accessing relevant data from diverse sources can assist educators and students in improving their English language proficiency.

Evidence demonstrates that this technique enhances students' learning speed and effectiveness, as well as the relevance of the information to their lives. In this study, Liu and Lu (2023) have devised and executed an experiment aimed at enhancing English listening skills. The experiment utilizes a wireless communication microcontroller, focus on VR education and the advancement of English pedagogy. The utilization of VR technology facilitated the creation of immersive learning environments, resulting in increased student engagement and improved teacher effectiveness. The integration of VR into the educational process is becoming increasingly important in furthering the use of technology in secondary schools. This trend toward virtualization and intelligence is critical for the modernization of education.

The utilization of AI robots, which are robots that operate based on AI, in the field of education has become a very promising subject of research due to the rapid and significant advancement of AI technology. AI robots have the potential to introduce innovative methods for curriculum development and teacher training, as suggested by a growing corpus of research. However, there has not been a thorough examination of the role and emphasis of artificial intelligence robots in education (AIRE) studies (Sharadgah & Sa'di, 2022).

The study by Gligorea et al. (2023) primarily focuses on the discussion of adaptive learning, teacher evaluation, online classes, and other applications of AI in the classroom. Subsequently, the author derives inferences on the impact of these findings on classroom instruction. This has significant implications for improving the educational experience for both teachers and students (Muthmainnah et al., 2023). Ultimately, it examines the various challenges that AI-driven educational applications may face and provides recommendations for leveraging AI to advance reforms in the education sector.

This study provides a synopsis of the material development curriculum that has recently been implemented in sharia economic law study programs in Indonesia. This also includes evaluation of course materials based on comments made by participants, who are students at universities in Indonesia who are enrolled in courses majoring in sharia economics law.

Outlined in the curriculum overview are objectives, structure, and organization, content, and assessment methods. The student teacher's written responses to the questionnaire form the curriculum evaluation. First, we want to find out whether curriculum material development helps students and lecturers at EFL universities produce creative learning plans. Second, we want to know the opinions of undergraduate students regarding EFL learning for English courses based on the generative artificial IoT. Third, we want to know what problems teacher educators might encounter when trying to create and implement materials development curricula in their own classrooms.

26.4 Methods

26.4.1 Research Methodology

This study employed a mixed-method approach, incorporating both quantitative and qualitative data. The quantitative data was derived from the questionnaire administered to the students studying English for bank and finance using AGIoT. The sample consisted of 19 economic law students who were in their second semester at a private university in Indonesia. The rationale for selecting students from specific semesters is that they have completed their General English class. Next, the qualitative data was obtained from the interview conducted with three respondents to ask their opinion about the EFL teaching materials based on AGIoT.

The participants were chosen to participate in the study to gain a deeper understanding of the implementation of English banking and finance through AGIoT class and to provide suggestions for improving the structure of the English banking and finance through AGIoT course based on their experience. Survey administered to the students was modified from Muthmainnah et al.'s (2024) questionnaire. Prior to distribution to the students, the questionnaire underwent validation by an expert and a pilot study was completed. Subsequently, the quantitative analysis of the acquired Google form questionnaire was conducted.

During the interview with one student, *bahasa* Indonesia was selected as the language of choice in order to obtain thorough data from the participant. The interview guide addressed the alumna's expertise in managing the ESP course and her recommendations for enhancing the English banking and finance through AGIoT course specifically for banking and finance. The interview was subjected to qualitative analysis and interpretation using the framework proposed by Miles and Huberman (1994). This framework involves four main steps: data collection, data display, data reduction, and conclusion or verification. The focus of this study was to examine the students' viewpoint regarding the utilization of AI robots in the classroom. The researchers employed a phenomenology study design that specifically examined the students' viewpoint regarding the utilization of AI robots in English classrooms.

The researchers categorized the data in this study into two distinct groups: qualitative and quantitative data. The qualitative data was derived from the outcomes of open-ended questionnaires (needs analysis), the evaluations of materials conducted by experts, students, and teachers (suggestions). The quantitative data encompassed the evaluations provided by specialists on the product, as well as the questionnaires completed by students and teachers regarding the product, and the scores achieved by students.

The researchers employed various instruments, including interview and questionnaires for students need and want to gather data for this study. The researchers employed open- and closed-ended questionnaires to conduct a need analysis and gather responses from both students and teachers. The questionnaire was provided with the materials topic rubric to evaluate the syllabus and lesson plan and provide recommendations. The product reviews were acquired based on recommendations from both the students and the English teacher.

To examining the data, the researchers categorized the data into qualitative and quantitative data. The qualitative data comprises open-ended needs analysis surveys and reviews, which include comments from professionals, students, and lecturer. The researchers gathered all the questionnaires, reviews, and observation notes and converted them into written form by transcription. The quantitative data comprises the product review scores provided, and the surveys completed by students and teachers regarding the survey. The researchers examined the data and categorized it according to its classification. Finally, the researchers examined and contrasted the findings derived from the qualitative and quantitative data, and then drew a conclusion.

26.4.2 Procedure of Development Banking and Financial EFL Materials

At this stage, the teacher assesses the students' quality and the required content. The teacher uses two functions to evaluate student progress and attributes. The first task is to assess and manage students' basic information, which includes their previous EFL learning experiences, family background, talents, and the feedback they provide to teachers during the learning process.

The second feature functions as a score manager for students. As learning continues, student score data accumulates over time through tests and exams. The score manager makes it easier for teachers to analyze student learning progress more comprehensively. When analyzing teaching materials, teachers may use existing databases or search the internet to gather information for the analysis and design of teaching materials.

Khang, Muthmainnah et al. (2023) found that the use of multimedia presentations, ICT, and AGIoT in educational materials often increases cognitive abilities and stimulates students' interest. Therefore, the system provides students and lecturers with a comprehensive collection of AGIoT resources for easy access. This database hosts many multimedia resources specially curated for educators, such as AI Cici tutor robot or ChatGPT, Copilot, Gemini, YouTube, or Instagram. Undergraduate students can enter keywords related to the desired theme, and then a variety of related multimedia materials will appear to choose from.

Teachers have the option to include these items in the teaching resources they create for undergraduate students. Additionally, due to the complex nature of internet hyperlink connections, lecturers and students often lose concentration when conducting web searches or AI apps. Simply put, hyperlinks found on the internet offer a variety of information. Instructors and students face challenges when searching for and utilizing materials in the teaching and learning process. Additionally, students spend a lot of effort filtering out irrelevant information.

Additionally, both lecturers and students may experience disorientation due to the many inter-connected pathways. To overcome this problem, the system offers a record feature that allows lecturers to easily save important material from the internet at any time during their online research and the probability that a lecturer will successfully find suitable resources or adequate multimedia assets through several internet searches is low. Therefore, in addition to a web browser, the system offers teachers a URL collector, a URL browser recorder, and a URL resource bank to assist them in searching and collecting online resources. The URL collector allows teachers to enter new websites that they frequently use, while also offering a keyword search function for URLs already stored in the system.

URL browser recorder is a tool that allows teachers to document the names and URLs of websites they access using the system. The URL resource bank contains a comprehensive collection of useful and diverse URLs. Teachers can easily retrieve information for designing teaching materials by accessing other websites via URLs provided in the data bank. The database stores two categories of URLs: users are interested in two types of material: (1) literature focused on educational theory or psychology, and (2) course-related information, such as lesson plans and design examples of teaching activities.

26.4.3 Instruments and Data Analysis

A survey was administered to students to ascertain their sentiments on utilizing the Evoce robot. There were three perspectives from which to examine the students' perceptions. The poll comprised three elements: utilization, students' enthusiasm, and the pedagogical content when utilizing the Cici virtual tutor robot as AGIoT-based materials. The initial component comprises a set of five questions designed to assess the extent to which students fully utilize and showcase the capabilities of the Cici virtual tutor robot. The second element comprises a collection of five elements pertaining to students' statements regarding their level of interest when utilizing the AGIoT for banking and finance materials. The third aspect pertains to the pedagogical content contained within the Cici virtual tutor robot, which aids undergraduate student in the acquisition of English language.

The scoring rubric is designed as a Guttman scale, where respondents indicate their choice as either "strongly agree, agree, neutral, disagree or strongly disagree" on the scale. Each affirmative response was assigned a value of 5, while the negative response was assigned a score of 1. The respondent score was determined based on the number of statements that were approved. Therefore, a higher score indicates a greater perception of behavior, while a lower score indicates a poorer perception of the use of Cici virtual tutor robot.

To assess the possibility of organizing the statements based on their tolerance level, it is necessary to establish the Coefficient of Reproducibility (CR) and Coefficient of Scalability (CS) and found that the overall score of a student is the sole reliable indicator for estimating the amount of their reaction pattern in the context of CR. A Guttman scale is regarded to meet the unidimensional and cumulative properties if its CS is at least 0.60 and its CR is at least 0.90. The questionnaires were subsequently assessed for data adequacy using a validity test employing the Likert scale.

The CR indicates the level of reliability of a measurement using a specific scale. This can be determined by the percentage of consistent replies that can be replicated based on the scale score used to describe the measurement. The criteria for adopting the CS are that they must be greater than 0.90. The CS is utilized to assess if deviations on the repeatability scale remain within acceptable thresholds. The criteria for adopting the CS are that it must be greater than 0.60 as shown in Table 26.1.

Table 26.1 EFL Teaching Materials for Banking and Finance through AGIoT Driven

No	Description
1.	Introduction to AI in Banking and Finance
2.	Application of AI in Risk Management
3.	AI for Financial Forecasting
4.	AI-Based Customer Service Solutions
5.	AI for Regulatory Compliance
6.	Achieving the SDGs through AI in Banking
7.	AI Challenges and Ethical Considerations
8.	Mid Semester
9.	Case Studies: AI Implementation in Banking
10.	AI and Financial Inclusion
11.	AI in Sustainable Finance
12.	Project Planning and Proposal
13.	Project Development and Implementation
14.	Project Presentation and Peer Evaluation
15.	Reflections and Future Directions
16.	Final Semester

26.5 Findings and Discussion

The findings of this study were derived from two instruments: a questionnaire and an interview. The following is the description of the outcome produced by those instruments.

26.5.1 Questionnaire Outcome

The questionnaire revealed several crucial aspects regarding the implementation of English for specific objectives for students studying bank and finance. The questionnaire typically includes two sections that inquire about the respondents' proficiency in English, their amount of experience with the language, their preferred class activities, and their interest in issues linked to the tourist department. The questionnaire had an open-ended question that allowed students to write down their preferred option if it was not listed among the options offered by the researchers (Khang & Gujrati et al., 2024).

The questionnaire revealed that a large number of students had been studying English for about seven years. They stated that they had acquired knowledge of English since they were in junior high school. Regarding improving their English language skills and developing banking and finance material, there are five strategies implemented. Strategies include watching movies, listening to music, taking English programs, and accessing more educational materials (YouTube and Instagram) and using AI technology.

The survey also contained questions about the critical skills necessary for their success, with a particular focus on the importance of oral communication skills as reported by students studying banking. The students emphasized the importance of speaking and listening skills, as they believed that having a high level of competency in these skills would enable effective communication with clients especially during bank internships. This is very relevant for students in the banking and finance fields because they will interact with consumers from various countries in the future.

Apart from that, it can facilitate their communication while working abroad. In addition, having proficient speaking and listening skills will greatly facilitate their performance during job interviews in the future. Several students emphasized the importance of understanding terminology related to banking and finance, AI technology as it allows them to communicate information effectively to English-speaking consumers by integrating AI-based technology as shown in Table 26.2.

Table 26.2 Questionnaire Data Results

Description	N	Minimum	Maximum	Mean	Std. Deviation
1. I am familiar with the concept of English teaching materials through AI for the banking and finance sector.	19	2.00	5.00	3.7368	.93346
2. I believe that frequently studying banking and finance material can improve your academic or professional life.	19	3.00	5.00	4.2105	.53530
3. I support specific topics or areas in banking and finance, such as Islamic Banking and Finance: A Study of the Principles and Practices of Islamic Banking and Finance, including Islamic Banking Products and Services.	19	4.00	5.00	4.3684	.49559
4. I agree with the Financial Technology (Fintech) material: exploration of technological innovations that are transforming the banking and financial industry, such as blockchain, artificial intelligence, and mobile banking.	19	3.00	5.00	4.1053	.65784
5. I find it easy to access banking and financial materials for learning purposes (e.g., textbooks, online resources, academic journals) using AI.	19	3.00	5.00	4.4211	.60698

(Continued)

Table 26.2   Questionnaire Data Results *(Continued)*

Description	N	Minimum	Maximum	Mean	Std. Deviation
6. I would prefer if the English material covered Banking and Economic Development: An Overview of the Relationship between Banking Sector Development, Economic Growth, and Financial Inclusion in Emerging and Developing Countries.	19	3.00	5.00	4.2105	.53530
7. How effective do you think existing banking and finance materials are in meeting your learning needs.	19	3.00	5.00	4.1053	.56713
8. The use of AGIoT (e.g., videos, infographics, and 3D images) is most helpful in understanding banking and financial concepts.	19	3.00	5.00	4.4211	.69248
9. I am motivated to use interactive or AI-powered learning tools to learn banking and finance.	19	3.00	5.00	4.3684	.59726
10. I am confident that I can apply banking and finance concepts in real-world scenarios	19	3.00	5.00	3.8947	.80930
11. The challenges I face when trying to study banking and finance are learning resources, the internet, material that is difficult to understand, and a learning environment that is not supportive.	19	2.00	5.00	4.0526	.91127
12. How do you think technology, such as AI, can improve the accessibility and effectiveness of banking and finance materials?	19	3.00	5.00	4.3158	.58239
13. I believe the special features or functions of AI-powered banking and finance learning tools are very interesting.	19	3.00	5.00	4.0526	.52427
14. I think AI-assisted English learning can help create a personalized learning experience tailored to individual learning styles and preferences.	19	3.00	5.00	4.0526	.62126

(Continued)

Table 26.2 Questionnaire Data Results *(Continued)*

Description	N	Minimum	Maximum	Mean	Std. Deviation
15. My confidence in learning English has increased with AI in banking and finance education.	19	2.00	5.00	3.9474	.70504
16. I believe English course material is very important for understanding banking and finance material.	19	2.00	5.00	3.9474	.70504
17. I find learning a language that specifically focuses on banking and financial terminology very interesting.	19	3.00	5.00	4.0526	.52427
18. In my opinion, integrating artificial intelligence technology into English learning can improve vocabulary related to banking and finance.	19	3.00	5.00	4.0000	.57735
19. In my opinion, banking and finance material has an impact on improving English language skills and thinking skills.	19	3.00	5.00	3.9474	.62126
20. English material is easy to understand and uses correct grammar and language that has high reproducibility.	19	3.00	5.00	4.1053	.56713
Valid N (list wise)	19				

We asked 19 people about their experiences with AI learning materials related to banking and finance and displayed their answers in a table of descriptive statistics. On a scale from 1 (strongly disagree) to 5 (strongly agree), participants rated the claims. The standard deviation shows how spread out the answers are, while the mean value shows how much agreement there is on average among the participants. When asked about their opinions regarding the usefulness and accessibility of AI-powered learning tools for banking and finance education, participants generally gave favorable responses.

Statements regarding the efficacy of AI in improving the learning experience, preference for certain subjects, motivation to use interactive learning tools, and ease of obtaining resources received very high mean scores. Comprehension problems, a lack of adequate resources, and a hostile classroom environment were also cited by participants as barriers. Based on these results, there seems to be a lot of enthusiasm for using AI to make English learning easier, expand finance and banking vocabulary, and encourage analytical and linguistic proficiency in these areas as shown in Table 26.3.

Table 26.3 shows a value with a standard deviation of 8.86975 and an average score of 82.3158. Descriptive statistics show that the majority of the 19 participants have a positive impression of the

Table 26.3   Mean Score of the Development Banking and Finance Materials for EFL

	N	Minimum	Maximum	Mean	Std. Deviation
Banking and finance	19	68.00	100.00	82.3158	8.86975
Valid N (list wise)	19				

development of AGIoT-based EFL banking and finance teaching materials as shown in Figure 26.1 (a, b, and c).

Based on the statistical data in Table 26.4, the Cronbach's Alpha a coefficient value of 0.940 is close to 1, for a total of 20 items, indicating that this measurement has high reliability according to statistical data. This high coefficient value indicates that the items tested, the AGIoT-based EFL teaching material development variable, are closely related and consistently measure the same basic construct or concept, indicating the existence of significant internal consistency.

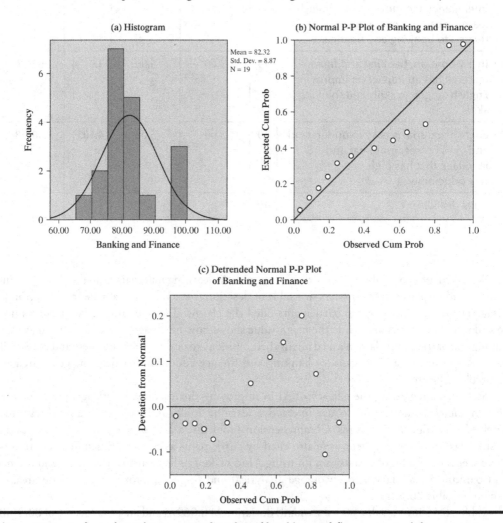

Figure 26.1   (a, b, and c) Histogram and P-plot of banking and finance materials.

Table 26.4 Reliability Statistics

Cronbach's Alpha	Number of Items
.940	20

26.5.2 Interview Results

The interview comprises a set of five inquiries pertaining to the students' experience studying English as well as her recommendations for English learning materials. The initial segment cantered on comprehending their encounter with acquiring English skills within the banking and finance sector. They asserted that English was a mandatory course in their department as she completed the class for two consecutive semesters. The initial semester was dedicated to the general English course, while the subsequent semester focused on professional English. Based on this information, we conducted a thorough examination of the syllabus available on the tourism website and discovered that the English course mentioned by the alumna is still being taught. Consequently, English remains a mandatory subject in the department.

For the second inquiry, we asked the alumna about the paramount English proficiency required by tourism students and the underlying significance behind it. Subsequently, the alumna emphasized that the primary focus for English language acquisition among tourism students should be on developing their speaking and listening skills. They emphasized that these abilities were crucial as tourism students will interact with consumers from many parts of the globe in their future professions. Consequently, it is imperative for them to possess proficient oral communication abilities in order to effectively interact with their clientele.

The respondents then proposed the essential content to be included in the course. She emphasized the importance of including additional content on tourism-related vocabulary and expanding the grammar material for both formal and informal communication. The linguistic components were recommended to be properly incorporated into the learning material based on the alumna's input. In addition, she suggested incorporating cultural elements into the course, such as non-linguistic characteristics, geography, and art.

When we inquired about the necessity of including those features, she explained that incorporating them would be advantageous for their future profession as a tour guide, particularly in relation to the non-linguistics specialization. She emphasized the importance of possessing non-linguistic abilities, particularly for individuals who lack the ability to effectively communicate or articulate ideas verbally in English. They can utilize motions to elucidate information for the customers. Therefore, she deemed it crucial to be included in the course.

The previous question concerned the student's recommendation for a potential enhancement in the execution of English courses. They proposed incorporating additional immersive role-playing exercises in an authentic setting to enhance their learning, such as in an actual tourist destination. Her own experience in a course that implemented a role-play activity, allowing students to engage in simulated scenarios at an actual tourist destination, motivated the notion. She expressed that the learning exercise was both enjoyable and advantageous, particularly for her English language skills. In addition, she emphasized that the learning activity should not place children in a stressful setting. The instructor should design a pleasurable educational exercise that enables the pupils to have an enjoyable and effective English language learning experience.

The needs analysis findings indicate that students studying finance and banking through AGIoT prioritize listening and speaking skills as the most crucial aspects of English language learning. ESP education should prioritize both skills equally throughout the syllabus without neglecting any other language skills in English.

Furthermore, the proactive involvement of the ESP for banking and finance instructor is crucial in designing a pleasurable educational experience for students. The utilization of enjoyable activities, together with the AGIoT effect, has been extensively documented in various research studies, enabling countless students to overcome their embarrassment and engage more actively in the process of producing meaning. The instructor must design activities that effectively engage the students, such as group discussions and role-playing exercises. The professor should give the students a chance to improve their skills by conducting activities in a real-world environment, like a tourist destination. Additionally, the lecturer must ensure that the classroom environment is conducive to learning English by creating a comfortable atmosphere for undergraduate students.

26.6 Analytics and Results

To ensure the design and development of teaching materials using AGIoT in accordance with student characteristics, student analysis was carried out. To meet the learning objectives outlined in the Merdeka curriculum, the design of EFL teaching materials in accordance with the curriculum of the sharia economics law study program, namely banking and finance, has been modified to comply with the competency standards of the national higher education qualification framework (KKNI).

Analyzing undergraduate students' need to learn English with specific topics of banking and finance includes, among other things, looking at micro-EFL skills (vocabulary and grammar) and macro-skills (listening, speaking, reading, and writing), technological literacy skills (AGIoT), knowledge, and their level of cognitive development. This analysis will be the basis for developing teaching materials based on AGIoT media and technology (Richards, 2015). To ensure the design and development of AGIoT-based banking and finance teaching materials in accordance with student characteristics, an analysis of the needs and desires of undergraduate students was carried out. To meet the learning objectives outlined in the independent curriculum, the design of English teaching materials for banking and finance has been modified effectively and efficiently according to the needs of the 21st century.

According to the results of the needs analysis from survey and interview, students majoring in tourism have the most urgent need to master fluent spoken and written English. English language courses should prioritize these two skills in the syllabus and lesson plan without ignoring other English language competencies. Culturally relevant content in banking and finance based on AGIoT, especially those that address linguistic specifics—that is, the way a person communicates with other people or customers through language—should also be included in the course outline.

According to Wang, Yasmin et al. (2023), culture not only helps us develop and strengthen our values and ideas but also educates us about important social norms, practices, traditions, and customs that are part of our communities. Students majoring in sharia economic law may benefit from linguistic specifics, as their future jobs may require them to communicate with individuals from various cultural backgrounds. To help students better understand the unique character of each location, the curriculum may also include elements of public speaking.

Furthermore, to create a pleasant learning experience for students, the active role of EFL lecturers is very important. Several studies have shown that the use of technology-based learning activities and friendly and communicative lecturers can help students overcome shyness and anxiety, increase their engagement, motivation, and self-confidence, and be actively involved in the process of creating meaning (Zaafour, 2024; Buelo et al., 2024; Abdelhalim, 2024).

Group projects and role-playing exercises, presentation projects using YouTube, mind mapping, quizzes, Instagram, and AGIoT are examples of the types of activities that lecturers must design to keep students' attention in class by incorporating modern media and technology. Instructors should facilitate opportunities for students to refine their skills by conducting activities in authentic and real banking and finance locations. Additionally, for students to learn English effectively, instructors must ensure that the classroom environment is conducive to their comfort.

Educational transformation usually involves AGIoT interactions between students and lecturers during the learning process. Students receive instruction through AGIoT platforms, including AI, VR, social media such as YouTube, Instagram, Pinterest, and mind mapping, even though they are physically close to the teacher in the same facility. AGIoT-based learning is largely dependent on the internet. It entails using online tools for educational purposes. Learning using AGIoT is a combination of learning that involves elements of technology with the aim of achieving authentic learning outcomes and conventional face-to-face learning. These concepts were created to help educators and students create a student-centered learning approach.

Therefore, the aim is to choose a learning style that appropriately suits students at a particular institution, especially when developing an English for Specific Purposes (ESP) banking and finance course in the sharia economics study program. Our EFL learning design for banking and finance has adopted the concept of blended learning, which is not a new approach. Lecturers traditionally leverage shared AGIoT resources and technologies. AGIoT learning is essentially the integration of multiple learning methods, learning styles, resource formats, and various technologies.

Students are given a schedule that requires them to attend some sessions physically at the university, while for other classes, they have the option to create their own schedule or follow a plan provided by the lecturer to complete their assignments online. At universities, technology is an integral element of undergraduate students' daily lives, and the teaching of core topics relies heavily on AGIoT-based methods. In this study, we have created interactive teaching resources that provide opportunities to use technology in English courses similar with Wan and Moorhouse's (2024) study.

Learning with a hyplex model (flexible hybrid) can be seen as a shift back to a teacher-centered approach, where the teacher still has the main task of organizing content, presenting it in a didactic way, providing assistance to students, and maintaining control. Therefore, instructors take on the role of course designers, whether or not they are qualified for this challenging responsibility. In this regard, we would like to describe the main procedures that a course designer must adhere to when formulating an ESP banking and finance course for a particular group of prospective experts in a particular field of study.

When building an ESP banking and finance course, whether online or face-to-face, it is important not to overlook three key steps. First, the course objectives were determined by conducting a learning needs analysis for banking and finance. Second, a relevant teaching theory was selected, namely constructivism. Third, appropriate teaching materials were selected by adapting actual texts. By following this procedure, course designers can create an ESP course that truly meets the needs of its intended learners.

The main findings of this research show that the AGIoT-based banking and finance teaching material design used by the researchers is very interesting for undergraduate students in sharia economic law study programs. This research uses a research and development research design, with one of the processes requiring an analysis of undergraduate students' needs and desires to study banking and finance. The product obtained from the conclusions of this research has succeeded in meeting the ideal criteria.

Apart from that, this product is also able to increase student motivation and achievement in the field of ESP for banking and finance programs. It is recommended to further develop certain language skills based on local knowledge. Indonesia has a wealth of local values that reflect its culture. This means that culture has a crucial influence on shaping the tactics used in the AGIoT-based EFL banking and finance teaching and learning process (Khang & Rath et al., 2023).

26.7 Conclusions

Based on the results, it seems that students thought the class material was quite cool. The curriculum aims to encourage students to think creatively by incorporating theoretical perspectives through reading assignments, incorporating small-scale research projects into material development, and ensuring everyone uses ICT. To add to the ongoing discussion about how teacher preparation programs can better equip future educators to serve as content creators, we offer the following suggestions. After completing the questionnaire and interviews, we came to some definite conclusions.

Important skills for students studying tourism include proficiency in listening and speaking. This skill is very important because it allows the individual to communicate effectively with clients in the future. They realized that they would mostly use English in their future professions, namely in travel companies and as receptionists. Apart from that, this also has important meaning. Including language components such as vocabulary and grammar allows students to construct English sentences proficiently. Incorporating cultural elements into learning content is very important. Examples include linguistic specifications, non-linguistic specifications, geography, and art. Additionally, it is important for students to engage in fun educational activities that will improve their command of the English language. Engaging educational activities can involve incorporating technology into the classroom, facilitating group conversations, and implementing role-playing exercises.

The research output successfully meets the criteria for effective learning materials, determined by its pedagogical implications. Students' motivations, desires, skills, and needs are clearly visible. Our material design should aim to align the options available in a particular context with the needs and preferences of learners. We emphasize the importance of aligning materials with the specific curriculum and adapting them to learners' experiences, realities, and first language for maximum effectiveness. Lecturers, in their role as designers of teaching materials, must have the ability to establish relationships between the knowledge possessed by students and the content outlined in the syllabus and learning plans. It is necessary to accurately translate technical words related to banking and finance content into the target language (Khang, Shah, & Rani, 2023).

References

Abdelhalim, S. M. (2024). From Traditional Writing to Digital Multimodal Composing: Promoting High School EFL Students' Writing Self-Regulation and Self-Efficacy. *Computer Assisted Language Learning*, 1–30. https://www.tandfonline.com/doi/abs/10.1080/09588221.2024.2322148

Al-khresheh, M. H. (2024). Bridging Technology and Pedagogy from a Global Lens: Teachers' Perspectives on Integrating ChatGPT in English Language Teaching. *Computers and Education: Artificial Intelligence*, 100218. https://www.sciencedirect.com/science/article/pii/S2666920X24000195

Al Yakin, A., Khang, A., & Mukit, A. (2023). Personalized Social-Collaborative IoT-Symbiotic Platforms in Smart Education Ecosystem. In *Smart Cities* (pp. 204–230). CRC Press. https://www.taylorfrancis.com/chapters/edit/10.1201/9781003376064-12/personalized-social-collaborative-iot-symbiotic-platforms-smart-education-ecosystem-muthmainnah-ahmad-al-yakin-alex-khang-abdul-mukit

Badrkhani, P. (2023). How a Catastrophic Situation Turns into an Exceptional Opportunity: Covid-19 Pandemic in Iran and Challenges of Online Education for New English Language Educators. *Interactive Learning Environments*, *31*(7), 4200–4218. https://www.tandfonline.com/doi/abs/10.1080/10494820 .2021.1956545

Bi, A., & Ye, S. (2024). The Application of Flipped Classroom Information Technology in English Teaching in the Context of 6G Network. *International Journal of Information and Communication Technology Education (IJICTE)*, *20*(1), 1–18. https://www.igi-global.com/article/the-application-of-flipped-classroom-information-technology-in-english-teaching-in-the-context-of-6g-network/ 338322

Buelo, R. J. V., Alcones, S., Aranas, D., & Austria, G. (2024). Assessing the Effectiveness of Electronic-Based Multimodal Instructional Approach in Improving Students' Oral Communication Confidence Using Kirkpatrick's Four Levels of Evaluation: Electronic-Based Multimodal Instructional Approach in Improving Students' Oral Communication Confidence Using Kirkpatrick's Four Levels of Evaluation. *International Journal of Curriculum and Instruction*, *16*(1), 129–161. https://ijci.globets.org/index.php/ IJCI/article/view/1423

Crompton, H., Edmett, A., Ichaporia, N., & Burke, D. (2024). AI and English Language Teaching: Affordances and Challenges. *British Journal of Educational Technology*. https://bera-journals.onlineli-brary.wiley.com/doi/abs/10.1111/bjet.13460

Dincer, A. (2020). Understanding the Characteristics of English Language Learners' Out-of-Class Language Learning Through Digital Practices. *IAFOR Journal of Education*, *8*(2), 47–65. https://avesis.omu.edu. tr/yayin/4927b0ad-7ff6-4adb-b5fb-7c0ab7a46919/understanding-the-characteristics-of-english-lan-guage-learners-out-of-class-language-learning-through-digital-practices

Genç, G., & Kırmızıbayrak, Ö. (2024). The Use of Web 2.0 Tools in English Language Learning: A Systematic Review. *Multidisciplinary Reviews*, *7*(5), e2024102. https://malque.pub/ojs/index.php/mr/ article/view/2057

Gligorea, I., Cioca, M., Oancea, R., Gorski, A. T., Gorski, H., & Tudorache, P. (2023). Adaptive Learning Using Artificial Intelligence in e-Learning: A Literature Review. *Education Sciences*, *13*(12), 1216. https://www.mdpi.com/2227-7102/13/12/1216

González-Pérez, L. I., & Ramírez-Montoya, M. S. (2022). Components of Education 4.0 in 21st Century Skills Frameworks: Systematic Review. *Sustainability*, *14*(3), 1493. https://www.mdpi. com/2071-1050/14/3/1493

Guo, X. R., Li, X., & Guo, Y. M. (2021). Mapping Knowledge Domain Analysis in Smart Education Research. *Sustainability*, *13*(23), 13234. https://www.mdpi.com/2071-1050/13/23/13234

Hoel, T., & Mason, J. (2018). Standards for Smart Education–Towards a Development Framework. *Smart Learning Environments*, *5*(1), 1–25. https://link.springer.com/article/10.1186/s40561-018-0052-3

Hsieh, H. C., & Hsieh, H. L. (2019). Undergraduates' Out-of-Class Learning: Exploring EFL Students' Autonomous Learning Behaviors and Their Usage of Resources. *Education Sciences*, *9*(3), 159. https:// www.mdpi.com/2227-7102/9/3/159

Hui, J., Zhou, Y., Oubibi, M., Di, W., Zhang, L., & Zhang, S. (2022). Research on Art Teaching Practice Supported by Virtual Reality (VR) Technology in the Primary Schools. *Sustainability*, *14*(3), 1246. https://www.mdpi.com/2071-1050/14/3/1246

Ikubanni, P. P., Adeleke, A. A., Agboola, O. O., Christopher, C. T., Ademola, B. S., Okonkwo, J., ... & Akinlabi, E. T. (2022). Present and Future Impacts of Computer-Aided Design/Computer-Aided Manufacturing (CAD/CAM). *Journal Européen des Systèmes Automatisés*, *55*(3).

Jagatheesaperumal, S. K., Ahmad, K., Al-Fuqaha, A., & Qadir, J. (2024). Advancing Education Through Extended Reality and Internet of Everything Enabled Metaverses: Applications, Challenges, and Open Issues. *IEEE Transactions on Learning Technologies*. https://ieeexplore.ieee.org/abstract/ document/10415252/

Jiang, R. (2022). How Does Artificial Intelligence Empower EFL Teaching and Learning Nowadays? A Review on Artificial Intelligence in the EFL Context. *Frontiers in Psychology*, *13*, 1049401. https:// www.frontiersin.org/journals/psychology/articles/10.3389/fpsyg.2022.1049401/full

Joshi, K., Kumar, R., Bharany, S., Saini, D. K. J. B., Kumar, R., Ibrahim, A. O., … & Medani, M. (2024). Exploring the Connectivity between Education 4.0 and Classroom 4.0: Technologies, Student Perspectives, and Engagement in the Digital Era. *IEEE Access*. https://ieeexplore.ieee.org/abstract/document/10412043/

Kamińska, D., Zwoliński, G., Laska-Leśniewicz, A., Raposo, R., Vairinhos, M., Pereira, E., … & Anbarjafari, G. (2023). Augmented Reality: Current and New Trends in Education. *Electronics*, *12*(16), 3531. https://www.croris.hr/crosbi/publikacija/resolve/croris/800307

Karataş, F., Abedi, F. Y., Ozek Gunyel, F., Karadeniz, D., & Kuzgun, Y. (2024). Incorporating AI in Foreign Language Education: An Investigation into ChatGPT's Effect on Foreign Language Learners. *Education and Information Technologies*, 1–24. https://link.springer.com/article/10.1007/s10639-024-12574-6

Kessler, G. (2020). Professionalizing Your Use of Technology in English Language Teaching. *Professionalizing Your English Language Teaching*, 163–173. https://link.springer.com/chapter/10.1007/978-3-030-34762-8_13

Khang, A., Gujrati, R., Uygun, H., Tailor, R. K., & Gaur, S. (Eds.). (2024). *Data-Driven Modelling and Predictive Analytics in Business and Finance: Concepts, Designs, Technologies, and Applications* (1st Ed.). Auerbach Publications. https://doi.org/10.1201/9781032618845

Khang, A., Inna, Semenets-Orlova, Alla, Klochko, Rostyslav, Shchokin, Rudenko, Mykola, Lidia, Romanova, & Kristina, Bratchykova. (2024). "Management Model 6.0 and Business Recovery Strategy of Enterprises in the Era of Digital Economy," In Khang, A., Gujrati, R., Uygun, H., Tailor, R. K., & Gaur, S. (Eds.), *Data-Driven Modelling and Predictive Analytics in Business and Finance* (1st Ed.). CRC Press. https://doi.org/10.1201/9781032618845-16

Khang, A., Muthmainnah, M., Seraj, P. M. I., Al Yakin, A., & Obaid, A. J. (2023). AI-Aided Teaching Model in Education 5.0. In *Handbook of Research on AI-Based Technologies and Applications in the Era of the Metaverse* (pp. 83–104). IGI Global. https://www.igi-global.com/chapter/ai-aided-teaching-model-in-education-50/326025

Khang, A., Rath, K. C., Satapathy, S. K., Kumar, A., Das, S. R., & Panda, M. R. (2023). Enabling the Future of Manufacturing: Integration of Robotics and IoT to Smart Factory Infrastructure in Industry 4.0. In Khang A., Shah V., & Rani S. (Eds.), *Handbook of Research on AI-Based Technologies and Applications in the Era of the Metaverse* (pp. 25–50). IGI Global. https://doi.org/10.4018/978-1-6684-8851-5.ch002

Khang, A., Shah, V., & Rani, S. (Eds.). (2023). *Handbook of Research on AI-Based Technologies and Applications in the Era of the Metaverse*. IGI Global. https://doi.org/10.4018/978-1-6684-8851-5

Konkol, P., & Dymek, D. (2024). Towards Education 4.0: Challenges and Opportunities. *Supporting Higher Education 4.0 With Blockchain*, 7–36. https://www.taylorfrancis.com/chapters/edit/10.4324/9781003318736-2/towards-education-4-0-pawe%C5%82-konkol-dariusz-dymek

Lei, B., Fathi, J., Noorbakhsh, S., & Rahimi, M. (2022). The Impact of Mobile-Assisted Language Learning on English as a Foreign Language Learners' Vocabulary Learning Attitudes and Self-Regulatory Capacity. *Frontiers in Psychology*, *13*, 872922. https://www.frontiersin.org/articles/10.3389/fpsyg.2022.872922/full

Li, G., & Liu, J. (2024). Improving Physical Education Through Innovative Multimedia Learning Platform and Data-Driven Instruction. *Soft Computing*, *28*(2), 1567–1584. https://link.springer.com/article/10.1007/s00500-023-09436-7

Li, R. (2024). Effects of mobile-assisted language learning on foreign language learners' speaking skill development. https://scholarspace.manoa.hawaii.edu/items/2813b22a-8e5e-4ee2-873d-aa66a87c4ce7

Liu, B., & Lu, Z. (2023). Design of Spoken English Teaching Based on Artificial Intelligence Educational Robots and Wireless Network Technology. *EAI Endorsed Transactions on Scalable Information Systems*, *10*(4), e12. https://publications.eai.eu/index.php/sis/article/view/3048

Liu, X., & Huang, X. (2022). Design of Artificial Intelligence-Based English Network Teaching (AI-ENT) System. *Mathematical Problems in Engineering*, *2022*. https://www.hindawi.com/journals/mpe/2022/1849430/

Marougkas, A., Troussas, C., Krouska, A., & Sgouropoulou, C. (2024). How Personalized and Effective Is Immersive Virtual Reality in Education? A Systematic Literature Review for the Last Decade. *Multimedia Tools and Applications*, *83*(6), 18185–18233. https://link.springer.com/article/10.1007/s11042-023-15986-7

Miles, M. B., & Huberman, A. M. (1994). *Qualitative Data Analysis: An Expanded Sourcebook*. Sage.

Mukhamediev, R. I., Popova, Y., Kuchin, Y., Zaitseva, E., Kalimoldayev, A., Symagulov, A., & Yelis, M. (2022). Review of Artificial Intelligence and Machine Learning Technologies: Classification, Restrictions, Opportunities and Challenges. *Mathematics*, *10*(15), 2552. https://www.mdpi.com/2227-7390/10/15/2552

Muthmainnah, M., Al Yakin, A., Mursidin, M., & Al Aqad, M. H. (2024). AI-Driven Content Developing and Designing for Teaching Materials of Digital Healthcare. In *Driving Smart Medical Diagnosis Through AI-Powered Technologies and Applications* (pp. 238–257). IGI Global. https://www.igi-global.com/chapter/ai-driven-content-developing-and-designing-for-teaching-materials-of-digital-healthcare/340371

Muthmainnah M., Obaid, A. J., Al Yakin, A., & Brayyich, M. (2023). Enhancing Computational Thinking Based on Virtual Robot of Artificial Intelligence Modeling in the English Language Classroom. In *International Conference on Data Analytics & Management* (pp. 1–11). Singapore: Springer Nature Singapore. https://link.springer.com/chapter/10.1007/978-981-99-6550-2_1

Ong, Q. K. L., & Annamalai, N. (2023). Technological Pedagogical Content Knowledge for Twenty-First Century Learning Skills: The Game Changer for Teachers of Industrial Revolution 5.0. *Education and Information Technologies*, 1–42. https://link.springer.com/article/10.1007/s10639-023-11852-z

Park, W., & Kwon, H. (2024). Implementing Artificial Intelligence Education for Middle School Technology Education in Republic of Korea. *International Journal of Technology and Design Education*, *34*(1), 109–126. https://link.springer.com/article/10.1007/s10798-023-09812-2

Pedro, F., Subosa, M., Rivas, A., & Valverde, P. (2019). Artificial intelligence in education: Challenges and opportunities for sustainable development. http://repositorio.minedu.gob.pe/handle/20.500.12799/6533

Pradas-Esteban, F. (2024). Digital Literacy in the EFL Classroom: Main Barriers and Implications. In *Educational Innovation to Address Complex Societal Challenges* (pp. 59–73). IGI Global. https://www.igi-global.com/chapter/digital-literacy-in-the-efl-classroom/340261

Rajaram, K. (2023). Future of Learning: Teaching and Learning Strategies. In *Learning Intelligence: Innovative and Digital Transformative Learning Strategies: Cultural and Social Engineering Perspectives* (pp. 3–53). Singapore: Springer Nature Singapore. https://link.springer.com/chapter/10.1007/978-981-19-9201-8_1

Ravshanovna, K. L. (2024). Enhancing Foreign Language Education Through Integration of Digital Technologies. *Miasto Przyszłości*, *44*, 131–138. http://miastoprzyszlosci.com.pl/index.php/mp/article/view/2374

Richards, J. C. (2015). Materials Design in Language Teacher Education: An Example from Southeast Asia. In *International Perspectives on English Language Teacher Education: Innovations from the Field* (pp. 90–106). London: Palgrave Macmillan UK. https://link.springer.com/chapter/10.1057/9781137440068_6

Rogti, M. (2024). The Effect of Mobile-Based Interactive Multimedia on Thinking Engagement and Cooperation. *International Journal of Instruction*, *17*(1), 673–696. https://e-iji.net/ats/index.php/pub/article/view/539

Sharadgah, T. A., & Saʼdi, R. A. (2022). A Systematic Review of Research on the Use of Artificial Intelligence in English Language Teaching and Learning (2015-2021): What Are the Current Effects?. *Journal of Information Technology Education: Research*, *21*. https://search.ebscohost.com/login.aspx?direct=true&profile=ehost&scope=site&authtype=crawler&jrnl=15479714&AN=160727726&h=4mKAmTOX7P3pP0jvRzpJNtZXM%2B0OrxRW9TIG%2FETRZ6pB2PeFEavmugpHJsGI5Hct9nmd0Ww%2FHjpkZClebbG4dg%3D%3D&crl=c

Tran, V. T. H. (2021). EFL teachers' Perceptions of the Significance of "Four Cs" and Their Suggestions to Enhance "Four Cs" for High School EFL Students in Vietnam. *International Journal of Science and Management Studies (IJSMS)*, *4*(5), 134–162. https://www.ijsmsjournal.org/2021/volume-4%20issue-5/ijsms-v4i5p112.pdf

Van Nguyen, T., Sit, H. H., & Chen, S. (2022). An Exploration of Developing ICT-Related Pedagogical Strategies in the Professional Development of EFL Teachers in Vietnam. In *Digital Communication and Learning: Changes and Challenges* (pp. 203–220). Singapore: Springer Singapore. https://link.springer.com/chapter/10.1007/978-981-16-8329-9_11

Volioti, C., Keramopoulos, E., Sapounidis, T., Melisidis, K., Zafeiropoulou, M., Sotiriou, C., & Spiridis, V. (2022). Using Augmented Reality in K-12 Education: An Indicative Platform for Teaching Physics. *Information*, *13*(7), 336. https://www.mdpi.com/2078-2489/13/7/336

Wan, Y., & Moorhouse, B. L. (2024). Using Call Annie as a Generative Artificial Intelligence Speaking Partner for Language Learners. *RELC Journal*, 00336882231224813. https://journals.sagepub.com/doi/abs/10.1177/00336882231224813

Wang, Y., Yasmin, F., & Akbar, A. (2023). Impact of the Internet on English Language Learning Among University Students: Mediating Role of Academic Self-Efficacy. *Frontiers in Psychology*, *14*, 1184185. https://www.frontiersin.org/articles/10.3389/fpsyg.2023.1184185/full

Wang, C., Zhang, M., Sesunan, A., & Yolanda, L. (2023). Technology-driven education reform in Indonesia: a look into the current status of the Merdeka Belajar Program. https://repositori.kemdikbud.go.id/30538/

Wijaya, T. T., Tang, J., & Purnama, A. (2020). Developing an Interactive Mathematical Learning media Based on the tpack Framework Using the hawgent Dynamic Mathematics Software. In *Emerging Technologies in Computing: Third EAI International Conference, iCETiC 2020, London, UK, August 19–20, 2020, Proceedings 3* (pp. 318–328). Springer International Publishing. https://link.springer.com/chapter/10.1007/978-3-030-60036-5_24

Wu, S., Cao, Y., Cui, J., Li, R., Qian, H., Jiang, B., & Zhang, W. (2024). A Comprehensive Exploration of Personalized Learning in Smart Education: From Student Modeling to Personalized Recommendations. *arXiv preprint arXiv:2402.01666*.

Younus Jasim, M., & Rawdhan Salman, A. (2023). Investigating the Impact of Multimedia and Mobile Applications in English Language Education. *Technology Assisted Language Education*, *1*(1), 54–73. https://tale.razi.ac.ir/article_2945.html

Zaafour, A. (2024). Incorporating Technology into CPBL to Enhance English Learning. *International Arab Journal of English for Specific Purposes*, *7*(1), 127–142. https://revues.imist.ma/index.php/IAJESP/article/view/46104

Zarrabi, M., Mohammadi, M., & Seifoori, Z. (2024). EFL Teachers' Professional Identity as a Predictor of Using Information and Communication Technologies: Practices, Challenges, and Solutions. *Technology of Education Journal (TEJ)*, *18*(1). https://search.ebscohost.com/login.aspx?direct=true&profile=ehost&scope=site&authtype=crawler&jrnl=20080441&AN=176086229&h=Pgkg3aFcikJWId3qva5MSFkuXnYkLjJFNXr1MJKm0EtuM1a41rpYEm8FSvC42VWNjtSgo6XT%2B30KOIzq5%2FySjg%3D%3D&crl=c

Zhao, Q., & Nazir, S. (2022). English Multimode Production and Usage by Artificial Intelligence and Online Reading for Sustaining Effectiveness. *Mobile Information Systems*, *2022*. https://www.hindawi.com/journals/misy/2022/6780502/

Index

A

Access control, 25, 102, 202, 208, 229, 298
Account management, 204
Accuracy, 65, 66, 67, 68, 71, 72, 73, 76, 77, 78, 86, 96,
    97, 100, 101, 117, 132, 133, 198, 200, 201,
    202, 204, 205, 206, 210, 227, 230, 231, 232,
    233, 235–239, 241, 254, 255, 256, 257, 294,
    304, 323, 336, 353, 380, 381, 386
Advanced Persistent Threat, 226
Agile, 33, 382, 388
Agriculture, 310, 312, 345, 370
AI algorithm, 96, 100, 101, 125, 126, 127, 129, 130,
    132, 133, 291, 292, 293, 298, 303, 304, 330,
    379, 380, 381, 383, 384, 386, 387
AI in banking, 121, 123, 125, 126, 127, 129, 130, 131,
    133, 134, 135, 292, 293, 295, 296, 334, 414,
    417
AI model, 102, 293, 295, 296, 297, 330, 336, 382
AI-driven Algorithm, 381, 386
AI-powered Algorithm, 379
Alexa, 315
Algorithm, 5, 18, 19, 28, 29, 30, 32, 33, 34, 35, 37, 38,
    39, 40, 41, 42, 43, 52, 57, 58, 59, 65, 66, 68,
    71, 73, 78, 86, 96–102, 106–114, 116, 117,
    120–133, 152, 168, 172, 174, 187, 198, 199,
    229, 234, 244, 254, 291, 292, 293, 297, 298,
    299, 301–304, 316, 322, 323, 327, 328, 330,
    331, 332, 333, 335, 379–388, 390–401, 410
Alibaba, 134, 297
Alternative Channel Services, 261, 262, 263, 264, 267
Amazon, 88, 90, 182, 315
Analytics, 24, 39, 46, 55, 58, 60, 63, 68, 88, 89, 90, 91,
    96, 97, 98, 99, 100, 101, 102, 103, 120–129,
    133, 134, 150, 152, 156, 157, 167, 169, 171,
    176, 199, 201, 217, 218, 221, 227, 231, 245,
    253, 258, 285, 287, 291, 299, 303, 326, 331,
    334, 342, 369, 375, 381, 385
Anova, 154, 155, 221, 223, 360
Anti-money laundering, 51, 96, 109, 155, 250, 251, 255,
    326, 331

API, 1, 2, 4, 6, 8, 10, 12, 14, 16, 18, 19, 20, 22, 23, 24,
    27, 28, 30, 32, 33, 34, 36, 38, 39, 40, 42, 43,
    46–56, 58, 59, 60, 62, 64, 65, 66, 68, 69, 70,
    72, 74, 75, 76, 77, 78, 83, 85, 87, 89, 91, 93,
    98, 100, 102, 108, 110, 112, 114, 115, 116,
    117, 120, 121, 122, 124, 125, 126, 128, 130,
    132, 133, 134, 135, 140, 142, 144, 148, 149,
    150, 151, 153, 155, 156, 157, 159, 160, 161,
    163, 164, 165, 167, 168, 169, 171, 172, 173,
    175, 176, 182, 184, 186, 188, 190, 191, 192,
    195, 196, 198, 199, 200, 202, 204, 206, 208,
    210, 214–218, 220, 221, 222, 228, 229, 230,
    232, 234, 236, 238, 240, 242, 244, 250–254,
    256, 258, 262, 264, 266, 267, 268, 269, 270,
    272, 273, 274, 277, 278, 279, 280, 282, 284,
    285, 286, 287, 290, 291, 292, 294, 296, 298,
    300, 302, 303, 304, 310, 312, 314, 316, 318,
    324, 326, 327, 328, 330, 332, 333, 334, 336,
    341, 342, 344, 346, 347, 348, 353, 354, 356,
    358, 360, 366–370, 372, 373, 374, 375, 378,
    379, 380, 382, 384, 385, 386, 388, 392, 394,
    396, 398, 400, 404, 405, 406, 408, 409, 410,
    412, 414, 416, 418, 420, 422
API integration, 49
ARIMA, 70, 98
Artificial Intelligence, 97, 99, 101, 103, 200, 209, 248,
    249, 251, 253, 255, 257, 336, 388, 415, 422
Assessment tool, 326
Asset management, 49, 51, 52, 55, 60, 163, 168, 326
ATM, 48, 84, 85, 86, 87, 88, 90, 91, 92, 93, 97, 139,
    171, 183, 185, 192, 236, 262, 315, 316, 347,
    354, 358, 383, 407, 420
Attachment, 354
Audience, 17, 19, 28, 33, 215, 343, 344, 345
Audit, 12, 42, 91, 131, 188, 198, 202, 205, 206, 208,
    244, 254, 257, 258, 284, 287, 348, 382, 383
Augmented reality, 348
Authentication, 5, 22, 23, 52, 100, 110, 111, 114, 130,
    182, 184, 187, 188, 229, 243, 280, 282, 283,
    284, 316, 317, 318, 342, 347, 348, 391, 392,
    395, 396, 397, 401

427

Automated decision-making, 130
Automated teller machine, 48, 183, 354
Automation, 11, 25, 55, 86, 90, 91, 93, 99, 101, 102,
103, 123, 124, 127, 152, 157, 168, 186, 195,
197–210, 216, 253, 254, 291, 294, 302, 303,
304, 323, 326, 336, 375, 384, 385, 406

B

Bangladesh, 169
Bank, 1, 2, 3, 5–19, 21–25, 47, 48, 49, 51, 52, 54–60,
68, 82, 83, 84, 85, 86, 87, 88, 89, 90, 91,
92, 93, 100, 120–135, 138–144, 147–176,
181–186, 188–199, 201–204, 206, 207, 208,
209, 210, 214–223, 226, 227, 228, 229,
231–239, 241–245, 248–255, 257, 258,
261–275, 277–287, 290–304, 308–318, 323,
325, 326, 328, 332, 333, 334, 335, 336,
340–349, 352–359, 361, 366, 370, 371, 372,
386, 387, 390–397, 399, 401, 403,
405, 411–422
Bank transfer, 181, 186
Banking, 1–11, 13, 15, 17, 19, 21, 22, 23, 24, 25, 47,
48, 49, 51, 54, 57, 58, 59, 68, 82, 83, 84, 86,
87, 88, 90, 92, 93, 100, 120–135, 138–144,
147–164, 166, 167, 168, 170–176, 181, 186,
188, 189, 192, 195, 196, 198, 199, 201, 202,
203, 204, 206, 207, 208, 209, 210, 214–223,
226, 227, 228, 229, 231–239, 241–245, 248,
249, 251, 253, 254, 255, 257, 258, 261–275,
277, 278, 279–287, 290–299, 301, 302, 303,
304, 308–318, 323, 325, 326, 328, 332, 333,
334, 335, 336, 340–349, 352–359, 361, 366,
370, 390–397, 399, 401, 403, 405, 411–422
Banking and finance, 7, 23, 24, 84, 86, 88, 90, 92, 93,
121, 122, 123, 124, 125, 126, 127, 128, 129,
130, 131, 132, 133, 134, 135, 147, 195, 196,
199, 203, 206, 207, 209, 210, 214, 226, 227,
228, 229, 231–235, 237, 239, 241, 242, 243,
244, 245, 290, 291, 292, 293, 294, 295, 296,
297, 298, 299, 301–304, 411, 414–418, 420,
421, 422
Banking industry, 84, 161, 168, 172, 174, 175, 176, 188,
216, 217, 248, 254, 258, 261, 263, 265, 267,
269, 271, 273, 275, 290, 308–315, 317, 323,
332, 346
Banking services, 48, 49, 57, 87, 92, 135, 138, 139, 140,
141, 143, 144, 149, 150, 192, 215, 261, 262,
264, 267, 269, 270, 271, 273, 274, 277–287,
295, 314, 315, 317, 341–347, 349, 352, 353,
354, 355, 356, 357, 358, 359, 361, 391
Big data, 46, 100, 167, 168, 249, 251, 252, 253, 309, 406
Big data analytics, 46, 167, 253
Binance, 56
Bitcoin, 47, 48, 53, 155, 157, 163, 176, 191
Blockchain, 1, 2, 5, 6, 7, 8, 9, 10, 11, 12, 13, 14, 15, 16,
17, 18, 19, 20, 21, 23, 24, 25, 43, 46, 47, 48,

49, 50, 51, 52, 53, 54, 55, 56, 57, 59, 60, 103,
149, 152, 153, 155, 158, 161, 167, 168, 169,
171, 172, 176, 189, 217, 218, 219, 220, 221,
228, 249, 250, 253, 279, 280, 282, 286, 287,
293, 302, 309, 310, 348, 415
Budgeting, 57, 64, 126
Business organization, 329
Businesses, 2, 16, 23, 24, 25, 46, 48, 49, 50, 51, 54, 55,
57, 64, 65, 92, 115, 149–159, 161, 164, 167,
168, 169, 171, 172, 174, 175, 181, 183, 184,
188, 195, 200, 201, 202, 215, 249, 263, 277,
287, 317

C

CAGR, 181, 184
Challenges, 2, 6, 8, 9, 18, 19, 23, 24, 28, 29, 30, 38,
39, 40, 41, 42, 43, 46, 47, 50–55, 58, 59, 62,
63, 64, 72, 74, 75, 76, 77, 78, 83, 84, 88, 90,
93, 97, 102, 112, 113, 114, 120–125, 127,
129–135, 139, 147, 151, 155, 156, 158, 160,
164, 165, 207, 215, 216, 217, 223, 228, 231,
234, 235, 242, 243, 244, 245, 248, 250, 251,
262, 263, 264, 278, 279, 281, 285, 286, 291,
298, 302, 304, 313, 314, 317, 318, 324, 329,
335, 336, 346, 348, 349, 352, 353, 354, 361,
368, 370, 371, 378, 379, 382, 383, 385–392,
401, 407, 408, 411, 412, 414, 416
Change management, 205, 207
Chart, 14, 46, 131, 236, 238, 300, 379
Chatbot, 49, 97, 126, 130, 199, 204, 206, 210, 216, 280,
282, 285, 286, 287, 291, 292, 294, 302, 303,
323, 325, 328, 332, 335, 341, 343, 348, 381,
384, 387
ChatGPT, 294, 412, 422
Cheques, 182, 186
China, 83, 134, 153, 169, 171, 175, 184, 252, 296
Classification, 412
Classroom, 404, 406, 410, 411, 417, 420, 421
Cloud, 25, 35, 40, 78, 83, 89, 113, 115, 169, 172, 174,
182, 203, 208, 226, 227, 228, 229, 231, 233,
234, 235, 237, 239, 241, 243, 245, 249, 250,
253, 255, 308, 316, 317, 324, 385, 392, 406
Cloud computing, 78, 169, 172, 174, 226, 228, 249,
250, 253, 385, 406
Cloud-based solutions, 35, 208
Clustering, 72, 98, 107, 301
Coefficient(s), 37, 143, 218, 219, 220, 221, 360, 413, 418
Cognition, 21, 57, 62, 63, 66, 67, 68, 72, 76, 77, 78, 90,
107, 114, 127, 130, 190, 191, 209, 223, 249,
251, 252, 280, 282, 283, 310, 328, 348, 369
Commercial bank, 19, 149, 155, 160, 217, 282, 352
Commodity price analysis, 63, 67, 78
Competition, 1, 19, 34, 40, 51, 52, 58, 125, 149, 153,
160, 169, 191, 262, 304, 314, 353, 354, 403
Complex calculations, 27, 116
Computer vision, 66, 253, 254, 290, 303, 316, 405

Confidentiality, 111, 132, 227, 235, 266, 268, 269, 270, 272, 273, 275

Consumer behavior, 65, 97, 99, 101, 139, 150, 171, 215, 332

Continuous learning, 133, 231, 298, 385

Convenience, 6, 9, 21, 52, 83, 135, 138, 139, 140, 141, 144, 157, 182, 189, 190, 191, 192, 261, 263, 277, 279, 280, 282, 283, 342, 356, 390

Convolutional neural networks, 62, 63, 65, 67, 69, 71, 73, 75, 77

Corda, 420

Correlation, 98, 141, 143, 218, 219, 221, 353, 355, 359, 361, 367, 375, 381, 400

Correlation analysis, 141

Cost savings, 33, 34, 49, 58, 102, 291, 294, 302

Costs, 7, 12, 16, 35, 36, 39, 41, 49, 50, 52, 56, 58, 59, 70, 87, 93, 101, 102, 103, 113, 123, 127, 128, 139, 151, 156, 161, 162, 163, 167, 190, 192, 201, 206, 216, 249, 251, 254, 262, 264, 280, 282, 287, 291, 294, 304, 314, 316, 318, 335, 352, 353, 381, 382, 384, 387

COVID-19, 1, 22, 25, 147, 181, 191, 192, 215, 279, 406

Credit cards, 48, 86, 90, 93, 155, 185, 189, 190

Credit risk, 57, 77, 99, 109, 128, 173, 290, 291, 292, 294, 296, 297, 299, 302, 370

Credit scoring, 7, 18, 19, 34, 43, 57, 60, 67, 96, 97, 99, 102, 109, 116, 124, 130, 131, 292, 294, 297, 325, 381

Crowdfunding, 19, 48, 150, 163, 172, 175

Cryptocurrency, 17, 25, 47, 48, 50, 53, 56, 76, 77, 163, 167, 175, 176

Cryptocurrency exchange, 56

Cryptographic, 2, 3, 4, 5, 11, 25, 28, 29, 34, 38, 40, 43, 110, 111, 112, 114, 188, 390, 391, 392, 395

Culture currency, 366, 367, 368, 375

Customer data, 12, 57, 86, 87, 90, 99, 100, 132, 228, 231, 232, 241, 245, 254, 280, 284, 291, 348, 382

Customer engagement, 58, 121, 125, 129, 309, 314, 318, 343, 380, 382, 387

Customer experience, 59, 90, 120, 121, 122, 123, 125, 126, 127, 134, 148, 158, 216, 218, 220, 262, 278, 279, 281, 285, 286, 290, 291, 293, 294, 296, 304, 309, 314, 315, 318, 335, 340, 341, 343, 344, 345, 346, 347, 348, 349, 367, 375, 378, 379, 384, 387

Customer relationship management, 332

Customer satisfaction, 43, 68, 139, 164, 199, 207, 263, 264, 265, 266, 267, 268, 269, 270, 271, 272, 273, 275, 279, 282, 283, 284, 286, 291, 293, 302, 303, 343, 344, 346, 353, 354, 355, 356, 357, 358, 359, 360, 361, 369, 374, 375, 387

Customer service, 1, 49, 87, 88, 92, 97, 99, 124, 130, 148, 155, 162, 199, 207, 208, 210, 216, 217, 218, 221, 263, 279, 280, 290, 292, 293, 303, 323, 327, 353, 367, 368, 375, 380, 381, 384, 385, 387, 414

Customer support, 101, 126, 144, 172, 199, 200, 202, 282, 286, 287, 335, 340, 341, 343, 344, 348, 356

Cutting-edge computing, 123

Cyber fraud, 144

Cybersecurity, 8, 40, 51, 52, 59, 60, 99, 102, 106, 131, 132, 150, 156, 168, 215, 226, 227, 228, 229, 231, 232, 233, 234, 235, 237, 239, 241, 243, 244, 245, 278, 279, 281, 284, 286, 287, 295, 298, 304, 336, 348, 391

D

Data analysis, 69, 70, 98, 107, 168, 172, 199, 231, 250, 299, 334, 413

Data analytics, 24, 46, 90, 91, 96, 97, 98, 99, 100, 101, 102, 103, 124, 150, 152, 156, 167, 171, 176, 199, 217, 218, 221, 253, 287, 342, 369, 385

Data collection, 8, 59, 69, 74, 86, 87, 89, 99, 132, 133, 141, 169, 204, 234, 235, 278, 383, 411

Data covernance, 102, 132, 133, 378, 383, 385

Data leak, 243

Data migration, 133

Data model, 3, 4, 24

Data preprocessing, 69, 74, 243

Data privacy, 41, 51, 52, 59, 60, 102, 111, 120, 121, 125, 131, 134, 150, 208, 227, 228, 230, 231, 232, 233, 234, 235, 236, 241, 245, 284, 286, 290, 295, 296, 298, 336, 344, 347, 348, 349, 379, 382, 383, 385, 388

Data process, 43, 86, 90, 102, 133, 200, 201, 202, 300, 304, 335

Data processing, 43, 86, 90, 102, 200, 201, 202, 300, 304, 335

Data protection, 39, 41, 51, 59, 235, 242, 278, 281, 284, 286, 296, 298, 348, 349, 382, 390, 391, 397, 401

Data quality, 63, 69, 74, 75, 78, 102, 132, 171, 202, 231, 295, 297, 304, 382

Data science, 46, 47, 49, 51, 53, 55, 57, 58, 59, 60, 78, 133, 296, 298, 304, 327, 385

Data scientist, 133, 298, 385

Data security, 23, 40, 41, 90, 93, 102, 121, 122, 131, 132, 188, 207, 242, 243, 340, 343, 348, 385, 401

Data storage, 6, 9, 344, 347

Data transformation, 390, 391, 392, 401

Data visualization, 98

Data volume, 207, 235

Database, 6, 7, 8, 9, 12, 21, 133, 165, 166, 184, 197, 208, 258, 329, 396, 397, 412, 413

Data-driven decision-making, 59, 336, 382

Dataset, 9, 27, 29, 33, 34, 38, 39, 41, 43, 65, 66, 68, 69, 70, 71, 72, 74, 75, 76, 77, 78, 96, 97, 98, 101, 107, 109, 123, 125, 127, 130, 131, 132, 134, 230, 233, 234, 235, 242, 243, 294, 299, 302, 304, 325, 327, 385

Debit card, 48, 85, 182, 183, 186, 189, 190, 191
Debt, 84, 86, 158, 165, 299, 312, 333
Decision support, 77
Decision tree, 66, 73, 299, 387
Decision-maker, 63, 69, 70, 234
Decision-making, 28, 29, 30, 38, 39, 41, 42, 56, 59, 62, 63, 64, 66, 67, 68, 73, 74, 76, 77, 78, 85, 89, 91, 96, 97, 98, 99, 100, 101, 102, 103, 107, 109, 112, 114, 117, 121, 123, 124, 130, 152, 165, 205, 208, 209, 244, 291, 294, 295, 299, 304, 314, 322, 323, 324, 325, 326, 327, 328, 335, 336, 344, 345, 348, 379, 380, 382, 383, 384, 385, 387, 388, 406
Decryption, 228, 391, 392, 393, 394, 395, 396, 397, 399, 400, 401
Deep learning, 66, 123, 316, 323, 386, 405
Deep neural network, 66, 386
Deloitte, 277, 285, 294, 296, 298
Demographic, 85, 100, 116, 126, 129, 140, 141, 142, 143, 173, 190, 222, 262, 263, 301, 312, 332, 341, 342, 357, 368, 370
Descriptive Statistic, 357, 358, 417
Determination, 265
Developer, 47, 49, 59, 97, 169, 197, 203, 385
Development, 1, 29, 30, 35, 36, 37, 39, 40, 41, 42, 46, 47, 49, 55, 58, 60, 68, 71, 74, 78, 83, 84, 87, 98, 102, 103, 107, 110, 112, 113, 114, 115, 122, 124, 125, 131, 133, 134, 144, 150, 152, 153, 156, 164, 166, 167, 168, 169, 171, 172, 176, 182, 190, 191, 195, 197, 200, 202, 203, 205, 209, 210, 215, 227, 232, 244, 245, 248, 249, 250, 254, 277, 278, 279, 285, 287, 294, 295, 302, 308, 309, 310, 311, 312, 313, 316, 317, 322, 323, 325, 330, 331, 334, 335, 336, 340, 341, 342, 345, 346, 347, 349, 352, 353, 354, 366, 368, 369, 370, 371, 373, 375, 383, 385, 386, 387, 388, 396, 403, 404, 405, 406, 407, 409, 410, 411, 412, 414, 416, 418, 420, 421
DiFi, 25, 160, 257, 391, 393, 395, 396, 397, 399, 401
Digital age, 126, 128, 187, 226, 291, 332, 378, 379, 387
Digital banking, 1, 2, 9, 135, 138, 139, 140, 141, 142, 143, 144, 171, 214, 217, 218, 219, 220, 221, 267, 279, 284, 285, 295, 340, 341, 342, 343, 344, 345, 346, 347, 348, 349, 352, 353, 391
Digital divide, 59, 349
Digital economy, 25, 46, 304, 308
Digital environment, 24
Digital finance, 336
Digital identity, 1, 2, 4, 7, 8, 9, 21, 22, 23, 25
Digital key, 22
Digital landscape, 290, 291
Digital literacy, 135, 139, 287, 343, 347, 348, 349
Digital natives, 280, 283, 286
Digital payment, 2, 60, 83, 139, 157, 181, 182, 183, 184, 185, 187, 189, 190, 191, 215, 217, 218, 221, 277, 281, 285, 287, 340, 341

Digital platform, 60, 171, 172, 343, 344, 346
Digital service, 1, 2, 175, 176, 330, 344, 348
Digital transformation, 48, 125, 149, 156, 164, 195, 214, 215, 217, 221, 222, 223, 254, 277, 278, 279, 281, 285, 286, 287, 291, 299, 308, 368
Digital world, 216
Digitalization, 1, 18, 153, 161, 175, 277, 279, 285, 341, 352, 353
Digitization, 1, 11, 48, 153, 164, 168, 186, 249
Distributed denial-of-service, 238
Distributions, 231, 244
Download, 336

E

E-banking, 263, 277, 278, 279, 280, 281, 282, 283, 284, 285, 286, 287, 314, 352, 353, 354, 355, 356, 357, 358, 359, 361
E-commerce, 181, 182, 183, 184, 192, 263, 315, 316, 343, 346
Economy, 25, 46, 49, 52, 57, 82, 83, 147, 150, 151, 156, 160, 163, 168, 175, 184, 190, 192, 285, 304, 308, 314, 340, 352, 353
Ecosystem, 24, 46, 49, 50, 51, 53, 84, 114, 125, 150, 152, 157, 161, 169, 181, 192, 196, 251, 279, 303, 315, 325, 332, 341, 379, 383, 396, 407, 422
Education, 24, 35, 42, 50, 135, 141, 144, 172, 192, 210, 223, 250, 287, 310, 336, 342, 344, 345, 348, 358, 383, 387, 388, 403, 404, 405, 406, 407, 408, 409, 410, 411, 412, 415, 417, 419, 420, 421, 422
Educator, 404, 405, 407, 409, 410, 411, 412, 421, 422
Effectiveness, 6, 9, 34, 63, 65, 69, 72, 76, 77, 102, 103, 134, 162, 168, 192, 199, 205, 215, 227, 231, 232, 233, 234, 235, 245, 258, 263, 264, 266, 267, 269, 270, 272, 273, 274, 304, 334, 345, 361, 373, 374, 375, 395, 397, 405, 406, 410, 416, 422
Efficiency, 16, 19, 21, 24, 25, 27, 28, 29, 30, 33, 36, 38, 39, 41, 43, 47, 49, 50, 52, 54, 56, 58, 59, 60, 64, 66, 68, 73, 75, 77, 87, 88, 92, 93, 96, 97, 101, 103, 120, 121, 122, 123, 125, 126, 127, 128, 130, 135, 150, 152, 156, 159, 160, 162, 172, 175, 189, 196, 197, 200, 201, 204, 205, 207, 214, 216, 218, 219, 220, 235, 241, 251, 254, 258, 264, 278, 280, 287, 290, 291, 299, 302, 303, 304, 310, 314, 315, 323, 325, 335, 336, 353, 375, 379, 380, 381, 384, 390, 391, 396, 397, 398, 400, 401
E-government, 22
E-learning, 410
Electronic, 1, 11, 21, 22, 48, 82, 126, 138, 139, 152, 157, 160, 166, 172, 181, 182, 184, 185, 186, 188, 189, 190, 192, 249, 262, 263, 277, 281, 308, 352, 353, 354, 355, 356, 409
Electronic fund transfer, 181, 182, 189
Electronic payment system, 152

Elliptic curve cryptography, 110
Email, 166, 182, 188, 197, 254, 261, 262, 263
Emerging market, 54, 60, 290, 297
Emotional intelligence, 130
Employee, 24, 40, 84, 87, 133, 183, 185, 191, 198, 207,
        208, 218, 220, 228, 252, 263, 264, 284, 287,
        342, 352, 356, 361, 366, 367, 368, 369, 370,
        371, 373, 374, 375, 385, 386, 388
Employer, 154, 183, 185
Encryption, 28, 29, 38, 39, 40, 51, 52, 60, 102, 106, 107,
        109, 110, 112, 113, 114, 132, 182, 184, 187,
        191, 202, 208, 216, 229, 230, 232, 234, 236,
        243, 251, 253, 284, 298, 342, 344, 347, 348,
        390, 391, 392, 393, 394, 395, 396, 397, 398,
        400, 401
English as a foreign language, 406
Enterprise resource planning, 166
Entrepreneur, 19, 83, 135, 153, 156, 166, 210, 217
Entrepreneurship, 83, 135, 156, 166
Ethereum, 25, 47, 53, 56, 191
Ethical AI, 290, 296, 336, 387, 388
Ethical considerations, 39, 55, 63, 64, 78, 102, 103, 111,
        121, 130, 279, 295, 296, 388, 414
Ethics, 97, 103, 244, 336, 369
Europe, 116, 132, 134, 161, 171, 173, 174, 284, 290,
        295, 296, 298, 345, 352
European Union, 132, 134, 174
Excel, 34, 38, 66, 68, 73, 115, 134, 200, 201, 202, 208,
        366, 367, 369, 373, 374, 375
Exchange rate, 62, 63, 64, 67, 71, 77, 173
Explainable AI, 103

F

Facebook, 166
Facial recognition, 21, 280, 282, 283, 348
Facilities, 144, 201, 262, 341
Federated learning, 103, 226, 227, 229, 230, 231, 232,
        233, 234, 235, 236, 237, 238, 240, 241, 242,
        243, 244, 245
Feedback, 42, 86, 126, 154, 282, 287, 342, 344, 346,
        349, 373, 382, 412
Finance, 7, 11, 13, 14, 16, 23, 24, 25, 27, 28, 29, 30,
        31, 33, 34, 35, 37, 38, 39, 40, 41, 42, 43,
        46, 47, 48, 49, 51, 52, 54, 55, 56, 60, 63,
        66, 67, 68, 72, 73, 74, 78, 82, 84, 86, 88,
        90, 91, 92, 93, 97, 101, 102, 106, 107,
        108, 110, 112, 113, 114, 115, 117, 120, 121,
        122, 123, 124, 125, 126, 127, 128, 129, 130,
        131, 132, 133, 134, 135, 147, 148, 151, 153,
        154, 156, 157, 158, 161, 163, 166, 168, 171,
        172, 175, 176, 184, 195, 196, 199, 201, 203,
        204, 206, 207, 209, 210, 214, 215, 226, 227,
        228, 229, 231–235, 237, 239, 241, 242, 243,
        244, 245, 248, 249, 262, 263, 280, 290–299,
        301, 302, 303, 304, 309, 310, 322, 323, 324,
        326, 327, 329, 334, 335, 336, 345, 347, 354,

370, 378, 379, 382, 383, 384, 387, 388, 411,
        413–422
Finance industry, 35, 101, 121, 122, 123, 124, 127, 128,
        130, 156, 199, 201, 209, 210, 290, 291, 293,
        295, 297, 299, 301, 303, 326
Finance operation, 42
Finance service(s), 27, 28, 29, 30, 31, 33, 35, 37, 39, 41,
        43, 82, 84, 86, 88, 90, 92, 206, 226, 227,
        229, 231, 233, 235, 237, 239, 241, 243, 244,
        245, 298
Financial compliance, 251
Financial forecasting, 62, 63, 64, 65, 66, 67, 68, 69, 70,
        71, 72, 73, 74, 75, 76, 77, 78, 116, 328, 414
Financial inclusion, 6, 9, 49, 52, 53, 54, 55, 57, 58, 60,
        168, 184, 190, 191, 216, 261, 278, 285, 287,
        290, 297, 304, 335, 340, 341, 342, 344, 346,
        347, 349, 370, 414, 416
Financial industry, 39, 40, 48, 49, 52, 58, 60, 62, 63, 68,
        75, 77, 78, 82, 84, 93, 96, 97, 99, 101, 102,
        103, 107, 108, 122, 147, 148, 151, 152, 153,
        154, 156, 161, 164, 171, 175, 192, 199, 202,
        215, 242, 291, 304, 324, 325, 326, 327, 328,
        329, 331, 335, 336, 369, 371, 378, 379, 385,
        415
Financial institutions, 2, 11, 15, 34, 35, 43, 48, 49, 52,
        55, 56, 58, 59, 64, 69, 77, 83, 84, 87, 92, 96,
        97, 99, 100, 101, 102, 103, 107, 108, 111, 112,
        117, 121–135, 151, 152, 153, 154, 160, 161,
        168, 169, 171, 172, 173, 174, 182, 186, 189,
        195, 196, 197, 199, 202, 204, 205, 207, 208,
        210, 216, 226, 227, 228, 232, 233, 245, 249,
        250, 251, 254, 262, 263, 278, 279, 281, 282,
        284, 287, 290–299, 302, 303, 304, 326, 327,
        340, 345, 353, 355, 366–375, 378–388
Financial literacy, 287, 343, 344, 345, 347, 349
Financial operations, 40, 41, 101, 161, 175, 197, 208,
        292, 323, 379, 380, 385
Financial planning, 21, 57, 157, 327
Financial risk, 34, 248
Financial sector, 27, 37, 54, 56, 60, 64, 97, 99, 100, 101,
        106, 107, 108, 109, 110, 111, 113, 115, 117,
        120, 121, 149, 150, 154, 160, 161, 167, 171,
        196, 204, 208, 215, 226, 227, 232, 233, 245,
        250, 277, 279, 281, 285, 286, 291, 295, 322,
        323, 324, 325, 327, 329, 331, 333, 335, 336,
        371, 373, 378, 379, 381, 383, 385, 386, 387
Financial services, 1, 2, 3, 5–11, 13, 15, 16, 17, 19, 21,
        23, 25, 43, 46, 49, 50, 51, 52, 54, 56–60,
        82, 84, 86, 93, 96, 97, 99, 102, 103, 121,
        122, 128, 131, 132, 133, 134, 135, 148,
        149, 150, 152–157, 160, 161, 163, 164, 167,
        168, 169, 172, 176, 182, 184, 196, 201, 215,
        216, 231, 262, 263, 277, 278, 287, 290, 291,
        293, 295, 296, 299, 303, 304, 309, 310, 314,
        323, 325, 332, 333, 335, 336, 340, 341, 342,
        346, 354, 367, 368, 375, 383, 384, 387, 388,
        390, 401

Financial solution, 46, 135, 148, 150, 172, 279, 282, 283, 287, 333
Financial stability, 52, 64, 86, 117, 153, 156, 161, 167, 168, 172, 295, 370
Financial technology, 1, 46, 147, 148, 149, 150, 152, 153, 154, 156, 161, 162, 167, 169, 176, 214, 215, 216, 217, 297, 309, 388, 415
Fintech/FinTech, 46, 47, 48, 49, 50, 51, 52, 53, 54, 55, 56, 57, 58, 59, 60, 83, 92, 93, 125, 134, 147–172, 174, 175, 176, 181, 192, 214, 215, 216, 217, 219, 221, 222, 223, 248, 249, 258, 277, 278, 281, 282, 285, 286, 287, 290, 296, 309, 312, 317, 327, 341, 347, 349, 388, 415
Fintech revolution, 149, 214, 215, 217, 219, 221, 223
Firewall, 188, 228, 229
Flexible learning, 407
Fluctuation, 16, 33, 41, 71, 73, 74, 83, 91, 292
Food, 85
Foreign exchange rate forecasting, 62, 64, 67
Fourth Industrial Revolution, 388
Framework, 5, 29, 34, 35, 39, 40, 41, 42, 50, 51, 52, 54, 55, 73, 78, 103, 112, 113, 115, 121, 122, 125, 126, 131, 132, 133, 151, 154, 155, 156, 167, 175, 176, 201, 210, 215, 217, 232, 236, 243, 244, 245, 250, 258, 262, 263, 277, 278, 279, 281, 286, 295, 324, 329, 334, 336, 347, 348, 349, 356, 357, 366, 378, 379, 383, 384, 385, 388, 391, 392, 396, 411, 420
Fraud detection, 18, 34, 43, 49, 55, 57, 67, 90, 93, 96, 100, 101, 102, 103, 107, 108, 109, 124, 127, 129, 130, 131, 167, 168, 172, 198, 204, 210, 216, 290, 291, 292, 293, 294, 297, 299, 300, 303, 327, 331, 332, 335, 381, 384, 386
Future outlook, 55, 348

G

Generative AI, 93
Gig, 152, 154
Global banking, 279
Google, 169, 202, 411
Google analytics, 169
Growth, 1, 2, 12, 24, 47, 50, 55, 59, 83, 103, 114, 120, 124, 147, 153, 154, 156, 160, 161, 162, 164, 169, 171, 173, 174, 181, 184, 196, 201, 216, 236, 262, 277, 278, 280, 282, 285, 286, 287, 291, 292, 304, 313, 315, 327, 340, 341, 342, 346, 347, 349, 361, 370, 371, 375, 379, 387, 407, 416

H

Hardware, 29, 30, 35, 39, 40, 41, 53, 75, 78, 89, 113, 115, 182
HBase, 165
Healthcare, 47, 50, 72, 172, 231, 322
Hong Kong, 175
Hospitality, 367
Hotel, 129
HRM Practices, 367, 369, 373, 374, 375
Human capital, 215, 373
Human resource, 125, 127, 166, 197, 249, 353, 366
Hybrid model, 63, 73, 74, 78, 404
Hypotheses, 357, 360, 361

I

IBM, 14, 35, 40, 56, 253
IBM Watson, 253
Identity verification, 12, 323
Incentives, 92, 144, 159, 164, 347
Incident response, 132
Income, 84, 116, 125, 130, 135, 141, 142, 151, 159, 160, 165, 171, 181, 184, 299, 328, 342
India, 21, 23, 83, 139, 144, 153, 175, 184, 190, 216, 217, 222, 310, 314, 318, 340, 341, 342, 343, 346, 349, 370
Information and communication technology, 144, 318
Information and Communications Technology, 407
Information security, 250
Information technology, 175, 249, 353, 390, 401, 404
Infrastructure, 22, 35, 39, 40, 54, 55, 56, 58, 87, 113, 115, 125, 133, 134, 135, 144, 157, 161, 164, 166, 169, 208, 242, 243, 244, 277, 286, 287, 293, 296, 298, 312, 314, 315, 316, 317, 332, 343, 346, 354, 356, 358, 370, 378, 384, 385, 407
Innovation, 21, 28, 41, 42, 43, 46, 47, 48, 49, 50, 51, 52, 54, 55, 56, 58, 59, 60, 82, 83, 88, 93, 96, 97, 102, 103, 113, 114, 120–126, 133, 134, 135, 139, 148, 150–156, 158, 159, 161, 163, 164, 167, 168, 169, 171, 187, 189, 191, 192, 195, 196, 203, 214, 217, 218, 220, 223, 244, 249, 250, 278, 279, 280, 281, 282, 285, 286, 287, 290, 291, 294, 297, 298, 299, 302, 303, 304, 315, 323, 332, 333, 336, 347, 349, 366, 368, 371, 374, 375, 378, 379, 382–388, 407, 408, 415
Innovation and development, 249, 279
Instagram, 412, 415, 421
Insurtech/InsurTech, 157, 161, 169, 171, 175, 293, 294
Integrity, 5, 40, 41, 47, 51, 52, 60, 69, 70, 110, 111, 131, 132, 133, 175, 182, 184, 227, 228, 232, 244, 245, 253, 300, 303, 366, 367, 368, 382, 383, 388, 395, 396, 401
Intelligence, 24, 46, 62, 84, 85, 96, 97, 99, 101, 103, 120, 122, 130, 152, 158, 167, 171, 172, 189, 200, 209, 214, 227, 228, 229, 230, 231, 233, 236, 245, 248, 249, 251, 253, 255, 257, 279, 280, 290, 309, 312, 313, 315, 322, 334, 336, 348, 369, 378, 384, 388, 405, 406, 410, 415, 417, 422
Internet of Things, 24, 82, 83, 84, 86, 88, 90, 92, 103, 168, 226, 286, 293, 308, 311, 312, 318, 403, 404

Intrusion Detection Systems, 228
Inventory, 65, 83, 91, 108, 312, 328
Investment, 11, 19, 20, 25, 28, 29, 30, 33, 34, 36, 37, 40,
    41, 43, 47, 49, 50, 52, 54, 55, 56, 57, 58, 64,
    67, 77, 92, 96, 97, 99, 103, 106, 107, 109, 115,
    116, 117, 121, 125, 129, 133, 134, 135, 149,
    153, 157, 163, 168, 169, 170, 171, 172, 175,
    176, 199, 210, 243, 245, 249, 287, 290, 292,
    293, 294, 295, 296, 299, 303, 317, 327, 329,
    330, 331, 333, 335, 336, 341, 345, 346, 347,
    352, 366, 370, 372, 382, 384, 385, 386, 388
Investment management, 49, 57, 163, 293, 294, 346
Investment strategies, 28, 30, 40, 58, 97, 107, 292, 293,
    294, 303, 333, 336, 345, 366
IoT applications, 309, 310, 311, 313, 314, 315, 317, 318
IoT-based systems, 310, 314, 315, 316, 317, 318

J

Job, 39, 101, 102, 103, 121, 127, 166, 175, 197, 202, 205,
    207, 208, 210, 304, 335, 336, 375, 385, 415,
    420
Job market, 304, 336

K

Know your customer, 7, 10, 11, 198, 291
Knowledge, 13, 23, 28, 35, 42, 55, 72, 73, 76, 78, 84,
    98, 99, 108, 113, 117, 120, 121, 139, 140, 150,
    152, 154, 159, 164, 200, 202, 210, 217, 230,
    233, 245, 287, 300, 314, 323, 324, 349, 355,
    356, 361, 375, 388, 403, 405, 406, 407, 408,
    409, 410, 414, 420, 422

L

Labor market, 385
Leadership, 368, 374, 375
Learning Ability, 77
Legacy Systems, 46, 130, 133, 134, 207, 243, 296, 298
Legal Risk, 50
Liar, 63, 135, 144, 404, 415
Lifelong learning, 408
Likert, 265, 353, 358, 413
Linear Regression, 357, 360
LinkedIn, 166
Liquidity Risk, 83
Loan processing, 93, 127, 201, 204
Loans, 12, 14, 15, 16, 93, 149, 154, 157, 158, 160, 161,
    172, 173, 175, 198, 255, 261, 262, 294, 326,
    370, 372

M

Machine learning, 34, 35, 38, 39, 49, 64, 65, 96–103,
    107, 108, 114, 120, 121, 123–130, 133, 134,
    150, 152, 156, 157, 168, 169, 171, 174, 187,

    199, 205, 209, 210, 216, 227, 229, 230, 231,
    234, 236, 243, 245, 251, 254, 287, 290, 298,
    316, 323, 326, 327, 331, 380, 381, 384, 385,
    386, 405, 410
Machine vision, 254
Manufacturing, 33, 34, 36, 37, 40, 41, 370
Market risk, 57, 128, 167, 173
Market trend, 34, 40, 58, 64, 65, 67, 68, 73, 97, 99, 100,
    101, 127, 303, 382
Marketer, 332
Marketing, 19, 36, 37, 58, 68, 83, 84, 86, 88, 100, 126,
    140, 144, 261, 302, 325, 327, 333, 354, 382
MasterCard, 12, 294
Mathematical model, 30, 33, 36, 116
Mean absolute error, 72
Mean squared error, 72
Message, 5, 190, 315, 318, 392, 393, 394, 398, 399
Metaverse, 404
Microfinance, 168, 172
Microsoft, 12, 40, 201, 202, 309, 313, 315
Mobile, 10, 21, 22, 30, 31, 32, 36, 46, 48, 51, 54, 82, 83,
    86, 88, 90, 92, 126, 129, 139, 148, 149, 152,
    154, 155, 156, 160, 161, 166, 168, 169, 171,
    172, 175, 181, 182, 184, 186, 189, 190, 191,
    192, 226, 228, 251, 262, 277, 279, 280, 282,
    283, 284, 285, 286, 297, 311, 315, 324, 329,
    340–346, 354, 356, 381, 390–397, 399, 401,
    405, 406, 409, 415
Mobile banking, 48, 51, 54, 88, 92, 129, 139, 160, 171,
    189, 226, 228, 262, 277, 280, 282, 283, 284,
    286, 340, 341, 390, 391, 392, 393, 394, 395,
    396, 397, 399, 401
Mobile payments, 149, 154, 155, 181, 186, 283
Mobile wallet, 10, 182, 190, 191, 192, 285, 341, 354
Modelling, 199, 209
Modified RSA, 391, 393, 395, 396, 397, 399, 401
Monetary, 101, 106, 107, 108, 110, 111, 112, 113, 114,
    115, 116, 117, 173, 300, 323, 334
Monitor, 10, 42, 49, 51, 60, 72, 84, 85, 86, 87, 90, 91,
    92, 93, 101, 103, 124, 129, 165, 167, 172, 187,
    197, 205, 208, 209, 218, 228–252, 254, 284,
    290, 291, 292, 295, 297, 312, 318, 330, 346,
    349, 382, 388
Motivation, 62, 63, 121, 164, 334, 417, 420, 421, 422
Multi-factor authentication, 229, 284, 391, 392, 401
Multimedia, 192, 404, 405, 412, 413
Multiple linear regression, 357, 360

N

Natural language, 73, 96, 120, 126, 134, 206, 209, 249,
    253, 254, 290, 302, 387, 405
Natural language processing, 73, 96, 120, 126, 134, 254,
    290, 302, 387, 405
Net present value, 117
Network, 6, 11, 12, 16, 17, 23, 24, 30, 53, 55, 56, 62, 63,
    65, 66, 67, 68, 69, 70, 71, 73, 75, 77, 82, 83,

84, 85, 86, 87, 100, 103, 108, 112, 134, 144, 150, 152, 155, 158, 163, 166, 169, 172, 182, 183, 185, 186, 187, 188, 189, 191, 201, 227, 228, 229, 230, 232, 233, 256, 263, 264, 308, 310, 311, 312, 318, 331, 332, 355, 386, 387, 391, 392, 395, 405, 409, 410

Neural, 62, 63, 65, 66, 67, 69, 70, 71, 73, 75, 77, 100, 108, 256, 332, 386

Neural network(s), 62, 63, 65, 66, 67, 69, 70, 71, 73, 75, 77, 100, 108, 256, 332, 386

NGO, 4, 19, 39, 43, 47, 55, 63, 64, 72, 78, 107, 108, 110, 125, 158, 160, 195, 210, 277, 335, 344, 349, 370, 382, 383, 388, 391, 392, 401, 407, 422

Non-fungible Tokens, 25, 48

O

Onboarding, 12, 172, 198, 378, 384

Online banking, 2, 22, 48, 138, 147, 150, 160, 181, 188, 262, 279, 352, 353, 356

Online platform, 168, 263, 345

Online transaction, 21, 22, 184, 280, 401

Open banking, 49, 59, 171, 189, 217, 218, 221, 279

Open-source, 155, 192

Operational risk, 57, 96, 116, 128, 249, 252

Operations, 6, 28, 30, 40, 41, 42, 53, 54, 66, 82, 84, 91, 101, 120, 121, 123, 124, 125, 128, 133, 139, 150, 151, 152, 156, 159, 161, 168, 172, 174, 175, 176, 196, 197, 198, 200, 201, 202, 205, 206, 208, 209, 210, 216, 228, 241, 249, 253, 254, 278, 291, 292, 304, 308, 312, 314, 317, 322, 323, 327, 328, 332, 369, 370, 379, 380, 385, 387, 390, 396, 401

Opportunities, 28, 40, 42, 46, 47, 50, 51, 52, 53, 54, 55, 57, 60, 75, 83, 84, 99, 102, 103, 106, 107, 114, 120, 121, 122, 123, 125–131, 133, 135, 147, 149, 150, 156, 164, 171, 184, 196, 209, 215, 216, 234, 245, 263, 277, 278, 279, 281, 283, 285, 286, 287, 291, 292, 293, 294, 303, 304, 330, 336, 352, 354, 371, 378, 379, 380, 382, 385, 386, 387, 388, 408, 410, 421

Outcome, 11, 12, 13, 14, 16, 17, 19, 32, 33, 59, 64, 65, 72, 73, 74, 112, 130, 131, 165, 199, 217, 234, 279, 299, 323, 329, 335, 344, 345, 374, 375, 382, 383, 385, 388, 397, 409, 412, 414, 421

P

Pakistan, 169

Payment system, 2, 52, 55, 86, 91, 139, 150, 152, 168, 181, 182, 186, 188, 190, 191, 215, 277, 281, 314, 343

PayPal, 147, 150, 182, 186, 252, 303, 386

Peer-to-peer, 6, 8, 47, 149, 150, 155, 156, 158, 163, 167, 172, 186, 316

Performance, 30, 33, 36, 63–66, 68–77, 84, 89, 90, 93, 96, 97, 116, 117, 124, 155, 160, 162, 164, 166,

197, 201, 205, 217, 218, 221, 222, 231, 234, 235, 236, 238, 241, 244, 249, 299, 313, 314, 324, 328, 353, 355, 356, 366–371, 373, 374, 375, 381, 397, 400, 401, 403, 404, 405, 409, 410, 415

Performance management, 366, 368, 369, 373, 374, 375

Personal computer, 143

Personalization, 58, 100, 217, 218, 221, 281, 282, 286, 333, 336, 343, 384

Phishing, 226, 227, 228, 232, 238

PIN, 2, 4, 6, 8, 10, 12, 13, 14, 15, 16, 18, 20, 22, 23, 24, 27, 28, 30, 32, 34, 36, 38, 39, 40, 42, 46, 47, 48–52, 54–58, 60, 62, 64, 66, 68, 69, 70, 72, 74, 75, 76, 78, 83, 85–89, 91, 92, 93, 97–103, 108, 110, 112–116, 121–126, 128, 129, 130, 132, 133, 134, 135, 140, 142, 144, 149–153, 155–161, 163, 165–171, 173, 174, 175, 181, 182, 184, 186–192, 196, 197, 198, 200, 202, 204, 206, 208, 210, 214, 215, 216, 218, 220, 222, 227, 228, 230, 232, 233, 234, 236, 238, 240, 242, 244, 245, 249, 250, 252, 253, 254, 255, 256, 258, 262, 263, 264, 266–274, 277, 278, 279, 280, 282, 284, 286, 291, 292, 294, 296, 297, 298, 299, 300, 302, 304, 308, 310, 312, 314–318, 324, 326–334, 336, 342–346, 348, 352, 354, 355, 356, 358, 360, 366–370, 372, 374, 375, 378, 379, 380, 382, 384, 385, 386, 388, 392, 394, 396, 398, 400, 403, 404, 405, 406, 408–412, 414, 416–422

Planning, 21, 42, 57, 63, 64, 65, 82, 86, 101, 129, 133, 157, 166, 168, 208, 210, 243, 315, 323, 326, 327, 373, 414

Platform, 1, 14, 16, 17, 19, 20, 21, 23, 24, 25, 40, 48, 49, 50, 51, 54, 55, 56, 57, 58, 59, 60, 87, 88, 89, 90, 99, 113, 115, 125, 129, 134, 139, 148, 150, 152, 157, 165, 166, 168, 171, 172, 181, 182, 183, 188, 192, 199–204, 207, 210, 230, 250, 251, 252, 263, 277, 281, 282, 285, 292, 294, 297, 302, 303, 311, 315, 316, 318, 333, 340, 341, 343–348, 354, 381, 382, 386, 390, 405, 406, 410, 421, 422

Policymaker, 50, 52, 83, 112, 121, 122, 215, 216, 227, 335, 336, 347, 349, 379, 383, 384, 387, 388, 409

Portfolio management, 58, 67, 99, 106, 107, 109, 114, 201, 327

Portfolio optimization, 27, 28, 29, 30, 31, 33, 35, 37, 38, 39, 40, 41, 42, 43, 100, 106, 107, 116, 117, 125, 292, 294, 299

Prediction, 38, 43, 62, 63, 64, 65, 66, 67, 68, 69, 70, 72, 73, 74, 75, 76, 77, 78, 98, 107, 108, 109, 114, 117, 123, 175, 244, 313, 325, 328, 330, 386

Predictive analytic(s), 58, 90, 97, 98, 99, 100, 101, 102, 103, 120, 121, 124, 127, 128, 129, 227, 231, 245, 291, 299, 303, 331, 334

PricewaterhouseCoopers, 206
Privacy, 1, 2, 7, 8, 9, 12, 23, 24, 40, 41, 51, 52, 55, 59,
        60, 74, 83, 84, 97, 99, 102, 103, 111, 113, 114,
        120, 121, 122, 125, 130–135, 144, 150, 151,
        152, 208, 227, 228, 229, 230, 231, 232, 233,
        234, 235, 236, 237, 238, 239, 241, 242, 243,
        245, 264, 266, 268, 269, 270, 272, 273, 275,
        279, 284, 286, 290, 295, 296, 298, 314, 318,
        336, 343, 344, 347, 348, 349, 353, 356–361,
        379, 382, 383, 385, 388
Probability, 257, 328, 406, 413
Problem-solving, 28, 29, 210, 322, 408
Processes, 7, 9, 10, 19, 24, 25, 28, 29, 33, 36, 39, 43,
        47, 48, 49, 52, 56, 58, 59, 68, 69, 76, 77,
        90, 93, 97, 101, 102, 103, 121, 123, 125,
        127, 132, 171, 172, 187, 188, 191, 195, 196,
        201, 202, 203, 204, 205, 206, 208, 209,
        210, 216, 227, 244, 245, 250, 251, 254, 278,
        286, 287, 290, 291, 295, 299, 302, 304,
        309, 310, 318, 322, 324, 325, 326, 327, 328,
        335, 341, 345, 348, 352, 354, 368, 378,
        379, 380, 382, 383, 384, 385, 388, 390,
        396, 401, 421
Product, 1, 2, 13, 14, 25, 34, 36, 37, 43, 49, 52, 57, 58,
        59, 60, 65, 68, 82, 83, 86, 87, 88, 91, 93, 96,
        100, 102, 103, 115, 123, 125, 126, 127, 131,
        134, 135, 148, 149, 152, 153, 154, 155, 158,
        159, 160, 162, 166, 169, 172, 176, 182, 183,
        201, 202, 204, 205, 206, 209, 251, 252, 253,
        261, 263, 278, 281, 282, 283, 291, 292, 293,
        294, 296, 302, 303, 308, 312, 314, 315, 317,
        323, 325, 327, 332, 333, 335, 341, 344, 346,
        354, 355, 356, 361, 366, 367, 368, 371, 373,
        382, 384, 412, 415, 421
Productivity enhancement, 294
Proof-of-authority, 53
Psychology, 413
Public-private partnership, 54, 287
P-value, 143, 219, 220, 222, 360, 361
Python, 395, 396

Q

Quality, 1, 32, 33, 37, 59, 63, 69, 74–78, 82, 102, 107,
        113, 130, 132, 133, 135, 140, 155, 171, 181,
        202, 207, 231, 243, 264, 266, 268, 269, 270,
        272, 273, 275, 295, 297, 304, 310, 314, 317,
        318, 332, 340, 341, 353, 354, 355, 356, 361,
        368, 369, 374, 375, 381, 382, 383, 403–408,
        410, 412
Quantum algorithms, 28, 29, 30, 33, 34, 38, 39, 41, 42,
        43, 108, 112, 113
Quantum computing, 27, 28, 29, 30, 31, 33, 34, 35, 36,
        37, 38, 39, 40, 41, 42, 43, 59, 103, 106, 107,
        108, 109, 110, 111, 113, 114, 115, 117
Quantum-resistant, 34, 38, 39, 40, 110, 112, 114
Quantum-safe cryptography, 28, 42

R

Random, 66, 71, 73, 111, 141, 299, 386
Random forest, 73, 299, 386
Real estate, 25, 50, 55, 121
Real-time application, 84
Real-time monitoring, 91, 93, 254
Real-time reporting, 253
Recurrent neural network, 71, 256
Regression, 65, 67, 71, 72, 98, 100, 116, 219, 220, 221,
        299, 357, 358, 360
Regression analysis, 65, 98, 100, 357, 358, 360
RegTech, 49, 60, 167, 169, 170, 171, 192, 253, 293,
        294
Regulatory challenges, 42, 50, 52, 160, 281, 382, 388
Regulatory compliance, 19, 40, 41, 42, 43, 50, 52, 58,
        59, 60, 74, 77, 96, 101, 102, 103, 110, 111,
        112, 122, 125, 127, 130, 131, 149, 150, 152,
        156, 166, 198, 201, 202, 204, 207, 228,
        230, 231, 242, 244, 245, 248, 249, 251,
        286, 291, 295, 296, 304, 326, 333, 375,
        387, 414
Regulatory measure, 134
Reinforcement learning, 66, 98, 386
Relevance, 8, 29, 63, 72, 74, 149, 410
Researcher, 28, 30, 63, 83, 121, 122, 139, 140, 154, 216,
        221, 326, 329, 392, 405, 406, 407, 409, 410,
        411, 412, 414, 421
Resource allocation, 28, 34, 42, 64, 127, 128, 291, 304
Responsiveness, 33, 210, 314, 353, 356, 357, 358, 359,
        360, 361, 381, 400
Retail, 87, 99, 125, 149, 151, 161, 182, 187, 189, 191,
        314, 318, 366
Return on investment, 37
Ripple, 56
Risk analysis, 28, 29, 42, 107, 108, 109, 116, 293, 326
Risk assessment, 28, 30, 33, 38, 41, 43, 57, 58, 67, 77,
        82, 93, 102, 103, 109, 115, 123, 128, 130,
        168, 210, 291, 292, 293, 294, 297, 299, 317,
        326, 334, 378, 384
Risk management, 14, 27, 29, 30, 37, 38, 39, 41, 42, 43,
        49, 55, 58, 62, 64, 67, 73, 74, 77, 99, 100, 101,
        102, 108, 122–128, 131, 149, 150, 152, 154,
        166, 167, 218, 220, 248, 249, 250, 251, 258,
        290, 291, 295, 299, 312, 314, 318, 323, 324,
        325, 326, 327, 328, 333, 334, 356, 381, 384,
        388, 414
Robo-advisor, 49, 58, 96, 99, 149, 167, 168, 292, 294,
        327, 330
Robotic, 103, 114, 172, 195, 197, 199, 201, 203, 205,
        207, 209, 253, 254, 294, 302
Robotic process automation, 103, 195, 197, 199, 201,
        203, 205, 207, 209, 253, 254, 294, 302
Robotics, 114
Robust, 33, 35, 39, 41, 43, 51, 63, 65, 67–73, 75, 78, 97,
        100, 110, 111, 131, 133, 138, 139, 187, 203,
        226, 227, 228, 230, 232, 233, 242, 243, 244,

245, 277, 280, 283, 284, 286, 287, 297, 298, 302, 342, 344, 346, 347, 348, 355, 359, 373, 378, 381–385, 388, 390, 391, 395, 396, 401
R-square, 219, 220
Rural population, 342
Russia, 139, 169, 336

S

Sales, 17, 19, 36, 37, 65, 83, 116, 157, 201, 261, 262, 382
SAP, 17, 120, 326, 407
SAS, 175
Secure sockets layer, 236
Security, 2, 5, 6, 7, 8, 9, 19, 21, 23, 24, 25, 34, 35, 38, 40, 41, 43, 46, 47, 49, 50, 51, 52, 55, 59, 60, 67, 83, 84, 85, 86, 90, 91, 93, 97, 99, 102, 103, 106–112, 114, 121, 122, 125, 130, 131, 132, 135, 138, 139, 140, 144, 150, 152, 156, 157, 168, 172, 182–185, 187–192, 200, 202, 203, 206, 207, 208, 215, 216, 226–239, 241, 242, 243, 244, 245, 250, 251, 253, 278–284, 286, 287, 293, 295, 297, 298, 304, 313, 317, 318, 322, 326, 331, 332, 336, 340, 342, 343, 344, 347, 348, 354, 356–361, 382, 383, 385, 386, 390–397, 399, 401
Self-sovereign identity, 2, 3
Sentiment analysis, 66, 67, 69, 96, 97, 127, 302, 325, 327, 328, 330, 334, 387
Service delivery, 126, 154, 158, 161, 261, 264, 266, 267, 269, 270, 272, 273, 274, 314, 335, 367, 368, 369, 374, 375, 378, 384
Services, 1, 2, 3, 5–11, 13, 15, 16, 17, 19, 21, 22, 23, 25, 27, 28, 29, 30, 31, 33, 35, 37, 39, 40, 41, 43, 46, 47, 48, 49, 50, 51, 52, 54–60, 82, 83, 84, 86, 87, 88, 90, 92, 93, 96, 97, 99, 100, 102, 103, 115, 120, 121, 122, 123, 125–129, 131–135, 138, 139, 140, 141, 143, 144, 148–158, 160–164, 167, 168, 169, 171, 172, 175, 176, 182, 183, 184, 190, 192, 196, 201, 206, 214–218, 220, 226, 227, 228, 229, 231, 233, 235, 237, 239, 241, 243, 244, 245, 253, 261, 262, 263, 264, 266–275, 277–287, 290–296, 298, 299, 303, 304, 308, 309, 310, 312, 314, 315, 317, 318, 323, 325, 327, 330, 332, 333, 335, 336, 340–349, 352–359, 361, 366, 367, 368, 369, 371, 373, 375, 378, 379, 382, 383, 384, 387, 388, 390, 391, 392, 401, 415
Small and medium enterprise, 285
Smart banking, 314
Smart city, 312
Smart contract, 6, 7, 9, 12, 13, 15, 16, 18, 20, 25, 47, 49, 52, 84, 153, 172
SMS, 4, 23, 24, 39, 42, 48, 53, 63, 71, 73, 75, 110, 111, 114, 187, 208, 229, 244, 284, 327, 344, 346, 347, 367, 368, 373, 375, 383, 388, 391, 392, 396

Social, 6, 8, 9, 21, 42, 47, 57, 59, 60, 63, 66, 67, 69, 76, 78, 83, 96, 98, 99, 112, 126, 135, 156, 166, 172, 181, 228, 229, 292, 297, 311, 314, 323, 327, 328, 330, 334, 335, 342, 345, 347, 381, 386, 409, 420, 421, 422
Social media, 57, 63, 67, 69, 76, 78, 96, 98, 99, 126, 166, 292, 297, 327, 328, 330, 381, 386, 421
Social media interaction, 126
Socioeconomic, 122, 134, 135
Software, 25, 35, 82, 91, 113, 156, 161, 168, 169, 171, 195, 197, 199, 200, 201, 202, 205, 209, 229, 252, 254, 302, 308, 327, 328, 357, 409
Soil, 53
Spectrum, 73, 148, 157, 299, 317, 333, 380, 397, 399
SPSS, 141, 357
Staff, 87, 102, 129, 133, 159, 165, 166, 195, 198, 251, 264, 335, 373
Stakeholder, 23, 24, 39, 42, 49, 50, 51, 52, 54, 74, 77, 97, 112, 121, 122, 130, 131, 133, 152, 205, 217, 227, 228, 243, 245, 258, 279, 300, 316, 333, 344, 347, 349, 356, 378, 379, 383, 384, 385, 387, 388
Standard deviation, 417
Start-ups, 277, 278, 281, 282, 286, 287
Stellar, 7, 16, 17, 57
Stock price, 62, 63, 64, 67, 71, 76, 78, 100, 299, 325, 330
Stock price prediction, 62, 63, 64, 67, 76, 78
Stock trading, 325
Streamline process, 49, 58, 101, 201
Supply chain, 28, 30, 32, 33, 34, 36, 41, 43, 47, 50, 56, 84, 91, 202, 228
Supply chain management, 30, 33, 47, 50, 202
Support vector machine, 66, 386
Sustainability, 53, 56, 60, 64, 65, 336, 341, 371, 379, 383, 387
Sustainable development, 340, 341, 345, 346, 347, 349
Systemic risk, 151, 173, 174, 226, 248, 251, 384

T

Talent acquisition, 130, 132, 296, 304, 369, 371, 373
Tax, 4, 22, 23, 37, 201, 248, 347
Teaching materials, 404, 405, 406, 407, 408, 409, 411, 412, 414, 415, 418, 420, 421, 422
Technological change, 162, 353, 385
Technological innovations, 120, 189, 415
Technology, 1, 2, 3, 5, 6, 7, 9, 21, 23, 24, 25, 28, 37, 39, 40, 41, 46–57, 59, 60, 82–87, 90, 92, 93, 98, 111, 112, 113, 115, 117, 121–125, 131–135, 138, 139, 140, 141, 143, 144, 147–158, 160, 161, 162, 164, 167, 168, 169, 171, 172, 174, 175, 176, 182, 185, 186, 187, 191, 192, 196, 200, 207–210, 214–221, 226, 248–254, 258, 261, 262, 263, 267, 277, 278, 279, 280, 282, 286, 292, 293, 297, 302, 303, 308–314, 317,

318, 323, 327, 329, 332, 335, 340, 345, 347, 348, 353, 354, 356, 375, 384, 387, 388, 390, 401, 404–410, 415, 416, 417, 420, 421, 422

Technology transformation, 138, 139, 141, 143

Telecommunication, 182, 188, 231, 262, 308, 317

Testing, 29, 85, 98, 165, 205, 287, 343, 347, 360, 384

Thematic analysis, 329

Theoretical foundation, 278, 410

Theoretical framework, 217, 324, 334

Time series analysis, 62–65, 68, 73, 98

Tokenization, 14, 16, 25, 47, 52, 55, 60, 191, 233, 302

Tourism, 419, 420, 422

Trading, 14, 25, 28, 34, 42, 43, 52, 55, 56, 57, 60, 68, 69, 71, 76, 77, 96, 97, 99, 106, 108, 109, 128, 155, 173, 201, 252, 290, 292, 294, 303, 322, 325, 327, 328, 329, 330, 331, 346, 354, 379, 380, 381, 386, 387

Traditional bank, 47, 48, 49, 52, 57, 58, 135, 138, 140, 147, 148, 149, 150, 152, 154–160, 162, 163, 164, 166, 168, 170, 172, 174, 176, 192, 195, 214–223, 261, 262, 264, 278, 285, 286, 290, 296, 309, 310, 326, 347, 348

Traditional banking adaptation, 149

Transaction data, 67, 107, 128, 129, 234, 292, 297, 299, 300, 301, 303, 331, 386, 396

Transformation, 40, 46, 48, 121, 125, 138, 139, 141, 143, 144, 149, 150, 151, 156, 162, 164, 195, 214, 215, 217, 221, 222, 223, 249, 250, 254, 267, 277, 278, 279, 281, 285, 286, 287, 291, 299, 304, 308, 322, 323, 325, 327, 329, 331, 333, 335, 336, 340, 368, 378, 379, 381, 382, 383, 384, 385, 387, 390, 391, 392, 397, 401, 403, 404, 421

Transformative impact, 56, 181, 204, 222, 283

Transforming, 33, 51, 55, 56, 69, 84, 101, 103, 120, 154, 163, 216, 264, 267, 293, 312, 331, 335, 384, 392, 401, 415

Transport layer security, 236

Transportation, 41, 84, 253, 312

Trust, 1, 2, 5, 7, 10, 16, 17, 25, 41, 49, 54, 59, 74, 78, 87, 99, 102, 111, 125, 128, 129, 133, 135, 139, 144, 149, 161, 183, 184, 187, 192, 227, 244, 245, 263, 278, 279, 283, 284, 286, 287, 304, 332, 333, 335, 343, 344, 348, 354, 361, 366, 367, 379, 383, 387, 388

Twitter, 166

U

Uber, 172, 411

Urban, 261, 265, 270, 271, 273, 274, 285, 341, 342, 348, 349, 408

URL, 413

USA, 34, 59, 85, 91, 117, 133, 135, 139, 140, 141, 143, 144, 148, 149, 153, 166, 174, 190, 206, 208, 267, 280, 308, 310, 314, 325, 335, 341, 344, 356, 367, 383, 394

User acceptance, 24

User experience, 135, 189, 343, 347

V

Variance, 38, 116, 122, 134, 218, 221, 222, 223, 358, 359, 360

Vehicle, 36, 90, 91, 293, 308

Virtual assistant, 97, 125, 130, 197, 291, 292, 296, 325, 332, 348, 381, 384, 387

Virtual reality, 405

Visa, 16, 56

Volatility, 16, 29, 38, 58, 65, 70, 76, 101, 116, 127, 128, 167, 173, 371

W

Waste management, 54

Wealth management, 48, 52, 86, 125, 129, 163, 295, 303, 341, 379

Wealthfront, 292, 294

Welfare, 21, 51, 151, 342, 403

Whatsapp, 17

Wi-Fi, 89

Workforce, 40, 42, 133, 200, 249, 298, 336, 368, 371, 385, 386

Y

YouTube, 412, 415, 421

Z

Z-score, 160